Traveling Through Time

Traveling Through Time

Edited by Laura R. Ashlee

Bureau of History
Michigan Historical Commission
Michigan Department of State

*T*his book is fondly dedicated to former Michigan Historical Commissioner Willard Wichers of Holland. He was the gentlest gentleman I have known.

CONTENTS

Foreword 9
Preface 11
Acknowledgements 13
Introduction 15
How To Use This Book 18
Alcona County 21
Alger County 21
Allegan County 22
Alpena County 25
Antrim County 25
Arenac County 27
Baraga County 27
Barry County 28
Bay County 31
Benzie County 33
Berrien County 35
Branch County 40
Calhoun County 45
Cass County 61
Charlevoix County 62
Cheboygan County 64
Chippewa County 65
Clare County 69
Clinton County 70
Crawford County 73
Delta County 75
Dickinson County 76
Eaton County 77
Emmet County 84
Genesee County 87
Gogebic County 95
Grand Traverse County 96
Gratiot County 99
Hillsdale County 100
Houghton County 102
Huron County 107
Ingham County 111
Ionia County 126
Iosco County 128
Iron County 129
Isabella County 131
Jackson County 132
Kalamazoo County 137

Kalkaska County 146
Kent County 146
Keweenaw County 156
Lake County 157
Lapeer County 157
Leelanau County 159
Lenawee County 162
Livingston County 168
Luce County 171
Mackinac County 173
Macomb County 182
Manistee County 190
Marquette County 193
Mason County 196
Mecosta County 198
Menominee County 200
Midland County 201
Monroe County 202
Montcalm County 203
Montmorency County 203
Muskegon County 204
Oakland County 207
Oceana County 225
Ontonagon County 225
Osceola County 226
Otsego County 226
Ottawa County 227
Presque Isle 236
Roscommon County 238
Saginaw County 239
St. Clair County 244
St. Joseph County 248
Sanilac County 252
Schoolcraft County 253
Shiawassee County 254
Tuscola County 262
Van Buren County 264
Washtenaw County 268
Wayne County 278
Wexford County 319
Out of State 321
Appendix 323
Photo Credits 326
Index 327

Foreword

The Michigan Historical Marker Program, along with the state's other history programs, became part of the Michigan Department of State under the state constitution of 1962-1963. Today, Michigan Historical Markers can be found throughout our villages and cities and along our highways—each one telling a special story—each one teaching a lesson about our history. Some commemorate past struggles; in Flint, for example there are three recalling the General Motors sit-down strike of 1937. Others, like the one at the Albert Kahn-designed Fisher Building in Detroit, celebrate our art and architecture. Still others honor individuals like Orsel McGhee, who successfully challenged the legality of residential neighborhood restrictive covenants based on race.

These particular markers are special to me, not only because of the stories they tell, but also because as Michigan's official historian, I participated in their dedications and was able to see, first-hand, the community pride and sense of achievement that each historical marker represents. Marker dedications, I might add, can also be just plain fun—like the unveiling of Detroit's Shrine Circus marker . . . by an elephant.

This is just a sampling of the stories that await you in *Traveling Through Time*. Read it in your easy chair, or keep it in your glovebox as a handy reference. Either way, it is sure to add interest to all your Michigan travels. And as you read it, I hope you will share my appreciation of the many hours of volunteer time given to this program by the members of the Michigan Historical Commission.

Richard H. Austin
Secretary of State

Preface

Since its creation, the Michigan Historical Commission has been responsible for designating and marking historic sites in Michigan. When the legislature passed Public Act 10 in 1955 and created the State Register of Historic Sites and the Michigan Historical Marker Program, the commission began the current program of actively recognizing sites, buildings, events, people and institutions that played a significant role in our state's development. Although the program at first marked only state-significant sites on Michigan's highways, many of our markers have been erected in communities to honor local history—Michigan markers can be found in Indiana, Kentucky, Maryland, Tennessee and France! These recognize Michigan's contributions outside the Great Lake State.

Over two thousand sites have been listed in the state register and at least half display markers. The earliest markers were purchased with state funds earmarked by the legislature for that purpose. However, for the last thirty years or so, the markers have been paid for by the people who apply for designation and wish to mark sites in their communities. History-related organizations, chambers of commerce, businesses, church congregations and private citizens donate money to purchase historical markers. Without their interest and diligence in fund-raising, Michigan's Historical Marker Program could not continue.

The Michigan Historical Commission is extremely pleased to see the publication of *Traveling Through Time: A Guide to Michigan's Historical Markers*. We are proud to have such a successful program and we enjoy sharing our history with Michigan residents and visitors. We hope you will enjoy traveling through Michigan's past.

John B. Swainson, President
Jerry D. Roe, Vice President
Elizabeth S. Adams
Esther Gordy Edwards
Ann Preston Koeze
Donald F. Wall

Acknowledgements

While reading volumes of Michigan Historical Commission minutes, I noted that the commission frequently discussed the need for a second edition of *Michigan Historical Markers*, which was published in 1967. It was not until the following people collectively approved and supported the idea of publishing a second historical marker book that work could actually begin. I would like to acknowledge the support of: Secretary of State Richard H. Austin, Special Affairs Deputy Dennis G. Neuner, the Michigan Historical Commission and State Historic Preservation Officer Kathryn B. Eckert.

A special thank you goes to Roger L. Rosentreter, *Michigan History Magazine* editor and the head of the Bureau of History's Publications Section, for his encouragement—and for bringing me tuna-fish sandwiches on Saturdays—and Paul Smyth for sharing his computer expertise, his patience and for helping me keep my sense of humor.

Many people authored the historical markers that appear in this book. George May, historic sites specialist for the Michigan Historical Commission, researched and composed the marker texts for the first ten years of the program. In 1974, with America's bicentennial celebration on the horizon, interest in Michigan's marker program grew, and a full-time staff-person was hired. Carolyn Torma coordinated the marker program from 1974 to 1976, Saralee R. Howard-Filler did so from 1976 to 1979, Robin S. Peebles served from 1977 to 1988, and I began my tenure in 1988. Throughout the life of the program other historic sites staff-members, including Donald Chaput, Catherine Ellis, William Lowery and Donna Stiffler, wrote texts when needed. Their contribution has also been significant.

Thanks to my colleagues in the Historic Preservation Section for their interest in promoting the erection of historical markers in order to educate and alert the public as to the value of historic properties worthy of preservation.

I also want to thank Robert Burg, JoAnn Carroll, Charles Cotman, Mary Patrick and Dale Reid, who spent their "after hours hours" searching for markers and verifying their locations, and Don Robinson, who with JoAnn, made numerous telephone calls to inquire, "Is the marker there? Where is it? How does it look?"

Thank you to Christopher Behmer who made heads **and** tails out of our chaotic records and created the first real "list" of markers. Thank you to Sharon McHaney and Carey Draeger for the time they spent proofreading, Mary Jo Remensnyder and Rose Ashlee for their clerical support, Diana Engle for her enthusiastic marketing of this book, Patrick Reed and Roger Rosentreter for their design talents and Stewart Ashlee for his rendering of the marker seal on page 17. Tiffany Reinhardt and Carrie Scupholm contributed to the publication in different capacities; their efforts are also appreciated.

Thanks to Charlotte Douthitt of Sewah Studios who provided the company's records of the Michigan Historical Markers that it manufactured over the last thirty years. Without these records we would have been unable to assemble the information for this book.

The people who sent illustrations for possible publication are too numerous to mention, but I want them to know that I appreciated their swift responses to my requests.

Lastly, I must acknowledge "marker hunters" Jim Brennan, Edward and Annemarie Herman and Eric Smith, who offered their assistance and confirmed that this publication was needed.

Introduction

"There's no history in Michigan." "All of America's history is back east." "If you want to see history, you've got to go to Europe." I have heard these statements so often that I want to hit people over the head with a piece of Michigan lumber! An exaggeration to be sure, but many people believe that American history began with the Pilgrims landing at Plymouth Rock, and ended with the conclusion of the Civil War at Appomattox Courthouse. Others value the relics at Canterbury, England, or the grandeur of Versailles, but disregard the events that directly influenced their own way of life. Did Massachusetts lead the nation in the production of copper, iron and lumber in the late nineteenth century? Was the assembly line developed in London, England?

Many Michiganians are unaware that European explorers came here only a half-century after the Pilgrims disembarked. The French first visited Sault Sainte Marie, in 1641. This state has a varied history that parallels the development of frontier America, yet is unique because of the topography and the people who settled here. The Great Lakes that make up Michigan's boundaries and the intricate network of inland lakes and rivers provided the means for transporting raw materials from America's interior to the early industrial centers in the east and to Europe. If we view America's past through Michigan's history, we will see that our country is in fact "the sum of its parts."

A record of Michigan's rich history exists in state historical markers. These wolverine-topped green and gold markers showcase topics of interest to everyone—even if you aren't a "history buff." Whether you are enthusiastic about baseball, skiing, science, aviation, music, agriculture, industry, black history, prehistory, war, religion, beer, temperance or the breakfast cereal that graces your table, there will be at least one marker of interest to you along a highway, in a city—and in this book.

Traveling Through Time is a collection of state historical markers erected since 1955. When the State Register of Historic Sites and the current Historical Marker Program began that year, the Michigan Historical Commission's goal was to erect markers in scenic turnouts and state parks where large numbers of people could read them. In October 1955 the first marker was dedicated at Michigan State University, recognizing it as the model for land grant colleges in the United States. Early markers commemorated the state's unique natural features and early history—the Great Lakes, fur trading, exploration and missionaries. Agricultural products and industry were also highlighted. Over the last thirty-six years the recognition of local history and our architectural history has become important as well, and markers can now be found sprinkled throughout Michigan's wilderness and concentrated in villages and cities.

Michigan history enthusiasts who appreciate more than "Great Man's History," demanded this book. At the end of my first day as Michigan's historical marker coordinator in April 1988, I counted four requests for lists of historical markers. A complete list was unavailable, but I told the callers that I would keep their name and address on file until something was available. Little did I know that those four requests were only the beginning! The calls kept coming in from scout leaders, chambers of commerce, reporters, students, teachers, travel agents, and on and on! In 1989, State Historic Preservation Officer Kathryn Eckert and I discussed the need for an updated marker book. The last book, published in 1967, had been out of print for at least a decade. Secretary of State Richard Austin and the Michigan Historical Commission supported the project, and now, at last, a publication is available to those many callers and the most diligent of all marker fans, whom I fondly refer to as "marker hunters."

During the hours that I spent compiling, typing and proofreading these marker texts, I learned and thought a lot about Michigan's past. I noted with surprise that Harriet Quimby, the first woman in the U.S. to obtain a pilot's license, was born in Coldwater. I wondered if Presque Isle lighthouse keeper Patrick Garrity ever felt isolated and suffered from cabin fever. I thought about how Michigan's buildings, the Greek Revivals in the southern Lower Peninsula and the stepped-gables of Holland, reflect the homelands of the first residents. Most of all I thought about the people who read historical markers. The parents who turn off the highway, either at their children's request—or with much protest from the back seat—and read the markers. They are parents like mine who detoured every time I spotted a sign that said "historical marker. . .memorial. . .or monument ahead." Neither of them have forgotten this, in fact they both reminded me of this—what some people consider "a quirk"—when I informed them that I was editing this book.

Laura R. Ashlee
State Register & Historical Marker Coordinator

How To Use This Book

The information presented in this volume is straightforward. Each historical marker record consists of two parts: (1) the marker text; and (2) the historic site information. The records are arranged alphabetically by county, the incorporated governmental unit in which the marker is located and by the exact title. Titles beginning with "The" have been alphabetized and indexed by the second word in the title, and proper names are by the **first** name. You will notice that some records have two titles; these are two-sided markers with different titles.

When searching for a specific community, identify the county and locate it in the Table of Contents. Once the county has been located, search the site information for each marker the your community. Remember that the markers are arranged **alphabetically** by the **incorporated governmental unit.**

A sample record is below:

Holland Harbor Lighthouse

The first lighthouse built at this location was a small, square wooden structure erected in 1872. In 1880 the lighthouse service installed a new light atop a metal pole in a protective cage. The oil lantern was lowered by pulleys for service. At the turn of the century a steel tower was built for the light, and in 1906 the present structure was erected. Named the Holland Harbor South Pierhead Lighthouse, it has a gabled roof that reflects the Dutch influence in the area. The lighthouse, popularly referred to as "Big Red," was automated in 1932. When the U.S. Coast Guard recommended that it be abandoned in 1970, citizens circulated petitions to rescue it. The Holland Harbor Lighthouse Historical Commission was then organized to preserve and restore this landmark.

Holland Harbor

When seeking a location for his Netherlands emigrant followers in 1847, the Reverend A. C. Van Raalte was attracted by the potential of using Black Lake (Lake Macatawa) as a harbor. However, the lake's outlet to Lake Michigan was blocked by sandbars and silt. Van Raalte appealed to Congress for help. The channel was surveyed in 1849, but was not successfully opened due to inadequate appropriations. Frustrated, the Dutch settlers dug the channel themselves. On July 1, 1859, the small steamboat *Huron* put into port. Here, in 1886, the government established the harbor's first life-saving station. By 1899 the channel had been relocated and harbor work completed. This spurred business and resort expansion. In 1900 over 1,095 schooners, steamers and barges used the harbor.

Location   Historic Site Name   Common Name

South Pier, Holland Harbor, Holland State Park, Park Township; Holland Harbor South Pierhead Lighthouse (Holland Lighthouse); L394; January 16, 1976; 1987

State Register Number   Date Registered   Year Erected

The **site location** consists of two parts, the physical location of the site and the municipality. When we began compiling the information, we started with the locations available in files. Some were extremely vague. Bureau of History staff then contacted local historical societies, chambers of commerce, municipalities and others to verify the location and presence of each marker. Approximately 80 percent of the locations were verified. In some cases we were unable to reach anyone who was knowledgeable of the marker's whereabouts. NOTE: Those markers that are no longer on site are denoted with an asterisk (*) preceding the location.

The **historic** and **common site names** were assigned when the sites were designated, therefore the common name may be outdated. Some of the historic and common site names contain the words "Informational Site" and "Informational Designation." Informational Sites are those specific sites that were listed because of their association with a significant structure that was formerly on the site, i.e. Fort Lernoult, or an event that occurred at a specific site. Informational Designations reflect the registration of an institution, person or event that is not associated specifically with the site where the marker is located, i.e., a marker honoring Spanish-American War nurse Ellen May Tower stands in a Byron park. Byron was Tower's home town, but the park was not associated with her.

Historic site numbers were assigned when the sites were designated; the registration dates are also included. In some cases these numbers and dates are lacking because a marker was inadvertently erected without the site being listed. The initials **HB** = Historic Building; **S** = State Significant; **L** = Locally Significant. In some cases letters follow the numerals in the site numbers. Beginning in 1978 sites were classified depending on whether a historic building was registered, or whether the site was registered for marking purposes only. Under the current policy, the "A" classification is reserved for those historic buildings, fifty years of age or older, that retain historical integrity and reflect the period in which they were built. The "B" classification is for those historic buildings, fifty years of age or older, that have suffered a loss of integrity, and the "C" classification is for Informational Sites or Informational Designations.

An index by marker title can be found at the back of the book. Historical markers with two titles are indexed under both titles.

Illustrations are captioned. The title of the marker related to the illustration is provided in italics at the end of the caption. Photo credits are on page 326.

The historical marker texts included in *Traveling Through Time* appear as they do on the markers. Grammatical revisions have been made in order to promote consistency among the entries in this book. Spelling errors have been corrected and factual errors that are known have been noted preceding the site information. The reader should keep two things in mind: (1) there may have been markers erected that we do not have record of; and (2) that the markers in this book are not definitive histories and factual errors have occurred.

Lake Superior covers over 31,700 miles. The resting place for many sunken ships, this inland sea reaches a depth of 1,333 feet. (*Lake Superior*)

Alcona

Greenbush School

Built in 1870, across from the township hall, Greenbush School is one of Alcona County's pioneer schools. It remained a part of the Alcona County educational system until 1947. The school began with twenty-five students, kindergarten through eighth grade. During the lumbering era, when Greenbush grew into a settlement of fifteen hundred people, the school served up to sixty students. The building was moved to its present location, next to the Township Hall, in 1979. A fire hall was built on its original site.

On Campbell Road, one-half block west of State Road, Greenbush Township; Greenbush School; L728A; August 3, 1979; 1987

Alger

Lake Superior

Le lac superieur the French called it, meaning only that geographically it lay above Lake Huron. In size, however, Lake Superior stands above all other freshwater lakes in the world. The intrepid Frenchman Brule discovered it around 1622. During the 1650s and 1660s French fur traders, such as Radisson and Groseilliers, and Jesuits, such as Fathers Allouez and Menard, explored this great inland sea. Within 250 years fur-laden canoes had given way to huge boats carrying ore and grain to the world.

Scott Falls Roadside Park, M-28, eleven miles west of Munising, Au Train, Au Train Township; Lake Superior Informational Designation; S121; January 19, 1957; 1957

Paulson House

Swedish pioneer Charles Paulson purchased one hundred acres of land here in 1884 and constructed this cabin for his family home. Built of hand-hewn cedar logs securely dovetailed at the corners, the house was occupied by Paulson and his wife until their deaths in 1925. At the turn of the century the three Paulson daughters were able to attend the district school, which met in the upper story. Today the restored Paulson House serves as a museum of pioneer life.

South of Au Train on USFS Road 2278 in Hiawatha National Forest (Sec. 6, T46N, R20W), Au Train Township; Paulson House; L176; February 11, 1972; 1972

Grand Marais

Grand Marais, which is among Michigan's oldest place names, received its name from French explorers, missionaries and traders who passed here in the 1600s. "Marais" in this case was a term used by the *voyageurs* to designate a harbor of refuge. In the 1800s, Lewis Cass, Henry Schoolcraft and Douglass Houghton also found the sheltered harbor a welcome stopping place. Grand Marais's permanent settlement dates from the 1860s with the establishment of fishing and lumbering. At the turn of the century Grand Marais was a boom town served by a railroad from the south. Its mills turned out many millions of board feet annually. Lumbering declined around 1910, and Grand Marais became almost a ghost town, but the fishing industry continued. Many shipping disasters have occurred at or near this harbor of refuge, which has been served by the Coast Guard since 1899. In 1942 the first radar station in Michigan was built in Grand Marais. Fishing, lumbering and tourism now give Grand Marais its livelihood.

Bay Shore Park, Grand Marais Avenue, Grand Marais, Burt Township; Grand Marais Informational Designation; S240; August 14, 1962; 1968

Lobb House

One of the most graceful houses in Munising, this structure, built in 1905-1906, was the home of Elizabeth Lobb. Madame Lobb, as she was affectionately known, gained her wealth from a mine that was discovered on property that she and her husband, Edward, owned in Marquette County. Thirteen years after the death of her husband, Madame Lobb erected this handsome residence. She and her son Nathaniel operated a large brickyard in nearby Hallston until 1910. The Alger County Historical Society purchased this structure for a museum in 1974.

203 West Onota Street, Munising; Lobb House (Lobb/Madigan House); L259; December 11, 1973; 1980

Allegan
Allegan County

Allegan County's name was coined by the noted student of the Indians, Henry Schoolcraft. The county was set off in 1831 and organized in 1835. Settlement of the county seat, Allegan, was promoted in 1835 by eastern capitalists who were attracted by the site's sources of water power. For many years steamboats plied the Kalamazoo between here and Saugatuck. Extensive lumbering by the pioneers cleared the way for farm production in which the county has been a leader.

Allegan County Courthouse, 113 Chestnut, Allegan; Allegan County Informational Designation; S226; November 14, 1961; 1962

Episcopal Church of the Good Shepherd

On June 15, 1858, the Episcopal Church of the Good Shepherd was organized; its parish was admitted into the Diocese of Michigan two years later. Built in 1866-1869, this Gothic structure was designed by Gordon W. Lloyd and first used for Divine Service on Palm Sunday, March 21, 1869. Bishop McCoskry performed the rite of consecration on April 8 of that same year. In 1886 the parishioners purchased the present tracker organ, which is still in use, and one of the few such organs left in this state today.

101 Walnut Street, Allegan; Church of the Good Shepherd (Allegan Episcopal Church) L243; July 26, 1973; 1971

The Second Street Bridge

This simply ornamented wrought-iron bridge was built in 1866. It replaced an earlier wooden one that had begun to fall into disrepair. Designed by the King Iron Bridge and Manufacturing Company of Cleveland, Ohio, the double-intersection Pratt truss bridge was completed at a cost of $7,532.25. Eighteen feet wide and spanning 225 feet of the Kalamazoo River, it is one of the largest extant bridges designed by the firm. Following a battle by city officials and local citizens to save the bridge from demolition, it was restored at a cost of $552,000 in 1983. The bridge was listed in the National Register of Historic Places in 1980.

Second Street at the Kalamazoo River, Allegan; Second Street Bridge; S549A; September 8, 1982; 1984

Ebenezer Reformed Church

Members of the First Reformed Church in Holland founded this congregation in 1866 to provide a place of worship for the settlers living southeast of town. Heavy immigration from The Netherlands prompted this move. The Dutch language was used exclusively at first, and some services in Dutch continued until 1937. Three buildings have been used for worship; the first church, dedicated in 1867, was destroyed by fire in 1883. Replaced immediately by a second structure, the third and present house of worship was dedicated in 1964.

A11048 Ottogan (Thirty-second Street), corner of Fifty-second Street, Fillmore Township; Ebenezer Reformed Church Informational Designation; L77; February 27, 1970; 1971

Graafschap Reformed Christian Church

Erected in 1862, this church was the center of the Dutch immigrant community. The first settlers in this area arrived in early 1847 led by the Reverend Albertus C. Van Raalte. In June of that year a separate group of seventy people from Graafschap Betheim, near the Dutch border, founded this village, which they named Graafschap. Joined by thirty-four other immigrants from Drenthe, The Netherlands, the villagers shared common religious views and spoke similar dialects. Before erecting a log church in 1849 near this site, these early settlers attended services conducted by Van Raalte in nearby Holland. Graafschap followed Van Raalte's example by affiliating with the Reformed Church in America in 1850. Seven years later the congregation severed that tie and reasserted its independence.

Side Two

Those who established this church were among thousands of Europeans who sought to escape religious and political persecution and economic depression by emigrating to America in the 1840s. Later Graafschap was one of the founding members of the Christian Reformed Church which bound itself closely to Dutch customs and ways of thinking, as evidenced by the fact that this church's parishioners continued to speak Dutch for two generations. This structure is made of hand-hewn timber and one of the roof beams spans its entire length. Although modified by the addition of educational facilities in 1922 and the expansion of the entry in 1937 and 1949, the main church structure remains intact. The Graafschap Christian Reformed Church is a noteworthy symbol of continuity in what is still a predominately Dutch-German-American community.

621 Church Street, on Forty-eighth Street, one mile west of Washington Avenue, Fillmore Towhship; Graafschap (Graafschap Christian Reformed Church); L483; December 14, 1976; 1977

Old Wing Mission

The main portion of this building was the residence of George N. Smith, a Congregational missionary to the Indians in this area and at Waukazoo's Village on nearby Lake Macatawa. The mission was named after an Indian convert. Built in 1844-1845 by Isaac Fairbanks, a government agricultural agent to the Indians, this house is the oldest structure in the vicinity. Nearby were a church and school, and some Indian dwellings. The first Dutch settlers in 1846-1847 lodged here and in the Fairbanks cabin on the knoll to the southeast. As the Dutch settlement grew, Smith and the Indians moved away and established a new village on Grand Traverse Bay. Isaac Fairbanks remained in this area and was active in the settlement of Holland.

5298 East 147th Avenue, between 52nd and 50th streets, Fillmore Township; Old Wing Mission; L70; December 8, 1967; 1969

Pier Cove

Surveyed in 1839, the village of Pier Cove was once hailed as "the busiest port between St. Joseph and Muskegon." Before the Civil War, Pier Cove was a bustling community and a major point for lumber distribution, with ships departing daily carrying tanbark and cordwood to Chicago and Milwaukee. With the exhaustion of the lumber supply in the late 1860s, the fire of 1871 and the coming of the railroad, the sawmill was moved to Fennville and Pier Cove's prosperity diminished. In the 1880s, however, fruit became a major shipping commodity. This site once overlooked the warehouse and two piers that revived the village's economy. In 1899 a freeze killed much of the local harvest and shipping at Pier Cove was reduced to passenger traffic. Commercial activity ceased in 1917.

Pier Cove Park, half way between 122nd Avenue and 124th Avenue on 70th Street (Lake Shore Drive), Pier Cove Informational Designation; L1628C; February 16, 1989; 1989

Oakland Christian Reformed Church

A Dutch settlement known as Oakland sprang up in this area about a decade after the founding of nearby Holland in 1847. Many residents worshipped with the Vriesland and Drenthe congregations until they formed their own churches. One group, North Overisel, had a church a half-mile to the north. Another group, East Overisel, worshipped in a schoolhouse to the southwest. In 1887 the two merged and built a church in the shape of a cross (Kruiskerk) by moving the North Overisel Church and using lumber of the East Overisel Church. The new church was named the Holland Christian Reformed Church of Doornspijk, after a small town in The Netherlands. In 1890 the name was changed to the Oakland Christian Reformed Church. The 1887 structure stood on this site until 1953, when the present building was erected.

4452 Thirty-eighth Street, Bentheim vicinity, Overisel Township; Christian Reformed Church of Doornspijk Informational Designation; L1318C; June 13, 1986; 1986

Overisel

Seeking religious liberty and better economic opportunity in a new land, the Reverend Seine Bolks and a congregation of about two dozen families left Hellendoorn, Province of

The soon-to-be-demolished Richardsonian Allegan County Courthouse, constructed in 1889-1890, looms over its replacement, completed in 1961. (*Allegan County*)

Overisel, The Netherlands, on August 18, 1847. The group wintered in Syracuse, New York, before continuing its journey to "Black Lake Country" (present-day Lake Macatawa) in Michigan. The Overisel settlers joined Dutch immigrants in the Holland settlement in June 1848. They selected land and pooled the gold they had brought with them to purchase two thousand acres of land from the government and speculators. Prices ranged from $1.25 to $3.00 per acre, and land assignments were determined by lot. The settlers then established the village of Overisel.

Overisel Reformed Church

The Dutch immigrants who established the Overisel congregation in June 1848 worshipped in homes until a log church was built in 1849. The congregation affiliated with the Reformed Church in America in 1850 and built a larger, frame church in 1851. This Greek Revival church was erected in 1866 and is one of the oldest extant Reformed church buildings in Michigan. The steeple was added in 1868. The value placed on education by the Overisel congregation is demonstrated by the unusually high number of members who have become ministers, missionaries, educators, scientists and other professionals. Among them was Dr. Gerrit J. Kollen, who was president of Hope College from 1893 to 1911.

A-4706 142nd Avenue, Overisel Township; Overisel Reformed Church; L1566B; June 30, 1988; 1988

All Saints Episcopal Church

An Episcopal parish was organized in Saugatuck on All Saints' Day, November 1, 1868. Services were held at various locations until 1873. In 1871 the parish purchased this property. Detroit architect Gordon W. Lloyd designed the Gothic Revival-style church building. Although services were first held on January 25, 1873, the church was not completed until 1874. After a period of decline that caused the parish to become a diocesan mission, full parish status was restored in 1946.

Gordon W. Lloyd

Gordon W. Lloyd (1832-1904) was among the Midwest's foremost church architects. He was trained at England's Royal Academy, under the tutelage of his uncle, Ewan Christian. Lloyd immigrated to the United States in 1858, settling in Detroit. In 1861 he designed Detroit's Christ Church. Among his other churches are Central United Methodist Church in Detroit, Grace Episcopal Church in Mount Clemens and St. Paul's Episcopal Church in Flint. The design of All Saints closely resembles that of his St. James Church of Grosse Ile.

252 Grand Street, SW corner of Hoffman Street, Saugatuck; All Saints Episcopal Church; L908A; April 24, 1981; 1983

Singapore, Michigan

Beneath the sands near the mouth of the Kalamazoo River lies the site of Singapore, one of Michigan's most famous ghost towns. Founded in the 1830s by New York land speculators who hoped it would rival Chicago or Milwaukee as a lake port, Singapore was in fact, until the 1870s, a busy lumbering town. With three mills, two hotels, several general stores, and a renowned "wildcat" bank, it outshone its neighbor to the south, "The Flats," as Saugatuck was then called. When the supply of timber was exhausted the mills closed; the once bustling waterfront grew quiet. The people left, most of them settling here in Saugatuck. Gradually, Lake Michigan's shifting sands buried Singapore.

Saugatuck City Hall, Butler Street, Saugatuck; Singapore Informational Designation; S191; April 16, 1958; 1958

Alpena

St. Bernard Catholic Church

In 1861, Bishop Frederic Baraga (1797-1868) trod through snow and icy waters from Sault Ste. Marie to Alpena where he founded a Catholic church. However, it was not until 1866 that Father Patrick Murray became the first resident pastor of the church dedicated to and named for St. Bernard. Father Murray was instrumental in the building of the first church structure, which was located almost directly opposite the current edifice. The foundation of this stone structure was laid in 1880. Three years later the church split into three parishes. The French parish, which kept the original structure, became St. Anne; the Polish became St. Mary; and the Irish retained the St. Bernard name and records. This structure, completed by the Irish in 1884, houses the oldest Catholic parish between Bay City and Cheboygan.

SE corner of Fifth and Chisholm streets, Alpena; St. Bernard Church (St. Bernard Catholic Church); L990A; February 18, 1982; 1983

World's Largest Cement Plant

Portland cement, so-called because it resembles in color stone from the Isle of Portland in the British Isles, was first produced in the United States in 1871, in Michigan in 1896. Because of Alpena's location in the midst of immense limestone deposits, the Huron Portland Cement Company, founded at Detroit in 1907, chose this site for its plant. Cement production began here in 1908. Able management and skilled workmen made this the world's largest cement plant. From Thunder Bay, ships of the Huron fleet deliver cement to all parts of the Great Lakes region.

Ford Avenue, roadside park east of Alpena, Alpena; Michigan's Cement Industry Informational Designation (Huron-Portland Cement Plant) S145; February 26, 1957; 1958

Antrim

Bellaire—The Antrim County Seat

The first pioneers of Antrim County settled along Grand Traverse Bay near Elk Rapids in the 1850s. Later settlers moved inland, and urged that the county seat be transferred from the bay shore closer to the geographical center of the county. After a close election in 1879, Keno, later named Bellaire, became the new county seat. Thus began a bitter controversy which was appealed to the state Supreme Court and lasted for twenty-five years. Although the courthouse square was purchased as early as 1879, the county building was not constructed until 1904-1905 after another vote. Designed by Jens C. Peterson, and built by Waterman and Price, the courthouse cost $30,000.

Bounded by Cayuga, West Court, North Broad and East Grove streets, Bellaire; Antrim County Courthouse; L274; April 5, 1974; 1974

Elk Rapids Iron Company

The brick ruin near this marker was the hearth of the Elk Rapids furnace, during the 1870s

Although built in 1904-1905, the Antrim County Courthouse was still "clockless" on July 4, 1919. (*Bellaire-Antrim County Seat*)

one of the nation's greatest producers of charcoal iron. Forty-seven feet high and twelve feet in diameter, it was begun in 1872 and produced the first blast of iron on June 24, 1873. The local logging firm of Dexter and Noble constructed the furnace, locating it in Elk Rapids to utilize the vast stands of hardwood timber which surrounded the town. The hardwood was converted to charcoal to fire the furnace, and iron ore was imported from the Upper Peninsula by freighter. Once the town's major employer, the furnace closed during World War I when the nearby forests were depleted, and cheaper smelting processes were developed.

Ames Street in the yard of the Elks River Inn Motel, Elk Rapids; Elk Rapids Iron Company Informational Site; S292; February 28, 1969; 1973

The Island House

Edwin S. Noble (1838-1922) designed and built this house for his family in 1865. Noble, an expert accountant, was associated with the Dexter-Noble Company, first as secretary-treasurer and later as a full partner. The company was involved in logging and the production of chemicals, flour and high-quality pig iron. It also operated a store and a brick yard. By 1882 the firm, then known as the Elk Rapids Iron Company, had become the largest employer in town. Edwin Noble, a driving force behind the iron company for over two decades, transformed a four-acre sand dune into this scenic island area by covering it with clay and dark loam and planting over sixty species of trees on it. He built a broad bridge over the river to connect the island with the town. In 1949 a part of the Island House became a public library.

Isle of Pines Drive, Elk Rapids; Noble, Edwin, House (The Island House); L648A; April 24, 1979; 1985

Township Hall

Designed by Charles H. Peale and built in 1883 near the site where the earliest white settler, Abram Wadsworth, had lived, the Elk Rapids Township Hall has served as a social and political center for over ninety years. Largely due to lumbering and related industries, the village was the most important economic force in the area. Located on Grand Traverse Bay, the prosperous community needed a permanent meeting place. Thus this hall was erected and has hosted theatrical, patriotic, school and township activities.

River Street, Elk Rapids; Elk Rapids Township Hall; L59; November 15, 1973; 1969

Village of Wetzell

On November 10, 1881, the *Antrim County Herald* ran an advertisement about the village of Wetzell that read: "New Town, New Store; Everything New!" Earlier that year the Wetzell brothers had platted the village and opened a sawmill. As the town grew the pine forests were depleted. In 1886, Frank Harding changed Wetzell into a company town when he converted the sawmill into a wood turning factory that utilized the area's abundant hardwood forests. Harding attracted millhands to the town by guaranteeing them "steady work, good wages, free stove wood, free rent and water." Wetzell boomed, but its prosperity was fleeting. By 1909 timber supplies were low, the factory operated sporadically and Harding decided to cease operations. Without a new industry to sustain it, Wetzell became a ghost town.

Corner of US-131 North and Satterly Lake Road, north of Mancelona, Mancelona Township; Wetzell, Village of, Informational Designation; L1618C; January 19, 1989; 1989

Arenac

Omer Masonic Hall

This church-like white frame structure with its graceful cupola was built in 1890 as the second Arenac County Courthouse. The first courthouse on this site burned the previous year. Omer had been a part of Bay County until Arenac was organized in 1883 and this city, then a village, became the county seat. Less than a decade later, voters made nearby Standish the county seat. The Grand Lodge of Free and Accepted Masons of the state of Michigan purchased this building in 1893 for the Omer Masonic Lodge; that group and the Order of the Eastern Star still hold meetings here. Surviving the disastrous fire of 1914, which swept through Omer's business district, this edifice housed the temporary headquarters of several firms. It is one of the city's oldest buildings.

Central Avenue (US-23), east of Main Road, Omer; Second Arenac County Courthouse (Omer Masonic Hall); L444; March 2, 1976; 1977

Baraga

Keweenaw Bay

This region's history is long and rich. Father Menard, the Jesuit missionary, wintered near what is now L'Anse in 1660-1661. Near here Father Baraga set up his mission in 1843. He and the head of the neighboring Methodist mission, the Reverend J. H. Pitezel, were good friends. Furs and fish figured prominently in the bay's early history as a source of economic wealth. In the 1880s and 1890s the area's timber was cut with Baraga and Pequaming being the centers of lumbering.

Baraga State Park on US-41, one-quarter mile south of Baraga, Baraga Township; Keweenaw Bay Informational Designation; S135; January 19, 1957; 1963

L'Anse-Lac Vieux Desert Trail

Near this spot ran the L'Anse-Lac Vieux Desert Trail, which crossed the interior of the Upper Peninsula of Michigan from L'Anse on Keweenaw Bay to Lac Vieux Desert on the

Wisconsin border. The trail was used in prehistoric times by Native Americans traveling to visit, hunt or trade. Father Rene Menard may have followed this route in 1661 as he traveled south from Keweenaw Bay, a trip from which he never returned. The trail was later used by fur traders, early surveyors and homesteaders. L'Anse and Lac Vieux Desert bands of Chippewa Indians used this trail into the twentieth century. Today, many segments of the L'Anse-Lac Vieux Desert Trail are unpaved roads that can be traveled by car.

*US-41 North, L'Anse; L'Anse-Lac Vieux Desert Trail Informational Designation; L1198C; November 15, 1984; 1985.

Zeba United Methodist Church

Early Methodist missionaries came to Kewawenon from Sault Sainte Marie by canoe, often a two-week trip. Among them was John Sunday, a Chippewa, who arrived in 1832 to educate and Christianize his fellow Indians. John Clark came two years later and erected a school and mission house. By 1845 this mission consisted of a farm and a church with fifty-eight Indian and four white members. A second church, erected in 1850, was dedicated by John H. Pitezel, who served here from 1844 to 1847.

Side Two

Indians from far and near came here to attend the annual camp meetings which began in 1880. The present frame church, known now as the Zeba Indian Mission church, was erected in 1888. Completely covered with hand-made wooden shingles, this structure has changed little since its construction. The Methodist minister of L'Anse serves the congregation. The Zeba Indian United Methodist church, the successor of the 1832 Kewawenon mission, is an area landmark.

Peter Marksman Road, three and one-half miles NE of L'Anse, L'Anse Township; Kewawenon Mission (Zeba United Methodist Church); L638A; January 29, 1979; 1979

Barry

Carlton Township Hall

Receiving its name from Carlton Township in western New York, this area was settled in 1836 by Samuel Wickham and George Fuller. The township was formally organized in 1842. This structure, built in 1867, is recognized by the Michigan Township Association as the fourth-oldest township hall in the state. A center of political and social activity, it is much the same as it was when completed and is still heated with a wood-burning stove.

M-43 west of M-66, Carlton Center, Carlton Township; Carlton Township Hall; L693A; August 3, 1979; 1982

Barryville

This village was settled in the mid-nineteenth century, and in 1857 a post office was opened. By 1860 a town of several blocks was established, and the businesses included a gristmill, hotel and sash factory. The gristmill, run by Melatiah J. Lathrop, was the principal industry for a number of years. The Grand River Valley Railroad bypassed Barryville in 1869, and soon population declined. One hundred people lived here in the early 1870s, but by the next decade only fifteen remained. The mill operated until the turn of the century.

Peace United Methodist Church, 6043 Scott Road, Castleton Township; Barryville Informational Designation; L86; November 6, 1970; 1971

Early Hastings

Barry County, organized in 1839, was named after U.S. Postmaster General William Barry. Hastings, the county seat, was platted in 1836 and chartered as a village in 1855. The present courthouse was completed in 1892. A newspaper was published here in 1851, and in 1869 the first railroad reached town. Dr. William Upjohn, founder of the pharmaceutical firm that bears his name, established his practice here after the Civil War and perfected a process for the commercial manufacture of the friable pill. Judge Ella C. Eggleston, one of the first women probate judges in the state, began her term of office here in 1919.

220 West State Street, SE corner of Broadway, Hastings; Barry County Courthouse (Barry County Courthouse/Early Hastings); S291; February 28, 1969; 1969

Governor Kim Sigler

Kim Sigler (1894-1953), a native of Schuyler, Nebraska, received his law degree from the University of Detroit in 1918. While attending law school, Sigler worked at Henry Ford's Highland Park plant. He first practiced law in Detroit, where he worked in the office of Edwin Denby, former secretary of the Navy, and Judge Arthur Webster. In 1922 his family moved to Hastings. A Democrat at that time, he was elected as Barry County prosecutor for three consecutive terms. In 1928 he unsuccessfully ran against Wilber M. Brucker for attorney general. In the late 1920s, Sigler took office as city attorney, serving in that capacity for over ten years. He returned to private practice and moved to Battle Creek in 1943.

Side Two

Kim Sigler's vigor and courtroom manner led to his selection as a special prosecutor for a grand jury probe of legislative graft in 1943. The success of this investigation gave him a statewide reputation. Though originally a Democrat, he won the Republican gubernatorial nomination and election in 1946. His was one of the largest gubernatorial majorities in the country that year. In office, he created the Department of Administration, effected changes in the Prison and Corrections Department and revitalized the unemployment compensation program and the Public Service Commission. However, he faced an uncooperative legislature and division within his cabinet. He was defeated for reelection in 1948. He died while piloting his own plane in a crash near Battle Creek on November 30, 1953.

Barry County Courthouse, 220 West State Street, Hastings; Sigler, Governor Kim, Informational Designation; S586C; January 22, 1987; 1987

Hastings Mutual Insurance Company

On April 5, 1885, the Michigan Mutual Tornado, Cyclone, and Windstorm Insurance Company became the first mutual windstorm company incorporated by the state of Michigan. Starting in a one-room office above Grant's store, the company occupied and outgrew five sites in Hastings. Locally the firm was called the Windstorm Company, while out of town it was known as the Hastings Company. In 1920 its name was formally changed to the Michigan Mutual Windstorm Insurance Company. On January 15, 1959, the company became a general mutual, taking the name Hastings Mutual Insurance Company. Over the years, the firm has expanded to write policies for commercial, home and farm property, workers' compensation, automobile and marine insurance.

404 East Woodlawn Avenue, Hastings; Hastings Mutual Insurance Company Informational Designation; S561C; June 15, 1984; 1984

Railroad Depot

Hastings was first linked with Jackson and Grand Rapids by the Grand River Valley Railroad in 1870. The Michigan Central Railroad leased the line that same year. At first located elsewhere, a passenger station was built on this site in 1882. In 1922 this brick structure was constructed with the aid of the Rotary Club. Passenger service was discontinued in 1959 and in 1968 the building was privately purchased. Restored and furnished in the style of the 1850s, it now houses law offices.

222 West Apple Street, NW corner of Church Street, Hastings; Hastings Railroad Depot; L285; July 26, 1974; 1974

Striker House

Built in the 1880s by Daniel Striker, this Queen Anne-style building was once considered the "handsomest residence in Hastings." Born in New York State in 1835, Striker moved as a child with his family to Michigan. He was elected to several offices in Barry County, became a lawyer, and in 1871-1875 was elected Michigan secretary of state. Striker was also widely known in banking circles. He died in 1898, and after the death of his wife in 1915 the house became a hospital, later a convalescent home.

321 South Jefferson Street, Hastings; Striker, Daniel, House; L88; November 6, 1970; 1971

Indian Landing-Charlton Park

In the early nineteenth century the Thornapple Band of Ottawa Indians established a village a short distance from Thornapple Lake. It was served in the 1840s by a Methodist mission and school conducted by the Reverend Mannaseh Hickey. Trails leading to Canada and the

Grand River intersected near the northeast end of the lake. In 1848 four Indian families purchased land here, remaining until their removal to northern Michigan about 1855. In 1936, Irving D. Charlton donated the land to Barry County for a park in memory of his parents and founded a museum with a large collection of pioneer artifacts. He served as director until his death in 1963.

Charlton Park, 2545 South Charlton Park Road, Hastings Township; Indian Landing-Charlton Park; L215; March 14, 1973; 1973

Putnam Public Library

Built in 1884-1885, this red-bricked Italianate structure was the home of Charles W. and Agnes Putnam. Mr. Putnam was a hardware merchant and banker; Mrs. Putnam taught music and was the first public school teacher in Nashville. Around the turn of the century, the Putnams hosted many elegant social events here. In 1921 they willed their home to Nashville for use as a public library. They established a $10,000 trust fund to begin its operation. The Woman's Literary Club launched the library in 1923.

327 North Main Street (M-66), north of Washington Street, Nashville; Putnam, Charles W., House (Charles W. Putnam Public Library); L801A; April 21, 1980; 1982

Thomas's Mill

In 1850, George Thomas operated a sawmill here, and in the next decade as settlers began to arrive he built a gristmill. The new village, also known as Gull Lake, was a few miles south of the Reverend Leonard Slater's Baptist Indian mission. Thomas dominated local affairs, being the leading merchant, the postmaster, a large land owner and a member of the state legislature. At the turn of the century, when the village was practically abandoned, Gull Lake became popular as a summer resort.

M-43, north end of Gull Lake Park, Prairieville Township; Thomas's Mill; L87; November 6, 1970; 1971

Parmelee United Methodist Church

In 1878 twelve persons organized the Parmelee Methodist Church. The small congregation met at various locations until 1884, when this church was built on land given to the Methodist Trustee Board by Oliver and Bernice Carpenter. On September 15, 1884, the congregation held its first services in the original portion of this Gothic-style wood-frame building. The following year the Reverend M. D. Marsh became the church's first resident pastor. In 1903, Clara Joels, daughter of the village's founder Erastus K. Parmelee, gave additional property to the church for a horse and buggy shed. In 1913 a basement was built beneath the church. In 1961 the final addition was completed.

Parmelee Road, east of Stimson, Thornapple Township; Parmelee United Methodist Church; L1367A; January 22, 1987; 1988

Scales's Prairie

In 1834, Louis Moran, member of a French family prominent in Detroit since the mid-1700s, purchased land here and opened a log tavern and trading post. An Indian settlement called Middle Village was nearby, on the trail from Gull Prairie to Grand Rapids. Moran moved to Grand Rapids about 1837 and his interests were taken over by nineteen-year-old Robert Scales of Kentucky. Since then the area has been known as Scales's Prairie although its namesake departed after a ten-year residence.

Corner of Adams and Norris roads, west of M-37, Thornapple Township; Scales's Prairie Informational Designation; L191; February 11, 1972; 1972

Woodland Town Hall

The area now known as Woodland Township was first settled in 1837 by Charles Galloway and Jonathan and Samuel Haight. In 1842 the state legislature set aside the township, which by then had several hundred residents. The area's level surface and fertile soil attracted farmers who specialized in fruit, wheat and vegetables. By 1867, Woodland's population had grown to about one thousand. On April 5 of that year, the township board voted to build a "town house." The building committee—consisting of George Cramer, George Davenport, Alson P. Holly, John Holbrook and Ira Stowell—drafted a plan, and construction began. The township board accepted the completed town hall and discharged the building committee three years later.

Side Two

30

In 1867 after agreeing to build a hall, the Woodland Township board purchased this property from Lawrence Hilbert. Building committee member George Davenport erected the frame for the Greek Revival structure and later built the front doors. S. S. Ingerson enclosed the building, and Ira Stowell, another member of the building committee, was responsible for the completion of the hall. The handsome structure, with its hand-hewn timbers, cost nearly $2,000. The two-story, thirty-by-forty-eight-foot hall has been used by the township, fraternal organizations, traveling shows, community programs and a school. By 1984 the town hall was the only virtually unaltered early building in the community. Heated by a free-standing wood stove, it was still used for the annual township meeting.

SW corner of East Broadway (M-43) and State Street, Woodland; Woodland Township Hall; L940A; August 22, 1981; 1984

Bowen's Mills

Settlement began here in the mid-1830s, and in 1850 a post office known as Gun Lake was established. The village, never over one hundred [in] population, contained a sawmill, general store, blacksmith shop and several other businesses. E. H. Bowen constructed the present gristmill in 1864 and in 1870 the name of the town was changed to honor its leading citizen. Bowen and his son William operated the mill, famous for its buckwheat flour, until 1912. Production continued until [the] mid-twentieth century.

Brigg's Road, two miles north of Chief Noonday Road, Yankee Springs Township; Bowen's Mills; L192; February 11, 1972; 1972

Yankee Springs Inn

Near here once stood one of the most famous inns west of Detroit. It was run by "Yankee Bill" Lewis, a New Yorker who came here in 1836. His establishment, located on the main road from Grand Rapids to Battle Creek and Kalamazoo, was an unimposing collection of log cabins, but the fame of his hospitality was such that as many as one hundred people often stayed at the tavern for a night. Sixty teams of horses could be stabled at a time. Stagecoaches stopped there to rest passengers and to change horses. After Lewis's death in 1853 new roads bypassed Yankee Springs. His inn soon closed.

Yankee Springs Road, one-quarter mile north of Duffy Road, Yankee Springs Township; Yankee Springs Inn (Yankee Springs Recreation Area); S159; September 17, 1957; 1958

Bay

Ogaukawning Church

Established in 1847, the Ogaukawning Indian Mission, the first church in present-day Bay County, served Chippewa Indians at the nearby Kawkawlin settlement. First ministered by Methodist missionaries, it soon came under Indian trusteeship and still remains so. This site has been the social and religious center of the community since the 1840s. Several Indian pastors officiated at the Kawkawlin Mission, the last in 1947.

Hidden Road at North Euclid Road, Bangor Township; Ogaukawning Church; L1526A; June 30, 1988; 1990

Saginaw Bay

This bay derives its name from the Sauk Indians who once dwelt by its shores. Adrien Jolliet, on his voyage down Lake Huron's western shore in 1669, first made it known to the white man. In the late 1800s an immense lumber industry flourished in the region. Schooners by the scores daily passed through the bay bringing to the sawmills more logs and hauling off cut lumber. The bay's waters for years also made fishing good business.

Bay City State Park, three miles north of Bay City on M-247, Bangor Township; Saginaw Bay Informational Designation; S14; October 30, 1956; 1957

Bay City

Although French explorers had visited this area in the 1600s, a permanent white settlement occurred only in the 1830s. During the Civil War period the lumber industry developed, reaching its peak in 1882. When the lumbermen left, coal mining, fishing, shipbuilding and the production of beet sugar provided the basis for Bay City's economic growth.

Sixth Street, Wenonah Park, Bay City; Bay City Informational Designation; S43; July 19, 1956; 1956

Sage Public Library

Henry W. Sage (1814-1897) founded the village of Wenona (later West Bay City) in 1863. A merchant and philanthropist, he was also a founder of the Sage, McGraw & Company saw-mill. In 1881 he donated property, building funds and $10,000 for books to West Bay City for this, its first public library. The structure was built in 1882-1883 at a cost of nearly $50,000. Charles Babcock of Cornell University designed the French Chateauesque-style building, and the local architectural firm of Pratt & Koeppe superintended the construction. The library was dedicated on January 16, 1884, in a ceremony presided over by Cornell's Moses Coit Tyler. Michigan Supreme Court judges, congressmen and state officials attended. Offering continuous public library service since 1884, the library was listed on the National Register of Historic Places in 1980.

100 East Midland Street, east of Winona Avenue, Bay City; Sage Library (Sage Branch Library of the Bay County Library System); L639A; January 29, 1979; 1984

Swedish Evangelical Lutheran Sion Church

During the 1870s, Swedish immigrants arrived in Bay County. By 1880 many Swedes had settled in West Bay City. In October of that year, fifty people organized the Swedish Evangelical Lutheran Sion Church, affiliated with the Augustana Synod. A year later, a church and parsonage were built here on land donated by lumberman Henry W. Sage. In 1938 the church was renamed Messiah Evangelical Lutheran Church. The present building was completed in 1956.

501 South Catherine Street, SW corner of Thomas and Henry streets, Bay City; Swedish Evangelical Lutheran Sion Church Informational Designation; L1779C; August 23, 1990; 1990

"Ten Hours or No Sawdust"

When Bay City's sawmills opened in 1885, mill owners notified workers that wages would be twelve to twenty-five percent lower than in 1884. On July 6, 1885, Bay City millhands began to walk off the job. Their slogan, "Ten Hours or No Sawdust," represented their demand for a ten-hour workday, higher wages and semimonthly pay. On July 9, 1885, D. C. Blinn, editor of Bay City's *Labor Vindicator* and a member of the Knights of Labor, held a rally at Bay City's Madison Park. After the rally, millhands left by barge for Saginaw, where they closed the mills the next day. The demands of the millhands were rejected, and the sporadic violence that followed led the mayors of Bay City and Saginaw to seek help from the state militia and private detectives.

Side Two

On July 14, 1885, Governor Russell A. Alger, a wealthy lumberman, came to Bay City to attempt to resolve the strike that had closed Bay City and Saginaw mills. From the steps of the Frazer Hotel, across the street from this site, he spoke to a crowd of millhands, warning against further violence. On July 29, Terence V. Powderly, Grand Master of the Knights of Labor, came to the valley. He urged the millhands to return to work with a ten-hour day and reduced wages. Nevertheless, the strike continued for several weeks, with support from the people of Bay City. The mill owners, however, remained intransigent, and by late September the strikers were defeated. The ten-hour workday went into effect on September 15, 1885, by an act of the state legislature, but wages remained low.

Water and Sixth streets, Bay City; Bay City's Sawdust Strike Informational Designation (Wenonah Park); L1413C; May 15, 1987; 1987

Beet Sugar Industry

The first successful beet sugar factory in Michigan was built in 1898 by the Michigan Sugar Company on Woodside Avenue in Essexville. A year later the Bay City Sugar Company built a competing factory across the street. The two plants merged in 1903 with the original plant closing down shortly thereafter. The name of the merged company was Bay City-Michigan Sugar Company, which was then shortened to Michigan Sugar Company. It operated continuously until 1929 and closed permanently in 1933. The company's early success sparked the construction of many other beet sugar plants. All were part of the drive which has made beet sugar vital to Michigan's economy. The present Monitor Sugar factory is the only beet sugar plant still in operation in Bay County.

North side of the 1100 block of Woodside Avenue, Essexville; Sugar Factories; S356; December 10, 1971; 1977

Beet Sugar

One of the first attempts in America to produce beet sugar was made in Michigan at White Pigeon late in the 1830s. The venture did not succeed though the future governor, John Barry, went to Europe seeking to learn its production methods. In 1888, Dr. Robert C. Kedzie of Michigan Agricultural College began encouraging farmers in the state to grow sugar beets. At Bay City in 1898 the state's first successful factory opened. Thereafter the Saginaw Valley became the sugar bowl of Michigan.

Two miles south of Bay City on M-13, in Veteran's Park, Portsmouth Township; Beet Sugar Industry Informational Designation; S129; January 19, 1957; 1957

Benzie

Benzonia College

In 1858, in what was then a remote wilderness, the Reverend Charles E. Bailey and four families from his Ohio Congregational parish founded Benzonia colony. It was to be an "educational Christian colony" modeled after the earlier Congregational settlements at Oberlin, Ohio, and Olivet, Michigan. As an integral part of the new community, Grand Traverse College was chartered in 1863. Its first building was erected on this corner. During the pioneer era it provided college preparatory work and teacher training. The school reorganized as Benzonia College in 1891. It supplied college-level education until 1900. Benzonia Academy was then maintained until changed conditions led to its closing in 1918. Benzonia College and Academy fulfilled the founders' dream of bringing educational opportunity to northern Michigan.

River Road, Benzonia Village Park, US-31, Benzonia; Benzonia College Informational Designation (Grand Traverse College); S245; July 10, 1963; 1964

Benzonia Congregational Church

Early in the 1850s Congregationalists came to this area to found the community of Benzonia and a Christian college. In 1860 the Reverend Charles E. Bailey, prime figure behind the organization of the community and college, helped organize the area's first church with eighteen members. Erected in 1884-1887, this Gothic Revival-style building served the congregation until 1968. In 1969 the building became the Benzie Area Historical Museum.

694 Grand Traverse Avenue, one block west of US-31, Benzonia; Benzonia Congregational Church (Benzie Area Historical Museum); L879A; February 23, 1981; 1983

Henry Bernstein's WPA mural, painted for the Frankfort Post Office in 1941, depicts the sinking of car ferry *Ann Arbor 4* on February 14, 1923. (*Car Ferries*)

Bruce Catton

Historian, author, editor, Bruce Catton (1899-1978) is best known for his two Civil War trilogies—*The Army of the Potomac* and *The Centennial History of the Civil War*. Born in Petoskey, Catton spent most of his childhood in Benzonia, where his father accepted a teaching position at Benzonia Academy. In 1906 he became the academy's principal. The Cattons lived in this building, which was the principal's home and the girls' dormitory. Catton had served in the navy and worked for newspapers and the federal government when, at the age of fifty-one, he published his first Civil War book, *Mr. Lincoln's Army*. In 1954 he became editor of *American Heritage* magazine and was awarded the Pulitzer Prize for *A Stillness at Appomattox*. He died at his Frankfort, Michigan, summer home in 1978.

Side Two

Bruce Catton's fascination with the Civil War began in Benzonia, where he grew up with Civil War veterans, who "gave a color and a tone, not merely to our village life, but to the concept of life with which we grew up." He was impressed by their certainty, their values and their faith in bravery, patriotism, freedom and the progress of the human race. He wrote, "I think I was always subconsciously driven by an attempt to restate that faith and to show where it was properly grounded, how it grew out of what a great many young men on both sides felt and believed and were brave enough to do." In the 1970s, Catton turned his thoughts to his native state, writing *Waiting for the Morning Train*, an account of the Michigan of his boyhood, and *Michigan: A Bicentennial History*.

891 Michigan Avenue, Benzonia; Bruce Catton Boyhood Home Informational Site (Benzonia Library); S560C; May 8, 1984; 1984

Mills Community House

This building was a girls dormitory erected in 1909 for the Benzonia Academy. Named Mills Cottage in honor of the Reverend Harlow S. Mills, pastor of the Benzonia Congregational Church from 1896 to 1916, it became the property of that church when the academy closed in 1918. Renamed Mills Community House, it hosts local gatherings and houses a public library. Its purposes are consistent with the educational and religious beliefs held by the town's early settlers.

891 Michigan Avenue, Benzonia; Mills Cottage (Mills Community House); 1977

Pacific Salmon

Since 1870 several unsuccessful attempts have been made to establish Pacific salmon in the Great Lakes. In 1966 at this site the Department of Conservation released coho fingerlings, hatchery-reared from eggs given by the state of Oregon. They migrated to Lake Michigan and fed on its enormous alewife population. Augmented by subsequent annual plantings, the coho became firmly established. By 1970 the sport fishery catch reached ten million pounds. Other species of Pacific salmon—the chinook and kokanee—were also successfully introduced to the Great Lakes area in the late 1960s. To complete their life cycle the salmon return to their home stream to spawn and then die. Millions of salmon are now planted each year. In 1973 the world's largest recorded coho, weighing over thirty-nine pounds, was taken at a state weir.

15210 US-31, Beulah; Platte River Hatchery; S417; February 22, 1974; 1974

Marquette's Death

On May 18, 1675, Father Jacques Marquette, the great Jesuit missionary and explorer, died and was buried by two French companions somewhere along the Lake Michigan shore of the Lower Peninsula. Marquette had been returning to his mission at St. Ignace which he had left in 1673 to go on an exploring trip to the Mississippi and the Illinois country. The exact location of Marquette's death has long been a subject of controversy. Evidence presented in the 1960s indicates that this site, near the natural outlet of the Betsie River, at the northeast corner of a hill which was here until 1900, is the Marquette death site and that the Betsie is the Riviere du Pere Marquette of early French accounts and maps. Marquette's bones were reburied at St. Ignace in 1677.

Cannon Park, Main Street, shore of Lake Michigan, Frankfort; Marquette's Death Informational Site; S272; June 11, 1965; 1965

Car Ferries on Lake Michigan

Lake Michigan, over three hundred miles long and up to eighty miles wide, blocked rail traffic between lower Michigan and Wisconsin, posing a serious problem to several Michigan lines in the late 1800s as logging revenues declined. In 1892 car-ferry operations from Lake Betsie to Kewaunee, Wisconsin, were begun by the Ann Arbor Railroad. This was the world's first use of car-ferries across such an expanse of open water. Other ferries were soon operating from Ludington, Grand Haven and Muskegon to terminals across the lake, thus forging a vital link in America's railroad network.

*Originally on River Road at Lake Michigan, Frankfort, now in the collections of the Michigan Historical Museum, Lansing; Car Ferries on Lake Michigan Informational Designation; S122; January 19, 1957; 1958

Berrien

The Morton House

This house, built in 1849 by Eleazar Morton and his son Henry, was occupied until 1936 by four generations of Mortons. The oak-framed barn was built in 1840. Members of the Morton family, pioneers in this area, were prominent in Benton Harbor's early development. The porch on the house was often called the "Indian Hotel" because Henry Morton allowed the Potawatomi Indians to sleep here on their way to St. Joseph to sell their baskets. J. Stanley Morton, president of the Graham and Morton Transportation Company, modernized the house and added the pillars in 1912. He left his home to the Benton Harbor Federation of Women's Clubs in appreciation of its civic work.

501 Territorial Road, Benton Harbor; Morton House/Indian Hotel (Benton Harbor Federation of Women's Club Building); L37; February 11, 1964; 1964

The Fruit Belt

Because of Lake Michigan's moderating effect, a narrow coastal strip from Indiana to Grand Traverse Bay, three hundred miles north, is blessed by a climate uniquely suited to fruit growing. This fact was observed by the 1840s when peaches already were being shipped from Berrien County to Chicago. Apples, cherries, berries, grapes, pears and plums added to the fame of the "fruit belt." One of the world's great fruit markets has developed here in Benton Harbor to provide an outlet for these bountiful crops.

Originally erected at Benton Harbor Fruit Market, SW corner of Bond and Eleventh streets, Benton Harbor. Present location is at the Benton Harbor Fruit Market, Territorial Road between Crystal Avenue and Euclid, Benton Township; Fruit Belt; S155; September 17, 1957; 1958

Andrews University

This, the oldest Seventh-day Adventist college and the pioneer in a world-wide system of Christian education, was chartered in 1874 at Battle Creek as Battle Creek College. It was moved to Berrien Springs in 1901 where its name was changed to Emmanuel Missionary College. The first classes here were held in tents. The old Berrien County Courthouse served as an administration building. Permanent buildings were erected by student labor. In 1960 the Adventists' Theological Seminary, founded in 1934, and the Graduate School (1957), were moved here from Washington, D.C., to join Emmanuel Missionary College under one charter as Andrews University. The name honors a pioneer Adventist author, administrator and missionary, John Nevins Andrews.

Labardy Road, Berrien Springs; Andrews University Campus; S250; September 13, 1963; 1965

Berrien Springs Courthouse

This building, a fine example of the Greek Revival style, was designed by Gilbert B. Avery in 1838. James Lewis, the contractor, agreed to complete the building by April 1839. Built almost entirely of whitewood, the courthouse has hand-hewn timbers almost one foot square and forty feet long. In 1894 the county seat was transferred to St. Joseph, and the courthouse soon passed into private hands. For a number of years it was used as an armory for the Berrien Springs Light Guard and as a center for community gatherings. In 1922 the building was purchased by the Seventh-day Adventist Church, and in 1967 Berrien

County repurchased the courthouse to ensure its preservation.

NW corner of Union and Cass streets, Berrien Springs; Berrien County Courthouse (Berrien Springs Courthouse); HB50; May 10, 1968; 1970

Morris Chapel Church

The local Methodist Episcopal Society, the oldest Methodist society in Berrien Township, was organized in 1840. In 1846 it voted to name its church in honor of Bishop Thomas A. Morris, then the head of the Methodist Episcopal Church in Michigan. This church, the congregation's second one, was built in 1867. In 1919 the basement was completed for community and social gatherings. Jessie Shilliday and Mattie Barnd bequeathed money for renovating both the exterior and interior of the church.

NW corner of Pucker Street and Chapel Road, Berrien Township; Morris Chapel (Morris Chapel Church); L732A; September 10, 1979; 1981

Bertrand

Nearby French and English trading posts were known as *parc aux vaches* or "cowpens" for the wild buffalo once found here. Joseph Bertrand, an early trader, married the daughter of a Potawatomi chief and through her acquired land in various Indian treaties. In 1833 this land was platted into the town of Bertrand, which soon included several large hotels and stores and a four-story warehouse—remarkable on the Michigan frontier. Bertrand became a stop for stages on the Detroit-Chicago Road, and in 1844 the Sisters of the Holy Cross founded their first American convent here. Failure of the railroads to pass through town, and the high price of lots, caused the decline of this expansive village and the financial ruin of its founder.

On Bertrand Road at the intersection of Bond Street, Bertrand Township; Bertrand Informational Designation; S286; February 17, 1967; 1967

Portage Prairie United Methodist Church

In 1887 the Reverend J. A. Frye sparked a religious revival that inspired the construction of this Gothic Revival church. Embellished with oak details, the church cost $7,200 and was debt-free upon its dedication. Its one hundred-foot steeple was removed in 1919 due to severe electrical storms. Evangelical pioneers had worshipped in a log schoolhouse until 1859, when they built a yellow brick church. That structure was replaced by the present church.

Side Two

Persuaded by reports of good land from the Reverend John Seybert, Bishop of the Ohio conference, the Jacob and David Rough families came to Portage Prairie from Pennsylvania in the spring of 1849. In 1851 they organized the Zion Evangelical Church. The denomination merged with the United Evangelical Church in 1922 and with the United Brethren Church in 1946. This church was renamed the Portage Prairie United Methodist Church in 1968.

2450 Orange Road, Niles vicinity, Bertrand Township; Portage Prairie Evangelical Church (Portage Prairie Methodist Church); L1368A; January 22, 1987; 1989

Moccasin Bluff

People have lived on the terrace between Moccasin Bluff and the St. Joseph River for eight thousand years. The first inhabitants stayed in small temporary camps as early as 6300 B.C. The residents of A.D. 500 traded with groups in Indiana and Illinois. Those living here six hundred to nine hundred years ago farmed and had more permanent villages. In 1977, Moccasin Bluff was listed on the National Register of Historic Places because of its archaeological importance.

Side Two

As white settlers began to farm and log the St. Joseph River Valley in the late 1820s, the federal government adopted a policy of moving local Potawatomi Indians west. This bluff is said to be named for Cogomoccasin, leader of one of the permanent Potawatomi villages. Riverboats were the valley's main source of transportation until, in 1881, the St. Joseph Valley Railroad was constructed along the route that became the Red Bud Trail.

Near Red Bud Trail, north of Buchanan, Buchanan Township; Moccasin Bluff Site (20BE8); S382; April 14, 1972; 1987

This Greek Revival building served as Berrien County's Courthouse from 1839 to 1894. In 1967 it became a museum. (*Berrien Springs Courthouse*)

New Buffalo Welcome Center

The nation's first highway Travel Information Center opened on May 4, 1935, on US-12 at New Buffalo, not far from here. Other states followed Michigan's lead, and by 1985 there were 251 travel information centers across the nation. The New Buffalo center was built by the Michigan State Highway Department, now the Michigan Department of Transportation, to welcome motorists entering the state via US-12. It was relocated at this site, with its more modern building, on April 6, 1972, after the I-94 freeway was completed. Michigan's state-wide travel information program, which began in 1935, includes staffed welcome centers and interpretive, promotional and informational displays at rest areas and roadside parks across the state.

I-94 East, near mile marker one, New Buffalo Township; Tourist Lodge Informational Designation; L1256C; July 23, 1985; 1986

The Chapin House

This Queen Anne-style house, completed in 1884, was the Henry A. Chapin family home until 1902. In 1932, when the city of Niles bought the property at auction for $300, the Chapin grandchildren stipulated that it be used only for civic purposes. Now serving as the Niles City Hall, the house is built of local brick and terra cotta tile. The interior is orna-mented with leaded glass windows and transoms, handcarved woodwork and stenciled ceil-ings. In 1939 the Works Progress Administration joined the carriage house to another outbuilding, thus creating the Fort St. Joseph Museum structure. The museum holds over ten thousand items, including Fort St. Joseph and Potawatomi Indian artifacts, local memorabilia and a collection of original drawings by Chief Sitting Bull.

Henry Austin Chapin

Henry A. Chapin (1813-1898) spent most of his early life in Ohio. He married Ruby N. Nooney in 1836 and settled in Edwardsburg, Michigan. In 1846, Chapin and S. S. Griffin opened the first general store in Niles. With his son Charles, Henry A. later established an insurance and loan agency. Their firm had interests in nearby paper mills and electric

37

companies and real estate in Alabama, Illinois and Michigan. The bulk of the family capital came from the discovery of iron ore in Michigan's Upper Peninsula. The Chapin Mine, near Iron Mountain, began operations in 1879. "Mr. H. A.," as he was known, received up to $300,000 yearly in royalties from the mine. Owing to the Great Depression, the Chapin Mine closed in 1934, after fifty-five years of continuous production.

508 East Main Street (US-31), NE corner of Fifth Street, Niles; Chapin, Henry A. (Niles City Hall/Fort St. Joseph Museum); L475; November 3, 1976; 1978

Ferry Street School

Constructed in 1867 at a cost of nearly $3,000, the Ferry Street School opened in January 1868, as Niles's school for "colored children." In 1870 the Niles school system was integrated, and this facility closed. It reopened as an integrated school in 1873. The west wing was added in 1903. From 1956 to 1975 the School for Exceptional Children was located here. In 1975 concerned citizens began restoring the original building to its nineteenth-century style. Nineteenth-century one-room schools in this community typically contained a woodburning stove, woodbox, water bench, coat pegs, wooden blackboards and long rows of desks. One teacher often taught two grades. Lessons were in reading, writing, spelling, numbers, declamation and geography—all with a moral. This school provides a link to schools of yesteryear.

620 Ferry Street, SW corner of Seventh Street, Niles; Ferry Street Elementary School (Ferry Street School); L477; November 3, 1976; 1980

Fort St. Joseph

The French fort built here in 1691 controlled southern Michigan's principal Indian trade routes. Missionaries and fur traders were here already. The fort became a British outpost in 1761. Two years later it was one of the forts seized by Indians during the uprising of Chief Pontiac. Still later, traders made it their headquarters. In 1781, Spanish raiders ran up the flag of Spain at the fort for a few hours.

South Bond Street, north of Fort Street, Niles; Fort St. Joseph Site (20BE23) S4; February 18, 1956; 1957

Four Flags Hotel

The Four Flags Hotel opened with much fanfare on July 6, 1926. The newly formed Niles Hotel Corporation had raised $350,000 to build a hotel on the site of the Pike House hostelry. Chicago architect Charles W. Nicol designed the hotel, which was touted as fireproof and modern. The hotel's name was the first to recall the four nations that asserted sovereignty over the area: France, Great Britain, Spain and the United States. According to local legend, Al Capone stayed at the Four Flags.

404 East Main Street, Niles; Four Flags Hotel (Four Flags Inn); L1643A; April 20, 1989; 1990

Ring Lardner

Sportswriter, humorist, sardonic observer of the American scene, Ring Lardner was born in the house across the street on March 6, 1885. Possibly the best-known American author in the 1920s, he began his career writing sketches of sporting events for the *Niles Sun* and later worked for papers in Chicago and New York, where he wrote a popular syndicated column. Beginning in 1914 the *Saturday Evening Post* began publication of a series of articles that were to become his best known work. Later entitled *You Know Me Al*, the articles were letters from an ignorant bush league baseball player to his friend and were among the first literary uses of American common speech. His death occurred in New York on September 25, 1933. Lardner's achievements were favorably compared to those of Mark Twain.

519 Bond Street, Niles; Lardner, Ring, House; S339; August 13, 1971; 1971

Saint Mary's

The Roman Catholic Church in Niles traces its origins to the Indian mission established at nearby Fort St. Joseph in the late 1600s. Re-established at Bertrand, three miles south of Niles, in the 1830s, the mission moved into town in 1849 and was renamed St. Francis's. In 1866 the cornerstone of the present building was laid and on December 11, 1870, the church was dedicated to St. Mary. Designed by Rufus Rose of Niles, with later modifications by Father John Cappon, the church was completed in 1890 with the construction of the Gothic tower. Father Cappon, known as the "parish's greatest benefactor," was a

Belgian-born priest who served as pastor for over thirty years. He gave generously of his large personal estate for many parish improvements.

211 South Lincoln, SE corner of Clay Street, Niles; St. Mary's Catholic Church; S344; October 1, 1971; 1972

Trinity Church

This is the oldest existing church structure in Niles, located in the oldest Episcopal parish in the Diocese of Western Michigan. The first Episcopal service in Niles was conducted by Bishop Philander Chase in 1832. The parish was organized in 1834. In that year there were fourteen houses in Niles. The first edifice, of frame construction, was built on this site in 1836 under the direction of the Reverend James Selkrig, the first rector. The present church was completed in 1858. On May 7, 1876, the Reverend Robert McMurdy presented 308 persons for confirmation. This is said to have been one of the largest such classes in American church history.

9 South Fourth Street, Niles; Trinity Episcopal Church; L62; April 6, 1966; 1966

Wesley United Methodist Church

In 1830 circuit riders from Ohio began preaching in Niles, using the barroom of a local hotel. In 1832 nine worshippers formed the Methodist class that grew to be the Wesley United Methodist Church. They dedicated their first house of worship in 1839, and by 1840 they had organized a Sunday School to teach reading and religion. In 1862 the congregation laid the cornerstone for the present sanctuary. The structure was completed in 1863. The Dodge brothers of motor car fame attended Sunday School here during Joseph S. Tuttle's twenty-eight-year tenure as Sunday School Superintendent. In 1920, out of gratitude for his teachings, John F. Dodge gave Tuttle a life lease to his home on Main Street.

Side Two

The cornerstone of this handsome Italianate-style church was laid in 1862. The pastor at that time was the Reverend William Sprague, who organized the first Methodist class in Niles in 1832. Sprague was presiding elder of the district for four years, a member of the U.S. Congress and a state Indian agent. The church's architect is believed to have been Rufus Rose of Chicago, who designed several other notable structures in Niles. Construction was under the general supervision of Cass Chapman of Niles. Measuring forty-six-by-seventy feet, the original edifice had two corner towers. The square pyramid-roofed tower remains, but the mansard-capped tower was removed in 1951. Over the years the church has had several additions and alterations, but the original wainscoting, woodwork and windows have been retained.

302 Cedar Street, Niles; Methodist Episcopal Church (Wesley United Methodist Church); L734A; September 10, 1979; 1982

Parc Aux Vaches—Madeline Bertrand Park

Known as *Parc aux Vaches*, or "cow pasture," this area was named by the French for the wild buffalo that once grazed here. Two major Indian trails crossed here: the Sauk Trail, also called the Old Chicago Trail, which linked Detroit and Chicago; and the Miami Trail, which linked the Grand and the Wabash rivers. About 1808, French fur-trader Joseph Bertrand established a post in this area. Bertrand married Madeline, said to be the daughter of Potawatomi Chief Topenebee. Under the 1821 Treaty of Chicago, which ceded much of the lower southwest corner of Michigan to the United States, this site was deeded to Madeline Bertrand. *Parc aux Vaches* is now part of Niles Township.

Berrien County Park visitors center, 3088 Adams Road (Ontario Road), Niles Township; Parc Aux Vaches Informational Designation (Madeline Bertrand Park); L1363C; December 5, 1986; 1987

St. Joseph's Mission

Here, in 1837, in the then-flourishing settlement of Bertrand, a fine brick church, dedicated to St. Joseph, was built to serve the Catholics of this area. In this church, on September 4, 1844, the habit of the Sisters of the Holy Cross was given for the first time in America. Those who received the habit were Sister Mary of the Holy Cross, Sister Mary of the Nativity and Sister Mary of Mount Carmel. The sisterhood opened a school this same year in a dwelling, which still stands a thousand feet to the north. This mission in the Detroit diocese was directed by the Reverend Edward Sorin, C. S. C., founder of the University of Notre Dame. In 1911 the church was torn down. Madeline Bertrand, wife of the town's founder, is among those buried in this historic cemetery.

North of Bertrand Road, south of Niles, Niles Township; St. Joseph Mission (St. Joseph Cemetery); S260; September 18, 1964; 1964

Burnett's Post

William Burnett, an American patriot from New Jersey, established a trading post on the bank of the St. Joseph River immediately east of this point between 1775 and 1782. He was the first permanent white resident of this area. He married Kakima, daughter of Chief Aniquiba and sister of Topenebee, principal chief of the Potawatomi nation. Burnett built a warehouse at the mouth of the St. Joseph on the site of old Fort Miami, another at the site of Chicago, and a third on the Kankakee River. In 1785 the British charged Burnett with "exciting sedition" among the Indians. He was arrested, sent to Montreal and Quebec, but not under guard, and at last released without trial. During the War of 1812 he disappeared, but his son James continued to manage the post until 1833.

East of Miller Drive and Langley Avenue on the western shore of the Saint Joseph River, St. Joseph; Burnett, William, Trading Post Informational Site; S234; March 13, 1962; 1965

Fort Miami

Here in November 1679, on the Miami River as the St. Joseph was then called, La Salle, the French explorer, built a fort as a base for his western explorations. He awaited the *Griffin*, the upper lakes' first ship. When the ill-fated vessel did not come he made his way on foot to Canada through lower Michigan's uncharted wilderness. He returned in 1681 to prepare for his great push down the Mississippi. A decade later the French built Fort St. Joseph, some twenty miles upriver near Niles.

Lake Boulevard and Ship Street, St. Joseph; Fort Miami; S6; February 18, 1956; 1956

Old St. Joseph Neighborhood

During the late nineteenth and early twentieth centuries, local river captains, mill owners, merchants and other professionals built homes in this neighborhood. Over one hundred of their homes remain. They exemplify popular architectural styles ranging from Spanish Colonial Revival to American Foursquare. Of particular interest are the elegant Queen Anne-style homes. The Old St. Joseph Neighborhood is recognized as a state historic district.

Three identical markers are located in the district consisting of State and Main streets and Lake Boulevard, St. Joseph; Old St. Joseph Historic District; L945A; September 17, 1981; 1984

The Dewey Cannon

This cannon, captured in the Spanish-American War by Admiral Dewey, was presented to Three Oaks when its citizens raised $1,400 for a memorial to the men of the battleship *Maine*. This was the largest contribution, per capita, of any community in the nation. "Three Oaks Against the World," a local paper proudly boasted. This park was dedicated October 17, 1899, by President William McKinley, and others. Presentation of the cannon took place on June 28, 1900. Guest of honor was Helen Miller Gould, called the Spanish-American War's "Florence Nightingale." Thousands of people were in attendance on each occasion.

Dewey Cannon Park, on Maple Street, two blocks north of M-60, Three Oaks; Dewey Cannon; S239; August 14, 1962; 1963

Branch

The Chicago Road

One of the great routes for the pioneers coming west was the Chicago Road. The survey of the road began at Detroit in 1825 and followed closely the Sauk Trail which Indians had marked and traveled for centuries before the coming of the white man. Because of its many curves the road was likened to "a huge serpent, lazily pursuing its onward course, utterly unconcerned as to its destination." Originally designed as a military highway linking the forts at Detroit and Chicago, the road proved to be more important in opening southern Michigan to settlement and as a westward land route enabling travelers to avoid the long voyage by boat around lower Michigan. By the 1830s pioneer families by the thousands each year were moving over this road in their wagons. By 1835 the Western Stage Company of Detroit was running two stages daily to Chicago. Much of the road was little more than an unimproved trail, making a trip over it an unforgettable and an uncomfortable experience. Buildings from that bygone age still stand along US-112, the Chicago Road's descendant.

Present-day US-12 and Prairie River Road (park one and one-half miles west of Bronson), Bronson Township; Chicago Road Informational Designation, The; S162; September 17, 1957; 1958

The City of Coldwater, 1861-1961

Potawatomi Indians ceded Coldwater Prairie to the United States in 1827. The Indians called it "Chucksewyabish," meaning "cold spring water." Coldwater is located at the junction of the Old Sauk and Fort Wayne Indian trails. The settlement's first house was built near this site in 1830 by Hugh Campbell. The first school was organized in 1832. Coldwater became a village in 1837, the county seat of Branch County in 1842, and a city on February 28, 1861. The State Home and Training School, dating back to 1871, is here. Coldwater has many fine old houses, legacies of the pioneers who built this city.

City park at intersection of US-12 and US-27, Coldwater; City of Coldwater Informational Designation; L19; April 14, 1961; 1961

First Presbyterian Church

Organized in 1837, the same year that Coldwater became a village, the local Presbyterian society held services in various quarters until 1844 when it erected its first church. It completed the present Romanesque Revival-style brick church in 1869 at a cost of $40,104. The 185-foot steeple, one of the highest in southern Michigan and the chief landmark of the city, was made possible by a gift from S. M. Seely. The Meneely bell came from West Troy, New York, in 1853. In early times, the church often served as a lecture and concert hall. Sojourner Truth, former slave and early women's rights activist, spoke here in 1877. This church building is now the oldest in the city still in use by its original denomination.

52 Marshall Street, NE corner of Marshall and Church streets, Coldwater; First Presbyterian Church (First United Presbyterian Church); L657A; June 15, 1979; 1987

Governor Cyrus Gray Luce

On this site lived Cyrus Gray Luce, twenty-seventh governor of Michigan. Born in Ohio in 1824, Luce moved to Branch County in 1849. He soon became involved in township, local and state politics, serving on the Board of Agriculture, in the legislature and as a member of the 1857 constitutional convention. In 1886 and 1888 he was elected governor on the

Harriet Quimby Pioneer Pilot USAirmail 50

In 1991 the U.S. Postal Service featured Coldwater-born aviatrix Harriet Quimby on a fifty-cent airmail stamp. (*Harriet Quimby*)

Republican ticket. He remained active in the farmer's Grange until his death in Coldwater in 1905.

NE corner of Division and East Washington streets, Coldwater; Luce, Governor Cyrus Gray, Home Informational Site, (Public Safety Building); S469; August 15, 1975; 1975

Michigan Library Association

The first formal step toward the founding of a state library association was taken by Mary A. Eddy, of the Coldwater Free Public Library, in a letter to Henry M. Utley of the Detroit Public Library on January 13, 1891. They had discussed this matter at the 1890 meeting of the American Library Association in New Hampshire. A state association, they believed, would be helpful to Michigan librarians unable to attend national library conferences. Working closely with Lucy Ball, Grand Rapids Public Library, they awakened a statewide interest and arranged the first Michigan meeting in Detroit, September 1, 1891. Mr. Utley became the association's first president.

10 East Chicago Street, between Division and Hudson streets, Coldwater; Clarke, Edwin R., Library [Michigan Library Association] (Coldwater Public Library); S275; March 9, 1966; 1966

State Public School at Coldwater

In 1871 the Michigan legislature authorized the building of a special state public school to furnish temporary support and instruction for dependent and neglected children between the ages of four and sixteen until they could be placed in homes or returned to their families. The school was opened in Coldwater on May 21, 1874. Once admitted, children participated in "family-like" life in cottages and a placing-out program. A third of each day was used for schoolwork, a third for recreation and entertainment, and a third for acquiring work skills. Children learned reading, spelling, counting, calisthenics, singing, cyphering and slate drawing. By the turn of the century, the facility had become the only home in Michigan admitting both normal and handicapped children.

Coldwater Regional Center

By an act of the state legislature the State Public School became the Michigan Children's Village in 1935. The facility then began to admit only children with mild mental impairments. Most of the former residents were transferred to the Michigan Children's Institute, established in Ann Arbor in 1935. In 1939 the Children's Village became the Coldwater State Home and Training School, and persons of all ages with more serious mental handicaps were admitted. By 1960 there were twenty-nine-hundred residents. During the 1970s, special education, training and living experiences in communities reduced the number of residents to less than seven hundred. Renamed the Coldwater Regional Center for Developmental Disabilities in 1978, the remodeled facility provides training programs for independent living and self-help.

620 Marshall Road, Coldwater; State Public School at Coldwater (Coldwater Regional Center); S540B; May 13, 1981; 1981

Wing House Museum

Lucius M. Wing (1839-1921), Civil War captain, county sheriff and prominent businessman, purchased this residence in 1882. That same year he served a term as mayor. Making notable contributions to the industrial, financial and social life of the city, he was the long-time president of a local bank, a manufacturer of cigars and founder of the Bon Ami Social Club. The house remained in the family for three generations until acquired by the Branch County Historical Society in 1974 for use as a historical museum.

Side Two

This impressive Second Empire-style home with mansard roof was constructed in 1875 for Jay M. Chandler (1850-1884) and his young bride Frances. On this site from 1847-1871 had stood the Parrish flouring mill. Jay, the fourth son of locally prominent Albert Chandler, followed his brothers into the family hardware business. Albert founded the *Coldwater Sentinel* and served as the city's first mayor. Jay Chandler sold his home to Lucius Wing in 1882.

27 South Jefferson Street, NE corner of South Jefferson and East Pearl Street, Coldwater; Wing, Lucius M., House (Chandler-Wing House); S445; October 17, 1974; 1979

Harriet Quimby

Harriet Quimby was born in the Coldwater area on May 11, 1875, to Ursula (Cook) and William Quimby. The Quimby family moved to Arroyo Grande, California, in 1884, then to San

Francisco. In 1902, Harriet became a journalist for the *San Francisco Dramatic Review*. She later wrote features for the *San Franciso Chronicle* and worked for the *Call-Bulletin*. In 1903 she went to New York City as a drama critic and feature writer of *Leslie's Weekly*. At the Belmont Park Aviation Meet in October 1910 she became fascinated with flying. At the Hotel Astor, mingling with the theater crowd, she met John Moisant, who was celebrating his victory at the meet. She soon began taking lessons at the Moisant School of Aviation in Mineola, New York. She later toured the United States, Mexico and Europe with the Moisant Fliers.

Side Two

Harriet Quimby, the first woman in the United States, and second in the world, to obtain a pilot's license, received Federation Aeronautique Internationale License No. 37 from the Aero Club of America on August 1, 1911. On April 16, 1912, Quimby became the first woman to cross the English Channel, flying from the Cliffs of Dover to Hardelot, France. She returned in triumph to the United States after being feted in Europe. In June she shipped her plane to Boston so that she could fly in the Harvard-Boston Aviation meet. On July 1 she flew the manager of the meet, William A. P. Willard, around Boston Light. During the flight, her Berliot plane was caught in turbulent air and nose-dived, plummeting both Willard and Quimby to their deaths in Dorchester Bay.

Branch County Memorial Airport, Coldwater Township; Quimby, Harriet Informational Designation; L1490C; January 21, 1988; 1988

Quincy Public Library

In 1906, Quincy businessman Charles W. Bennett and steel entrepreneur Andrew Carnegie both offered to build a library in Quincy Township. Carnegie required that the township provide the land and name the building after him. Bennett's only stipulation was that his name not appear on the building. He agreed to provide in his will both land and funds for a library. Upon the sudden death of Bennett's son construction of the library began ahead of schedule in March 1910.

The State Public School at Coldwater, opened in 1874, housed and educated dependent and neglected children like those pictured here. (*Coldwater Regional Center*)

Side Two

Dedicated on November 1, 1910, this building represents the generosity of two Quincy citizens, Charles W. Bennett and Quincy State Bank President Melvin S. Segur. Segur gave the funds necessary to begin construction immediately after the sudden death of Bennett's son Charles A. Bennett. The elder Bennett wished the library to be built as a memorial to his son. The township was given title to both the land and the building and has provided for the maintenance of both since that time.

11 North Main Street, just north of US-12, Quincy; Quincy Township Public Library (Quincy Public Library); L1508A; April 25, 1988; 1989

Union City Furnace

On March 17, 1847, the Union City Iron Company was incorporated with leading citizens of the town as stockholders. The company was formed to produce iron from the bog and kidney iron ore deposits in Union and neighboring townships. A furnace was built, and in May 1847, it produced what was apparently the first iron made from Michigan ores. Earlier Michigan iron furnaces used imported pig iron. The percentage of iron in southern Michigan's ores was too small, however, to make their use profitable. Thus, in a few years Union City's pioneering furnace ceased making pig iron and turned to the production of plows.

Coldwater Road, south of Union City, Union Township; Union City Iron Furnace; L28; February 14, 1963; 1963

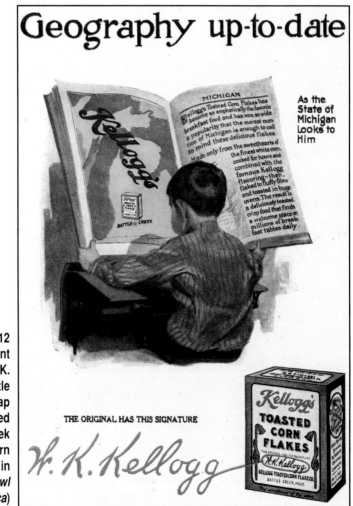

As this 1912 advertisement boasts, W.K. Kellogg put Battle Creek on the map when he founded the Battle Creek Toasted Corn Flake Company in 1906. (*Cereal Bowl of America*)

Calhoun

Albion College

Methodists obtained a charter for Spring Arbor Seminary from the Territorial Council of Michigan in March 1835. Later the institution was established in Albion on land donated by Jesse Crowell, a leading Albion pioneer and benefactor. In 1841 the cornerstone was laid for the first building, and in 1843 the institution opened as the Wesleyan Seminary. In 1861 the power to confer degrees was obtained and the school named Albion College. Support from the Methodist Church, a large endowment and private sources have contributed to its growth as a strong liberal arts college.

Ingham Street and Michigan Avenue, Albion; Albion College Informational Designation; S212; May 1, 1959; 1959

Birthplace of Famed Song

It was in the spring of 1911 that two freshmen at Albion College, Byron D. Stokes and F. Dudleigh Vernor, wrote the words and music for a song they called "The Sweetheart of Sigma Chi." The song made a hit with their fraternity brothers, and requests of copies came in from other chapters. Within a few years the melody and lyrics of "The Sweetheart of Sigma Chi" had become familiar to people around the world.

Albion College Campus, South Hall, Albion; Birthplace of Famed Song Informational Designation; S216; May 1, 1959; 1959

Birthplace of "The Old Rugged Cross"

"The Old Rugged Cross," one of the world's best-loved hymns, was composed here in 1913 by the Reverend George Bennard (1873-1958). The son of an Ohio coal miner, Bennard was a lifelong servant of God, chiefly in the Methodist ministry. He wrote the words and music of over three hundred other hymns. None achieved the fame of "The Old Rugged Cross," the moving summation of his faith. "I'll cherish the Old Rugged Cross, Till my trophies at last I lay down; I will cling to the Old Rugged Cross, And exchange it some day for a crown."

1101 East Michigan Avenue, Albion; Birthplace of Old Rugged Cross Informational Site, (Delta Tau Delta Fraternity); S215; May 1, 1959; 1959

The First Home

The first house at what was then known as the "Forks of the Kalamazoo" was erected near this site by Tenney Peabody, a New Yorker. To this cabin with its thatched roof of grass from the banks of the nearby Kalamazoo River, Albion's first settler brought his wife and seven children on March 4, 1833. This courageous pioneer used three yoke of oxen and two wagons to bring his family from New York. He helped form the company organized to build the town, named Albion after a town in New York.

303 East Erie Street, Albion; First Home in Albion Informational Site (Peabody, Tenney, House); L13; August 25, 1960; 1960

Gardner House Museum

Augustus P. Gardner (1817-1905), a wealthy hardware merchant, built this Victorian-style house in 1875. A three-story, thirteen-room mansion with a mansard roof, it was Gardner's home until his death in 1905. In 1966, after decades of neglect, the house was purchased by the Albion Historical Society. Restored, it houses a local museum. Five of the rooms are furnished as a nineteenth-century home, and the remainder feature permanent and rotating exhibits. This house is among the last of its type in this area.

509 South Superior Street, Albion; Gardner, A. P., Mansion (Gardner House); L97; January 22, 1971; 1981

Holy Ascension Orthodox Church

In 1904 the Albion Malleable Iron Company began recruiting workers for its foundry. The arrival of six Russians from New York City marked the beginning of Albion's "Foreign Colony." By 1915 the Foreign Colony had grown to around six hundred people of several East European nationalities, most of whom were Orthodox Christians. Initially, a visiting priest from Detroit conducted Albion's Orthodox services, but by 1915 permission to build an

Orthodox church had been granted. A fund drive within the city raised $5,000. The cornerstone was laid on April 30, 1916, and the church was consecrated on Thanksgiving Day of that year. Holy Ascension Church was the only non-Greek Orthodox parish in south-central Michigan until the late 1950s.

810 Austin Avenue, Albion; Holy Ascension of Christ Orthodox Church; L966A; November 16, 1981; 1982

Mother's Day in Albion

On May 13, 1877, the second Sunday of the month, Juliet Calhoun Blakeley stepped into the pulpit of the Methodist-Episcopal Church and completed the sermon for the Reverend Myron Daugherty. According to local legend, Daugherty was distraught because an antitemperance group had forced his son to spend the night in a saloon. Proud of their mother's achievement, Charles and Moses Blakeley encouraged others to pay tribute to their mothers. In the 1880s the Albion Methodist church began celebrating Mother's Day in Blakeley's honor.

Mother's Day

The official observance of Mother's Day resulted from the efforts of Anna Jarvis of Philadelphia. In 1868 her mother had organized a Mother's Friendship Day in a West Virginia town to unite Confederate and Union families after the Civil War. Anna Reeves Jarvis died on the second Sunday in May 1905. In 1907 her daughter began promoting the second Sunday in May as a holiday to honor mothers. Following an act of Congress in 1914, President Woodrow Wilson proclaimed the second Sunday in May Mother's Day.

Corner of Ionia and Erie streets, Albion; Mother's Day in Albion Informational Designation; L1723C; March 15, 1990; 1990

The Observatory

The Albion College Astronomical Observatory was built in 1883-1884 at the urging of Dr. Samuel Dickie, who later became president of the college. Dickie helped raise $10,000 to build and equip the facility. The observatory still harbors its original telescope, transit circle, sidereal clock and chronograph. The building has housed classrooms, a bookstore, faculty offices and the West Michigan Methodist Conference archives. In 1984 it was refurbished as the college Ethics Center.

Cass Street, Albion College Campus, Albion; Albion College Astronomical Observatory; S566A; January 25, 1985; 1985

Battle Creek City Hall

Ernest W. Arnold designed this Beaux-Arts Classical-style city hall "to harmonize with the post office" located directly across Division Street. It was built in 1914 by Seirn B. Cole Construction at a cost of $305,000. The building's interior is embellished with marbleized columns and trim and cherry millwork. Two stained-glass windows, one of which depicts the original city seal, highlight the stairwells. The city hall was listed on the National Register of Historic Places in 1984.

103 East Michigan Avenue, Battle Creek; Battle Creek City Hall; L1103A; August 12, 1983; 1989

Battle Creek House

The Battle Creek House, a stagecoach stop and the social and political hub of the settlement from 1836 to 1866, stood here. The balconied, three-story inn was destroyed by a fire late in the 1860s. In 1870, Daniel Reily put up a "solid brick" building housing stores, offices, and, from 1903 to 1931, the Central National Bank. It was known as the C. E. Thomas Block between 1892 and 1956. Remodeling by [the] Peoples Savings and Loan Association in 1957 left the basic structure unchanged.

2 West Michigan Avenue, Battle Creek; Battle Creek House (Stagecoach Stop Site); L8; June 26, 1959; 1959

Battle Creek Post Office

The second Battle Creek Post Office, one of Albert Kahn's earliest commissions, opened in 1907. He designed the structure with reinforced concrete supports, an innovation he later used in his internationally renowned factory designs. The building's stone trim and repeating arches exemplify Second Renaissance Revival architecture. The post office became the Calhoun County Hall of Justice in 1978. The structure was listed on the National Register of Historic Places in 1972.

67 East Michigan Street, Battle Creek; Battle Creek Post Office; S405; May 17, 1973; 1989

Battle Creek Sanitarium

The Battle Creek Sanitarium opened in 1866 as the Western Health Reform Institute. The institute was founded on health principles advocated by the Seventh-day Adventist Church. In 1876, Dr. John Harvey Kellogg became the medical superintendent at the sanitarium. Kellogg's many innovations included the use of radiation therapy for cancer patients and the invention of flaked cereal. The sanitarium burned in 1902; the following year a six-story Italian Renaissance Revival-style building, designed by Dayton, Ohio, architect Frank M. Andrews, was constructed. Kellogg's brother W. K. Kellogg worked at the sanitarium for twenty-six years before leaving to establish the Battle Creek Toasted Corn Flake Company. The Battle Creek Sanitarium is listed on the National Register of Historic Places.

Percy Jones General Hospital

In 1928 the Battle Creek Sanitarium was enlarged with a fourteen-story "towers" addition and dining room annex designed by M. J. Morehouse of Chicago. After the stock market crashed in 1929, business declined; the facility went into receivership in 1933. The sanitarium continued to occupy the site until 1942 when the U.S. Army purchased the buildings and established the Percy Jones General Hospital, named for an army surgeon whose thirty year career included commanding ambulance units during World War I. The hospital specialized in neurosurgery, plastic surgery and the fitting of artificial limbs. Approximately 100,000 military patients were treated at the hospital before it closed permanently in 1953. In 1954 the building became the Battle Creek Federal Center.

74 North Washington Avenue, Battle Creek; Battle Creek Sanitarium (Battle Creek Federal Center); S597A; September 7, 1989; 1990

Beckley Cemetery

In 1833, Joseph W. Stewart, a native of New York, settled in the Oak Openings area of western Calhoun County. Recognizing a need for a cemetery in the neighborhood he set aside a portion of his land for this purpose, offering the plots without charge. When a new law in 1859 required each township to make provisions for burials, Stewart turned his property over to Battle Creek Township. In later years this area became known as Beckley Corners after Ira Beckley, another early settler.

Helmer and Beckley roads, Battle Creek; Beckley Cemetery; L211; September 29, 1972; 1973

Beckley School

This country schoolhouse, one of a vanishing type, was built in 1859 and named after Ira Beckley, an early settler. During the first year, thirty-three pupils used a library of forty-two books for a seven-month session. Instruction was offered in grades one through eight, but attendance was irregular in the early years. The maple trees, which now surround the building, were planted by order of the district school board in 1866. Beckley School provided education for neighborhood children until 1957.

3019 Beckley Road, at Helmer Road, Battle Creek; Beckley School (Battle Creek Township No. 5 Schoolhouse); L82; August 27, 1970; 1970

Cereal Bowl of America

This is Battle Creek, where the leading producers of ready-to-eat cereals are located. Early attempts to process grains into appetizing new foods for Sanitarium guests revolutionized the eating habits of people everywhere. "Made in Battle Creek" was the magic phrase used by over forty cereal manufacturers here in the early 1900s. Millions the world over enjoy the benefits and conveniences of packaged breakfast foods today. Cereals from "Foodtown, U.S.A." have made Battle Creek one of the best known cities of its size in the world.

Bailey Park, NE Capital Avenue at M-78, Battle Creek; Breakfast Food Industry Informational Designation; S131; January 19, 1957; 1958

Del Shannon

In late 1960 the Hi-Lo Club, located on this site, "rocked" when the Charlie Johnson Band played "Runaway" for the first time. Johnson, whose real name was Charles Westover, was born in Grand Rapids and raised in Coopersville. In 1960, Westover (1934-1990) signed with Detroit's Big Top Records and adopted the stage name Del Shannon. According to the

New York Times, Shannon's 1963 recording of "From Me To You" was the first American release of a Lennon and McCartney song. His last hit was "Sea of Love" in 1982.

"Runaway"

Del Shannon wrote the lyrics for "Runaway" and recorded the song in New York on January 21, 1961. "Runaway" was released on the Big Top label and debuted on March 6, 1961. One month later Shannon sang "Runaway" on the "American Bandstand" television show. The song hit the top of the pop charts on April 24, 1961, and remained there for four weeks. "Runaway" sold over six million copies. In 1986, Shannon re-recorded the song as the theme for the "Crime Story" television series, which aired from 1986 to 1988.

45 Capital Avenue SW, SE corner of Hamblin and Capital, Battle Creek; Del Shannon/Runaway Informational Site (Hi-Lo Club, Former site of [vacant]); S616C; June 21, 1990; 1990

First Baptist Church

The First Baptist Church, oldest church in Battle Creek, was organized in April 1835, with nineteen charter members. Meetings were held in the log schoolhouse the first few years. The present site was bought from Sands McCamley in 1843 for $275. The first building, completed in 1850, was replaced in 1871 by the present sanctuary at a cost of $26,500. Many members signed notes for the indebtedness. In 1957 an educational building was erected. The church was remodeled in 1959.

80 East Michigan Avenue, Battle Creek; First Baptist Church; L9; August 9, 1959; 1960

James and Ellen White

James S. and Ellen G. White were among the founders of the General Conference of the Seventh-day Adventist Church, which was organized in Battle Creek in 1863. Long participants in the Adventist movement, they came to Battle Creek in 1855 when the Adventist press was moved there. James served as minister, author, editor and General Conference president. Ellen, a prophetess, reportedly experienced over two thousand visions. Married in New England in 1846, both were involved in the founding of publishing, medical and educational institutions. After James's death in 1881, Ellen traveled to organize Adventist churches in Europe, Australia and the American South and West. She is widely known for her writings on health, education, family life and the Bible, and is one of the most translated American authors. She died in 1915.

Oak Hill Cemetery, 255 South Avenue, Lot No. 320, Battle Creek; White, James and Ellen G., Grave Site (Oak Hill Cemetery); L1252C; July 23, 1985; 1986

Kimball House Museum

Three generations of doctors made this structure their home. The attractive Victorian house was built by Dr. Arthur H. Kimball in 1886. Kimball, a city health official, came to this area in 1883. His son, Arthur S. Kimball, became Battle Creek's first pediatrician, founded the local chapter of the American Red Cross and established clinics for the poor. Arthur S. Kimball, Jr., gained national recognition for his work in the treatment of tuberculosis. In 1966 heirs of the Kimball family donated the property to the Junior League for use as a museum.

196 Capital Avenue, Battle Creek; Kimball House; L469; September 21, 1976; 1986

The Log Schoolhouse

Near this spot, facing the Indian Trail, the village's first public school was erected in 1834. Built of logs, its floor, desks and benches were constructed of lumber floated down the river from Bellevue's sawmill. Warren B. Shepard, the first teacher, had a dozen pupils. The pioneers paid eighty dollars for their schoolhouse, using it also for religious services, debates and other meetings. Sometimes friendly Potawatomi Indians dropped in to watch the strange doings.

East State and Monroe streets, Battle Creek; Log School House; L7; June 5, 1959; 1959

Methodism in Battle Creek

The first Methodist class in this area met in the home of Daniel Thomas in 1833. Three years later services were being held in the log schoolhouse. In 1841 the first structure for religious services in the village was built by the Methodists 150 feet to the north. On this site

Coeducation pioneer Mary Bryant Mayo was born on her family's Convis Township farm in 1845. Today, that farm remains in the Bryant family. (*Bryant Farm*)

a brick edifice with spire and tower was built in 1859. The sanctuary could seat six hundred and had a large pipe organ. The present building, entirely new, was completed in 1908.

114 East Michigan Avenue, Battle Creek; Methodism in Battle Creek (First United Methodist Church); L5; May 1, 1959; 1959

Michigan Central Depot

The Michigan Central Railroad Depot opened on July 27, 1888. Rogers and MacFarlane of Detroit designed the depot, one of several Richardsonian Romanesque-style stations the Michigan Central built between Detroit and Chicago in the late nineteenth century. Thomas Edison as well as Presidents William Howard Taft and Gerald Ford visited here. The depot was acquired by the New York Central Railroad in 1918, Penn Central in 1968 and Amtrak in 1970. The depot was listed on the National Register of Historic Places in 1971.

West Van Buren, Battle Creek; Michigan Central Railway Station (Penn Central Railway Station/New York Central Railway Station); S317; November 6, 1970; 1989

St. Thomas Episcopal Church

In 1839, Battle Creek's first Episcopal service was conducted. Regular services were held in the schoolhouse after 1841 by the Reverend Montgomery Schuyler, then Rector at

Marshall. In appreciation he was given a team of horses. In 1842, Bishop Samuel Mc-Coskry confirmed six candidates, and a parish was organized. A brick building on this site was consecrated on June 11, 1848. It was replaced by the present edifice thirty years later.

72 Capital Avenue Northeast, Battle Creek; St. Thomas Episcopal Church; L6A; May 1, 1959; 1959

Seirn B. Cole House

This flamboyant Arts and Crafts style-house was constructed in 1912. Its first resident, Seirn B. Cole (1861-1947), was a native of New Jersey. He and his wife, Elizabeth Farmer, lived in Detroit before they moved here where Cole was the contractor for the Battle Creek City Hall. Cole eventually became one of the city's most active contractors. By the time he retired in 1934, his contributions to the city's architecture included the Ralston-Purina Plant, the Masonic Temple, the Battle Creek High School and the YWCA. During his fifty-year career, he also worked on the Ypsilanti Stone Water Tower and schools throughout the state. Cole was a civic leader. He was a thirty-second degree Mason and a charter member of the Battle Creek Country Club.

276 Capital Avenue NE, Battle Creek; Cole, Seirn B., House; L1369A; January 22, 1987; 1988

Seventh-day Adventists

Battle Creek is closely identified with Adventist history. The first church built by Seventh-day Adventists was erected here in 1855 and the General Conference organized in 1863. The denomination's first world headquarters, publishing house, sanitarium, school and college were in Battle Creek. The "Dime" Tabernacle, seating thirty-two-hundred, built on this site in 1878 with contributions from members throughout the nation, burned in 1922 and was replaced in 1924 by this building.

19 North Washington at Van Buren Street, Battle Creek; Seventh-day Adventist Church; S218; October 14, 1959; 1959

Union Pump Company

In 1884, A. E. Preston, John Heyser, Edward Keet and James Gridley opened a small machine shop in the basement of a wagon shop. There they manufactured woodworking and ironworking machinery. The company was incorporated on May 22, 1885, when D.W. Lovell joined the founders. In 1893 the company relocated here. By 1894 the firm, originally known as the Union Manufacturing Company, was capitalized as $75,000 and wholly engaged in the manufacturing of steam pumps. The present name, Union Pump Company, was adopted in 1959.

*87 Capital Avenue SW, Battle Creek. Building razed. New location of marker undetermined; Union Manufacturing Company; L1225C; March 28, 1985; 1985

Veterans Hospital No. 100

World War I created the need for increased medical care for returning soldiers. Veterans Hospital No. 100, a five-hundred-bed neuropsychiatric facility that opened in 1924 on the grounds of Fort Custer, originally consisted of twenty-two Neo-Georgian structures in a crescent shaped arrangement. Like other Veterans Bureau facilities of the time, the hospital was built from standardized floor plans at a cost of nearly $3 million. When erected on the grounds of Fort Custer, trenches, sand dunes and barren soil dominated the site. Between 1927 and 1930, ninety-four hundred trees were planted on the 675-acre site, including English walnut trees transplanted from the Battle Creek Sanitarium that were originally grown at Mt. Vernon, Virginia.

5500 Armstrong Road, Battle Creek; Veterans Hospital No. 100, Camp Custer (Battle Creek V.A. Medical Center); S603A; December 20, 1989; 1991

W. K. Kellogg

At the age of fourteen, Will Keith Kellogg (1860-1951) began working as a salesman for his father's broom business. Later, he worked with his brother, Dr. John Harvey Kellogg, at the Battle Creek Sanitarium. In 1894, John, assisted by Will, developed a successful cereal flake. It was first served to the patients at the sanitarium and later sold by the Sanitas Food Company. In 1906, W. K. Kellogg launched his own food company to sell Toasted Corn Flakes cereal. The company grew to be the largest manufacturer of ready-to-eat cereals in the world. Kellogg's early personal philanthropies included assistance to rural teachers, to

British children orphaned by war, to the blind and to a number of hospitals and medical programs. In 1930 the W. K. Kellogg Foundation was established to promote the health and well-being of children. Today, it is among the world's largest philanthropic organizations.

Kellogg Company

Will Keith Kellogg founded the Battle Creek Toasted Corn Flake Company in 1906. He manufactured his first boxes of cereal in a three-story building on Bartlett Street at the rate of thirty-three cases per day. In 1907 the original factory building was destroyed by fire, and part of the present structure was erected on this site. Kellogg Company sold more than one million cases of cereal in 1909, and by 1911 the company's advertising budget had reached $1 million. In 1917 production capacity reached nine million boxes per day. In 1980, United States production of Kellogg's ready-to-eat cereals required more than 110,000 bushels of corn, 225,000 pounds of bran, 9,000 bushels of wheat and 12,000 pounds of wheat germ each day. By its seventy-fifth anniversary in 1981, Kellogg Company had forty-seven plants operating in twenty-one countries.

235 Porter Street, Battle Creek; Battle Creek Toasted Corn Flake Company (Kellogg Company); S541B; May 13, 1981; 1987

Ward Mill Site

In 1845, Joseph M. Ward (1822-1902) joined William Fargo in a livery and freight business, located on the corner of State and Jefferson streets. In 1849, Ward bought an interest in a woolen mill on the nearby creek, which he operated until 1860. The next year he converted the mill to flour production. Ward's son Frank (1860-1936) and E. C. Hinman (1852-1906) took over the business in 1882. Hinman left the business in 1888, and Frank Ward moved to Detroit in 1897. Joseph resumed control of the business until his death.

Ward Building Site

In 1905, Frank and Charles Ward erected a six-story steel and masonry building here, on the site of the Ward flour mill, in memory of their father, Joseph M. Ward. The *Battle Creek Sunday Record* quoted authorities at the Michigan Commercial Insurance Company who stated that the "Ward Skyscraper" was the "only absolutely fireproof office building in Michigan." It housed many prosperous businesses, a business school and the Athelstan social club. The Ward Building was razed in 1987.

Capitol Avenue, north of State Street at the Battle Creek, Battle Creek; Ward Mill-Ward Building Informational Site; L1792C; October 12, 1990; 1991

Bryant Farm

This farm has remained in the Bryant family since 1844 and retains much of its original Civil War-era appearance. The ruins of stone fences erected without mortar still stand as a rare reminder of early settlement. Mary Bryant Mayo (1845-1903), Michigan's pioneer leader in coeducation, was born here. During the latter part of the nineteenth century she was very active in the Grange movement and traveled throughout the Midwest exhorting farm women to improve their lives through education.

Side Two

The Grange's purpose was to show farmers that their happiness depended upon education as well as prosperity, and Mary Mayo "had the power of reaching those who dwell in the farm house." Perry Mayo, her husband, who had gained prominence by being elected state senator in 1887-1888, encouraged her efforts. In 1900, Mary was instrumental in establishing the first women's dormitory, the Women's Building, on the Michigan State University campus. Thirty-one years later that university built a new women's dormitory and named it in honor of Mary Mayo.

12557 L Drive North, east of Twelve Mile Road, Convis Township; Mayo, Mary (Bryant), Birthplace (Bryant Farm); L591; April 4, 1978; 1978

Hasbrouck House

Mathew Hasbrouck (1814-1883), a native of New Paltz, New York, settled near Marshall in 1837. In 1841 he had this house built in the style of his ancestral home in New Paltz. The Huguenot floor plan, featuring two entrances and the possibility of separate living units, is rare in Michigan. Hasbrouck's ancestors were among the French Huguenots, who came to North America to escape religious persecution in the sixteenth and seventeenth centuries.

In 1921, Harold C. Brooks, the father of Marshall's historic preservation movement, purchased this house, built by Jabez Fitch in 1840. (*Fitch-Gorham-Brooks House*)

The Huguenot Society of Michigan was organized in this house in 1937.

18600 Sixteen Mile Road, Convis Township, one mile north of I-94; Hasbrouck, Mathew, House; L1169A; June 15, 1984; 1985

The Hawkins Farm

In 1836 the Hawkins family was among the first to settle Convis Township. Asahel Hawkins, who had emigrated from Vermont, began with 80 acres of government land and steadily increased his holdings until they reached 240 acres. After his death in 1881, his son Asahel Myron Hawkins, the first white baby born in Convis Township, took over the farmstead. He raised a variety of crops and livestock and held several civic offices, including township supervisor, clerk, highway commissioner and justice of the peace. His son Schubail Frank Hawkins ran the farm until 1933. In 1942 the farm was converted to turkey production, and in 1968 the fourth, fifth and sixth generations of Asahel Hawkins's descendants opened a turkey restaurant on the farm.

18935 15-1/2 Mile Road, Convis Township; The Hawkins Farm Informational Designation; L1253C; July 23, 1985; 1986

First Presbyterian Church

The First Presbyterian Church of Homer was organized with thirty-four members under the direction of the Reverend Elijah Buck in 1838. Shortly afterwards, services were held in the "Session House," which served the group until 1853, when the existing sanctuary was built. In 1886 the narthex was added and the church was remodeled under the guidance of architect L. D. Grosvenor. The architectural style is Renaissance Classical, showing some influence of Sir Christopher Wren.

309 South Sophia Street, Homer; First Presbyterian Church; L934A; July 17, 1981; 1985

Homer Fire Station

This brick structure with arched windows and a decorative cornice was built in 1876, five years after Homer incorporated as a village. A fire station, jail and city offices initially occupied the building, which is located in the center of the commercial district. Shortly after its construction, townspeople used the facilities for public meetings and theatricals. Now attached to the new fire station and municipal offices, it is the oldest public building in Homer.

128 East Main Street, Homer; Homer Fire Station; L439; January 16, 1976; 1977

Marengo Pioneer Cemetery

This site on Territorial Road was a gift of Seeley Neal (1778-1862) from 640 acres acquired from the government in 1831. Neal, a veteran of the War of 1812, built the first log house in the township. His was the first family to locate in the settlement later named by him, Marengo. He built a sawmill on the Kalamazoo River, and was a member of the commission that helped to locate and survey the Territorial Road.

West Michigan at Twenty-one Mile Road (five miles west of Albion), Marengo Township; Marengo Pioneer Cemetery; L1; May 1, 1959; 1959

American Museum of Magic

Presto-Change-O! From saloon to billiard parlor, to clothing store, to bakery, to museum, this edifice, built in 1868, has known many transformations. Since April Fools' Day 1978 it has housed a unique collection that celebrates the magician's arts of wonder and delight. Michigan's link to magic is no illusion for nearby Colon, a center of magic manufacturing, was once home to famed magician Harry Blackstone, Sr., (1885-1965), whose memorabilia is displayed here.

107 East Michigan Avenue, Marshall; Faust Block (American Museum of Magic); L1240A; June 20, 1985; 1985

Butler-Boyce House

This handsome Italian Villa, with paired arched windows, is adorned with combined cupola and railing. Edward Butler (1814-1881) merchant, banker and first treasurer of Calhoun County, built the residence in 1858-1861 on land once owned by author James Fenimore Cooper. William D. Boyce (1860-1929), founder of the Boy Scouts of America, purchased the house and sixty acres as a summer home in 1894. For many years it was the home of Myron B. and Anne Ells. Mrs. Ells founded the Marshall Historical Society in 1961.

W. D. Boyce

William D. Boyce, a Chicago publisher, founded the Boy Scouts of America. Boyce first became acquainted with the scouting movement while in London in 1909. He lost his way in the midst of heavy fog, and was rescued by a Boy Scout who took him to the address he had been seeking. Offering the young boy a tip, he was told that Boy Scouts did not accept money for doing a good deed. Impressed by this organization, Boyce returned home with pamphlets, badges and a uniform. He incorporated Boy Scouts of America, now Scouting/USA, on February 8, 1910.

1110 Verona Road, Marshall; Butler-Boyce House; L690A; June 15, 1979; 1979

Calhoun County Fair

First held in 1839, the Calhoun County Fair has continued to this day as one of Michigan's foremost agricultural attractions. Floral Hall, the oldest building on the fairgrounds, was constructed in 1860 in the then-popular octagon style. The wings were added at later dates. Designed originally for the display of flowers and farm produce, the building still plays a major role at one of the state's oldest county fairs.

Between Fair Street and Washington Avenue, east of Marshall Avenue, Marshall; Calhoun County Fair; L196; February 11, 1972; 1977

Capitol Hill School

This 1860 building is the last of three Gothic Revival schools in Marshall. The name comes from its location on a site proposed for the Michigan state capitol. Donated to the Marshall Historical Society by the Board of Education in 1967, it is today a children's museum with a restored nineteenth century classroom. It is listed in the Historic American Buildings Survey and the National Register of Historic Places.

603 Washington Street, Marshall; Capitol Hill School (Fourth Ward School); L113; April 23, 1971; 1973

Charles T. Gorham

Gorham (1812-1901) came to Marshall in 1836 from New York State. First a merchant, he became a banker and in 1865 organized the First National Bank of Marshall, now the Michigan National Bank. He was a defendant in the famous Crosswhite fugitive slave case. A vice-president of the first Republican Convention at Jackson in 1854, Gorham later was a state senator. During the 1870s he served the United States as minister to The Netherlands and then as assistant secretary of the interior.

Michigan National Bank, 124 West Michigan, Marshall; Charles T. Gorham Informational Designation; S491; November 3, 1976; 1977

First Baptist Church

The Reverend Thomas Z-R. Jones, a traveling missionary, began visiting the Marshall area in 1838. On January 15, 1840, he helped organize the First Baptist Church of Marshall with eight members. The group erected this church in 1850-1851. They enlarged and remodeled it in 1876 with plans provided by Benjamin J. Bartlett of Chicago. The handsome Romanesque church, now the oldest church edifice in the city, features rounded-arch stained glass windows and an early example of a modified Akron (semicircular) seating plan.

305 North Superior Street, Marshall; First Baptist Church; L1226A; April 23, 1985; 1986

Fitch-Gorham-Brooks House

Built by Jabez S. Fitch in 1840, this handsome residence became the home of Charles T. Gorham, prominent Marshall citizen, in 1848. Harold C. Brooks purchased the house in 1921 and contracted with landscape architect Jens Jensen to design the grounds. The Reverend John D. Pierce and Isaac E. Crary planned the Michigan public school system in 1834 under the oak now by the west entrance. This Greek Revival structure with five-column arrangement and side entrances reflects the New York heritage of this city's early settlers.

Harold C. Brooks

Harold Craig Brooks (1885-1978) was Marshall mayor from 1925 to 1931, patron and philanthropist. His interest in city beautification set a standard for preservation and adaptive use as early as 1921. He owned and protected more than a dozen Marshall buildings. Brooks is responsible for the design of the Marshall Post Office, the conversion of the Old Stone Barn into Town Hall and presentation of the Brooks Memorial Fountain to the city. He donated land for veterans, the airport, recreational uses and funds for education and hospital facilities.

310 North Kalamazoo Avenue, Marshall; Fitch, Jabez S., House (Brooks, Harold C., House); S512A; January 29, 1979; 1979

Governor's Mansion

State Senator James Wright Gordon built this Greek Revival house in 1839, the year he introduced a bill to make his town state capital. Land near his house had been selected for the capitol grounds. Marshall's hopes were not fulfilled but Gordon became lieutenant-governor in 1840, and acting governor in 1841 upon the resignation of William Woodbridge. In 1967 the property was deeded to the Mary Marshall Chapter of the Daughters of the American Revolution.

621 South Marshall Avenue, Marshall; Governor's Mansion (Capitol Hill House); L197; February 11, 1972; 1972

Grand Army of the Republic

In 1866 northern Civil War veterans organized the Grand Army of the Republic to fight for veterans' pensions and other benefits. Michigan's first chapter was formed the next year. National membership peaked in 1890 with 409,489 men, while Michigan's rolls crested in 1889 with more than 21,000 members. In its heyday, the G.A.R. was a powerful political pressure group. The society also provided food and clothing for indigent widows and orphans. The last state encampment was held in 1948.

The G.A.R. Hall

Marshall's Civil War veterans organized a Grand Army of the Republic chapter in 1883. They built this handsome red-brick structure as their headquarters in 1902. It was named for Marshall's Corporal Calvin Colegrove, color-bearer for the Michigan First Infantry, who was killed at the first Battle of Bull Run on July 21, 1861. The memorial hall, built at a cost of $3,000, served C. Colegrove Post No. 166 until the late 1930s. In 1977 the Marshall Historical Society purchased it for one dollar to house its archives.

West Michigan Avenue at Exchange Street, Marshall; G. A. R. Hall; L1051A; January 27, 1983; 1983

Honolulu House

Abner Pratt settled in Marshall in 1839 and in the 1850s became chief justice of the state supreme court. In 1857-1859 he was United States Consul to the Sandwich (Hawaiian) Islands. Returning home he built this house in 1860 to recreate the island atmosphere. Teak and ebony were used, and murals on the walls depicted tropical plants and animals. In 1887 the interior was changed but the opulent style of the exterior, unique in the Midwest, has survived.

107 North Kalamazoo Street, Marshall; Pratt, Abner, House (Honolulu House); HB42; February 17, 1965; 1972

Isaac E. Crary House

Michigan's first congressman lived here from the early 1840s until his death in 1854. Located on lots one and two, original plat, lower village, the house was a wedding gift from his father-in-law, Judge Abner Pratt. Arriving here in 1831, Crary was a member of Michigan's first constitutional convention. He was three times elected to Congress, and twice to the legislature. In 1961 the building became the office of [the] Marshall Savings and Loan Association.

107 North Park Street, Town Square, Marshall; Crary, Isaac E., House; S397; March 14, 1973; 1973

James A. Miner

James A. Miner, born in Marshall in 1842, began studying law in Clinton, Iowa, in 1860. Completing his studies in Marshall, he was admitted to the Calhoun County bar in 1863. There he was circuit court commissioner (1866-1870) and prosecuting attorney (1870-1874). His office was in this building from 1869 to 1873. His 1876 partnership with Francis A. Stace created one of the county's largest law firms. President Benjamin Harrison appointed him a Utah territorial justice in 1890, and he was elected the state's first chief justice (1896-1903). He died in 1907.

156 West Michigan Avenue, Marshall; Miner, James A., Office; L898B; February 23, 1981; 1981

John D. Pierce Homesite

On this foundation stood the log house of the Reverend John D. Pierce. Born in New Hampshire, Pierce moved to Marshall in 1831, where he founded the Congregational church. In 1834 he and Isaac Crary designed Michigan's school system, and from 1836 to 1841, he served as the state's and the nation's first superintendent of public instruction. Pierce died in 1882 and is buried in Marshall's Oakridge Cemetery, honored by a monument erected by Michigan schoolteachers.

314 West Mansion, Marshall; Pierce, Reverend John D., Home Site (Pierce-Ludington House); S454; February 21, 1975; 1975

Ketchum Park

In 1831, Sidney and George Ketchum located here on Rice Creek. This first settlement in Marshall consisted of a water-powered sawmill and log cabins. Until the twentieth century this was an important industrial area, containing at various times a malt house, plow foundry and flour mill. The latter was in operation until 1960. Ketchum Park is now a memorial to the first settlers of Marshall.

South Marshall Street at Montgomery Street, Marshall; Ketchum Park; L198; February 11, 1972; 1972

Lieutenant George A. Woodruff

Lieutenant George A. Woodruff (1840-1863) graduated from West Point in only three years

Abner Pratt, U.S. consul to present-day Hawaii (1857-1859), built Marshall's most recognizable building in 1860. (*Honolulu House*)

because of the start of the Civil War. Young Woodruff served valiantly in the battles of the Army of the Potomac. At Gettysburg he was mortally wounded while defending the center of the Union line with his First United States Field Artillery (Battery I) against Confederate General George Pickett's charge on July 3, 1863. Lingering through the night, George A. Woodruff died the following day.

Side Two

After learning of the death of his son, the Honorable George Woodruff, a well-known Calhoun County judge, traveled to Gettysburg to bring young George's body back to this city. Last rites for the gallant Civil War veteran were held in Marshall and he was buried here in Oakridge Cemetery. His brother William was killed in the Battle of Petersburg and subsequently buried in the Gettysburg National Cemetery, in Gettysburg, Pennsylvania.

Oakridge Cemetery, 614 Dibble Street, Marshall; Lieutenant George A. Woodruff Informational Site; L654B; April 24, 1979; 1979

Marshall

Founded in 1831 by Sidney Ketchum and settlers from New York and New England, the town was named in honor of Chief Justice John Marshall. Townsmen Isaac Crary and the Reverend John Pierce planned in 1834 the innovative Michigan public school system. Marshall's early hopes of becoming state capital were not rewarded, but the coming of the Michigan Central Railroad in 1844 increased prosperity and the town remained a rail center until the 1870s. In 1863 the Brotherhood of Locomotive Engineers was founded here. Many of the citizens held strong abolitionist views, and in 1847 they prevented the return of fugitive slave Adam Crosswhite to Kentucky. The architectural excellence of Marshall's homes is known through the Midwest.

Town Square, West Michigan Avenue (city property south of the Honolulu House), Marshall; Marshall Informational Designation; S375; February 11, 1972; 1972

National House

Erected by Andrew Mann in 1835, this structure is reported to be the first brick building in Calhoun County. National House was also known as Mann's Hotel. It served travelers passing through Marshall and hosted political and community gatherings. Over the years it has been called, among other names, the Acker House and Facey House. Its varied history includes use as a wagon and windmill factory. This two-story, low-gabled building has been restored to its original appearance and use as an inn.

102 South Parkview, Marshall; National House (National House Inn); L434; January 16, 1976; 1977

The Old Stone Barn

Built by William Prindle in 1857, this landmark served as a livery stable for over sixty years. It also saw brief use as a stagecoach stop for the lines connecting Coldwater with Lansing. By 1928 it had become an unsightly gas station. Purchased through the efforts of Mayor Harold C. Brooks, its conversion into a city hall by architect Howard Young was completed in time for Marshall's centennial celebration of 1930.

323 West Michigan Avenue (South Kalamazoo at Fountain Circle), Marshall; Prindle, William, Livery Stable [Old Stone Barn], (Marshall Town Hall); L216; March 14, 1973; 1973

Oliver C. Comstock, Jr.

Oliver C. Comstock, Jr. (1806-1895) built this Gothic Revival house between 1849 and 1856. Comstock, born in Fairfield, New York, migrated to the Marshall area in 1836. He left a well-established medical practice in Trumansburg, New York, to start anew on the Michigan frontier. Later that year, he erected the first brick business building in Calhoun County on Exchange Street. It housed his pharmacy and office.

Side Two

Oliver C. Comstock, Jr., served as the state's third superintendent of public instruction (1843-1845). In 1847 he was one of the abolitionists who prevented Kentucky slaveholders' taking the fugitive slave family of Adam Crosswhite. In 1848 he and several prominent Marshall citizens were convicted and fined for conspiracy to harbor the fugitives. Comstock was superintendent of the construction of the Michigan Central Railroad between Jackson and Kalamazoo and a founder of the Michigan Pioneer and Historical Society.

203 South Marshall Avenue, Marshall; Comstock, Oliver C., Jr., House (Comstock-Sargent House); L783B; February 27, 1980; 1980

Pioneer School

The city of Marshall was platted in 1830 by Sidney Ketchum, a land speculator from Clinton County, New York. In 1832 townsfolk erected their first public building, a modest frame schoolhouse, on land donated by Isaac E. Crary, who became one of the fathers of the Michigan public school system. During its early years, the schoolhouse also served as a church for three denominations, the circuit court of Calhoun County and, during the cholera epidemic, a hospital.

Side Two

In 1833, Marshall's first village officials were elected at a meeting held in the pioneer schoolhouse. The building served the community as a school until 1843. William Venn built a house on this property in the early 1860s and moved the old schoolhouse to the rear of the lot. There it was used as a barn. The schoolhouse was demolished in 1871 when the First Presbyterian Church purchased the property for a manse. The church sold the property in 1880 and repurchased it in 1914.

200 West Mansion, Marshall; Marshall Public Schools Pioneer School House Informational Site; L1393C; March 19, 1987; 1987

Postmasters

Until the Civil Service reforms of 1883, one became a postmaster through a federal political appointment. Thus, postmasters were usually prominent political leaders of the local community. In 1831, George Ketchum, cofounder of the city of Marshall, became this area's first postmaster. In 1833 he was followed by the Reverend John D. Pierce, who later became Michigan's first state superintendent of public instruction. Through the years a stagecoach operator, a banker, a physician, a mayor and a newspaper publisher have served the community as postmasters.

Howard F. Young

Howard F. Young (1889-1934), a native of Allegan, designed this Marshall post office building in 1932. Young studied engineering at the University of Michigan and was involved in construction work in Albany, New York, Detroit and Kalamazoo. His interest in restoring Greek Revival architecture is evident in his Marshall projects, which include the restoration

Michigan's first congressman, Isaac E. Crary (left), and the Reverend John D. Pierce, founded Michigan's Public School System in 1834. (*State School System*)

of the Harold C. Brooks and other homes and the conversion of Marshall's livery stable into a town hall. Young also designed the Brooks Memorial Fountain.

202 East Michigan Avenue, Marshall; United States Post Office; L989A; January 13, 1982; 1982

Railroad Union Birthplace

In April 1863 a meeting held here at the home of Jared C. Thompson led directly to the organization of the Brotherhood of the Footboard. Under the leadership of Marshall's William D. Robinson, founder and first Grand Chief Engineer, fifty-four locals were established in the next sixteen months. Renamed the Brotherhood of Locomotive Engineers in 1864, the union grew to over eighty thousand members by the mid-twentieth century.

633 West Hanover, Marshall; Thompson, Jared C., House (Railroad Union Birthplace); L282; April 5, 1974; 1974

Sam Hill House

Samuel W. Hill, legendary figure of the northland, surveyed the Great Lakes' harbors in 1840-1844 and worked with Dr. Douglass Houghton on the first geological survey of the Upper Peninsula in 1845. He was later involved with the sale of land and the building of roads and canals in the area. For many years he directed some of the most successful copper mines of the Lake Superior region. Twice elected to the state legislature, Hill retired to this house in 1875. He died in 1889.

139 West Mansion Street, Marshall; Hill, Sam, House; L283; July 26, 1974; 1974

Schellenberger Tavern

German immigrant Jacob Schellenberger built this structure as both a home and tavern. A stone cutter by trade, Schellenberger obtained sandstone from along the nearby Kalamazoo River for the building, which he completed around 1840. Because of its proximity to the river, Indians reportedly stopped here enroute to Detroit trading posts. Now a private residence, the structure features the low-pitched roof and wide entablature characteristic of Greek Revival architecture.

507 West Hanover, Marshall; Schellenberger Tavern; L473; November 3, 1976; 1977

Schuler's

A hotel or inn has occupied this site since 1870. Here stood The Exchange, which became

The Johnson House in 1892. The Painter family erected the present brick building in 1895 then known as The Royal. Albert W. Schuler, Sr., purchased the hotel in 1924 and renamed it The Schuler. Ten years later the edifice became a restaurant, which the Schuler family continues to operate. Located in a city noted for its wealth of historic buildings, Schuler's features a longstanding tradition of fine food.

115 South Eagle Street, Marshall; Win Schuler's Inn; L458; August 6, 1976; 1977

Sidney Ketchum (1797-1862)

Sidney Ketchum, a land surveyor, was born in Clinton County, New York. Seeking a new home and hoping to found a town, Ketchum explored central lower Michigan in 1830. Later that year he obtained government grants for the land on which most of Marshall now stands. He named the town in honor of U.S. Chief Justice John Marshall. Ketchum founded the county's first bank in 1836 and built the city's first Methodist church in 1838.

Marshall House

This handsome structure was built in 1838 by Sidney Ketchum, founder of Marshall. For many years it was one of the largest and most elaborate hotels outside of Detroit. The then three-story structure, known as the Marshall House, had forty bedrooms and a dining room with a seating capacity of 150. Suffering from competition with a newly erected local inn, the hotel closed in 1859. The building reopened in 1864 as the Perrin Collegiate Institute, a boarding and day school for girls. It now houses a mortuary.

100 Exchange Street, Marshall; Marshall House (Antique Centre); L784B; February 27, 1980; 1980

State School System

In 1834-1835, Isaac E. Crary (1804-1854) and John D. Pierce (1793-1882) planned Michigan's public school system, which influenced educational policy throughout America. Their most important contribution was the establishment of a separate department of education run by a superintendent—an innovative effort to introduce uniform schooling in Michigan. Crary and Pierce specified that certain land revenues go to the state, not the townships, for education. They also designated Michigan's general college fund for the financially ailing University of Michigan. Later in 1862, Congress adopted this state's method of using land revenues for schools, a plan which benefited Michigan Agricultural College in East Lansing. Using ideas from Prussian educators and New England schools, Michigan's school system aided the growth of this frontier area.

Isaac E. Crary and John D. Pierce

When attorney Isaac E. Crary came to Marshall in 1832 from Connecticut, he became fast friends with another transplanted easterner, the Reverend John D. Pierce. Interested in government and education, these two men in 1834-1835 planned Michigan's public school system. The proposed system became law in 1835 when Crary headed the education committee of the state's inaugural constitutional convention. The following year Pierce was appointed state superintendent of education—the first such position in America. Crary, who later was a state legislator and the first United States representative from Michigan, and Pierce continued to battle for educational plans including free schools. Dying in 1854 and 1882 respectively, Crary and Pierce were buried in Oakridge Cemetery, Marshall.

100 East Green Street, Marshall; Marshall Middle School; S503; January 19, 1978; 1978

Thomas J. O'Brien

Thomas J. O'Brien (1842-1933), a graduate of Marshall High School and the University of Michigan Law School, practiced law here in the First National Bank of Marshall Building from 1865 to 1876. He was appointed minister to Denmark in 1905 by President Theodore Roosevelt. During his tenure, he began negotiations for the U.S. purchase of the Danish West Indies, now the U.S. Virgin Islands. In 1908, O'Brien became ambassador to Japan and, in 1911, ambassador to Italy. He resigned from diplomatic service in 1913 and resumed his law practice.

117 East Michigan Avenue, Marshall; First National Bank of Marshall (Smithfield-Banques Antique Store); L1794A; November 15, 1990; 1991

Trinity Episcopal Church

Trinity parish was organized in 1836. Early services were held in a log schoolhouse. The

Reverend Samuel Buel assumed duties as the first pastor in 1838. This native Marshall sandstone building, with its Victorian interior, was completed in 1864 at a cost of $9,982. The architect was Gordon W. Lloyd of Detroit, and the builder was Nathan Benedict of Marshall. The Marshall Historic Home Tour originated here as a kitchen tour sponsored by the Trinity churchwomen.

Montgomery Schuyler

Trinity's second minister, Montgomery Schuyler (1814-1896), was born in New York City. He came to Marshall in 1835, entered a hardware business, began a Sunday school and helped found Trinity. He was ordained and made pastor of Trinity Episcopal Church in 1841. In 1842 he founded St. Thomas's Church, Battle Creek. He founded St. John's parish in Buffalo, New York, in 1845 and was rector and dean of Christ Church in St. Louis, Missouri, from 1854 to 1896. He is buried in Marshall's Oakridge Cemetery.

101 East Mansion Street, Marshall; Trinity Episcopal Church; L786A; February 27, 1980; 1980

William W. Cook

For thirty-three years this was the home of William Wallace Cook, prolific writer of dime novels. Heroes such as Frank Merriwell, Nick Carter and Buffalo Bill were his speciality. Employed by Street and Smith serial publishers, Cook's problems in turning out quantities of material on a tight schedule were described in the autobiographical account, *The Fiction Factory*. He later systematized his writing technique in *Plotto, A New Method of Creative Fiction*. Born in Marshall in 1867, Cook returned in 1900 and resided here until his death in 1933.

603 North Kalamazoo, Marshall; Cook, William Wallace, House; L218; March 14, 1973; 1973

The Starr Commonwealth Schools

In 1913, Floyd Starr purchased forty acres of land on Montcalm Lake to found Starr Commonwealth for Boys, a nonprofit home and residential school for wayward, delinquent and neglected boys. At that time, the only building on the property was an old barn in which Starr and the first two boys stayed until the first structure was completed. Today, 155 boys are served on a three-hundred-acre campus encompassing facilities built with private contributions. Services to youth were expanded with the founding of the Van Wert, Ohio, campus in 1951 and the merger with the Hannah Neil Center for Children in Columbus, Ohio, in 1978. Focusing on positive support in the character development of troubled children by providing a well-founded academic, social and spiritual exposure, Starr Commonwealth is now a nationally recognized child care organization.

Floyd Starr

Floyd Starr, originator of the credo, "There is no such thing as a bad boy," was born in Decatur, Michigan, on May 1, 1883. After graduating from Marshall High School, he worked for several years in a half-way house in St. Louis, Missouri. Returning to Michigan, he obtained his bachelor of arts degree from Albion College in 1910. Fulfilling a lifetime dream to someday adopt fifty boys, Starr founded Starr Commonwealth for Boys in 1913. "Uncle Floyd," as he was affectionately called by his boys, earned the respect of court officials, coworkers and students for his successful work with homeless, neglected and delinquent boys. He received numerous citations for his humanitarian efforts. Starr retired from active leadership of Starr Commonwealth in 1967, but provided guidance until his death on August 27, 1980, at the age of ninety-seven.

Twenty-six Mile Road (Starr Commonwealth Road), between I-94 and Michigan Avenue, one-half mile south of exit 119, Sheridan Township; Starr Commonwealth for Boys; S544A; July 17, 1981; 1982

Harvey Randall House

This Queen Anne house was built in 1898 for Tekonsha businessman Harvey N. Randall (1859-1917) and his wife, dressmaker Adell Warboys Randall (1863-1943). Randall prospered as a produce, livestock and hardware merchant. By 1905 he established the Harvey N. Randall Company, which dealt only in hardware. Adell served as the company's secretary-treasurer. Randall held positions as the village president, school board trustee and director of the First State Bank of Tekonsha.

103 East North Street, Tekonsha; Randall, Harvey N., House; L1473A; November 20, 1987; 1991

Cass

Cass County Courthouse

Completed in 1899, this wooden frame building with limestone veneer is the third courthouse to serve Cass County. The Territorial Government of Michigan established the county in 1829 and named it after then-Governor Lewis Cass. Two years later Cassopolis became the county seat. The Board of Supervisors built this first courthouse in 1835 away from the Public Square. The area's rapid growth necessitated the erection of a second courthouse on the Public Square in 1841. Nineteen years later some county offices moved across the street to a building called "The Fort." The inconvenience of two separate facilities and the dilapidated condition of the second courthouse led to construction of the present building. With a wing added in 1976, it remains the seat of justice in Cass County.

110 North Broadway, Cassopolis; Cass County Courthouse; L487; December 14, 1976; 1977

Episcopal Church

The first recorded Episcopal gathering in Cass County was conducted by Bishop Philander Chase in 1832. In 1858, under the auspices of the Trinity Church of Niles, the first Episcopal services in Dowagiac were held. In 1897 the Reverend R. H. F. Gairdner of Niles helped establish St. Alban's Mission. The mission rented this property. After St. Alban's Mission dissolved in 1903, a small group of Episcopalians continued to meet informally until 1911, when St. Paul's Mission was formed. The mission first leased this structure, then purchased and remodeled it in 1913. On June 8, 1915, St. Paul's was established as a parish of the Diocese of Western Michigan. The consecration of this building as an Episcopal church was held on December 17, 1919.

St. Paul's Church

Under the leadership of Justus Gage (1805-1875), this structure was built in 1859 as a Universalist church. Completed at a cost of $3,000, it is Dowagiac's oldest public building. At the time of completion, it was the town's only auditorium. Women's rights advocates Victoria Woodhull, Belva Lockwood, Anna Shaw, Mary Livermore and Susan B. Anthony spoke here, as did black civil rights supporter Sojourner Truth. Performers appearing in the auditorium included Ole Bull, the Norse violinist. Episcopalians first met here in 1897. The Romanesque-style exterior has remained virtually unchanged; however, the interior was remodeled extensively in 1959 when Dom Francis Bacon, O.S.B. (1903-1967), added mosaics and decorations reminiscent of very early churches.

306 Courtland Street, Dowagiac; First Universalist Church of Dowagiac (St. Paul's Episcopal Church); L1028A; September 8, 1982; 1984

District Schoolhouse

This late-Victorian schoolhouse was built in 1874-1875. Constructed at a cost of $3,000, it is made of locally manufactured yellow and red brick. The 1882 Cass County history described it as "the best rural schoolhouse in the State." Its two classrooms could accommodate 110 pupils. The school was used until the local district was absorbed into the Constantine School District in 1959. In 1964 the building became the township hall, and in 1972, the Mason Union Branch of the Cass County Library.

17049 US-12, Mason Township; Mason District No. 5 Schoolhouse (Mason Township Hall); L821A; June 10, 1980; 1981

Smith's Chapel

The first Methodist church in Milton Township was organized in 1839. The following year, this church was built and named Smith's Chapel to honor Canon Smith, who had contributed generously to the construction of the church. Smith, a native of Delaware, bought land here in 1829 and settled on it in 1831. The chapel is one of the oldest Methodist churches in southwestern Michigan. In 1967 regular church services were discontinued. Milton Township purchased the structure in 1972. It now serves as a wedding and funeral chapel.

Redfield Road between Brush and Fir roads, Milton Township; Smith's Chapel (including the cemetery grounds); L652A; April 24, 1979; 1981

Poe's Corners

In 1835, George Poe (1779-1851) emigrated from Crawford County, Ohio, and settled on land deeded to him by the U.S. government. Within two years he acquired 520 acres of land in Newberg Township. Many members of the Poe family settled in this vicinity, and it became known as the Poe Neighborhood and Poe's Corners. In 1838 the first recorded burial, that of Rachel Everhart, occurred in Poe's Cemetery, located on one corner of George Poe's farm. The First Regular Baptist Church of Newberg, also known as Poe's Church, was organized in 1841; a church was erected in 1858. School District No. 2, known as Poe's School, was created in 1856. In 1957 the school district merged with the Marcellus School District; the school building became the Newberg Township Hall in 1958.

Intersection of Patterson Hill Road and Born Street, Newburg Township; Poe's Corners Informational Designation; L1817C; March 21, 1991; 1991

The Underground Railroad

Vandalia, prior to the Civil War, was the junction of two important "lines" of the "Underground Railroad." Slaves fleeing through Indiana and Illinois came to Cass County, where Quakers and others gave them shelter. Fugitives seeking a refuge in Canada were guided to "stations" to the east. Many stayed here and built a unique Negro rural colony. Slave-hunting by Kentuckians in 1847 led to legal action and increased North-South tensions.

Bonine Elk Park, M-60, one-half mile west of Vandalia, Penn Township; Underground Railway Informational Designation; S137; January 19, 1957; 1957

Sacred Heart of Mary Catholic Church

Chief Leopold Pokagon and his tribe of Potawatomi Indians built a log church here in 1838 and deeded the forty acres of land on which it stood to the Catholic Bishop of Detroit. Pokagon, who came to Silver Creek Township from his village outside of nearby Niles, was buried on this site in 1841. During the early 1840s the Holy Cross Fathers of Notre Dame in Indiana ministered to the Indians. In 1844, Father Theophile Marivault became the church's permanent priest; he was followed by Father Louis Baroux who served most of the years from 1847 to 1870 and was buried here in 1897. In the mid-nineteenth century many Irish immigrants settled in the vicinity and attended this parish. The white frame church built in 1861 burned in 1886 and was immediately replaced by this present structure.

SE corner of Leach and Priest roads, Silver Creek Township; Sacred Heart of Mary Catholic Church; L348; January 16, 1976; 1977

Newton House

Designed by Christian Haefner in the 1860s, this house belonged to George Newton, a state legislator. The cupola, projecting eaves and symmetrically grouped windows distinguish its architecture. This building is located in the 580-acre densely timbered Fred Russ Experimental Forest, which Michigan State University used as a forestry school after receiving it as a gift in 1942. The Cass County Historical Commission has restored this elegant structure.

20689 Marcellus Highway, Volinia Township; Newton, George, House; L367; November 14, 1974; 1977

Charlevoix

Horton Bay

Named for pioneer settler Samuel Horton, this village was founded as a lumbering community in 1876, complete with sawmill, shanty boys, boarding house, company store, blacksmith shop and draft horses. The store and many early buildings still stand. After the timber was gone, three fine restaurants opened: Dilworth's, The Waffle Shop and The Red Fox Inn. Young Ernest Hemingway frequently came here to fish and camp on "The Point." This area is the setting for several of his famous "Nick Adams" short stories. Hemingway was married here in 1921.

Bay Township Hall, corner of Lake Street and Boyne City Road, Bay Township; Horton Bay Historic District; S463; November 12, 1975; 1977

Boyne City United Methodist Church

In 1874 the Reverend Andrew Wiggins and twelve pioneers organized the Methodist Episcopal Church of Boyne City, near Deer Lake. In 1883, Zachariah Morgan and his wife, Mary, donated land on which to build a church. The first church was built on this site in 1894. In 1905 teams of horses were used to haul the church away to make room for the present structure. The Grand Rapids architectural firm of Osgood and Osgood designed this church, which was completed in 1906 at a cost of $13,000.

324 South Park Street, Boyne City; Boyne City United Methodist Church; L1443B; August 21, 1987; 1989

Mormon Kingdom

About twenty miles northwest of here is Beaver Island. In 1847, James Strang set up a colony for his followers, dissenters from the main body of Mormonism. Strang crowned himself "King James in 1850. Hatred of the sect by non-Mormons led to the Battle of Pine River in 1853 at present-day Charlevoix. On June 16, 1856, because they hated his authoritarian rule, some of Strang's subjects mortally wounded him. Later in the summer, mainlanders drove the Mormons from Beaver Island.

James Strang, Beaver Island's self-proclaimed monarch, established a Mormon colony there in 1847. (*Mormon Kingdom*)

City Dock Park, on US-31, Charlevoix; Mormon Kingdom Informational Designation; S136; January 19, 1957; 1957

Greensky Hill Mission

Here in the 1840s the Chippewa Indian missionary, Peter Greensky, established a Protestant mission in an area where legend says Indian chiefs once held their councils. New trees have been planted in an arrangement similar to that of the trees that made up the original council circle. Mission services first were held in a rude building of boughs and bark. In the 1850s the Indians built the present church. It is a fine example of the old log style construction with hand-hewn timbers and notched corners. Windows, doors and much of the lumber were brought by canoe from Traverse City to Pine Lake (now Lake Charlevoix) and then carried two miles to this site. Methodist services for the Indian congregation have been held here regularly to the present.

NE of Charlevoix at junction of Old US-31 and County Road 630, Hayes Township; Pine River Indian Mission (Greensky Hill Mission); L26; November 17, 1962; 1964

Mormon Print Shop

This building was erected in 1850, by James Strang and his followers. Here during the 1850s, these Mormon dissenters published religious works and two newspapers, the *Northern Islander* and the *Daily Northern Islander*. Strang's group had settled on Beaver Island in 1846 after breaking away from the Mormons led by Brigham Young. In 1850, Strang was declared "king" of his community, which made up the majority of the population on the island. In 1856, Strang was fatally shot by two disenchanted followers. In the wake of the assassination, an angry mob from the mainland stormed Beaver Island destroying buildings and forcing the Mormons to flee. At that time, this print shop was ransacked. It later became a boardinghouse. Today it serves as the headquarters for the Beaver Island Historical Society.

NW corner of Forrest and Main streets on Beaver Island, St. James Township; Strang, James, Print Shop (Mormon Print Shop); HB32; February 19, 1958; 1977

Cheboygan

Jacob J. Post House

Cheboygan businessman Jacob J. Post built this Queen Anne-style house in 1886. The residence was designed by Frederick W. Hollister of Saginaw and reflects Post's prominence in the community. A New York native, Post received a medical discharge from the Union army in 1863. He then worked in a general store where he learned the merchant trade. In 1872, Post and his wife, Cornelia, settled in Cheboygan. Here he opened Cheboygan's first hardware store and founded the First National Bank of Cheboygan.

528 South Huron, Cheboygan; Post, Jacob J., House; L1622A; February 16, 1989; 1990

Old Cheboygan County Courthouse

When Cheboygan County was organized in 1853, the courthouse was located in Duncan (now a part of the city of Cheboygan). In 1860 the county board of supervisors moved the county seat to Inverness Township and purchased this property from Bela Chapman. This courthouse, built by J. F. Watson in 1869 at a cost of $3,000, held its last circuit court session in 1899. Since then it has served as a fire station, a church and a community center.

229 Court Street, Cheboygan; Cheboygan County Courthouse (demolished); L417; September 15, 1975; 1980

St. Mary Church

Father Andrew D. Piret, a priest serving the Mackinac Island mission, celebrated the first mass of the St. Mary's congregation in the home of Charles Bellant in 1852. Four years later, the parish built a temporary chapel on Peter McDonald's farm on the Cheboygan River. In 1862 the parish's first confirmation was conducted by Bishop Frederic Baraga. Visiting priests and bishops served the parish until 1868, when Father Charles DeCeuninck became its first resident priest. In 1870 the parish completed its present church building. In 1895 the French-speaking members of the parish established St. Charles Parish, and the Polish-speaking members founded St. Lawrence Parish.

120 North D Street, Cheboygan; St. Mary Catholic Church; L899A; March 16, 1981; 1987

Mackinaw City

In 1634, Samuel de Champlain sent Jean Nicolet from Quebec to explore this area and make peace with the Ottawa and Ojibwa Indians. French traders were in the area in 1673, but they left when conflict with the Indians ensued. The French returned in 1715 and established Fort Michilimackinac, which they occupied until the English took over in 1761. The English abandoned the fort in 1781, during the American Revolution, and re-established it at Mackinac Island. In 1857, Edgar Conkling and Asbury Searles platted the present village of Mackinaw City. The village developed commercially with the arrival in 1881 of the Michigan Central Railroad, which terminated here. The Grand Rapids and Indiana Railroad arrived in 1882. Mackinaw City was officially incorporated as a village in December 1883.

Side Two

This site was the terminus of the Dixie Highway, the Mackinaw Trail, the East Michigan Pike and the West Michigan Pike. The East and West pikes were mapped out in 1913 as gravel and dirt roads. Concrete construction began in the 1920s. Private auto clubs began making trips on the West Michigan Pike, which extended from Chicago to Mackinaw City, in 1913. The first trip, from St. Joseph to Mackinaw City, marked the beginning of an annual event that continued until 1919. Beginning in 1916 the East Michigan Pike was used for touring. Groups from Detroit came up this eastern route. Until the Mackinac Bridge was completed in 1957, the State Highway Department managed a ferry system that transported those arriving by these routes across the Straits of Mackinac.

Marina Park, at Central and Huron avenues, Mackinaw City; Mackinaw City Informational Designation; L1414C; May 15, 1987; 1987

Old Mackinac Point Lighthouse

This light is opposite the turning point for ships making the difficult passage through the

Straits of Mackinac, one of the business crossroads of the Great Lakes. McGulpin's Point light, two miles to the west, had been established in 1856, but it was not visible from all directions. In 1889, Congress appropriated funds for the construction of a steam-powered fog signal here, which went into operation on November 5, 1890. Construction of the light tower and attached keeper's dwelling began, and the light was first displayed on October 25, 1892. Heavy iron and brass castings were used throughout the structure, and the light was visible to ships sixteen miles away. In operation until 1958, the lighthouse is now a maritime museum.

Michilimackinac State Park, North Huron Avenue, Mackinaw City; Mackinac Point Lighthouse; S377; April 14, 1972; 1972

Old Mill Creek

In 1780 the British garrison at Fort Michilimackinac moved to Mackinac Island as a safer location during the American Revolution. Robert Campbell built a sawmill on this site to furnish lumber for the new fort and settlement. His sawmill and dam were one of the earliest industrial enterprises in northern Michigan. The complex later included a grist mill, an orchard, a blacksmith shop, a warehouse and several homes. Michael Dousman purchased the site in 1819 and continued to operate the mill until 1839. By 1867 the buildings were gone and the site had fallen into disrepair. In 1975 the Mackinac Island State Park Commission acquired the site. It opened its recreated working sawmill to the public in 1984.

Four miles SE of Mackinaw City on US-23, Old Mill Creek State Historic Park, Mackinaw Township; Campbell, Robert, Mill (Old Mill Creek State Historic Park); L1154; March 20, 1984; 1984

Inland Waterway

The glaciers of the last Ice Age retreated to the north some 25,000 years ago, leaving behind the lakes that rank as Michigan's most notable geographical feature. Among the state's largest inland lakes is Burt Lake, named after William A. Burt, who, together with Henry Mullett, made a federal survey of the area from 1840 to 1843. By following the Cheboygan River, Mullett Lake and Indian River to Burt Lake, then up Crooked River to Crooked Lake, Indians and fur traders had only a short portage to Little Traverse Bay. Thus they avoided the trip through the Straits. Completion of a lock on the Cheboygan in 1869 opened this inland waterway to the Cheboygan Slack Water Navigation Company, whose vessels carried passengers and freight until railroads put it out of business. Day-long excursions over these waters became popular with tourists.

Burt Lake State Park, Old US-27, near I-75 and M-68, Tuscarora Township; Inland Waterway Informational Designation; S127; January 19, 1957; 1957

Michigan Central Depot

In 1881, John M. Sanborn surveyed land owned by Daniel McKillop and platted the village of Torrey. That year a post office opened here under the name "Wolverine." In 1882 the village was replatted as Wolverine. By the turn of the century, lumbering made Wolverine a boom town. The original land survey had included a right-of-way for the Michigan Central Railroad (MCRR). Early in the 1880s Wolverine became part of the MCRR's Mackinaw Division. Four passenger trains ran daily. By 1903 scheduled runs increased to six as tourism to the Straits developed. The MCRR promoted northern Michigan as "curative of hayfever, asthma, bronchial and lung affections." Around 1906 this depot opened, providing modern conveniences for travelers.

100 Railroad, Wolverine; Michigan Central Railroad Depot; L1696A; December 20, 1989; 1991

Chippewa

Fort Drummond

Forced by the Treaty of Ghent to evacuate the fort they had captured on Mackinac Island during the War of 1812, the British selected this island as an alternate military post. The stronghold was close to the traditional Indian gathering point at the Straits of Mackinac in order to sustain English control of the Indians and the Upper Great Lakes fur trade. Built by Colonel Robert McDonall and his men, Fort Drummond and the nearby village at Collier's Harbor were maintained for more than a decade. The British abandoned their stronghold in

1828, six years after Drummond Island was ruled United States territory. Now summer cottages occupy this rocky countryside and only a few ruined chimneys survive as reminders of the conflict between British and American sovereignty in the Old Northwest.

West end of Drummond Island at the ferry boat landing, NW shore of the St. Marys River, Drummond Township; Fort Colyer (Fort Drummond); S109; November 27, 1956; 1977

Elmwood

Appointed Indian agent in 1822, Henry Rowe Schoolcraft (1793-1864) requested that the government provide a suitable structure to house the agency. Obed Wait, designer of Michigan's territorial capitol in Detroit, directed the construction of this building. Nearly one hundred feet in length when completed in 1827, the Federal-style building originally had a two-story central unit flanked by two single-story wings. While at Elmwood, Schoolcraft, explorer and ethnologist, collected materials for his pioneering works on Indian culture, which scholars still use. These inspired Henry Wadsworth Longfellow's "Song of Hiawatha." Charles T. Harvey lived here during the mid-1850s when he supervised the building of the canal and locks at Sault Ste. Marie. Elmwood's substantial alterations during the past 150 years reflect its varied uses and inhabitants.

Originally located at 705 East Portage Avenue, Sault Ste. Marie; house and marker moved to 417 Water Street, Sault Ste. Marie; Schoolcraft House/Indian Agency (Elmwood); HB6; September 25, 1956; 1977

Indian agent John Johnston settled with his Indian wife in the Sault Ste. Marie area in 1793. (*John Johnston House*)

Fort Brady

On July 6, 1822, a battalion of American troops under Colonel Hugh Brady reached the Sault, thereby reconfirming the assertion of American authority over this region made by Lewis Cass in 1820. Fort Brady was built here by year's end. The French and Indians living at the little village now recognized that this remote outpost was truly part of America. The fort was removed in 1893 to a new site chosen by General Phil Sheridan.

Fort bounded by the Corps of Engineers Service Plaza on the north, Portage Street on the south, Brady Street on the east and Bingham Street on the west, Sault Ste. Marie; marker located on Water Street; Fort Brady (20CH51); S88; August 23, 1956; 1956

John Johnston House

A native of Ireland and a Protestant, John Johnston (1762-1828) arrived on the Lake Superior frontier in the early 1790s. He married the daughter of a powerful Chippewa chief and settled here in 1793. Johnston's knowledge of the Chippewa and the Great Lakes region made him a central figure in the development of this frontier. His original house was a hospitable meeting place for explorers, surveyors, trappers, traders and Indians. Loyal to the British, Johnston aided them in taking the American fort on Mackinac Island in 1812. In retaliation, American troops burned Johnston's house in 1815. He soon rebuilt it. This surviving portion erected about 1822, in part to house his daughter Jane and her husband, Henry Rowe Schoolcraft, is a reminder of Johnston's pivotal role in the area's transition from British to American control.

Originally located at 415 Park Place, Sault Ste. Marie; house and marker moved to 415 Water Street, Sault Ste. Marie; Johnston, John, House; HB34; February 19, 1958; 1977

Lake Superior State College

In 1946 the state of Michigan assumed control of New Fort Brady, and presented it to the Michigan College of Mining and Technology, now Michigan Technological University. The Houghton-based school, forced to expand by the enrollment of returning veterans, adapted the old Army buildings to college classrooms, residence halls and offices. Not until 1964, with the completion of Crawford Hall, did the campus have a building constructed for educational purposes. The school's curriculum, which at first duplicated the main campus's engineering program, was broadened. On January 1, 1970, the school became a separate and autonomous four-year institution called Lake Superior State College.

West Easterday Road near the intersection with Meridian Road, Sault Ste. Marie; Lake Superior State College; L382; February 21, 1975; 1976

Larke Road

Until 1962, Three Mile (Larke) Road was known simply as Larke Road. In 1876, Henry Larke (1824-1900) became the first settler along this road, making his home about one and one-half miles west of this site. He had emigrated from Canada, where he farmed and made wooden pumps. From 1876 until 1897, Larke operated a dairy farm near this site. His son Richard and daughter-in-law Lena maintained the farm until the 1940s. Around the turn of the century, a local glacial deposit and the local rural school were named in honor of the Larke family.

About one-quarter mile from exit 392 on business I-75, corner of Three Mile Road and Eighth, Sault Ste. Marie; Larke Road Informational Designation; L986B; January 13, 1982; 1982

Methodist Indian Mission

Several Methodist ministers were active in missionary work in the "Soo" area in the 1830s. John Sunday, an Indian preacher from Canada, began mission work in the Indian settlement at the Sault Ste. Marie Rapids around 1831. The Reverend John Clark followed in his steps two years later. Then a church and log schoolhouse were erected. In 1833, Peter Marksman, son of an Indian medicine man, was converted to Christianity and later became an esteemed minister of the Detroit Annual Conference. By 1834 the school had thirty-five students, and three "Methodist classes" were organized with forty Indians and nineteen whites. The Michigan Conference sent William H. Brockway to the mission as superintendent in 1839. Here he remained for ten years, serving most of that time as chaplain for Old Fort Brady.

Side Two

John H. Pitezel and John Kahbeege continued the ministerial work at this settlement having come to the "Soo" in 1843. Pitezel arrived at what was a flourishing school and a farm with nearly fifty cultivated acres of land. He served as superintendent of the Methodist Indian District from 1848 to 1852, with missions as far away as Minnesota. A mission house was built in 1849 at Naomikong on Whitefish Bay. Little Rapids had been the focal point of the mission, for here were the farm, mission house, chapel and needed supplies. As more white settlers came to the "Soo" in the 1850s, many of the Indians moved away. By 1861, Methodist mission work in the area was concentrated at Iroquois Point near Sault Ste. Marie. The Methodists sold the mission land here in 1862.

Near Rotary Park and turnoff to Sugar Island Ferry, Riverside Drive, Sault Ste. Marie; Methodist Indian Mission (Sault Ste. Marie Golf Course); L633A; October 9, 1978; 1979

New Fort Brady

When Sault Ste. Marie expanded and its canal was widened, the riverfront site of Fort Brady was abandoned for a higher, more strategic site selected by General Philip Sheridan. Work began in 1886, and the new fort was opened in 1893. From this hilltop, New Fort Brady guarded the copper and iron ore enroute from the mineral regions of western Lake Superior through St. Mary's Ship Canal. Although never under attack, its troops were called up in 1894 during civil unrest, but primarily they protected the canal until the Second World War, when fifteen thousand soldiers were stationed here. In 1944 the National Guard assumed these responsibilities and New Fort Brady was closed. Camp Lucas, a small section of the fort was reactivated briefly during the Korean Conflict.

Lake Superior State University Library parking lot off Ryan Street, Sault Ste. Marie; New Fort Brady; S305; July 17, 1970; 1976

Sault Ste. Marie

This city, the oldest in the Midwest, grew up about the mission of Fathers Dablon and Marquette, founded in 1668 on the banks of the rapids through which Lake Superior's waters commence their long journey seaward. In 1641, Fathers Jogues and Raymbault of Sainte

Marie Mission near Georgian Bay, came here and applied the name Sault de Sainte Marie, or "rapids of Saint Mary," to the waters. Popular usage shortens it to "the Soo."

Rest area on I-75, five miles south of Sault Ste. Marie, Soo Township; Sault Ste. Marie; S29; February 18, 1956; 1957

St. Mary's Pro-Cathedral

In 1853, Pope Pius IX separated the Upper Peninsula from the Diocese of Detroit and established a vicariate apostolic. Reverend Frederic Baraga, a missionary from L'Anse, became vicar apostolic and made St. Mary's Church his headquarters. In 1857 the vicariate became a diocese, Baraga was named "Bishop of the Sault" and the log church known as St. Mary's became a cathedral. With the onset of mining, settlements sprang up in the western Upper Peninsula. Faced with the task of serving these remote parishes, Bishop Baraga obtained the pope's permission to move the seat of the diocese to Marquette. In May 1866, Baraga left St. Mary's and the parish became the pro-cathedral parish. In 1881 the present Gothic Revival-style church, designed by Joseph Connolly of Toronto, was erected.

320 East Portage Avenue, Sault Ste. Marie; St. Mary's Pro-Cathedral; S595A; July 20, 1989; 1990

Johnston Homesite

In 1864, John McDougal Johnston, his wife, Justine, and their six children homesteaded this island. His father was a famous Sault Ste. Marie fur trader and his mother was the daughter of an Ojibway chief. He served as an interpreter for his brother-in-law, Henry R. Schoolcraft, the Indian agent. After twelve years on Rains Island, John and Justine moved to a farm near the Sault. Two children, Anna Marie, known as Miss Molly, and Howard, remained to farm the homestead. In 1892 birch bark cabins were built on this site to house visitors. Miss Molly called the spot Ononegwud, an Indian name for Happy Place. The land was given to the Neebish Pioneer Association in memory of the Bagnall family in 1974 to preserve as the Johnston Conservation area.

Sailor's Encampment, Neebish Island, Soo Township; Johnston Homestead Informational Site; L389; April 4, 1975; 1975

Emerson

Once a thriving hub of pine lumbering, Emerson is now a fishing hamlet. Just one mile south of the mouth of the Tahquamenon River (immortalized in Longfellow's poem "Hiawatha"), this settlement overlooks picturesque Whitefish Bay. The village was founded by Kurt Emerson, a lumberman from the Saginaw Bay area, in the 1880s. Emerson erected a sawmill and in 1884 sold his establishment to the Chesbrough Lumber Company. Milling and lumbering operations ceased in 1912, at which time commercial fishing became the economic bulwark of the community.

M-123, one-quarter mile south of Tahquamenon River, Whitefish Township; Emerson Informational Designation; L725B; August 3, 1979; 1980

Post Office

This post office opened just six years after Whitefish Point was settled in 1871 as a landing for the then abundant lumber supplies and as a commercial fishery. Permanent residents received their mail from Sault Ste. Marie. During the summer months, mail was delivered by boat three times a week. In severe winter weather, dog teams hauled the mail twice a month. In service for nearly a century, this post office provides a link with days before lumbermen cut down tall stands of pine trees. The office here ceased operations in 1973.

Intersection of Whitefish Point and Wildcat roads, Whitefish Township; Whitefish Point Post Office (Biehl's General Store); L724B; August 3, 1979; 1979

Shelldrake

Legend has it that Lewis Cass, governor of the Territory of Michigan, and his party of nearly one hundred camped here on their search for the source of the Mississippi River in 1820. This area, once a bustling lumbering community, was first settled in the mid-nineteenth century. Shelldrake is now a sleepy resort and hunting place. Few of the weatherbeaten buildings that once faced the long boardwalk remain. This settlement is a reminder of the area's lumbering era.

Old Shelldrake Road (private road now—abandoned—inaccessible to public), Whitefish Township; Shelldrake Informational Site; L727B; August 3, 1979; 1980

Whitefish Point Lighthouse

This light, the oldest active on Lake Superior, began operating in 1849, though the present tower was constructed later. Early a stopping place for Indians, *voyageurs* and Jesuit missionaries, the point marks a course change for ore boats and other ships navigating this treacherous coastline to and from St. Mary's Canal. Since 1971 the light, fog signal and radio beacon have been automated and controlled from Sault Ste. Marie.

Eleven miles north of the intersection of M-123 and Whitefish Point Road, Whitefish Township; Whitefish Point Lighthouse; L272; February 22, 1974; 1974

Whitefish Township

In 1849 the Whitefish Point lighthouse was put into service. Soon after the township was organized in 1888, lumber towns such as Emerson and Shelldrake emerged at the mouth of the Tahquamenon and Shelldrake rivers. Paradise was established in 1925. In the 1920s lumbering declined and fires burned the cutover land, creating a rich soil for blueberries. Cranberry and blueberry cultivation as well as commercial fishing on Whitefish Bay sustained the area's economy.

M-123, two miles south of the intersection of Whitefish Point Road, Whitefish Township; Whitefish Township Informational Designation; L1733C; March 15, 1990; 1990

Clare

Harrison

The Flint & Pere Marquette Railway Company platted this area in 1879 and presented a parcel to the county. This site became the Clare County seat in November of that same year. Named for President William Henry Harrison, the village was incorporated in 1885 and officially became a city in 1891. Harrison was noted at the turn of the century for its thriving lumber mills. Prominent lumbermen in the vicinity included Frederick Miller, Ephraim B. Rought and William and Samuel Wilson, who built and operated several mills on the Budd Lake shoreline.

Lake Street and Budd Lake, Harrison; Harrison, Clare County Seat; L635B; December 21, 1978; 1979

Logging Railroads

Michigan's lumbermen found many areas were too far from rivers for logs to be taken to the mills in the spring drive. After 1870 the logging railroad came into increasing use as the means of opening these regions. The Lake George and Muskegon Railroad here in Clare

The railroad revolutionized the logging industry. The Lake George and Muskegon Railroad helped open up Clare County's timberlands. (*Logging Railroads*)

County began hauling logs seven miles to the Muskegon River in 1877. New steam saw-mills soon went up near these narrow-gauge lines because of the steady supply of timber that the logging trains furnished. Shown above is the Shays train, a type specially designed for use on the logging railroads.

Highway Park, old US-27, seven and one-half miles north of Clare, Hatton Township; Logging Railroads; S28; February 18, 1956; 1957

Clinton

Gunnisonville

Purchasing 160 acres of farm land from the government, Elihu Gunnison first settled this site, originally known as Gunnison, in 1835. This settlement, which its inhabitants often called "four corners," had a general store owned and operated by Boyden Hubbard. After being appointed postmaster, Hubbard opened the Gunnisonville Post Office in 1891 and operated it in his store. In 1901 rural mail service was initiated in this vicinity, and the old post office was discontinued. In spring of 1890 the townspeople established the community band, which performed for religious, educational and social gatherings; the following year, a bandstand was erected. During the later part of that decade, the Gunnisonville Band participated in several state band tournaments.

Side Two

The Gunnisonville School was initially a center for social, religious and educational activities. It served as a school for nearly a century and a quarter, first being established in 1836 and continuing to operate, though only as a kindergarten in latter years, until 1963. The present one-room schoolhouse, the fourth to stand on this site, was constructed in 1907. It was refurbished as a living educational museum by the joint efforts of the Gunnisonville Restoration Committee and the Lansing School District in 1975. The Methodist Episcopal Church, now the United Methodist Church, was organized in 1862. Seven years prior to this, the local cemetery was established. In 1888 the present church edifice was completed and dedicated on November 4.

SE and NE corners of Clark (Bath) and Wood roads, one mile west of US-27, DeWitt Township; Gunnisonville Historic District; L449; May 11, 1976; 1979

Philip Orin Parmelee

Philip Orin Parmelee, noted early aviator, lived a tragically brief but venturesome life. Born in 1887 in Matherton, Michigan, Parmelee grew up in nearby St. Johns, Clinton County, where he developed a keen interest in mechanical devices. This led him to join the Ohio flying school run by Orville and Wilbur Wright. After training he went on to become a famous flier for the Wright Exhibition Team. Fascinated with aircraft, Parmelee was the first pilot to transport merchandise, drop live test bombs from a plane and search from the air for criminals.

Side Two

Nicknamed "Skyman," Parmelee held world endurance, speed and altitude records, and performed at flying exhibitions. During one such flight on June 1, 1912, in North Yakima, Washington, Parmelee's plane crashed and he was killed, ending a promising career dedicated to the then perilous adventure of flying. He was buried in East Plains Cemetery in Clinton County. By constant experimentation with their primitive planes, Parmelee and other early fliers contributed to a science of aviation which was the forerunner of today's sophisticated and safe air travel.

Capital City Airport terminal, North Grand River Avenue, Lansing vicinity, DeWitt Township; Parmelee, Philip, Informational Designation; L566; November 7, 1977; 1978

Rochester Colony

In 1836 a Rochester, New York, association purchased land here and by winter several families were settled in newly built log homes. Methodist circuit riders in 1837 organized a class which became [the] center of the three-county Mapleton circuit. In 1841 the settlement was renamed Duplain and the colonists began working for better schools and roads. The Duplain Methodist Church was built in the mid-1850s as a center for community worship.

Pioneers from Rochester, New York, settled in Clinton County in 1835 and established what became known as the Rochester Colony. (*Rochester Colony*)

Methodist Church, Maple Road north of Colony Road, between Watson and Harmon roads, DuPlain Township; Rochester Colony (Duplain) Informational Designation; L83; September 23, 1970; 1970

Joshua Simmons II

Joshua Simmons II, Revolutionary War veteran, is buried in this cemetery. He was born on a Massachusetts farm in the early 1760s. In 1778 he volunteered to fight the British and served with various units in Massachusetts for about two years. In 1790 he married Ruth Andrews. Later the family migrated to western New York. His wife died in 1806 leaving Joshua to raise their eight children. In the 1830s his younger son David settled in this area. Joshua joined him and at his death in 1840 was buried here on his son's land.

North Eagle Cemetery, Grange Road, south of Howe Road, Eagle Township; Simmons, Joshua II, Burial Place; L347; September 17, 1974; 1974

Greenbush United Methodist Church

The Reverend William Benson organized a Methodist class for this area in 1849. The class, which had seven members, held its first worship service in a log school south of Eureka. Later it met in the Sherwood School and the Keystone Grange Hall. Following a revival service conducted by the Reverend James Connolly in 1895, the class decided to build a permanent church. The present frame church was completed at a cost of nearly $4,000 and dedicated on August 28, 1898.

NW corner of Scott and Marshall roads, Greenbush Township; Greenbush United Methodist Church; L1370A; January 22, 1987; 1988

Village of Ovid

In 1836 inhabitants of Ovid, Seneca Falls County, New York, began to settle this fertile farm area. Among them were Samuel Barker, who built his log cabin in "Section 6"; Jabez Denison, noted for his prowess in killing bears; and William Swarthout, who put up his home by the Maple River, which passes through the town. Land given to the Detroit, Grand Haven and Milwaukee Railway determined the location of Ovid's depot. The incorporated village of Ovid dates from 1869, when 227 voters were involved in its first election. Businesses, houses and factories rapidly grew in number. Lumber, general merchandise, cabinets, musical instruments and carriages were among the wares carrying the Ovid stamp. Main Street became and continued to be a center of activity for village residents and others in the area. In 1980, Ovid claimed 1,712 residents.

First Congregational Church of Ovid

On February 13, 1871, twenty-two persons began Ovid's First Congregational Church. The next year this structure was erected. George Fox served as master carpenter. Its first minister was the Reverend William Mulder. Originally located at High and Park streets, the church was pulled here by oxen in 1899 and turned to face Main Street. It was enlarged for a growing congregation, which came to be "one of the most powerful social forces in the county." In 1943, Ovid's Congregational and Methodist societies merged, using both their buildings until 1972. In 1979 the church became a private residence. This Ovid landmark, whose octagonal belfry tower holds a melodious 1876 bell, is listed on the Historic American Buildings Survey and the National Register of Historic Places.

222 Main Street, SE corner of Pearl Street, Ovid; First Congregational Church of Ovid; L114; April 23, 1971; 1985

St. John's Church

In 1858 twelve persons organized St. John's Church. During the Civil War the membership dispersed; the congregation reorganized in 1864. They built their first church in 1867. Shortly after the close of Easter evening services in 1893 the church burned. Detroit architects Rogers and MacFarlane designed the present Neo-Gothic church, which was built the following year. The congregation celebrated the first service in the new church on Easter Sunday 1894.

Mead and Walker streets, St. Johns; St. John's Episcopal Church; L880A; February 23, 1981; 1990

Michigan's Capitol

Ahead lies Lansing, capital of Michigan. In 1835, when the state was organized, Detroit was the capital, as it had been when Michigan was a territory. The capital, after much debate, was moved to its present, more centrally located site in 1847. The city of Lansing did not exist at that time, and the first capitol, completed by 1848, was built in a wilderness. Today, Lansing is the center for state government and also for major industries. Michigan State University is in East Lansing.

Rest area on eastbound I-96 west of Lansing, Watertown Township; Michigan's Capital; S268; April 27, 1965; 1965

Westphalia Settlement

In October 1836 the Reverend Anton Kopp and five other men from Westphalia, Germany, arrived in New York. They traveled to Detroit by way of the Erie Canal. Advised to settle in the Grand River Valley, the Reverend Kopp and Eberhard Platte went to the Ionia land office and on November 10, 1836, purchased 560 acres of Clinton County farmland. The original land owners were Anton Cordes, Joseph Platte, John Hanses, William Tillman and John Salter. Leaving Detroit, these men walked along the Dexter Trail to Lyons. There, they hired William Hunt, a trapper and fur trader, to guide them to their land holdings. They named their settlement Westphalia in honor of their homeland. It was the first German-Catholic settlement in central Michigan.

St. Mary's Parish

In 1836, Bishop Rese of the Detroit Diocese appointed a German emigrant priest, Anton Kopp, to head the Westphalia Mission. Mass was being celebrated in the homes of the new community's founding settlers by 1837. These early worshippers, members of the first parish for German-speaking Roman Catholics in central Michigan, completed their first permanent structure, a modest log church, in 1838. It was followed by a larger frame structure in 1847. Known as St. Peter's Church, that structure was replaced in 1869 with a church constructed of brick from Westphalia's brickyard and black walnut from its forests. The new church, dedicated as St. Mary's Church, served the parish until it was destroyed by fire in 1959. The present church, erected on the site of the original log church, was dedicated on May 28, 1962.

201 North Westphalia Street, two blocks north of Main Street, Westphalia; St. Mary's Church/Westphalia Settlement Informational Designation; L1325C; July 17, 1986; 1986

Crawford

Beginning of State Reforestation

A concern over the depletion of Michigan's forests led in 1899 to the creation of a forestry commission. In 1903 the first state forest was set up by the legislature on cut-over, burned-over lands in Roscommon and Crawford counties. The same year also saw the start of organized forest fire protection and the establishment of Higgins Lake Nursery at its present site. Thus began the program of reforestation in Michigan.

Higgins Lake Nursery, County Road 200, one-half mile east of Old US-27, one-quarter mile north of Roscommon County line, Beaver Creek Township; Beginning of State Reforestation Informational Site; S143; February 26, 1957; 1958

Chief Shoppenagon

Chief David Shoppenagon was born in Indianfields, a Chippewa Indian Village in the Saginaw River Valley. In 1795 his grandfather, also a Chippewa chief, was among the Indians who met with General Anthony Wayne at Fort Greenville, Ohio, and signed a treaty

Grayling, now extinct in Michigan, once populated Michigan's streams and drew sportsmen to northern Michigan. *(Michigan Grayling)*

that ended forty years of warfare in the Ohio Valley. Shoppenagon arrived in the Grayling area from the Saginaw Valley during the early 1870s. He trapped, hunted and was a guide for sportsmen throughout the northern Lower Peninsula.

Shoppenagon's Homesite

Chief David Shoppenagon had a house near this site, though he spent much of his time along the lakes and rivers of the area. Whites called him "Old Shopp" and welcomed his campfire tales of bear and deer hunts. He made canoes and paddles by hand and was a river guide in the area. In the early 1900s, a local inn, the area's cork pine and maple flooring company were named for Chief Shoppenagon. The chief died on Christmas Day 1911. He was believed to be 103 years old.

Chief Shoppenagon, born in the Saginaw River Valley, moved to Grayling in the 1870s. (*Chief Shoppenagon*)

Old US-27/I-75 intersection at AuSable River near the bridge, Grayling; Shoppenagon, Chief David, Home, Informational Site; L757B; December 12, 1979; 1981

Michigan Grayling

Although fishermen had been catching this fish in such rivers as the Manistee, Pere Marquette and Au Sable for some years, its classification as true grayling came only in 1864. The thrill of landing this fish drew sportsmen from the country over as railroads entered northern Michigan in the 1870s. The town of Grayling was the center for fishing trips on the Au Sable. Habitat changes following deforestation were making Michigan grayling rare by about 1900, and by about 1930 they were extinct.

Side Two

While now extinct in Michigan, members of the grayling family are found in Montana, Europe and the Arctic. The grayling are related to the trout and salmon and are distinguished by a thyme-like odor and a long wavy dorsal fin, a superb mark of beauty. Measuring from twelve to fifteen inches, the Michigan grayling lived in cold, swift streams and were a gamy fish and delicious as food.

North Down River Road at the east branch of the Au Sable River north of Michigan Avenue, at the Grayling State Fish Hatchery, Grayling; Michigan Grayling; S144; February 26, 1957; 1958

Officer's Club

The Camp Grayling Officer's Club and the land on which it is constructed were given to the state of Michigan by Rasmus Hanson, a successful Grayling businessman who made his fortune in the white pine forests. In 1913 he also donated 13,760 acres of land to the state for the training of the militia which became known as the Hanson Grant. The Officer's Club, built in 1917, has since served as the focal point for the social and formal functions of the Michigan National Guard Officer Corps. Reminiscent of the architecture that is typical of southern military structures, the colonnaded veranda and symmetrically spaced dormers set into the low hipped roof are common to militia camps and army posts erected at the turn of the century.

Building Number 311, Howe Road, Grayling Township; Camp Grayling Officers Open Mess; S508; August 24, 1978; 1980

32nd Red Arrow Division

After American entry into World War I in 1917, President Woodrow Wilson ordered all of Michigan's National Guard to Camp Grayling. Eight thousand of these troops then went to Texas where they joined Wisconsin soldiers to form the Thirty-second Division. Arriving in France in 1918, the division earned the name "Red Arrow" for its swift assaults through German lines. During World War II the Thirty-second Red Arrow Division fought courageously in the Pacific Theatre and received a commendation from General Douglas MacArthur.

*Camp Grayling, vicinity of stone mess hall, Grayling Township; 32nd Red Arrow Division Informational Designation; S499; April 15, 1977; 1977

Delta

Little Bay De Noc

The Noquet (or Noc) Indians, who once lived along these shores, gave this bay its name. Here at Sand Point, in 1844, Douglass Houghton came with his party of government surveyors to chart the land to the north. In 1864 the first ore dock was built on the shore of this deep harbor, from which the ores of all three of Michigan's rich iron ranges have been shipped. Escanaba, which was incorporated in 1866, was one of the earliest lumbering centers in the Upper Peninsula. Sawmills were built here as early as 1836. Up the west shore of the bay, Gladstone was founded in 1887 by Senator W. D. Washburn to serve as a rail-lake terminal. Here, as at other points such as Ford River, Masonville, Rapid River and Garth, the major source of income was timber products.

Escanaba municipal dock, Ludington Street, Escanaba; Little Bay de Noc Informational Designation; S147; April 2, 1957; 1957

Ludington Hotel

In 1864, E. Gaynor built the Gaynor House hotel, which he renamed the Ludington House in 1871 after lumberman Nelson Ludington. In the late 1880s proprietor John Christie enlarged the hotel and renamed the establishment the New Ludington Hotel. An advertisement in the 1893 *Michigan Gazetteer and Business Directory* read, "New Ludington Hotel—The Largest and Only Hotel In the City Having Baths, Steam Heat and Electric Call Bells—$2.00 per day." The hotel exemplifies Queen Anne resort architecture, popular in the 1880s and 1890s.

223 Ludington Street, Escanaba; Ludington Hotel (The House of Ludington); L881A; February 23, 1981; 1990

Indian Trail

The trail that begins here was one of the most important in the Upper Peninsula. The Noquets, an Algonquian tribe, lived in this area and used the trail in their frequent travels between Lake Michigan and Lake Superior. In places the trail is deeply worn from centuries of use. Beginning in the early 1800s, the Northwest Fur Company and the American Fur Company established posts at Grand Island, near the Lake Superior end of the trail. Traders, lumbermen and others continued to use this route until a county road was built. The U.S. Forest Service has reconstructed the trail and maintains it for hiking and riding.

West side of County Road 509, north of US-2 and south of Bills Creek, Masonville Township; Grand Island Indian Trail Informational Designation; S281; May 4, 1966; 1968

Escanaba River: The Legend

This is the land of the Chippewa Indians and the legendary Hiawatha. Indian villages existed along the banks of the river, and Indians were living here when the first white men came to this region in the 1600s. The Indians named the river for the flat rocks over which it runs. In *The Song of Hiawatha*, Longfellow described how Hiawatha "crossed the rushing Escanaba" in pursuit of Mudjekeewis, whom he slew to avenge the death of his mother. The last Indian lands in the Upper Peninsula were ceded to the United States in 1842. This closed an era that began about ten thousand years ago.

Escanaba River: The Lumbermen

A short distance upriver from this marker, Alden Chandler built the first sawmill about 1835. Another mill was built in the early 1840s where this power dam now stands. Government surveyors were surprised to discover these mills and a small settlement here in 1844. These mills were all water-powered. The region was at first famous for its vast white pine forests. Lumber sawed here helped build Chicago and rebuild that city after the great fire of 1871. Hardwood flooring in large quantity was also produced here. At the turn of the century the I. Stephenson Company, with mills at the river mouth, was the largest producer of lumber in the world.

Opposite Pioneer Trail Park, behind the Department of Natural Resources building, US-2 & 41 (M-35), one mile north of Escanaba, Wells Township; Saw Mills (Smith Brother's Mill); L63; May 4, 1966; 1967

Dickinson

Menominee Iron Range

This range, named for the Menominee River which runs through part of it, is one of three great iron ore districts in the Upper Peninsula. In 1846, William A. Burt—the discoverer of the Marquette Iron Range—noted signs of iron ore in the Crystal Falls area. In 1849 federal geologist J. W. Foster found ore near Lake Antoine, and two years later he and J. D. Whitney confirmed Burt's report on the Crystal Falls district. The first mining activity began in 1872 at the Breen Mine, where ore had been discovered in the 1860s by the Breen brothers, timber cruisers from Menominee. Development of the range was delayed until a railroad could be built from Escanaba. The Breen and Vulcan mines shipped 10,405 tons of ore in 1877 when the railroad was built as far as Quinnesec. By 1880 it reached Iron Mountain and Florence, and in 1882 tracks were laid to Crystal Falls and Iron River. Twenty-two mines had made shipments of ore that year. A few crumbling ruins are all that remain of most of them, but in subsequent decades many more mines were developed which have produced vast amounts of ore for America's iron and steel mills.

Fumee Park, one mile east of Quinnesec on US-2, Breitung Township; Menominee Iron Range Informational Designation; S85; August 23, 1956; 1958

The Ardis Furnace

Inventor John T. Jones of Iron Mountain recognized the economic potential of the low-grade iron ore of the Upper Peninsula. He developed a method for processing the ore and built an experimental furnace in 1908, named for his daughter Ardis, to test his theory. The furnace, a huge metal tube lined with firebrick, was placed on an incline and charged with ore. The whole device was rotated by electric motor, with iron suitable for mill use discharged from the lower end of the tube. The experiment was plagued with financial and mechanical problems, and by the close of World War I the Ardis was dismantled, Jones moving to other mining endeavors. Elements of the Jones method were later incorporated into successful processing operations for low-grade iron ores.

*Northeast corner of Aragon and Antoine streets, Iron Mountain; Ardis Furnace; L148A; August 13, 1971; 1972

Built in 1890-1891 and fashioned after pumps in Cornwall, England, the Cornish Pump lifted two hundred tons of water per minute at the Chapin Mine. (*Cornish Pump*)

Carnegie Library

While in Iron Mountain on business during 1901, Andrew Carnegie saw the need for a library on the Menominee Iron Range, which was then a prospering area. He donated $15,000 for this building. Serving the community for over seventy years, the Neo-Classical Revival structure, designed by James E. Clancy, was one of the earliest Carnegie libraries in the Great Lake State. In 1971 this edifice became the Menominee Range Museum, featuring the history of its namesake.

300 Ludington Street, Iron Mountain; Menominee Range Historical Museum (Carnegie Public Library); L501; February 7, 1977; 1979

Cornish Pump

When the E. P. Allis Company of Milwaukee built this pump in 1890-1891, it was heralded as the nation's largest steam-driven pumping engine. On January 3, 1893, the massive engine, designed by Edwin C. Reynolds, began lifting 200 tons of water per minute at "D" shaft of the Chapin Iron Mine. In 1896 underground conditions shifted the engine out of alignment and it was dismantled. The Oliver Iron Mining Company purchased and rebuilt it at shaft "C" of the Ludington Mine in 1907. It dewatered the combined Chapin, Ludington and Hamilton mines until 1914, when it was replaced by electric pumps. Patterned after similar pumps used in tin mines in Cornwall, England, the Cornish Pump boasts a flywheel forty feet in diameter, which weighs 160 tons and averaged ten revolutions per minute. The pump was listed in the National Register of Historic Places in 1981.

Kent Street and Kimberly Avenue, Iron Mountain; Chapin Mine Steam Pump Engine (The Cornish Pump); S273; February 19, 1958; 1983

Maria Santissima Immacolata

In the late nineteenth and early twentieth centuries Italian immigrants came to Iron Mountain to work in the iron mines. In 1890, Italian Catholics from the community's north side organized what was popularly known as "the Italian Church." That year they built a frame church near this site. The church burned in 1893 and was rebuilt. In April 1902, Father G. Pietro Sinopoli arrived here. Within two months he formed a church building committee. Four thousand dollars was raised and in June Father Sinopoli began excavating the foundation. The church was completed in December and dedicated to Mary Immaculate of Lourdes on January 1, 1903.

Mary Immaculate of Lourdes Church

This church reflects the heritage and building techniques of the Italian immigrants who erected it. The church, with its bell tower fashioned after a campanile, is strikingly reminiscent of Renaissance parish churches in Italy. Father G. Pietro Sinopoli, the parish priest, is thought to have designed the building. Masons and volunteers hauled sandstone from a quarry one mile south of here to build the exterior walls. The Menominee Stained Glass Works created at least three of the windows, including the choir loft window designed by Father Sinopoli. The church was listed in the National Register of Historic Places in 1990.

500 East Blaine Street, Iron Mountain; Immaculate Conception Church (Mary Immaculate of Lourdes); L661A; June 15, 1979; 1990

Norway Spring

In 1878 a sawmill was erected here as the first industry in the Norway-Vulcan area. John O'Callaghan was owner of this mill, which supplied early mining lumber needs until 1902. This spring was caused by a 1094-foot hole drilled in 1903 by the Oliver Mining Company in a search for iron ore. The hole cuts several steeply dipping porous strata that trap water at higher elevations to the north. The difference in elevation causes pressure; this pressure is released by the drilled hole, demonstrating the principle of the artesian well. On the slope to the north are the obscure workings of the Few and Munro mines, operated in 1903-1922, now owned by the Ford Motor Company.

US-2, just west of Norway, Norway Township; Norway Spring; L66; June 2, 1966; 1966

Eaton

Eaton County

Named for John H. Eaton, Secretary of War under Andrew Jackson, Eaton County was set off in 1829. Bellevue, where the county's first settlement took place in 1833, was platted by Isaac E. Crary and John D. Pierce, fathers of Michigan's public school system. Most of the early settlers were Yankees. The county was organized in 1837. Charlotte, which was built on a prairie near the center of the county, became the county seat. Maple sugar soon was a famous county product.

100 West Lawrence Avenue at Cochran and Bostwick streets, Charlotte; Eaton County Courthouse; S190; April 16, 1958; 1958

First Congregational Church of Charlotte

This handsome brick church was completed in 1881. Seven persons organized the congregation in 1851 in nearby Carmel Township. Moving to Charlotte the next year, they held services in the wooden courthouse and in 1856 built the city's first place of worship, "The Basswood Church" on Bostwick Avenue. In 1873 construction of the present church began. Members made contributions to assure its finish. Local businessman Joseph Musgrave donated exterior brick originally purchased for his own home.

106 South Bostwick, SW corner of Lawrence, Charlotte; First Congregational Church; L187; February 11, 1972; 1978

Gresham United Methodist Church

Members of the Gresham United Methodist Church first worshipped in a school and in homes. In 1879, Palmer and Rebecca McDonald gave this site on which to build a church. In order to erect the church, people in the community donated logs which were cut at Dade Merriam's sawmill. The building's pointed-arch windows and steeply pitched roof exemplify the prevalence of Gothic Revival elements in rural church architecture. The church was completed in 1881.

5055 Mulliken Road, NW corner of Gresham Highway, Chester Township; Gresham United Methodist Church; L1489A; January 21, 1988; 1989

Delta Center Methodist Church

In 1837, Methodists in Delta Township began meeting in a log schoolhouse. Served by circuit riders, they organized as a Methodist class in 1842 with two families. The class grew, and in 1865 the Reverend J. Gulic became its first appointed minister. On June 6, 1867, a Ladies Aid Society was formed to raise funds to build an adequate place of worship. The church, completed in 1873, was significantly enlarged in 1926 and 1954. During a special church conference in the summer of 1962, delegates from Delta Center and nearby Bethel and Millett voted to merge their three churches. The first meeting of the newly formed church was held at the Delta Center Methodist Church on June 24, 1962. The name Trinity Methodist Church was adopted on July 5, 1962.

Side Two

The original white frame church that stood just northwest of the present church was designed and built by Darius B. Moon, a native of Delta Township, in 1873. Members of the congregation donated labor and much of the building material. The 30' x 50' structure, which cost $340, served area Methodists for 110 years. When completed, it was a crisp, clean, simple rectangular building with a central entrance and rectangular windows. It was topped by a square, louvered belfry, with bracketed cornice and turned finial capping. The last regular worship service in the frame church was held on March 10, 1968. The congregation used the old church as a fellowship hall until it was razed on May 18, 1983.

7533 West St. Joseph, Delta Township; Delta Center Methodist Church Informational Designation; L1120C; October 27, 1983; 1984

Delta Mills

Erastus S. Ingersoll settled here in 1836 and constructed a water-powered sawmill. A gristmill was added, and in 1840 a resident wrote that people came from twenty miles around to have their flour made. A school modeled after Oberlin College was chartered as "Grand River Theological Seminary," but never opened. Platted as Grand River City in 1841, the village was commonly called Delta Mills after the township and main industry. The mills operated into the twentieth century.

Delta Mills Park, Old River Trail, SW of Delta Mills, Delta Township; Delta Mills Informational Designation; L201; April 14, 1972; 1972

Delta Mills Schools

On this site in 1839, residents of Delta Township built their first school. A one-room wood frame structure, it could seat sixty-five. In 1940 the building was remodeled and a second

The shade, a collection of animals and a museum attracted "pleasure seekers" to the Grand Army Park on McAuliffe's Island in the Grand River. (*Island Park*)

classroom was added. Although the township district was annexed to the Grand Ledge School District in 1956, grades one through eight continued to be taught in the old building until 1958. That year, the old schoolhouse was replaced with a modern structure, which served students until 1982.

6816 Delta River Drive, Delta Township; Delta Mills School Informational Site; L1080C; March 22, 1983; 1983

Delta Township

Musgrove Evans platted this area in 1827. The first settlers, Erastus and Sally Ingersoll and their twelve children, did not arrive until 1835. The township was organized in 1842. At the first township meeting, citizens chose the name Delta and elected Ingersolls to nine of the nineteen township offices. They also appropriated "$100 for bridges and roads" and decreed that bulls and boar hogs must be fenced in. By 1887 the area was mainly supported by farming and grist and sawmills. The clapboard township hall, erected in the mid-1870s, served the township until 1955. A combination fire chief's residence and township hall was built to replace it on the site of the old Soper one-room schoolhouse, one mile north of the earlier structure.

Delta Charter Township

Between 1940 and 1987, Delta Township's population zoomed from 2,618 to nearly 28,000, and its state tax evaluation increased from $1.48 million to $475 million. Charter status, attained in 1962, helped fuel an explosion that gave Delta the moniker "fastest growing township in Michigan." Local government services are now directed from this building, which was completed in 1970. As farms became residential subdivisions and apartment complexes, the township created an extensive recreation facility. The Sands Moon House, a log cabin built around 1855, was moved to Woldumar Nature Center in 1980, when a large industrial plant was built on its original site. There it became a walk-in demonstration museum commemorating Delta's early pioneers.

7710 West Saginaw Highway, Delta Township; Delta Township Informational Designation; L1458C; September 26, 1987; 1987

First Presbyterian Church

In 1846, Congregational services were conducted by the Reverend Joseph Smith in the home of one of Windsor Township's earliest residents, Nathan Pray. In 1875 nineteen years after the town of Dimondale was platted around the mill of Isaac Dimond, the Congregationalists and Presbyterians jointly built this structure. The community's first church, it was formally purchased by the Presbyterians in 1877.

162 Bridge Street, SW corner of Quincy, Dimondale; First Presbyterian Church; L390; April 4, 1975; 1975

Underhill Store

Isaac M. Dimond purchased four thousand acres of land here in 1837. In 1850 he built a dam on the Grand River to furnish power for a sawmill and gristmill, platting the village of Dimondale in 1856. This building was constructed that year and is the oldest store in town. Owned at first by Myron Crofts, it was purchased in 1883 by Elias Underhill and taken over by his son, Rufus, in 1900. Vacant since the 1920s, the store was purchased for restoration in 1972.

106 Jefferson, Dimondale; Underhill Store; L246; September 7, 1973; 1973

Michigan's war governor Austin Blair began his political career as Eaton County clerk. (*Austin Blair*)

Austin Blair

Civil War governor Austin Blair (1818-1894) came to Jackson, Michigan, from New York in 1841. In 1842 he moved his law practice to Eaton Rapids. At that time the area was made up mostly of farmers, and Blair was paid for his legal services with produce and firewood. He lived in a frame house that once stood near this site. In 1843, while a resident of this town, he was elected Eaton County clerk. Poverty and the deaths of his infant daughter and his wife led him to resign as county clerk in 1844 and return to Jackson.

Side Two

Austin Blair began his political career in 1842 as Eaton County clerk. In 1846 he was elected to the Michigan House of Representatives. He was selected as Jackson County prosecutor in 1852, and from 1855 to 1856 he served in the state senate. In 1861, Blair became governor of Michigan, a post he held for two terms. While in office he personally raised about $100,000 to equip the First Michigan Volunteer Infantry Regiment. He represented Michigan as a U.S. congressman from 1867 to 1873 and was a University of Michigan regent from 1882 to 1890.

248 East Main Street at the corner of Spicer, Eaton Rapids; Blair, Austin, Home, Informational Site (Warner, Hart & Peters Law Offices); S558C; February 15, 1984; 1984

Island Park

This island, owned and operated by J. D. McAuliffe from 1872, was hailed as "a shady retreat for pleasure seekers . . . with a fine collection of animals and a museum of rare specimens." In 1897, Eaton Rapids bought it for a city park. From 1908 to 1929 the Eaton County Battalion of the G.A.R. held its annual encampment at what was then named Grand Army Park. Summer concerts, reunions and picnics brought many here over the years. A group formed in 1973 to save the island from erosion served to refocus attention on this spot.

Middle of the Grand River, Downtown Eaton Rapids; Island Park; L286; July 26, 1974; 1974

Red Ribbon Hall

The Eaton Rapids Reform Club under the leadership of Isaac N. Reynolds, built this temperance hall in 1878. Affiliated with the national Red Ribbon movement, over a thousand local men knotted red ribbons in their lapels after pledging to abstain from all alcoholic beverages, and adopted the motto, "Dare to do right." The building served as a cultural center, and, at the turn of the century, as an opera house. Since 1924 it has been a Masonic Hall.

314 South Main Street, Eaton Rapids; Red Ribbon Hall (Masonic Temple Building); L361; November 14, 1974; 1975

"The Saratoga of the West"

Eaton Rapids became a popular health resort when mineral water was discovered in 1869. Attracted by advertisements boasting of its curative powers, thousands came for treatment. The water was also bottled and shipped across the country. In 1874, Anderson House was erected on this site as the town's most elegant hotel. The mineral water heyday had passed when it burned in 1911, although a bath continued to operate until 1962.

101 South Main Street, Eaton Rapids; Anderson House (Saratoga of the West); L360; November 14, 1974; 1975

Center Eaton United Methodist Church

On November 30, 1878, the local Methodist class purchased land for a church from Benjamin and Catherine Spotts for $25.00. Church men cut and hewed the logs for the building. The Reverend B. E. Paddock dedicated the church on November 10, 1881. Luren D. Dickinson, governor of Michigan from 1939 to 1940, taught Sunday school here both before and during his tenure as governor. From 1918 to 1955 the church sponsored Lulu Tubbs, a missionary in Southern Rhodesia, which became Zimbabwe.

2145 Narrow Lake Road, Eaton Township; Center Eaton United Methodist Church; L1371A; January 22, 1987; 1987

Fitzgerald Park

Migrant Indian tribes led by the famous Chief Okemos called this area "Big Rocks." They came here in early spring to tap the sugar maples. Later, the beauty of the ledges and woods attracted the Grand Ledge Spiritualist Camp Association which, in 1894, established a summer campground and erected the large pavilion which still stands. Thousands of spiritualists came here for summer encampments until the turn of the century. In 1919 the

The Sunfield chapter of the Grand Army of the Republic, a post-Civil War social and support organization for Union veterans, built this meeting hall in 1899. (*G.A.R. Hall*)

city of Grand Ledge bought the property and named it Riverside Park. The pavilion was used for dances, roller skating and basketball. During World War II, it housed a factory. This park's name commemorates Grand Ledge native Governor Frank D. Fitzgerald who died in office in 1939. The pavilion was refurbished as a summer theater by the Grand Ledge Improvement Association in 1955.

3808 Grand Ledge Highway, Grand Ledge; Riverside Park Informational Site (Fitzgerald Park); L593; April 4, 1978; 1978

Governor Frank D. Fitzgerald Home

Here lived Frank D. Fitzgerald who served his first term as governor from 1935-1936. His second term, starting in January 1939, was cut short by his death in this house in March of that year. Born in Grand Ledge in 1885, Fitzgerald earned wide respect from local citizens. A Republican, he was secretary of state 1930-1934. State chief executive during some tumultuous Depression years, Fitzgerald advocated government reorganization measures including a civil service system for state employees.

Side Two

Governor Fitzgerald acquired this house during his first gubernatorial term. At that time the state did not provide an official mansion; thus Fitzgerald used this home as the governor's residence. Out of office 1937-1938, he planned his successful re-election campaign from here. Lansing architect Edwyn C. Bowd designed the residence in 1907. It was built for $18,000. The house was set on a high foundation. The tile roof, massive chimneys and rounded bay windows, are Romanesque style.

219 West Jefferson Street, between Harrison and Adams streets, Grand Ledge; Fitzgerald, Governor Frank, House; S511A; December 21, 1978; 1979

Second Island

Graced by the natural beauty of these soaring sandstone ledges, Grand Ledge was once famous for its Seven Islands Resort, a recreation area centered on this island from 1870 to 1910. At the turn of the century the ledges made this city one of the most popular resort areas in lower Michigan. Excursion trains brought thousands to enjoy this area which featured steamboat rides, a boat livery, a hotel and vaudeville theater, mineral wells, a roller coaster and fishing. In 1976 the Grand Ledge Area Bicentennial Commission erected the band pavilion.

Second Island, the Grand River, Grand Ledge; Seven Islands Resort Informational Designation; L592; April 4, 1978; 1978

Olivet College

On February 24, 1844, the Reverend John J. "Father" Shipherd and thirty-nine followers arrived by ox-cart on this wilderness hilltop, driving their herds before them. They felt God had directed them to this oak grove for the purpose of founding a coeducational Christian college open to students of all races. First chartered as Olivet Institute, the school received its charter as a college in 1859. For over a century it has given a broad liberal arts education, with strong support from the Congregational church. Many alumni have gone forth "Pro Christo et Humanitate."

Burrage Library, NE corner of College Avenue and Main Street, Olivet; Olivet College Informational Designation; S186; March 19, 1958; 1960

The Potterville United Methodist Church

The Potterville United Methodist Church was organized after the Reverend Hiram Nichols held a revival meeting in Potterville in 1867. The congregation appointed a building committee in 1875 and began work on the church in the spring of 1877. George M. Potter donated the land for the church, which was dedicated on February 3, 1878. The church took its present name after the Methodist Church merged with the Evangelical United Brethren Church in 1968.

Side Two

When constructed in 1877, the church seated three hundred people. Its main entrance was at its southeast corner. From 1920 to 1923 the church was remodelled and enlarged under the guidance of head carpenter John Griffith. Much of the original woodwork on the windows and gables was removed; however, the stained glass windows and the bell were left intact. The church also retained its L-shape, frame structure and high gable roofs.

105 North Church Street, NW corner of Vermontville Highway, Potterville; Potterville Methodist Episcopal Church (Potterville United Methodist Episcopal Church); L1296B; February 28, 1986; 1987

G.A.R. Hall

The Samuel W. Grinnell Post No. 283 was granted its charter by the Grand Army of the Republic (G.A.R.) on October 6, 1884. The post operated until 1934, at which time it was disbanded. Members built this hall in 1898-1899. Dedicated in October 1899, it contains flags, medals, photographs and other mementos of the Civil War and of the Sunfield veterans of that war. Furniture, ritual equipment and records of this G.A.R. post are also kept here. In 1899 members planted the three maple trees at the front of the property, dedicating them to the memory of Generals Grant, Sheridan and Sherman. The two cannon on either side of the hall were brought to Sunfield by the G.A.R. in 1900.

Side Two

The G.A.R. was founded in 1866 as a veterans association to assist Union veterans and their widows and orphans. The G.A.R. and several of its allied orders have used this hall since its completion in 1899: Samuel W. Grinnell Post No. 283, G.A.R. (1899 to 1934); Woman's Relief Corps No. 62 (1899 to 1925); Samuel W. Grinnell Camp No. 17, Sons of Union Veterans, U.S.A., (1918 to 1925); Helen Edwins Tent No. 30, Daughters of Union Veterans of the Civil War (beginning in 1926); and Curtenius Guard Camp No. 17, Sons of Union Veterans of the Civil War (beginning in 1983). In 1987 the hall was owned by the Daughters of Union Veterans of the Civil War. This marker was dedicated on Memorial Day (May 30) during the Michigan Sesquicentennial.

115 Main Street, Sunfield; Sunfield Grand Army of the Republic Post No. 283 Hall; L735A; September 10, 1979; 1987

First Congregational Church

Reverend Sylvester Cochrane, a Congregational minister from Vermont, first conceived of a settlement in Michigan after a visit here in 1835. Returning home he formed a group called the Union Colony, which settled in Vermontville the next year. The colonists were religiously oriented, and one of their stated purposes in settling here was to "remove the moral darkness," which they thought pervaded the West. Church services were first held in a log cabin and later in the academy across the street. The present church was dedicated in 1864. The building strongly resembles certain New England meetinghouses of the late eighteenth century, especially in its roof framing of roughly hewn timbers and in much of the interior woodwork.

341 South Main Street at West Main, Vermontville; First Congregational Church; HB54; June 27, 1969; 1970

Opera House

Vermontville Opera House, completed in 1898, is still the main center of community activities. The two-story red brick structure with cut stone foundation, and an off-center tower over the front entrance, was constructed with funds solicited from the township and village. Stage plays, political events, social gatherings and religious services have taken place here. L. Vern Slout and his players, one of Michigan's oldest tent companies gave first and last performances in this opera hall, now used in part as a public library.

West side of South Main, between First and Second streets, Vermontville; Vermontville Opera House; L435; January 16, 1976; 1978

Vermontville Academy

In 1836 a group from Vermont known as the Union Colony settled here. The members were determined that their children should receive a good education. The Vermontville Academical Association was formed, constructed this building and opened it for classes in the winter of 1844-1845. Vermontville was advertised as an ideal location for an academy, since there was little to distract the students from their work. Because most of the colony were Congregationalists, their minister also served as the academy teacher. Religious services were held here until 1864 when the church across the street was completed. Town meetings were held in the academy, and in 1853 Vermontville's first general store opened on the ground floor.

North Main and East Main streets, Vermontville; Vermontville Chapel and Academy (First Congregational Chapel); HB55; June 27, 1969; 1970

Vermontville United Methodist Church

A Methodist class was organized in this area in 1845. Early worship services, held in private homes and local schools, were conducted by preachers traveling the Eaton circuit. In 1859 the Michigan Methodist Conference made Vermontville a separate charge and installed the Reverend Josiah Fowler as its pastor. In 1862 this church was constructed at a site two miles northeast of this location. It was moved here in 1877. After the completion of repairs and renovation, including the addition of a belfry and tower, the church was rededicated on this site on January 8, 1878. The handsome Late Victorian-style church with its pointed-arch stained-glass windows is the home of one of the town's oldest religious organizations.

108 North Main Street, Vermontville; Vermontville Methodist Episcopal Church (Vermontville United Methodist Church); L1218B; February 26, 1985; 1986

Emmet

Stafford's Bay View Inn

J. W. Howard completed this spacious inn in 1887, naming it the Woodland Avenue House because of its proximity to that street. Later he called the hotel the Howard House. In 1923 the popular resort became the Roselawn in honor of Horace Rose, innkeeper at that time. Renamed the Bay View Inn, this building is now Stafford's Bay View Inn and is one of the oldest seasonal hotels in continuous operation in the area. Carved out of deeded railroad property next to the village of Petoskey in 1875, the summer colony of Bay View began as a religious retreat. Then it became a cultural and educational center complete with a college and Chautauqua series. This inn is a center of hospitality in the swirl of local summer activities.

East side of US-31, at Woodland Avenue, NE of Petoskey, Bay View vicinity, Bear Creek Township; Bay View (Bay View Association); S151; June 5, 1957; 1978

Bliss Pioneer Memorial Church

The congregation of the East Bliss United Brethren Church was organized in 1880. During the pastorate of the Reverend Edward McFarland, this Carpenter Gothic-style church was erected. It was dedicated on May 4, 1903. The congregation flourished until 1923, then declined. Financial difficulties forced it to disband in 1949. Former members purchased the church from the United Brethren Conference in 1965 and renamed it Bliss Pioneer Memorial Church. Memorial Day and fall homecoming services are held in it annually.

Sturgeon Bay Trail, one-quarter mile west of Pleasant View Road (County Road 81), Bliss Township; Evangelical United Brethren Church (Bliss Pioneer Memorial Church); L778A; February 27, 1980; 1981

Pioneer Picnic Park

A Pioneer Association was formed in 1915 at Round Lake, also known as Lark's Lake, to preserve the natural beauty of these grounds for posterity and as a memorial to the settlers of northern Emmet County. Annual picnics honoring the pioneers were held until 1932, with programs that featured singing, recollections of early days, speeches and contests. The association deeded the park to Emmet County in 1950.

Lark's Lake Park (Round Lake Park), one and one-half miles south of Beckon Road 66, between Lark's Lake and Canby roads, Center Township; Pioneer Picnic Park; L142; August 13, 1971; 1971

Ephraim Shay

The many-sided house across the street, sheathed in steel plates, was built for Ephraim Shay, inventor of the Shay locomotive operated by a gear drive mechanism. Its great traction power and ability to operate on tight curves made it a favorite with logging and mining firms. Built in Lima, Ohio, thousands of Shays were operated by railroads throughout the world. Several were used on Shay's Hemlock Central railroad, which began here and ran about fifteen miles to the north. Shay, born in Ohio in 1839, was an inveterate mechanic. He built the Harbor Springs waterworks and later donated it to the city. His firm experimented with boats and automobiles, and one winter he built sleds for the children of the town. In 1888, Shay moved to Harbor Springs, where he died in 1916.

SW corner, Main and Judd streets, Harbor Springs; Shay Complex (Ephraim Shay House/Shay Locomotive); S248; August 8, 1963; 1970

In 1882, Ephraim Shay built his hexagonal house entirely of metal, except for the cut-stone foundation, and heated it with steam produced in his workshop. (*Ephraim Shay*)

Holy Childhood of Jesus School

This Indian school was founded in 1829 by Father Pierre Dejean, who came here with two teachers, Miss Elizabeth Williams and Joseph L'Etorneau. The Indians built a church and the first school building, a hewn-log structure, forty-six-by-twenty feet. The school was both a boarding and a day school, with twenty-five boarders in its initial enrollment of sixty-three Indian boys and girls, who were taught, in French, the three "R's" and vocational skills. Father Dejean was followed in 1831 by Father Frederic Baraga, the future "Apostle of the Ottawas and Chippewas." Under the Franciscan Fathers, who arrived in 1884, and the School Sisters of Notre Dame, who came in 1886 the school continues to serve the state and community, caring for Indian children.

School campus grounds, NW corner of West Main and State streets, Harbor Springs; Holy Childhood of Jesus Church and School; S259; May 5, 1964; 1964

Harbour Inn

Built around the turn of the century as the Ramona Park Hotel, this building initially included the tower, lobby, dining area and about thirty guest rooms. The large east wing was added in 1929. The history of the inn reflects the growth of Harbor Springs as a resort area. Called Little Traverse until 1881, Harbor Springs had small but flourishing lumbering and fishing industries in the latter half of the nineteenth century. Its deep harbor, pollen-free air and scenic woods attracted summer residents. After the lumbering boom ended, seasonal dwellers and tourists continued to frequent the village, which incorporated as a city in 1932. Two nearby ski areas opened in the 1950s bringing winter visitors. Renamed Harbour Inn in 1962, this hotel which was originally a summer resort, now operates year-round.

1157 Beach Road, west of Menonaque Beach, Little Traverse Township; Ramona Park Hotel (Harbor Inn); L355; October 17, 1974; 1977

Passenger Pigeons

At one time Michigan was a favorite nesting ground for the passenger pigeons. Vast quantities of beechnuts and other food attracted them. Each spring immense flocks arrived, literally darkening the skies hours at a time as they flew over. Here at Crooked Lake a nesting in 1878 covered ninety square miles. Millions of birds were killed, packed in barrels and shipped from Petoskey. Such wanton slaughter helped to make the pigeon extinct by 1914. The conservationist's voice was heard too late.

Passenger Pigeons
(*Ectopistes Migratorius*)

At one time North America's most numerous bird, the passenger pigeon was particularly abundant in the Upper Mississippi Valley. The mature male was about sixteen-inches long. Less colorful and big was the female. In 1914 the last known survivor of the species died.

State of Michigan fish hatchery, 3377-1/2 Oden Road, one mile west of Oden on US-31, Littlefield Township; Passenger Pigeons Informational Designation; S138; January 19, 1957; 1957

Fort Michilimackinac

This fort, built about 1715, put French soldiers at the Straits for the first time since 1701. French authority ceased in 1761 when British troops entered the fort. On June 2, 1763, during Pontiac's Uprising, Chippewa Indians seized the fort, killing most of the

Martha, the last known surviving passenger pigeon, died in captivity in 1914. (*Passenger Pigeons*)

small force, and held it a year. When the British moved to Mackinac Island in 1781 this old fort soon reverted to the wilderness.

Fort Michilimackinac State Park, Straits Avenue, Mackinaw City; Fort Michilimackinac; S11; February 18, 1956; 1979

Michigan's First Jewish Settler

Ezekiel Solomon, a native of Berlin, Germany, who had served with the British army, arrived at Michilimackinac in the summer of 1761. He is Michigan's first known resident of the Jewish faith. Solomon was one of the most active Mackinac fur traders until his death about 1808. He was one of those who narrowly escaped death in the massacre of 1763. During the Revolutionary War, he and other hard-pressed traders pooled their resources to form a general store. In 1784 he was a member of a committee of eight formed to regulate the Mackinac-area trade. Ezekiel Solomon's business often took him to Montreal where he is believed to have been buried and where he was a member of Canada's first Jewish congregation, Shearith Israel.

Fort Michilimackinac State Park, Straits Avenue, Mackinaw City; Ezekiel Solomon Informational Designation; S249; August 8, 1963; 1964

Little Traverse Bay

For centuries this region has been the home of Ottawa Indians, whose warriors and orators fought bravely to retain their land. Around 1700 a mission was built by French Jesuits at the famous *L'Arbre Croche* villages, which stretched from Cross Village to Harbor Springs. Petoskey, named for Chief Petosega of the Bear River Band, was first settled in 1852 by Andrew Porter, a Presbyterian missionary. With the coming of the railroad in 1873 it changed rapidly from primitive settlement to one of America's leading summer resort cities. Bay View, the adjoining summer colony, was established in 1875.

Sunset Park on US-31, one mile west of Petoskey, Resort Township; Little Traverse Bay Informational Designation; S166; September 17, 1957; 1959

Genesee

Clio Depot

In 1862 the Flint Pere Marquette Railroad built its original 26.1-mile section of track from Saginaw to Mount Morris. It selected Clio, originally known as Varna, as a railroad station location. The area around Varna was covered with white pine. The railroad thrived on the shipment of logs, lumber and wood products. In 1873, Varna changed its name to Clio and this frame depot was built. As the surrounding forests were cleared, rich farmland became available. By 1881, Clio had a population of 550 and boasted a blacksmith shop, a flour mill, a shingle mill, a grain elevator and numerous general stores. Between 1880 and 1915, as many as eight passenger trains stopped at the station each day and hundreds of carloads of freight were shipped each year. The station was used by the railroads until 1960. In 1977 it was purchased by the Clio Area Historical Association.

300-308 West Vienna Road, Clio; Clio Depot (Clio Depot of the Flint and Pere Marquette Railroad Line); L586; April 4, 1978; 1985

Dibbleville

Clark Dibble came here from New York State in 1834 and laid claim to forty acres of government land. Known as Dibbleville, this area was Fenton's original business district. It encompasses the A. J. Phillips Library, two churches and two commercial blocks. Most of the edifices date from the last four decades of the nineteenth century and retain notable architectural details. One structure in this district was built by Robert Le Roy in 1837 shortly after he and William Fenton purchased Dibbleville and named it Fentonville. The village became Fenton in 1863.

District roughly bounded by Mill Street, South Leroy, East Shiawassee, East Elizabeth, West Shiawassee and South Adelaide, Fenton; Fenton Old Town Historic District; L437; January 16, 1976; 1977

Fenton House

Constructed soon after the Detroit and Milwaukee Railroad reached town in 1855, this hotel has been a favorite resting and dining spot for over a century. It was said in 1883 that the guests were "entertained in a style unsurpassed in many large cities." The interior decor of the hotel is much as it was at the turn of the century. However, the exterior was altered by the destruction of the front porch in 1904 by a team of runaway horses. The Fenton House is one of the oldest hotels in continuous operation in Michigan.

302 North Leroy Street, NE corner of First Street, Fenton; Fenton House; L164; December 10, 1971; 1972

Fenton United Methodist Church

In March 1837 the Reverend Washington Jackson formed a Methodist congregation in Dibbleville (present-day Fenton) at the home of Levi Warren. Warren donated land and the first church was built in 1853. Its brick walls collapsed during the construction of a basement. A new brick church was built in 1869 and it burned in 1929. In 1930 the congregation laid the cornerstone for the present church, the third on this site. After delays during the Depression, this Neo-Gothic church was dedicated in 1938.

119 South Leroy Street, between Ellen and Caroline streets, Fenton; Fenton United Methodist Church; L1387A; March 19, 1987; 1989

Charles W. Nash

This Queen Anne-style house, built circa 1890, was owned by automotive pioneer Charles W. Nash (1864-1948). Born in Illinois, Nash worked on area farms before forming a successful hay-processing firm, "Adams and Nash," in 1882. He was hired by the Flint Road Cart Company as a cushion stuffer at one dollar a day in 1890. He later became general manager and vice president of the Durant-Dort Carriage Company, general manager of the Buick Motor Company (1910) and president of Buick and the General Motors Corporation (1912). In 1916 he formed the Nash Motor Company.

307 Mason Street, Flint; Nash, Charles W., House Informational Site; L1397C; March 19, 1987; 1988

Civic Park

In 1916, as a flood of new workers for Flint's automobile factories caused housing shortages, the directors of the Flint Board of Commerce formed the Civic Building Association. The association had built 133 houses on four hundred acres of farmland by December 1917, when a slump in the automobile industry and World War I slowed construction. After the 1918 Armistice, General Motors Corporation agreed to complete the project. The Dupont Company, General Motors' controlling shareholder, organized the Modern Housing Corporation, which added 280 acres and constructed 950 homes in less than nine months. At the peak of construction, Dupont employed forty-six hundred people. Postwar house prices ranged from $3,500 to $8,000. A typical home had five or six rooms, a slate roof, an open porch and a basement. Curved streets, planned park areas and tree-lined boulevards added to the attractiveness of the community.

Roughly bounded by Welch and Brownell boulevards, Trumbull Avenue, Dupont and Dartmouth streets, Flint; Civic Park Historic District (Civic Park Historic Residential District); S543B; May 13, 1981; 1982

Community Presbyterian Church

The Community Presbyterian Church grew out of the Civic Park community, which General Motors established in 1919 through its Modern Housing Corporation to provide housing for its Flint workers. Several Presbyterian families in the area first met in December 1919 for a Christmas party, and by 1921 the group had grown so large that a formal Presbyterian church was organized. The Reverend Orville H. Wood became the first installed pastor in 1922 and served until his death in 1949. The congregation's first building was an old construction barracks located at the corner of Hamilton and Chevrolet. The basement of the present Gothic-inspired edifice was completed in 1924, and the sanctuary, in 1927. The stately blond-brick structure features stone trim and leaded glass windows.

2505 Chevrolet Avenue, Flint; Community Presbyterian Church; L926A; May 13, 1981; 1982

Court Street United Methodist Church (First Methodist)

In 1834 circuit rider Bradford Frazee held the first Methodist service in Flint. The following year, William Brockway, of the Saginaw Mission, established regular services in Wait Beach's barroom. In 1836 the class of nine persons organized as the Flint River Mission in a room above the Stage and Wright store. In 1841 the Genesee County Board of Commissioners deeded this property to what became the First Methodist Episcopal Church, the oldest organized religious group in the city. The congregation's first church, built in 1842, burned in 1861. Its second one was razed in 1888 to build a third, which burned in 1892. The present church was dedicated in 1894. The Church House was dedicated in 1929.

225 West Court Street, Flint; First Methodist Episcopal Church (Court Street United Methodist Church); L736A; September 10, 1979; 1986

Flint Road Cart Factory

This one-story mill was built in the early 1880s as part of an unsuccessful effort to diversify the Flint Woolen Mills. In 1886, J. Dallas Dort and Billy Durant began leasing it to manufacture road carts. By the end of its first year of operation, their Flint Road Cart Company had produced four thousand vehicles. The company later expanded to produce four-wheeled carriages, wagons and, for a short time, bicycles. The company ceased carriage manufacturing in 1917, and this building and other surrounding factories were converted to the manufacture of the Dort Motor car.

Durant-Dort Carriage Factory No. 1

Built in 1888 this building exemplifies the dramatic growth of the Flint Road Cart Company, which became the Durant-Dort Carriage Company. During the 1890s, Durant-Dort expanded its Blue Ribbon line to include Webster Vehicle farm wagons, the Victoria Vehicle Company's mail-order business and the Diamond Buggy Company. By 1900, Durant-Dort was the largest volume producer of horse-drawn vehicles in the United States. In 1906, its peak year, it employed one thousand people and produced fifty thousand vehicles.

301-311 Water Street, Flint; Flint Road Cart Factory - Durant-Dort Carriage Factory No. 1 Informational Site; L1395C; March 19, 1987; 1988

The Flint Sit-Down

On December 30, 1936, Fisher Body workers struck this plant as the sit-down strikes against General Motors continued. Their primary objective was union recognition. Violence

erupted on January 11, 1937, as an attempt was made to halt food deliveries to the strikers. The street became a battlefield as gunfire, flying debris, tear gas and high pressure water hoses became assault weapons. Sixteen strikers and eleven police officers were wounded. Governor Frank Murphy ordered the National Guard into Flint on January 12. On February 11, 1937, the strike ended when General Motors accepted the United Auto Workers as bargaining agent for all UAW members. A new era in American labor relations was born as the old open-shop policy of industry gave way to a more modern labor-industry relationship designed to promote justice, stability and mutual interests.

South Chevrolet Avenue, Flint; Flint Sit-Down Strike of 1936-37 (Site of) (Fisher Two); S497.b; February 7, 1977; 1980

The Flint Sit-Down

On February 1, 1937, the wave of sit-down strikes against General Motors broadened as Chevrolet Plant No. 4

Crowds (top) and national guardsmen (bottom) gathered at Flint's General Motors Corporation plants where operations were crippled by strikes in late 1936 and early 1937. (*Sit-down Strike*)

was seized. The United Auto Workers' strategy was a diversionary strike at the nearby Plant No. 9 to draw company personnel to that point while the true target, Plant No. 4, was secured. As a battle between unionists and company guards took place inside Plant No. 9, other strikers captured the key Plant No. 4. Pickets outside were aided by the Women's Emergency Brigade, which fended off police until strikers inside secured the vital plant. Since all Chevrolet engines were produced in Plant No. 4, elimination of this supply would close Chevrolet operations nationwide. On February 11, 1937, the strike ended as General Motors recognized the UAW as bargaining agent for its members. This represents one of the most significant events in labor history.

300 block of South Chevrolet Avenue, Flint; Flint Sit-Down Strike of 1936-37 Informational Site (Chevrolet Four Plant); S497.c; February 7, 1977; 1980

The General Motors Sit-Down Strike

Starting December 30, 1936, this building was occupied for forty-four days by striking members of the United Auto Workers. The strikers, acting in concert with other plants that were closed or to be closed by sit-downs, asked for recognition of the union as sole bargaining representative for all hourly-rated employees of General Motors Corporation. Court injunctions and threats of eviction by both the sheriff of Genesee County and the Flint Police Department did not sway the strikers from their goal. An agreement was reached in Detroit on February 11, 1937, that changed relationships between the company and its employees. This settlement led to complete unionization of the auto industry in ensuing years and added stability for workers and company.

4300 South Saginaw, Flint; Flint Sit-Down Strike of 1936-37 Informational Site (Main Office of Fisher Body Plant One); S497.a; February 7, 1977; 1980

Genesee County Courthouse

Genesee County was organized on March 8, 1836. The previous year the territorial legislature had stipulated that the county seat would be located on the west side of the Saginaw Turnpike "on lands recently deeded by John Todd and wife" to Wait Beach. Beach would in turn donate two acres of land to the county for "a courthouse and public square, one acre of ground for a burial ground, two churches and two school lots of common size." The first courthouse and jail was constructed on this site in 1839. In 1866 an inmate in the jail burned the structure. The second courthouse, completed in 1867, was replaced by a more spacious building in 1904. That courthouse also burned. On August 31, 1926, the present Neo-Classical-style structure, designed by Fredrick D. Madison, was dedicated.

920 South Saginaw Street, SE corner of Court Street, Flint; Genesee County Courthouse and Jail; L1678A; September 7, 1989; 1989

Glenwood Cemetery

Glenwood Cemetery was established in 1857. It is one of only a few mid-nineteenth-century Michigan cemeteries to feature a rolling landscape with winding roadways. The original cemetery, the western section of the present grounds, displays a broad range of historic funerary art. The focal point of the eastern portion, developed in 1925, is a granite Neo-Classical-style public mausoleum. Among those buried in Glenwood are: Jacob Smith, Flint's first white settler; Governors Henry H. Crapo and Josiah Begole; Lieutenant Governor William M. Fenton; William A. Patterson and James Whiting, carriage and automobile builders; J. Dallas Dort, co-founder of the Durant-Dort Carriage Company and Dort Motor Company; and philanthropist Charles S. Mott and Harlow Curtice of the General Motors Corporation.

2500 West Court Street, between Barlett Place and Forest Avenue, Flint; Glenwood Cemetery; S593A; January 21, 1988; 1989

Henry Howland Crapo

Near this site stood the home of Henry Howland Crapo (1804-1869). Born in Massachusetts, Crapo in 1858 moved his family to Flint, where he had invested in timber land. Here, he developed a prosperous lumbering business, which became one of the largest and most successful in the state. In 1863-1864 Crapo turned his attention to railroading. He was instrumental in the construction of the Flint & Holly Railroad and served as its president until 1868. Originally a Whig, Crapo became a Republican early in his political career. He became mayor of Flint in 1860 and a state senator in 1863. In 1864 he was chosen as Michigan's thirteenth governor. He was reelected to that post in 1866. Fearing that localities would burden themselves with debt, Crapo opposed measures that permitted communities to subsidize railroads. He died in Flint in 1869.

Willson Park

Willson Park was originally laid out by Governor Crapo as a garden in the early 1860s. Shaped like an amphitheater, it had winding paths and steps bordered with flowering shrubs, perennials, evergreens and original forest trees. Friends said it was "a garden of surprises, since no one knew what finely arranged display would appear at the next turn in the path." The garden also contained an octagonal latticed summer house, which stood in the park for many years. Following Governor Crapo's death, the house and garden were maintained by his son-in-law Dr. James C. Willson, after whom the park is named. After Dr. Willson's death in 1912, his son George offered the site to the public. It is now part of the campus of the University of Michigan-Flint.

Corner of First and Clifford avenues, Flint; Crapo, Governor Henry Howland, House Informational Site; S579C; May 8, 1986; 1986

Jacob Smith

The first permanent structure erected on this site was probably the trading post built in 1819 by Jacob Smith, the founder of Flint. Fluent in English, French, German and a half-dozen Indian languages, Smith represented the Chippewa nation at the Great Council held in 1819. At that council, the Indians ceded six million acres of land to the federal government. Five sections of that land, including this site, were reserved for Smith's children. In 1873, Smith's daughter Louisa Payne and her husband, Chauncy, donated this site to the First Baptist Church of Flint. The group worshipped here in a white clapboard sided church from 1873 to 1889. Around 1892, Stephen Crocker built five houses in this area, including this vernacular Queen Anne-style building.

Fred A. Aldrich

Fred Aldrich (1861-1957) moved into this house in 1894. A native of Van Buren County, Aldrich had come to Flint at age eight, when his father purchased the *Flint Globe* newspaper. In 1880, Aldrich established the *Otter Lake Enterprise* newspaper in northeast Genesee County. In 1889 he began working for his childhood friend, William C. Durant, as a clerk at the Flint Road Cart Company. He became secretary of the Durant-Dort Carriage Company upon its incorporation in 1896. He was the only secretary of that company and its successor, the Dort Motor Car Company, which closed in 1924. As a banker, Aldrich was instrumental in building the Durant and Flint Tavern Hotels. A prominent civic leader, he helped found the Community Chest, the local American Red Cross chapter and the Flint Improvement Fund.

221 West First Avenue, Flint; Jacob Smith/Fred A. Aldrich Informational Site; L1396C; March 19, 1987; 1988

St. Michael Roman Catholic Church

In 1834, Daniel O'Sullivan, a teacher from Ireland, moved to Flint and began teaching religion to students after school. Together with two traveling priests he convinced Bishop LeFevre to build a church in Flint. That church became St. Michael Roman Catholic Parish. In 1848 the parish completed its first church on land donated by Chauncey S. Payne. When this church became too small, the parish built its second church in 1883 under the leadership of Father Timothy J. Murphy. In 1924 fire destroyed the sanctuary of that church. Monsignor Patrick Dunigan had it rebuilt that same year. Monsignor Earl V. Sheridan led the construction of the third church in 1964. It was dedicated in 1966.

Side Two

Father Charles DeCeuninck, the third pastor of St. Michael, organized the parish's first school in 1856. The first permanent school building was completed in 1872. In 1877 the Sisters of the Immaculate Heart of Mary began staffing the school. The rectory became their convent. The parish built a new school in 1928, and a new rectory in 1938. A new convent for the Sisters was completed in 1950. The school was enlarged in 1954. In 1940 the Franciscan Sisters came to Flint and were given the Holy Angels Convent on the St. Michael property. In 1970 the school merged with other area Catholic schools and the convent belonging to the Sisters of the Immaculate Heart of Mary became a Parish Religious Education Center.

609 East Fifth Avenue, Flint; St. Michael Roman Catholic Church (St. Michael Roman Catholic Church); L1491C; January 21, 1988; 1988

St. Paul's Episcopal Church

The Reverend Daniel Brown came to this area in 1839 to help form a new Episcopal parish. He became the first rector of St. Paul's in 1840 when it received canonical sanction. The congregation met in a temporary chapel and then in a small church before the present structure was started in 1872 through efforts of the Reverend Marcus Lane. This massive Gothic Revival building was designed by Gordon Lloyd of Detroit. The limestone, donated by a quarry in Flushing, was transported by members to the site. On August 24, 1873, the first service was held in this church. St. Paul's was consecrated in 1882 when the Reverend William Seabrease was rector. Memorials in the church honor eminent citizens of Flint's past, including carriage makers and auto pioneers.

711 South Saginaw Street, Flint; St. Paul's Episcopal Church; L371; December 18, 1974; 1977

"The Vehicle City"

Flint, platted in 1836, became known as the "Vehicle City." The production of road carts reached 150,000 annually. Due to the foresight of its vehicle manufacturers Flint has become second only to the Detroit area in production of motor vehicles. A. B. C. Hardy made fifty Flint Roadsters in 1903. In 1904 the Buick Motor Car Company produced thirty-seven cars at its new Flint plant. In 1905, W. C. Durant, of the Durant-Dort Carriage Company, became head of Buick. He incorporated the General Motors Company in 1908 with Buick as its first automobile. In a few years Chevrolet, Fisher Body, AC Spark Plug and other auto parts makers also were established in Flint.

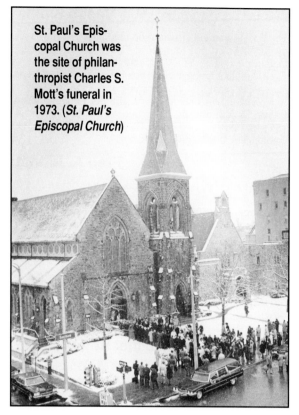

St. Paul's Episcopal Church was the site of philanthropist Charles S. Mott's funeral in 1973. (*St. Paul's Episcopal Church*)

Flint City Hall, 1101 South Saginaw, Flint; The Vehicle City Informational Designation; S180; February 19, 1958; 1961

Whaley House

The central portion of this handsome Victorian home was built in the late 1850s. Several prominent Flint families lived in it before Robert J. Whaley purchased it in 1884. Whaley, a local lumberman and banker, remodeled the house extensively. Three bays, the library alcove and a west-end addition were among the exterior changes. The interior was enhanced by adding ornate woodwork and colorful tiled fireplaces. In 1925, Whaley's wife endowed the house, making it a home for elderly women. In 1975 it became a public museum.

Robert J. Whaley

Robert J. Whaley was born in Castile, New York, in 1840. He moved to Wisconsin with his family in the 1840s, then returned to New York. There he met and married Mary McFarlan of Flint. Whaley and his bride moved to Flint in 1867. Here, he joined his father-in-law in lumbering and later banking. He purchased this gracious structure in 1884. Serving as president of Flint's Citizens Bank for forty-one years, Whaley was also a trustee for the Michigan Charitable Schools, a Mason, an Elk and a 1912 Democratic candidate for state treasurer. He died in 1922.

624 East Kearsley Street, SE corner of East Street, Flint; Whaley, Robert J., House (Whaley Historical House); L502; February 7, 1977; 1982

William C. Durant

William Crapo Durant (1861-1947), one of Flint's most important historical figures, was a pioneer in the development of the American auto industry. Durant's vehicle ventures began in 1886, when, with a borrowed $1,500, he bought the rights to build a two-wheeled road cart. Nine years later the Flint Road Cart Company, begun by Durant and his partner, Dallas Dort, became the Durant-Dort Carriage Company. Durant took over Flint's tiny Buick Motor Company in 1904. He turned it into the largest American producer of automobiles by 1908, and, on Buick's success, founded General Motors in September of that year. In 1911 he and Louis Chevrolet founded the Chevrolet Motor Company, which combined with General Motors seven years later. Parting with General Motors in the 1920s, Durant founded Durant Motors Company and its subsidiaries but went bankrupt during the Depression. He died in New York City.

Durant-Dort Carriage Company

William C. Durant and his business partner, J. Dallas Dort, completed this building in 1896.

It was originally the headquarters of the Durant-Dort Carriage Company, one of the largest volume producers of horse-drawn vehicles in the United States at the turn of the century. Many of the decisions that led to the birth of General Motors, now the world's largest automobile manufacturer, took place here. After the carriage firm ceased operations in 1917, this building was headquarters of the now defunct Dort Motor Car Company until 1925. The Durant-Dort Carriage Office Building is the last structure in Flint linked to "Billy" Durant's pioneer efforts in automobile manufacturing. It was listed in the National Register of Historic Places in 1975.

316 West Water Street and 307 Mason Street, Flint; Durant-Dort-Nash Historic District; L343; September 17, 1974; 1978

William C. Durant began his automotive industry career in 1886.
(William C. Durant)

Brent Creek United Methodist Church

This structure was completed and dedicated as the Brent Creek Methodist Protestant Church in the fall of 1891. There were sixteen members. The church, which was originally located slightly west of this site, was moved here in 1940. The Gothic-inspired wood-frame building has undergone only minor changes since its relocation. Changes include stained-glass windows, interior paneling, and asbestos shingle siding. It has served the community continuously since its organization. It became a United Methodist Church in 1968.

10412 West Mount Morris Road, Flushing Township; Brent Creek Methodist Protestant Church (Brent Creek United Methodist Church); L904B; March 16, 1981; 1982

Harrison Homestead

In 1835, Rufus and Sarah Harrison settled on this property, traveling by ox team from Detroit. It was said their farm was the first in Flushing Township to be cleared. Harrison died in 1856, and the farm was acquired by William Schram, his son-in-law. Schram and his wife, Harriet, continued to reside here until the early twentieth century. The nearby well is thought to be the original, although the covering is modern.

1570 Main Street, Flushing Township; Harrison Homestead (Sigma Nu Fraternity House); L221; May 17, 1973; 1973

Congregational Church

In 1833 eleven people established the First Congregational Church of Grand Blanc. The congregation, which held its early services in homes and, later, schoolhouses built their first house of worship in 1855. They replaced it with this modest red brick structure in 1885. The building served the Congregationalists for eighty-three years; its last worship service was on October 6, 1968. Purchased by the city of Grand Blanc in 1967, it became the home of municipal offices and a museum.

203 East Grand Blanc Road, Grand Blanc; Congregational Church of Grand Blanc (Grand Blanc City Hall); L935A; July 17, 1981; 1982

Davison Farmstead

Jonathan Davison (1795-1865), a native of Livingston County, New York, purchased 160 acres of land here in 1831. His son, John W. Davison, a farmer and carpenter, completed the rear portion of the present structure in 1855. He enlarged it to its present size in 1870. After his father's death in 1865, John acquired the property and built a barn, a dairy house and a large structure that contained a blacksmith and carpenter shop and a granary. In 1986 the 135-acre farm was still owned and operated by the Davisons' descendants.

3305 East Hill Road, one-half mile east of Saginaw Street (M-54), Grand Blanc Township; Davison, John West, Farmstead; L1138A; January 20, 1984; 1986

First Baptist Church

As Americans settled the wilderness areas of Michigan, religious services were often the first community concern. Beginning in 1831, traveling preachers visited this area, holding revival and prayer meetings, and starting new congregations. One of the earliest Protestant churches between Pontiac and the Mackinac area was the First Baptist Church of Grand Blanc founded on June 1, 1833. Two preachers from Pontiac helped organize the society. It was kept alive and active after the preachers moved on by Daniel Williams, Alfred Brainard and John Tupper, all of whom were deacons from New York State. Meetings were held in barns, homes and schools until this site was selected in 1843. Completed in 1851, this simple white frame church was dedicated on May 21 by the Reverends T. H. Facer and Joseph Gambell.

6101 South Saginaw, south of Edward Street, Grand Blanc Township; First Baptist Church; L300; July 26, 1975; 1976

William Ray Perry House

In 1894, William Ray Perry built this house on the farm that was purchased by his father in 1829. The Queen Anne house displays Eastlake ornamentation. Perry's forebearers had arrived in New England in 1650. In 1825, Edmund Perry, William's great-uncle, moved his immediate family from Rhode Island to the Grand Blanc area; other family members followed. The Perry's were the township's second pioneer family, and this vicinity became popularly known as the "Perry Settlement."

6025 Perry Road, Grand Blanc Township; Perry, William Ray, House (Perry House); L1680B; September 7, 1989; 1990

Linden Mills

The Linden Mills were a vital source of this village's economic growth. The first mill, located on the land granted to Consider Warner, was used to cut lumber. From 1845-1850 Seth Sadler and Samuel W. Warren, local residents, erected both a saw and grist mill. Operating along with the earlier facility, this complex was called the Linden Mills. The grist mill continued to function for over a century until the machinery was dismantled and sold at auction in 1956. The village then purchased the building for municipal offices and a public library.

Tickner Street, Linden; Grist Mill, Linden Mills (Linden Mill); L160; October 29, 1971; 1979

Linden Presbyterian Church

The First Presbyterian Society of Linden was founded under the direction of the Reverend Thomas Wright on May 8, 1860. It had eight charter members and was the first religious society to be established in the village of Linden. The Linden Presbyterians held their services in homes, halls and stores for three years until they completed this building. They held their dedication on October 21, 1863. The original church bell sits one hundred feet to the east.

119 West Broad Street, Linden; Linden Presbyterian Church Informational Site; L1263C; August 22, 1985; 1985

First United Methodist Church

First United Methodist Church, one of the oldest congregations in Genesee County, began with services held in Lewis Buckingham's home in 1836. The Reverend Luther D. Whitney a Flint circuit rider, and nine other people, organized the congregation in 1838. Their first church, built in 1850, was moved to Genesee Street in 1865-1866. The Reverend Seth Reed, a patriarch of Michigan Methodism, dedicated the congregation's present Gothic Revival church on January 31, 1886.

808 Genesee Street, SE corner of Church Street, Mount Morris; First United Methodist Church; L1444B; August 21, 1987; 1988

Voiture 1116-40-et 8

During World War I the capacity marking stenciled on French box cars (*voitures*) was "*40 et 8*"—forty men (*hommes*) and eight horses (*chevaux*). "Forty and eight" became a symbol of comradeship among the American veterans of that era. In 1920 a Philadelphia group of American Legionnaires organized the first *Societe Des 40 Hommes Et 8 Chevaux*. Soon there were chapters across the nation. In 1933 this chapter, "Voiture 1116-40-et-8," was chartered in Genesee County.

G-3255 East Mount Morris Road, Mount Morris; Voiture 1116-40 et 8 Informational Designation; L1166C; May 8, 1984; 1985

Mason's Tavern

Daniel Mason, a native of New Hartford, New York, built this structure as a stagecoach inn and tavern around 1850. It soon became a popular stagecoach stop along the route of the Flint and Fentonville Plank Road Company, which was established in 1849. From 1853 to

1871, Mundy Township's first post office was also housed here. The tavern and post office continued to operate until shortly after the Flint and Pere Marquette Railway came to the area. In 1879, Mason sold the property and moved to Flint, where he died in 1880. The tavern later became a private residence.

7500 Fenton Road, near the SE corner of Grand Blanc Road, Mundy Township; Mason's Tavern; L1132A; November 30, 1983; 1986

Gogebic

Gogebic Iron Range

The Gogebic was the last of the three great iron ore fields opened in the Upper Peninsula and northern Wisconsin. Beginning in 1848 with Dr. A. Randall, federal and state geologists had mapped the ore formations almost perfectly long before any ore was mined. One geologist, Raphael Rumpelly, on the basis of his studies in 1871, picked out lands for purchase, which years later became the sites of the wealthy Newport and Geneva mines. The first mine to go into production was the Colby. In 1884 it shipped 1,022 tons of iron ore in railroad flat cars to Milwaukee. By 1890 more than thirty mines had shipped ore from this range. Many quickly ran out of good ore and had to close. Others took their places as richer ore bodies were found. Virtually all mining here has been underground, as attested by many shafts and "cave-ins." The soft hematite ores common on this range usually have been sent in ore cars to Ashland and Escanaba, there to be loaded in ore boats and taken to America's steel mills.

Memory Lane Park (roadside park on US-2, one mile east of Bessemer), Bessemer Township; Gogebic Iron Range; S83; August 23, 1956; 1957

Norrie Park

This recreational area was named in honor of A. Lanfear Norrie, who in 1882 began to explore for iron ore on the Gogebic Range. His discovery resulted in the opening of the Norrie Mine in Ironwood. Soon other mines, such as the Ashland, Aurora, Pabst and Newport, were booming in these bustling locations. Ironwood is said to have been named after the mining "captain," James Wood, who was nicknamed "Iron" Wood. After a destructive fire in 1887, the community was rebuilt.

Norrie Park Road (Alfred Wright Boulevard), south of Ironwood, Erwin Township; Norrie Park; L12; April 13, 1960; 1960

Curry House

Here lived Solomon S. Curry, pioneer in the mining industry of the Ironwood area. Curry, a progressive, broad-minded man, was also instrumental in the building of the city of Ironwood, which through his efforts, grew from a wilderness to one of the major cities in northern Michigan. A Democrat, Curry was elected state representative in 1874 and was a candidate for lieutenant governor in 1896. Restored to its original appearance, the Curry House has Tiffany windows, nineteenth century light fixtures and ornate woodwork.

631 East McLeod Avenue, SE corner of Day Street, Ironwood; Curry, Solomon S., House (Kornwolf's Antiques); L560; November 7, 1977; 1978

Ironwood City Hall

This building served as city hall for Ironwood, which was settled in 1885 as the commercial center of the Gogebic iron mining district. Ironwood incorporated as a city in 1889 and erected the building a year later. Designed by George Mennie, this structure of Lake Superior sandstone and brick initially contained a jail, fire station, library and city offices. Then fire and police departments occupied the building exclusively. Firemen have hung their hoses to dry from the eighty-five-foot tower.

McLeod Avenue and Norfolk Street, Ironwood; Ironwood City Hall (Ironwood Fire Hall and Police Station); L399; May 14, 1975; 1977

Newport Hill

On this site, on October 8, 1871, geologist Raphael Pumpelly of Harvard University discovered one of the iron ore formations that created Gogebic County's "boom era." The

Newport Mine, named for Pumpelly's home in Rhode Island, began operations in 1884—the Geneva Mine in 1887. By the closing of the mines in 1966, 255 million tons of iron ore had been shipped from Gogebic County, and 67 million for adjoining Iron County Wisconsin.

Across from No. 1 Newport Heights, off of Country Club/Bonnie Road, Ironwood; Pumpelly, Raphael, Discovery of Iron Ore Formation Informational Site (Newport Hill/Newport-Bonnie Mine); S523B; August 3, 1979

Copper Peak: Chippewa Hill

At an altitude of more than 1,500 feet, 300 feet above the surrounding terrain, this location was the southern-most area in Michigan to offer a prospect of producing copper in commercial amounts. The Chippewa Copper Mining Company began work here in 1845, sinking a still-visible tunnel into the granite rock. No copper was ever produced, although around 1900 the Old Peak Company made further explorations. In 1970 a 280-foot ski slide, the highest in the world, was completed on the peak in time for the western hemisphere's first international ski flying tournament here. Skiers record flights of nearly 500 feet from this slide.

North Black River Valley Parkway (County Trunk 519, Ottawa National Forest, Ironwood Township; Copper Peak/Chippewa Hill (Chippewa Bluff/Old Peak); S324; January 22, 1971; 1974

Grand Traverse

Interlochen

Ottawa Indians once lived in the pine forest between lakes Wahbekaness and Wahbekanetta. In the late 1800s white men came and cut the pines, leaving only a small forest between

This interior view of the Traverse City Opera House, designed by E. R. Prahl of Pontiac, shows the grandeur that greeted Traverse City's theater-goers. (*City Opera House*)

The Northern Michigan Asylum was built in 1885. The hospital is listed in the National Register of Historic Places. (*The Traverse City Regional Psychiatric Hospital*)

the lakes. This virgin pine was purchased in 1917 by the state and became part of one of the first state parks. When the lumber era ended, the Wylie Cooperage mill occupied the Indian village site, making barrels until the hardwood ran out. Willis Pennington's summer hotel, opened in 1909, was popular with fishermen until automobiles and better roads drew them elsewhere. Then in 1918, Camp Interlochen, one of Michigan's first girls' recreation camps, was opened, followed in 1922 by Camp Pennloch for boys. In 1928, by arrangement with Willis Pennington, Joseph E. Maddy and Thaddeus P. Giddings established the National High School Orchestra Camp. It grew rapidly in scope, size and reputation, becoming the National Music Camp in 1931, and affiliating with the University of Michigan in 1942. Interlochen Arts Academy was chartered in 1960 to provide year-round training in the creative arts.

In front of the Stone Center on the campus of Interlochen Music Camp, just east of the intersection of M-31 and M-137, Green Lake Township; Interlochen (Interlochen Music Camp); S225; November 14, 1961; 1962

City Opera House

In 1891 three brothers-in-law—Anthony Bartak, Charles Wilhelm and Frank Votruba—built this 1,200-seat Victorian opera house. Designed by E. R. Prall of Pontiac, the opera house was the first facility in Traverse City to use electric lights. It has a forty-three-foot ceiling, hardwood maple floors and excellent acoustics. Built as a meeting hall and auditorium, the opera house hosted concerts, traveling plays, vaudeville shows, high school graduations, dinners and balls.

Side Two

In 1920 a motion picture firm leased the opera house and closed it to avoid competition with its own film theaters. The building was used briefly during the Depression for a WPA project creating miniature city buildings. In 1971 it was listed on the national and state historic registers. In 1978 the City Opera House Heritage Committee began raising money to restore the structure. In 1980 the opera house was given to Traverse City by the descendants of one of the original owners, Frank Votruba.

106-112 Front Street, Traverse City; City Opera House; L162; October 29, 1971; 1985

Congregation Beth El

This simple white frame structure featuring gable roof ends with spindle work is the oldest synagogue building in continuous use in Michigan. It was constructed in 1885 on land donated by Perry Hannah, Traverse City lumber magnate who contributed to many religious and civic institutions. Julius Steinberg, Julius Levinson and Solomon Yalomstein were the first trustees of Beth El. Unchanged in appearance, the building has served the Jewish community in the Grand Traverse area for almost a century.

312 South Park Street, Traverse City; Congregation Beth El; L421; October 21, 1975; 1977

Grand Traverse Bay

French traders named this bay when they made "the long crossing"—*la grande traverse* — across its mouth. Chippewa and Ottawa tribes fought in this region. Peter Daughtery's Indian Mission, established in 1839 at Old Mission, paved the way for white settlers. Founded in 1847, Traverse City was for years an important center of lumbering. Subsequently, it has become famous as the nation's cherry capital.

Clinch Park, Traverse City; Grand Traverse Bay Informational Designation; S42; July 19, 1956; 1957

Grand Traverse County Courthouse

Grand Traverse County was officially organized in 1851. Its first courthouse and jail were built in 1854 for $600 on land donated by the lumbering firm Hannah, Lay and Company. The courthouse, a wooden structure, burned in 1862. The county used rented quarters until 1900. In 1898 the county accepted plans for the present brick and stone structure submitted by architects Rush, Bowman and Rush of Grand Rapids. The building, placed on the site of the original courthouse, was completed in 1900 at a cost of $35,665. In 1975, after an intensive campaign led by County Historical Society President Jennie Arnold, citizens voted to remodel the building. The renovation was completed at a cost of $1.7 million, and the structure was rededicated on July 4, 1981.

SW corner of Boardman and Washington streets, Traverse City; Grand Traverse County Courthouse; L297; July 26, 1974; 1986

Ladies Library Association

On July 28, 1869, eight Traverse City women organized the Ladies Library Association. In 1878 the association purchased its first building at 205 East Front Street. In 1909 the association sold that building and retained Fred E. Moore as architect and E. E. Buckner as contractor to build the present structure. The cornerstone and time capsule were put into place on July 23, 1909. This building was used as a library until 1949. It served the city until 1983. In 1986 it was renovated for private law offices.

216 Cass Avenue, Traverse City; Ladies Library Building; L1309A; May 8, 1986; 1987

Novotny's Saloon

In 1886, Antoine Novotny, one of the Bohemian founders of this community, built a bar on this site. Novotny's Saloon was the social center of the city's south side and headquarters of the Traverse City Hustlers semi-pro baseball team. In 1939 the business was purchased by William H. Dill, and the name changed to Dill's. In the ensuing years, the adjacent meat market and vegetable stand were added to the pre-existing establishment. The second floor was the home of both the Salvation Army and a dance hall. On April 22, 1978, a fire destroyed the original wood frame building. This near replica of that structure, which was completed ten weeks later, continues to be one of Traverse City's social centers.

423 South Union Street, Traverse City; Novotny's Saloon Informational Site (Dill's Olde Towne Saloon); L737B; September 10, 1979; 1980

Traverse City Regional Psychiatric Hospital

The Northern Michigan Asylum (now the Traverse City Regional Psychiatric Hospital) was organized in 1881. It opened on November 30, 1885, with 43 residents. Dr. J. D. Munson was the facility's superintendent for its first thirty-nine years. The original buildings served five hundred residents. By 1959 the facility had 1.4 million square feet of floor space and housed 2,956 residents. The institution's farms and its processing and manufacturing facilities covered over a thousand acres and made it nearly self-sufficient. Between 1885 and 1985 it served over 50,000 residents. After 1960, with advances in treatment and community services, the need for in-patient facilities declined. In 1985, 150 beds served the area's acute and intensive psychiatric needs.

Bounded by C&O RR tracks, Division and Eleventh streets, Elmwood Avenue, Orange and Red drives, Traverse City; Northern Michigan Asylum (Traverse City Regional Psychiatric Hospital); S573C; October 26, 1985; 1985

Gratiot

Alma College

On October 26, 1886, the Presbyterian Synod of Michigan accepted an offer by Ammi W. Wright of Alma of thirty acres of land, containing two buildings, and a gift of $50,000 from Alexander Folsom of Bay City, for the purpose of establishing Alma College. The synod had resolved: "We will, with God's help, establish and endow a college within our bounds." A charter was granted by the state of Michigan, April 15, 1887. Classes began September 12, 1887. In the first year there were ninety-five students and nine faculty members. Here the Presbyterian Church has fostered the pursuit of learning to the glory of God and to the dignity of men.

700 block West Superior Street, Alma; Alma College Informational Designation; S181; March 18, 1961; 1961

Michigan Masonic Home

In November 1885 the Michigan Masonic Home Association was established to raise funds for a home and health care facility for aged Masons. In 1891, Michigan's first Masonic Home, located on Reed's Lake near Grand Rapids, was opened. When fire destroyed it in 1910, Alma businessman and philanthropist Ammi W. Wright donated the former Alma Sanitarium as a replacement. The Masons used that structure for twenty years. In 1929 the Masons began construction of a new home on this 116-acre site. The first residents moved into the new facility in 1931. Since 1931 several additions have combined to create this diverse residential and nursing care facility operated by the Grand Lodge of Free and Accepted Masons of Michigan.

1200 Wright Avenue, Alma; Michigan Masonic Home; S567A; May 21, 1985; 1986

Gratiot County

This county was named for General Charles Gratiot, builder of Fort Gratiot at Port Huron in 1814. A few Chippewas and other Indians lived in the area in 1831 when the county was laid out. A Lutheran Indian mission was set up in 1846 near what is now St. Louis. Settling of the county began in the same year. In 1856 the county government was organized, Ithaca being selected as county seat. Agriculture and industry combine to give Gratiot County a stable economy.

Center Street, Courthouse Square, Ithaca; Gratiot County Courthouse; S176; September 15, 1957; 1958

Michigan's Petroleum Industry

In 1860, State Geologist Alexander Winchell reported that oil and gas deposits lay under Michigan's surface. First commercial production was at Port Huron where twenty-two wells were drilled, beginning in 1886. Total output was small. Michigan's first oil boom was at Saginaw, where production began in 1925. About three hundred wells were drilled here by 1927, when Muskegon's "Discovery Well" drew oil men the country over to that field. The Mount Pleasant field, opened in 1928, helped to make Michigan one of the leading oil producers of the eastern United States. Mount Pleasant became known as the "Oil Capital of Michigan." Efforts of the industry itself resulted in excellent state laws regulating petroleum output. Well depths range from one thousand to six thousand feet. New wells are constantly opened as exploration continues.

*Erected at the rest area on southbound US-27, north of Alma, Pine River Township; now in the collections of the Michigan Historical Museum, Lansing; Michigan's Petroleum Industry; S130, January 19, 1957, 1958

Lumberjack Park

In 1926 when George Beck of Ithaca learned that one of the last stands of white pine in Gratiot County was going to be cut, he called on local lumberjacks and rivermen to buy the threatened forty-acre tract and preserve it as a memorial. The woodsmen organized the Lumberjack and Riverdrivers Association and in 1927 purchased the land for $3,000. They elected Otis Terpening as their first president that year. By 1945 the mortgage had been fully paid through membership fees, donations and fund-raising dinners.

Side Two

The Lumberjacks and Riverdrivers Association minutes of October 18, 1934, explained: "We shanty boys are growing old and our ranks keep getting thinner year by year, but when our day is ended we know our children's children still can gather on this spot where the shanty boys have built their final camp." The bunkhouse and cook shanty were completed in 1930, the pavilion by 1931, and the caretaker's house in 1947. The park also features a band shell, a playground area and a nature trail.

Lumberjack Road, about one and one-half miles north of M-46, Riverdale, Seville Township; Lumberjack & Riverdrivers Association Park (Lumberjack Park); S545B; January 11, 1982; 1982

Hillsdale

College Baptist Church

This church was incorporated as the First Free Will Baptist Church on November 24, 1855. The congregation met at the Hillsdale College Chapel until the present church was constructed in 1867-1868. This Romanesque building was designed by a Chicago architect using sketches of European cathedrals prepared by Wayland Dunn. Wayland was the son of Professor Ransom Dunn, the pastor at the time of construction. The only alteration of the exterior has been the loss of the southeast spire, which was toppled by the wind in 1871.

204 North Manning, Hillsdale; First Free Will Baptist Church (College Baptist Church); L1275A; November 26, 1985; 1987

Hillsdale

The plat for the village of Hillsdale was filed in July 1839, though the first settlement probably occurred a few years previously. Before that time this area had been inhabited mainly by a band of Potawatomi Indians led by their chief, Baw Beese. Jonesville was the first county seat, but Hillsdale gained this distinction in 1843 due to its more central location and the completion of the Michigan Southern Railroad to the town. The first Hillsdale County Fair was held on this site in 1851. Hillsdale College opened for classes in November 1855, and the city received its charter in April 1869.

Courthouse Square, Howell Street, Hillsdale; Hillsdale County Courthouse; S294; April 10, 1969; 1969

Hillsdale College

In 1844 a group of Freewill Baptists organized Michigan Central College at Spring Arbor. This college was the first in Michigan to grant degrees to women. Moved to Hillsdale in 1853 and chartered by the legislature in 1855, the school was renamed Hillsdale College under an independent board of trustees, its only controlling organization. The charter opened the institution "to all persons . . . irrespective of nationality, color or sex."

Front Campus, Hillsdale; Hillsdale College; S230; January 16, 1962; 1968

St. Anthony's Catholic Church

The origins of Catholicism in Hillsdale County date to the 1840s when Irishmen who worked

Central Hall at Hillsdale College dominates the campus of this liberal arts institution, the first in Michigan to grant degrees to women. (*Hillsdale College*)

for the Southern Railroad settled here. In 1853 the Reverend Joseph Kindekens of Adrian and eighty-five people organized St. Anthony's parish. The former Presbyterian church, which was located on this site, became the first house of worship. In 1858 the Reverend Charles Ryckaert became the first pastor and built a rectory. After the Reverend Peter Slane arrived in 1878, the old church was razed to make way for the present one. On June 15, 1884, Bishop Casper Borgess dedicated this spired Gothic Revival church. St. Anthony's Church remains the only Catholic parish in Hillsdale County.

11 North Broad Street, Hillsdale; St. Anthony Roman Catholic Church; L1645A; April 20, 1989; 1991

Grace Episcopal Church

William N. Lyster, Irish-born missionary, preached in Jonesville in 1836, and Darius Barker organized the parish in 1838. A church featuring Classical and Gothic styling was begun in 1844 and consecrated by Bishop Samuel McCoskry in 1848. Panelling and furniture made from black walnut are still in place. William Walton Murphy, a founder and vestryman, was Abraham Lincoln's consul-general to the German city of Frankfurt.

360 East Chicago Street, Jonesville; Grace Episcopal Church; L84; January 6, 1971; 1972

Grosvenor House

Completed in 1874, this structure of High Victorian Italianate design is one of the most magnificent residences in Michigan. The interior, an excellent example of a living museum of the 1870s, contains thirty-two rooms with twelve-foot ceilings. Other striking features are eight Italian marble fireplaces each of a different color, walnut window valances with carved Egyptian heads and a sweeping balustrade staircase. Despite the fact that electricity was installed in 1915, this house still retains several gas-operated globe lights.

Side Two

Elijah E. Myers designed this residence for Ebenezer Oliver Grosvenor (1820-1910). An eminent Jonesville citizen and banker, Grosvenor was also a prominent Republican statesman. He served two terms as state senator and treasurer, one term as lieutenant governor and seven years as a University of Michigan regent. He was also vice-president and presiding officer of the State Building Commission responsible for the erection of the Michigan State Capitol in 1874-1879, which Myers also designed.

211 Maumee Street, Jonesville; Grosvenor, E. O., House (Gamble House); S500; April 15, 1977; 1978

Congregational Church of Litchfield

Twenty charter members, led by the Reverend Elisha Buck, established this church on July 14, 1839. Founded as a Presbyterian mission, it was reorganized under the congregational polity by the Reverend J. J. Bliss in 1844. At first, worship services were held in a local school, which was also used by the Baptists and Methodists of Litchfield. This red brick, Gothic-style structure was the second building erected by the congregation. Completed in 1870, it is the oldest extant church in Litchfield. Its stained-glass windows were installed in 1910. In 1888 the Christian Endeavor Society, an ecumenical youth organization, held its first Michigan meeting here.

203 North Chicago Street, Litchfield; Litchfield Congregational Church; L814A; June 10, 1980; 1984

Mosherville Church

The Mosherville Church was built in 1861-1862 on land donated by Joseph and Mary Riggs. Originally part of the Litchfield circuit of the Methodist Episcopal Church, it became the home church of a separate circuit in 1870. The Ladies Aid Society was organized in 1891. In 1893 a bequest from Kate C. Brower allowed the society to enlarge the church, adding the Kate C. Brower Memorial Chapel. The church has held weekly nondenominational services since 1943.

Mosherville School

Mosherville's first school opened in 1847. In 1857-1858 the community erected a frame schoolhouse. It was replaced by this building in 1872 at a cost of $2,800. The oldest school in Scipio Township, it originally had two rooms serving grades one through ten. Later, as an eight-grade school, its well-kept yard and out-buildings, organization, furnishings and supplies earned it the status of "standard school." The school closed in 1967 and later became the home of the Ladies Aid Society.

North Street, Scipio Township; Mosherville Church and School Complex; L653A; April 24, 1979; 1980

Houghton

Calumet Theater

One of the first municipal theaters in America, the Calumet opened on March 20, 1900, "the greatest social event ever known in copperdom's metropolis." The theater contained a magnificent stage and elegant interior decorations, including an electrified copper chandelier. For over a decade, Copper Country audiences witnessed the broad panorama of American legitimate theater, and many prominent stage personalities, both American and European, trod the boards of the Calumet. By the 1920s, motion pictures replaced live theater, and,

Damp, dusty and dark describe the underground world of Michigan's copper mines, like the Houghton and Keweenaw county mines in the Upper Peninsula. (*Copper Country*)

subsequently, live drama returned to the Calumet. The reopened community theater resumed its position as a focal point of civic pride for the people of Calumet and the Copper Country.

340 Sixth Street, Calumet; Calumet Theatre (Calumet Civic Auditorium); L112A; April 23, 1971; 1973

Italian Hall

On December 24, 1913, area copper miners had been on strike for five months. The miners were fighting for better pay, shortened work days, safer working conditions and union recognition. That day, during a yuletide party for the striking miners and their families, someone yelled, "Fire!" Although there was no fire, seventy-three persons died while attempting to escape down a stairwell that had doors that opened inward. Over half of those who died were children between the ages of six and ten. The perpetrator of the tragedy was never identified. The strike ended in April 1914.

Side Two

The Italian Hall was built in 1908 as the headquarters for Calumet's benevolent society. The society, organized along ethnic lines, encouraged and financially aided immigrants and provided relief to victims of hardship. Following the 1913 Christmas Eve tragedy, the hall continued to be used for nearly five decades. The two-story red brick building was razed in 1984. Through the efforts of the friends of the Italian Hall and Local 324 of the AFL-CIO, the site of the building became a memorial park, dedicated to the people who lost their lives in 1913.

Near the corner of Seventh and Elm streets, Calumet; Italian Hall Disaster Site (Demolished) (Italian Hall Disaster Site); L1337C; September 16, 1986; 1987

St. Paul the Apostle Church

St. Joseph Roman Catholic Church was established in 1889 by Slovenian immigrants who

Designed by the architectural firm of Saarinen and Swanson, Old Main opened as the primary building of Suomi College in 1900. (*Suomi College*)

came to this area to work in the mines of the Copper Country. The wood frame church erected by the parish in 1890 was destroyed by fire in 1902. The following year this elegant Romanesque church, designed by Erhard Brielmaier of Milwaukee, was begun. It was completed at a cost of $100,000 in 1908. Built of locally-quarried Jacobsville sandstone, the structure displays Cathedral-type stained-glass windows from the Ford Brothers Glass Studio of Minneapolis. Its interior features a beautifully painted sixty-five-foot nave. In 1966 four parishes consolidated, making this building their church and changing its name to St. Paul the Apostle.

301 Eighth Avenue, Calumet; St. Joseph Roman Catholic Church (St. Paul the Apostle Catholic Church); L1089A; June 23, 1983; 1986

Suomi Synod

On March 25, 1890, nine Lutheran congregations, representing twelve hundred Finnish immigrants, assembled at Trinity Lutheran Church in Calumet and organized the Finnish Evangelical Lutheran Church In America—Suomi Synod. Four pastors and seventeen laymen from congregations in Calumet, Hancock, Jacobsville, Republic, Ishpeming, Negaunee and Ironwood, Michigan, as well as Savo, South Dakota, chose the Reverend Juho K. Nikander as the first president of the synod. By the 1920s the synod had become a national church body with 153 congregations and thirty-six thousand members. In 1963 it merged with Lutheran churches of Swedish, German and Danish descent to form the Lutheran Church In America. The Calumet congregation, Faith Lutheran Church, is a continuation of the Finnish, Swedish and Norwegian group that met in Trinity Lutheran in 1890.

Faith Lutheran Church, Depot & Laurium streets, Calumet; Suomi Synod Informational Designation; L1714C; January 16, 1990; 1990

Suomi College

In the 1880s large numbers of Finns immigrated to Hancock to labor in the copper and lumber industries. One immigrant, mission pastor J. K. Nikander of the Finnish Evangelical Lutheran Church of America, headquartered in Hancock, wanted to ensure seminary training in America. He had observed that Swedish and Finnish immigrants along the Delaware River did not train new ministers, and he feared a loss of Finnish identity. In 1896, Nikander founded Suomi College. The college's role was to preserve Finnish culture, train Lutheran ministers and teach English. During the 1920s, Suomi became a liberal arts college. In 1958 the seminary separated from the college. Four years later the Finnish Evangelical Lutheran Church of America merged with other mainstream Lutheran churches.

Old Main

Suomi College was founded in 1896 by the Finnish Evangelical Lutheran Church of America. The cornerstone of Old Main, the first building erected at Suomi College, was laid on May 30, 1898. Jacobsville sandstone, quarried at the Portage Entry of the Keweenaw waterway, was brought here by barge, cut and used to construct Old Main. Dedicated on January 21, 1900, it contained a dormitory, kitchen, laundry, classrooms, offices, library, chapel and lounge. The burgeoning college quickly outgrew this building, and in 1901 a frame structure, housing a gym, meeting hall and music center was erected on an adjacent lot. The frame building was demolished when Nikander Hall, named for Suomi's founder, J. K. Nikander, was constructed in 1939. The hall was designed by the architectural firm of Saarinen and Swanson.

Suomi College Campus, 601 Quincy Street, Hancock; Suomi College Building (Old Main); S211; February 12, 1959; 1991

Houghton County

Organized in 1845, Houghton County once comprised the entire Keweenaw Peninsula. Eagle River was its first county seat. In 1861, after the state legislature split the county into

Houghton became the county's governmental center in 1861. This High Victorian court-house was dedicated in 1887. (*Houghton County*)

Keweenaw and Houghton, the village of Houghton became the new seat of Houghton County government. Finnish settlers were predominant in the county. There were also Scandinavians, as well as Cornish, Germans and French Canadians. Jobs were plentiful since Houghton County was the center of the copper boom. In 1874, Michigan produced 88 percent of the nation's copper, of which Houghton County mines supplied 79 percent. Two years later, Michigan copper production peaked at 90 percent of the nation's output. The Michigan Mining School opened in Houghton in 1886. In 1964 it was renamed Michigan Technological University.

Houghton County Courthouse

The opulent High Victorian design of the Houghton County Courthouse testifies to the prosperity that the copper boom brought to the area in the late nineteenth century. The building's irregular form and polychromatic exterior make it one of Michigan's most distinctive nineteenth-century courthouses. The red sandstone trim and copper roof were products of the Upper Peninsula. The architect, J. B. Sweatt, was from Marquette. Originally from Chicago, Sweatt typified the many architects who worked in Houghton and participated in the building rush that occurred during the copper boom. Dedicated on July 28, 1887, the courthouse replaced a frame structure constructed in 1862.

401 East Houghton Street, Houghton; Houghton County Courthouse; S431A; July 26, 1974; 1989

Michigan Tech

In 1885 the Michigan Mining School was established here by the state. Classes were held in temporary quarters until 1889 when Hubbell Hall was erected. Situated ideally in the midst of the Upper Peninsula's booming mining industry, the school soon ranked as one of the world's best mining colleges. Renamed Michigan College of Mining and Technology in 1927, it now offers work in all the major fields of engineering and science.

(Original marker, erected in 1957, replaced with revised marker in 1966)

Michigan Tech

In 1885 the state established a mining school here in America's first great metal mining region. As the Michigan College of Mines, it achieved world-wide renown as a center of education and research in mining, metallurgy and geology. In 1927 and again in 1964 its name was changed and its scope was broadened to meet industry's expanding needs. Under its present name, Michigan Technological University, it enrolls men and women in undergraduate and graduate programs in its original subjects and in many other branches of engineering, science, business, forestry and the liberal arts.

On the campus of Michigan Technological University between the library and Fisher Hall, Houghton; Michigan College of Mining and Technology Informational Designation; S93; September 25, 1956; 1966

St. Ignatius Loyola Church

The roots of the Catholic Church in the Portage Lake area are associated with Bishop Frederic Baraga, the "Snowshoe Priest," who dedicated the original St. Ignatius Loyola Church on July 31, 1859. Before the erection of that building, Catholics in Houghton worshipped in a boarding house and later a school. The present structure was completed in 1902, after four years of construction, under the direction of Father Anton Ivan Rezek. Father (later Monsignor) Rezek came as pastor in 1895 and remained in that position for fifty-one years. One of the most imposing edifices in Houghton, St. Ignatius Loyola Church features rock-faced sandstone facades. Beautiful stained-glass windows and an elaborate Gothic altar adorn the breathtaking interior.

703 East Houghton Avenue, Houghton; Saint Ignatius Loyola Church; L568A; December 8, 1977; 1979

Trinity Episcopal Church

Many of the Cornish miners, storekeepers and mining captains who immigrated to this area during the Copper Country mining boom (1842-1860) were Anglicans. On July 17, 1860, the Reverend Samuel A. McCrosky, Episcopal Bishop of Michigan, met with nine Houghton and Hancock businessmen to establish a parish. The group held its first public worship services on September 15, 1860. At its first vestry meeting, on July 13, 1861, the name Trinity Church was adopted. The present Jacobsville sandstone church was completed in 1910. Located on the site of an earlier wooden church, the present building has an interior design influenced by the Oxford Movement. The sanctuary's attractive wood carvings are the handiwork of Aloysius Lang of Oberammergau.

200 Pewabic Street at the corner of Montezuma, Houghton; Trinity Episcopal Church; L1319A; July 17, 1986; 1987

The Copper Country

Long before Columbus reached America, Indians extracted native copper in the Lake Superior region and worked it into articles which were used by tribes throughout the continent. French explorers learned of the vast copper deposits but were not able to mine the metal. In 1771 an English group tried without success to mine copper near the Ontonagon Boulder, a huge mass of native copper weighing three tons. In 1841, Douglass Houghton's survey of copper resources was printed. Prospectors by the hundreds soon flocked here. Boom towns sprang up. The Phoenix was the first real mine to begin operation, but the Cliff was the first to show a profit. Soon miners were tapping the rich deposits all along the Keweenaw Peninsula's backbone. Until 1887 this was the country's leading center of copper production. This has been virtually the only area in the world with any substantial native copper production. Copper is found in combination with other elements at the White Pine Mine where a great new mining operation began in the 1950s.

Roadside park off US-41 just north of Airport Road, midway between Hancock and Calumet, Quincy Township; Copper Country; S30; July 19, 1956; 1957

Finnish Lutheran Church

In 1886 a group of Finnish immigrants banded together to organize the Jacobsville Finnish Lutheran congregation. Early worship services were held in various locations until 1888, when this simple frame structure was built. In 1890 the congregation helped organize the Finnish Evangelical Lutheran Church-Suomi Synod. In 1891 the church was placed atop its stone foundation, and in 1892 its tower and bell were added. The well-preserved church, one of the oldest remaining structures in the community, retains its original furnishings, kerosene lamps and wood stove. It has neither electricity nor plumbing. In 1952 the congregation and church property became part of the Gloria Dei Lutheran congregation of Hancock. In the 1980s the church continued to be used for summer vesper services.

Jacobsville

The first settler in this area was George Craig, Sr., who arrived in the mid-nineteenth century. However, the unincorporated community of Jacobsville did not spring into being until 1884, when John H. Jacobs of Marquette opened his sandstone quarries in the vicinity. The quarries provided high quality red stone for buildings throughout North America and abroad from 1884 to 1919. During this time, some 800,000 tons of stone were shipped for such projects as the first Waldorf-Astoria in New York. The community, populated mostly by Finns, reached its peak about 1897, when it had eight hundred inhabitants. The Finnish Lutheran congregation, founded in 1886, was a major factor in preserving the Finnish culture and ethnic solidarity that was still present a century later.

West of Jacobsville, Torch Lake Township; Jacobsville Finnish Lutheran Church; L532; June 6, 1977; 1987

Huron

St. Mary of Czestochowa Roman Catholic Church

The Polish refugees who immigrated to Dwight Township in the 1840s in order to escape Prussian domination worshipped at St. Michael's Catholic Church in Port Austin. In 1903, in an effort to retain their Polish identity, they established their own parish and built St. Mary of Czestochowa church, named for "the Queen of Poland." The parishioners built the wood frame structure on land purchased from Frank and Rosa Koroleski. Father J. Trzetrzynski was the first pastor. After that church burned on May 29, 1932, construction began on the present cobblestone and brick building, which was dedicated on May 28, 1933. Father Henry Podsiad directed the building of this church, which is reminiscent of polish Romanesque churches.

107

Rzymsko Katolicki Kosciół Matki Boskiej Częstochowskiej

Polacy, którzy by uniknąć jarzma pruskiego, wyemigrowali z Polski po 1840 roku do Dwight Township, modlili się w kościele Św. Michała w Port Austin. W roku 1903, starając się utrzymać swoją polskość, załozyli wlasną parafię i zbudowali kościół Matki Boskiej Częstochowskiej, zwanej "Królową Polski". Parafianie wznieśli drewniany budynek na ziemi zakupionej od Franciszka i Róży Koroleskich. Ks. J. Trzetrzynski był pierwaszym proboszczem.

29 Maja 1932 roku, kościół spłonął. W następstwie, rozpoezęto budowę obecnego budynku wzniesionego z kamienia i cegly, przypominającego poliskie kościoly romanśkie. Pracami budowlanymi kościoła kierował Ksiądz Henryk Podsiad.

Poświęcenia dokonano 28 maja 1933 r.

Moeller Road east of Hellems Road, Kinde vicinity, Dwight Township; St. Mary of Czestochowa (Saint Mary of Czestochowa Roman Catholic Church); L849A; November 2, 1980; 1989

Bay Port Fishing District

The Gillingham Fish Company was established in 1886; the Bay Port Fish Company, in 1895. At their peak in the 1920s and 1930s, they shipped tons of perch, walleye, herring, whitefish and carp to New York and Chicago in refrigerated railroad cars. Once known as one of the largest fresh water commercial fishing ports in the world, Bay Port retains a commercial fishery that operates much as it did in the past. Bay Port also offers sport fishing, water skiing, ice fishing and hunting.

Public access off M-25 at the end of Promenade Street, Bay Port, Fairhaven Township; Bay Port Commercial Fishing Historic District; S458; February 21, 1975; 1986

Great Fire of 1881

Small fires were burning in the forests of the Thumb, tinder-dry after a long, hot summer, when a gale swept in from the southwest on September 5, 1881. Fanned into an inferno, the fires raged for three days. A million acres were devastated in Sanilac and Huron counties alone. At least 125 persons died, and thousands more were left destitute. The new American Red Cross won support for its prompt aid to the fire victims. This was the first disaster relief furnished by this great organization.

Roadside Park on M-25, one-half mile south of the junction of M-25 and M-142, Bay Port, Fairhaven Township; Great Fire of 1881; S141; January 19, 1957; 1957

Stagecoaches

Stagecoaches played an important part in developing the Midwest. Michigan's frontier "fever" peaked in the decade from 1830 to 1840 with a 600 percent population increase. Stagecoaches attempted to fill the demand for fast and relatively comfortable transportation. Early stagecoach travel was slow and rough but improved with better built roads. The inns and taverns on the stage routes were a welcome relief in Michigan. This stepping stone, which once led to the famous Bay Port Hotel, is all that remains from the stagecoach era in Bay Port.

NE corner of Cedar and Second streets, Bay Port, Fairhaven Township; Stagecoach Travel in Michigan Informational Designation; L541; August 12, 1977; 1978

Frank Murphy

Frank Murphy was associate justice of the U. S. Supreme Court from 1940 until his death in 1949. His earlier career included service as a judge in the Detroit Recorder's Court and instructor in law at the University of Detroit in the twenties. In the following decade he was mayor of Detroit, U. S. governor-general in the Philippines, governor of Michigan and attorney general of the United States. Governor Murphy's stand during the 1937 sit-down strike received national attention when he refused to send troops to remove workers from the factories. As an associate justice, Murphy wrote many of the Court's opinions concerning civil liberties. In Thornhill v. Alabama (1940), Murphy clarified labor's right to strike, holding that peaceful picketing was a manifestation of freedom of speech. Murphy died on July 19, 1949, and is buried in Harbor Beach.

During the 1860s, Ohio Congressman, later president, James A. Garfield was a frequent guest of Charles and Maria Learned. (*Charles Learned*)

Side Two

1890-Born, Harbor Beach, on April 13; 1914-Graduated from University of Michigan Law School; 1917-19, Army officer, World War I, service in Germany; 1919, Law studies, London and Dublin; 1920-23, first Assistant U.S. District Attorney, Eastern Michigan District; 1922-27, Law instructor, University of Detroit; 1923-30, Recorder's Court Judge, Detroit; 1930-33, Mayor of Detroit; 1933-36, Governor General, Philippine Islands; after the islands achieved commonwealth status, he became U. S. High Commissioner; 1937-38, Governor of Michigan; 1939-40, Attorney General of the U. S.; 1940-49, U.S. Supreme Court Justice; 1949, Died at Detroit, on July 19. Buried in Rock Falls Cemetery, Harbor Beach.

142 South Huron Street, between Broad and State streets, Harbor Beach; Murphy, Frank, Birthplace; S285; February 17, 1967; 1967

Owendale

In 1882, as three new railroads began to lay track in Huron County, two cousins from Saginaw, John G. and John S. Owen, bought land in the Columbia Swamp. The following year, they opened a sawmill to harvest the native oak. John G. Owen hired Quincy Thomas, a civil engineer, to survey a town site in 1887. The streets, alleys and parks were dedicated to the public for their perpetual use, and the village was named Owendale. The sawmill burned in 1896, and the Owendale area turned from lumbering to agriculture.

Village Park, Sebewaing Road (Main Street), Owendale; Owendale Informational Designation; L383; April 4, 1975; 1976

Pigeon Depot

The Pigeon Depot was constructed in 1908 and served two railroad lines. In 1883 the Pontiac, Oxford and Port Austin Railroad, a north-south line, had been extended to Caseville and a depot was built at Berne, one mile north of here. Around 1886 the Saginaw, Tuscola and Huron Railroad built tracks through the Tamarack Swamp and crossed the north-south line at this point. This railroad stop became known as Berne Junction. Berne's population quickly dwindled as people moved to the junction where they established Pigeon in 1888. The Pontiac, Oxford and Port Austin line became the Pontiac, Oxford and Northern and later the Grand Trunk Railroad. The Saginaw, Tuscola and Huron was absorbed by the Pere Marquette Railroad and then by the Chesapeake and Ohio Railroad. The Pigeon Depot presently serves as the Pigeon Historical Society Museum.

59 South Main, Pigeon; Pigeon Depot; L1439A; August 21, 1987; 1989

Charles G. Learned

A native of New York, contractor Charles G. Learned helped build New York City's waterworks system and the Erie Canal. Around 1857, Learned and his brother-in-law purchased several thousand acres of pine land in Michigan's Thumb area. Two years later, Learned and his wife, Maria Raymond, came to Port Austin and bought a house and three acres at this site. Learned's cutover pine land became a two-thousand-acre farm where he prospered as an agriculturalist and dairy farmer. With profits from his lumbering and farming enterprises Learned enlarged and updated this house in the French Second Empire style. In the 1860s, Ohio congressman, later president, James A. Garfield, a family friend, was a frequent guest here. From 1931 to 1979 the house served as the Mayes Inn and Tower Hotel. It was listed on the National Register of Historic Places in 1984.

8544 Lake Street, Port Austin; Learned, Charles G., House (The Tower Hotel); L815A; June 10, 1980; 1990

Port Hope Chimney

This chimney was built in 1858 by John Geltz. It is all that remains of the lumber mill established that year by William R. Stafford. Port Hope grew up around the mill. For a score of years this town was a center of lumbering in the Thumb. It also became an important producer of salt. In 1871 and again in 1881 the mill, the docks and possessions of hundreds of people were destroyed by fire. This chimney is a monument to these pioneers who by their courage and industry developed this area.

Huron Street; Stafford Park, off M-25, Port Hope; Stafford, W. R., Saw Mill Informational Site; L21; July 17, 1961; 1962

The Indian Mission

Here, on July 1, 1845, three Lutheran missionaries, Reverend Johann J. F. Auch, Reverend J. Simon Dumser and Reverend George Sinke, arrived. The Lutheran leader, Reverend Friedrich Schmid, sent them from Ann Arbor to evangelize the Chippewa Indians. A log chapel was built here later that summer. In 1849, Reverend Mr. Auch ferried lumber from lower Saginaw to Shebahyonk on Wild Fowl Bay, seven miles north of Sebewaing. A mission house was built there and dedicated June 27, 1849. Reverend J. F. Maier had charge of the mission. By 1854 the Indians had left these parts. The mission house was sold. A century later, it was moved to this site and established as a museum. It is now maintained by the Michigan District of the Lutheran Church—Missouri Synod.

590 East Bay Street (Sebewaing Road, east of M-23, Sebewaing Township; Indian Mission (Luckhard Museum/Luckhard Indian Mission/Sebewaing Indian Mission); L24; July 19, 1962; 1962

White Rock School

Named after a boulder in Lake Huron that was used as a landmark in the Indian Treaty of 1807, the village was settled about 1860. Destroyed in the Great Fire of 1871, the town was soon rebuilt, including a schoolhouse. The present building was constructed in 1909. At that time twenty-five pupils attended, and the teacher was paid forty dollars a month. White Rock School continued in use until 1968. The Huron County Historical Society acquired the property in 1970 for a historical museum.

On White Rock Road (M-25), eleven miles south of Harbor Beach, Sherman Township; White Rock School; L202; April 14, 1972; 1976

Ingham

Alice B. Cowles House

The Alice B. Cowles House, built in 1857, is the oldest building on the Michigan State University campus. Built as a "Farm Cottage" on Faculty Row from bricks made of clay from the banks of the Red Cedar River, it was originally the official residence of the president of Michigan Agricultural College. After 1874 it was used as faculty housing, as Department of Education offices and as a residence for female students. In 1941 it again became the official home of the president. After World War II, it was remodeled using funds from the estate of alumnus Frederick Cowles Jenison and named for Jenison's mother, Alice B. Cowles. Jenison's grandfather, Albert Cowles, had been a student in the college's first class in 1857 and had helped gather the materials for the building.

Side Two

Cowles House was centrally located on the campus of the nation's oldest land grant institution, Michigan Agricultural College. Constructed in 1857, it was one of four cottages, designed by architect J. J. Scott of Toledo, Ohio, to house college faculty and their families. Joseph R. Williams, president from 1857 to 1859, was its first resident. In 1874 a new house on the site now occupied by Gilchrist Hall became the president's residence and Professor William James Beal moved into Cowles House with his wife Hannah and daughter Jessie. A pioneer botanist, Beal is credited with the first documented account of hybrid corn experimentation. Due to the many modifications of Cowles House over the years, only the stone foundation and two walls of the original structure remain visible.

1 Abbott Road, south side of West Circle Drive, Michigan State University campus, East Lansing; President's House/No. 4 Faculty Row (Cowles House); S572B; September 25, 1985; 1988

Bigelow-Kuhn-Thomas House

By 1986 this Greek Revival house was the only privately-owned pre-Civil War house still used as a residence in East Lansing. Horace Bigelow (c. 1822-1891) built it in 1849. According to the 1874 *Atlas of Ingham County*, Bigelow was "a farmer, stock and wool grower, and breeder of Essex hogs." He was also a member of the Marble School Board. His daughter Jennie Kuhn (1853-1925), long-time secretary of the Marble School Board, lived in the house all of her life.

334 North Hagadorn Road, corner of Ann Street, East Lansing; Bigelow-Kuhn House; L629; August 24, 1978; 1987

Michigan's first historical marker was erected at Michigan State University on the site of College Hall (top); Women's Program students learned farming skills. (*Michigan State University*)

Harry J. Eustace Hall

Famous horticulturist and educator Liberty Hyde Bailey designed this building as the first separate horticulture laboratory in America. Completed in 1888, the structure contained rooms for classes and botanical experiments. It exemplified Bailey's pioneering work in scientific investigation of plant life. Its present name commemorates Harry J. Eustace, former professor and chairman of the Horticulture Department. The Honors College now occupies the structure.

West Circle Drive, across from Morrill Hall and Olin Health Center, Michigan State University campus, East Lansing; Horticultural Laboratory Building (Eustace Hall); S327; March 3, 1971; 1977

Michigan Automobile Dealers Association

In 1920 the Michigan Automotive Trade Association was founded in Detroit. On May 19, 1921, the group was incorporated with the following officers: G. S. Garber, president; H. H. Shuart, secretary; and Clark Graves, treasurer. The association's purpose is to promote and protect the interests of franchised automobile dealers. In 1937 the association moved from Detroit to Lansing and changed its name to the Michigan Automobile Dealers Association. The 100th anniversary of the first gasoline-powered automobile patent was celebrated in 1986. To commemorate this milestone, President Ronald Reagan proclaimed 1986 the "Centennial Year of the Gasoline Powered Automobile." In Michigan's sesquicentennial year, 1987, the association had 850 members.

1500 Kendale Boulevard, off of Shiawassee, East Lansing; Michigan Automobile Dealers Association (Michigan Automobile Dealers Association); L1338C; September 16, 1986; 1987

Michigan State University-Founded 1855

On this site stood College Hall, first building in the United States erected for the teaching of scientific agriculture. Here began the first college of its kind in America, and the model for land grant colleges established under the Morrill Act of 1862. This act granted lands for the endowment of colleges to provide for "liberal and practical education . . . in the several pursuits and professions in life."

Michigan State University campus, West Circle Drive, across from the Main Library, East Lansing; College Hall Informational Site (Beaumont Tower); S1; March 25, 1955; 1955

St . Thomas Aquinas Roman Catholic Parish

Founded in 1940 by Bishop Joseph H. Albers, St. Thomas Aquinas was the largest parish in the Diocese of Lansing by 1988. The first Catholic parish established in East Lansing, it also served Okemos, Haslett and Bath. The church took its name from the scholar St. Thomas Aquinas because it originally served as the Michigan State University parish. During the pastorate (1943-1978) of Monsignor Jerome V. MacEachin, the present church site was purchased. The parish school was opened in 1949 and the present church was dedicated in 1968. It features a mosaic of the Miracle at Cana of Galilee and a forty-five-foot-high faceted glass window depicting salvation history as seen through the mind of St. Thomas Aquinas.

Monsignor Jerome V. MacEachin

Affectionately known as Father Mac, the Reverend Monsignor Jerome V. MacEachin (1904-1987) was associated with Lansing-area Catholics for nearly forty-five years. A native of Ubly, he was ordained as the first superintendent of schools for the Diocese of Lansing (1940-1955). He became pastor of St. Thomas Aquinas in 1943. He founded the parish grade school in 1949 and St. John Student Center at Michigan State University in 1957. He was a lecturer in theology at MSU from 1943 to 1966. His loves in life were Catholic schools, MSU, the Knights of Columbus and the state police. All his life he sought to do some spiritual good for each person he met whether young or old, without regard to creed.

955 Alton Road, south of Saginaw Highway, East Lansing; St. Thomas Aquinas Parish & Father J. V. MacEachin Informational Designation; L1502C; February 25, 1988; 1988

Central United Methodist Church

The first recorded Methodist meeting in Lansing was held in 1845 when the Reverend Lewis Coburn preached in the log cabin of Joab Page of North Lansing. In 1850 a Methodist class (congregation) was formed in what is now central Lansing. Its first leader was Reverend Resin Sapp, chaplain of the Michigan legislature. Services were held at Representative Hall in the old state capitol. The same year, the state deeded land at the corner of Washington Avenue and Ottawa Street to the First Methodist Episcopal Church under Public Act No. 231 of 1848. That land was subsequently turned over to the Central Methodist Episcopal Church, which built its first building in 1863. The present Romanesque-style edifice was erected in 1888-1889 and is perhaps the only church designed by Elijah E. Myers, architect of the State Capitol.

215 North Capitol Avenue, Lansing; Central Methodist Episcopal Church (Central United Methodist Church); L790A; March 19, 1980; 1981

Church of the Resurrection

On June 15, 1922, the Most Reverend Michael J. Gallagher, bishop of Detroit, sent Father John A. Gabriels to Lansing to establish a Catholic parish east of the Pere Marquette railroad tracks that would include East Lansing, Okemos and Haslett. Father Gabriels named the parish Resurrection, because he believed this was the most important event in Christ's life and the cornerstone of Christianity. He celebrated the first Mass on Christmas morning 1922 in the basement church, which would become a school. In 1926 two stories were added with classrooms for eight grades. Five Dominican sisters were the first teachers. Parishioners worshipped in the basement church until the present church was built in 1952.

Monsignor John A. Gabriels

In 1906, John A. Gabriels (1881-1960) was ordained a Catholic priest. In 1922 he came from Detroit to establish a new parish and become chaplain of the Boys Vocational School. He became a highly respected citizen of Lansing. He was chaplain of the Michigan State Police, a member of the Knights of Columbus, Chamber of Commerce, a popular Old Newsboy, and established Father John's Fund for Needy Children. In 1934 he delivered Lansing's first radio-broadcasted Mass. The programs became weekly in 1937. Father Gabriels was bestowed the title Right Reverend Monsignor in 1944. In 1956 he was honored at a testimonial banquet by many civic leaders including the governor of Michigan. Father John loved and served all people. He was well-known as a leader, story teller, radio preacher and convert maker.

1529 East Michigan Avenue, Lansing; Church of the Resurrection and School (Church of the Resurrection School); L1632A; March 16, 1989; 1991

First Presbyterian Church

This church, Lansing's first congregation to affiliate nationally (with the Marshall Presbytery), was founded on December 17, 1847. It was organized by the Reverend Calvin Clark, an agent for the American Home Missionary Society. There were four members. The first pastor, the Reverend W. W. Atterbury, served from 1848 until May 1854. The congregation held its early services in a school, the legislative chambers of Lansing's first capitol, an inn and a storage building called "God's Barn." It built its first permanent home, Lansing's first church edifice, in 1852.

Side Two

The congregation's first church, at the intersection of Genesee Street and Washington Avenue, housed the first bell in Lansing in its fifty-five-foot tower. The bell was purchased with money raised by church women and was installed in 1856. For years it awakened Lansing, announced noon hour and curfew and alerted firemen. The congregation's second church, at the intersection of Capitol Avenue and Allegan Street, was built in 1889. The church on this site, begun in 1947, was completed in 1953. The Molly Grove Chapel was added in 1984.

211 North Chestnut Street at Ottawa Street, Lansing; First Presbyterian Church Informational Designation; L1471C; October 23, 1987; 1987

The Grand River

The Grand River and its valley were formed by the melting of the continental glacier that retreated from this area some twelve thousand years ago. Known by Chippewa Indians as *Washtanong* (further country) and by the French as *le Riviere Grand*, the Grand is Michigan's longest river. From its headwaters in northern Hillsdale and southern Jackson counties, it flows 270 river miles and drops 460 feet in elevation before entering Lake Michigan at Grand Haven. Together with its tributaries, it drains a 5,570-square-mile watershed, including all or part of eighteen counties. Lansing is located in the upper portion of the river basin where the Grand changes direction from northward to westward. The Red Cedar River, one of seven major tributaries, enters one mile upstream from here.

Grand River History

The Grand River has been an important resource and travel route throughout Michigan's past. To the Indians, the Grand River provided a route for travel and trade and a valley for hunting and agriculture. Seventeenth-century French explorers were the first Europeans to see the river. In the eighteenth century French, British and American fur traders canoed the Grand and its tributaries. The journal of Detroit fur trader Hugh Heward, who passed by this site in 1790, is thought to be the first written record of travel near present-day Lansing. In the mid-nineteenth century the Grand became an important means of transportation for logs and lumber. In the twentieth century the waters of the Grand have been used for industrial and agricultural production, as well as recreation.

East bank of the Grand River in Riverfront Park, between Shiawassee and Saginaw streets, Lansing; The Grand River Informational Site (Riverfront Park); S617C; July 19, 1990; 1990

Grand Trunk Depot

Constructed in 1902, this castle-like building with its square tower was the Lansing station for the Grand Trunk Western Railroad until 1971. For decades passengers streamed through its doors. Here servicemen left for and returned from military duty. Children and adults alike associated this depot with the excitement of travel and vacations. The city's joys and sorrows were reflected in this rail station; greetings and good-byes were its most vital ingredients. But gradually rail travel ebbed. Renovated as a restaurant in 1972, the building's exterior remains unchanged. Gerald R. Ford from Michigan, the thirty-eighth president of the United States, dined here during a "whistle stop" campaign tour on May 15, 1976.

1203 South Washington Avenue, south of Main Street, Lansing (marker inside of building); Grand Trunk Western Rail Station, Lansing Depot ; L521A; April 11, 1977; 1978

John T. Herrmann House

This English Tudor house was built in 1893 for John T. Herrmann, a Lansing tailor. Herrmann immigrated to Lansing from Bernsberg, Germany, in 1872 with his wife, Katharine, and two children, Henry and Christian. In 1878, John Herrmann opened the Herrmann Merchant Tailor Shop. After Herrmann's death in 1898, his sons took over the business. Designed by Lansing architect J. Arthur Bailey, this house remained in the Herrmann family until Lansing Community College purchased it in 1966 and renamed it the Herrmann Conference Center.

520 North Capitol Avenue, Lansing; Herrmann, John T., House (Herrmann Conference Center); L1430A; July 23, 1987; 1987

The Kerns Hotel Fire

At 5:30 A.M. on December 11, 1934, the fire alarm outside the Kerns Hotel sounded. The 211-room, four-story brick hotel that stood on this site had 215 registered guests. Before the last embers of the fire were extinguished, thirty-two people were known dead and forty-four, including fourteen firemen, had been injured. Two of the injured people died later. Among the dead were seven Michigan legislators and five unidentified people. Many guests escaped by descending four fire ladders, and eight people jumped into life nets. However, the fire spread through the hotel's wooden interior so rapidly that many people were trapped in their rooms. Seventy-two members of the ninety-seven-man Lansing fire force fought the fire using eight of the force's eleven pieces of fire apparatus.

The Box 23 Club

The firemen who fought the Kerns Hotel fire were aided by the Lansing and Michigan State Police, the Red Cross, the Salvation Army, the Volunteers of America and citizen volunteers, who brought the firemen hot drinks and dry gloves. Some of those volunteers later decided to form a club to support the work of the Lansing Fire Department. The club took its name from Fire Alarm Box 23, at Ottawa and Grand, from which the first alarm for the Kerns Hotel fire was sounded. The Box 23 Club was formally organized on December 11, 1937, the third anniversary of the fire. Its membership, which is limited to twenty-three people, pledges to support the Lansing Fire Department and to provide aid at fires when requested to do so by the Fire Department officer in charge of the fire.

This building, which looks more like a school than the seat of state government, was Lansing's first capitol, built in 1847. (*Lansing's First Capitol*)

East side of Grand Avenue between Michigan Avenue and Ottawa Street, Lansing; Hotel Kerns Informational Site ; L1468C; October 23, 1987; 1987

Lansing Becomes the Capital City

The territorial courthouse that served as Michigan's first state capitol was completed in Detroit in 1828. However, Michigan's first constitution made Detroit a temporary capital and said that a permanent site should be chosen by 1847. As the deadline approached, nearly every town in Michigan was proposed. James Seymour, a land speculator with a mill in what is now North Lansing, campaigned for Lansing Township, pointing out its location equidistant from Detroit, Monroe, Mt. Clemens and the mouths of the Grand and Kalamazoo rivers. The house voted on thirteen sites before selecting Lansing; and the senate voted fifty-one times before it accepted the house's recommendation that the wilderness township with less than one hundred people become the new state capital.

Lansing's First Capitol Building

Early in 1847, three commissioners were appointed to select an appropriate site for the capitol in Lansing. The contract for construction was awarded on June 3, 1847. Building materials were shipped by boat on the Grand River or by rail from Detroit to Jackson and by wagon on cut trails through the woods to Lansing. Gradually, the capitol rose on this site. It was described as "a churchlike little structure of wood, painted white." The building measured sixty feet by one hundred feet, was two stories high and had a cupola. A white picket fence set it off from the surrounding forest. It contained legislative and supreme court chambers, an office for the governor, a few other offices and a library. Completed in late 1847, it was used until the present capitol was completed in 1879.

South Washington Square, on boulevard between Allegan and Washtenaw streets, Lansing; First Capitol in Lansing Informational Site (F. W. Woolworth Company); S587C; March 19, 1987; 1987

Lansing City Market

Dancing and fiddling heralded the opening of the Lansing City Market on August 25, 1938. Built by the Granger Construction Company, and partly financed by the Works Progress Administration and the Public Works Administration, the market typifies Depression-era municipal projects. The first city-sponsored market opened at North Grand Avenue and

East Shiawassee Street in 1909 after the North Side Commercial Club blocked off Turner Street twice a week and showed the city council that a farmers' market could succeed.

333 North Cedar Street, Lansing; Lansing Municipal Market (Lansing City Market); L1517A; May 19, 1988; 1988

Lansing Community College

Lansing Community College was established on April 8, 1957, by the Lansing Public Schools. It opened that fall with 425 students and sixteen faculty members. It offered civil, mechanical and electronic technologies, as well as practical nursing and apprenticeship programs. In 1961 the college began year-round operation. The Lansing Community College District was formed by a vote of area citizens in 1964. The Board of Trustees was organized and six members were elected at that time. The first off-campus learning center was established in 1971. In its thirtieth year of operation, the college provided lifelong education and training in more than two hundred academic programs to a student body numbering over forty-three thousand.

419 North Capitol, Lansing; Lansing Community College Informational Designation; L1449C; August 21, 1987; 1987

Malcolm X Homesite

Malcolm X, born Malcolm Little in Omaha, Nebraska, in 1925, lived on this site in the 1930s. His early life was marked by the violent death of his father, the Reverend Earl Little, on the Michigan Avenue streetcar tracks. Under severe economic stress, the family was separated, and in 1937, Malcolm was sent to Mason. After a public school teacher discouraged his ambition of becoming a lawyer, Malcolm at fifteen, left for Boston and New York. He became involved in street crime and was arrested in Massachusetts. In prison he was converted to the teachings of Elijah Muhammad and read widely in history and philosophy. He also developed an understanding of black self-hatred and came to see his years in Lansing as common to black experience. Released in 1952, he joined his family in Detroit, and began his new life as a Muslim. When his talent for

Side Two

preaching was recognized, he moved to New York to head Temple Eleven. He founded the Nation of Islam's weekly newspaper, *Muhammad Speaks*, and traveled the country organizing new temples among its followers. In 1959 a television program brought him to

Malcolm X, a leader of black nationalist movements in the early 1960s, lived in Lansing as a child. (*Malcolm X*)

public attention as the principal minister of the Nation. Preaching black pride and autonomy, he openly articulated the extent of racial discontent in our society. He broke with the Nation in 1964 and founded Muslim Mosque, Incorporated. A trip to Africa in the same year helped him enlarge his thinking on international problems. By 1965 when he was assassinated, he had become an eloquent spokesman for the oppressed everywhere. His influence continues through his recorded speeches and *The Autobiography of Malcolm X*, a landmark of twentieth century social thought.

4705 South Logan, Lansing; Malcolm X Home Informational Site ; S455; February 21, 1975; 1975

Michigan Dental Association

The Michigan Dental Association was organized on January 8, 1856, by fourteen dentists who met in Detroit at the office of Hiram Benedict and Lorain Christopher Whiting. According to the American Dental Association, it was the first state dental society in the country. At this meeting the dentists established bylaws and membership qualifications. "One must be twenty-one, a practicing member of the profession, possess 'a good English education,' and have unexceptionable moral character." In the 1860s and 1870s the association advocated a dental school in the state. At this time few dentists received formal training. In 1875, after almost twenty years of effort, the state legislature appropriated money to establish a dental school at the University of Michigan.

230 North Washington Square, Lansing; Michigan State Dental Association Informational Designation; L1640C; March 16, 1989; 1989

Michigan Education Association Building

When completed in 1928, this building marked the Michigan Education Association's seventy-fifth anniversary. The Lansing architectural firm of Warren Holmes-Powers Company designed the Neo-Georgian structure. The symmetry, limestone quoining, projecting entrance and the broken pediment topping the center second-story window typify the style. The Michigan Education Association (MEA) was organized in 1847 in Ann Arbor. By the 1960s operations expanded and a larger facility was needed. In 1964 the organization moved to new offices. The MEA Building has housed many different enterprises. In 1988 it became the headquarters of the Michigan Association of Counties.

Michigan Association of Counties

On February 1, 1898, township and city officials met in the capitol and founded the Michigan State Association of Supervisors (MSAS). The group served as a liaison between the legislature and county government, and worked for statewide rather than parochial interests. In the 1950s a director was hired and an office opened in a quonset hut at Michigan State University in East Lansing. In 1957 the Institute for Local Government merged with the MSAS. That year offices were relocated to Lenawee Street in Lansing. In December 1969 the group adopted the name Michigan Association of Counties. The association acquired this building in 1988.

935 North Washington Avenue, Lansing; Michigan Education Association Building (Lindsey Centre); S626A; October 27, 1983; Michigan Association of Counties Informational Designation; November 17, 1991; S625C; 1991

Michigan Licensed Beverage Association

After the repeal of prohibition in 1933, some Michigan tavern owners and liquor dealers organized trade associations including the Progressive Liquor Alliance and the Royal Ark No. 2. In 1939 these two organizations agreed to merge. The following year the Michigan Table Top Congress was organized. The group headquartered in Detroit until it moved to Lansing in 1946. In 1947 the Association of Michigan Tavern Owners and Operators joined the Table Top Congress. The organization became a lobbyist on behalf of the hospitality industry. It soon led the campaign to repeal a law that prohibited women from tending bar in cities of fifty thousand or more residents unless they were the bar owner's daughter or wife. In 1963 the organization was renamed the Michigan Licensed Beverage Association.

534 South Walnut, Lansing; Michigan Licensed Beverage Association Informational Designation; L1676C; July 20, 1989; 1989

Michigan Manufacturers Assocation

Since its 1902 founding, the Michigan Manufacturers Association has dealt with many important business issues. Beginning in 1908, the MMA organized employers to establish a system for compensating injured workers. In 1912, based on a proposal authored by the MMA, Michigan's first Workers Compensation Act became law. In 1943 the Michigan Manufacturers Association became the first such association in the nation to offer group insurance programs to its members.

Side Two

In 1902 the Michigan Manufacturers Association (MMA) held its first meeting in the chamber of the Michigan House of Representatives. The MMA is a voluntary, non-profit organization dedicated to promoting the welfare of Michigan industry and providing information to manufacturers about such ongoing concerns as taxation, workers' compensation and unemployment insurance. In 1952 the MMA established an office in Lansing so that constant contact with the legislative process could be maintained.

124 East Kalamazoo Street, east of Washington Avenue, Lansing; Michigan Manufacturers Association Informational Designation; L1459C; September 26, 1987; 1987

Michigan Pharmacists Association

On November 14, 1883, seventy-seven druggists met in the state capitol to organize the Michigan State Pharmaceutical Association. Jacob Jesson of Muskegon led the effort to establish a professional association to participate in national professional organizations and secure legislation to regulate drug distribution and pharmacist licensure. By 1886 the association boasted 971 members. It changed its name to the Michigan Pharmacists Association in 1973.

815 North Washington Avenue, between Oakland and Saginaw streets, Lansing; Michigan Pharmacists Association Informational Designation; L1194C; September 24, 1984; 1986

Michigan Retail Hardware Association

With the philosophy, "in union there is strength," twenty Michigan hardware retailers convened in Detroit on July 9, 1895, and organized the Michigan Retail Hardware Association. Frank S. Carlton of Calumet was elected the first president. The group worked toward the enactment of state and national legislation on behalf of the retail, wholesale and manufacturing trades. The first success was the passage in 1897 of a state mechanics lien law.

Side Two

Hardware retailers in attendance at the association's organizational meeting in 1895 were: R. B. Bloodgood, C. F. Bock, L. B. Brockett, F. S. Carlton, Thomas Harvey, George W. Hubbard, T. Frank Ireland, H. C. Minnie, J. H. Moyes, John Popp, J. B. Sperry, N. B. Wattles, Henry C. Weber, S. L. Boyce & Son, Casper Gnau & Company, Edwards & Chamberlin, Foster, Stevens Company, John W. Jochim Company, McDonnell Hardware and Scott Brothers & Delisle.

4414 South Pennsylvania at Cavanaugh, Lansing; Michigan Retail Hardware Association Informational Designation; S628C; February 21, 1991; 1991

Michigan School for the Blind

Michigan began educating the blind in 1859 at Flint's Michigan Asylum. In 1879 the legislature established the Michigan School for the Blind, which opened here on September 29, 1880, with thirty-five students. The next year, five students were its first graduates. At first, students learned by lecture/demonstration, but in 1884-1885 the school introduced braille reading and writing. The first deaf/blind student was enrolled in 1887. By the 1950s the school boasted its largest enrollment, three hundred children in kindergarten through grade twelve. Student activities have included music, drama and track. In 1961 and 1963 student wrestlers won class B state championships.

Administration Building

In 1880 the Michigan School for the Blind moved from Flint to this site, the former home of the Michigan Female College and the Institute for Oddfellows. This structure, often called Old Main, has served as the focal point of the forty-acre campus of the Michigan School for the Blind. The monumental, three-story Neo-Classical Revival-style building was designed by Edwyn A. Bowd (1865-1940) of Lansing. It originally housed the entire student body and school offices. Enlarged and remodeled several times, the E-shaped brick and limestone structure retains its architectural beauty.

715 West Willow Avenue, intersection of Grand River and Pine streets, Lansing; Michigan School for the Blind; S575A; April 10, 1986; 1986

Michigan Sheriffs' Association

In December 1877 twenty-four county sheriffs met in Lansing and formed the Michigan State Sheriffs Association—committed to devising "ways and means for assisting each other in the detention, arrest and conviction of criminals." In 1893 the group joined other law enforcement officials and formed the Michigan Association of Police, Sheriffs and Prosecuting Attorneys. In 1931 the sheriffs incorporated independently as the Michigan Sheriffs' Association.

515 North Capitol Avenue, Lansing; Michigan Sheriffs' Association Informational Site; S620C; November 15, 1990; 1991

Michigan Society of Professional Engineers

On May 10, 1946, forty-five engineers from around the state met to organize the Michigan Society of Professional Engineers, which was incorporated on September 30, 1946. Michigan was the twenty-fourth state to organize such a society. The society promotes licensure of engineers as a safeguard to the public's life, health and property. It includes engineers in government, industry, private practice, construction and education. In 1987 the society had 2,550 members.

215 North Walnut Street, one block west of Capitol Avenue, Lansing; Michigan Society of Professional Engineers Informational Designation; L1378C; January 22, 1987; 1987

Morgan B. Hungerford House

This Late Victorian house, designed by Darius B. Moon, was built by Morgan B. Hungerford in 1880. Hungerford (1830-1903) had arrived in the area in 1858. He farmed a large tract of land in what is now west Lansing and served one term as justice of the peace for Lansing Township. In 1958, Lansing realtor Marguerite Moore restored the house as a residence and office. It became an administrative office building of Blue Cross and Blue Shield of Michigan in 1984.

602 West Ionia Street, corner of Pine Street, between Sycamore and Chestnut streets, Lansing; Hungerford, Morgan B., House; L1185A; August 24, 1984; 1987

North Presbyterian Church

On October 19, 1863, fourteen members of Lansing's First Presbyterian Church signed the articles of association creating the Franklin Street Church Society. The society acquired a lot for a church from James Turner, a merchant and leading Methodist, with the proviso that the Presbyterians would supply Lower Town (now North Lansing) with gospel preaching. The first Franklin Street Presbyterian Church was dedicated on this site on October 3, 1865.

Side Two

Built in 1915-1916 on the site of the congregation's first church, the Franklin Avenue Presbyterian Church was constructed to accommodate North Lansing's growing population. Edwyn Bowd, Lansing's leading architect of public buildings in the early twentieth century, designed the church and manse. The extensive Arts and Crafts detailing is unusual among Michigan churches of this period. The congregation changed its name when Franklin Avenue became Grand River Avenue in 1934.

108 West Grand River Avenue, Lansing; Franklin Avenue Presbyterian Church (North Presbyterian Church); L1353A; December 5, 1986; 1988

Optometric Association

The state's professional optometry organization was founded as the Michigan Optical Society in Muskegon in 1896. Benson W. Hardy, Jay W. Gould, Ernest Eimer, Nelson K.

This Oldsmobile advertisement boasted that the Runabout was so simple to drive, even "ladies and children" could "readily understand its mechanism." (*Ransom Eli Olds*)

Standart and Emil H. Arnold were its first directors. In 1904 the group was incorporated as the Michigan Society of Optometrists. It became the Michigan Optometric Association in 1945. The group moved its headquarters to Detroit in 1944 and to Lansing in 1956. Ninety years after its founding, the association included 670 practitioners of optometry.

530 West Ionia Street, corner of Pine Street, Lansing; Michigan Society of Optometrists Informational Designation ; L1408C; April 28, 1987; 1987

Ransom Eli Olds

Born in Geneva, Ohio, Ransom E. Olds came to Lansing in 1880. He worked in his father's machine and repair shop, where he experimented with small steam engines. In 1887, Olds drove, for a distance of one block, Lansing's first automobile, an experimental steam vehicle. He continued to work with steam, gasoline and electric power. Eventually, he produced a gasoline-powered vehicle that seated four persons and could do eighteen miles per hour on level ground. On August 21, 1897, Olds, Edward W. Sparrow, Eugene F. Cooley, Arthur C. Stebbins, Samuel L. Smith, Frank G. Clark, Fred M. Seibly and Alfred Beamer formed the Olds Motor Vehicle Company, the forerunner of the Oldsmobile Division of General Motors. As general manager, Olds was authorized to "build one carriage in as nearly perfect a manner as possible." Four vehicles were produced that first year.

Curved Dash Oldsmobile

On a site southwest of here, production of the Curved Dash Oldsmobile Runabout began on December 16, 1901. The model was first produced in Detroit in 1900, but much of the assembly was shifted to Lansing after a fire destroyed the Detroit plant. The Curved Dash, built from 1900 to 1904, was the first car to carry the name Oldsmobile. With a sixty-six-inch wheelbase, it weighed about 650 pounds; it was powered by a one-cylinder, seven-horse-power engine and cost $650. It was the first car built using a progressive assembly system. The company produced 425 vehicles in 1901, 2,500 in 1902, 4,000 in 1903 and 5,508 in 1904. For a time the Runabout was the best-selling model in the United States. In 1905 it inspired Gus Edwards to write the song "In My Merry Oldsmobile."

920 Townsend Street at the corner of William Street, Lansing; Birthplace of Oldsmobile Division Informational Site; S590C; May 15, 1987; 1987

Rogers-Carrier House

Lansing architect Darius B. Moon built this Queen Anne-style house in 1891 for realtor H. M. Rogers. Purchased by Lansing merchant M. R. Carrier in 1905, the house was occupied by the Carrier family until 1964. In 1966, Lansing Community College bought the structure. Students of the architectural studies center began restoring it in 1982. The restoration included redesigning and reconstructing the turret that previously had been removed.

528 North Capitol Avenue, Lansing; Rogers, Herbert M., House (Rogers-Carrier House); L1140A; January 20, 1984; 1987

Sophie Turner House

Sophie Scott Turner (1856-1941), a member of one of Lansing's pioneer families, built this house in 1927. Turner was considered one of the city's largest land-holders, owning vast acreage in Lansing Township and around Potter Park and Mount Hope Cemetery. This Colonial Revival house, with its broad veranda, has been compared to George Washington's home, Mount Vernon. The Michigan Historical Museum was housed here from 1943 until 1979. In 1980, Lansing Community College acquired the property.

Lansing Community College Campus, 505 North Washington Square, Lansing; Turner House; L1691B; November 16, 1989; 1991

State Bar of Michigan

The State Bar of Michigan was established by the legislature in 1939 as an organization dedicated to improving the administration of justice and the delivery of legal services. Every lawyer licensed to practice in Michigan is required to be a member. The organization is under the supervision of the Michigan Supreme Court. Before 1935 lawyers could join the Michigan State Bar Association, which was organized in 1890. The State Bar made this building its headquarters in 1950. A four-story addition was completed in 1979. The State Bar of Michigan's guiding principle, expressed by its first president, Roberts P. Hudson, is "No organization of lawyers can long survive which has not for its primary object the protection of the public."

306 Townsend Street, Lansing; The State Bar of Michigan Informational Designation; S588C; April 28, 1987; 1987

In 1982 preservationists joined state government leaders in a campaign to restore the ultimate symbol of Michigan's government—the State Capitol. (*State Capitol*)

State Capitol

This edifice, the center of government since 1879, is Michigan's third capitol. It replaced the frame building that was erected nearby in 1847 when the capital was removed to Lansing from Detroit. Construction began in 1872 on the new building designed by Elijah Myers. It cost $1,510,130 to build, and was dedicated January 1, 1879, at a meeting addressed by six of Michigan's governors.

Erected in 1956, in collections of the Michigan Historical Museum, replaced 1980.

State Capitol

The state capitol of Michigan, rededicated in its centennial, 1979, is the third structure to serve as the symbolic and functional center of state government. In 1837, when statehood was attained, the old Michigan Territorial Courthouse in Detroit became the first capitol. Twelve years later, the legislature voted to move Michigan's seat of government to Lansing where a new capitol was erected. That frame building was soon found inadequate. Then in 1871, Governor Henry P. Baldwin recommended the construction of a new capitol and the legislature concurred. It was completed at a cost of nearly $1.5 million.

Side Two

Michigan's present state capitol building was first dedicated in 1879 at the inaugural ceremony of Governor Charles M. Croswell. This classically styled structure, designed by Elijah E. Myers, has a 267-foot spired dome. It represents over six years of planning and construction. Michigan's resources are exhibited in the copper, slate and white pine used throughout the structure. Built to house the governor's office, the legislature, supreme court and other state functions, the building has been substantially renovated over the years to meet changing needs.

Intersection of Capitol and Michigan avenues, Lansing; Michigan State Capitol (State Capitol); HB1; February 18, 1956; 1980

Town of Michigan

In 1847, required by Michigan's 1835 constitution to choose a permanent capital site within the first decade of statehood, the legislature voted to move the capital from Detroit. Convinced that the governmental seat should be in the state's interior, legislators voted to relocate in Ingham County's unsettled Lansing Township. Citizens viewed the choice with skepticism—believing the decision was a joke that backfired. The capital commission platted the "Town of Michigan" in 1847 and chose a site bounded by Washington and Capitol avenues and Allegan and Washtenaw streets for a temporary capitol building. When the legislature met that year, many members were forced to lodge in private homes; others made their beds on the capitol floor. During that session, the legislature renamed the capital city Lansing.

Lansing

The town of Michigan was platted in 1847 as the state capital. In April the state legislature considered renaming the capital Pewanogowink, Swedenborg or El Dorado, but chose Lansing, after John Lansing, an American Revolution hero. At that time the capital was a wilderness fraught with wolves and a "brain fever" (spinal meningitis) epidemic. In 1859, Lansing was incorporated as a city. During the 1870s, Lansing's lyceums and literary societies hosted author Mark Twain and actor Edwin Booth. The 1847 capitol, considered "an old rattle trap," was replaced by the present building in 1879. Primarily an agricultural community, Lansing developed as a manufacturing center in the 1890s. In 1897, Ransom Eli Olds organized the Olds Motor Vehicle Company, Michigan's first operating automobile company.

City Hall, 124 West Michigan Avenue, NE corner of Michigan and Capitol avenues, Lansing; Lansing (Town of Michigan) Informational Designation ; S629C; March 21, 1991; 1991

Trinity A.M.E. Church

Trinity African Methodist Episcopal Church of Lansing is the oldest black church in the city. Its first services were held in a building on North Washington Avenue. The church, formally organized by the Reverend Mr. Henderson of the British Methodist Episcopal Church in 1866, was first called the Independent Methodist Episcopal Church. In 1875 it was reorganized as Bethel A.M.E. Church. In 1902, upon the death of the Reverend George R. Collins, the pastor for many years, the church was renamed the George R. Collins A.M.E. Church. It was incorporated in 1906. The church received its present name, Trinity A.M.E. Church, in 1964.

Side Two

During the church's first decade, the congregation purchased a small frame building and moved it to a site on the 100 block of North Pine Street. In 1877 a modest brick church was erected near the original site. It served the congregation for eighty-eight years. In 1965 the congregation was forced to relocate to make room for the State Capitol Complex building project. Selling its downtown property to the state, Ingham County's oldest black congregation then moved to this ten-acre tract, where it built a church and a parsonage. Starting with twenty-one members, the church had over four hundred members by its one hundredth anniversary in 1966.

3500 West Holmes Road at Waverly, Lansing; Collins Memorial A.M.E. Church (Trinity A.M.E. Church Congregation); L987B; January 13, 1982; 1983

Turner-Dodge House

Gracefully situated high on the bank of the Grand River, this Classical Revival-style mansion, built in 1858, was the home of prominent Lansing merchant James Turner (1820-1869). In 1899, Turner's son-in-law Frank L. Dodge (1853-1929) bought and enlarged it. The three-story building, designed by Lansing architect Darius Moon, features stately wooden Ionic columns and a decorative cornice. Its interior, with its large classical doorways and several fireplaces, is adorned with beveled and leaded French windows. After remaining in the family for a century, the property was purchased by the Great Lakes Bible

College in 1958. In 1974 the city of Lansing acquired it for a park. The site was listed on the National Register of Historic Places in 1972.

Side Two

James Turner, a Lansing pioneer, originally owned this property. A native of New York, Turner came to Lansing in 1847 from nearby Mason, where he was a merchant. He immediately opened a general store in the Seymour House, the first hotel in north Lansing. He was appointed deputy state treasurer in 1860 and elected to the state senate in 1866. Interested in education, he helped found the Misses Rogers' Seminary, later called the Michigan Female College (1855-1869). He was also active in the construction of plank roads and railroads in the Lansing area. Frank L. Dodge married Turner's daughter Abby in 1888 and purchased this house from Turner's widow in 1899. Dodge, a Democrat, was elected to the state legislature in 1883 and 1885. He was city alderman for twelve years and was active on several civic boards.

100 East North Street at James, Lansing; Dodge Mansion (Turner-Dodge House); 1980

Wolverine Boys' State: The American Legion

On November 28, 1937, the board of directors of The American Legion established Wolverine Boys' State. American Legion departments in other states, including Ohio and Indiana, had existing programs. The American Legion sought to teach citizenship and leadership to boys by training them in the fundamental principles of American government. Individual legion posts sponsored local boys who were "mentally alert, vigorous and enthusiastic and honest and thrifty." The first Boys' State was held at Michigan State College (present-day Michigan State University) in East Lansing. Posts sent eight hundred boys at a cost of $12.50 each for the ten-day event. In 1946, Boys' Nation was organized.

Wolverine Girls' State: American Legion Auxiliary

In 1941 the women of the American Legion Auxiliary established Wolverine Girls' State. The organization's original purpose was "to find and develop girls who show inherent tendencies toward leadership." The first Girls' State meeting was held in June 1941 at the University of Michigan in Ann Arbor. The eight-day program included sessions on entertaining, etiquette, drama, nursing, art and music appreciation and citizenship. In 1952, to accommodate women's changing roles, the auxiliary shifted the organization's focus to inform girls about "the duties, privileges, rights and responsibilities of American citizenship and self-government." Girls' Nation was established in 1947.

212 North Verlinden, SE corner of Verlinden and Ottawa streets, Lansing; Wolverine Boys' State/Wolverine Girls' State Informational Designation; S618C; August 23, 1990; 1990

Woodberry-Kerns House

Darius Moon, prominent turn-of-the-century Lansing architect, designed this Queen Anne house in 1896 for Chester E. Woodberry, founder of the Lansing Capitol Savings & Loan Association. The structure's last residential owner was William G. Kerns who owned the Kerns Hotel, which stood on North Grand Avenue. Kerns's family sold the house to the Michigan State Medical Society in 1951. Extensively remodeled in 1951, the house is one of the few remaining structures designed by Moon. It became the state headquarters of the Michigan Democratic party in 1977.

606 Townsend Street, corner of Hillsdale, Lansing; Woodberry-Kerns House (Hart-Kennedy House); L766A; January 18, 1980; 1981

Michigan Millers Mutual Insurance Company

Founded in 1881 by flour mill owners from ten mid-Michigan communities, the Michigan Millers Mutual Fire Insurance Company was among the first millers' cooperative fire insurance companies in America. Its first policy was issued to company president D. L. Crossman of Williamston on October 26, 1881. By the turn of the century, Michigan Millers offered other types of insurance as well. During the Great Depression the company continued to grow, and in 1933, it established its Western Department in Glendale, California. The firm shortened its name to Michigan Millers Mutual Insurance Company in 1954.

Side Two

Michigan Millers Mutual Insurance Company has headquartered in Lansing since it was founded in 1881. The company built its first office in 1890 at 120 West Ottawa Street, and erected its second, the Mutual Building, at 208 North Capitol Avenue in 1929. One-hundred-year-old millstones imbedded in the concrete sidewalk outside of the building serve as reminders of the company's origins. Michigan Millers continued to grow through the 1940s and 1950s. Its present office, designed by Childs and Smith of Chicago, was built in 1956-1957. The building's symbolic link to the company's origins is the 1858-vintage steam pumper fire engine, encased in glass on the front lawn.

2425 East Grand River, East Lansing vicinity, Lansing Township; Michigan Millers Mutual Fire Insurance Company Informational Designation; L1567C; June 30, 1988; 1988

Plymouth Congregational Church

Congregational churches originated with the Puritan and Separatist churches of New England. Soon after "Michigan" (present-day Lansing) was chosen as the site of the state capital in 1847, the Reverend S. S. Brown, a Congregationalist with the Connecticut Home Missionary Society, came to Lansing and, together with seven members, formed a Congregational society. Local Congregationalists and Presbyterians cooperated under the national Plan of Union of 1801, which encouraged the two denominations to worship together. In 1864, Lansing Congregationalists established Plymouth Church, named for its New England origins. Plymouth Church founded two daughter churches, Pilgrim Congregational in 1892 and Mayflower Congregational in 1903.

Side Two

When Lansing Congregationalists established the Plymouth Church in 1864, services were held in the Senate chambers of Michigan's first capitol building in Lansing. In 1865 a chapel was erected at the corner of Washtenaw Street and Capitol Avenue. That building was later moved to a site at the corner of Allegan and Townsend streets purchased for the church by Cortland Stebbins. In 1877 a monumental Gothic Revival church was dedicated on that site. The *Detroit News* reported that capitol architect Elijah Myers considered it "one of the finest churches in the United States." The structure, with its 160-foot steeple, tragically burned on February 25, 1971. Rooms at the neighboring YWCA served as a temporary sanctuary. The present church was dedicated on October 12, 1975.

2001 East Grand River Avenue, East Lansing vicinity, Lansing Township; Plymouth Congregational Church Informational Designation; L1641C; March 16, 1989; 1989

First Baptist Church

On April 12, 1839, eight people met in the Leslie schoolhouse and organized the First Baptist Church. Elijah K. Grout, a charter member, became the church's first pastor in November 1841. Between 1856 and 1858 this church, the first built in Leslie, was constructed. In 1887-1888 the building was raised, and a basement was built. The exterior was then clad with brick giving the building its present Gothic Revival appearance. In 1966 a wooden cross replaced the church's spire.

204 East Bellevue, Leslie; First Baptist Church of Leslie (Leslie First Baptist Church); L1656A; May 18, 1989; 1991

Ingham County Courthouse

Named for Samuel Ingham, secretary of the treasury under Andrew Jackson, Ingham County was organized in 1838. In 1840, Mason became the county seat. The town's wide public square had been designed as the county's political and business center. The first county offices were on the sides of the square built at this location. The present building, completed in 1904, was described as a "temple of justice." Governor Fred Warner, speaking at the dedication, called it "a meeting place for farmers, mechanics, business and professional men." The courthouse has been the center of Ingham County's activities throughout the twentieth century. In 1971 the building was placed on the National Register of Historic Places.

Corner of Jefferson and Ashley streets, Mason; Ingham County Courthouse; L117; May 18, 1971; 1972

John Rayner House

This handsome brick structure, said to be the oldest remaining house in Mason, is one of the most elaborate and best preserved Greek Revival houses in Ingham County. Pioneer John Rayner, a native of New York State, began construction of this farmhouse in 1840. The original Rayner farm totaled 320 acres. The ponds in the park opposite this site were dug to supply ice for early Mason. The remaining outbuilding contains a blacksmith shop and an icehouse. The twin sons of Chief Okemos played here with Rayner's oldest son, William. The Rayner family had a major impact upon early Mason, owning the slaughterhouse, ice ponds and the Rayner Opera House. At the time of his death in 1879, John

The Ingham County Courthouse, designed by Lansing architect Edwin Bowd, was dedicated by Governor Fred Warner in 1904. *(Ingham County Courthouse)*

Rayner was called "one of the most opulent men of the county," having acquired thousands of acres of land in Ingham and adjacent counties.

725 East Ash Street, Mason; Rayner, John, House; L668A; June 15, 1979; 1980

Haslett

Settlement on Pine Lake, now Lake Lansing, began in the 1830s, but real growth came after the opening of the Chicago and Northwestern Railroad in 1877. Easy access prompted the Nemoka Spiritual Association to begin in 1883 the first of a long series of summer camp meetings. James H. Haslett was a leader of this group, and in 1895 the village was renamed in his honor. In the early part of the twentieth century the Lake Lansing area became Lansing's summer vacation and entertainment haven.

6101 Marsh Road, Meridian Township; Haslett Informational Designation; L154; October 1, 1971; 1971

Stockbridge Town Hall

Designed by Elijah E. Myers, the Stockbridge Town Hall was constructed by Mitter & Heuderlong in 1892. This stately Romanesque structure was built to house local township offices and a community center. In addition to local township business, the hall has also been the setting for lectures, musicals and numerous social gatherings. It was listed on the National Register of Historic Places in 1980. A federal grant and local taxes provided the money for the massive restoration that was completed in 1982.

123 South Clinton Street, corner of East Main, Stockbridge; Stockbridge Town Hall; L431; November 21, 1975; 1987

White Oak

The settlements of White Oak, Ingham, Wheatfield and Leroy were organized as Ingham Township by the legislature on March 11, 1837. On April 2, 1837, the first township meeting was held at the home of Caleb Carr. White Oak separated from Ingham Township and organized on March 21, 1839. Daniel Dutcher hosted the first meeting of the new township at his home. Until the erection of this hall in 1877, townspeople held meetings in their homes. This building is dedicated to those pioneers who established White Oak Township.

1002 South Stockbridge Road (M-52), north of M-36, White Oak Township; White Oak Township Hall; L531; June 6, 1977; 1978

Grand River Trail

The old Grand River Indian Trail, now US-16, became a plank road in 1848. A toll gate and Red Bridge Post Office were located here. Nearby were homes of John Mullett, pioneer surveyor, and John Forster, explorer [and] north Michigan mine pioneer. Michigan State University, [the] first U. S. land grant college, and Lansing, the capital of Michigan, lie to the west.

Roadside Park on Grand River Avenue [(M-43) previously US-16] at Red Cedar River, approximately four miles west of Williamston, Williamston Township; Grand River Trail Informational Designation; S31; July 19, 1956; 1956

St. Katherine's Chapel

This building was erected about 1887 for John Forster, an early surveyor in the Lake Superior Copper Country. In 1888 the chapel, named in memory of Forster's daughter Kitty, was presented to the Protestant Episcopal Diocese of Michigan. Simple in design and workmanship, the chapel seems to be the work of an unsophisticated country builder. The interior is completely panelled with naturally finished pine with black accents.

4650 Meridian Road, Williamston Township; Saint Katherine's Chapel; HB52; February 23, 1969; 1969

Williamston Center United Methodist Church

The Williamston Center United Methodist Church is the outgrowth of a Methodist class that met in a local schoolhouse before this structure was completed. On November 5, 1877, members of the congregation pledged money to build this church. Merrit Andress deeded the church site to the congregation, and G. S. Brower was the builder. The handsome Greek Revival church, which cost $1,500, was completed in 1879. Sunday School classrooms were added in the 1920s; and a modern kitchen and restroom facilities, in 1960.

SW corner of Zimmer and Haslett roads, Williamston Township; Williamston Center United Methodist Church; L1015A; May 20, 1982; 1984

Ionia

Alvah N. Belding Library

Alvah N. Belding erected this library in 1917-1918 as a memorial to his parents, Hiram and Mary Wilson Belding. Alvah and his brother Hiram began peddling silk around Belding (then Patterson's Mills) in 1858. With the help of their brother Milo they began the internationally known Belding Brothers & Company in 1863. Michigan's first silk mill was erected here in

1886 and operated until 1932. This library, which cost $50,000, was dedicated and presented to the city of Belding on May 14, 1918. It is the only structure built by the Beldings still being used for its original purpose. An example of Classical Revival architecture, the limestone structure features a Spanish-tile roof. Its interior contains trim of marble, oak and pine.

302 East Main Street, Belding; Belding, Alvah N., Memorial Library; L816A; June 10, 1980; 1981

The Roadside Table

Here on old US-16 in Boston Township, Ionia County, the first picnic table along a highway right-of-way was placed in 1929 through the initiative of Allan Williams, county engineer. The table was built of salvage planks formerly used for guardrails. The idea immediately caught on and was adopted by the State Highway Department. The Ionia County Road Commission made the state's tables until the work became too great. The roadside table became an emblem of Michigan's hospitality, one which has been widely emulated by states the nation over.

Grand River Avenue, east of Morrison Lake Road, near Saranac, Boston Township; First Roadside Table Informational Site; S253B; December 10, 1963; 1964

Fred W. Green

Governor of Michigan, 1927-1931, Fred W. Green was born in Manistee in 1872 and grew up in Cadillac. A partner in the Ypsilanti Reed Furniture Company, he moved the business to Ionia in 1904. Attracted to politics, he served twelve terms as mayor of Ionia and ten years as treasurer of the Republican State Central Committee. While mayor, he had this handsome Mission-style house built, completing it in 1924. An avid sportsman, his administration was characterized by an expanding fish planting program and acquisition of seven state parks. In 1931 he returned to private life and to his favorite pastimes, hunting and fishing. He died in 1936 near Munising.

320 Union Street, Ionia; Green, Governor Fred W., House; S408A; July 26, 1973; 1973

Ionia Church of Christ

In Merritt's Hall on January 24, 1859, the Reverend Isaac Errett and forty-three members signed the original charter of the Ionia Church of Christ (First Christian Church). The first church of this denomination had been founded in nearby Muir in 1856. In 1861, James A. Garfield, later the twentieth president of the United States, was a

Governor Fred Green, served as Michigan's political leader from 1927 to 1931. (*Fred W. Green*)

guest speaker at a revival meeting held by the church. The site of the present church was purchased in 1864. The basement was completed in 1867. Services were held there until the church was completed in 1873. Patterned after Romanesque models in the east, the church displays the influence of Philadelphian architect Samuel Sloan. The E. H. Stafford Company of Ionia designed and built the wooden pews. In 1889 the church was enlarged. Its stained glass windows were installed in 1917.

130 East Washington Street, Ionia; Ionia Church of Christ [Ionia First Christian Church] (Disciples of Christ); L1170A; June 15, 1984; 1986

Ionia County Courthouse

Completed in 1885, the Ionia County Courthouse is the largest structure ever built of Ionia sandstone. The handsome three-and-a-half-story courthouse replaced an 1840s hall of justice, which had become inadequate for the county's needs. David W. Gibbs (1836-1917), of Toledo, Ohio, designed the 120' x 80' Classical Revival structure. The $42,380 courthouse was financed by a special tax levy, which was approved in 1883. The first county offices moved into the new building in January 1886 and court was first held in it in late February of that year. Formal dedication services were observed on July 3, 1886. The interior is adorned with black and white marble floors, oak wainscoting, fourteen marble fireplaces and a massive walnut and butternut staircase.

1000 East Main Street, Ionia; Ionia County Courthouse; L448A; March 2, 1976; 1983

St. John's Episcopal Church and Parish House

The St. John's Episcopal parish was established on February 4, 1841. Under the leadership of the Reverend Melancthon Hoyt, the parish constructed its first church, now the parish house, that same year. Built on land donated by Ionia's founder, Samuel Dexter, the building was the first church in Ionia County and is thought to be the second-oldest Episcopal building in Michigan. It was consecrated on April 24, 1842, by the Reverend Samuel McCoskry, the first bishop of Michigan. In 1882-1883 the present brick church was erected at a cost of $7,334.89. This Gothic-style structure, with English Cathedral glass windows, was consecrated on July 2, 1890, by the Right Reverend George de Normandie Gillespie, the first bishop of Western Michigan.

107 West Washington at the corner of Kidd Street, Ionia; St. John's Episcopal Church and Parish House; L913A; April 24, 1981; 1983

White's Bridge

This picturesque covered bridge, one of the last of its kind in Michigan, was built in 1867 by Jared N. Brazee and J. N. Walker, builders of several covered bridges in this area. The name of the bridge derives from the White family, a prominent pioneer family. The crossing of the Flat River here was known as White's Crossing before the first primitive bridge was built. In 1840 a bridge of log-corduroy construction was erected. It was replaced by this covered bridge, costing $1,700. It is of the through-truss type with a gable roof. The hand-hewed trusses are sheeted over with rough pine boards. Wooden pegs and hand-cut square iron nails are used to secure the various parts of the bridge. White's Bridge has been in constant use since 1867, proof that it was well made.

Whites Bridge Road over the Flat River, south of Four Mile Road, Keene Township; White's Covered Bridge; L42A; February 17, 1965; 1965

Smyrna

In 1843, Calvin Smith became the first white settler in the area. N. G. Chase opened a store here the following year. When Dr. Wilbur Fisher, the area's pioneer physician, began operating a rural post office in 1848, he named the community Smyrna after a Greek city. The village, platted as Mount Vernon, was also called Mount Vernon Mills. In the 1880s, with a population of three hundred, Smyrna had a hotel on this site, plus saw and flour mills, a foundry, three blacksmith shops, two churches and a wagon shop.

4972 Whites Bridge Road, Otisco Township; Village of Smyrna Informational Designation; L1063C; January 27, 1983; 1983

Saranac

In 1836, when Saranac was settled, the upper Grand River Valley was a promising but un-developed area. The soil was fertile; Lake Creek provided water power; and the river was navigable to Grand Rapids. The town grew slowly until 1857, when the coming of the Detroit and Milwaukee Railroad made Saranac a shipping center. Local products included such items as flour, lumber, hides, felloes, barrels and staves. As the forests disappeared, manufacturing declined, and agriculture gradually became the dominant industry.

Entrance to Scheid Park, Main Street, between Fuller Street and Jackson Road, Saranac; Village of Saranac Informational Designation; L76B; June 27, 1969; 1970

Iosco

Alabaster

This area is named after a variety of gypsum, discovered offshore by Douglass Houghton in 1837. Prospectors soon began searching for other gypsum deposits, and this quarry was opened in 1862 by B. F. Smith. Used at first as fertilizer and as an ingredient in plaster, gypsum is now used principally in the manufacture of wallboard. A fire in 1891 destroyed the operation but it was rebuilt in time to supply material for the main buildings at the Chicago Columbian Exposition of 1893. These buildings, with marble-like walls, earned the exposition the title, "White City," and greatly expanded gypsum sales. Incorporated into the U.S. Gypsum Company in 1902, this quarry has helped to make Michigan a leading producer of gypsum for over a century.

U.S. Gypsum Company Quarry, intersection of Benson and Turtle roads, Alabaster Township; Alabaster Quarry; S247; August 8, 1963; 1972

The Louis Chevalier Claim

In 1823, Louis Chevalier, a French-Canadian trader, was granted 500 arpents (640 acres) of land by the United States government. This land, located on the AuSable River, extends northwesterly in a long, narrow, French ribbon-farm manner. It still appears on maps of Au-Sable Township. From around 1820 to the mid-1830s, Chevalier bartered trade goods for furs, fish and game brought in by Chippewa and white trappers, hunters and fishermen in this locality. He conducted his trade near this site from a hand-hewn log blockhouse. Although he left the area in 1833, ruins of the structure were still visible in 1867. Chevalier's trading post is regarded by many as the first business of consequence in Iosco County.

295 Harbor Street, AuSable, AuSable Township; Louis Chevalier Claim Informational Site; L830B; July 29, 1980; 1980

Lumbering on the Huron Shore

Lumbermen swarmed into this area during the latter half of the 1800s, attracted by some of the finest pine forests in North America. From Tawas City, where the first sawmill was built in 1854, north to Alpena, about twelve billion board feet of timber were cut between 1866 and 1896. Each spring the AuSable, the Thunder Bay, and the other rivers of the region were filled with logs being driven to the sawmills. To the lake ports lumber boats came in the summer to carry the lumber away to help build the nation.

Harbor Refuge Boat Ramp, off US-23, Baldwin Township; Lumbering on the Huron Shore Informational Designation; S32; July 19, 1956; 1957

Pioneer Cemetery

This township cemetery began in 1870 with the purchase of the land from William and Rosina Dommer, by Daniel E. Fries, Herman Dommer, B. F. Chappell and William M. Webster, officers of Grant Township. Stages on the Tawas-Manistee line passed these grounds over the Iosco & Ogemaw State Road. One of the stagecoach stops was the Sand Lake House, one and one-half miles to the east. This marker commemorates not only the old highway and the cemetery, but also the many unmarked graves of early settlers.

Old State Road west of Sand Lake, Grant Township; Grant Township Cemetery (Pioneer Cemetery); L33; June 18, 1963; 1963

Dock Reserve

"Oscoda and AuSable are Wiped Off The Map!" headlined the July 12, 1911, *Detroit Free Press*. The day before, forest fires, fanned by thirty-mile-per-hour winds, had destroyed these "twin cities" and killed four people. Refugees fled to this beach without money or possessions; some spent the night on the beach near the Dock Reserve, or in Lake Huron waiting to be rescued. The lumber barge, *Niko*, and the Detroit and Mackinac Railroad carried the victims to Tawas, East Tawas and Port Huron, where they received food, clothing and shelter.

Beach at end of Michigan River Road, Dwight and Park streets, Oscoda Township; The Dock Reserve Informational Site (Oscoda Township Beach); L1576C; July 21, 1988; 1988

Iron

First Roadside Park

In 1918 the Iron County Board of Supervisors approved the recommendation of the road commission, through its engineer-manager, Herbert F. Larson, to purchase this 320-acre tract of roadside virgin timber and to dedicate it as a forest preserve. The following year Iron County established Michigan's first roadside park and picnic tables. This was quite likely America's first such facility. Since then similar parks have been provided by most states for the comfort and enjoyment of the traveling motorist.

Iron County Park, US-2, four miles east of Iron River, Mapleton vicinity, Bates Township; First Roadside Park Informational Site; S213; March 19, 1958; 1964

Helmeted safety crews guarded the welfare of iron miners throughout the U.P. ranges. Iron County deposits were the first discovered in the Menominee Range. (*Iron County*)

Iron County

This county was set off in 1885 from Marquette and Menominee counties. Iron ore deposits, which gave the new county its name, were the first on the Menominee Iron Range to be discovered. Shipping of ores began in 1882 when the railroad came in. Iron River was the first county seat, but in 1889, after a celebrated struggle, the government was shifted to Crystal Falls. Logging, which began in 1875, has been second only to mining in Iron County's economy.

Side Two

J. C. Clancy designed this Richardsonian Romanesque-style building which was completed in 1891. Constructed of regional materials, including reddish stone columns quarried from the nearby Paint River and yellow clay bricks, the courthouse commands a view of the city's main street and the valley below. The structure featuring a domed courtroom with original furnishings continues to serve a county built from "the iron and the pine."

Iron County Courthouse front lawn, west end of Superior Avenue, Crystal Falls; Iron County; S179; January 24, 1958; 1977

Iron Inn

Erected in 1906, this hotel is said to be the first brick commercial building in the city. The Iron Inn is known for a Prohibition-era incident, which occurred in February 1920. Here local attorney Martin McDonough challenged the right of federal Prohibition officer A. V. Dalrymple to arrest, without a warrant, people involved in a wine-making operation. This confrontation was part of the eight-day "Rum Rebellion" against federal policies of seizure relating to Prohibition. It resulted in the reaffirmation of due process in Iron County.

202 West Adams, Iron River; Iron Inn (Iron Inn Hotel); L376; December 18, 1974; 1977

MacKinnon House

Donald C. MacKinnon built this house, said to be one of the oldest frame houses in the area, in the mid-1880s. He came to the vicinity in 1878 with W. H. Selden, founder of Stambaugh, seeking iron ore. Platting the village of Iron River in 1881, Donald and his brother Alexander filed claims for the first mines, the Nanaimo and the Beta, and helped bring in the railroad in 1882. Donald MacKinnon also served as the first village president. His daughter Sara, born in 1894, married Martin McDonough, an attorney involved in the 1920 "Rum Rebellion" incident.

*411 North Ninth Street, Iron River; MacKinnon, Donald C., House (demolished); L350A; September 17, 1974; 1978

Indian Village

Here, in October 1851, U.S. surveyor Guy H. Carleton discovered an Ojibwa (Chippewa) Indian village, cemetery and campground. Chief Edwards, last ruler at Chicaugon Lake, received a patent for this land in 1884. Selling it in 1891, he and his wife Pentoga, for whom this area is named, moved to the Lac Vieux Desert area. By 1903 only a few burial houses and a brush fence remained from the ancient village. Iron County engineer Herbert Larson, Sr., convinced the county to buy the property and restore it as a park honoring the area's first inhabitants. It was dedicated in 1922.

County Road 639 (Pentoga Trail), Pentoga Park, at the south end of Chicaugon Lake, Stambaugh Township; Ojibwa Indian Village and Burial Ground; L342; September 17, 1974; 1980

Isabella

Central Michigan University

Privately organized by citizens of Mount Pleasant in 1892, Central became Michigan's second state-supported normal school in 1895. This met a long-felt need for a state school in this region. At first the college was designed to prepare rural and grade school teachers. In the next three decades, however, the school grew into a four-year teachers college. Progress and growth since then have been even more notable in terms of standards, enrollment, facilities and educational goals. Central had become a multi-purpose institution by the 1940s, and in 1959, by legislative act, it achieved university status.

Adjacent to Warriner Hall on campus, Mount Pleasant; Central Michigan University; S113B; January 19, 1957; 1962

Central Michigan University

Founded in 1892 as a private institution, Central Michigan Normal School and Business Institute held its first classes on this site. The institution became a state normal school in 1895. After several changes in name, the school became Central Michigan University in 1959.

201 South Main Street, Mount Pleasant; Central Michigan University, First Class; L69B; March 1, 1968; 1968

Doughty House

Built about 1865 this oldest remaining house in Mount Pleasant was purchased by Wilkinson Doughty in 1869. An early hardware and dry goods merchant, Doughty was a town trustee, and a founder of Central Michigan Normal School, now Central Michigan University. A carefully preserved example of balloon-frame pioneer architecture, the house has remained in the family since Doughty's death in 1909. It was listed on the National Register of Historic Places in 1974.

301 Chippewa Street, Mount Pleasant; Doughty House; L223A; May 17, 1973; 1975

Indian Cemetery

In the 1850s the Methodist Episcopal (Indian) Church established the Bradley Mission School and Indian Cemetery in this area. The cemetery served the mission until the late 1860s. Only a few grave markers are visible, and it is not known how many Indians were buried here. The best-known Indian buried here was Chief Shawshawwawnabeece (1817-1868). As leader of the Saginaw Swan Creek and Black River Band of Chippewa, he signed the Treaty of 1855, which set aside six adjoining townships of land in Isabella County for his tribe.

1475 South Bamber Road, north of Pickard Road, south of River Road, on the south side of Mission Creek, Mount Pleasant; Mission Creek Cemetery (Indian Cemetery); L1298; April 10, 1986; 1987

Sacred Heart Academy

In 1889, Sacred Heart Academy was organized as a school for St. Charles Church, which was established in 1872. That year a new church was built here and the parish was renamed Most Sacred Heart of Jesus. Father John J. Crowley moved the old church to an adjacent lot and used it as a school, which was run by Dominican Sisters. Saginaw architect Clarence W. Cowles designed this building, constructed in 1908. The addition was built in 1955; the elementary school in 1964.

316 East Michigan Avenue, Mount Pleasant; Sacred Heart Academy; L1657A; May 18, 1989; 1990

Saint John's Episcopal Church

A mission was organized in Mount Pleasant in 1876, and in 1882 the present building was begun. Local businessman William N. Brown contributed most of the building funds, and the bricks and lumber were made in his plants. The interior design of St. John's was adopted from a chapel on the English estate of the Duke of Devonshire. The Right Reverend George D. Gillespie consecrated the church in a three-hour ceremony on January 10, 1884, after which parishioners repaired to a local hotel for a ten-course dinner.

206 West Maple Street, Mount Pleasant; St. John's Episcopal Church; L189A; February 11, 1972; 1972

Schoolhouse

In 1891, Congress established the Mount Pleasant Indian Industrial School and appropriated $25,000 for land and buildings. Local citizens contributed an additional $3,400 for the land. First occupied on June 30, 1893, the school building contained eight classrooms and an auditorium. The school, emphasizing academics and vocational training, operated until 1934, with an average enrollment of three hundred. That year the property was transferred to the state of Michigan becoming the Mount Pleasant branch of the Michigan Home and Training School.

Harris Street, campus of Mount Pleasant Regional Center for Developmental Disabilities, Mount Pleasant; United States Indian School School Building; S574A; January 17, 1986; 1987

Power House

The Shepherd Village Power House was built in 1908-1909. It housed the community's first electric plant and water pumps. The thirty-five-kilowatt dynamo, driven by a coal gas engine, operated from 1909 to 1912. From 1913 to 1925 outside power was transmitted through the facility. In 1925, Consumers Power Company purchased the village distribution system, and the Power House ceased operations. Part of the building was used as a village council hall until 1957. The Shepherd Area Historical Society began using it in 1982.

314 West Maple Street, Shepherd; Shepherd Village Power House; L914A; April 24, 1981; 1985

Jackson

Brooklyn Presbyterian Church

Thirteen lay members founded the First Presbyterian Church of Brooklyn in 1838. The Reverend C. W. Gurney became the church's first installed pastor in 1841. Dedicatory services for the church were held on October 7, 1845. Built with hand-hewn beams and pegged timber, this is now the oldest church building in Brooklyn. The original simple Greek Revival structure with its square belfry measured forty-by-sixty feet. The church was remodeled in 1901 and enlarged twice in subsequent years.

160 North Main Street, Brooklyn; Brooklyn First Presbyterian Church (Brooklyn United Presbyterian Church); L853B; November 2, 1980; 1982

Brooklyn's Founder

This village was founded by the Reverend Calvin Swain who filed the first land claim on June 16, 1832. Elder Swain, who had been a chaplain in the War of 1812, was a Baptist minister and the postmater in Adamsville, New York, before coming to Michigan at the age of fifty-four. By 1833 he had established a settlement and a sawmill here. The town was called Swainsville until August 5, 1836, when the name Brooklyn was adopted by vote of the town meeting. Mr. Swain was the postmaster until 1841. He founded Baptist churches at Brooklyn, Woodstock and Napoleon. He died in 1856 and is buried in Oak Grove Cemetery in Napoleon.

Village Square on M-50, Brooklyn; Brooklyn's Founder Informational Designation; L29; February 14, 1963; 1963

The Jackson Area

The pioneers in the 1830s by the tens of thousands traveled west over the Territorial Road (roughly parallel to I-94). Many of them stopped in the Jackson area to take up land. Jackson County was named after Andrew Jackson and organized in 1832. The principal settlement, Jackson, founded in 1829, was first called Jacksonopolis and later Jacksonburgh. Located near the head of the Grand River, Jackson has always been an important transportation center. One of America's most famous political conventions took place in this city on July 6, 1854, when fifteen hundred persons from throughout Michigan assembled "under the oaks" and organized a new party which they named the Republican party. This area is

St. Mary Star of the Sea Church was built 1923-1926 according to a design by Frederick Spier. St. Mary's elaborate interior is spectacular. (*St. Mary Star of the Sea Church*)

the home of Michigan's oldest and largest state prison and many diversified industries.

*Rest Area, westbound I-94, west of Mount Hope Road, Grass Lake Township; Jackson Area, The, Informational Designation; S233B; January 16, 1962; 1964

Wellman General Store

This triple-brick Victorian-style structure, built in 1886 by Newton Sears and Milford Tanner, exemplifies small town midwestern general stores of the 1880s. In 1891, Ernest Wellman and his mother bought out Tanner's interest. The following year, Ernest married Hattie Tripp. The couple ran the general store for thirty-seven years. Under later ownership, the store was associated with the Red and White grocery chain.

205 Main Street, Hanover Township; Wellman General Store; L740A; September 10, 1979; 1974

Austin Blair

For over a half century Civil War governor Austin Blair (1818-1894) was a resident of this city. Born in Tompkins County, New York, Blair moved to Jackson in 1841. He began his law practice and was admitted to the Michigan bar in October of that year. After a brief residence in Eaton Rapids (1842-1844), he returned to Jackson. Originally a Whig, Blair joined the Free Soil party in 1848. In 1854 he was a leader of the over three thousand delegates who met in Jackson and founded the Republican party, the immediate goal of which was to stop the further extension of slavery in the territories. Blair served as a delegate to the Republican National Convention in Philadelphia in 1856 and chaired the Michigan delegation at the national convention in Chicago in 1860. In 1860 and again in 1862 he was elected governor of Michigan on the Republican ticket.

Side Two

Austin Blair began his political career in Eaton Rapids, where he was elected Eaton County clerk in 1842. As a member of the Michigan House of Representatives (1846-1849), he served on the Judiciary Committee and was a leading supporter of the 1846 law to abolish capital punishment. He also introduced legislation to enfranchise black citizens. He was elected Jackson County prosecutor in 1852, and served in the state senate from 1855 to 1856. Elected governor in 1860 and in 1862, Blair personally raised about $100,000 to organize and equip the First Michigan Volunteer Infantry Regiment, which was the first western force to respond to Lincoln's call for troops. During the close of his active political life, Blair was a United States congressman (1867-1873) and a University of Michigan regent (1882-1890). He died in Jackson in 1894.

Greenwood Park, 600 Greenwood Avenue, Jackson; Governor Austin Blair Informational Designation; S559C; February 15, 1984; 1984

Ella Sharp Museum

In 1855, Abraham Wing purchased this farm for his widowed daughter Mary. Within a year she married Dwight Merriman, and under their guidance, "Hillside" became a model farm, with over six hundred acres of orchards and cultivated fields. In 1881 their first and only surviving child, Ella, married John C. Sharp, attorney and later state senator. Ella died in 1912, leaving the farm to the city of Jackson as a park. The house was opened as a museum in 1965.

3225 Fourth Street, Jackson; Sharp, Ella, House (Ella Sharp Farm Museum-Tower Barn); L147; August 13, 1971; 1975

First Baptist Church

In 1834 thirteen Jackson pioneers established the Barry-Jackson Baptist Church in Sandstone Township. Five years later the Reverend David Hendee and seventeen members of that church formed the First Baptist Church in Jackson. Meetings were held in several locations until 1868, when construction began on the present church. J. R. Lewis provided the plans and specifications for this Romanesque Revival-style structure. When a lack of funds resulted in repeated construction delays, "Uncle Ben" Mosher, a member of the building committee, agreed to erect the walls free if the materials were supplied. A donation from four church members in 1871 assured the structure's completion. The church was eventually dedicated on March 10, 1872.

201 South Jackson Street, Jackson; Jackson First Baptist Church; L1171A; June 15, 1984; 1989

First State Prison

This was the original site of Michigan's first state prison, approved by the legislature in

On July 6, 1854, antislavery men converged in Jackson to form a new political party. They met outside under oak trees and formed the Republican Party. (*Under the Oaks*)

1838. A temporary wooden prison, enclosed by a fence of tamarack poles, was built on sixty acres donated for that purpose here. In 1839 the first thirty-five prisoners were received. A permanent prison was built three years later. Beginning in the 1880s under Warden H. F. Hatch a greater emphasis was placed on the education and rehabilitation of prisoners. After 1934 the inmates were housed in the new prison north of Jackson.

National Guard Armory, north end of Mechanic Street, Jackson; First State Prison; S178; January 24, 1958; 1958

St. John's Church

Constructed in 1857, St. John's is the oldest Catholic Church in Jackson and was the only church of this denomination in the city until 1901. Bishop Peter Paul LeFevre laid the cornerstone for this structure in 1856. St. John's began as a mission in 1836 and officially became a parish twenty years later. At that time Father Charles Moutard, the first resident pastor, led the congregation, then predominately Irish in origin. The potato famine of 1845 in Ireland forced thousands of Irish to the United States. Many of these immigrants settled in mining towns such as Jackson. During the early 1870s this edifice was enlarged, a school was added and nuns first came here as teachers and workers. This church now includes people of many ethnic backgrounds. St. John's continues to serve the city of Jackson.

717 Cooper Street, SE corner of Ganson Street, Jackson; St. John's Church; L587; April 4, 1978; 1978

St. Mary Star of the Sea Church

In 1880, Bishop Casper Henry Borgess of the Detroit Diocese approved the establishment of a second Catholic parish in the city of Jackson. The cornerstone ceremony for the parish church was held on July 4, 1881. The present limestone Romanesque structure, erected in 1923-1926, was designed by Frederick Spier of Detroit. One of the towers houses the twenty-seven-hundred-pound 1902 bell from the parish's first church. The edifice also features stained-glass windows imported from Innsbruck, Austria, and Italian Carrara marble altars and communion rails. The confessionals and sacristy cases were built using the pews of the first building. During the parish's growth, from 124 members at its founding to 3,800 at the time of its centennial, it has had only six pastors.

NE corner of Wesley and South Mechanic streets, Jackson; St. Mary Star of the Sea Church; L885A; February 23, 1981; 1981

St. Paul's Episcopal Church

On December 8, 1838, the founders of St. Paul's Parish met and began the task of drafting the Articles of Organization for a "new Protestant society." The Parish of St. Paul's Church was officially established with the signing by twenty-two persons of the Articles of Organization on January 12, 1839. Its first house of worship, a small frame church completed at a cost of $2,500 by vestry member Lemuel S. House, was consecrated on October 20, 1840. By 1850 the group had outgrown its original home, and plans were begun to build a larger church. Designed by Buffalo architect Calvin N. Otis, the new Romanesque Revival church, was consecrated on January 11, 1853. Remodeled and expanded several times, it is one of the oldest Episcopal church structures in southern Michigan.

309 South Jackson Street, SE corner of Washington, Jackson; St. Paul's Episcopal Church; L1221A; March 28, 1985; 1986

Under the Oaks

On July 6, 1854, a state convention of antislavery men was held in Jackson to found a new political party. *Uncle Tom's Cabin* had been published two years earlier, causing increased resentment against slavery, and the Kansas-Nebraska Act of May 1854, threatened to make slave states out of previously free territories. Since the convention day was hot and the huge crowd could not be accommodated in the hall, the meeting adjourned to an oak grove on "Morgan's Forty" on the outskirts of the town. Here a state-wide slate of candidates was selected, and the Republican party was born. Winning an overwhelming victory in the elections of 1854, the Republican party went on to dominate national politics throughout the nineteenth century.

NW corner, Second and Franklin streets, Jackson; Under the Oaks (Birth of the Republican Party) Informational Site; S15; February 18, 1956; 1972

Spring Arbor College

The Michigan institutions of higher education have had their roots here. The predecessor of

Albion College, Spring Arbor Seminary, was chartered in 1835. Michigan Central College, founded in 1844, was located here until its removal in 1855 when it became Hillsdale College. Spring Arbor College was opened by Free Methodists in 1873 as an academy with elementary and secondary grades. In 1928 the elementary program was discontinued when a junior college was officially introduced. The high school was terminated in 1961 when a senior college was proposed. In September 1963, the first junior class was accepted into the regionally-accredited four-year liberal arts college. Throughout its history, the Spring Arbor faculty and students have been dedicated to "the serious study of the liberal arts, commitment to Jesus Christ as a perspective for learning and participation in the campus community and the contemporary world."

Spring Arbor College Campus, Main Street (M-60), Spring Arbor Township; Spring Arbor College Informational Designation; S246; July 10, 1963; 1963

Jameson Farm

James M. Jameson, a native of New York State, became a pioneer settler of Springport in 1835. A school teacher, justice of the peace and township supervisor, he eventually acquired four hundred acres of land here, which he farmed until he left the area in 1876. The Jameson Farm produced wheat, corn and oats. By the mid-1850s Jameson had built what is said to be the first brick home in Springport. The elaborate Greek Revival house has remained virtually unaltered through the years. In 1979 it was listed in the National Register of Historic Places.

10220 North Parma Road, NW corner of Pope Church Road, Springport, Springport Township; Jameson, James M., Farm (Daly Farm); L999A; March 18, 1982; 1982

McCain School

This typical one-room schoolhouse was built for School District No. 2 of Summit Township in the 1880s. Named for a school board member, McCain School is the second schoolhouse erected on this site. The first was built in the early 1850s shortly after the land was set aside for school purposes. The rear lean-to addition was completed in 1899. The building operated as a school until 1956. It later served as a social center. In 1976 it was renovated as a studio apartment.

3517 McCain Road, east of Robinson Road at Ganton Drive, Summit Township; McCain School; L884A; February 23, 1981; 1981

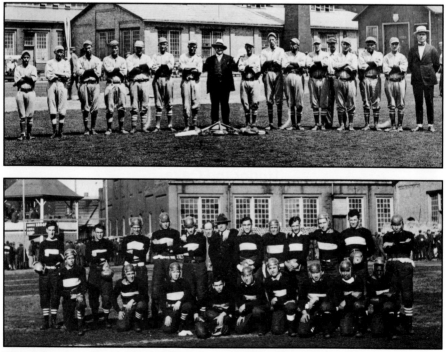

Recreation was viewed as rehabilitation at Jackson State Prison. These team photos were taken in the early twentieth century. (*First State Prison*)

Kalamazoo

Barn Theatre

The Barn Theatre, originally constructed in 1943 by Robert M. Cook as a dairy barn, is the home of Michigan's oldest resident summer stock theater. Such theaters use a group of actors who perform consecutive productions of different shows. Founded in 1946 as The Village Players, the company first used the Community Hall in Richland. It began renting this barn in 1949 and purchased it in 1954. The company was incorporated as The Barn Theatre, Inc. on July 12, 1949. It became an Equity (union of professional stage actors) theater in 1951. The company has performed over three hundred plays and musicals and played to over one million patrons.

13319 Augusta Drive (Highway M-96), Charleston Township; Barn Theatre; L1107A; August 12, 1983; 1985

Daniel B. Eldred House

In 1835, New York native Daniel B. Eldred built this house, which is believed to be the earliest frame dwelling in Climax. Eldred's house, with its delicate Federal entrance, was the site of the first Climax Township meeting in 1838. Eldred first came to the area in 1831 with his father, Judge Caleb Eldred, to found a new settlement. He is credited with naming the area Climax Prairie because he said it "climaxed" the end of their search.

216 East Maple, Climax; Eldred, Daniel B., House (Wolfsalger or Sheldon); L1681B; September 7, 1989; 1990

The Kalamazoo Region

Kalamazoo is an Indian word said to mean "boiling water." Originally it was applied to the river that flows northwesterly to Lake Michigan. A trickle of settlers in the late 1820s became a torrent in the 1830s as the region's fertile prairies, oak openings, bottom lands and ample sources of water power became known. The village of Bronson, founded in 1829 by Titus Bronson, is now the city of Kalamazoo. Here Lincoln made his only known Michigan speech. J. Fenimore Cooper wrote about the area in *Oak Openings*. Kalamazoo College, founded in 1833, Nazareth College (1897) and Western Michigan University (1903) are here. Once famous for its celery and its stoves, Kalamazoo is now known for many products including paper and drugs. The nation's first permanent pedestrian mall was opened in the downtown section in 1959.

Three identical markers: 1) *Rest Area, westbound I-94 near Galesburg, Comstock Township, 2) Rest Area, eastbound I-94, Oshtemo Township, 3) *Rest Area, southbound M-131, Alamo Township; Kalamazoo Region Informational Designation; S222; July 17, 1961; 1964

Cooper Congregational Church

This church was built in 1856 with money raised from the sale of family church pews—a popular fund-raising method used in New England and New York. Ephraim Delano, George Delano, George Hart, A. R. Allen, A. W. Ingerson, Allen Chappell and John Walker built the church on land donated by Barney and Eliza Earl. The cornice returns, triangular pediments and square louvered belfry, containing a bell cast by Meneely and Kimberly of Troy, New York, reflect the church's Greek Revival styling.

Side Two

In 1843 the Reverends Mason Knappen and Ova Hoyt organized the Cooper Congregational Church with families from New York and Vermont. Church founders included Laura Blanchard, John and Betsy Borden, Mace, Nancy and John Borden, Matilda Delano, David Deming, Eliza Earl, Lydia Hart, Fidelia Pratt, William and Susan Lyman and Almon and Phoebe Monroe. These members first worshipped in a log schoolhouse at Cooper Centre. The present church was erected in 1856.

8071 Douglas Avenue, between C and D avenues, Cooper Township; First Congregational Church of Cooper; L1445B; August 21, 1987; 1989

DeLano Homestead

William Smith DeLano (1819-1901) was a southwestern Michigan pioneer settler. He built this modest Greek Revival-style house in 1858. A native of western New York State,

137

A 1980 tornado destroyed Kalamazoo's *A.U.V.* Auditorium, built in 1898 as the home of the German Workingmen's Benevolent Association. (*A.U.V. Auditorium*)

DeLano came to the area with an uncle in 1837. He first worked clearing farms for neighbors. In 1843, at the age of twenty-three, he purchased 40 acres and began the family farmstead. By 1854, DeLano owned over 100; by 1880 he had 235 acres. Over the years, DeLano's sons continued to purchase neighboring lands. The family eventually acquired over 600 [acres]. Members of the family lived on the farm until 1963. For several years afterwards, the house was neglected. In 1968 the Kalamazoo Nature Center acquired the structure and most of the original DeLano farm. The farmhouse was restored and opened to the public in 1975.

555 West E Avenue, between Douglas and North Westnedge avenues, north of Kalamazoo, Cooper Township; DeLano, William S., House (DeLano Homestead); L432; November 21, 1975; 1982

Congregational United Church of Christ

This congregation has held services continually since 1832. In 1852 it was formally organized as an offshoot of the First Presbyterian Church of nearby Comstock. Later that year the church's name was changed to the First Congregational Church. It became the Congregational United Church of Christ in 1960. This Greek Revival-Italianate structure, one of the oldest church buildings in Kalamazoo County, has been altered only slightly since it was built in 1861.

22 Church Street, Galesburg; First Congregational Church (Congregational United Church of Christ); L767A; January 18, 1980; 1980

A.U.V. Auditorium

Completed in 1898, this huge building, with its elegant ballroom, replaced the old hall of the German Workingmen's Benevolent Association or *Arbeiter Unterstutzungs Verein (A.U.V.)*. Organized in Kalamazoo in 1866, this association offered aid, insurance and recreation to its members. By 1904 it was one of over eighty *A.U.V.* affiliates in Michigan. Although greatly altered, with the original spires removed, the building continues to be a reminder of the state's German heritage.

*137 Portage, Kalamazoo; *A.U.V.* Auditorium (demolished) (German Workingmen's Benevolent Association Building); L488; December 14, 1976; 1977

David S. Walbridge

Born in Vermont in 1802, David S. Walbridge became one of Kalamazoo's most distinguished citizens. He moved here in the early 1840s and was a founding member of the First Presbyterian Church. Active in the business community, Walbridge set up a general store, bought a large flour mill, and invested in flat boats and plank road construction to transport his goods. His deep interest in Whig politics led to his participation in the first state Republican convention in Jackson, where he was named permanent chairman of the meeting. Elected to Congress in 1855, he served until 1858. His other offices included terms as postmaster and state legislator. After years of service to his party and to Michigan, David S. Walbridge died in Kalamazoo in 1868.

202 South Kalamazoo Mall, Kalamazoo; Walbridge, David, Informational Site; S462; January 16, 1976; 1976

East Hall

In 1903 the state legislature provided for the creation of Western State Normal School, the forerunner of Western Michigan University, a publicly-funded institution of higher learning. Donating money, services and land, the city of Kalamazoo worked with the State Board of Education to develop this campus. The Olmsted Brothers, well-known landscape architects, laid out a prominent site on Prospect Hill, and E. W. Arnold of Battle Creek designed this Georgian Revival complex as Western's official home. Construction began in 1904, and the first portion of East Hall, the Administration Building, was dedicated in 1905. By 1909 the remainder of the building was completed, and some five hundred students from all over the state attended classes at the college. East Hall symbolizes the cooperation between school and community.

Oakland Drive, Western Michigan University campus, Kalamazoo; East Hall; S510; October 9, 1978; 1978

Edward Israel Arctic Pioneer

Near here is the grave of Edward Israel, who went on the nation's first polar expedition, led by Lieutenant Adolphus W. Greely. The team set out in 1881 for Ellesmere Island in the Arctic Ocean. Expedition scientist was Israel of Kalamazoo, age twenty-two, a recent graduate of the University of Michigan. He collected valuable astronomical information and assisted Greely in many administrative chores. Disaster struck in 1883 when the relief ship was sunk en route. After a severe winter, eighteen of the twenty-five expedition members died. Israel died on May 27, 1884. The entire city of Kalamazoo, with mixed sorrow and pride, honored Israel when the body was returned in August of that year.

Mountain Home Cemetery, bounded by Main Street, Ingleside Terrace and Forbes Street, Kalamazoo; Edward Israel Arctic Pioneer; 1972

Epaphroditus Ransom

The only resident of Kalamazoo to be elected governor of Michigan during its first 150 years, Epaphroditus Ransom lived and farmed on this site. Born in Massachusetts in 1796, Ransom came to Michigan in 1834. An attorney, he soon became the area's first circuit court judge, riding horseback through the wilderness to hear cases. In 1836 he was appointed associate justice of the Michigan Supreme Court, and in 1843 he became the court's chief justice. A declaration he issued in 1840 prevented the removal of the Catholic Potawatomi from their southwestern Michigan lands. In 1848, Ransom was the first governor to be inaugurated in Lansing, which had just become the state capital.

Side Two

During Epaphroditus Ransom's gubernatorial term (1848-1850), the Kalamazoo Regional Psychiatric Hospital was established. Following his term as governor, Ransom became the first president of the Michigan Agricultural Society, which was instrumental in the creation of both the Michigan State Fair and Michigan State University. He was also a regent of the University of Michigan (1850-1852), a founder of the village of Augusta and a state representative (1853-1854). In 1857, President James Buchanan appointed Ransom receiver of the Kansas Osage Land Office in Fort Scott, Kansas. He died in Kansas in 1859. His body was returned to Kalamazoo, where it was interred in Mountain Home Cemetery.

Epaphroditus Ransom was the first governor inaugurated in the new capital of Lansing. (*Epaphroditus Ransom*)

401 South Burdick Street, Kalamazoo; Governor Epaphroditus Ransom Informational Site (*Kalamazoo Gazette*); S569C; May 21, 1985; 1987

First Baptist Church

Constructed in 1853, this is the oldest church building in Kalamazoo. Titus Bronson, the city's founder, donated this site on Church Square. The Baptist faith reached the Kalamazoo River Valley in 1826 when missionary Leonard Slater preached to the Indians. In 1836 fourteen settlers led by Jeremiah Hall, a Baptist minister from Vermont, met in the home of Ezekiel Ransom to organize the First Baptist Church.

Side Two

The history of the First Baptist Church and Kalamazoo College are closely interwoven. The same year that the church was organized, the Reverend Jeremiah Hall persuaded the Michigan and Huron Institute, now Kalamazoo College, to settle in this city. The second pastor, Dr. James H. B. Stone, was an early president of the college and many of his successors in that office have been active in this congregation. Over the years the First Baptist Church has served as the parent church of several parishes in outlying areas.

315 West Michigan Avenue, Kalamazoo; First Baptist Church; L338; January 16, 1976; 1977

First United Methodist Church

In 1830 the Reverend James T. Robe, a young Methodist circuit rider, delivered the first sermon in the village of Bronson, later Kalamazoo, at the home of the town's founder, Titus Bronson. After his appointment to the Kalamazoo Mission in 1832, Robe preached throughout a circuit that extended from Niles to Allegan. In 1833 the Reverend Richard C. Meek formed a local Society of Methodists, and this eight-member congregation became Kalamazoo's first organized church.

Side Two

The Kalamazoo Methodist Society met first in the home of George Patterson and later in a schoolhouse. The congregation built its first church in 1842 at Academy and Church streets. A second church, built in 1866, burned in 1926. Ernest Batterson, a church member and architect, designed the present Late Gothic Revival building, dedicated in 1929. An educational wing was added in 1949. The congregation assisted in founding a number of area Methodist churches.

212 South Park Avenue, Kalamazoo; First United Methodist Church; L1528A; June 30, 1988; 1988

First Women's Club in Michigan

This building, completed in 1879, is the first in the nation erected for the use of a women's club. The Ladies' Library Association, organized in January 1852, grew out of a reading club started in 1844. It was the first women's club in Michigan and the third in the United States. Mrs. Lucinda H. Stone, who is known as the "mother of women's clubs," helped to found this club. The association has had a continuous existence from its organization.

333 South Park Street, Kalamazoo; Ladies Library Association Building; S221; April 15, 1961; 1961

Indian Fields

This locality, known as Indian Fields, was the site of a large Potawatomi village. The tract included about four square miles. The early white settlers found here fine examples of the famed garden beds. A short distance southwest of this terminal a tribal burial ground was located. Here during the War of 1812 the families of warriors fighting with the British against the Americans were concentrated, and American soldiers are said to have been held as prisoners.

Mounted on the Kalamazoo Municipal Airport terminal, Kalamazoo; Indian Fields Informational Designation; S46; August 23, 1956; 1961

Kalamazoo Celery

A Scotsman named Taylor grew the first celery in Kalamazoo in 1856. Diners at the Burdick Hotel regarded it with curiosity. Cornelius De Bruyn, a gardener, who came here from The Netherlands in 1866, developed the modern type of celery from the earlier soup celery. Other Dutch farmers by 1872 were turning the Kalamazoo mucklands into fields of celery. J. S. Dunkley sold medicines and condiments made of celery. Soon Kalamazoo celery was known the nation over. Michigan has been a leading celery producer ever since.

Intersection of Crosstown Parkway, Balch and Park streets, Kalamazoo; Kalamazoo Celery Informational Designation; S133; January 19, 1957; 1958

Kalamazoo College

This school, Baptist in origin, was chartered in 1833 by the Territory of Michigan as the Michigan and Huron Institute and held its first classes in 1836. Instruction of college level has been given here longer than at any other Michigan school. In 1845 the present campus was purchased. The right to confer degrees was granted in 1855. This pioneer school has won national renown as a liberal arts college with special honor in teaching of the sciences.

Erected in 1957, replaced in 1983

Kalamazoo College was chartered as a Baptist school in 1833. These coeds, members of the Kappa Pi Society, posed for this group portrait in 1907. (*Kalamazoo College*)

Kalamazoo College

The first classroom building for the Michigan and Huron Institute, now Kalamazoo College, was erected on this site between June and September of 1836. The charter bill for the school had been introduced in the Michigan Territorial Legislative Council on January 18, 1833, and signed into law by Governor George B. Porter on April 22, 1833. Village pledges supplied funds for the two-story frame classroom structure, which was the start of Michigan's first church-related college.

1200 Academy, Kalamazoo; Kalamazoo College Informational Designation; S101; September 25, 1956; 1983

Kalamazoo Gazette

Founded in 1833 as the weekly *Michigan Statesman and St. Joseph Chronicle*, this newspaper, edited by Henry Gilbert, followed the United States Land Office when it moved from White Pigeon to Kalamazoo in 1835. It first appeared as the *Kalamazoo Gazette* on January 23, 1837. On March 26, 1872, under Andrew J. Shakespeare, it became a daily publication. In 1925 the *Gazette* moved to its present location. It celebrated its 150th anniversary of publication in 1987, the year of the Michigan sesquicentennial.

401 South Burdick Street, Kalamazoo; *Michigan Statesman and St. Joseph Chronicle* Newspaper Informational Site; L1399C; April 28, 1987; 1987

Kalamazoo School Case

Near here, in 1858, Kalamazoo's first high school was opened. Fifteen years later the right of the school board to levy taxes to support a high school was challenged. A unanimous decision of the Michigan Supreme Court, rendered by Justice Thomas M. Cooley in 1874, affirmed an opinion of Kalamazoo Circuit Judge Charles R. Brown that upheld this right. As a result the way opened for free high schools in Michigan and also in other states.

Community Education Center, NE corner of Westnedge and West Vine streets, Kalamazoo; Kalamazoo School Case of 1874 Informational Designation; S153; September 17, 1957; 1959

Kalamazoo State Hospital

Until the 1840s the mentally ill received little therapy and often were neglected. Upon recommendation of Governor Epaphroditus Ransom, the legislature, in 1848, established Michigan's first state institution for the treatment of mental patients. Kalamazoo was chosen as the site in 1850. Construction of the first building began in 1854, but it was not completed for five years. The first patient was admitted on April 23, 1859. The superintendent, Dr. Edwin H. Van Dusen, anticipated many methods of treatment that later won general acceptance. Linda Richards, America's first trained nurse, was superintendent of nurses here, 1906-1909. This hospital was the first in Michigan to open an outpatient psychiatric clinic and to begin a home-boarding program. Adoption in 1910 of the name Kalamazoo State Hospital, replacing the original name, Michigan Asylum for the Insane, symbolized a new concept of mental illness.

1210 Oakland Drive, between Wheaton Avenue and Howard Street, Kalamazoo; Michigan Asylum for the Insane; S244; March 12, 1963; 1964

Lincoln at Kalamazoo

On August 27, 1856, here in this park, Abraham Lincoln, then an obscure lawyer, spoke to a rally for John Fremont, the Republican presidential nominee. This was the only time that Lincoln addressed a Michigan audience. The event was almost unnoticed in the press. Some Republicans felt the speaker was too moderate on the antislavery issue. Four years later Michigan's vote helped put Lincoln into the White House.

Bronson Park, Kalamazoo; Lincoln at Kalamazoo Informational Site; S44; July 19, 1956; 1957

The Peninsula Building

Originally designed for the Peninsula Restaurant, this three-story brick structure was built by Nicholas Baumann in 1874. The elegant ethnic restaurant gave way to the Franklin and Folz clothing store in 1884. After Franklin and Folz moved in 1924, the building housed a succession of businesses including a stove company, a department store, a book bindery and a hotel. It became the headquarters for the W. R. Biggs/Gilmore agency in 1973. Severely damaged by a 1980 tornado, the building was completely rehabilitated in 1980-1981.

111 Portage Street, Kalamazoo; Peninsula Building; L1000A; March 18, 1982; 1984

Pioneer Cemetery

South Westnedge Street Park is actually Kalamazoo's first cemetery. The pioneer leader, Cyren Burdick, and his wife, Mary Ann, in 1833 donated this land as a common burial ground. From this time until 1862 hundreds of pioneer settlers were buried here in what was then known as South West Street Cemetery. Later an unknown number of bodies were removed to other cemeteries in the village. In 1884, after years of neglect, Kalamazoo's pioneer cemetery was converted into a park.

South Westnedge, between Wheaton and Minor streets, Kalamazoo; Pioneer Cemetery Informational Site (South Westnedge Street Park); L10; March 24, 1960; 1960

South Street Historic District

This tree-lined neighborhood, today nestled between the business district and college campuses, recalls a quiet but prosperous Kalamazoo at the turn of the century. The street was platted in 1841. Its beautifully preserved houses, which were built between then and 1915, reflect the spectrum of fashionable domestic architecture of the period with the Italian Revival style most prevalent.

Side Two

Many prominent middle class families lived in this neighborhood, which runs two blocks along South Street. Here were the homes of professors, lawyers, journalists, businessmen and others active in the civic, commercial and professional life of Kalamazoo. Today the district houses community service organizations as well as businesses and families, thereby retaining its traditional cultural and civic orientation.

516 West South Street, between Oakland Drive and Westnedge Avenue, Kalamazoo; South Street Historic District; L206; June 16, 1972; 1974

The Stuart House

This historic house was built in 1858 for United States Senator Charles E. Stuart. As one of the leading lawyers and Democratic politicians of his day, Stuart naturally desired a house befitting his position. Thus it included tile and marble from Italy, stenciled and wood-paneled walls, tiffany light fixtures, a great ballroom and Kalamazoo's first indoor bathroom! Stables and beautiful gardens were found on the estate. Stuart died in 1887. The Tau Kappa Epsilon fraternity acquired the house in 1956.

427 Stuart Avenue, Kalamazoo; Stuart, Charles E., House (Tau Kappa Epsilon House); L57; November 18, 1965; 1966

Stuart Neighborhood

There are three "Stuart Neighborhood" historical markers located within the historic district.

Stuart Neighborhood

Marker One

Homes of this neighborhood reflect the individuality and at times the economic status of their original owners. These homes, designed in the architectural styles of the mid- and late nineteenth century, range from the fashionable Queen Anne, most popular during that era, to the Renaissance-style architecture, which also flourished at this time. Many of the residences feature Italian, Gothic and Greek influences. This district is one of the city's earliest suburbs.

Marker Two

Charles Stuart, politician and lawyer, initiated this residential area with the building of his Italianate house in 1858. Illinois Senator Stephen Douglas visited the Stuart home, which was one of the first on the west edge of the village of Kalamazoo. Later, as the neighborhood developed around that site, Stuart opened Douglas Avenue, which he named in honor of his guest. Most of the early residents of this area, then a suburb, were prosperous businessmen and self-employed craftsmen.

Marker Three

Wealthy merchants and businessmen, seeking an escape from the hurried life of downtown

The Stuart Neighborhood/Henderson Park Historic District, with its 322 buildings, is one of Kalamazoo's six National Register historic districts. (*Stuart Neighborhood*)

living, built this prosperous neighborhood in the latter half of the nineteenth century. Movement to the suburbs gained in popularity after the 1850s, but lack of transportation hindered rapid development. The early suburbanites were mostly well-to-do and could afford to be a few minutes late to work if their buggies got stuck in the mud or snow. With the installation of horse-drawn trolleys in the 1880s, the middle class began to move here.

District is roughly bounded by the Michigan Central Railroad, Forbes, West Main, North, Elmwood and Elm streets, Douglas, Kalamazoo and Grand avenues, Kalamazoo; Stuart Neighborhood/Henderson Park Historic District (Stuart Historic District); L565; November 7, 1977; 1978

The Upjohn Company

The Upjohn Pill & Granule Company was founded on this site in 1886 by Dr. William E. Upjohn and his three brothers—Dr. Henry U., Frederick L. and Dr. James T. Upjohn. The pill-making factory began in the basement of a commercial block, where the Upjohn brothers turned out their specialty, "friable pills." By year's end the company employed twelve people, manufactured 186 different medicinal formulas and had moved to a new building on Farmer's Alley. In 1888 the company moved again, this time to Lovell Street, where it celebrated a century of operations in 1986. The Upjohn Company (renamed in 1902) is a worldwide provider of pharmaceutical, agricultural and chemical products, and health-care services.

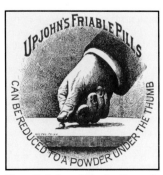

The Upjohn Pill & Granule Company was established in 1886. (*The Upjohn Company*)

William E. Upjohn

Dr. William E. Upjohn (1853-1932), founder of the Upjohn Company, was known as Kalamazoo's "First Citizen" because of his active role in the community. He helped institute the commission-manager form of government and served as the city's first mayor under the new system (1918-1921). He helped direct the construction of Bronson Hospital (1904) and several area churches (1926). He also established the Kalamazoo Foundation (1925) and the W. E. Upjohn Institute for Employment Research (1932). His belief in the "happy use of leisure time" led him to donate land for Upjohn

Park (1919), to help fund an "Art House" (1928) and a municipal golf course (1929) and to build the Civic Auditorium (1931).

Kalamazoo Mall, south of the intersection of South Street and Burdick, Kalamazoo; UpJohn Company Informational Designation; S582C; July 17, 1986; 1986

Western Michigan University

Established by legislative act in 1903 as Western State Normal School, the first classes were held in 1904. The first permanent building, completed in 1905, overlooked the city from Prospect Hill. By the 1920s Western had become one of America's leading teachers' colleges. Starting in 1934 general degree work was offered. An expansion program on the west campus began in 1944. Increasing enrollment and the addition of new departments and courses during the 1940s and 1950s made Western a multi-purpose institution and led to its designation as a university by an act of the legislature in 1957.

Western Michigan University campus, Kalamazoo; Western State Normal School Historic District (East Campus/Western Michigan University); S117; January 19, 1957; 1957

Harris Family

Among the earliest pioneers of Oshtemo Township was a black family, that of Enoch and Deborah Harris. Born in the East in the late 1700s, they settled in the Ohio wilderness about 1810. Moving westward with the advancing frontier, they claimed land near here in 1831. Early accounts agree that Harris planted the first apple orchard in the area, and their daughter was said to be the township's first bride. Farming over two hundred acres, Harris won the respect of his fellow settlers. He died in 1870 and was buried here, one-quarter mile east of his farm.

SE corner of Eleventh Street and Parkview Road (M Avenue), just west of Kalamazoo city limit, Oshtemo Township; Harris Family Burial Site (Genesee Prairie Cemetery); L245A; July 26, 1973; 1973

Community Library

The Ladies Library Association raised the funds to build this Classical Revival-style building, which was completed in 1910. After serving as a private library for thirty-eight years, it was sold first to the Richland Rural Agricultural School (1948) and then to the First Presbyterian Church (1959). In 1981 the Richland Community Library Board purchased it. Through a community fund-raising campaign, the building was renovated and became the public library for Richland Township in 1983.

8951 Park Street, Richland; Ladies' Library Building (Richland Community Library Building); L1189A; September 24, 1984; 1987

The First Presbyterian Church

Settlers from Hudson, Ohio, came to the Richland area (then known as Gull Prairie) in 1830. A year later a Presbyterian congregation was organized. Established under the 1801 Plan of Union adopted by the Presbyterians and Congregationalists for churches west of New York, the church originally served both denominations. The early "Presbygationalists" worshipped in log homes of the settlers until they built their first house of worship, a wood frame structure completed in 1837, on this site.

Side Two

Dedicated on February 27, 1861, during the pastorate of Milton Bradley, this is the First Presbyterian congregation's second church. William Doolittle and Stephen Patrick built the Greek Revival frame edifice with its round-headed Italianate doors and windows at a cost of $7,000. The original bell cracked and was replaced by the present one in 1881. Until 1886 a slender ornate steeple stood thirty feet higher than today's tower. The interior was altered in 1952, but the original pews remain.

8047 Park Street, Richland; Richland First Presbyterian Church; L835A; October 2, 1980; 1981

W. K. Kellogg House

W. K. Kellogg (1860-1951) founded the Toasted Corn Flake Company of Battle Creek in 1906. In 1925, Kellogg and his second wife, Dr. Carrie Staines, a physician at the Battle Creek Sanitarium, commissioned Benjamin and Benjamin of Grand Rapids to design a summer house here. Their picturesque estate included this Neo-Tudor manor house, a windmill, a greenhouse, a stable, a boathouse, a combined guest house, garage and chauffeur's residence and a caretaker's house. Marshall Field and Company of Chicago decorated the interior. From 1944 to 1950 the estate served as a rehabilitation center for the Percy Jones Army Hospital in Battle Creek. In 1952 the W. K. Kellogg Foundation gave the property to Michigan State College (now Michigan State University), which developed it as the Kellogg Gull Lake Biological Station.

3700 Gull Lake East Drive, Hickory Corners vicinity, Ross Township; Kellogg, W. K., House (Eagle Heights/W. K. Kellogg Biological Station); S605A; February 15, 1990; 1991

Fanny M. Bair Library

Fanny M. Bair, a member of one of Vicksburg's pioneer families, built this library and presented it to the Ladies Library Association on November 21, 1902. Charles A. Fairchild of Kalamazoo designed the building with "modern conveniences" like electric lighting and running water. The Ladies Library Association administered the library until ownership was transferred to the village of Vicksburg in 1948.

120 West Maple Street, Vicksburg; Bair, Fanny A., Library (Vicksburg Community Library); L1481A; December 17, 1987; 1989

Kalkaska

Excelsior Town Hall

Twenty-five years after the township's organization in 1875, Excelsior's citizens decided to build a town hall. In 1901 they purchased this site from Edwin Wagenschutz for $100 and with plans costing only $7, erected this structure for $1,085. The simple frame building continues to serve as the town hall. From 1907 to 1926 the hall also housed Excelsior High School, the first rural high school in Michigan established under the law of 1901.

Corner of County Road 571/612 and Wagenschutz Road, Excelsior Township; Excelsior Town Hall; L288; July 26, 1974; 1974

Rugg Pond Dam

In 1904, Ambrose E. Palmer founded the Kalkaska Light and Power Company and built a dam and power plant at Rugg Pond where the two branches of the Rapid River meet. Palmer reportedly commissioned farmers to bring wagonloads of stone to the pond to construct the foundation of the dam. This plant supplied electricity to the village of Kalkaska and surrounding areas. The pond was named for R. F. Rugg, a prominent local businessman. According to legend, Ernest Hemingway spent a night fishing from the Rugg Pond Dam powerhouse.

Side Two

In 1950, Consumers Power Company purchased the former Kalkaska Light and Power Company hydroelectric plant, located at Rugg Pond Dam. Consumers Power sold the dam to Kalkaska County for one dollar in 1953. In 1980 the Army Corps of Engineers condemned the dam. Two years later concerned citizens formed Save Rugg Pond Natural Area to restore the dam and preserve the area. Local contributions, grants and monies from the Kammer Land & Trust Fund have been used to maintain this scenic area.

Off Valley Road, north of Hanson (Hill) Road, Rapid River Township; Rugg [Antrim] Pond Dam (Rugg Pond Dam); L1158A; May 8, 1984; 1990

Kent

Ada Covered Bridge

An act of the legislature in 1867 authorized Ada Township to borrow up to $3,000 for the purpose of building or repairing bridges in the township. This bridge was built about that time, apparently by William Holmes. The design for the trusses was patented by Josiah Brown in 1857. A timber bearing his name was uncovered during repair work. The bridge has been threatened by floods a number of times. It is said that farmers used to drive wagons loaded with stone onto the bridge during high water to hold it to the foundation. The bridge was closed to automobile traffic in 1930 and restored by the Kent County Road Commission in 1941.

NOTE: Present bridge is a reconstruction. Across the Thornapple River at Bronson Street, Ada Township; Ada Covered Bridge (demolished); L75; May 9, 1969; 1974

Alpine Township Hall

In 1847, Alpine Township was set apart from Walker Township at a meeting held in a schoolhouse in present-day Comstock Park. Edward Wheeler was elected supervisor. Subsequent meetings were held in a log school one-half mile east of here on the Wheeler farm. In 1855, Wheeler deeded a parcel of land adjacent to this site to the township for the establishment of a cemetery. Around 1860 this hall was built at the geographic center of the township to house the area's governmental and community activities. The Grange, organized by local farmers in 1874, met here until 1878 when they built their own hall one mile west of here. In 1961 a new township office was erected and this structure was vacated. The township restored the hall in 1987. Two years later it opened as a museum.

SE corner of Seven Mile Road and Walker Road NW, Alpine Township; Alpine Township Hall; L1417A; June 10, 1987; 1990

Byron Township Hall

Byron Township Hall was built in 1876. Byron Center had been platted four years earlier from the Samuel S. Towner farm, which was located in the geographic center of the township. The hall housed the township library until 1963 and continued to house government offices until 1986. The International Order of Odd Fellows held a ninety-nine year lease on the second story of the building beginning in 1877. The Byron Center Historical Society purchased and restored the building in 1986.

Side Two

In 1896, William Jennings Bryan, the "silver-tongued orator," spoke here while stumping the country as the Democratic presidential candidate. Gerald R. Ford often met here with his constituents during his thirteen terms as Michigan's Fifth District congressman. The Byron Township Hall served as a forum for political speeches and provided space for community activities such as dances, weddings, meetings and church services. It became the Byron Township Historical Museum in 1987.

2506 Prescott Street, Byron Township; Byron Township Hall (Byron Center Township Hall); L1451A; September 26, 1987; 1990

David Kinsey Home

David Kinsey, the founder of Caledonia village, settled on this site on April 13, 1856. He replaced his temporary lodging, a board shanty, with a plank house shortly after he arrived. Occasionally, Indians would be found sleeping on the first floor wrapped in blankets. In 1872-1873, Kinsey built a brick house, which stood here until a fire in 1976 gutted it. The owners completed the restoration and reconstruction of the building in 1988, which included the addition of a summer kitchen built from parts of an old barn.

Side Two

David Kinsey was born in Dumfries, Ontario, Canada, on August 22, 1830. In 1855 he came with his brother Isaac to Gaines Township. Kinsey laid out and platted the village of Caledonia, where he settled. Kinsey started a farm on this site, which was crossed by the Grand Valley Railroad in 1870. He offered two village lots to the man who would build the first house in Caledonia. He also offered two lots for the site of the United Brethren Church. He died on his farm in May 1892.

6087 100th Street, west of Kinsey Boulevard, Caledonia; Kinsey, David, Home; L478; November 3, 1976; 1988

Cascade Christian Church

Established in 1864, the Cascade Christian Church is the oldest of its brotherhood in Kent County. Alfred Stow and his parents, Zebulon and Edytha, who settled in the area in the early 1860s, led the efforts to organize the church. The Stows had also been instrumental in founding a Christian church in Summit County, Ohio. In 1864 they invited a friend, Elder Alanson Wilcox, to the area to preach. Through his efforts, the church was founded with sixteen charter members. At the time of the church's centennial, in 1964, the membership numbered over four hundred. The present church structure was completed in 1965. The

Ethelbert and Charles Fox, brothers and partners in a lumbering firm, built this Heritage Hill landmark in 1884-1886. (*The Castle*)

original church is still used for Sunday services, weddings, funerals and group gatherings.

Orange Street, near the intersection of Cascade Road and Twenty-eighth Street, Cascade Township; Cascade Christian Church (Cascade Christian Church Chapel); L852A; November 2, 1980; 1982

John Isaac Cutler House

In 1853, John and Christina Cutler and their ten children came to this area from New York and founded the town of Cutlerville. In 1891, Cutler's son John Isaac built a three-story brick house. The interior was embellished with hardwood and heated by a gas furnace. In 1910 the Cutlers sold the home and farm to what became the Pine Rest Christian Hospital Association. The former residence was its first treatment center. In 1979 it was renovated and renamed The Homestead.

300 Sixty-eighth Street SE, Gaines Township; Cutler, John Issac House (Pine Rest Christian Hospital); L1575B; July 21, 1988; 1989

Aquinas College

Aquinas had its beginning in 1887 as the Novitiate Normal School of the Dominican Sisters of Marywood. In 1922 it became Marywood College of the Sacred Heart. When the college was moved downtown in 1931, it became the coeducational Catholic Junior College. It began operating as a four-year college in 1940 and was named in honor of the great medieval theologian and philosopher, Saint Thomas Aquinas. Aquinas is primarily a liberal arts college. It was moved to this campus, the former Lowe estate, in 1945.

1607 Robinson Road SE, near Fulton Street, Grand Rapids; Aquinas College Informational Designation; S235; April 18, 1962; 1962

Calvin College and Seminary

These schools are institutions of the Christian Reformed Church, a denomination founded in 1857 in western Michigan by Dutch immigrants whose religious roots lay in the Calvinist Reformation. The seminary began in an upper room of a school building on Williams Street, Grand Rapids, in 1876. From 1892 to 1917 it was located on Madison Avenue. Thereafter it was moved to the Franklin Street campus, where Calvin College, emerging from its preparatory-school attachment to the seminary, became in 1921 a four-year, degree-granting institution. The present campus, Knollcrest Farm, was acquired in 1956. Development of it began in 1959. These related schools, which emphasize liberal arts and theological education, are dedicated to preparing youth for the service of God.

Calvin College campus, 3205 Burton Street, just west of M-37 (Beltline Avenue), Grand Rapids; Calvin College and Seminary; S228B; January 16, 1962; 1965

The Castle

Designed by local architect William G. Robinson, this castle-like edifice was constructed in 1884-1886 for Colonel E. Crofton Fox and his brother Charles. Built of granite block imported from Scotland, this house is a fine example of Chateauesque-style architecture. A Heritage Hill landmark, this house features leaded and stained-glass windows, and a metal stair dormer superbly crafted to resemble stone. Its interior is adorned with parquet flooring in the entry hall and a carved oak staircase. It was refurbished as a restaurant in 1978.

Side Two

The Fox brothers, Ethelbert Crofton (1852-1904) and Charles (1853-1915), local lumber barons, built this structure as their home. These brothers were partners in a Grand Rapids lumbering firm, Osterhout, Fox & Company, and accumulated vast wealth. Appointed to the State Military Board by Governor Cyrus Luce in 1887, E. Crofton, a colonel, was twice elected president of that organization. He was also associated with banking and was treasurer of the City Board of Trade. Charles was a founder of the Michigan Trust Company, established in 1889.

455 Cherry Street SE, Grand Rapids; The Castle; L691A; July 24, 1979; 1979

Central Reformed Church

Central Reformed Church was formed on April 23, 1918, by the merger of the first two Reformed churches in the Grand Rapids area: the First Reformed, an English-speaking church organized in 1840; and the Second Reformed, a Dutch speaking church established in 1849. The new congregation chose to worship in the home of the First Reformed Church on the corner of Fountain and Barclay streets. On October 31, 1919, the Reverend John A. Dykstra became the church's first pastor.

Side Two

Central Reformed Church, established in 1918, had nearly six hundred members by 1920. Dynamic growth led to the building's enlargement in 1922. Fire destroyed the sanctuary in 1953. The congregation worshipped in Central High School and the former Grace Episcopal Church until this structure was completed in 1957. Designed by Eggers and Higgins of New York, the building reflects English and American Georgian church architecture of the late seventeenth and early eighteenth centuries.

10 College Avenue NE, Grand Rapids; Central Reformed Church Informational Designation (Central Reformed Church); L1683C; November 20, 1987; 1989

First (Park) Congregational Church

First Marker

On September 18, 1836, twenty-two persons founded one of the first Protestant congregations in Grand Rapids. Initially a Presbyterian parish, it was reorganized under the Congregational polity in 1839. The congregation occupied a former Roman Catholic chapel from 1842 to 1869. The present brick Gothic structure, completed in 1869, is the second-oldest existing church building in the city. Additions were made in 1916 and 1950. The church was listed in the National Register of Historic Places in 1982.

First (Park) Congregational Church

Second Marker

On September 18, 1836, twenty-two persons, under the direction of the Reverend Silas

William Haldane, Grand Rapids' first cabinet maker, arrived in the mid-1830s. Within fifty years, the city was the furniture capital of the nation. (*Furniture Industry*)

Woodbury of Kalamazoo, founded one of the first Protestant congregations in Grand Rapids. Initially a Presbyterian parish, the church was reorganized under the Congregational polity in 1839, with the Reverend James Ballard as pastor. For the next two years, services were held in various structures around town. During 1842-1869, the church occupied a wooden, former Roman Catholic chapel on the corner of Division and Monroe. The present church was completed in 1869. First (Park) Congregational Church was instrumental in founding a Reformed Protestant Dutch, a Presbyterian and ten Congregational churches in the area.

Side Two

This handsome yellow brick Gothic-style structure is the second-oldest existing church building in Grand Rapids. Erected between 1867 and 1869, it was designed by A. Barrows of Adrian, Michigan, and Chicago. Among the church's notable features are its Tiffany stained-glass windows and its stately corner tower. The unusual second-floor worship area is adorned with delicate art work and an ornately carved wood reredos designed by Alois Lang. The church complex now consists of the original 1867-1869 church, a 1916 fellowship hall and a 1950 addition comprising a narthex, chapel, offices and church school rooms. The church was listed on the National Register of Historic Places in 1982.

10 East Park Place NE, Grand Rapids; First (Park) Congregational Church; L850A; November 2, 1980; 1985

Furniture Industry

The first cabinet maker in Grand Rapids was William Haldane, who in 1837 set up a shop in his home at the corner of Pearl and Ottawa streets. During the ensuing decades Grand Rapids attracted increasing numbers of furniture craftsmen. Under able business management Grand Rapids had developed into the furniture capital of America by the 1880s. Buyers the world over come for the furniture markets, first held in 1878. Grand Rapids today ranks among the leaders of the industry in quality, style and design.

Public Museum, 133 Washington Street SE, Grand Rapids; Furniture Industry Informational Designation; S132; January 19, 1957; 1958

Ladies Literary Club

In 1870 six women who had been meeting for a year to study history, organized Grand

Rapids' first Ladies Literary Association. The group was also instrumental in opening the first public library in the city that same year. In 1882 the association incorporated as the Ladies Literary Club of Grand Rapids. It built this Richardsonian Romanesque-style meeting house for $6,000 in 1887. Designed by William G. Robinson, it is one of the earliest Michigan structures built as a women's club.

61 Sheldon Street SE, Grand Rapids; Ladies' Literary Club; L120; May 18, 1971; 1983

May House

This house was built in 1908-1909 for local clothier Meyer S. May and his wife, Sophie Amberg. Frank Lloyd Wright designed the house in the Prairie style. It was his first major commission in Michigan. May was the son of Abraham May, founder of A. May and Sons clothing store. In 1906, Meyer became president of the store, which was the first in the nation to display clothes on Batts hangers. Meyer May lived here until his death in 1936. The house was used as a private residence until 1985. In 1986, Steelcase Incorporated began the complete restoration of the house, its interior and grounds.

450 Madison SE, Grand Rapids; May, Meyer, House; L1342A; October 23, 1986; 1987

McCabe-Marlowe House

Built between 1865 and 1870 by James and Hanna Gallup, this Victorian-style villa is one of the oldest homes in the Heritage Hill Historic District. Gallup and his family lived here until 1896. The house was later owned by several prominent Grand Rapids residents, including the James Wylie family (major contributors to the Grand Rapids Foundation), the Ennis P. Whitley family and the Alexander M. Campbell family. In 1945 the house was purchased by Marie McCabe and her niece Wilma McCabe Marlowe. Both women taught science at Grand Rapids Junior College until the 1950s. They opened their home as a social and cultural gathering place for students, faculty and community leaders. The Grand Rapids Junior College Foundation acquired the property in 1980 so that the house could continue to be used in the tradition begun by Marie McCabe and Wilma Marlowe.

74 Lafayette NE, Grand Rapids; Gallup, James, House (McCabe-Marlowe House); L915A; April 24, 1981; 1986

Saint Andrew's Cemetery

On August 5, 1852, Father Charles Louis DeCeuninck purchased ten acres of land for the formation of Saint Andrew's Cemetery. The land was deeded to Bishop LeFevre on December 7, 1852. It was the first permanent Catholic cemetery in Grand Rapids. Louis Campau, the founder of Grand Rapids, and his wife, Sophie DeMarsac Campau, are buried in Saint Andrew's. Also buried here are Father Andrew Viszoczky, an early priest of Grand Rapids and the pastor of Saint Andrew's Church, and John Clancy, a lumberman and philanthropist.

Prince Street between Madison and Union avenues, Grand Rapids; Saint Andrew's Cemetery; L1593C; September 21, 1988; 1989

Sixth Street Bridge

The Massillon Bridge Company of Ohio built this $31,000, four-span bridge for Grand Rapids in 1886. The rust-resistant wrought iron used in its four Pratt trusses accounts for its durability. In 1921 the western truss was shortened when the west bank canal was filled in. In 1975 the bridge was slated for demolition, but concerned citizens convinced authorities to save it. This structure, the longest, oldest remaining metal bridge in Michigan, was listed in the National Register of Historic Places in 1976.

Spans the Grand River between Newberry and Sixth Street, just north of I-196, Grand Rapids; Sixth Street Bridge; S479; June 18, 1976; 1981

Valley City Milling Company

In 1884, William N. Rowe, Conrad G. Swensberg, M. S. Crosby and R. M. Lawrence founded the Valley City Milling Company in Grand Rapids. The company, which at first milled flour, expanded to include horse feed in 1893. Incorporated in 1894, it remained in Grand Rapids until 1923, when fire destroyed its facilities. In 1924 the company moved to Portland. It began producing dog food in 1931. Company brands included Lily White Flour, Rowena Dog Diets, Rowena Quality Feeds and Rolling Champion Self-rising Flour. Manufacturer of commercial feed and dog food ceased in 1958. The company continued to make flour until it sold its flour brands to a Nebraska firm in 1970. In 1973 the Valley City Milling Company opened a mobile home park in Portland.

Erected at 299 Bristie Street, just outside the Portland city limits; relocated at the corner of Front Street and Fulton Street, Grand Rapids; Valley City Milling Company Informational Designation; L1125C; October 27, 1983; 1986

Vandenberg Center

Vandenberg Center encompasses 12.5 acres lying to the northeast of this site. It was part of the land originally registered on September 19, 1831, by Louis Campau, Grand Rapids' first permanent settler. Campau platted the village of Grand Rapids, running his streets at right angles to what was known as upper Monroe Avenue, now Monroe Mall. Just to the north, on land purchased from Campau, land surveyor Lucius Lyon platted the village of Kent, laying the streets squarely on the compass. There was no direct connection between the two street plans until 1873. Vandenberg Center was once the site of industry, commerce, hotels and government offices. The federal urban renewal program of the 1960s cleared the area, providing space for the new city-county complex, the Gerald R. Ford Federal Building and other office structures.

Arthur Vandenberg, one of Michigan's most influential U.S. senators, helped draft the United Nations charter in 1945. (*Vandenberg Center*)

Arthur Hendrick Vandenberg

Arthur H. Vandenberg was born in Grand Rapids on March 22, 1884. Poverty forced him to work a variety of jobs as a youth, but by 1906 he was editor of the *Grand Rapids Herald*. In 1928, Governor Fred Green appointed him to the United States Senate, a position he held until his death in 1951. In the 1930s, Vandenberg fathered the Federal Deposit Insurance Corporation (FDIC) and supported isolationism. However, during World War II he decided that international involvement was unavoidable, and in 1945 he helped draft the United Nations Charter. A lifelong Republican, he was a post-war advocate of bipartisan foreign policy. He led senate support of aid to Greece and Turkey and the Marshall Plan. His "Vandenberg Resolution" paved the way for the North Atlantic Treaty Organization and the Military Assistance Program.

1 Vandenberg Center, Grand Rapids; Arthur H.Vandenburg Informational Designation; L1438C; July 23, 1987; 1987

Veterans' Facility

The Michigan Veterans' Facility (formerly the Michigan Soldiers' Home) was authorized by Act 152 of the Public Acts of 1885, which provided for the establishment of a home for disabled Michigan veterans. This act resulted from the efforts of Civil War veterans who were members of the Grand Army of the Republic. The home was dedicated in December 1886 with speeches by Governor Russell A. Alger, Governor-elect Cyrus G. Luce, former Governor Austin Blair and various legislators. The need for nursing care was soon realized, and in 1891 an 80-bed hospital and an 80-bed annex were added to the 320-bed main building. A 30-bed unit for women dependents was built in 1893. In 1894 the fountain and the Civil War soldiers statue in the cemetery were completed. They are the only remaining structures of that period. A new hospital was built in 1909.

Side Two

These buildings served Civil War veterans until 1938, when the last resident veteran of that conflict died. Veterans of the Spanish-American War and World War I were then being admitted, making construction of the Mann and Rankin buildings necessary. By 1965, World War II and Korean War veterans were using the facility in such numbers that a new concept of services was needed. This was realized in 1975, as increasing numbers of Vietnam veterans required assistance, with the completion of a new building to replace many of the oldest structures. At the time of its centennial celebration, in 1986, the Michigan Veterans' Facility, with the support of an employee network, veterans' organizations, the Board of Managers and volunteers continued to serve the physical, emotional and spiritual needs of many of Michigan's disabled and needy veterans.

Veterans' Cemetery

In April 1886 the Board of Managers of the Michigan Veterans' Facility set aside five acres for a cemetery. The Grand Rapids posts of the Grand Army of the Republic dedicated the cemetery on Memorial Day, May 31, 1886. The original cemetery was designed in the form of a Maltese cross with 262 grave sites in each of its four sections. In 1894 a granite statue of a Civil War soldier was placed in the center of the cross. By the time of its centennial in 1986, the cemetery had recorded over four thousand burials of veterans and their dependents.

3000 Monroe Avenue NW, Grand Rapids; Michigan Soldiers' Home (Michigan Veterans' Facility); L1254C; July 23, 1985; 1986

Villa Maria

Villa Maria was founded by the Sisters of the Good Shepherd in 1904 as a haven for destitute young women. Many girls came here seeking shelter from negligent or abusive families; in later years some were referred by social service agencies. Villa Maria's mission was not only to educate, but to teach self-discipline and offer the women a new start. Residents learned a variety of skills so that they could become independent. The home was first located on Bridge Street and moved to the present site in 1904. In 1985 it became a retirement center.

1315 Walker NW, Grand Rapids; Villa Maria Complex (Industrial, Penitent, Chapel and Monastery Buildings); L1603A; December 15, 1988; 1989

In 1871, Jared Bresee of Ada built the Fallasburg Bridge over the Flat River. It is one of only three covered bridges surviving in Michigan. (*Fallasburg Covered Bridge*)

153

Voigt House

This elegant and perfectly preserved Victorian mansion was built for Carl G. A. Voigt in 1895. Voigt came to Grand Rapids in 1870 and ran a mill and dry goods store with W. G. Herpolsheimer. In 1902, when the partnership ended, Voigt took over the milling works. The house, designed by eminent local architect, William G. Robinson, was inspired by the chateaux at Chenonceaux, France. The interior is opulently furnished with original possessions of the Voigt family. In 1972, a year after the death of the last occupant, Ralph Voigt, the house became a public museum.

115 College Avenue SE, Grand Rapids; Voigt, Carl G. A., House; S419A; February 22, 1974; 1977

Robert W. Graham House

In 1873, Robert W. Graham designed and built this Italianate structure as a two-family residence. A native of England, Graham settled in Lowell in 1858. Here he worked as a brick mason, a farmer and a merchant. Graham's son Ernest, an architect, designed notable buildings in Chicago; Washington, DC; New York City; Cleveland and London. The Graham House was deeded to the city in 1954. In 1922 the public library moved into its west wing. The east wing became the headquarters of the local YMCA in 1960.

323-325 Main Street, Lowell; Graham House (Lowell Library); L126; June 19, 1971; 1982

William Hyser

William Hyser (1826-1909), pioneer surgeon and Civil War captain, came to Plainfield Township in 1850, when it was a lumber center. In 1852 he built this Greek Revival house as a home and an office for his medical and civic duties. He was at various times township clerk, school inspector and supervisor, and justice of the peace. The house has also served as a stagecoach station and a post office. In 1976 it was moved to its present site. The only remaining structure from the original Plainfield village, it is now restored as a museum.

Austerlitz Post Office

Plainfield was first settled in 1838. Its post office, known as the Austerlitz office because there was a Plainfield post office elsewhere, was established in 1843. It was later housed in this structure for a short time. At first mail came by horse; in 1848 it began to come by stagecoach; and in 1876, by rail via nearby Belmont. In the days before envelopes, letters were folded and closed by sealing wax and other means. The Austerlitz office operated until 1913 when it was consolidated into the one at Belmont.

6440 West River Road, west of Northland Drive and the Rogue River, Plainfield Township; Hyser House (William Hyser-Austerlitz Post Office); L582; February 23, 1978; 1981

Alton Pioneer Village

In the early 1830s the settlement known as Alton grew up in this vicinity. A log schoolhouse, the first in the township, was built on this corner in 1839. In 1842, Gideon Hendricks and Newcomb Godfrey organized the Christian Church Society, and in 1868 the society built this structure. The Honorable Walter White, justice of the peace for the village, served as the area's first postmaster from 1851 to 1866. W. H. Keech and his wife, Jenny (Carver), ran the general store that later served as the post office.

Side Two

Alton was a thriving village in the years following the Civil War. Porter's flour mill was built in 1865. By 1870, Edmund Ring had a sawmill a half-mile west of Alton Corners. There he made wooden farm wagons and rakes until around 1900. In 1880 the community boasted a cooper, three blacksmith shops, two carriage repair shops, two shoemakers, a general store, a cabinet maker and a machinery dealer. Alton began to lose population around 1900 after the Pere Marquette Railroad, which ran to nearby Moseley and Lowell, bypassed the village.

Intersection of Three Mile and Lincoln Lake roads, Vergennes Township; Alton Pioneer Village; L1580C; July 21, 1988; 1988

John Wesley Fallas House

John Wesley Fallas built this house in 1842 in the village which bears his family name. Fallas platted the village on land he purchased from the U.S. government in 1839. That year, after a bridge had been built across the Flat River, he constructed a three-story sawmill with a chair factory on the top floor. In 1840 he built the first gristmill in the area next to his saw-mill on the river. He used lumber from his sawmill to build this house, the oldest Greek Revival-style structure in the township.

John W. Fallas

John Wesley Fallas was born in 1812 at Nelson, New York, where his parents, William and Hannah (Stone) Fallas, had lived since leaving Massachusetts in 1804. After spending his childhood at Dryden, New York, he moved to Michigan in 1837, and the rest of the family followed. In 1841, John went back to New York to marry Phoebe Brown. After the couple's return to Fallasburg they had two sons, Henry B. and Charles Wesley Fallas. John and his wife lived in this house until their deaths in 1896 and 1891 respectively.

13893 Covered Bridge Road, Vergennes Township; Fallas, John Wesley, House; L1348B; October 23, 1986; 1988

Fallasburg Covered Bridge

John W. and Silas S. Fallas settled here in 1837, founding a village, which soon boasted a chair factory, sawmill and gristmill. About 1840 the first of several wooden bridges was placed across the Flat River, but all succumbed in a short time to high water and massive spring ice jams. Bridge builder Jared N. Bresee of Ada was given a contract in 1871 to build the present structure. Constructed at a cost of $1,500, the bridge has latticework trusses made of white pine timbers. As in all covered bridges, the roof and siding serve to protect bridge timbers from rot. Repairs in 1905 and 1945 have kept the bridge safe for traffic for one hundred years.

Covered Bridge Road, east of Fallasburg Park Road, over the Flat River, Vergennes Township; Fallasburg Covered Bridge (Fal-lasburg Covered Bridge); S197; February 12, 1959; 1971

Fallasburg Pioneer Village

Fallasburg was settled in 1837 by two brothers from Tompkins County, New York. In 1839, John Wesley Fallas purchased the northwest quarter of Section 24 and laid plans for a vil-lage. His brother, Silas S., also purchased land at that time. Other family members soon fol-lowed, making the long journey in covered wagons. John W. built a sawmill on the east bank of the Flat River in 1839. In it he established a chair factory that was a forerunner of the Kent County furniture industry. He soon added a gristmill.

Side Two

Fallasburg was a prosperous lumber town, boasting over one hundred inhabitants by 1850. At one time, it offered a hotel and an inn that served as a regular stop on the stagecoach route between Grand Rapids and Ionia. The town also had two general stores, two shoe and harness shops, a post office, a distillery and several blacksmith shops. This structure, the Fallasburg School, was built in 1867. The focal point of the town, it was the site of town meetings, box socials, funerals and church services.

North of Covered Bridge Road, south of McPherson Road, Vergennes Township; Fallasburg Pioneer Village; L1265C; August 22, 1985; 1987

Vergennes United Methodist Church

In 1843 a group of twelve emigrants from New England and western New York State founded the First Methodist Episcopal Church of Vergennes. Originally part of the circuit running from Grand Rapids to Boston, Michigan, the group first met at the log house of An-thony Yerkes. Later it used the Yerkes and Bailey log schools. Surnames of many of the pioneer parishioners—Fairchild, Kerr, McPherson, Odell, Bieri, Anderson—still graced the church's rolls in 1986.

Side Two

In the early 1860s the Vergennes Methodist congregation decided to build a permanent place of worship and appointed Charles Collar, A. R. Hoag and T. Crakes to the building committee. In 1864, Smith Bailey, a prominent local farmer, donated the land for the church. Completed in 1864 the white clapboard structure, with its simple design, reflects the eastern origins of its founders. By 1986 the church had been in continuous service for over a century.

NE corner of Bailey and Parnell roads, Vergennes Township; Vergennes United Methodist Church; L574; January 19, 1978; 1986

Beginning in 1844, Fort Wilkins was manned to protect copper interests and miners. Abandoned in 1870, the fort is now a museum. (*Fort Wilkins*)

Keweenaw

Fort Wilkins

As soon as miners began to enter the Copper Country, appeals were made to the army for protection from resentful Indians. Thus, in 1844, Fort Wilkins was built. Two companies of infantry stood guard at this early copper mining and shipping center. In 1846, during the Mexican War, the force was withdrawn. It was replaced only from 1867 to 1869.

*NOTE: Fort abandoned 1870; Fort Wilkins State Park, Grant Township; Fort Wilkins; S33; July 19, 1956; 1957

Lake Shore Drive Bridge

This bridge, completed in 1915, was one of two bridges erected simultaneously by the Michigan State Highway Department across the Eagle River. The second was located in

The Wisconsin Bridge and Iron Company of Milwaukee constructed this state highway bridge over the Eagle River in 1915. (*Lake Shore Drive Bridge*)

nearby Phoenix. Prior to 1915 a Pratt through truss bridge crossed the fifty-three-foot gorge here. It deteriorated and was replaced with this structure. The highway department designed the bridge, which was constructed by the Wisconsin Bridge & Iron Company of Milwaukee. The Smith-Byers-Sparks Company of Houghton provided the concrete abutments for this steel riveted Warren deck truss bridge, which is 139 feet long. The main span measures 105 feet long and 17 feet wide. In 1990 this bridge was converted to pedestrian use when the adjacent timber bridge opened.

Eagle River

In 1843 the Lake Superior Copper Company purchased several land leases for mining. Two years later the Cliff Mine, alleged to be "the first great copper mine in the Western Hemisphere," was opened by the Pittsburgh & Boston Company. The mines attracted large numbers of Germans, Cornishmen and Irishmen and gave rise to other industries. On August 29, 1846, the *Lake Superior News and Miners' Journal* boasted that Eagle River had "the appearance of a thriving village." In 1850, Prussian immigrant Frank Knivel opened the Knivel Brewery, and in 1862 the Eagle River Fuse Company was established southeast of here on the river. The company manufactured twenty-five thousand feet of fuse per day for use in the mines. In 1861, Keweenaw County was set off from Houghton County and Eagle River became the county seat.

Lake Shore Drive at the Eagle River, Eagle River, Houghton Township; Lake Shore Drive Bridge (M-26 Bridge); S613A; May 10, 1990; 1991

Lake

Lake County

This county was originally set off in 1840 and first named *Aishcum* after a well-known Potawatomi chief. In 1843 the name was changed to Lake. For three decades it was attached to neighboring counties until 1871 when settlement was sufficient to warrant organization. Baldwin, the county seat, was settled in 1872. The county's forests helped make Michigan a leading lumbering state. Farming and the tourist industry are the chief activities. Wildlife is abundant.

County Courthouse, Baldwin; Lake County Informational Designation; S184; February 19, 1958; 1958

Brown Trout

On April 11, 1884, the first recorded planting of brown trout (*Salmo pariole*) in the United States was made into the Pere Marquette River system by the Northville, Michigan, Federal Fish Hatchery. The trout eggs from which the planting of forty-nine hundred fry was made had been obtained from Baron Friedrich Von Behr of Berlin, Germany, by Fred Mather, superintendent of the Cold Spring Harbor Federal Fish Hatchery at Long Island, New York. Some brown trout eggs had been shipped to the United States and distributed to various fisheries in the country for observation in 1883, but the Northville station was the first to stock American waters with the fish. From this beginning, the species (known in Germany as *Bachforelle*) has become widely established throughout the United States.

Two and one-half miles south of Baldwin on M-37, Pleasant Plains Township; Brown Trout Informational Designation; L1145C; February 15, 1984; 1984

Lapeer

Columbiaville Depot

In the nineteenth century, railroads provided the prime transportation link between small villages and the rest of the country. The first Columbiaville depot was built near this site in 1872. In 1893, William Peter (1824-1899) replaced that structure with this small Romanesque-inspired depot with its rounded-arch, beveled-glass windows. Peter, Columbiaville's dominant merchant and a millionaire lumber baron, built the new depot in an effort to spur the development of the village and assure the continued growth of his many businesses. By prior agreement, he gave the building to the Detroit-Bay City Railroad Company in exchange for having a line run through the community. The property was deeded to the company for one dollar in 1893. It served as a train station until 1964. The depot now houses the Columbiaville Rotary Club and a public library.

4643 First Street, Columbiaville; Detroit-Bay City Railroad Company Columbiaville Depot (Columbiaville Rotary Club and Public Library); L750A; October 23, 1979; 1981

United Methodist Church

This handsome Romanesque structure was completed in 1897 for the Methodist Protestant Church of Columbiaville. Local Methodists, with the assistance of circuit riders, had organized the church some forty years earlier. In 1865 the congregation erected a parsonage. They held church services there until 1880, when their first church was built. That early church was struck by lightning and burned in 1896. The following year, this red brick church was completed on the same site at a cost of $3,000. It has also been used for school graduation and baccalaureate ceremonies and other community gatherings.

4696 Pine Street, Columbiaville; Columbiaville Methodist Episcopal Church (Columbiaville United Methodist Church); L1162A; May 8, 1984; 1986

The William Peter Mansion

This structure, completed in 1896, was the home of William Peter (1824-1899). Peter, a prominent Columbiaville businessman, was a rags-to-riches character. Around 1847 he came to the area from Germany via New York State, a penniless immigrant. Immediately he began working in a local sawmill. He invested his earnings in large tracts of land and platted the village of Columbiaville in 1871. From 1879 to 1899, Peter developed the community. He built a gristmill, a woolen mill, houses for his workmen, a school, a church and several commercial buildings. Most of Columbiaville was owned and dominated by him. His wife, Roxanna, planned this Italianate residence, which still displays its original hardwood floors and decorative woodwork in oak, mahogany, walnut, cherry and maple.

4707 Water Street, Columbiaville; Peter, The William, Mansion (Peter-DeWitt House); L751A; October 23, 1979; 1981

Dryden Depot

The area now known as Dryden was settled in 1834. By 1880 it was a hamlet of about three hundred people. A marketing center surrounded by rich farm land, it turned to the railroad to increase its prosperity. Its citizens, spurred by the local Ladies Library Association, contributed $11,000 to help defer construction costs in order to bring the railroad to Dryden. On October 3, 1883, the Pontiac, Oxford and Port Austin Railroad passenger train rolled into town. Over five hundred spectators, the Thornville cornet band and a cannon were on hand to salute the train.

Side Two

This modest board-and-batten structure was erected in 1883 as a depot on the Pontiac, Oxford and Port Austin Railroad (known as the Pollyann and later named Pontiac, Oxford and Northern). As with most small-town depots, it soon became the center of community activity. In 1884 it was the setting of a gala "leap year" party. Purchased by the Grand Trunk in 1909, the station continued to be used for passenger service until 1955 and as a freight agency until October 9, 1973. It was moved here in 1979 and opened as a museum in 1981.

Railroad Street, north of Main Street, Dryden; Grand Trunk Railroad Depot (Dryden Depot); L460; August 6, 1976; 1985

Ladies Library Hall

The Ladies Library Association was established in 1871 to provide reading material at a small cost to the community. In the beginning the association only allowed married women to be members and charged an annual fee of one dollar. The women of the association were also involved in charitable works, such as giving aid to Northern Michigan victims of fire in 1881. The association built this Italianate structure in 1885 for $1,500. The first floor contained the library, dining room and kitchen. The second floor hall, which includes a stage, continues to be used for plays and community meetings. Dryden Township accepted the building in 1974 and made it the public library.

5480 Main Street, Dryden; Dryden Ladies Library Association Hall (Ladies Library Hall); L669A; June 15, 1979; 1988

General Squier Park

Major General George Owen Squier (1865-1934) was a noted soldier and scientist. Graduating from West Point in 1887, he subsequently led the United States Signal Corps. He was also Chief of the Army Air Service during World War I and military attache in London during the postwar period. Working in the capacity of science, he discovered the multiplex telegraph system, which made him world renowned. The general held membership in the National Academy of Sciences, London Physical Society and the Royal Institute of Great Britain. Although he was denied royalties because of his army affiliations, Squier continued to contribute to the world of invention and discovery. He perfected much of his work at his country estate, which he opened as this free public park for the people of the community.

Side Two

General Squier held a great love for his community and showed this by establishing a country club in 1918 for the people of the entire area. The club was originally known as the "Golden Rule Club" for the general's only rule was that visitors should leave the grounds and equipment as they found them. In 1918, Squier purchased the old mill, built in 1871, and converted it into a cottage. In 1919 a building known as Forest Hall was constructed and served as the main meeting, dance and banquet area of the park. Other structures include a variety of rustic shelters, teahouses and a look-out tower. The general spent many hours of creative work in the tower as well as offering its use to the public. Lapeer County Parks, Recreation and Conservation Commission now administers this quaint little country club.

4725 South Mill Road, Dryden Township; Dryden Community Country Club-General Squier Historic Park; L534; June 6, 1977; 1978

Lapeer County

Set off by Governor Cass in 1822, this county took its name from the French *La Pierre*, a translation of the Indian name for the Flint River. Settlers began to arrive in 1828. The county seat, founded in 1831, was also named Lapeer. Organization of the county government took place in 1835. This courthouse, built in 1839, is the oldest one still in use in Michigan. Farming is the county's principal economic activity, and it was here that the first local Grange in Michigan was founded in 1872.

Courthouse Square, Nepessing Street, M-21, Lapeer; Lapeer County Courthouse; S175; September 17, 1957; 1958

Pioneer Bank

Pioneer Bank was founded in 1885 as a state bank, and reorganized in 1889. President Frederick Howard, Vice President Albert Sholes and Cashier Charles W. Ballard were bank officers. In 1903 this lot was purchased from Sholes, and soon after the board selected Bay City architects Clark & Munger to design new offices. A bank was partially constructed, but it burned before completion. The present classical-inspired structure replaced the original and opened in 1906. In 1982 the bank was listed in the National Register of Historic Places.

4046 Huron Street, North Branch; Pioneer State Bank No. 36 (Pioneer Bank); L752A; October 23, 1979; 1991

Leelanau

Greilickville

This village was first known as Norristown, in honor of Seth and Albert Norris who opened a gristmill here about 1853. In the mid-1850s Godfrey Greilick and sons, natives of Bohemia, built a small, water-powered sawmill. The steam-powered Greilick Brothers mill replaced this in a few years. Until its destruction by fire about 1907 the mill was one of the most important on Grand Traverse Bay, cutting in 1883 8.5 million feet of hardwood lumber. Other industries in the nineteenth century included a brickyard, brewery [and] tannery. When the Manistee and Northeastern Railroad entered town in 1892 the station was called Greilicks, and soon the village also took this name. Population peaked at about two hundred, and in 1902 the post office was discontinued.

129 West Bay Shore Drive, Elmwood Township; Greilickville Informational Designation; L214; November 27, 1972; 1973

The intricate metal grave markers at St. Wenceslaus Cemetery demonstrate the settlement's Bohemian heritage. (*St. Wenceslaus Church and Cemetery*)

Empire Lumber Company

The Empire Lumber Company operated from 1887 to 1917, dominating this once-booming lumber town. Empire, incorporated in 1895, derived its name from the schooner *Empire*, which was icebound here during a storm in 1865. George Aylsworth operated the first mill between 1873 and 1883. Potter and Struthers built a second mill in 1885, which T. Wilce Company purchased in 1887. Called the Empire Lumber Company, it expanded to one of the largest and best equipped hardwood mills in the area, capable of producing up to twenty million feet of lumber a year. Docks, several businesses and a railroad sprung up in Empire. Destroyed by fire in 1906, the mill was quickly rebuilt. The mill burned again in 1917. With most of the nearby virgin timber gone, the mill was not replaced. Empire is now a picturesque village near the Sleeping Bear Dunes National Lakeshore.

Village Park, Niagra Street, Empire; Empire Lumber Company Informational Designation; L567; November 7, 1977; 1978

Early State Parks

By the end of World War I, with the rapid growth of the recreation industry in Michigan, a need for a state-wide parks system had arisen. In 1919 the State Park Commission was established. D. H. Day State Park, honoring the commission's chairman, was the first park that it set up. When state parks were transferred to the Conservation Department in 1921 over twenty other sites had been acquired, most of them, like D. H. Day State Park, beautifully located on lake shores.

Sleeping Bear Dunes National Lakeshore, four miles west of Glen Arbor, near the junction of M-109 and M-22, Glen Arbor Township; Early State Parks Informational Site; S173; September 17, 1957; 1957

Omena Presbyterian Church

In 1839 the Reverend Peter Dougherty founded Old Mission, the first Protestant mission in the Grand Traverse area. The church, comprising Indians and whites, was organized in 1843. After 1850 the Indians were allowed to buy land; they and the church moved to Omena, or New Mission in 1852. This church, resembling those of New England was built and dedicated in 1858. Since the 1880s it is used mostly in summer. It remains relatively unchanged from the original.

M-22, Leelanau Township; Grove Hill New Mission Church (Omena Presbyterian Church); S350; October 29, 1971; 1974

St. Wenceslaus Church and Cemetery

In the 1860s and 1870s settlers from Bohemia (now part of Czechoslovakia) came to this area and worked at the Leland Lake Superior Iron Foundry and the Gill sawmill. Catholics attended Mass at Holy Trinity Church in Leland until the church burned in 1880. In 1890 the first St. Wenceslaus Church was built and the cemetery established. Ornate metal grave markers reflect the Bohemian heritage, as do the names Bourda, Houdek, Hula, Jelinek, Kalchick, Kirt, Kolarik, Korson, Kovarik, Maresh, Novotny, Reicha and Sedlacek, which appear in the cemetery. The church membership doubled by 1908. In 1914 volunteers hauled bricks and other materials to this site and built the present church. This Late Gothic Revival church was completed during that year.

Intersection of County Roads 626 (Kolarik Road) and 637, Leelanau Township; St. Wenceslaus Roman Catholic Church and Cemetery; L1671A; July 20, 1989; 1990

Leland Historic District (Fishtown)

This commercial fishing district has provided a livelihood for residents of the town for over a century. Fishermen reached the fishing grounds of Lake Michigan by way of the Leland River (Carp River) using small sailboats until the introduction of primitive gas-powered oak boats around 1900. Small fishing shanties and related buildings such as ice and smoke houses were constructed during the peak years of the industry, which spanned the first three decades of the twentieth century. Now gray and weather-beaten, some still serve their original purpose. Other buildings in the district date back to Leland's lumbering and iron smelting era in the latter half of the nineteenth century. Leland continues to be a commercial fishing area as well as the headquarters for transportation to the Manitou Islands.

Roughly bounded by the park, Main Street, Avenue A and the harbor, Leland Township; Leland Historic District (Fishtown); S407; June 28, 1973; 1977

Great Lakes Sport Fishery

Great Lakes sport trolling was pioneered off Northport in the early 1920s. Traverse City native George Raff was the first to discover that lake trout could be caught by trolling in Grand

The shanties lining the Carp River in Leland in this 1930s photograph of "Fishtown" were converted to shops to support a new industry—tourism. (*Leland Historic District*)

Traverse Bay's protected waters. Prior to this, trout fishing was mainly a commercial enterprise, in which large quantities of the species were caught by net. Traverse City restaurant owners eagerly bought Raff's catches. Starting with one small boat, about sixteen feet long, Raff later began the area's first sports charter service. He charged each angler one dollar an hour, and guaranteed success. Methods he and his wife, Nell, developed for catching trout and other game fish species have spread throughout the Great Lakes.

Side Two

Sport trolling for lake trout almost vanished in the 1940s due to over-fishing by commercial netters and sea lamprey attacks on the trout. Chemicals finally controlled the lampreys, while state laws outlawed gill nets. In the 1960s, the Michigan Fishery Commission planted coho and Chinook salmon for a new sport fishery. Using the methods developed near Northport in the 1920s, plus other techniques—such as using piano wire, wooden and metal reels and lures made from tin cans and bicycle spokes—trollers again began catching salmon, brown and lake trout and steelheads throughout most of the Great Lakes. In 1981 sport fishing brought Michigan over $3 billion dollars in tourist revenues and attracted 700,000 licensed anglers in the Great Lakes.

Village Marina, 105 Rose, Northport; Great Lakes Sport Fishery Informational Designation; L1167C; May 8, 1984; 1984

Lenawee

Adrian College

Chartered on March 28, 1859, Adrian College traces its origins back to a Wesleyan Methodist theological institute founded at Leoni, Michigan, in 1845. This institution later became Michigan Union College. Strongly antislavery in its sentiments, the school was moved to Adrian in 1859 through the efforts of the antislavery leader and educator, Reverend Asa Mahan, who was elected first president of the new Adrian College. The college was transferred to the Methodist Protestant Church in 1868, and here for seventy-one years, leaders of this denominational union of American Methodism resulted in the establishment of the Methodist Church. Adrian College is affiliated with this great church body.

110 South Madison, Adrian; Adrian College; S227; January 16, 1962; 1962

Adrian Union Hall

In 1863, Charles M. Croswell (Michigan governor 1877-1881) formed an association to construct a new theater. An 1866 bird's-eye view of Adrian shows the completed exterior. Originally designated the Adrian Union Hall, by 1887 it was called Croswell Opera House. The theater hosted such performers as Maude Adams, Edwin Booth, Mrs. Patrick Campbell, Charles Frohman, Victor Herbert and the Gilmore Band, Joe Jefferson, Thomas W. Kean, James Whitcomb Riley, Otis Skinner and John Philip Sousa. In 1921 the interior of the building was renovated to show motion pictures. In 1967 the building was rescued by the Adrian Foundation from threatened demolition. Its care was then entrusted to the new Croswell Opera House and Fine Arts Association.

129 East Maumee Street, between Broad and Main streets, Adrian; Adrian Union Hall-Croswell Opera House; S478; March 2, 1976; 1986

County Courthouse

Lenawee County was first settled in 1824 at Tecumseh, which the Territorial Legislature subsequently made the county seat. Pioneers, mostly from upper New York State, then established Blissfield and Adrian, the latter called Logan. The largest Indian tribe in the area was the Potawatomi. In 1838 the first state legislature moved the Lenawee seat of justice from Tecumseh to Adrian. The first courthouse in Adrian was built in 1837 but burned in 1852. Immediately purchasing this site, formerly the western terminus of the Erie and Kalamazoo Railroad, the county erected a temporary courthouse. The present Romanesque-style edifice was completed in 1885 and features round-arched entrances and an ornate tower. Its exterior is also adorned with classic reliefs and terra-cotta trim. Since 1885 this impressive structure has been the seat of Lenawee County government.

301 North Main Street, Adrian; Lenawee County Courthouse; L365; November 14, 1974; 1981

162

St. John's Lutheran Church

The Reverend William Hattestaedt helped organize St. John's Lutheran Church in 1847. Until their first church was completed in 1849, the original congregation, fourteen German families, met in a church that belonged to the Episcopalians. Services were held every three to four weeks until 1850, when the Reverend Phillip J. Trautman was installed as the first full-time pastor. On July 1, 1861, the congregation laid the cornerstone for the present church. The structure was dedicated on June 29, 1862. It was enlarged in 1896. The handsome stained-glass windows depicting Bible stories were installed in 1914. Since its organization, St. John's Lutheran Church, the mother church of the denomination in Adrian, has held continuous services.

121 South Locust Street, NE corner of Church Street, Adrian; St. John's Lutheran Church (St. John's Lutheran Church); L887A; February 23, 1981; 1982

St. Joseph Hospital and Home for the Aged

In the old elm farmhouse that once stood on this site, six Dominican nuns opened the St. Joseph Hospital and Home for the Aged on May 20, 1884. They were sent by Mother Hyacinth Scheininger, prioress of Holy Rosary Convent in New York City, at the request of Father Casimir Rohowski, pastor of Adrian's St. Joseph Church. From 1884 to 1896 the St. Joseph Hospital cared for 138 patients and eighteen orphans, who in 1887 were accommodated in a larger facility. In 1896 the hospital was closed and converted into the St. Joseph Academy. It later became the center of the present Motherhouse of the Adrian Dominican Sisters. The farmhouse was demolished in 1926.

1269 Siena Heights Drive, Adrian; St. Joseph Hospital and Home for the Aged Informational Designation; L1178C; June 15, 1984; 1984

St. Joseph's Catholic Church

German immigrants desiring to practice Catholicism in their native language founded St. Joseph's parish in 1863. Father John G. Ehrenstrasser became the first pastor in 1865. This handsome brick and stone church, the second house of worship for this parish, was constructed at a cost of $30,000 and dedicated on October 13, 1879, by Bishop Casper H. Borgess. While St. Joseph's tranquil interior has seen several changes, its stately exterior has been altered only slightly in over a century.

415-419 Ormsby Street, Adrian; St. Joseph's Roman Catholic Church (St. Joseph Catholic Church Complex); L671A; June 15, 1979; 1980

Blissfield Hotel

Located on the site of a log tavern constructed around 1839, this three-story brick hotel with semi-circular windows was built in 1875, fifty-one years after Blissfield was settled. William Drew built this structure and named it Drew's Hotel. The community held dances on the third floor known as Drew's Music Hall. Called the Pennsylvania House at the turn of the century, this hotel was a popular gathering place for sports enthusiasts who fished on the nearby River Raisin. Later it became Coon's Tavern and is now called the Blissfield Hotel in which is located the Steam Inn. The village grew up around this intersection, first as an agricultural processing and trade center, then as a rail station on the Lake Shore & Michigan Railroad and now as a major cattle shipping and feeding area.

102 West Adrian Street, Blissfield; Blissfield Hotel (demolished); L459; August 6, 1976; 1977

Carpenter House

This Greek Revival mansion was built in 1851 for David Carpenter, one of Lenawee County's most prominent early residents. Born in New York State, he moved to Blissfield in 1838, and became a wealthy farmer and merchant. After his death in 1891, the house served as a private residence until 1960, when it became a restaurant. The building's only major exterior alteration has been the addition of second story wings and porches.

424 West Adrian Street, Blissfield; Carpenter, David, House (Hathaway House); L136; August 13, 1971; 1975

Erie & Kalamazoo Railroad

The first railroad operated west of the Alleghenies, the Erie and Kalamazoo, was chartered on April 22, 1833, to connect Port Lawrence (later named Toledo) with the Kalamazoo River via Adrian. A horse-drawn car made the first trip from Toledo to Adrian on November 2, 1836, running on strap iron strips spiked to oak rails. From 1852 to 1857 the line, then a

Peter Dederichs of Detroit designed St. Joseph's Catholic Church, an Italian Renaissance Revival church, built in 1879. (*St. Joseph's Catholic Church*)

part of the Michigan Southern Railroad, was a link in the only unbroken rail route from the East Coast to Chicago. As a part of the Lake Shore and Michigan Southern, the New York Central, the Penn Central and the Conrail systems, "The Old Road," as it continued to be known, carried passengers until November 1956. The trackage in the Blissfield area later became the property of the state of Michigan.

Side Two

In addition to being the first railroad built west of the Allegheny Mountains, the Erie and

Kalamazoo was in 1837 the first line west of the Alleghenies to operate a steam locomotive. Built in Philadelphia, the locomotive, the "Adrian No. 1," was brought west via the Erie Canal and Lake Erie. When the locomotive ran out of wood or water, passengers had to scour the countryside for them. A simple round trip between Toledo and Adrian took one day. The Erie and Kalamazoo was also the first western line to operate as an interstate railroad, to carry U.S. mail and to build a branch line. As a separate corporation, the Erie and Kalamazoo existed as a leased railroad, paying regular dividends to its shareholders, for more than 125 years.

Note: The Erie and Kalamazoo was not the first railroad built west of the Alleghenies. 424 West Adrian Street, Blissfield; Erie and Kalamazoo Railroad Informational Designation (David Carpenter House); L1146C; February 15, 1984; 1986

First Presbyterian Church

This church was organized in 1829, one of the oldest Presbyterian groups in the state. The sanctuary, completed in 1849, is largely the work of the Reverend John Monteith, who preached here 1845-1855. A graduate of Princeton Seminary, he came to Michigan in 1816. In that year he founded the first Protestant society in Detroit. In 1817 he became the first president of the University of Michigan. After his service in Blissfield, he retired from active ministry.

306 Franklin Street, NW corner of Maple Street, Blissfield; First Presbyterian Church of Blissfield; S271; June 11, 1965; 1966

St. Joseph's Church

St. Joseph's Church originated as a missionary church during the 1850s. Priests from Adrian, Clinton, Manchester, Tecumseh and Monroe served the parish until the first resident priest arrived in 1954. The original church, which is still part of the present structure, was constructed in 1854 by Irish pioneers. In 1863 the first Mass was held in the church. The tower and stained-glass windows were added in 1911. In 1928, Father Joseph Pfeffer from St. Mary's in Manchester served here and oversaw the enlargement and remodeling of the church to its present form. The transept was built and nave enlarged, transforming the church to a cruciform plan. The red tile roof, the tower and the use of mosaic, tile and wrought iron in the interior give the church its Spanish Mission flavor.

St. Joseph's Shrine

As part of the 1928 expansion of St. Joseph's Church, a shrine—inspired by the grotto at Our Lady of Lourdes in France—was designed. In 1932 work began on the fourteen outdoor stations of the cross, which depict scenes of the *Via Dolorosa* (the sorrowful way), that Jesus walked to Calvary. The footpath begins at a replica of Pontius Pilate's palace then winds past balconied houses, through the judgment gate and ends at Christ's tomb. The crucifixion scene is sculpted from Carrara marble. Two Mexican artisans, Dionicio Rodriquez and Ralph Corona, under the supervision of Leo Ouelette, sculpted the steps, archways and railings from wet cement to resemble stone and timber.

8743 US-12, Brooklyn, Cambridge Township; St. Joseph's Church and Shrine; S611A; April 19, 1990; 1991

The Walker Tavern

This historic building, a link with the bygone pioneer era, dates back to 1832. Here, at the junction of the Chicago Road and the road from Monroe, a small inn was opened by Sylvester Walker of Cooperstown, New York. Before long the Walker Tavern was a famed stopping-place for stagecoaches and the hundreds of pioneer wagons that passed here daily. Daniel Webster and James Fenimore Cooper were among the noted guests who stayed at this storied inn, which was also a center for the community. In the early days church services were held in the barroom. In 1921, Frederic Hewitt purchased the tavern, restoring it as a museum.

NOTE: Daniel Webster's and James Fenimore Cooper's presence at Walker Tavern is undocumented. *Erected at the junction of US-12 and M-50, Cambridge Township; Walker Tavern; HB16; February 19, 1958; 1959

Beginning in the 1840s, the Walker Tavern housed travelers along the Chicago Road. (*Walker Tavern*)

The Erie & Kalamazoo Railroad was chartered in 1833 to connect Lake Erie at Toledo, Ohio, and the Kalamazoo River at Adrian, Michigan. (*Erie & Kalamazoo Railroad*)

Clinton United Methodist Church

Here stands Michigan's oldest Methodist church building in continual use. In 1835 members of the Methodist Episcopal Church of Clinton purchased this land. They began construction in 1837 and by 1843 raised sufficient funds for the completion of this church with its thick brick walls and German stained-glass windows. In 1897 the tower was added; twenty years later the north wing was built. This pioneer church remains an inspiration to Methodists throughout the state.

SE corner of Tecumseh and Church streets, Clinton; Clinton United Methodist Church; L506; February 7, 1977; 1977

Clinton Woolen Mill

The Clinton Woolen Mill was a vital part of the economy of this area for over ninety years. Clinton's original mill was completed in 1867 at a cost of $95,000. Fire destroyed that structure in 1886. In less than a year, the mill was back in operation in the present building, the second to be erected here. The mill had the necessary equipment and skilled workers for making wool and for complex dye processing. One of the last woolen mills in the area, this company discontinued operations in 1957.

303 West Michigan Avenue (US-12), Clinton; Clinton Woolen Manufacturing Company; L655B; April 24, 1979; 1979

Site of the Clinton Inn

The Sauk and Potawatomi Indians first traversed this main thoroughfare as a portion of the Sauk Trail. It became a military road after Congress appropriated funds in the 1820s for survey and construction of a route from Detroit to Chicago. Built about 1830 on this site, the Clinton Inn served travelers on the Chicago Road who journeyed by stagecoach, covered wagon and horseback. Originally called the Eagle Hotel, the inn became the Union Hotel during the Civil War and lodged soldiers coming to and from the front. Walter Hubbell Smith purchased the inn in 1864. His daughter and heir, Mary Ella Smith, sold the building in 1927 to Henry Ford who moved it to Greenfield Village. There the inn was restored and reopened in 1929.

Clinton

Early settlers who came here from New York via the Erie Canal named this community in honor of DeWitt Clinton, the governor of their native state. First settled in 1829, Clinton became an important center of trade because of its location on the Chicago Road at the River Raisin. Only a decade after its settlement, the village had ten general stores, several blacksmith shops and a hardware store. Five religious groups organized and built churches during this era. In 1832, Clinton's first school was established; four years later a flouring mill began operation. A railway with wooden rails constructed about 1837 ran for a few years and by 1857 it had steel tracks. In order to utilize local wool production, village businessmen organized the Clinton Woolen Mills in 1866, which employed many area people until closing in 1957.

Clinton Village Offices, 119 East Michigan Avenue, Clinton; Clinton Inn Informational Site ; L474; November 3, 1976; 1977

St. John's Episcopal Church

In 1835, under the leadership of the Reverend William N. Lyster, this church was founded as St. Patrick's Episcopal Church. The Reverend Lyster had organized a church in nearby Tecumseh in 1833, and this church was a mission of that pioneer parish until 1836. In 1853 the parish voted to change its name to St. John's Episcopal Church. Completed in 1835, this is the oldest remaining Episcopal church building in Michigan. Its hand-hewn beams, wainscoting and stained-glass windows all date back to 1835.

122 East Church Street, Clinton; St. John's Episcopal Church; L875B; January 8, 1981; 1984

Davenport House

In 1834, Henry W. Sisson of New York settled here and built a log tavern, located on Evans Lake where the Chicago Road enters the Irish Hills. The tavern was purchased in 1839 by John Davenport, who owned the property until 1864. During this time the present building was constructed. Known as Lancaster House from 1864 to 1884, the building was later to serve as a general store and post office. As late as 1900 stagecoaches stopped here regularly.

1280 US-12, at Evans Lake, east of Walter J. Hayes State Park, Franklin Township; Davenport House (Bauer Manor); L123; May 18, 1971; 1971

Wooden Stone School

In 1850 the Reverend Robert Wooden built this school, located in Cambridge School District No. 6. It is an example of early fieldstone construction, commonly found in the southern part of the Lower Peninsula. The school closed in 1955, and in 1979 was condemned by Cambridge Township. A group of citizens convinced the township to postpone demolition; in 1983 the site was deeded to the Wooden Old Stone School Association. The group restored the schoolhouse in 1989.

NE corner of Stephenson Road and Hawkins Highway, Onsted; Cambridge Sixth District School (Stone School); L672A; June 15, 1979; 1989

Palmyra Presbyterian Church

Sixteen persons from Presbyterian congregations in Tecumseh, Blissfield and Adrian founded this church in 1836. The following year, the Reverend John Walker became their minister. They held services in a schoolhouse on the west side of the River Raisin. In 1842-1843 the congregation erected its first church. In 1861 the present structure was completed. Much of the labor and materials were donated. Originally designed in the form of a New England meetinghouse, the building has been remodeled several times.

6730 Palmyra Road, NE corner of Rouget Road, Palmyra Township; Palmyra Presbyterian Church (Palmyra Community United Presbyterian Church); L1284B; November 26, 1985; 1986

La Plaisance Bay Pike

In 1832 the federal government appropriated funds for survey and construction of a road, which was to begin at La Plaisance Bay, near Monroe. The road was to pass through Tecumseh, and join with the Chicago Road at Cambridge Junction. The road was completed in 1835. A few years later several boggy sections of the road were covered by oak planks. During early statehood years, thousands of settlers bound for western Michigan used this route.

Tecumseh Community Center on M-50, near the Monroe County line (US-23), Ridgeway Township; La Plaisance Bay Pike Informational Designation; S269; May 12, 1965; 1966

Evans House

Musgrove Evans built this dwelling in 1826. It is the oldest frame house in Tecumseh and believed to be the oldest still standing in Lenawee County. Evans was a pioneer settler in this area. He platted the village of Tecumseh, served as its first postmaster and probate judge and helped to organize Michigan's first temperance society. Used as an inn and home, the Evans House was moved to this location in 1886 from the northeast corner of Ottawa Street and Chicago Boulevard. However, its appearance has changed little over the years.

409-411 East Logan Street, NE corner of Maumee Street, Tecumseh; Evans, Musgrove, House; S351; October 29, 1971; 1980

Al Meyers Airport

The Al Meyers Airport is a privately owned airport designed for public use. It was established in 1939-1940 by a twenty-seven-year-old airman, designer and manufacturer, Al Meyers (1908-1976). When World War II broke out, Meyers received a contract to build planes for pilot training under the Civilian Pilot Training Program. He selected Tecumseh for his production site. His government contract ended just prior to the close of the war; however, he continued to manufacture planes for private use until 1966. This field, originally the Tecumseh Municipal Airport, was renamed Al Meyers Airport in 1975. The airport is still privately owned and is used for transporting manufactured goods and for the restoration of all types of airplanes, especially the Meyers plane.

Side Two

Al Meyers, a native of Allenhurst, New Jersey, settled in this area in 1939, after accepting a government contract to manufacture planes for pilot training. Prior to that he had visited the area as a barnstormer, selling airplane rides and performing aerobatics to raise money to build a prototype plane for the private flyer. In 1941 he formed the Meyers Aircraft Company. After the war, the company produced the Meyers 145 and four series of the Meyers 200, one of the most advanced private planes of its time. The company manufactured aluminum boats to help finance the production of these planes. In 1966 the Meyers 200 was sold to North American Rockwell, and production moved to Albany, Georgia. The boat division was sold in 1977. Proceeds from the sale were used to start the Allen H. Meyers Foundation.

Macon Road and Tecumseh-Clinton Highway, NE of Tecumseh, Tecumseh Township; Tecumseh Airport Informational Site (Al Meyers Airport); L1415C; May 15, 1987; 1987

Woodstock Manual Labor Institute

Prior Foster, an Ohio Negro, began this school "in the woods" in 1844 and four years later it was incorporated. Designed to serve "colored people and others," the institute taught a full range of subjects and was one of the nation's first integrated schools. The students worked in the fields and orchards to help support the school. Soon eight buildings were on the grounds. More than fifty students were in attendance, using a library of two thousand volumes. A fire in 1855 destroyed the main building, and the school was discontinued during the Civil War. The educational pioneering was continued by Foster's grandson, Dr. Laurence Jones, founder of the well-known Piney Wood School in Mississippi in 1909.

18123 Greenleaf Road, Woodstock Township; Woodstock Manual Labor Institute; S297; November 14, 1969; 1970

Livingston

Old Town Hall

Settled in 1832 by Maynard Maltby, this community was originally called Ore Creek for the stream that flows through it. In 1838 its name was changed to Brighton. It was incorporated as a village in 1867 and as a city in 1928. In 1878 the village council voted to build this hall. Local contractor James Collett completed it in 1879. The hall originally housed village council offices, a voting room, a jail and a firehouse. Its one-room weekend library grew into the public library that it housed for all but nine years from 1927 to 1981.

202 West Main Street, Brighton; Brighton Town Hall (Old Town Hall); L1010A; April 29, 1982; 1983

St. Paul's

When the Reverend William A. Clark, D.D., purchased his land in Brighton Township, he set aside an acre as a church site and established a cemetery near it. In 1837 he organized an Episcopal group and conducted its first services in his orchard. The group worshipped in rented quarters for over forty years before it erected this church. Ernest W. Arnold designed the English-style structure, which was built by local contractor James Collett. The church was completed in 1881. Reverend Clark's son John officiated at the first service.

200 West St. Paul Street, Brighton; St. Paul's Episcopal Church; L1011A; April 29, 1982; 1983

Kinsley S. Bingham

Twenty-five-year-old Kinsley Bingham left his New York home in 1833 saying: "Give me $500 and let me go to Michigan and I'll be governor in two years." He settled here, constructing this handsome Greek Revival house in 1842. Bingham's boast was not exaggerated, since he was elected to the legislature in 1836, serving five terms, and was U.S. congressman from 1847 to 1851. Adamantly opposed to slavery, he broke from the Democratic Party of the Fugitive Slave Act of 1850. The Republican Party chose Bingham as its candidate for governor in Jackson's famous "Under the Oaks" convention of 1854. Six months later he took office as the nation's first Republican governor, and in 1856 he was reelected. Becoming U.S. senator in 1859, Bingham died here on October 5, 1861.

13270 Silver Lake Road, between Kensington (Peer) and Dixboro roads, Green Oak Township; Bingham House; S406; June 28, 1973; 1973

In 1833, Kinsley Bingham said, "Give me $500 and let me go to Michigan and I'll be governor in two years." (*Kinsley Bingham*)

Spanish-American War Regiments

This was once the summer camp of Michigan's National Guard. Here in 1898 the five regiments, which were recruited in the state during the war with Spain, were organized. Ten men volunteered for every one who could be accepted. Two of the units, the Thirty-third and Thirty-fourth Michigan Infantry, saw action in Cuba during June and July 1898, in the fighting around Santiago. The Thirty-first Regiment served in the occupation of Cuba. The Thirty-second and Thirty-fifth remained in the United States. Of the nearly 6,700 men who served in these regiments 250 were fatalities. Most of these deaths resulted from disease, not from battle action.

Entrance to Island Lake State Park, two and one-half miles east of Brighton, Grand River Avenue, Green Oak Township; Spanish-American War Regiments Informational Designation; S134; January 19, 1957; 1957

Hamburg

The year 1831 marked the arrival of Hamburg's first settlers—Felix Dunlavey, Jesse Hall, Calvin Jackson, Cornelius Miller and Heman Lake—and their families. In 1835, Ann Arbor merchant E. F. Gay and Amariah Hammond purchased thirty acres of land in this area, constructed a dam and built the area's first sawmill. By 1837 the two men had sold their interests to the Grisson brothers, who had emigrated from Hamburg, Germany, in 1834. The Grissons also managed a store, a gristmill and a hotel. In 1837 the village of Hamburg was platted, and in 1840 its post office was established. John Grisson was the first postmaster. One hundred and fifty years after its founding, the village of nine hundred residents boasted a historic Episcopal church, a volunteer fire department, several stores and factories, a library, a cemetery and a township hall.

Edwin B. Winans

Edwin B. Winans (1826-1894) was the first Democrat to be elected governor of Michigan after the Civil War. Serving a two-year term starting in 1890, he instituted the secret ballot system. A native of New York, Winans moved to Livingston County, Michigan, at the age of eight. He attended Albion College and the University of Michigan Law School before leaving the state to seek his fortune in the California gold rush. In 1858 he returned to Michigan and

A training camp at Island Lake was the first taste of the military for Michigan's Spanish-American War recruits. (*Spanish-American War Regiments*)

purchased a four-hundred-acre farm in Hamburg. He enjoyed an active political career, serving as state representative (1861-1864), constitutional convention delegate (1867), township supervisor (1872-1873), Livingston County probate judge (1877-1881) and congressman (1883-1886). He died at his Winans Lake estate in Hamburg Township in 1894.

Outside Hamburg Cemetery, corner of Hamburg and Strawberry Lake roads, Hamburg Township; Governor Edwin B. Winans Informational Designation; S583C; July 17, 1986; 1986

St. Stephen's

This building is one of the oldest Episcopal churches in Michigan. St. Stephen's parish was organized in 1844, and construction of the church began almost immediately. Hiram Raymond of Hamburg was the contractor, and building funds were solicited in the East and in Europe. Donations were received from Hamburg, Germany, the native city of some parishioners. The clean, delicate lines of the church and the interesting tower make this one of the state's most intriguing churches.

10585 Hamburg Road, at the corner of Stone Street, Hamburg Township; St. Stephen's Church (St. Stephen's Episcopal Church); L78; February 27, 1970; 1970

Florence B. Dearing Museum

Hartland Township was settled in 1831. On this site distinguished early citizens Robert and Chauncey Crouse operated a general mercantile business. In 1891 this town hall was built. The hall later served as a fire station and center for community life. In 1970 it became the Florence B. Dearing Museum, honoring the librarian who collected and assembled memorabilia from the Hartland area.

3503 Avon Street, at the corner of Crouse Street, Hartland, Hartland Township; Hartland Town Hall; L411; August 15, 1975; 1976

Hartland Music Hall

This structure was constructed in 1858 as the Hartland First Congregational Church. It was purchased in 1929 for $500 by the Hartland Consolidated School Foundation, established by John Robert Crouse, Sr. In 1932 the remodeled building became the Hartland Music Hall, dedicated to promoting a creative, social and educational environment for the then rural community. The hall has been used for music festivals, plays, weddings and, since 1933, the annual presentation of Handel's *Messiah*.

3619 Avon Street, SE corner of George Street, Hartland, Hartland Township; Hartland First Congregational Church (Hartland Music Hall); L768A; January 18, 1980; 1986

Tom Walker's Gristmill

This mill, one of the last water-powered gristmills to operate in Michigan, was built in 1869. It was purchased by Tom Walker and John Browning for $10,000 in 1878. From then on the Walker family was involved with the mill for three generations. Tom Walker, a grandson, took over the mill's operation in 1926. Until he retired in 1969 and sold the mill, he ground grain for no more than seven cents a bag.

8507 Parshallville Road, junction of Cullen Road, Hartland Township; Tom Walker's Grist Mill (Parshallville Mill); L279; April 5, 1974; 1974

Ann Arbor Railroad

Howell raised $20,000 in 1885 to induce the Toledo, Ann Arbor & Northern Michigan to enter town. Many believed the town, already served by one railroad, would boom with a second line. Early in 1886 a right-of-way dispute erupted in an armed brawl between workmen of the two lines. The case was mediated in favor of the TAA&NM, and in the summer of 1886 this depot was built. The line was renamed the Ann Arbor Railroad in 1895.

126 Wetmore Street, between Michigan Avenue and Chestnut Street, Howell; Toledo, Ann Arbor and Northern Michigan Railroad Station (Ann Arbor Railway Station); L94; December 11, 1970; 1971

County Courthouse

Albert E. French designed this two-and-a-half-story brick and stone building. This edifice, completed in 1890, shows influence of Richardsonian architecture and has maintained many of its original Victorian furnishings. Peter and Marie Cowdry donated the land for the courthouse square with the provision that it revert to their heirs if no longer used for a courthouse. Local citizens presented the clock to the county as a gift. The people of Livingston County voted in 1976 to restore their courthouse, which is an area landmark.

200 East Grand River Avenue, Howell; Livingston County Courthouse; L391; April 4, 1975; 1978

St. John the Baptist Catholic Church

Irish immigrants founded a Catholic mission in Livingston County in 1843. The following year, two acres of land were purchased here and a log structure was erected for worship services. As the congregation grew it required a larger facility, and a frame structure was built onto the log church in later years. In 1868 the log portion was removed and the west end of the present corbeled brick building was erected. The cornerstone was consecrated at that time. In 1873 the frame segment was detached, moved across the road and used for services during construction of the present Gothic Revival structure. The church became a parish in 1974. Originally known as St. James, the St. John the Baptist congregation is the oldest Catholic congregation in Livingston County.

1991 Hacker Road, SW corner of M-59, Osceola Township; St. John Catholic Church and Cemetery; L598; May 17, 1978; 1982

Tyrone Township Hall

Tyrone Township was settled in 1834, and Joseph M. Becker was elected as the first township supervisor in 1838. Township meetings were held in the homes of the townsfolk until 1887, when this hall was erected on Hartland Road at a cost of $640. Locally referred to as the town house, it served as a gathering place for township business, elections and 4-H activities until a new hall was constructed in 1967. In 1975, as a bicentennial project, the town house was relocated, restored and rededicated on this site.

10408 Center Road, three-quarters of a mile east of US-23, Tyrone Township; Tyrone Township Hall; L704A; August 3, 1979; 1980

Luce

Helmer House Inn

Erected in 1881-1882 this two-and-a-half-story structure was built as a mission house and manse by Newberry's Presbyterian church. It served as a mission station until 1888, when

Gaylord Helmer—first postmaster and village deputy sheriff—purchased it for use as a general store and hotel. In 1894 the village of Helmer became a stagecoach mailstop and Gaylord Helmer added a second structure to accommodate more travelers.

Side Two

Charles and Jeanie Fyvie purchased the Helmer House Inn and store in 1904. The store housed the post office until 1920, when rural free delivery (RFD) was instituted. The Fyvie family continued to live here and operate the store and hotel until 1950. Following nearly three decades of disrepair and neglect, in 1981 the building received new windows, doors, porch, roof and stone facing and was reopened as a hotel to commemorate its centennial.

RD #3-County Road 417, one-half mile south of Highway 44, Lakefield Township; Helmer General Store and Resort (Helmer House Inn); L981A; January 11, 1982; 1983

Life Saving Station

Here stood the Two-Hearted River Life Saving Station, built in 1876. This station, like many others on the Great Lakes, was of the second class—erected at a cost of $4,790 and manned by volunteer crews. The facility, a simple two-story building with a small lookout tower, housed a lifeboat and other necessary equipment for recovering endangered sailors. An average crew consisted of six to eight experienced surfmen. In 1915 the Life Saving Service was integrated into the U.S. Coast Guard.

Side Two

Several shipwrecks occurred near the mouth of the Two-Hearted River, also referred to as the Twin River and the Big Two-Hearted River. Among these were the *Cleveland* (1864), the *W. W. Arnold* (1869) and the *Sumatra* (1875). After construction of the lifesaving station here in 1876, the lifesavers were responsible for brave rescues in the *Satellite* (1879) and the *Phineas S. Marsh* (1896) disasters. The station was decommissioned in the 1930s and the structure was razed in 1944.

Two-Hearted River Forest Campground, east of County Road 423, McMillan Township; Two-Hearted River Life-Saving Station Informational Site; L758B; December 12, 1979; 1980

Jail & Sheriff's Residence

Constructed in 1894, this graceful Queen Anne-style structure served as the Luce County jail and sheriff's residence for over seventy years. The Peninsular Land Company donated the site. The architectural firm of Lovejoy and DeMar, from Marquette, designed this sturdy edifice made of rough-hewn Jacobsville sandstone. The Luce County Historical Society rescued this building from demolition in 1975 and restored it as the Luce County Historical Museum, which opened in 1976.

411 West Harrie Street, Newberry; Luce County Sheriff's House and Jail (Luce County Historical Society); L408; August 15, 1975; 1980

The U.S. Life Saving Service arrived on the Great Lakes in 1879. Lifesaving crews used the breeches buoy to transport stranded sailors to shore. (*Life Saving Station*)

Mackinac

Bois Blanc Island

On August 3, 1795, Chippewa Chief Matchekewis ceded Bois Blanc to the United States as part of the Treaty of Greenville. The cession also included most of Ohio, part of Indiana, sixteen strategic sites on Michigan waterways and Mackinac Island. During the War of 1812, U.S. Navy Captain Arthur Sinclair's fleet took shelter at the island while waiting to attack the British at Fort Mackinac. In 1880 the island provided a haven to alleged murderer Henry English who escaped from Pennsylvania authorities before his trial. He was apprehended on Bois Blanc by Pinkerton agents, returned to Pennsylvania and acquitted. During the twentieth century, Bois Blanc's wilderness supported a lucrative lumber industry before giving way to tourism. Although primarily a resort in 1990, the island had forty-five permanent residents.

Side Two

Bois Blanc Island, known as "Bob-lo" to area residents, is twelve miles long, six miles wide and has six lakes. In 1827 the United States government platted the island. The U.S. Coast Guard established a life-saving station at Walker's Point in 1890. The following year the Pointe Aux Pins Association was formed. In 1908, on behalf of the association, President Walter B. Webb hired the Mason L. Brown Company, a Detroit surveying firm, to plat and record the Pointe Aux Pins subdivision. Pointe Aux Pins was the first resort community on the island. Much of Bois Blanc Island is state-owned forest land containing White and Norway pines that tower two hundred feet tall. As recently as the 1950s, Bois Blanc provided lumber to Mackinac Island where woodcutting is prohibited.

Ferry Dock, Bois Blanc Township; Bois Blanc Island Informational Designation; L1752C; May 10, 1990; 1990

The Northernmost Point of Lake Michigan

About a mile west of here is the northernmost point of Lake Michigan. This geographical location is of historical importance because the act of Congress, which created the territory of Michigan in 1805, used it to mark the western boundary of this new frontier governmental unit. The boundary line ran up the middle of Lake Michigan "to its northern extremity, and thence due North to the northern boundary of the United States." West of this line the Upper Peninsula in 1805 was part of Indiana Territory. In 1818, Michigan's boundary was pushed west to the Mississippi River. All of the U.P., along with what is now Wisconsin and part of Minnesota, came within the limits of the territory.

Roadside park on US-2, three miles east of Naubinway, Garfield Township; The Northernmost Point of Lake Michigan Informational Designation; S258; April 14, 1964; 1965

The British built Fort Mackinac during the American Revolution. The fort was garrisoned, at different times, by both British and American troops until 1895. (Fort Mackinac)

Epoufette

Epoufette has been a fishing village since 1859, when Amable Goudreau, born in Quebec around 1824, established a commercial fishery. More than a century after his death in 1882, some of his descendants continued fishing operations. Father Edward Jacker, then serving the St. Ignace and Mackinac Island missions, visited Epoufette in August 1875. He reported a thriving fishery, with nets as far as forty miles distant, which kept two coopers busy from dawn to dusk making barrels for shipment of salted fish to distant markets.

US-2 scenic turnout overlooking Epoufette Bay, Hendricks Township; Epoufette Informational Site; L1255C; July 23, 1985; 1986

Battlefield of 1814

Here in this area on August 4, 1814, an American force battled the British in a vain attempt to recapture the island, which the British had seized at the outbreak of the War of 1812. Coming ashore at what is known as British Landing, the Americans under Colonel George Croghan soon ran into strong resistance as they advanced inland. An attempt to outflank the British line was repulsed by Indians hidden in thick woods and resulted in the death of Major Andrew Holmes. Croghan withdrew when he found that he could not defeat the British.

Near Wawashkamo Golf Club, Mackinac Island; Battlefield of 1814 Informational Designation; S188; March 19, 1958; 1958

Beaumont Memorial

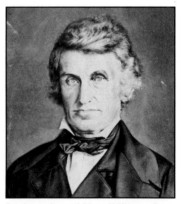

On June 6, 1822, Alexis St. Martin (1804-1880), a French Canadian, was accidentally shot in the stomach at this American Fur Company retail store. Dr. William Beaumont, M.D. (1786-1853), army surgeon at Fort Mackinac, nursed him back to health. Although St. Martin's physique was not impaired, his stomach wound refused to heal, leaving an opening through which the doctor could observe the digestive process. Beaumont convinced St. Martin to become the subject of a medical study of digestion and wrote several articles on the findings from these experiments. St. Martin married and fathered seventeen children. He out-lived Beaumont by twenty-seven years. The Michigan State Medical Society acquired the retail store in 1947 and, after building this memorial to Dr. Beaumont in 1953, gave the structure to the Mackinac Island State Park Commission.

During the 1800s, William Beaumont pioneered the study of digestion. (*Beaumont Memorial*)

Market Street at Fort Street, Mackinac Island; Beaumont's Medical Discovery (Beaumont Memorial); S19; February 18, 1956; 1982

Biddle House

This house is probably the oldest on the island. Parts of it may date from 1780. A deed to the property, upon which a one-hundred-dollar down payment was made in 1822 by Edward Biddle, was obtained by him in 1827 from the then owner. Biddle was a cousin of the Biddles of Philadelphia and a leading trader and citizen. For years he lived here with his Indian wife. The house is an example of the Quebec rural style. It is listed in the Historic American Buildings Survey and was restored by the Michigan Society of Architects and the building industry in 1959.

Market Street, Mackinac Island; Biddle House; HB2; July 19, 1956; 1960

British Cannon

Early on the morning of July 17, 1812, British troops set up a cannon on this height overlooking Fort Mackinac. This move, coupled with the size of the British forces, resulted in the American garrison's surrender.

Rear of Fort Mackinac, high ground north of the fort, Mackinac Island; British Cannon Site Informational Designation; L2; February 12, 1959; 1959

British Landing

Here, during the night of July 16-17, 1812, a small force of British regulars and several hundred *voyageurs* and Indian allies from St. Joseph Island landed. They occupied a height

Indians who visited the post at Fort Mackinac were housed in this dormitory, completed in 1838. It later served as the island's custom house and a school. (*Indian Dormitory*)

that overlooks Fort Mackinac and demanded its surrender. Lieutenant Porter Hanks, commander of the American garrison of fifty-seven soldiers, had not known that war had been declared. Realizing that resistance was hopeless and might provoke an Indian massacre, Hanks capitulated without a fight.

NW shore of Mackinac Island, Mackinac Island; British Landing; S187; March 19, 1958; 1958

Early Missionary Bark Chapel

According to descriptions by Jesuit missionaries, the bark chapels, which they built among the Indians of the Great Lakes, looked like this. In such primitive huts, far from civilization, the courageous French "blackrobes" lived and sought to turn the minds of the savages to Christianity. One of this illustrious company, Father Claude Dablon, from the mission of Sault Ste. Marie, and later superior general of the Jesuits in Canada, wintered on Mackinac Island in 1670-1671 and carried on missionary work here. It is to the memory of these heroic pioneer priests that this reconstruction of a bark chapel is dedicated.

*Erected on Fort Street, north of Main, near sidewalk to fort, Mackinac Island; Early French Missionary Chapel; HB36; May 1, 1959; 1959

Fort Holmes

Here in 1812, on the island's highest point, a blockhouse and stockade were built by the British and named Fort George. It was the bulwark of British defenses in 1814 when the American attack was repulsed. After the war the Americans renamed the post in honor of Major Holmes, who was killed during the American assault in 1814. The fort was not maintained by the Americans, however. The present blockhouse is not the original building.

Fort Holmes Road, north of the business district, Mackinac Island; Fort Holmes; S79; September 25, 1956; 1959

Grand Hotel

Opened on July 10, 1887, the Grand Hotel was built by the Grand Rapids & Indiana and the Michigan Central railroads and the Detroit & Cleveland Navigation Company through the efforts of Senator Francis B. Stockbridge. It is built of Michigan white pine. With its magnificent colonial porch, longest in the world, it is a classic example of gracious living in Victorian days. One of the outstanding landmarks on the Great Lakes, it is the world's largest summer hotel.

Grounds of the Grand Hotel, West Bluff, Mackinac Island; Grand Hotel; HB10; July 12, 1957; 1958

In 1887 the Grand Hotel opened as the most opulent of Michigan's resort hotels. The Grand is one of Michigan's twenty-eight National Historic Landmarks. (*Grand Hotel*)

In 1817, John Jacob Astor located the offices of the American Fur Company in the Market Street home of firm associate Robert Stuart. (*Market Street*)

Historic Fort Mackinac

Mackinac Island has been called the most historic spot in the Middle West. Fort Mackinac was first built by the British in 1780-1781. It was not until 1796, thirteen years after the end of the Revolutionary War, that the British relinquished this fort to the Americans. At the outbreak of the War of 1812 the British seized the island and built Fort George. This fort, which you see to the north beyond the Rifle Range, was renamed Fort Holmes by the Americans who reoccupied the island in 1815. Troops garrisoned Fort Mackinac until 1895.

Mackinac Island; Fort Mackinac; S189; February 19, 1958; 1958

Indian Dormitory

The Treaty of 1836 was one of the earliest attempts to consider the Indian problem in a humanitarian way. The treaty provided for "a dormitory for the Indians visiting the post." The building, completed in 1838, was designed by Henry R. Schoolcraft, author of the treaty. For ten years it served as a guest house for Indians, mostly Chippewa, who came to the island to receive their annual allotments. From 1848 to 1867 the building was used for a variety of purposes, including that of a U.S. Customs House. In 1867 it became the Mackinac Island School, serving in this capacity until 1960. It was purchased by the Mackinac Island State Park Commission in 1964. The building was restored in 1966 to conform with the original Schoolcraft plans.

Huron Street next to Marquette Park, Mackinac Island; Indian Dormitory; HB45; February 17, 1965; 1966

Island House

Constructed for Charles O'Malley about 1852, this building was one of the first summer hotels on Mackinac Island. Captain Henry Van Allen, a Great Lakes skipper, purchased the hotel in 1865. He later moved it from the beach to its present location. By the 1880s the Island House was known as "The best family hotel on the island." Following the death of her parents, Mrs. Rose Van Allen Webster became proprietor about 1892. She was the wife of Colonel John Webster, who she had met during the 1870s when he was stationed at Fort Mackinac. Mrs. Webster added the large wings in 1895 and 1912, retaining ownership until her death in 1938. The Island House still serves as a resort hotel.

Huron Street, Mackinac Island; Island House; L217; March 14, 1973; 1973

During the early 1800s, John Jacob Astor's American Fur Company dominated fur trading in the Great Lakes. Astor is considered the nation's first millionaire. (*Market Street*)

Lake View Hotel

Originally known as the Lake View House, this is one of the oldest continuously operated hotels on Mackinac Island. Reuben Chapman built the structure in 1858. After his death in 1860, the hotel was operated by his wife, Maria. In 1880 the Chapmans' daughter Jeannie and son-in-law Claude C. Cable purchased the structure. They later changed the name to the Lake View Hotel. In the 1890s, as Mackinac Island became a midwestern tourist mecca, the hotel was enlarged and the two large towers were added. The restaurant and bar were built in 1969 and expanded in 1975. The original portion of the hotel is a well-preserved example of vernacular resort architecture. The handsome building is accented by an open, wood-columned porch with a modified hipped roof and a raised basement.

SW end of Huron Street, Mackinac Island; Lake View House (Lake View Hotel); L982A; January 13, 1982; 1985

Little Stone Church

The Union Congregational Church, affectionately called Little Stone Church, was established in 1900 by eleven charter members. Local residents and summer visitors donated funds for its construction. The cornerstone was laid on August 2, 1904. This structure was built of Mackinac Island stones in an eclectic Gothic style. Its handsome stained-glass windows, installed in 1914, tell the story of the Protestant movement on the island. Open only during the summer, this church has been a landmark to visitors and a popular wedding site.

Cadott Street, Mackinac Island; Union Congregational Church (Little Stone Church); L644A; March 28, 1979; 1979

Mackinac Conference

On September 6, 1943, Michigan's Republican United States senator, Arthur H. Vandenberg, chaired the meeting of the Post War Advisory Council. Republican National Committee Chairman, Harrison Spangler, created the council to draw up a foreign policy plank for the 1944 party platform. Fearing a split between isolationists and internationalists, Spangler wanted a unified policy statement on treaty ratification and the proposed world peace organization. The resulting plank cleared the way for later Republican congressional support of the United Nations and ultimately the North Atlantic Treaty Organization. Among those attending the public sessions were Governors Warren of California, Dewey of New York, Kelly of Michigan, Green of Illinois and Senator Robert A. Taft of Ohio.

Grounds of the Grand Hotel, Mackinac Island; Mackinac Conference Informational Site (Grand Hotel); S468; August 15, 1975; 1975

Mackinac Island

In 1670 a Jesuit priest, Father Claude Dablon, wintered here. The British in 1781 made it a center of their military and fur-trade activity. The island was occupied by the Americans in 1796. Held by the British during the War of 1812, it became the hub of Astor's fur empire after 1817. Mackinac was already becoming a popular resort when fur trading declined during the 1830s.

Market Street near city hall, Mackinac Island; Mackinac Island Informational Designation; S34; July 19, 1956; 1956

Market Street

During the peak of the fur trade this street bustled with activity. Each July and August Indians, traders, and trappers by the thousands came here with furs from throughout the Northwest. In 1817, John Jacob Astor's American Fur Company located its headquarters here. Furs valued at $3 million went through the Market Street offices in 1822. After 1834 the trade moved westward.

Market Street, Mackinac Island; Market Street; S40; July 19, 1956; 1956

Mission Church

This is one of Michigan's oldest Protestant churches. It was built in 1829-1830 by the

Fur trader Robert Stuart (with wife Eliza, left) and U.S. Indian Agent Henry R. Schoolcraft were lay leaders in the Mission Church. (*Mission Church*)

First visited by missionaries, then the center of the British fur trade and military activities, Mackinac Island attracted resorters as early as the 1830s. (*Mackinac Island*)

Presbyterian flock of Reverend William M. Ferry, founder in 1823 of a nearby Indian mission. Robert Stuart and Henry Schoolcraft were lay leaders. About 1838 private owners bought the building. It is judged Michigan's best example of the New England Colonial church style.

Huron Street, corner of Truscott Street, Mackinac Island; Mission Church; HB3; July 19, 1956; 1957

Old Agency House

Here stood the federal Indian agent's home. The most famous of the Indian agents is Henry R. Schoolcraft, student of Indian ways whose work inspired the poem "Hiawatha." In the early 1870s the house burned.

*Huron Street, Mackinac Island; Agency House Informational Site; L3; February 12, 1959; 1959

Round Island Lighthouse

The Round Island Lighthouse, seen south of this site, was completed in 1895. Operating under the auspices of the United States government, this facility was in continuous use for fifty-two years. It was manned by a crew of three until its beacon was replaced by an automatic light in 1924. A sole caretaker occupied and operated the station from 1924 to 1947. Following the construction of a new automatic beacon near the breakwater off the south shore of Mackinac Island, the lighthouse was abandoned. The United States Forest Service now supervises the structure, which is located in the Hiawatha National Forest. The lighthouse serves as a sentinel for the past, reminding visitors of the often precarious sailing and rich history of the Straits of Mackinac.

Foot of Huron Street, in the municipal park adjacent to the Iroquois Hotel, overlooking the Round Island Lighthouse, Mackinac Island; Round Island Lighthouse Informational Designation; L107; April 23, 1971; 1978

Skull Cave

According to tradition this is the cave in which the English fur-trader Alexander Henry hid out during the Indian uprising of 1763. The floor of the cave, he claimed, was covered with human bones, presumably Indian.

Garrison Road, Mackinac Island; Skull Cave; L4; January 12, 1959; 1959

Trinity Church

Episcopal services on Mackinac Island date from 1837, when a Bishop preached in the Mission Church. For many years the congregation met in the post chapel at Fort Mackinac and

Many of Fort Mackinac's more recent visitors have admired the same view that these Victorian ladies enjoyed . This photograph was taken around 1900. (*Mackinac Island*)

in the courthouse. In 1873 a parish was organized, and in 1882 this church building was constructed. Its furnishings include an altar of hand-carved walnut, and two chancel chairs made by soldiers at the fort.

Fort Street, Mackinac Island; Trinity Episcopal Church; L73; July 11, 1968; 1968

Wawashkamo

In 1898, Chicago cottagers founded the Wawashkamo Golf Club. By 1900 the club had been incorporated and the clubhouse had been built on the site of the 1814 Battle of Mackinac Island. *Wawashkamo* is Indian for "Crooked Trail." Golf course architect Alex B. Smith left the natural features of the site unaltered in his design for these true nine-hole Scottish links. Wawashkamo Golf Club is Michigan's oldest unchanged private nine-hole golf links.

British Landing Road, Mackinac Island; Wawashkamo Golf Club; S550A; September 8, 1982; 1983

Across the Peninsula

Old Portage Road, which ends near here, has been used to cross the peninsula since this shore was first settled. It closely parallels the Indian trail, which was the way of the trapper and traveler in the seventeenth and eighteenth centuries.

Roadside Park on US-2, just west of St. Ignace, near intersection of Old Portage Road, Moran Township; Portage Road Informational Designation; L31; April 11, 1963; 1964

Gros Cap and St. Helena Island

French fishermen who came to Gros Cap (on the shore below) early last century also participated in its offshore settlement, St. Helena Island, where ships obtained wood fuel and other supplies. There in 1850, Archie and Wilson Newton set up a fishing and shipping business. The community thrived for more than thirty years.

Park on US-2, six miles west of St. Ignace, Moran Township; Gros Cap and St. Helena Island Informational Site; L22; January 19, 1961; 1962

Lake Michigan

This lake, the sixth largest in the world, was discovered in 1634 by Jean Nicolet, who explored this north shore to Green Bay but found no Orientals as the French in Quebec had hoped he would. The general size and outline of the lake was established in the 1670s by Marquette and Jolliet. They named it Lake Michigan. Its elongated shape was an obstacle to transcontinental expansion, but its waters soon proved a real boon to commerce.

US-2, west of St. Ignace near Gros Cap, Moran Township; Lake Michigan Informational Designation; S120; January 19, 1957; 1957

Fort de Buade

This fort was built by the French near here within a decade after Marquette had established his mission in 1671. Its name was that of the family of Frontenac, the French Governor for North America. Until Detroit was founded in 1701, this was the most important French post west of Montreal. The fort's commandant had charge of all other French forts in the west. Also known as Fort Michilimackinac, it was the first of three forts, which were to bear this name in the Straits area.

St. Ignace Municipal Building, State Street, St. Ignace; Fort de Buade; S98; September 25, 1956; 1958

Mackinac Straits

Nicolet passed through the straits in 1634 seeking a route to the Orient. Soon it became a crossroads where Indian, missionary, trapper and soldier met. From the 1600s through the War of 1812 first Frenchman and Englishman, then Briton and American fought to control this strategic waterway. In 1679 the Griffin was the first sailing vessel to ply these waters. The railroad reached the straits in 1882. Until the Mackinac Bridge was opened in 1957, ferries linked the north and south.

I-75 Rest Area and Visitors Center, just north of Mackinac Bridge exit, St. Ignace; Mackinac Straits; S82; August 23, 1956; 1958

St. Ignace

Pere Marquette established in 1671 the Mission of St. Ignace. French troops soon after built Fort Buade. The state's second oldest white village guarded the straits while serving as the most important French fur post in the Northwest. By 1706 both the fort and mission were abandoned. Only in the nineteenth century did lumbering and fishing revive the town.

State Ferry Dock No. 1, St. Ignace; St. Ignace Informational Designation; S41; July 19, 1956; 1957

St. Ignace Mission

In 1671 the mission of St. Ignace was established so that the Christian message could be brought to several thousand Indians living on this shore. The founder was Father Jacques Marquette, the Jesuit missionary. In 1673 he left on his great journey to the Mississippi Valley. He never returned to his mission before he died in 1675. Two years later his bones were reburied here beneath the chapel altar. In 1706, after French troops had abandoned the fort, the chapel was destroyed.

500 North State Street, St. Ignace; Father Marquette Burial Site (Marquette Mission Park and Museum of Ojibwa Culture); S92; September 25, 1956; 1958

Macomb

Moravian Road

In 1782 marauding American militia massacred nearly one hundred Christian Delaware Indians at their village in eastern Ohio. Seeking refuge, the Delaware settled on the Clinton River two and one-half miles north of here on land granted by the Chippewa. In time the settlement numbered over one hundred, ministered to by the Moravian missionaries. This highway, the first interior road in Michigan, was laid out in the winter of 1785-1786 to connect the village with the fort at Detroit, twenty-three miles away. At the close of the American Revolution the Chippewa withdrew their land grant, and in April 1786 the mission was closed. Some of the members returned to Ohio and others moved to Canada.

Clinton Grove Cemetery, Cass Avenue near Moravian Drive, north of Harrington Boulevard, west of Mount Clemens, Clinton Township; Moravian Mission Informational Designation; S142; January 19, 1957; 1972

Edsel & Eleanor Ford House

Edsel Ford, president of the Ford Motor Company for many years, and his wife, Eleanor Clay, completed this eighty-seven-acre estate in 1927. Architect Albert Kahn derived the design from precedents in Cotswold, England, and many of the building materials, including the staircase, paneling and fireplaces, were brought from old English homes. Noted landscape architect Jens Jensen developed the grounds. The Fords were collectors of art and antiques and benefactors of local and national institutions. Edsel was instrumental in the creation of the Ford Foundation in 1936. He died here on May 26, 1943. His wife, who lived here until her death on October 19, 1976, endowed the property and directed it be maintained for public use.

1100 Lakeshore Drive, Grosse Pointe Shores; Ford, Edsel and Eleanor, House (Lakeview, Gaukler Point); S498; February 7, 1977; 1980

Selfridge Field

Selfridge, Michigan's first real airport, began operations as a training base in July 1917. It has progressed to a leading role in America's air arm. It is often called "The Home of Generals" because Selfridge has been a springboard to success in the careers of 145 air force generals. It is named for Lieutenant Thomas E. Selfridge, the nation's first military pilot. In 1908 he was killed while flying with Orville Wright, becoming America's first military casualty of powered flight.

Roadside M-59 near Mount Clemens, Harrison Township; Selfridge Field (Selfridge Air Force Base); S168; September 17, 1957; 1958

"The Thing"

Thomas Clegg (1863-1939) and his English-born father, John, built "The Thing," the first recorded self-propelled vehicle in Michigan (and perhaps the country) in 1884-1885. The Thing, driven by a single cylinder steam engine with a tubular boiler carried in the rear, seated four. The vehicle was built in the John Clegg & Son machine shop here in Memphis. It ran about five hundred miles before Clegg dismantled it and sold the engine to a creamery. The shop was razed in 1936, just a short time before Henry Ford offered to buy it for Greenfield Village.

On Boardman at Cedar Street, Memphis; Thomas Clegg and First Auto Informational Designation; L824B; June 10, 1980; 1981

Alexander Macomb

In 1818, Territorial Governor Lewis Cass proclaimed the third Michigan County to be called Macomb. At that time the young general was commander of the Fifth Military Department in Detroit. Born in that city in 1782, son of prominent local entrepreneurs, Macomb had entered the U.S. Army in 1799. He had gained national renown and honor during the War of 1812 for his victory at Plattsburg in September 1814 over a far superior force of British invaders. Later as chief army engineer he promoted the building of military roads in the Great Lakes area. From May 1828 to his death in June 1841, Macomb served as commander in chief of the army. He is buried in the Congressional Cemetery in Washington, D.C. His birthday, April 3, is honored as Macomb County Heritage Day.

West edge of Courthouse Plaza, intersection of Gratiot Avenue and Macomb Street, Mount Clemens; Macomb, Alexander, Informational Designation; S418; February 22, 1974; 1974

Carnegie Library

Mount Clemens's Carnegie building was erected in 1904 and was the first Carnegie Library built in Macomb County. It is one out of 1,681 such libraries across the United States financed by Andrew Carnegie, the industrialist and philanthropist. The columns, stairs and large windows of this Neo-Classical design make the structure one of the distinguished public edifices in this vicinity. This site is part of the original land granted in 1811, private claim number 141, to Christian Clemens, founder of Mount Clemens. Initially used as a public library, this facility has an outstanding local history and genealogy collection. In 1969 the Carnegie building became the Art Center, a community-based nonprofit organization, which fosters the visual arts through exhibits, classes and tours in the area.

125 Macomb Street, Mount Clemens; Carnegie Library (Art Center); L575; January 19, 1978; 1978

Crocker House

The first mayor of Mount Clemens, Joshua Dickinson, built this Italianate house in 1869. His daughter Katherine (1849-1882), the great-granddaughter of city founder Christian Clemens, and his son-in-law George M. Crocker (1848-1918) moved into it after their marriage in 1870. Crocker, a former prosecuting attorney and justice of the peace, became mayor upon Dickinson's death. The Crocker family owned the house until 1921. Originally

Hotel Medea and Mineral Baths,
European Plan, Rooms $1.00 per day and up,
Moderate priced Cafe.

Mount Clemens's Medea Hotel (top) was razed in 1990. The Clementine had met the same fate some years before. (*Mount Clemens Mineral Bath Industry*)

located on the corner of Walnut and Market streets, the house was moved to New Street in 1908 to make room for a new post office. Slated for removal or demolition in 1975, it was rescued by the Macomb County Historical Society, which moved it to Union Street in 1976 for use as a local history museum.

15 Union Street, Mount Clemens; Crocker House (Macomb County Historical Society Museum); L181; February 11, 1972; 1988

Grace Episcopal Church

The Episcopal Diocese of Michigan sent Edward Magee to Mount Clemens in 1849. The interest generated by this missionary visit culminated a year later when the Grace Episcopal congregation was formed. In December of that year Michigan's first Episcopal bishop, the

Right Reverend Samuel McCoskry, conducted services in the courthouse. Six members were confirmed and Magee was ordained. In 1870 this simple Gothic Revival church was built.

115 South Gratiot Avenue, NE corner of Church Street, Mount Clemens; Grace Episcopal Church; L412; August 15, 1975; 1976

Mount Clemens Mineral Bath Industry

For seven decades, Mount Clemens was internationally renowned as a mineral bath resort city. In 1865 the first well was sunk to obtain brine for salt production. Because of the high cost of separating the salt from the various other minerals and elements in the water, this process proved unprofitable. In the fall of 1870, however, a local mill operator, Dorr Kellogg, decided to bathe in the warm, sulfurous water. Impressed with its therapeutic qualities, city businessmen were inspired to invest in a bathhouse. Known as the Original Bath House, it was completed in 1873. At the turn of the century, nine bathhouses and over thirty hotels operated in Mount Clemens. Owing to the Great Depression and increasing use of internal medicine, this "spa era" ended by 1940.

McArthur Park/City Arboretum, North River Road, Mount Clemens; Mount Clemens Mineral Bath Industry Informational Designation; L643B; March 28, 1979; 1979

Thomas Edison

While working as a railway newsboy on the Detroit-Port Huron line, Tom Edison often stopped in Mount Clemens. He made friends with station agent J. U. Mackenzie and in 1862 saved Mackenzie's young son from death by a train. In gratitude Mr. Mackenzie taught Tom Edison railroad telegraphy. From his training Tom became a qualified railroad telegrapher and worked during the 1860s at this occupation. Some of his earliest inventions were based on the telegraph.

198 Grand Street, at Cass Avenue, Mount Clemens; Grand Trunk Western Railroad, Mount Clemens Station (Mount Clemens Railroad Depot); L239; May 17, 1973; 1973

A young Thomas Edison sold newspapers to Grand Trunk passengers. (*Thomas Edison*)

Zion Church

Organized on July 3, 1854, Zion Evangelical Lutheran Church was the first German Protestant congregation in Mount Clemens. Its founding trustees were John Rossow and Abraham Devantier from Prussia, John William Miller and Carsten Roecker from Hanover, and John Charles Reimold and John George Murthum from Wuerttemberg. Zion Church operated as a free congregation, welcoming all Christians. It served primarily German-speaking Catholic and Protestant immigrants, including Lutherans, Calvinists and Huguenots. Worshipping at first in the Macomb County Courthouse, the congregation purchased this site, the former Methodist Academy, in 1862. The nave of the present brick sanctuary was built by Minard Barr in 1880. The tower and transepts were added in 1895.

Side Two

The itinerant ministers who served Zion Church in its formative years were Methodist, Lutheran and Evangelical. The first resident pastor was the Reverend William Kies (1862-1864). He was followed by the Reverend Hermann Gundert (1864-1903), who contributed $4,000 of his own money to help fund the tower and transepts of the present church building. It was not until the 1920s, during the pastorate of the Reverend F. A. Roese (1903-1926), that English became the language of the worship service and of church records. In the early twentieth century, the congregation turned to humanitarian work. Lead by the Reverend Jacob Wulfmann (1927-1949), the congregation helped support the Evangelical Deaconess Hospital and the Evangelical Home for Children and Aged in Detroit. In 1961 the church received its present name, Zion United Church of Christ.

68 New Street, Mount Clemens; Zion Evangelical Church (Zion United Church of Christ); L1251A; July 23, 1985; 1986

New Baltimore

French explorers led by Pierre Yax first settled this area now known as New Baltimore in

1796. Chippewa Indians inhabited this vicinity then. Fabian Robertjean made the first government land purchase in 1820. Twenty-five years later, Alfred Ashley of Mount Clemens came here and built the first sawmill and dock, and in 1851, platted the village of Ashley. He also managed a hotel and general store, opening the first post office in his store in 1852. German pioneers arrived here in 1853 clearing land along the Salt River for their settlement. Renamed New Baltimore in 1855, this area was incorporated as a village in 1867 and as a city in 1931. New Baltimore is a popular place for fishermen and hunters and is noted for its expansive shoreline dotted with summer cottages and homes.

St. John's Lutheran Church

In 1863, during the stormy days of the Civil War, Lutheranism had its beginning in the New Baltimore area. Seven German families made up the original congregation of St. John's Lutheran Church, holding worship services in the home of Fritz Turkow. Five years later the worshipers moved to an old chapel, which was rented from the Baptists. In 1870 the Lutherans erected this structure on property given by Gilbert Hatheway in January of 1869. Services and religious instruction were offered only in German until 1916 when English was introduced with one English service a month. German services were discontinued in 1934. St. John's houses a Hinners mechanical action organ, which was acquired in 1905.

51161 Maria Street, New Baltimore; St. John's Lutheran Church; L636A; December 21, 1978; 1979

Richmond Center for the Performing Arts

Built in 1887, this structure formerly served as the First Congregational Church. When the congregation merged with St. Paul's Evangelical and Reformed Church in 1973, it sold the building to the Richmond Community Theatre. That group adapted the interior for reuse as a theater and carefully restored the exterior. The building is a significant example of Gothic Revival architecture. The Richmond Center for the Performing Arts was listed on the National Register of Historic Places in 1975.

69619 Parker at the corner of Churchill, Richmond; First Congregational Church (Richmond Center for the Performing Arts); L393; April 4, 1975; 1988

Village of Romeo

Originally known as Indian Village, Romeo was platted in 1830 on the former winter campgrounds of a band of Chippewa Indians. Nathaniel Taylor, Ashael Bailey and a Major Larned laid out the village, which was incorporated in 1838. Named Romeo by Taylor's wife, Laura, the village became an agricultural and mercantile center. Many of its early settlers were from New England and upstate New York. In 1835 the Romeo Academy was established, and in the 1840s the Romeo Branch of the University of Michigan opened in the village. The many examples of nineteenth-century architecture that remain in the village led Michigan and the federal government to list Romeo as a historic district in 1970.

Corner of Main and Church streets, Romeo; Village of Romeo Informational Designation; L1424C; June 10, 1987; 1988

Erin United Presbyterian Church

Under the leadership of the Reverend Harry N. Bissell of Mount Clemens, several families organized the First Presbyterian Church of Erin in 1860. The original thirteen members held their first services in a small schoolhouse. They were the first congregation in this community to conduct services in English. In early 1861, Thomas Common donated the present site to the church. The first church on this site, which cost less than $500, was completed in October 1861. The congregation built a new church here in 1930 and added a more modern sanctuary onto it in 1967. Dedicatory services for the expanded church were held on September 17, 1967. The church's name was changed to the First Presbyterian Church of Roseville in 1929 and to the Erin United Presbyterian Church in 1953.

30000 Gratiot Avenue, Roseville; Erin United Presbyterian Church; L906B; March 16, 1981; 1983

Sacred Heart Church

On June 1, 1861, the Reverend Amandus Van Den Driessche, from the Detroit Diocese, helped establish a Catholic mission at Utica Junction (now Roseville). The Sacred Heart mission, composed of Irish, German, Belgian and French families, completed its first permanent church, a modest log structure, with seating for three hundred, in 1864. The mission became a parish in 1872. The next year, the parish purchased land for a cemetery. In

1915 expansion of the Detroit to Port Huron interurban railway necessitated moving the church building to the east. The basement of the current church was constructed in 1930, but the great Depression and World War II delayed construction of the upper church until 1950.

18430 Utica Road, Roseville; Sacred Heart Roman Catholic Church; L1354A; December 5, 1986; 1987

Blossom Heath Inn

Mathew Kramer, a hotelier and yachtsman, built this roadhouse in 1911, naming it the Kramer-hof. In 1920 the building was sold to William McIntosh, who renamed it the Blossom Heath Inn and added two large wings, which included an ornate ballroom. Blossom Heath was one of the most luxurious roadhouses in Michigan. Nationally known big bands, such as Ben Pollack's, drew people from Detroit and Canada. Blossom Heath became notorious for illegal drinking and gambling during Prohibition and the Depression. After McIntosh's death in 1930, the road-house was run by his heirs. By the late 1930s, the heyday of roadhouses was over, and in 1943 Blossom Heath was sold. The building fell into disuse, but in 1946 the village of St. Clair Shores purchased it. On May 19, 1946, it reopened as a civic center with village offices in the north wing. It became the St. Clair Shores Recreation Center in 1957.

24800 Jefferson Avenue between Nine and Ten Mile roads, St. Clair Shores; Kramerhof Roadhouse (Blossom Heath Inn); L705A; August 3, 1979; 1982

Lake Saint Clair (*Lac Sainte Claire*)

French explorers discovered and named Lake Saint Clair on August 12, 1679. Among the party of thirty-four men were voyageur Rene-Robert Cavelier, Sieur de la Salle and Roman Catholic friar Father Louis Hennepin. Aboard the *Griffin*, the first sailing vessel on the Upper Lakes, the group sailed from the Niagara Falls area on August 7, 1679, and entered the Detroit River on August 11. They reached Lake Saint Clair the following day and named it *Lac Sainte Claire* in honor of Sainte Claire of Assisi whose feast day fell at that time. It was Sainte Claire who established the order of Franciscan nuns, the Order of the Poor Claires. Government officials and map makers later changed the spelling to the present form of Saint Clair. This led to some confusion as to the true original of the name of the lake.

Lac Ste. Claire Park, Eleven Mile Road just east of Jefferson Avenue, St. Clair Shores; Lac Sainte Claire Informational Designation; S520B; June 15, 1979; 1979

Selinsky-Green House

In 1868, when this area was covered with small farms, Prussian immigrants John and Mary Selinsky bought farmland in Erin Township and built this salt-box house using solid log con-struction covered with clapboard. The Selinskys gave the house to their daughter Ernestine when she married John Green in 1874. The property was owned by their descendants until 1974. Moved to this location in 1975 because of the construction of I-696, this house is now restored as a museum.

22504 Eleven Mile Road, just east of Jefferson Avenue, St. Clair Shores; Selinsky-Green House; L618; July 26, 1978; 1978

Holcombe Beach

Near this site in 1961 archaeologists from the Aboriginal Research Club and the University of Michigan uncovered evidence of an early Paleo-Indian settlement. Here about eleven thousand years ago these first prehistoric dwellers in the Great Lakes region inhabited a lake shore. Excavations of artifacts and bones reveal that for food the Paleo-Indians hunted Barren Ground caribou, a species suited to the tundra-like terrain of that era. As their en-vironment changed, these Indians were forced to adapt to new ways of living. Different climate and sources of food required modified tools and methods of subsistence and the Paleo-Indian pattern of life developed into the culture of the Early Archaic people. The site known as Holcombe Beach is a reminder of basic changes in Michigan's physical and biological environment over the ages.

Intersection of Metropolitan Parkway (Sixteen Mile Road) and Dodge Park Road, Sterling Heights; Holcombe Site (20MB30) (Heritage Junior High School); S309; July 17, 1970; 1977

Upton House

Constructed in 1866-1867, the William Upton House is one of the oldest surviving nineteenth-century brick dwellings in Sterling Heights. Italianate in style, the house features a reconstructed open porch topped by a second-story balustrade, a cupola, period chimneys and refurbished window units. According to oral tradition, the interior building materials were imported from England. Most farmsteads of this era were constructed of wood; the brick used on this one demonstrates the affluence of its builder. By 1891 the Upton farm consisted of 138 acres. Upton farmed the land and sold fish from the Clinton River. When the exterior restoration of the house was done in 1981-1982, the interior was adapted for use as public offices.

Side Two

William Upton, a wealthy farmer and merchant, built this stately Italianate house in 1866-1867. Born in 1835 in Leicestershire, England, Upton came to this country with his parents in the fall of 1841. The family lived in Detroit for several years before settling in Sterling Township in 1845. In 1861, William married Sarah Jeanette Aldrich. He built this house on his farm, where he, his wife and their children lived until 1891, when they moved to Utica. There, Upton purchased a three-story business block from which he sold Shropshire sheep and ran a successful mercantile and real estate business until 1897. In 1904 fire destroyed the Upton Block. Shortly afterwards, William moved to Rochester, Michigan. He died in 1923 at the age of eighty-eight.

40433 Utica Road, Sterling Heights; Upton, William, House (Upton House); L1127A; October 27, 1983; 1985

St. Lawrence Parish of Utica

In May 1866 the Reverend Amandus VanDenDriessche of Detroit recited Utica's first Catholic Mass. Forty Irish families at Utica Junction (present-day Roseville) formed what became a mission of Sacred Heart Parish. On August 15, 1874, Bishop C. H. Borgess dedicated St. Lawrence Parish's first church. Four years later a cemetery was consecrated one-half mile north of here. In 1904 a fire swept through Utica, destroying the church. Parishioners worshiped in homes and a rented hall until a new church was built in 1908. The present Neo-Romanesque church was designed by Detroit architect Arthur DesRosiers and erected in 1951. The broad nave seats eight hundred people. St. Lawrence Parish remains the oldest religious community in Utica.

44633 Utica Road, Utica; St. Lawrence Parish of Utica Informational Designation; L1799C; November 15, 1990; 1991

Detroit Memorial Park Cemetery

Detroit Memorial Park Cemetery was organized in 1925 to serve the rapidly expanding post-war Detroit black population. Concerned with the indignities and poor quality of service received by the black community, several distinguished Detroiters established the cemetery to provide reasonably priced and dignified burials. This was the first black-owned and operated business of its kind in the state. Its incorporators included Charles Diggs, a mortician and acknowledged founder, and Dr. Aaron Toodle, a druggist and first president. By careful management the cemetery corporation survived the Great Depression and expanded into financial services. Famous inventor, Elijah McCoy, is buried here among doctors, lawyers, ministers, teachers and business, civic and political leaders.

4280 East Thirteen Mile Road, between Ryan and Mound roads, Warren; Detroit Memorial Cemetery; L392; January 16, 1976; 1976

Governor Alex J. Groesbeck

Son of a pioneer Dutch-French family, Groesbeck was born in Warren Township near the corner of Mound and Twelve Mile roads in 1872. His father's election as sheriff in 1880 caused the family to move to Mount Clemens. In 1893, Alex graduated from the University of Michigan and began a long and distinguished legal career in Detroit. After serving as state attorney general from 1917 to 1920 he became governor for the first of three successive terms in 1921. His Republican administrations were noted for governmental reorganization, prison reform and expansion of state highways. Highway M-97 was subsequently named after him. In 1927 he returned to Detroit, retaining active interest in public affairs until his death in 1953.

Alex J. Groesbeck became governor of Michigan in 1921. (*Governor Alex J. Groesbeck*)

Intersection of Mound and Twelve Mile roads, main entrance of the GM Technical Center, Warren; Governor Alex J. Groesbeck Birthplace Informational Site; S284; February 17, 1967; 1974

Surveyor William Austin Burt patented the solar compass in 1836. In 1847 he established the northern Michigan-Wisconsin boundary. (*William Austin Burt*)

Village of Warren

Pioneers, mostly farmers, from New England settled the Warren area in 1832. Virgin forests supplied logs for the sawmills, which were located on Twelve and Fourteen Mile roads. A strap railroad, one of the first of its kind in Michigan, connected the settlement to Detroit and Utica. By 1875 the community had two churches, a school and several business establishments. It was called Beebe's Corner after John L. Beebe, who operated the toll gate for the plank road that led to Detroit. In 1893 the predominately German community voted to incorporate as a village, electing Dr. J. D. Flynn as president. Though work and cultural activities draw residents into the Detroit metropolitan community, Warren retains its individual identity in its historic churches, homes and business establishments.

Intersection of Mound and Chicago roads, Warren; Original Village of Warren Informational Site; L833B; August 27, 1980; 1982

Simpson Park Campground

In the early nineteenth century Methodists began holding camp meetings, an outgrowth of their early revivals. Revival services were held during the winter months, and late summer was generally reserved for the district camp meeting. Simpson Park Campground was

189

begun as the Romeo District Summer Camp for the Methodist Episcopal Church in 1865. It is one of the oldest camp meetings in continuous service in Michigan. The Reverend John Russell, district presiding elder, was its founder. (In 1869 he also helped found the Prohibition party.) During the late 1860s families came from over fifty miles away to gather under the foliage for three weeks of almost uninterrupted religious exercises.

Side Two

Since the late 1890s, Simpson Park Campground has been operated by a private association made up predominantly of United Methodists. In 1907 it was reorganized and the Reverend William G. Nixon was elected its first president. A tabernacle was built and named in his honor in 1910. Many of the children and young people who have attended camp meetings have become preachers and missionaries as well as camp leaders. Today only ten-day camps are held. The meetings are less rigid than in the 1860s, and social and recreational activities are included. The annual Simpson Park Camp Meeting is held during the first two weeks of August. The original camp of thirteen acres has grown to forty-four acres.

70199 Campground Road, Washington Township; Simpson Park Campground; L927B; May 13, 1981; 1981

William Austin Burt

Near this site lived William Austin Burt, inventor, legislator, surveyor and millwright. Born in Massachusetts in 1792, Burt settled in this area in 1824, after spending several years in Erie County, New York. There he had been a justice of the peace, a school inspector and a postmaster. In Michigan he worked as a land surveyor and a millwright, building over eight mills. He was a member of the Michigan Territorial Legislature in 1826-1827. He served as Mount Vernon's first postmaster (1832-1856), a Macomb County Circuit Court judge (1833-1853), a state legislator (1853) and a deputy U.S. surveyor (1833-1853). Between 1833 and 1857 he and his five sons won acclaim for their accurate work on public land surveys. In 1857, Burt moved to Detroit, where he died in 1858.

Side Two

America's first patented typewriter was constructed by William Austin Burt in 1829 in a workshop located on this site. It was also here that Burt built the solar compass, patented in 1836, which was the prototype for those used today. Burt's compass became an indispensible instrument for surveying because it used the sun instead of the magnetic north as a fixed reference and was therefore unaffected by the magnetic fields of iron ore deposits. Burt also received a patent for an Equitorial Sextant. Among Burt's other accomplishments were the establishment of the northern point of the Michigan principal meridian in 1840; the discovery of the Marquette iron ore range in 1844 and the establishment of the northern portion of the Michigan-Wisconsin boundary in 1847. In 1852 he assisted in surveying the route for the Soo Canal.

Stoney Creek Metropark, 4300 Main Park Road, Washington; Burt, William Austin, Homesite; S0570C May 21, 1985; 1986

Manistee

The Bottle House

John J. Makinen, Sr. (1871-1942), built this house out of over sixty thousand pop bottles, most of which came from his business, the Northwestern Bottling Works. The bottles were laid on their sides with the bottom ends to the exterior. A native of Finland, Makinen moved to the area in 1903. He completed the house in 1941 but died before his family moved into it. In 1980 the building was purchased by the Kaleva Historical Society, which renovated it to house the Kaleva Historical Museum.

14551 Wuoksi Avenue, near Kauko, Kaleva; Makinen, John J. Sr., Bottle House (Kaleva Historical Museum); L983A; January 13, 1982; 1983

Kaleva

Finnish immigrants founded this little village in 1900. The name Kaleva is derived from the Finnish epic poem *Kalevala*. The poem was the source of street names in the original plat.

The Evangelical Lutheran Church, known today as the Bethany Lutheran, was organized on January 12, 1902. On that same day the Temperance Society "Kalevatar" was organized. The Temperance Hall was built that year and served as a place of worship until 1913 when the church was built and as a community center until 1933. About the same time the Youth Society was organized, and a hall for meetings was built in 1904. The Finns took pride in their cultural heritage, founded a lending library and instilled in their children a love for music, books and God and country. In 1901 the Finnish Publishing Company moved here from Brooklyn, New York, and the original building still stands.

Side Two

Among the pioneers arriving in Kaleva in 1900 were the families of John Haksluoto, Jacob Lemponen, Kalle Hendrickson, Matti Kemppainen, Antti Myllyla and John Palomaki. These settlers were mostly farmers and manual laborers. They possessed a distinctive quality of perseverance known as *sisu*. Life was a struggle. After arriving here, many were forced to clear land for homes and crops. Most homes had a sauna, and to a Finn, there is nothing comparable for reviving an overworked body and spirit. These pioneers along with people of other ethnic origins contributed considerably to the development of Maple Grove Township, Manistee County, and to the culture and agriculture of Michigan. Today, Kaleva is a thriving community with profitable businesses and farms, good schools and modern facilities.

Wuoski Avenue, at intersection of Aura, Kaleva; Kaleva Informational Designation; L524; April 15, 1977; 1978

First Congregational Church

William Le Baron Jenney, eminent Chicago architect known as the "father of the skyscraper," designed this beautiful Romanesque church. Completed in 1892, it features vibrant stained-glass windows, two of which are of Tiffany design. The soaring rafters form a canopy over the curved hand-carved pews in the luminescent and graceful interior. Lumber, salt and shipping industrialists of the late nineteenth century attended and supported this distinctive house of worship.

412 Fourth Street, between Oak and Maple streets, Manistee; First Congregational Church; L253; November 15, 1973; 1977

Holy Trinity Episcopal Church

St. Paul's Mission was organized in 1869. It was formally incorporated as Holy Trinity Episcopal Church in 1888, the same year this structure was completed and dedicated. The Reverend Richard R. Upjohn of Chicago was responsible for the Norman design of rough-hewn limestone and sandstone. This is one of the oldest Manistee churches still holding regular worship services.

410 Second Street, Manistee; Church of the Holy Trinity; L674A; June 15, 1979; 1981

Manistee Fire Hall

In early October 1888, the Manistee City Council hired Frederick Hollister of Saginaw, the architect of Manistee's principle school, to design a fire hall to replace the original station, which was constructed in 1872-1873 on Filer Street. Later that month the *Manistee Democrat* predicted that the city's new fire hall would be "a model of convenience and usefulness." Constructed of brick, cut stone and French plate glass, and trimmed with galvanized iron, this Romanesque Revival-style building was constructed by the local firm of Brownrigg and Reynolds at a cost of $7,516. The dome is covered with copper. The hall opened in June 1889 when Manistee's first "fire truck," a horse-drawn steam engine, was brought from the original hall.

281 First Street, SW corner of Hancock, Manistee; Manistee Fire Hall; L1647A; April 20, 1989; 1990

Our Saviour's Lutheran Church

Organized as a Scandinavian congregation in 1868, Our Saviour's became a Danish church in 1875 and served the American Evangelical Lutheran Synod until 1962. First used for worship in 1869, the building escaped damage in the Fire of 1871 and was completed with the addition of the tower in 1888. Danish architectural features are present, particularly the weather vane-topped spire, and the Danish language was used in services until [the] mid-twentieth century. Our Saviour's is now a museum of Danish life in America.

300 Walnut Street at Third Street, Manistee; Danish Lutheran Church (Our Saviour's Evangelical Lutheran Church); L119; May 18, 1971; 1972

The Manistee Fire Hall, with its copper-topped dome, appears quite elegant by modern standards for housing fire engines. (*Manistee Fire Hall*)

Ramsdell Theatre

Thomas Jefferson Ramsdell—pioneer lawyer, state legislator and civic leader—built this theater between 1902 and 1903. Many traveling companies played here and praised the features that made it unique among the playhouses of the era. Theatrical artist Walter Burridge painted the main curtain utilizing the theme "A Grove Near Athens." The dome and lobby murals were the work of Thomas Ramsdell's son Frederick. Public-spirited citizens saved the landmark from demolition in the early 1920s. It was acquired by the city of Manistee in 1943. The Manistee Civic Players have helped to preserve its architecture and interior decor. The Ramsdell Theatre was listed on the National Register of Historic Places in 1972.

101 Maple Street, Manistee; Ramsdell Theatre; L124; June 19, 1971; 1980

Great Fire of 1871

On October 8, 1871, the day the famous Chicago fire began, equally terrible fires broke out on Lake Michigan's east coast in forests parched by a hot, dry summer. The flames were fanned by high winds. In a few hours most of Holland and Manistee lay in smoldering ruins, a fate other coastal towns barely escaped. The fires swept on across the state, clear to Lake Huron, destroying some two million acres of trees. Relief for the thousands of victims came from all over Michigan and the nation.

Orchard Beach State Park, two miles north of Manistee on M-110, Manistee Township; Great Fire of 1871 Informational Designation; S140; January 19, 1957; 1957

In the 1920s early preservationists saved the Ramsdell Theatre from demolition. The city of Manistee acquired the theater in 1943 . (*Ramsdell Theatre*)

Marquette

Cliffs Shaft Mine

Opened by the Iron Cliffs Company in 1879, the mine was acquired by the present owner, the Cleveland-Cliffs Iron Company, in 1891. The Cliffs Shaft was the nation's largest producer of hard, specular hematite, a type of iron ore. Over twenty-six million tons were mined, and since 1887 ore was shipped every year but one. The mine was also one of the largest of Michigan iron mines, its sixty-five miles of tunnels running under most of Ishpeming and plunging to a depth of 1,358 feet. As late as the 1930s, there were eight iron mines in Ishpeming. The Cliffs Shaft was the last of these, and its closing in 1967 marked the end of an era.

504 Spruce Street, Ishpeming; Iron Cliffs Company (Cleveland Cliffs Iron Company); S398; March 14, 1973; 1973

Ishpeming: Historic Ski Center

The sport of skiing was introduced to America in the nineteenth century by Scandinavian immigrants. The first ski club in Michigan and one of the first in the country was formed at Ishpeming in 1887. It held its first public ski meet on February 25, 1888. The longest jump was one of thirty-five feet. Since then this city has produced many famous ski jumpers who have gained their experience on renowned Suicide Hill. Here in this city the National Ski Association was formed on February 21, 1904. The National Ski Hall of Fame and Ski Museum is located here because of Ishpeming's historic role in developing skiing in America.

610 Palms on US-41, between Second and Third streets, Ishpeming; Birthplace of Skiing in America Informational Designation (National Ski Hall of Fame); S139; January 19, 1957; 1957

193

Father Marquette Park

Serving as priests, explorers, cartographers, linguists, farmers, scientists and chroniclers, Jesuit missionaries introduced Christianity to the Great Lakes region. Among them was Father Jacques Marquette. Born in Laon, France, he came to Quebec in September 1666. In 1671 he and Chippewa Indians who had been forced eastward by the Sioux established St. Ignace mission at the Straits of Mackinac. From there Marquette and Louis Jolliet set out on their voyage to the Mississippi River in the spring of 1673. Ill before the journey began, Marquette died on the return trip, on May 18, 1675. Indians from St. Ignace later brought Marquette's remains to a chapel on this site where they were rediscovered in 1877 by Father Edward Jacker.

501 South Front Street, Marquette; Father Marquette Park (Father Marquette Park); S585C; December 5, 1986; 1987

First Steam Railroad in Upper Peninsula

On this site in 1852, the Green Bay and Lake Superior Rail-Road began the survey which led to the construction of the first steam railroad in the Upper Peninsula. The railroad ran from Marquette to the Jackson and Cleveland iron mines fourteen miles away. In 1855 the building of the railroad along the previously surveyed route was begun by the Iron Mountain Railroad Company. By 1857 it was hauling ore from the mines to Marquette. It later became part of the Duluth, South Shore and Atlantic Railroad, which has operated since 1961 as the Soo Line. This railroad, and others like it, carried millions of tons of ore, the basic raw material for the rapidly developing steel industry in the United States.

Lakeshore Boulevard at the foot of Washington Street, Marquette Harbor, Marquette; Point of Beginning of First Survey of Upper Peninsula Railroad Informational Site; S477; January 16, 1976; 1977

Marquette County Courthouse

This Neo-Classical Revival structure, designed by Charlton & Gilbert of Marquette, was constructed in 1902-1904 at a cost of $210,000. Built of local sandstone, it is the second courthouse to occupy this site. In a case tried here in 1913, President Theodore Roosevelt won a libel suit against Ishpeming newspaper publisher George Newett and was awarded six cents, "the price of a good newspaper." Another case tried here inspired *Anatomy of a Murder*, a novel by Ishpeming resident John D. Voelker. In 1959 the courthouse was the setting of the motion picture based on the novel. The picture was directed by Otto Preminger and the musical score for the movie was written by Duke Ellington. The courthouse was renovated in 1982-1984 at a cost of $2.4 million.

400 South Third Street, Marquette; Marquette County Courthouse; S486; August 6, 1976; 1985

This illustration of "Norwegian Sport at Ishpeming, Michigan" appeared in the March 12, 1892, issue of *Harper's Weekly*. (*Ishpeming: Historic Ski Center*)

Northern Michigan University

Established by the legislature in 1899 as a normal school to provide teachers for the Upper Peninsula, Northern opened with thirty-two students, six faculty members and Dwight B. Waldo as principal. A four-year collegiate program was introduced in 1918 and the first bachelor of arts degree was conferred two years later. In the 1950s, Northern became a multi-purpose institution placing emphasis on instruction, service and research. In 1960 it established its own graduate program leading to the master of arts degree. Serving an ever-increasing student body, Northern in 1963 achieved university status through an act of the legislature.

In front of the University Center, Northern Michigan University campus, Marquette; Northern Michigan University Informational Site; S115; January 19, 1957; 1966

Sam Cohodas Lodge

This lodge, built for Russian immigrant Sam Cohodas, symbolizes the Upper Peninsula's ethnic diversity. Finnish craftsmen erected this massive lodge in 1934, according to plans by local architect and Swedish immigrant David Anderson. The rustic log lodge is built of materials gathered within a fifteen-mile radius of this site. Cohodas was one of the nation's leading fruit wholesalers. The Sam Cohodas Lodge was listed in the National Register of Historic Places in 1991.

Sam Cohodas

In 1903, Sam Cohodas (1895-1988) and his family left present-day Byelorussia, U.S.S.R., joining his father, who had come to Marinette, Wisconsin, in 1900. Like many Jews, the Cohodases fled the eastern European pogroms. Cohodas, his father and brothers worked in an uncle's produce business. In 1915, Sam and his brother Harry began their own retail and wholesale company in Michigan's Copper Country. Under Sam's direction, the business boomed nationally. This lodge, erected in 1934, served as his wilderness camp from 1935 to 1972.

County Road IM near US-41, Negaunee vicinity, Michigamme Township; Cohodas, Samuel, Lodge (Michigamme Lake Lodge); L1728A; March 15, 1990; 1991

Jackson Mine

On this spot on September 19, 1844, William A. Burt, a deputy government surveyor, was the first to discover the great Lake Superior iron ore deposits. Peculiar fluctuations in his magnetic compass led Burt to ask his men to seek the cause, and they soon returned with pieces of iron ore from outcroppings in the area. Next year prospectors from Jackson, Michigan, led by Phil M. Everett, arrived at the Carp River. Marji-gesick, a Chippewa chief, guided members of the party in June to this location where he showed them iron ore in the roots of a fallen pine tree. As a result of this discovery the Jackson Mining Company, of which Everett was a founder, began taking out ore here in 1847. Thus was born the Lake Superior area's great iron mining industry.

Miners Park, 820 Maas Street at US-41 and Maple, Negaunee; Jackson Mine; S2; February 18, 1956; 1957

Marquette Iron Range

The first of the immensely rich Lake Superior iron ore deposits to be discovered and mined were those of the Marquette Iron Range. In 1844, William A. Burt and his surveying party discovered outcroppings of iron ore south of Teal Lake. This area soon became the first and has remained the chief center of the range's mining. In 1847 real production was underway at the Jackson Mine. Operations at the early mines were confined to ores at or close to the surface. Underground mining began after the Civil War when shafts were sunk. A forge built on the Carp River produced iron blooms in 1848. The pioneer furnace at Negaunee, built in 1857-1858, was the first actual blast furnace. Most ore has been shipped out to be smelted. When the Iron Mountain Railroad was built in 1857 ore could be moved easily to Marquette. Here at the pocket docks, the first of which was built in 1857, the ore was loaded aboard ships and carried through the Soo Canal to the growing industrial centers in the East. Copper, gold, silver and lead have been mined here but in small amounts only, leaving iron supreme.

City Park, at US-41 and Maple Street, Negaunee; Marquette Iron Range; S35; July 19, 1956; 1957

Few courthouses "go Hollywood!" The 1959 film *Anatomy of a Murder* was based on a Marquette County crime and set in the courthouse. (*Marquette County Courthouse*)

Mason

A Bygone Lumbering Town

Two centuries after Father Marquette's death not far from here in 1675, timber from this area's forests helped build America. Among the lumbering towns of the region was Hamlin, located on the Big Sable River at this site. Lumber from the sawmill was hauled by mule cars on a transway to long piers on Lake Michigan. In 1888 the mill dam broke. The released waters wiped out the little village.

Hamlin Dam area at Ludington State Park, M-116, Hamlin Township; Ghost Town of Hamlin Informational Site; S91; September 25, 1956; 1957

Armistice Day Storm

On November 11, 1940, a severe storm swept the Great Lakes area. As it crossed Lake Michigan, ships and seamen fought to reach safety away from its blinding winds and towering seas. Between Big and Little Points Sable the freighters *William B. Davock* and *Anna C. Minch* foundered with the loss of all hands. The crew of the *Novadoc*, driven aground south of Pentwater, battled icy winds and water for two days before being rescued by local fishermen. At Ludington the car-ferry *City of Flint 32* was driven ashore, her holds flooded to prevent further damage. Elsewhere lives were lost and ships damaged in one of Lake Michigan's greatest storms.

Stearns Park, between Stearns Outer Drive and Lakeshore Drive, Ludington; Armistice Day Storm Informational Designation; S318; November 6, 1970; 1971

S. S. Pere Marquette 18

At least twenty-nine persons died when this vessel sank in Lake Michigan twenty miles off the Wisconsin coast on September 9, 1910. One of the Ludington carferry fleet, the 350-foot *S. S. Pere Marquette 18* was traveling from this port to Wisconsin. About midlake a crewman discovered the ship was taking on vast amounts of water. The captain set a direct course for Wisconsin and sent a distress signal by wireless. He and the crew battled for four hours to save the boat but she sank suddenly. All of the officers and many of the crew and passengers perished, among them the first wireless operator to die in active service on the Great Lakes. The *S. S. Pere Marquette 17*, aided by other ships who also heeded the

196

wireless message for help, rescued more than thirty survivors but lost two of her own crew. The exact cause of this disaster remains a mystery.

Stearns Park, between Stearns Outer Drive and Lakeshore Drive, entrance to walkway leading to Ludington Harbor's north breakwall, Ludington; *S.S. PERE MARQUETTE* Informational Site; L484; December 14, 1976; 1977

Marquette's Death

Father Jacques Marquette, the great Jesuit missionary and explorer, died and was buried by two French companions somewhere along the Lake Michigan shore on May 18, 1675. He had been returning to his mission at St. Ignace, which he had left in 1673 to go exploring in the Mississippi country. The exact location of his death has long been a subject of controversy. A spot close to the southeast slope of this hill, near the ancient outlet of the Pere Marquette River, corresponds with the death site as located by early French accounts and maps and a constant tradition of the past. Marquette's remains were reburied at St. Ignace in 1677.

South Lakeshore Drive, Pere Marquette Park, bottom of Shrine, Ludington vicinity, Pere Marquette Township; Marquette's Death Site Informational Site; S278; April 6, 1966; 1966

Scottville

White settlers came to this area around 1860. In 1876 a station on the Flint and Pere Marquette Railroad opened. In 1879, James Sweetland built a sawmill adjacent to the railroad, which precipitated the establishment of a post office for the community of Sweetland. He sold the mill a year later to the firm of Crowley and Scott. Sweetland was informally known as Mason Center because of its location at the county's geographical center. In 1882, Hiram Scott and Charles Blain platted the village. According to legend, the men determined the name of the village with the toss of a coin. Scott won the toss and named the village

Father Jacques Marquette and Brother Louys Le Boeme established the first Jesuit mission in Michigan among the Chippewa at Sault Ste. Marie in 1668. (*Marquette's Death*)

Scottville. Charles Blain named the streets, the first of which were Blain, Crowley, State and Main. Scottville was incorporated as a village in 1889 and as a city in 1907. Today Scottville remains the agricultural center of Mason County.

Downtown Pedestrian Mall, 100 South Main, south of the intersection of US-10 & US-31, Scottville; Scottville Informational Designation; L1677C; July 20, 1989; 1989

Mecosta

Ferris Institute

This college was founded in 1884 by Woodbridge N. Ferris as the Big Rapids Industrial School. His objective was to provide low cost, practical training for all with a real desire to study, regardless of a lack of previous formal education. The school began with rented quarters and fifteen students. The first courses were commerce and college preparatory work. Programs in trade-technical work, pharmacy and teacher training followed. A pioneer school of its kind, it became a state school in 1949.

Erected in 1957, replaced in 1965.

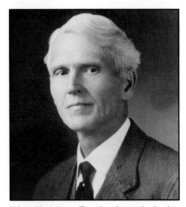

Ferris State College

This college was founded in 1884 by Woodbridge N. Ferris as the Big Rapids Industrial School, renamed Ferris Institute in 1895. His objective was to provide low cost, practical training for all with a real desire to study, regardless of a lack of previous formal education. The school began with rented quarters and fifteen students. The first courses were commerce and college preparatory work. Programs in trade-technical work, pharmacy and teacher training followed. A pioneer school of its kind, Ferris became a state college in 1949. By action of the legislature in 1963, it was renamed Ferris State College.

Woodbridge Ferris founded the Big Rapids Industrial School in 1884. (*Ferris Institute*)

Ferris State University campus, corner of State Street and Campus Drive, Big Rapids; Ferris Institute Informational Site; S114; January 19, 1957; 1965

First United Methodist Church

The First United Methodist Church was designed by W. E. N. Hunter, a Detroit architect who specialized in church designs. The domed Beaux Arts-style building reflects a trend in using Early Christian architectural forms of the fourth and fifth centuries in early twentieth century churches. This church was completed in 1907 and retains its original semicircular auditorium plan interior and stained-glass windows. The north window depicts the insignia of the Epworth League, a Methodist youth organization.

Side Two

In 1865 the Reverend W. J. Aldrich organized the first congregation in Big Rapids; it became the Methodist Episcopal Church in 1867. That year a frame church was built on this site. For many years the building served as a community center and was shared by members of the Presbyterian church. The present structure was dedicated on May 26, 1907. In February 1911 a fire damaged much of the building. The church reopened in time for Easter services on April 16.

304 Elm Street at Warren Avenue, Big Rapids; First United Methodist Church; L1418A; June 10, 1987; 1989

Mineral Well

In 1890, Alf Clark, who hoped to find oil at this site, found instead mineral water. Baths or drinks of Clark's Red Cross Electric Mineral Water were said to cure many maladies. By 1893 the Big Rapids Mineral Water Company was marketing the water on the East Coast and using it in its bath house on West Maple. In 1896, having changed its product name to Natural Medicinal Water, the firm built a bandstand next to the bathhouse. Twenty warm, soothing mineral baths cost five dollars. The water was bottled in a plant on North State Street.

The 1905 prospectus of the Yo-Landa Mineral Springs Company envisioned using Clark's mineral water in soft drinks, automobile anti-freeze and curative drinks. But scientific medicine, exemplified by the Ferris State College School of Pharmacy, which opened in 1893, was beginning to challenge elixirs. In 1912 the last local effort to market Clark's water failed. Its plant became Pioneer Publications' home in 1971; and in 1979 the well site became part of Ferris State, whose offerings include degrees in pharmacy, optometry and allied health.

Ferris State University Racquet Facility grounds, east of 14300 Northland Drive (Old 131/State Street); Big Rapids Clark's Mineral Water Informational Site; L1119C; September 21, 1983; 1983

Old Mecosta County Jail

Big Rapids became the county seat in 1859 and incorporated as a city in 1869. This building, antedated by two other jails, served as the county jail and sheriff's residence from 1893 until 1965. The oldest public structure in the original plat of the village of Big Rapids, it features gable and hip roofs and turrets characteristic of Queen Anne-style architecture. The adjacent grounds have been used for a park and for concerts.

220 South Warren Avenue, Big Rapids; Mecosta County Jail; L384; February 21, 1975; 1980

St. Andrew's Episcopal Church

St. Andrew's Parish was organized in 1870, when Michigan's logging industry was flourishing. Among its early members were George Stearns, the mayor and Thomas Lazell, the police magistrate. The simple white pine Gothic Revival church was built by the congregation, and dedicated on January 21, 1872. Part of the Western Michigan Diocese since 1874, St. Andrew's has served the Big Rapids community for over a century.

323 South State Street, corner of Locust, Big Rapids; St. Andrew's Episcopal Church; L414; August 15, 1975; 1976

Paris Fish Hatchery

Opening in 1881, the Paris Fish Hatchery was the state's second fish-rearing agency. This area was selected because of its abundant sources of water and excellent railroad connections. The Paris Fish Hatchery was a major supplier of salmon and brown trout fingerlings. Fish in milk cans painted a distinctive red were shipped throughout the state in railroad baggage cars, the most famous of which was the "Wolverine," which was used from 1913 to 1938, when motorized vehicles began to dominate shipment. The Works Progress Administration (WPA) renovated and expanded the facility in the mid-1930s. It continued to operate until 1964, when it was closed by the Department of Natural Resources. The site was acquired by the Mecosta County Park Commission in 1973, refurbished as a park and reopened in July 1976.

Paris Park, Old US-131 (Northland Drive), between Twenty-two Mile and Twenty-three Mile roads, Green Township; Paris Fish Hatchery; S506; February 23, 1978; 1980

Negro Settlers

In the 1860s, Negroes from southern Michigan, Ohio and Ontario settled this region as farmers and woodsmen. Some of them moved to new villages in Mecosta and Isabella counties. Schools and churches founded in the area were integrated. Among these was the Wheatland Church of Christ, established in nearby Remus in 1869. Their pioneering spirit provided a unity that led to the first Old Settlers' Reunion at this lake in the 1890s, a get-together which is still held annually.

School Section Lake Park, intersection of Nine Mile Road and Ninetieth Avenue, Morton Township; Negro Settlers Informational Designation; L81; July 17, 1970; 1971

Wheatland Church of Christ

Wheatland Church of Christ, also known as the Cross Church, is the oldest Disciples of Christ church built mainly for and by blacks in western Michigan. Thomas Cross (1826-1897), who with five other members founded the church in 1870, was its first elder. Early services were held in the Gingrich and Cross schoolhouses. When the congregation decided to build a church in 1883, Cross donated the land and loaned it the funds. In 1968 the church became an independent nondenominational organization.

3025 Eleven Mile Road, SW corner of M-66, Wheatland Township; Church of the Disciples (Wheatland Church of Christ); L1002A; March 18, 1982; 1988

The Mecosta County Jail and Sheriff's Residence, built in 1893, was threatened with demolition in the 1970s. Public pressure to the contrary saved the building. (*Old Mecosta County Jail*)

Menominee

Chappee Rapids

Stanislaus Chaput, a French-Canadian fur trader sometimes called Louis Chappee, became the first settler at the mouth of the Menominee River in the early 1800s. He fought, along with most of the Green Bay traders, in the British attack on Fort Mackinac during the War of 1812. After the war he traded extensively in the northern Wisconsin region, working for John Lawe, Green Bay fur magnate. Forcibly deposed from his old location in 1824 by rival traders William Farnsworth and Charles Brush, Chaput moved a few miles upstream and built a fortified trading post at the foot of the rapids. Until Chaput's death in the 1850s the post at the rapids was a center of trade for the surrounding villages of Menominee Indians.

Five miles west of Menominee, on River Road (County Road 581), Menominee Township; Chappee Rapids Informational Designation; S343; October 1, 1971; 1972

Menominee Area

This was the home of the Menominee Indians. Nicolet, the french explorer, visited them in

German immigrant Charles Meyer founded the Wisconsin Land and Lumber Company in 1883. Meyer's office is now the IXL Museum. (*Hermansville*)

1634 on his futile search for Cathay. Conflict over fishing rights brought on the Sturgeon War here between the Menominee and Chippewa tribes. During the 1700s this became a center of the fur trade. Until 1910 when the forests were cut Menominee was the Upper Peninsula's main lumber port. Its timber helped rebuild Chicago after the 1871 fire.

Menominee Tourist Center, US-41 north of interstate bridge linking Wisconsin to Michigan, Menominee Township; Menominee Area Informational Designation; L84; August 23, 1956; 1957

Hermansville

Charles J. L. Meyer of Minden, Germany, migrated to America in 1849 and continued his family tradition of woodworking by founding a plant in Fond du Lac, Wisconsin, for the manufacture of sash, doors and blinds. In 1878 he bought pine timberlands and founded the town of Hermansville to supply lumber to his Fond du Lac factories. The village was named for his son Herman, the first postmaster, and the township was named for Meyer. His son-in-law George Washington Earle of Tully, New York, helped bring the Wisconsin Land and Lumber Company, which Meyer started in 1883, through difficult times. Earle led the company to preeminence by producing precision finished hardwood flooring on machines which Meyer had designed and manufactured. The flooring factory closed in 1943.

US-2, near intersection of County Road 388, Meyer Township; Hermansville (Wisconsin Land and Lumber Company Town); L345; September 17, 1974; 1979

Midland

Midland County Courthouse

In 1831 the first white settlers in the area built a fur trading post near this site, called "Little Forks" by the Indians. When Midland County was organized in 1850, sixty-five people lived here. In 1856, Henry C. Ashmun, the county's first prosecuting attorney, was authorized to locate a courthouse, and he chose this site. The original courthouse served until 1926. In 1919, Mayor Joseph A. Cavanagh proposed that a new courthouse be built at this site. Voters approved a $225,000 bond issue in 1920 and, in gratitude for the war effort of area servicemen, invited the Midland American Legion to make its home here at the courthouse. Herbert H. Dow, founder of The Dow Chemical Company, provided additional funds and materials. Dr. Dow laid the cornerstone on March 29, 1925. This courthouse was occupied on January 1, 1926.

Side Two

Architect Bloodgood Tuttle of Detroit and Cleveland designed this courthouse in rustic Tudor Revival style. A portion of the exterior is magnesite stucco, a building material developed in 1925 by The Dow Chemical Company from Midland's vast underground brines. Donald Gibb of Dow worked with noted Detroit artist Paul Honore to develop the new "plastic mosaic" material. Ground glass was used instead of sand and silex in the magnesite stucco to give the murals their unusual color and sparkle. Using a palette knife, Honore created the layered, three-dimensional exterior murals of life-sized Indians, lumbermen and traders, illustrating the history of Midland County, and the mural in the Circuit Courtroom depicting an Indian Council. All of the exterior building materials are said to have originated in Midland County.

301 West Main Street, Midland; Midland County Courthouse; L1235A; May 21, 1985; 1989

The Upper Bridge

When completed in 1908 the Upper Bridge, today known as the Currie Parkway Bridge, replaced its wooden predecessor as the main crossing over the Tittabawassee River. The Joliet Bridge and Iron Company of Illinois constructed the bridge for $7,500. It is a 140-foot-long steel Pratt through-truss bridge. In 1955 the Karl B. Robertson Bridge, built one-quarter mile to the south, succeeded the Upper Bridge as the city's main river crossing. In order to preserve the Upper Bridge, the city added an independent structural arch in 1988.

Currie Parkway over the Tittabawassee River, Midland; Upper Bridge (Currie Parkway Bridge); L1581A; August 18, 1988; 1991

Monroe

St. Patrick Church

Irish and German immigrants first came to this area, known as Stony Creek, in the 1840s. The settlement was also called Athlone, after a city significant in Ireland's military history. Redemptorist missionaries served Catholics here from 1847 until 1855. On March 17, 1847, they celebrated the dedicatory Mass of their first church, which was built of logs donated by parishioners. On June 26, 1860, the cornerstone was laid for the present church; six months later the church was completed. Built in the Round-Arch mode, it once had a lofty spire surrounded by finials. On December 27, Bishop LeFevre appointed Father Desiderius Callaert the first resident pastor of Stony Creek, and St. Patrick's gained the full status of a parish.

2996 West Labo Road, east of Exeter Road, Carleton vicinity, Ash Township; Saint Patrick's Catholic Church; L1685A; October 10, 1989; 1991

Lake Erie

Named for the Erie Indians, this was the last of the Great Lakes discovered by white men. The French were exploring the upper lakes as early as 1615, but they avoided the region to the south, which was the realm of hostile Iroquois Indians. Then in 1669, Adrien Jolliet entered Lake Erie from the Detroit River and followed the north shore eastward. The final link was added to the mighty inland waterway so vital in Michigan history.

'Erected at the entrance of Sterling State Park, Park Road, east of M-50, east of Monroe city limits, Frenchtown Township; Lake Erie Informational Designation; S118; January 19, 1957; 1957

Michigan: Historic Crossroads

Because of its location in the heart of the upper Great Lakes, Michigan has been a historic crossroads. Its waterways and trails were favorite routes of Indians many centuries ago. French explorers first entered Michigan about 1620. By 1700 forts at several key points guarded this vital link between French colonies to the east and to the west and south. In 1760-1761 the British won control of Michigan. Not until 1796 did they withdraw in favor of the Americans, who had been awarded the area in 1783 at the end of the Revolutionary War. During the War of 1812, Michigan was one of the most fiercely contested areas. It was admitted as a state in 1837.

Michigan: Twenty-sixth State

When Michigan in 1837 became the twenty-sixth state admitted to the Union, only the southern part of lower Michigan was settled. Farming was the chief economic activity. In the next fifty years the remainder of the state was populated. Logging of the state's magnificent forests made Michigan America's lumbering capital during the 1880s and 1890s. Mining of the great Upper Peninsula copper and iron ore deposits made Michigan a leading producer of these minerals during most of this period. With the development of the automobile and other industries, Michigan became a manufacturing giant among the states of the United States and of the world.

Toledo Beach, east of I-75, exit 9 (Otter Road), near Monroe, Frenchtown Township; Michigan Historic Crossroads Informational Site; S165; September 17, 1957; 1958

Monroe

Monroe, founded about 1784, is one of Michigan's oldest settlements. It was first called Frenchtown after its original settlers. It was the scene of the River Raisin Massacre during the War of 1812. Renamed Monroe in 1824, it later anchored the Michigan Southern Railroad and became famous for its glass and paper. General George Custer made his home here.

Erected at Plum Creek Park, South Telegraph Road, Monroe Township. Now on exhibit at the Monroe County Historical Museum, 126 South Monroe Street, Monroe; Monroe County Informational Designation; S36; July 19, 1956; 1957

Peter Seitz Tavern & Stagecoach Inn

In 1856, German immigrant Peter Seitz built this house as a residence and stagecoach inn on North Custer plank toll road. Early stagecoaches were pulled by teams of up to four horses. The plank roads were constructed of wooden boards to aid travel during the "muddy season." The tavern was a popular meeting place for area residents as well as stagecoach travelers. It offered lodging, food, spirits and entertainment. Dances and other social and community gatherings were held in the second-floor ballroom. Here residents began plans that led to the founding of St. Matthew's Lutheran Church in 1860. Used as an inn until around the turn of the century, the structure was converted into a single-family home in 1899.

8941 North Custer Road, just west of Ida Maybee Road, Raisinville Township; Seitz Inn (Peter Seitz House); L753A; October 23, 1979; 1980

Montcalm

Greenville

In 1844, John and Deborah Green and their children moved to Montcalm County from their native New York. He purchased land, which now comprises more than half the town, and erected a dam and sawmill on this site. As the town grew, it became the commercial center of the county serving the expanding white pine lumber industry along the Flat River. Green financed many of the early businesses, and so when the city was chartered in 1871, Green's Village was officially named Greenville in honor of its founder.

Flat River Historical Museum, 213 North Franklin Street, South bank of the Flat River, Greenville; Greenville Informational Designation ; L413; August 15, 1975; 1976

Montmorency

Big Rock

Natural features have often played a role in the naming of communities. One such settlement was Big Rock. Named after a massive boulder, this hamlet was located at the crossroads of present-day M-32 and Thornton Road. Seth Gillet became the first postmaster in 1882. By 1902 a general store owned by Briley Township pioneer William Remington housed the post office. At that time a church and school, a grange hall, a sawmill and a blacksmith shop were also located in Big Rock. The post office closed in 1920.

M-32 West at Thornton Road, Briley Township; Big Rock Informational Designation; L1808C; January 17, 1991; 1991

Muskegon

Central United Methodist Church

The first Protestant society in Muskegon began as a mission station served by itinerant preachers. In 1843 the Reverend M. Warring held Muskegon's first service in Martin Ryerson's boardinghouse. Deacon Abner Bennett, a black lay preacher, and his wife, Mary, a former servant of President James K. Polk, formed the White Lake Sunday School. Bennett frequently preached in Muskegon. The church was formally organized on November 20, 1856.

Side Two

In 1859, Muskegon Methodists built their first church at Clay and Jefferson streets. Congregationalists met in the church, which also served as the county court. In 1887 a larger church was built on the same site. The present Neo-Gothic-style church, built in 1928-1930, was designed by denominational architect, Thoralf M. Sundt of Philadelphia. This Indiana limestone church seats one thousand persons. The tower rises one hundred feet.

1011 Second Street, Muskegon; Central United Methodist Church; L1659A; May 18, 1989; 1990

Hackley House

This three-story wood-frame building is one of Michigan's most splendid examples of Queen Anne architecture. With juxtaposition of masses created by roof lines, chimneys, tower and porte-cochere it has become a symbol of Muskegon. Fifteen stained-glass windows add to the elegance of the structure, and the interior decoration includes hand-stenciled walls and ceilings, carved woodwork and seven tiled fireplaces. The house is testimony to Hackley's wealth, and to an era when Muskegon was known as "Lumber Queen of the World."

Side Two

Charles H. Hackley (1837-1905) came to Muskegon in 1857. Though he had only seven dollars when he arrived, he was worth $12 million at the time of his death. He made his fortune in lumber, and when lumber declined, he administered the Chamber of Commerce program that rebuilt Muskegon into a center of industry. His gifts and endowments to the community totalled over $6 million and supported parks, statuary, schools, local churches, a hospital and a public library.

484 West Webster Avenue, Muskegon; Hackley, Charles H., House; HB58; April 24, 1970; 1988

Hackley Public Library

On May 25, 1888, Muskegon lumber baron Charles H. Hackley announced that he would donate a library to the city. Hackley stipulated that the facility be "forever maintained as a library." Patton and Fisher of Chicago, one of six firms invited to submit plans for the library, designed the Richardsonian Romanesque-style building. The library was constructed of Maine granite and trimmed with Marquette sandstone. The reading room windows depict Shakespeare, Goethe, Longfellow and Prescott.

Side Two

Muskegon citizens celebrated the laying of the Hackley Public Library cornerstone on May 25, 1889, the anniversary of Charles Hackley's donation of the library. It was the first annual celebration held in recognition of Hackley. The previous year the board of education had resolved that classes would be suspended annually on May 25 in Hackley's honor. On October 15, 1890, the completed library was dedicated. The lot, building and furnishings amounted to a $175,000 gift.

316 West Webster Avenue, Muskegon; Hackley Public Library; S606A; February 15, 1990; 1990

Hume House

Built in 1887-1889, this massive Queen Anne-style house served the Thomas Hume family through four generations. The architect for this, as well as the Hackley House, was David S. Hopkins of Grand Rapids. The structure behind the two buildings was shared by both families. Known as the City Barn, it reflects the features of each house. Though larger than the Hackley House, the Hume House is less pretentious in detail. One hundred years after completion, the Hackley and Hume Historic Site was administered by the Muskegon County Museum.

Side Two

Thomas Hume (1848-1920) was the business partner of Charles H. Hackley from 1881 to 1905. An Irish immigrant, Hume came to Muskegon in 1872 and began working as Hackley's bookkeeper. After Hackley's death, Hume was instrumental in transforming Muskegon from a lumber town to a major manufacturing center. At the time of his death in 1920, he was serving as an officer with the Amazon Knitting Company, Shaw Electric Crane Works, Sargent Manufacturing Company, Chase-Hackley Piano Company, the Stand Malleable Company and the Hackley National Bank.

During the 1880s, Thomas Hume built his residence, a premier example of Queen Anne architecture, adjacent to the home of his partner Charles Hackley. (*Hume House*)

472 West Webster Avenue, Muskegon; Hume House; L144; August 13, 1971; 1988

Muskegon Business College

Woodbridge N. Ferris founded the Ferris Business College in October 1888. Ferris had also founded what is now known as Ferris State University in Big Rapids three years earlier. The college was initially established as a proprietary school of business. Since its founding, it has been owned by various individuals and undergone several name changes. Since 1926 the college's prominent owners and managers have been the Jewell family. In 1965 the name became Muskegon Business College and the institution began granting associate degrees. In 1969 the school was chartered by the state of Michigan as a non-profit institution. After merging with Baker College of Flint and Owosso, Muskegon Business College began granting the Bachelor of Business Administration degree in 1987.

College courtyard off of Apple Avenue at Spring Street, Muskegon; Ferris Business College Informational Designation (Muskegon Business College); L1501C; February 25, 1988; 1988

Old Indian Cemetery

This cemetery was already established when the first white man came to the area. It is believed to have been used by the Ottawas as early as 1750 and is known to have been a burial ground from 1806 to 1854 for both Indians and settlers. The Daily-Badeau trading post existed from 1830 to 1848 on the shore of Muskegon Lake below the cemetery. Louis B. Badeau purchased Lot 2, containing the cemetery and much of downtown Muskegon, in 1839. This was the starting point for all the early surveys in the area. Near here Martin Ryerson set up his first sawmill. He obtained title to the cemetery, and in 1926 his son, Martin A. Ryerson, deeded it to Muskegon with the stipulation that it be maintained in perpetuity.

Morris Avenue between First and Second streets, Muskegon; Indian Cemetery; L20; June 13, 1961; 1964

Pinchtown

Pinchtown was officially known as "Ruddiman's Addition to the city of Muskegon" when it was platted by William Ruddiman in 1873. Township Clerk James Robinson gave the settlement its common name because it was pinched between the village of Lakeside and the city of Muskegon. On March 12, 1895, the Michigan legislature passed a bill, signed by

Governor John T. Rich, that annexed Pinchtown to the city. Pinchtown was bounded by Lakeshore Drive, Laketon Avenue, Ruddiman Creek and a gully. A shopping district occupied this site from the 1890s to 1950s.

Side Two

Some of Muskegon's earliest lumber mills were located in Pinchtown. In 1842, Joseph Stronach built a sawmill west of here on Muskegon Lake at Ruddiman's Creek. In 1844, George and John Ruddiman purchased the mill. In 1848 the mill was swept away in a flood, and the Ruddimans rebuilt it the following year. Newcomb McGraft and Anthony Schuyler Montgomery purchased the mill in 1875. In 1890 the mill burned. Standard Oil Company (present-day Amoco) tanks and docks occupied the site from 1924 to 1991.

SE corner of Laketon Avenue and Lake Shore Drive, Muskegon; Pinchtown Informational Designation; L1822C; April 11, 1991; 1991

Torrent House

This thirty-one room mansion, built for $250,000 in 1891-1892, was the home of John Torrent (1833-1915), pioneer lumberman, alderman, justice of the peace and Muskegon mayor for three terms. A successful entrepreneur, Torrent owned shingle, saw and lumber mills in Muskegon, Manistee, Ludington, Whitehall, Traverse City and Sault Ste. Marie, equipping them all with the most modern machinery. Over the years, this structure also housed a mortuary, hospital and the local Red Cross headquarters. In 1972 the city purchased the house to prevent its demolition.

315 West Webster Avenue, Muskegon; Torrent House (Muskegon Osteopathic Hospital); L129; June 19, 1971; 1980

Muskegon Log Booming Company

Muskegon was the largest center of lumbering on Lower Michigan's west coast. From the 1850s to the 1890s an immense amount of timber was floated to this port down the Muskegon River and its tributaries. In 1864 the Muskegon Booming Company was formed to sort the logs and raft them to the mills. Here at the upper end of Muskegon Lake was the great storage boom where the logs, each identified by its owner's log mark, were sorted into pens as fast as they floated in. They were then chained together into rafts which were towed to the mills by the company's tugboats. In thirty years the company delivered over ten billion board feet of logs.

Richards Park, Old US-31, south of North Muskegon, Muskegon Township; Muskegon Log Booming Company Informational Site; S90; August 23, 1956; 1958

Jean Baptiste Recollect Trading Post

Near this site, on the shore of Muskegon Lake, stood the first Indian fur trading post in Muskegon County. It was established in 1812 by Jean Baptiste Recollect, a French fur trader believed to be this area's first white settler. Jean Recollect remained here for about a year when a new manager took over. The Muskegon post operated as a successful business enterprise for many years. Remains of the chimney of Recollect's station were visible as late as 1836.

SE corner of Ruddiman and Bear Lake Road, North Muskegon; John Baptiste Recollect Trading Post Informational Site; L726B; August 3, 1979; 1980

Lebanon Lutheran Church

During the mid-nineteenth century, immigrant Swedes, Norwegians and Danes settled in this area. In 1868 they organized a Scandinavian Lutheran Church with the Reverend T. H. Ward as pastor. On June 2, 1872, the Swedish members of the congregation withdrew to become part of the Augustana Synod and formed the Swedish Evangelical Lutheran Lebanon Church of Whitehall. A theological student, V. A. Youngberg, was called as the new church's first pastor. The Swedes met in the Scandinavian Church until 1877, when they built this Gothic-inspired church using lumber cut from the surrounding woods and milled in the Covell-Stapes mill. Services were held in Swedish until the early 1930s. In the 1980s the neighborhood around the church was still known locally as Swedentown.

1101 South Mears Avenue, corner of Market Street, Whitehall; Swedish Evangelical Lutheran Church of Whitehall (Lebanon Evangelical Lutheran Church); L1064A; February 10, 1983; 1985

Oakland

Roseland Park Mausoleum

The Roseland Park Mausoleum was the largest public mausoleum in the United States when it was dedicated in 1914. Designed by Detroit architect Louis Kamper (1861-1953), the classically inspired, two-story building contains thirteen hundred crypts. Before designing this structure, Kamper traveled to Europe to study noted mausoleums there. The interior of this building is faced with Vermont marble and classically detailed with double-tier Doric columns in the entrance lobby and in the main hall. Skylights enhance its lighting.

NW corner of Twelve Mile Road and Woodward Avenue, Berkeley; Roseland Park Mausoleum (Roseland Park Mausoleum); L1060A; January 27, 1983; 1986

The Academy of the Sacred Heart

Responding to a request from the Antoine Beaubien family, five religious of the French order of the Sacred Heart came from New York to Detroit in 1851. The religious opened a school on Jefferson Avenue in June of that year with ten day-students and three orphans. From 1851 to 1861 the school occupied three different locations on Jefferson Avenue. In 1861 the religious erected a new school there. It operated for fifty-seven years. From 1918 to 1958 the school was located on Lawrence Avenue. In addition to their Detroit endeavors, the religious operated a boarding school in Grosse Pointe Farms from 1885 to 1969. In 1958 the Detroit school was moved to Bloomfield Hills. It is the oldest continuing school among the members of the Independent Schools of Michigan.

1250 Kensington Road, north of Wattles Road, Bloomfield Hills; Academy of the Sacred Heart Informational Designation; L1156C; March 20, 1984; 1984

Bagley Inn

This frame structure, completed in 1833, is the second home of Bagley's Tavern. Amasa Bagley first established the tavern in the 1820s in a log cabin. He came to this area in 1819 with his family and four other settlers. He was appointed associate judge of the Oakland County Court in 1820. Shortly afterwards Bagley and William Morris, the area's first sheriff, set up a brickworks and a saw and grist mill. However, they were best known for Bagley's Tavern, which hosted social and political functions.

101 West Long Lake Road, just west of Woodward Avenue, Bloomfield Hills; Bagley Inn ; L570; December 8, 1977; 1979

Seymour Lake Methodist Episcopal Church

The local Methodist society, organized in 1837 at the house of Joseph Shurter, met in residences and schoolhouses for nearly four decades. In 1871, Irene Gibbs donated this land for its use. The church's cornerstone was laid on May 29, 1874. Lumber for the $4,000-structure was hauled from Kings Mill near Lapeer. The builders were George Brock, Charles Tolfree and J. K. Wolfe. The building has been used as a house of worship and a community gathering place since its dedication on October 27, 1874.

3050 Sashabaw Road, NW corner of Seymour Lake Road, Brandon Township; Seymour Lake Methodist Episcopal Church (Seymour Lake United Methodist Church); L1176B; June 15, 1984; 1987

Byers Homestead

Two generations of the Byers family have resided at this site, said to be the home of the first white settler in Commerce Township. Abraham Walrod came here in 1825 from New York State and built a log cabin in what is now the village of Commerce. The present Early Victorian frame house erected prior to 1850 replaced the cabin. Now a country store, the barn is believed to have been a blacksmith shop. Other buildings on these grounds include a chicken coop and pantry. Traversed by the Huron River, the area attracted settlers, many of whom came westward via the Erie Canal, which opened in 1825. Inhabitants named their village Commerce hoping that its early growth would signal the beginning of a business center. Now a quiet residential village, the community features this picturesque and historic homestead.

213 Commerce Road, just west of Carroll Lake Road (South Commerce Road), Commerce Township; Byers Farm; L280; April 5, 1974; 1977

Commerce Roller Mill

The Commerce Roller Mill, built in 1837 by Amasa Andrews and Joseph and Asa Farr, harnessed the water power of the Huron River. It served the farm communities of western Oakland County for ninety years, closing in 1927. The mill's owners included Milton Parshall (circa 1900) and Isaac Lutz (circa 1920). With its undershot water wheel, the Commerce mill was the center of commercial activity in the township throughout the nineteenth and early twentieth centuries. The mill processed flour and ground feed for farmers' livestock. It was destroyed by fire in 1939. Only the excavations for the mill race, the mill flume and the stone foundations of the mill buildings remain. The site was developed as an interpretive historic area in 1984.

Commerce Road (Sleeth Road), just west of the intersection of Carroll Lake Road, Commerce, Commerce Township; Commerce Roller Mill (Commerce Mill Race Park); L1155; March 20, 1984; 1984

Commerce United Methodist Congregation

A Methodist Episcopal class, which later became a church society, was organized in Commerce in 1838. For many years, it was part of the Farmington Circuit. The Reverend Daniel C. Jacokes was the church's first circuit minister. Religious meetings were held in a schoolhouse until the society erected its first church in 1842. In 1854, Commerce, with its seventy-one members, was made the head of a circuit. The congregation organized a Sunday School in 1855 and an Epworth League for youth in 1891. The Ladies Aid Society, organized in 1885, hosted maple sugar and lawn socials to supplement its dues of five cents a month. By 1915 the local Presbyterian and Baptist congregations had disbanded, leaving the Methodist society as the sole church in Commerce.

Side Two

In 1842 the Methodist Episcopal congregation of Commerce erected a modest Greek Revival frame church at the northwest intersection of Commercial and Ponderosa streets. Logs for the church, including oak for the frame, were hauled to Lapeer to be sawed. The land for the church had been purchased a year earlier for $75. The cost of the church was $1,200. The handsome structure was moved to its present location in 1957 and enlarged. The original portion, presently used as a chapel, is easily distinguished by its towering steeple, a replica of the original one. Known as the Commerce United Methodist Church, the structure is recognized as the oldest Methodist church building in Oakland County and one of the oldest in Michigan.

1155 West Commerce Road, SW corner of Bogie Lake Road, Commerce Township; Commerce Methodist Episcopal Church (Commerce United Methodist Church); L1297B; February 28, 1986; 1986

Four Towns Methodist Church

Four Towns received its name because it is near the point where the townships of West Bloomfield, Commerce, Waterford and White Lake meet. In 1866 a frame schoolhouse was built here, on land donated by Nathan R. Colvin. From that year until 1930 the building served both as a school and church. Since then the building has been used primarily for church activities.

6451 Cooley Lake Road, Union Lake vicinity, Commerce Township; Four Towns Methodist Church; L61; March 9, 1966; 1966

First Quaker Meeting

In the 1820s members of the Society of Friends played a key role in the settlement of several Michigan communities. Farmington was founded in 1824 by Arthur Power, a Quaker from Farmington, New York. In 1831 what was apparently Michigan's first formal Quaker Meeting was organized at Farmington. Power in 1832 gave the land for the meetinghouse and the old Quaker Cemetery located one-half mile west of here on Gill Road. Earlier, in 1828, these Friends opened a school. This industrious group provided the nucleus around which the present city and township developed. The Quakers were also active in the antislavery movement. Farmington had a station on the Underground Railroad.

Farmington Municipal Building, Grand River Avenue, one block west of Farmington Road, Farmington; First Quaker Meeting Informational Designation; S266; March 23, 1965; 1965

Governor Fred M. Warner

This large white Civil War-era house in the center of Farmington's historic district has been the residence of the Warner family for many decades. Here lived Fred M. Warner, governor of Michigan from 1905 to 1911. Born in England in 1865, Warner spent most of his life in this city and served as its state senator from 1895 to 1898. An agriculturist and businessman, he established in 1889 the first of his thirteen cheese factories. From 1901 to 1904, Warner was secretary of state. Then he was elected to the first of three terms as state chief executive. This Republican governor championed many Progressive Era programs including regulation of railroads and insurance, conservation, food inspection, child labor laws, direct primary elections and woman's suffrage. Warner died in 1923, leaving a legacy of reform-minded years.

35805 Grand River Avenue, Farmington; Warner, Governor Fred, House; S371; February 11, 1972; 1979

Aldrich House

Royal Aldrich, a native of Farmington, New York, built this two-story Greek Revival farmhouse around 1840. His father, Esek, had purchased the 320-acre site from the United States government in 1823. Esek never lived here, but sold the property to Royal, who settled here in 1839. The house retains its original clapboard siding, interior woodwork, doors and hardware. It is supported by fourteen-inch to sixteen-inch walnut beams and a cobblestone basement foundation.

31110 Eleven Mile Road, east of Orchard Lake Road, Farmington Hills; Aldrich, Royal, House (Basil, Flora House); L953A; October 16, 1981; 1982

The Botsford Inn

This historic inn, the oldest in Michigan still providing food and lodging, was built as a home in 1836 by Orrin Weston. In 1841 it was converted into a tavern by Stephen Jennings. Known as the Sixteen Mile House, it was the stagecoach stop here in Clarenceville on the Grand River plank road, which followed an Indian trail that went on to Lake Michigan. Milton C. Botsford in 1860 acquired the inn. It became a popular meeting place for drovers, farmers and travelers to and from Detroit. Henry Ford, who had first seen the inn while courting his future wife, Clara, in a horse and buggy, purchased the inn from the Botsfords in 1924 and restored it. The Fords operated it until 1951.

28000 Grand River Avenue, Farmington Hills; Botsford Inn; HB24; February 19, 1958; 1962

David Simmons House

A native of Ontario County, New York, David Simmons moved to this area around 1827. Here he farmed, eventually acquiring 156 acres of land. He built this Greek Revival house around 1843. It features a fieldstone foundation, hand-hewn timbers and pegged joints. Its interior retains the original triple-facet woodwork with six-sided moldings around the doors and windows of the dining room. Although the house has been enlarged over the years, portions of the 1840s section are still visible.

22000 Haggerty, Farmington Hills; Simmons, David, House; L964A; October 16, 1981; 1988

Eber Durham House

This attractive Greek Revival house was built in 1845 by Stephen Jennings, an early owner of the Sixteen Mile House (now the Botsford Inn). He built the house as a wedding gift for his daughter Jane when she married Eber Durham. A civic-minded individual, Durham served the community as a highway commissioner, justice of the peace and drain commissioner. In 1924, Henry Ford purchased the house and restored it as a private residence. It was moved to this site in 1983.

35835 Thirteen Mile Road, Farmington Hills; Durham, Eber, House ; L1202A; December 19, 1984; 1986

Glen Oaks

This graceful English-style stone clubhouse, completed in 1925, was designed by Butterfield and Butterfield of Farmington. In 1923 developers began the Oakland Subdivision housing development. The clubhouse and its adjoining nine-hole public golf course were part of that development. During the 1925-1926 school year, the clubhouse was used as a school while a new district school for the area was being completed. The original dining room was extended in 1952 and again in 1968. After passing through several owners, the golf course and clubhouse were purchased by the Oakland County Parks and Recreation Commission in 1978. The commission has restored much of the imposing slate-roofed clubhouse, the focal point of the Glen Oaks County Park.

30500 West Thirteen Mile Road, just east of Orchard Lake Road, Farmington Hills; Glen Oaks Country Club Clubhouse (Glen Oaks Country Golf Course); L960A; October 16, 1981; 1986

Lawrence Simmons House

Constructed in 1861, this is one of the three houses that Livonia farmer Joshua Simmons had built for his three sons. Lawrence Simmons, for whom this house was built, lived here for twelve years. He, like the elder Simmons, was a farmer. The house was designed by local carpenter and architect Sergius P. Lyon, who was also an undertaker, a stove manufacturer and founder of the Farmington Universalist Church. The handsome Victorian-style stone structure displays seven different "gingerbread" designs in the trim.

33742 Twelve Mile Road, west of Farmington Road, Farmington Hills; Simmons, Lawrence, House (Simmons-Russell House); L1110A; August 12, 1983; 1985

Lemuel Botsford House

Lemuel and Lucy Botsford were Quakers. From Salisbury, Connecticut, they moved to Lyons, New York, and in 1836 to Farmington's Quaker settlement. In 1837 the Botsfords built this Greek Revival house on what became known as Botsford Hill. The house was on a 240-acre working farm. Their son Milton built an identical residence on the other side of the valley. Milton, the oldest of their ten children, was owner and proprietor of the Botsford Inn, Michigan's oldest continuously operating inn.

24414 Farmington Road, Farmington Hills; Botsford, Lemuel, House (Botsford-Wallaert House); L955A; October 16, 1981; 1988

Nardin Park United Methodist Church

In 1927 the Nardin Park Methodist Episcopal Church was formed by a merger of two Detroit churches: the Ninde Church, organized in 1886, and the Grand River Avenue Church, established in 1891. The following year an educational building and gymnasium were constructed on a site across West Chicago Boulevard from Nardin Park. The Depression delayed construction of the sanctuary. In 1937 a building campaign began. The Kresge Foundation donated $50,000. The completed sanctuary was dedicated in 1943. In 1963 the congregation sold the building to the Ebenezer African Methodist Episcopal Church. The present church was dedicated on October 17, 1965.

29887 West Eleven Mile Road, Farmington Hills; Nardin Park United Methodist Church Informational Designation; L1771C; July 21, 1990; 1990

Stephen Yerkes Rodgers House

Stephen Yerkes Rodgers built this Greek Revival-style house in 1834. The carved fretwork in the pilasters flanking the door are reminiscent of a design in Asher Benjamin's *The Practical House Carpenter* (Boston, 1830). Stephen Yerkes Rodgers was the nephew of Joseph Yerkes, the patriarch of one of Oakland County's pioneer families. For over a century and a half, the house has been owned continuously by descendants of Joseph Yerkes.

39040 Nine Mile Road, Farmington Hills; Stephen Yerkes Rodgers House (Barber House); L557; November 7, 1977; 1989

Theron Murray House

In 1831, Oakland County pioneers Theron and Rebecca Murray purchased eighty acres of land from the U.S. government including this site. This Greek Revival house and the barn, constructed around 1835, were built of hand-hewn poplar beams with wooden pegs. From 1942 to 1958, Charles W. Malpass owned the house as well as a parcel directly across Halsted Road. That forty-acre pasture served as a landing strip for private planes. Malpass allegedly named the house "Upson Downs."

30943 Halsted Road, Farmington Hills; Murray, Theron, House (William Dornan House); L962A; October 16, 1981; 1989

Franklin Village

Founded in 1824-1825, Franklin received its present name in 1828. [The] first postmaster was Dr. Ebenezer Raynale, state legislator and physician. The William Huston store, opened in 1830, was the forerunner of a business center that later included the famous Broughton Wagon Shop, the Van Every Mills, now "Ye Olde Cider Mill," several taverns, two distilleries and two churches. The village also was a station on the Underground Railroad. Franklin still has the appearance and atmosphere of an early Michigan village.

Village Green, Franklin Road between Carol and Wellington Streets, Franklin; Franklin Village Informational Designation; L11; March 25, 1960; 1960

Franklin Village School

Michigan's Territorial Council passed a law in 1827 requiring every township with fifty or more inhabitants to establish a school. Thus, the following year, the first school in Southfield Township was erected in Franklin Village. Sophie Gotie taught twenty-nine students in a log schoolhouse located near the still extant house of early settler Daniel Broughton. Franklin Village built a new school in 1845 at the foot of School Hill on property deeded by Wintrop Worthing. On this site in 1869 a third school was constructed on land given by wealthy postmaster A. A. Rust. After that building burned in 1922, the village erected the present school on this same location. The Franklin School District No. 3, Southfield Township, joined the Birmingham Public Schools in 1945.

32220 Franklin Road, at the corner of Romany, Franklin; Franklin School; L584; January 19, 1978; 1978

Methodist Episcopal Church of Highland Station

Highland's Methodist Episcopal Church was organized in 1865. Lester and George St. John built this structure in 1886 on three lots donated by J. B. and Betsey Crouse. In 1946 the former Hickory Ridge School was added to the Victorian church with the south portion completed in 1957. The township purchased the building in 1980 and meticulously renovated and expanded it, repeating the Venetian glass insets in the oriel windows and the ornate scroll-saw trim of the original. It was rededicated as a library in 1982.

205 West Livingston Road, Highland, Highland Township; Highland United Methodist Church (Highland Township Library); L902A; March 16, 1981; 1988

Rowe House

Squire and Dolly Rowe, who settled here in 1835, built this elegant, cut fieldstone house in 1855. The solid cobblestone, beaded mortar joint construction is highlighted by the pleasing and sophisticated use of delicate scrollwork under the eaves and by the smooth chiseled quoins, lintels and sills. Squire Rowe grew to a position of prominence in the community. After twenty-five terms as township supervisor, he served in the state legislature in 1865, the year before his death.

2360 Lone Tree Road, between Hickory Ridge and Milford roads, Milford vicinity, Highland Township; Rowe House; L351; September 17, 1974; 1975

Battle Alley

This historic district was once the scene of frequent brawls. In 1880 an uproar between local rowdies and workers of a traveling circus rendered so many bruised, beaten and jailed that this street was thus named "Battle Alley." Carrie A. Nation, "Kansas saloon smasher," came to Holly on August 28, 1908, at the request of the local prohibition committee. Wielding her umbrella, she strode through the alley's bars bellowing about the "Demon Rum" and its sins. In 1910, Battle Alley became the first brick street in the village.

Marker located at the corner of Battle Alley (Martha Street) and Broad Street in the district comprised of 102 South Broad Street; 125-127 and 201 South Saginaw; 106, 108, 109, 111, 117 Battle Alley, Holly; Battle Alley (Battle Alley Historic District); L602; May 17, 1978; 1978

Crapo Park

Henry Howland Crapo (1804-1869)—wealthy lumberman, Republican, state senator (1863-1864) and governor of Michigan (1865-1868)—owned prosperous lumberyards in Holly, Fenton and Flint. Lumber and railroads were essential elements in the development of this area. In 1863-1864, Crapo was instrumental in developing the Flint to Holly Railroad, which linked this part of the state to the rest of the country. The eighteen-mile line was among the first to use steel rails in the United States and was funded entirely by private subscriptions. This park, named for Governor Crapo, is on the site of his Holly lumberyard. The property, owned by the Chesapeake and Ohio Railroad, has been leased by the village of Holly since 1918.

Crapo Park, bounded by Martha Street (Battle Alley), Washington Street and railroad tracks, Holly; Crapo Park Informational Site; L832; July 29, 1980; 1980

Holly's Town Hall

Holly's Town Hall has been a center of community activity since it was built in 1892. Holly Township in Oakland County was formally organized in 1838, and the village of Holly was incorporated in 1865. The two local governments decided to join efforts in building a town hall after their nearby rival, Fenton in Genesee County, erected a hall in the late 1880s.

Township voters approved the idea in 1889, village voters in 1890. The two governments shared equally in the planning and funding of the $3,000 project. The hall has been used for municipal offices, a fire station, a jail, a polling place and as a setting for social, cultural and political gatherings. Village offices remained here until 1958; township offices, until 1982.

102 Front Street, NW corner of South Saginaw, Holly; Holly Town Hall; L1261A; August 22, 1985; 1985

Fred A. Baker House

In 1890, Fred A. Baker, an attorney and former state legislator, purchased 320 acres of land in Royal Oak Township. He developed the land into the Black Meadow Dairy Farm, one of the area's largest dairies. This Colonial Revival house was built in 1896 on his farm across LaSalle Street. It was moved to this site in 1916 when Baker and several associates formed the Baker Land Company and subdivided the farm into the Bronx Subdivision, one of the city's oldest neighborhoods.

10505 LaSalle Boulevard, Huntington Woods; Baker, Fred A., House (Huntington Woods Public Library); L1360B; December 5, 1986; 1990

Sashabaw Cemetery

Although burials were made here as early as 1836, it was 1849 before residents of Sashabaw Plains formed Sashabaw Burial Association for purposes of "fencing, improving, ornamenting and keeping the burying ground . . . in proper repair." A center alley was created and the price of lots set at one dollar. The association meets annually and maintains the cemetery. A sizeable addition was authorized in 1949.

5331 Maybee Road, east of Sashabaw Road, Independence Township; Sashabaw Cemetery; L58; June 6, 1966; 1966

Sashabaw United Presbyterian Church

This church structure, one of the oldest in the Detroit Presbytery, was erected by a church building society which was organized on January 20, 1855. A fine example of the classic New England church, it was built and furnished for $3,000. It was dedicated in June 1856 as the house of worship for the First Presbyterian Church of Independence. The congregation had been organized in 1840 under the Plan of Union as the Church of Orion and Independence. Because of a small membership, the church in 1932 was dissolved. When Sashabaw United Presbyterian Church was organized in 1946, this building became its house of worship. The original steeple was restored and the building carefully preserved.

5331 Maybee Road, east of Sashabaw Road, Independence Township; Sashabaw Presbyterian Church; L38; September 18, 1964; 1965

Lake Orion Methodist Church

Methodist missionaries preached here in the 1820s and in 1833 a class was organized. Services were held in homes and schoolhouses, and in 1853 several denominations combined to build a union church. The cornerstone of the present building was laid in 1872, and the church was dedicated on June 14, 1873. Members donated time and materials to reduce the cost to $7,000. To escape a noisy railroad the church was moved to its present location in 1901.

140 East Flint Street, SW corner of Slater Street, Lake Orion; Lake Orion Methodist Church; L212; September 29, 1972; 1973

Predmore House

This Carpenter Gothic-style house was built in 1879 for Joshua C. Predmore (1837-1912). A Civil War veteran, Predmore was on guard duty at the White House the night President Lincoln was assassinated. He was mustered out of the service in 1868. Returning to Lake Orion, he became a merchant, running a general store for forty years. Predmore held local offices from village president to councilman and was township clerk at the time of his death. The restored house features three original lattice archways and two oak fireplaces, one in the front parlor and one in the living room.

244 North Broadway, SW corner of Church Street, Lake Orion; Predmore, Joshua C., House; L709A; August 3, 1979; 1982

Hibbard Tavern

Aaron Phelps, pioneer settler and first postmaster of Milford, built this Greek Revival residence between 1836 and 1838. It was one of the first frame structures erected in the village. New York immigrant Ira Hibbard purchased the house and transformed it into a tavern in the early 1840s. It served the Milford community for many years as a tavern, stagecoach inn and mail drop on the Pontiac-Howell stage line. During the 1860s, the tavern was converted back into a private residence.

115 Summit near Union Street, Milford; Hibbard Tavern (Lancaster House); L650A; April 24, 1979; 1980

Oak Grove Cemetery

Oak Grove Cemetery, established in May 1845, was formally named in May 1871. When it was officially designated as the township cemetery, the remains from the area's "old burying ground," begun on the corner of Mill and Washington streets in 1832, were moved to it. Elizur Ruggles, Milford's first white settler, and veterans of the war of 1812 and the Civil War are buried here. The site has an early potter's field near the Huron River. The cemetery vault, built to thwart grave robbers and provide a place to store remains during hard winters, dates back to 1885. In 1980 the vault was restored and a new fieldstone entrance was built. The original cemetery, which covered 12.76 acres, has expanded over the years to encompass 15.6 acres.

1055 Garden Road, Milford Township; Oak Grove Cemetery; L743A; September 10, 1979; 1981

Samuel White Homestead

This Greek Revival farmhouse, built by Samuel White, shows the influence of the people from upstate New York who first settled this area. The deed to the property was signed by John Quincy Adams. Built around 1840, the house retains its original architectural features. The classic entrance, friezes and returns are typical of the style. Heavy native beams support the house, which rests on a fieldstone foundation. The barn, part of the working farm until 1956, was converted to a house in 1980.

Colonel Samuel White

The Samuel White family was one of the first to settle in Novi Township. White (1794-1870) and his wife, Amanda (1799-1869), immigrated to this area from Royalton, New York, in 1827. White had recently retired from the army, ending a career that included service in the War of 1812. A prosperous farmer, White was the second supervisor of Novi, a delegate to the 1835 Michigan Constitutional Convention and active in numerous other civic endeavors. He built this house for his wife and four children around 1840.

46040 Nine Mile Road, between Beck and Taft roads, Novi; White, Samuel, House; L891A; February 23, 1981; 1984

Chief Pontiac

A pleasant tradition, unsupported by history, says that Pontiac once lived on Apple Island here in Orchard Lake. This great Indian chief was born around 1720, probably in the Ottawa village on the Detroit River. A friend of the French, Pontiac was angered by the British rule, which began in 1760, and plotted its overthrow. In 1763 he led the Indians of the area in an attack on Detroit while other tribes, who were inspired by him, rose against the British in the West and overwhelmed every fort save Fort Pitt and Niagara. Pontiac's siege of Detroit failed. With it, this greatest of Indian uprisings also failed. In 1769, Pontiac was killed by another Indian in Illinois. He probably was buried in St. Louis, Missouri. The city of Pontiac was named in his honor.

Orchard Lake Public Fishing Site, corner of Pontiac Trail and Orchard Lake Road, Orchard Lake Village; Chief Pontiac Informational Designation; S177; January 24, 1958; 1958

Orchard Lake Chapel

Early settlers here were devout Christians, and from 1825 were served on occasion by itinerant preachers. Later Colin and Caroline Campbell had this chapel built on land donated by Peter Dow to accommodate the influx of summer visitors. It was dedicated on July 18, 1874. Early worshippers often arrived by steamboat. Since 1943 the permanent congregation has been known as the Orchard Lake Community Church, Presbyterian.

5171 Commerce Road, between Hiller and Orchard Lake roads, Orchard Lake Village; Orchard Lake Chapel; L284; July 26, 1974; 1974

Howarth School

John Howarth provided the land on which this Greek Revival schoolhouse was built in 1859. The building served the community as a place of worship for the Howarth United Methodist Church and as an Oakland County school. The Methodists moved to a new building across the road in 1898; however, the building was used as a school until 1955 when the Orion Township school system was consolidated. The church then acquired the building for its vacation Bible school and its annual Christmas bazaar.

4040 Bald Mountain Road at Silver Bell Road, west of Squirrel Road, Gingleville vicinity, Orion Township; Howarth United Methodist Church School (Howarth School); L1059A; January 27, 1983; 1988

Ortonville Methodist Episcopal Church

In June 1850 an eleven-member Methodist class was organized here as the Hadley Circuit of the Detroit District. B. F. Prichard was the pastor; M. H. Filmore, the class leader; and James Shaw, the presiding elder. That year the group built a stone church on Washburn Road, which it used until the present church was erected just north of this site in 1879. That church was moved here in 1887 and enlarged and remodeled in 1961. The oldest church building in Ortonville, it has a gable roof and a center bell tower.

93 Church Street, Ortonville; Ortonville Methodist Episcopal Church (Ortonville United Methodist Church); L1066B; February 10, 1983; 1988

Clinton Valley Center

The Clinton Valley Center has served southeastern Michigan for one hundred years and is the second oldest hospital for the mentally ill in the Great Lake state. Since opening in 1878, the center has employed seven superintendents. This institution was originally named Eastern Michigan Asylum; it became Pontiac State Hospital in 1911 and adopted the name Clinton Valley Center in 1973. The different names symbolize changing concepts in the treatment of mental illness. The first patient was admitted on July 31, 1878, a day before the official opening. Treating 222 patients at its start, this hospital now serves nearly 800 patients. It has advanced from a custodial institution to a modern treatment center which offers many kinds of therapy necessary for different emotional illnesses.

Side Two

Elijah E. Myers, a renowned Michigan architect, designed the original hospital structure in 1875. Charles Anderson, a local architect, was responsible for the master plan of several of the residences. Smith, Hinchman and Grylls, of Detroit, drew up plans for the 1907 chapel building which is still extant. Patients using the extensive grounds for agriculture, dairy and cattle breeding projects were a familiar sight to the citizens of Pontiac. The Clinton Valley Center trains psychiatrists, nurses and other health care workers. Receiving a World's Fair Award in 1894 for "evidence of excellent fire protection, detached cottages for each sex and a training school for attendants," this center continues to provide modern facilities for the mentally ill.

140 Elizabeth Lake Road, Pontiac; Eastern Michigan Asylum Historic District (Clinton Valley Center); S437; September 17, 1974; 1978

The Courthouse

The first Oakland County courthouse, built about 1824, was located on the corner of Saginaw and Huron streets on land given by the Pontiac Company. The log first story housed the jail, while the frame second story was occupied by the courtroom and sheriff's residence. Following several attempts to remove the county seat from Pontiac, a new courthouse was opened on the same site in 1858. This was replaced in 1905 by a three-story building of gray Cleveland sandstone. By the 1950s, population pressure and demand for increased services forced new construction. A more expansive site near the city's western limits, on which some county buildings were already located, was enlarged for the Oakland County Service Center. Ground for the present courthouse was broken on September 21, 1959.

Oakland County

A proclamation of Territorial Governor Lewis Cass organized Oakland County and designated Pontiac as the county seat on March 28, 1820, although the boundaries had been established on January 12, 1819. At that time this area was a wilderness, with the Indian trail from Detroit to Saginaw the main artery of settlement. Farming was the chief occupation in early times, and by mid-century the county led the state in agricultural production. The numerous lakes were a major attraction to settlers and vacationers, and today Oakland County has many public parks which serve urbanized southeastern Michigan. Once the home of the Michigan Military Academy, the county now has a number of outstanding educational facilities. Automobile manufacture has long been important here and remains the major industry.

Oakland County Courthouse, 1200 North Telegraph, just north of Elizabeth Lake Road, Pontiac; Oakland County; S274; November 18, 1965; 1970

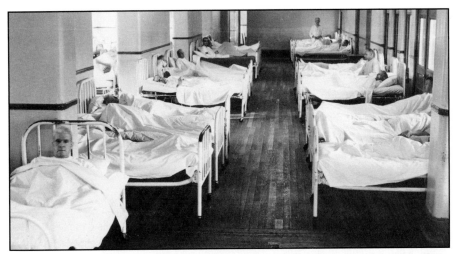

This 1950s photo shows crowded conditions at the Pontiac State Hospital. Elijah Myers designed the hospital, which opened in 1878. (*Clinton Valley Center*)

First Baptist Church

This church, Michigan's oldest Baptist church, was begun in 1821 by a small band of pioneers who came to Pontiac through the forest and swamp from Mount Clemens. In 1824 the Reverend Elkanah Comstock became the church's first pastor. The congregation met in homes, the schoolhouse and the courthouse until it dedicated its own building in 1841. In 1896 the church moved to its present location. Fifty-five years later on July 1, 1951, this building was dedicated. The church's large missionary program is well known.

34 Oakland Avenue at Saginaw Avenue, Pontiac; First Baptist Church; L17; March 18, 1961; 1961

First Methodist Episcopal Church

As early as 1820 itinerant Methodist preachers came to Pontiac, and in 1828 a society was organized by the Reverend William T. Snow in the home of Ira Donelson. The small group later met in a school and the courthouse until it was able in 1842 to build its first church at the corner of Pike and Perry. The present building was begun in 1861 and dedicated in 1864. The First Methodist Church, as it became following the 1939 Uniting Conference, is the "mother" of Methodist churches in Pontiac.

14 Judson Street, Pontiac; First Methodist Episcopal Church; L15; March 18, 1961; 1961

First Presbyterian Church

Organized February 26, 1824, by nine men and four women under the leadership of missionary Eldad Goodman at John Voorheis's home in Bloomfield Township, the congregation met during its early years in Pontiac and for a time in Auburn. In 1844 a brick church, forty-by-seventy feet, on the northwest corner of Huron and Saginaw was completed. In 1868 members subscribed funds for a building on the present site. It burned in 1914. The present church was begun in 1918 and was dedicated in 1924.

SE corner of West Huron and Wayne streets, Pontiac; First Presbyterian Church; L14; March 18, 1961; 1961

Franklin Boulevard Historic District

Built between 1845 and 1930, this neighborhood of ninety-three structures retains a turn-of-the-century appearance with its mix of Greek Revival, Italianate, Queen Anne, Stick Style and Colonial Revival architecture. During Michigan's early period of industrial growth (1880-1920), prominent leaders of Michigan's timber, mining, publishing, carriage and automobile industries made their homes in this area. Most notably, the 1848 Italian Villa-style Myrick-Palmer House located at 2323 West Huron Street was home to Charles H. Palmer, a nineteenth-century educator and copper miner. Also significant was 269 West Huron Street, home to Oliver Leo Beaudette, whose father founded the O. J. Beaudette Body Company, believed to be the first to use metal on automobile bodies.

Y.W.C.A., 269 West Huron, Pontiac; Franklin Boulevard Historic District; L1307C; April 10, 1986; 1986

Oak Hill Cemetery

On June 1, 1822, the Pontiac Company gave the citizens of Pontiac the first land for a village cemetery. It was "to be occupied and used forever as a burying ground." In 1839 when Captain Hervey Parke was employed by the village to survey Outlot 9 of the original plat of the village, Oak Hill Cemetery was laid out. Many of the early pioneers who had been buried near the intersection of Saginaw and Huron streets and on private property were reinterred here after 1839. The cemetery contains the Buckland Memorial Chapel, built of Berea sandstone in 1898 by Don Carlos Buckland in memory of members of his family. Among the monuments of note are those of Major General Israel B. Richardson, Governor Moses Wisner and David Ward. Acreage across Mount Clemens (renamed University) and Paddock streets was added to the original site as the need for increased space arose.

Side Two

Occupying the highest point of land in Pontiac, Oak Hill Cemetery has served the city throughout its history. Colonel Stephen Mack, who managed the Pontiac Company and was in 1818 one of the village's first settlers, was reinterred here, as was his daughter, Lovina, who was the first white settler to die in Pontiac. Mack's grave is one of six belonging to veterans of the American Revolution. Twenty-seven Civil War soldiers also lie here, including Governor Moses Wisner, Major General Israel B. Richardson and Brigadier General Joseph T. Copeland. Other historic figures interred here include the Reverend Isaac Ruggles, a pioneer missionary in Michigan, and lumberman David Ward. In more recent times, World War I Congressional Medal of Honor veteran Dr. Harold A. Furlong was buried here.

216 University Drive at the intersection of Douglas, Pontiac; Oak Hill Cemetery; L1450C; August 21, 1987; 1987

"Pine Grove"

This was the home of Moses Wisner and his wife, Angeolina Hascall. From 1859 to 1861, Wisner served Michigan as governor. He was born in New York, came to Michigan in 1837 and shortly established a successful law practice. In 1844 he purchased this property and in 1845 began construction of the main section of the house. He brought Angeolina here as a bride. Wisner planted various kinds of pine native to Michigan on the premises. During the Civil War he organized and commanded the Twenty-second Michigan Infantry. He died in Kentucky in 1863. He bequeathed the homestead to his wife who lived here until her death in 1905. Wisner's daughter and granddaughter maintained "Pine Grove" until its purchase in 1945 by the Oakland County Historical Foundation as a center for Oakland County history.

405 Oakland Avenue, NW of North Johnson Road, Pontiac; Wisner, Moses, House (Pine Grove); HB7; September 25, 1956; 1961

St. Vincent de Paul Catholic Church

St. Vincent de Paul parish, established in 1851 by Bishop Peter Paul LeFevre, once included all of Oakland County and parts of Genesee, Lapeer and Macomb counties. The parish's first house of worship, the Academy Building, was first a private school and later a branch of the University of Michigan. In 1866 the church was moved from North Saginaw Street to Oakland Avenue at Lafayette. The parish grew as increasing numbers of Irish and German Catholic immigrants came to Pontiac to work in industry and farming. The Reverend Fridolin Baumgartner, pastor from 1876 to 1894, organized the fund-raising for and the construction of the present church. Nearly five thousand people celebrated as its cornerstone was laid on September 6, 1885.

Side Two

Detroit architects John M. Donaldson and Walter Meier designed this Victorian Gothic church. Upon its dedication on September 18, 1887, a fourteen-coach excursion train brought spectators and clergy from Detroit to Pontiac to celebrate. Bishop Casper Henry Borgess and Father Fridolin Baumgartner presided over the ceremony. A sixty-six hundred-pound bell, cast by H. Stuckstede and Company, was installed in the bell tower of the church in 1890. The St. Frederick School building, added in 1897, was replaced by the present structure in 1923. The school was staffed by the Sisters, Servants of the Immaculate Heart of Mary, Monroe, until it closed in 1969. The rectory was built in 1895; the parish hall in 1911.

150 East Wide Track Drive at Whittemore, Pontiac; St. Vincent de Paul Catholic Church, School and Convent; L1403A; April 28, 1987; 1988

Masonic Block

Built in 1899-1900, the Masonic Block was designed by Edward R. Prall. The Rochester

The church to the left of the cattle ready for market, served the congregation of the First Presbyterian Church from 1868 until it burned in 1914. (*First Presbyterian Church*)

Building Association raised funds for the project. Among its leaders were William Clark Chapman, general manager of Western Knitting Mills and twentieth village president; Enos R. Mathews, ninth village president and former Avon Township supervisor; and Harvey J. Taylor, a local hardware dealer and farmer. The building's earliest tenants included the Rochester Savings Bank, the U.S. Post Office and the Free and Accepted Masons.

NE corner of Main and East Fourth streets, 400-404 Main Street and 111-115 East Fourth Street, Rochester; Masonic Block; L1442A; August 21, 1987; 1988

Rochester

The area known as Rochester was settled in 1817 by James Graham. It was the first permanent settlement in present-day Oakland County. The community was named in honor of Rochester, New York, where many of its pioneer settlers once lived. In 1819 the first industry in this vicinity was founded when William Russell, Benjamin Woodworth, Alexander Graham and John Hersey erected a water-powered sawmill. In 1826, Lewis Cass, territorial governor of Michigan, together with Austin E. Wing and Charles Larned, platted the village, which was incorporated in 1869 and became a city in 1967. Abundant sources of water and the advent of the railroad contributed to the development of woolen, flour, saw and paper mills in the region. The Rochester area is now a major cultural center and includes Oakland University, Michigan Christian College and the Leader Dog School for the Blind.

400 Sixth Street, Rochester; Rochester Informational Designation; L759B; December 12, 1979; 1980

Rochester Opera House

Built in 1890, the Opera House Block opened with the First National Bank and Norton Pharmacy on its ground floor. On November 7, 1890, a grand opening dance launched the upper-level opera house as Rochester's social and cultural center. Until 1933 plays, movies, lectures, dances, reunions, commencements—even boxing matches—filled the calendars, but never an opera. In 1987 this Richardsonian-style landmark, with its sixteen-foot ceilings and stained-glass windows, was restored.

340 Main Street, Rochester; Opera House (Lytle's Pharmacy); L1756A; June 21, 1990; 1991

Township Hall

Avon Township, the site of the first settlement in Oakland County, was organized in 1835. This white clapboard building was erected in 1880 as the township hall. Its alterations reflect the area's industrial and commercial growth. Initially constructed as a single-story building, the hall was enlarged by raising the roof eight feet and adding a second story in the early 1930s. In 1962 a north wing was also constructed. Avon Township Hall is one of the few public structures built prior to 1900 that still stands in Oakland County.

407 Pine Street, Rochester; Avon Township Hall (Avon Charter Township Hall); L642B; March 28, 1979; 1980

Clinton-Kalamazoo Canal

This canal, conceived at the peak of the era of canal-building, was part of Michigan's internal improvements program which was announced in 1837. The Clinton-Kalamazoo Canal would make it possible to cross southern Michigan by boat from Lake St. Clair to Lake Michigan. On July 20, 1838, construction began at Mount Clemens amid much fanfare. Hard times, however, soon made it difficult to sell bonds to finance the canal. When the excavation reached this point in 1843, the money ran out and all work ceased. With the coming of railroads, support for the canal vanished. The completed part was little used.

Rochester-Utica Recreation Area, one mile east of Rochester, off John R and Bloomer roads, Bloomer State Park, Rochester Hills; Clinton-Kalamazoo Canal; S96; September 25, 1956; 1957

Meadow Brook Hall

Home of Alfred G. and Matilda Dodge Wilson (widow of John Dodge), this Tudor-style mansion was built 1926-1929. William E. Kapp of Smith, Hinchman & Grylls designed the hall, incorporating details from famous homes of England. Mr. and Mrs. Wilson deeded the hall and its fourteen hundred-acre estate to Michigan State University in 1957 to found what is now Oakland University. The hall opened to the public in September 1971 as a conference and cultural center of the university.

Oakland University Campus, 480 South Adams Road, south of Walton Boulevard, Rochester Hills; Meadow Brook Hall (Meadow Brook Estate); S492; November 3, 1976, 1979

Stoney Creek Village

Lemeul Taylor and his family became Stoney Creek's first settlers in 1823. The next year a sawmill and a gristmill, along with a distillery and blacksmith shop were built. Next came a hotel and a woolen mill. Joshua Van Hoosen's family settled here in 1836, when he was six years old. In 1853, after seeking wealth in California's gold fields, Joshua returned to Stoney Creek, purchased the family farm and married Sarah Taylor, granddaughter of Lemuel. One of their daughters, Bertha Van Hoosen (1863-1952), became an internationally known surgeon. Their granddaughter Sarah Van Hoosen Jones (1892-1972) earned a doctorate in genetics and operated the family estate as a model dairy farm from 1923 until 1952, when she deeded about three hundred acres to Michigan State University.

1005 Van Hoosen Road at Runyon Road, Rochester Hills; Stoney Creek Village Informational Site; L174; December 10, 1971; 1982

Moses Wisner, governor from 1859 to 1861, built the main section of this Greek Revival house in 1845 and welcomed his bride, Angeolina, home soon after. (*Pine Grove*)

Winkler's Mill

A sawmill, dam and gristmill were built here in 1825 by John Hersey, one of the first settlers in the county and a founder of the villages of Rochester and Stony Creek, nearby. From 1870 to 1920 this mill was operated by Joseph Winkler. In a single year, 1880, Winkler ground 2,504 barrels of wheat and some 694,000 pounds of cornmeal, feed and buckwheat flour.

Mill originally located at 6381 Winkler Mill Road, burned, marker currently on display at the City of Rochester Hills Museum, 1005 Van Hoosen Road, Rochester Hills; Winkler's Mill; L72; July 15, 1968; 1968

Rose Township Hall

Rose Township was created by legislative act on March 11, 1837. Its organizational meeting was held at the house and tavern of David Gage. The township held meetings at the tavern until 1881, when the present structure was built by local carpenter William Miller. The Rose Township Board held its first meeting here in March 1882. From 1898 to 1958 the Rose Mission, organized by the Ladies Aid Society of Rose, held regular Sunday morning worship services here.

204 Franklin Street, Rose Center, Rose Township; Rose Township Hall; L1026B; July 20, 1982; 1987

First Baptist Church of Royal Oak

Several members of this church were significant to its early development. In 1839 charter member Hamlet Harris, "a free colored person" according to the 1840 census, donated twenty-five dollars towards the construction of the first church. In 1876, Athalinda Phelps donated the land, and the Reverend Silas Finn provided his labor and half of the money required to build a second church. When membership was low at the turn of the century, Anna B. Quick held meetings to maintain the church charter. This marker was erected in 1989, the church's one hundred fiftieth year.

Side Two

In January 1839 twenty people organized this congregation, ten of whom were baptized in the Red Run Creek. The Baptists built the first church in Royal Oak in August of that year near Main and Third streets. All subsequent churches have stood on the present site on Main Street where the second church, known as the "Greek Cross Church," was built in 1876. The Tabernacle followed in 1918, the first brick sanctuary in 1921 and the adjacent educational building in 1950. The present sanctuary was erected in 1965.

309 North Main Street, Royal Oak; First Baptist Church of Royal Oak Informational Site; L1610C; December 15, 1988; 1989

John Almon Starr

John Almon Starr (1828-1895) and his wife, Nancy Quick (1831-1895), built this house in 1868 from bricks fired in Almon's tile factory. Almon and his parents had emigrated to Michigan from Richmond, New York, in 1831, the same year Nancy was born in Royal Oak Township. Almon and his father, Orson Starr, manufactured animal bells until 1866, when Almon started his brickyard and tile works at this location, later known as Starr Corners. The house was occupied by the Starr family until 1967.

Saginaw Trail

The Saginaw Trail, running from Detroit to Saginaw through Pontiac and Flint, was originally an Indian trail. In 1816, [the] Michigan territorial government authorized the building of a road from Detroit to Saginaw along the trail. Part of the trail in Oakland County is now Woodward Avenue and Dixie Highway. Evidence of the original Saginaw Trail's path through Royal Oak is still visible as a depression in the ground running northwesterly across the property adjacent to the John Almon Starr House.

3123 Crooks Road, Royal Oak; Starr, John Almon, House (Almon Starr House); L1278A; November 26, 1985; 1988; Saginaw Trail Informational Designation; S164; September 17, 1957

Orson Starr Home

Orson Starr (1803-1873) and his wife, Rhoda Gibbs Starr (1806-1853), built this home in 1845. Five generations of the Starr family lived here until 1964. The house was purchased by the city of Royal Oak in 1976. Orson Starr came to this area in 1831 and began manufacturing cowbells in a factory located just north of this site. He continued this trade for forty years. The cowbells, products of Royal Oak's first industry, were stamped with Starr's trademark and are now prized by collectors.

3123 North Main Street between Bloomfield and Lawrence avenues, Royal Oak; Starr House; L465; August 6, 1976; 1985

Royal Oak Methodist Episcopal Church

On May 3, 1918, the *Royal Oak Tribune* boasted that, "architecturally and artistically," the new Methodist Episcopal Church was "the achievement of a master mind." William E. N. Hunter, a Detroit architect and Methodist who designed many Protestant churches, provided the plans for this Collegiate Gothic-style church, now known as First United Methodist Church. The Methodist Episcopal congregation was the first church organized in Royal Oak. It was established in 1838, and five years later its members built a wood-frame church on this site. In 1894 the frame church was replaced with one built of bricks manufactured and donated by Edwin A. Starr. By 1915 a new church was needed to accommodate the growing membership. The education wing was added in 1928.

8320 West Seventh Street, Royal Oak; First United Methodist Church; L1562A; June 30, 1988; 1990

Royal Oak Woman's Club

Erected in 1839, this building was originally a small frame Baptist church. The village purchased it for a town hall in 1914 and used it for municipal purposes until 1923, when the Royal Oak Woman's Club acquired it. The club, founded in 1902 as a women's study group, has relocated the structure twice. In 1923 when the building was remodeled as a Tudor-style structure, a cobblestone fireplace was installed. This is the oldest building in the city of Royal Oak.

404 South Pleasant Street, Royal Oak; First Baptist Church (Royal Oak Woman's Club); L679A; June 15, 1979; 1985

Congregation Shaarey Zedek

In 1861, at the beginning of the Civil War, seventeen followers of Traditional Judaism withdrew from the Beth El Society in Detroit to found the "Shaarey Zedek Society." In 1877 the membership constructed the first building in Michigan to be erected specifically as a synagogue, at Congress and St. Antoine. In 1913 as the first Conservative Jewish congregation in the Detroit area, Shaarey Zedek was one of the founding congregations of the United Synagogue of America. Since the nineteenth century, members of the congregation have played leading roles in Michigan, the nation and in world Jewry. Congregation Shaarey Zedek has worshipped in six different structures since its founding and continues to transmit its heritage from generation to generation. The congregation moved to Southfield in 1962.

27375 Bell Road, Southfield; Congregation Shaarey Zedek Informational Designation; L1365C; December 5, 1986; 1987

Lawrence Institute of Technology

Lawrence Tech was chartered in 1932 by the Lawrence brothers, Russell E. and E. George. The institution was located in Highland Park on Woodward Avenue until 1955 when it was moved to this campus. Lawrence Tech began with the College of Engineering, later adding the College of Industrial Management, College of Architecture and Technical Institute. The institution pioneered in 1935 in developing the four-quarter plan. It is a non-profit, self-owned institution.

Original marker erected 1963, replaced in 1986.

Lawrence Institute of Technology

Lawrence Tech was chartered in 1932 by the Lawrence brothers, Russell E. and E. George. The college was located in Highland Park on Woodward Avenue until 1955, when the first building opened on this campus. Lawrence Tech, founded as an undergraduate college of engineering, later added programs in architecture, management, arts and science, and various technological fields. The college pioneered in scheduling evening programs for working students and in 1935 developed the four-quarter academic calendar. "Theory and Practice" has been the motto of the college since its founding. Application of classroom theories to real situations involving the community of Michigan industries has been its goal. Lawrence Institute of Technology is a nonprofit independent college.

2100 West Ten Mile Road, Southfield; Lawrence Institute of Technology Informational Designation; S223; November 7, 1961; 1986

Pioneer Cemetery

Upon the death of his daughter in 1832, John Thomas donated part of his farm to the township to form a public burying ground. He gave an adjacent parcel to the Presbyterians who built a church there in 1837. Although nonsectarian, the cemetery became known as the United Presbyterian Church Cemetery. All but seven graves date from the nineteenth century. One of Southfield's first settlers Isaac Heth is buried here. The last interment was in 1926.

Lahser Road, north of West Ten Mile Road, Southfield; Pioneer Cemetery; L1476A; November 20, 1987; 1989

Southfield Cemetery

Thaddeus Griswold sold several parcels of his farm to settlers who used the land for burial grounds. In 1847 these "proprietors" donated the land to the board of health which established a township cemetery. The most heroic figure memorialized here is Harry J. Brooks, a test pilot for the Ford Motor Company, who, in 1928, set a world distance record while flying the "Ford flivver." On the return flight he crashed into the Atlantic. His remains were never found, but a headstone marks his place in the Brooks family plot.

23520 Civic Center Drive, Southfield; Southfield Cemetery; L1477A; November 20, 1987; 1989

Southfield Town Hall

The Southfield Town Hall was built between 1872 and 1873 to house the government of Southfield Centre, also known as the Burgh. The hall was the site of elections, public meetings and social events. Township officials continued to conduct business here until 1958 when the city of Southfield was organized. The township shared the building with the city until 1965. The hall is one of few historic buildings in Southfield and is the anchor in "the Burgh," the city's historic district.

26082 Berg Road, Southfield; Southfield Town Hall; L1709A; January 6, 1990; 1990

"Witch's Hat" Depot

In the late nineteenth century, the community of South Lyon was served by three rail lines operating from the 1871 Pere Marquette depot, which burned in 1908. By the time this one-story Queen Anne depot was erected by the Grand Trunk Western railroad system in 1909, only two lines came to South Lyon. Featuring a rounded front and a conical roof, the wood-frame structure served as a passenger station until 1955. The city of South Lyon acquired the depot in 1975 and in 1976 moved it to this site. In 1981 the station began its service as the Witch's Hat Depot Museum and a community center.

300 Dorothy Street in McHattie Park, South Lyon; Grand Trunk and Western Railroad Depot (Witches Hat Depot); L943B; August 22, 1981; 1984

Barn Church

Built by William Lakie as a dairy barn in 1912, this structure is now a church. At one time the electric interurban railway ran past this barn and picked up milk cans gathered from surrounding farms. After the Presbyterian Church purchased the building in 1928, they removed the silo and added a steeple and an appropriate entranceway. Thus the barn was adapted as a church with the hay loft becoming the chancel. The massive yet graceful lines of the former barn, now a Unitarian church, befit the spirit of a traditional house of worship.

4230 Livernois Road, north of Wattles Road, Troy; Barn Church (Troy Presbyterian Church); L507; February 7, 1977; 1978

Historic Green

The city of Troy has set aside this area for historic structures. Located here is the 1832 Greek Revival home of pioneer Solomon Caswell, moved from its original site. Nearby is Troy's 1927 township hall. This building is a replica of a Dutch Colonial inn near Troy, New York, and was the town hall until 1966. At the rear of this brick structure, now the Troy Historical Museum, are other restored buildings from past eras. The Historic Green is a symbol of continuity for a community first settled in 1821.

60 Wattles Road at Livernois Road, Troy; Troy Historic Green Informational Site; L762B; January 18, 1980; 1980

The Kresge Foundation

Sebastian Spering Kresge established this foundation in 1924 on the twenty-fifth anniversary of the company he had organized in Detroit. The foundation's sole donor, he remained

The Grand Trunk Western Railroad erected this depot in 1909. The Queen Anne conical roof has earned the building the name "Witch's Hat" Depot. (*Witch's Hat Depot*)

chairman of the board until retiring in 1966, shortly before his death. Grants of over $175 million in its first fifty years have aided established institutions to build facilities for teaching, research, healing and the arts. In 1984 the foundation moved to this site.

3215 West Big Beaver Road, one quarter mile west of Coolidge Road, Troy; The Kresge Foundation Informational Designation; S426; July 26, 1974; 1974

The Polar Bears

In the summer of 1918, President Woodrow Wilson, at the urging of Britain and France, sent an infantry regiment to north Russia to fight the Bolsheviks in hopes of persuading Russia to rejoin the war against Germany. The 339th Infantry Regiment, with the first battalion of the 310th Engineers and the 337th Ambulance and Hospital Companies, arrived at Archangel, Russia, on September 4, 1918. About 75 percent of the fifty-five hundred Americans who made up the North Russian Expeditionary Forces were from Michigan; of those a majority were from Detroit. The newspapers called them "Detroit's Own"; they called themselves "Polar Bears." They marched on Belle Isle on July 4, 1919. Ninety-four of them were killed in action after the United States decided to withdraw from Russia but before Archangel's harbor thawed.

Side Two

In 1929 five former "Polar Bears" of the 339th Infantry Regiment returned to north Russia in an attempt to recover the bodies of fellow soldiers who had been killed in action or died of exposure or disease ten years earlier. The group was selected by the members of the Polar Bear Association under the auspices of the Veterans of Foreign Wars. The trip was sponsored by the federal government and the state of Michigan. The delegates recovered eighty-six bodies. Fifty-six of these were buried on this site on May 30, 1930. The Polar Bear monument was carved from white Georgian marble; the steps, from white North Carolina granite. The black granite base symbolizes a fortress, and the cross and helmet denote war burial.

621 West Long Lake Road at Crooks Road, White Chapel Cemetery, Troy; Burial site of 339th Infantry Regiment; L1516C; April 25, 1988; 1988

S. S. Kresge Company

Sebastian Spering Kresge founded the firm in 1899 in Detroit. His guidance during its formative years was responsible for its initial success. By 1916 when it was incorporated in

Michigan, the company numbered 150 units. Innovative and careful management insured its continued growth. Since the introduction of the rapidly expanding Kmart division in 1962, the firm has become one of the world's leading mercantile chains. In 1972 the firm's international headquarters was located here.

3100 Big Beaver Road, Troy; S.S. Kresge Company Informational Site; S425; July 26, 1974; 1974

Troy Corners

The city of Troy was an unclaimed wilderness when Johnson Niles moved here with his family from New York in 1821. As a farmer, carpenter, innkeeper and merchant, Niles did much to develop the area, offering advice and encouragement to the settlers who followed. By 1834 the township included over eleven hundred inhabitants and the thriving village of Troy Corners had grown out of Niles's original settlement. Niles became Troy's postmaster and supervisor, and served in the Michigan legislature as a representative and later as a senator. His original home, a log cabin, was replaced by this house, built a few years after Niles arrived.

Intersection of Square Lake and Livernois roads, Troy; Founding of Troy Corners Informational Site (Troy Corners); L71; May 5, 1968; 1968

Wattles House

Harry Bennett Wattles purchased this house in 1876 about thirty years after its construction and added a veranda and a second story in 1909. Settling in Troy around 1837, the Wattles family has been active in civic and social affairs. Here on this property, once known as Sunnycrest Dairy, Wattles began to use progressive farming methods. His registered Jersey cows won numerous prizes. This house, Wattles, and his descendants who have lived here, provide Troy with the legacy of a community-minded family.

3864 Livernois Road, south of Wattles Road, Troy; Wattles House; L522; April 11, 1977; 1978

Stonecrest

This land served as the local schoolhouse site from 1836 to 1895. The original schoolhouse situated here was built of hewn logs and oak shakes. Stonecrest was constructed as a one-room schoolhouse in 1860. The teacher at Stonecrest in 1868-1869 was Joseph B. Moore, who later sat on the Supreme Court of Michigan and was the son of the builder of the school, Jacob J. Moore. Stonecrest is built of native stones, which were broken, faced and laid up in quicklime mortar. The building is situated on the highest point within the original

The Polar Bears, an American infantry regiment sent to Russia to fight the Bolsheviks in 1918, returned and marched on Belle Isle on July 4, 1919. (*The Polar Bears*)

village of Walled Lake as platted by Jesse Tuttle in 1836. It became the home of the Commerce Township Area Historical Society in 1980.

207 Liberty Street at Market Street, Walled Lake; Walled Lake School (Stonecrest); L890A; February 23, 1981; 1981

Hathaway-Hess Farm

The Hathaway-Hess Farm originated as the homestead of Jonathan Owen Hathaway, who migrated from New York to Oakland County with his parents in 1830. In 1861, Hathaway and his wife, Marcy C. Dewey, acquired an eighty-acre parcel of land in Waterford Township. In 1902, Hathaway's granddaughter Myrtle Hathaway married William Hess, an early investor in the Fisher Body Company. Following William's retirement in the 1930s, the Hesses devoted their lives to the family farm. Here they operated a successful dairy known as the Lone Cedar Farm, and raised champion sheep and Jersey and Hereford cattle. Myrtle Hess died in 1985. She bequeathed the family farm to Waterford Township and stipulated that the land be used as a park. In 1989, Waterford Township dedicated the Hess-Hathaway Park.

825 South Williams Lake Road, Waterford Township; Hathaway-Hess Farm (Lone Cedar Farm); L1682B; September 7, 1989; 1990

St. Patrick Church

This white clapboard edifice was built by Irish immigrants in 1840. It is believed to be the oldest existing frame Catholic church building in the Lower Peninsula. This area was one of the earliest in Michigan to be settled by Irish immigrants who arrived during the 1830s. The parish was organized in 1839 with about thirty members. Their numbers increased when the potato famine of 1845 in Ireland forced thousands of others to the United States. Having outgrown this tiny structure by the 1880s, the congregation traveled to Pontiac, Milford and other areas until approximately 1950, when a permanent parish was established here in Union Lake. Maintaining its original floors, walls and windows, this edifice is still used for ceremonial purposes. Today, the surrounding neighborhood is known as the "Dublin" area.

Union Lake Road at Hutchins Road, White Lake Township; St. Patrick's Catholic Church; L518; April 11, 1977; 1978

Wixom Cemetery

The Wixom Cemetery has been in continuous use since 1838, when it was established as the South Commerce Burial Ground. The first burial, however, that of an infant named Israel Barrett, occurred in 1835. Two hundred thirty-three of the graves date from the nineteenth century and contain the remains of most of Wixom's pioneers, including the Alonzo Sibley and Ahijah Wixom families. Alonzo Sibley donated the land for the cemetery, located across Maple Road from the Reverend Wire's home where funeral services were held in the parlor. The wrought-iron gate and fence along Wixom Road was erected in 1899. The sexton's shed was restored in 1981. It was constructed of cuspid block containing colored glass, a process used primarily between 1900 and 1930. The cemetery is presently owned and maintained by the city of Wixom.

NE corner of North Wixom and West Maple roads, Wixom; South Commerce Burying Ground (Wixom Cemetery); L1464A; October 23, 1987; 1989

Wixom-Wire House

This house was built in the early 1850s by Lucy Wixom, widow of Ahijah Wixom, one of the town's founders. Its first residents were the Reverend and Mrs. Samuel Wire. He was the pastor of the Free Will Baptist Association of Commerce. The house originally consisted of a parlor, a bedroom, a loft and a basement. The Wires used their home for church and funeral services. Caskets rested in an alcove in the parlor, whose wide door on the north was added so that the caskets could easily be moved to the cemetery across the street. In 1897 the Tiffin family purchased the house. They added the kitchen and porch in the 1920s. Sons William and Charlie continued to live in the house until 1975, when they died at the ages of 95 and 105. In 1975, the Wixom Historical Society acquired the home for restoration and the creation of [a] museum.

687 North Wixom Road, Wixom; Wixom-Wire House (Tiffin House); L1067A; January 31, 1983; 1985

Oceana

Veterans' Day Storm

The most disastrous day in the history of Lake Michigan shipping was Armistice (now Veterans') Day, November 11, 1940. With seventy-five-mile-per-hour winds and twenty-foot waves, a raging storm destroyed three ships and claimed the lives of fifty-nine seamen. Two freighters sank with all hands lost, and a third, the *Novadoc*, ran aground with the loss of two crew members. Bodies washed ashore throughout the day. As night fell, a heavy snow storm arrived. Rescue efforts by the Coast Guard and local citizens continued for three days after the storm. Three Pentwater fishermen were later recognized by the local community and the Canadian government for their bravery in rescuing seventeen sailors from the *Novadoc*.

Graveyard of Ships

The twenty-mile span of Lake Michigan between Little Point Sable, at Silver Lake, and Big Point Sable, north of Ludington, has earned a reputation as the "Graveyard of Ships." Beginning with the loss of the *Neptune* in 1848 through the Armistice (now Veterans') Day Storm of 1940, nearly seventy vessels have gone down in these treacherous waters. Gales and November snow storms have made navigation of this part of the lake a sailor's nightmare. Significant among the losses near Pentwater Harbor were the schooner *Wright* in 1854, the *Minnie Corlett* and the *Souvenior* in 1875, the *Lamont* in 1879 and the tug *Two Brothers* in 1912. The freighters *William B. Davock*, *Anna C. Minch* and *Novadoc* were all lost on November 11, 1940.

Village of Pentwater Memorial Marina, 421 South Hancock Street (BUS-31), Pentwater; Veterans Day Storm-Graveyard of Ships Informational Designation; S571C; May 21, 1985; 1986

Ontonagon

Porcupine Mountains

From Lake Superior the main range of mountains looks like a crouching porcupine, thus their name. Machinery, rock dumps and old adits are ghostly reminders of forty mining ventures in the years from 1846 to 1928, none of which succeeded. Some logging took place

Forty mining ventures failed in the "porkies" between 1846 and 1928. In 1945 a state park was created to preserve the beauty of this range. (*Porcupine Mountains*)

around 1916. As late as 1930 a few trappers eked out a living here. Finally in 1945 the area was made a state park to preserve its virgin splendor.

Porcupine Mountain State Park, Mead Copper Mine Picnic Area, M-107, ten miles west of Silver City, Carp Lake Township; Porcupine Mountains Informational Designation; S167; September 11, 1957; 1958

Osceola

"Unto a New Land"

Swedish immigrants, anxious to escape famine and an unsympathetic government, flowed into the Midwest frontier of America from the 1870s to 1890s searching for land and work. Railroads and lumbering industries offered attractive opportunities to these immigrants. The Grand Rapids & Indiana Railroad sent the Reverend J. P. Tustin to Sweden to recruit laborers for construction of its line. As an inducement, the railroad donated eighty acres to the Swedish colony of New Blekinge (Tustin). Swedes swarmed to this vicinity building the railroad, logging the forest and laboring in the sawmills. As the forest became depleted, many moved on but others became permanent settlers whose descendants still reside here. Children of these settlers have in this century gone across the country to make their contributions to America.

Old US-131 near Tustin, about ten miles south of Cadillac, Burdell Township; Swedish Immigration Informational Designation; S519B; June 15, 1979; 1979

Congregational Church

The First Congregational Church of Hersey was formally organized in 1870. Services were held in a local schoolhouse for three years. Delos A. Blodgett—early explorer, prominent lumberman and first settler of the area—donated land and lumber for this church, which was built in 1873-1874 at a cost of $3,000. It features handsome leaded-glass windows and a pyramidal steeple. Michigan white pine graces both the exterior and interior, including a hand-made pulpit.

216 South Main at the corner of Fourth, Hersey; Hersey Congregational Church (United Church of Christ); L682A; June 15, 1979; 1980

North Evart United Methodist Church

German settlers of this Osceola County farming community began holding evangelical services in the home of John J. Arndt in 1872. Later, services were held in a log house a quarter mile west of here. The church society was formally organized in 1882. The present church, originally named Emanuel Evangelical Church, was built at a cost of $2,500 and dedicated on November 9, 1884. The name changed in 1968 to reflect the merger of the Evangelical and Methodist societies.

Ninetieth Avenue, SW corner of Nine Mile Road, Evart vicinity, Osceola Township; Emanuel's Church [Evangelical Association] (North Evart United Methodist Church); L1179A; July 20, 1984; 1986

Otsego

Otsego County

First named Okkuddo when it was set off in 1840, this county was renamed Otsego in 1843 after a New York county and lake by that name. It is said to mean "clear water." Settlement did not begin until the late 1860s when lumbering was started. Otsego Lake, the first village, was founded in 1872 and became county seat in 1875 when the county was organized. Gaylord was settled in 1874 and named county seat in 1877. Farming and the tourist industry are now the chief businesses.

225 West Main (M-32) at Otsego Avenue, Gaylord; Otsego County Informational Designation; S219; February 17, 1960; 1961

Ottawa

Blendon Landing

In the mid-nineteenth century a site called Blendon Landing was located in this vicinity on the Grand River. Blendon was organized in 1854 and named for the Blendon Lumber Company. A logging train hauled timber seven miles from the pine forest to the landing for shipping. White pine and hardwoods were transported from here and used to manufacture ships, railroad cars and guns. Blendon's sawmill, logging operations and shipyard sustained a community of about two hundred people in the early 1860s. The sawmill burned in 1864 and by 1870 the railroad was abandoned. By 1912, Blendon was deserted. In 1965, Grand Valley State College professor Richard E. Flanders began excavating the Blendon Landing site as part of the university's archaeology program. Blendon Landing is owned by the Grand Valley State University Club.

Lake Michigan Hall, Grand Valley State University campus, Blendon Township; Blendon Landing Informational Designation; L1743C; April 10, 1990; 1990

Jenison Museum

Jenison is named for a pioneer family of English descent. Lemuel Jenison, son of a Revolutionary War soldier, came to the Grand River Valley from New York in 1835 with his family. Among the seven children born to Lemuel and his wife Sara, were four daughters and three sons, Hiram and twins Luman and Lucius. Lemuel died in 1837. The care and support of the family fell on the eldest son, then twenty-four, and the twins who were fourteen. Sara died in 1841. The Jenison brothers, initially lumbermen, later branched out in other ventures. They donated land for roads, schools and churches. Hiram, who served as the first Georgetown Township supervisor, died in 1889. Lucius and Luman, who were business partners, both died in 1899, and much of their estate was left to Margaret Husband who built this house.

Side Two

Margaret Husband was bookkeeper for, and legatee of, the Jenison twins. She built this landmark house at the turn of the century as a memorial to the twins. This two-story mansion, with massive fieldstone foundation, has ten rooms, curved plate glass windows in the turret, and leaded and beveled glass doors. Margaret Husband left the house to her daughter Bessie Husband Hanchett who died in 1960. Subsequently, the house was purchased by the C. W. Tiffany family, who began the restoration process later taken up by the Jenison Historical Association. In 1971 the Georgetown Township board voted to try to save the house, which had been purchased by the Department of State Highways and Transportation for demolition. Through the efforts of these historians, the State Highway Commission voted in 1975 to leave the Jenison Museum on this site.

28 Port Sheldon Drive, NE corner of Main Street, Jenison vicinity, Georgetown Township; Tiffany House (Hanchett House); L209; June 16, 1972; 1978

Central School

The first Central School was built in 1871. The Grand Haven Tribune hailed the belfry-topped school as "the finest in the state" and "the pride of every citizen of Grand Haven." The newspaper blamed arsonists for burning the school on May 5, 1901, and stated that more than one man would "contribute his services to a lynching bee, if the firebug had been detected." A second school, built on this site in 1902, housed over six hundred students in grades kindergarten through twelve. That school burned in 1963. The bell from the school was salvaged, but not usable. The following year the present elementary school opened. In 1965 the local Methodist church donated a bell from its old church so that the school could continue its tradition of ringing a school bell to call students to class.

106 South Sixth Street, Grand Haven; Central Schools Informational Site; L1655C; April 20, 1989; 1989

Grand Haven

This town began as a fur trading post established by Rix Robinson in the 1830s. Robinson, an agent for the America Fur Company, used this as one of his leading western Michigan

227

posts. The Reverend William M. Ferry came here in 1834 from Mackinac to work with Robinson in developing a town. The Grand Haven Company was formed, and lots were platted and sold. By 1837 the town had more than two hundred inhabitants. A heavy influx of settlers in the 1840s caused the decline of the fur trade. Lumbering soon became the leading activity, and by the 1870s there were several sawmills, a shingle mill and a sash and door factory in the community of six thousand. Grand Haven became a popular health resort in the late 1800s, famous for its magnetic mineral spring.

*Rix Robinson Park, located at M-31, near the Grand Isle Marina, Grand Haven; Grand Haven Informational Designation; S289; March 1, 1968; 1968

Grand Trunk Depot

This depot was constructed in 1870 as the western terminus of the Detroit, Grand Haven and Milwaukee Railroad. This line was later owned by the Grand Trunk Western Railroad. The station served Grand Haven as a passenger depot until passenger service between Detroit and Grand Haven ended in 1955. The city of Grand Haven purchased the property in 1967 and leased the depot to the Tri-Cities Historical Society. The rehabilitated structure was reopened as a historical museum in 1972.

1 North Harbor Avenue at the foot of Washington, Grand Haven; Grand Trunk Railroad Depot (Tri-Cities Historical Society Museum); L785A; February 27, 1980; 1981

Highland Park Association

On May 10, 1886, the city of Grand Haven leased sixty acres of land to the newly founded and incorporated Highland Park Association for the purpose of establishing a resort community. Most of the fifty-one original members of the association were prominent local businessmen; however, in its first century of maintaining the park, the association expanded to include cottage owners from across North America. Their cottages are nestled on Nipissing Age dunes and among hardwood forests characteristic of the eastern shores of Lake Michigan.

Side Two

By 1923 the Highland Park Association consisted of over one hundred cottages, miles of boardwalk and a hotel. The boardwalks, many of which remain, provide access to the dunes while protecting them. At the park's centennial there were ninety-eight cottages, but the once stately hotel was destroyed by fire in 1967. This unique environment is a climax dune habitat with a variety of wildflowers, small animals and migratory birds. The biological and geological landscape of Highland Park provides a recreational and educational resource for all visitors.

Highland Drive, Grand Haven; Highland Park Summer Resort Informational Site; L1308C; April 10, 1986; 1986

The Cappon House

Completed in 1874, this Italianate home was built by John R. Kleyn for Isaac Cappon. Erected in the aftermath of the devastating Holland fire of 1871, the Cappon House is one of the finest extant homes in the city. It remained in the Cappon family until the death of Isaac's daughter Lavina in 1978. Its furnishings were willed to the Netherlands Museum, which with the help of the city, acquired the property in 1981. Volunteer groups have restored and preserved the elegant home.

Isaac Cappon

Isaac Cappon (1830-1902) emigrated from The Netherlands to the United States in 1847. After a brief stay in Rochester, New York, he came to Michigan's Holland Colony in 1848. Here he worked as a laborer in a local tannery. In 1857 he helped found the Cappon & Bertsch Leather Company, one of Holland's leading nineteenth-century industries. When Holland incorporated in 1867, Cappon became its first mayor. He held that office for four subsequent, but not successive, terms. Cappon was prominent in both church and civic affairs.

228 West Ninth Street, Holland; Cappon, Isaac, House; L1134A; November 30, 1983; 1984

Central Avenue Christian Reformed Church

In 1865, The Holland Church, the city's first Christian Reformed congregation, was founded. In 1866 the group bought this lot on what was then Market Street and moved a school here to use as a church. The following year the congregation built a new church and adopted the name True Dutch Reformed Church. It became popularly known as Market Street Church. By 1899 the street and the church were renamed Central Avenue. The present church was built in 1952.

1 Graves Place, NW corner of Graves Place and Central Avenue, Holland; Central Avenue Christian Reformed Church Informational Designation; L1780C; August 23, 1990; 1991

Dutch in Michigan

On February 9, 1847, the Reverend Albertus C. Van Raalte and a band of Hollanders founded the city of Holland. Within two years the other four original colonies—Graafschap, Zeeland, Vriesland, Overisel—had also been established. Plagued by illness and not accustomed to the task of clearing a wilderness, the settlers found their first year a hard one, but their suffering was to be repaid in the bountiful days ahead.

Centennial Park, bounded by River Avenue, Tenth Street, Central Avenue and Twelfth Street, Holland; Dutch in Michigan Informational Designation; S89; 1957

This "mother and son from Holland" appeared in the October 24, 1891, issue of *Harper's Weekly*. (*Dutch in Michigan*)

First United Methodist Church

When the Reverend Albertus Christian Van Raalte and the first Dutch settlers came to Michigan in February 1847, they were aided by two Methodists who had settled earlier in the Holland area. George Harrington, Sr., brought the Dutch settlers from Allegan by ox cart; and Isaac Fairbanks welcomed them to his cabin, where they stayed during the building of their own log homes. Later, in 1861, Fairbanks and Harrington helped found the Holland Methodist Episcopal Church (now First United Methodist Church), which became the

Built of native stone and locally manufactured brick in 1889, this house was the home of Henry Kremers, a Holland physician, and his wife, Alice. (*The Netherlands Museum*)

Van Raalte Hall is one of several buildings at Hope College that honor Dutch settlers. The Reverend Albertus C. Van Raalte (inset) founded Holland in 1847. (*Hope College*)

first English-speaking church organized in the Holland community. In 1986 the congregation celebrated its 125th anniversary at this site, its fourth church home.

57 West Tenth Street, Holland; First United Methodist Church Informational Designation; L1350C; October 23, 1986; 1986

Hope Church: Reformed Church In America

In 1854, seven years after Dutch settlers came to this area, the Reformed Church in America established an English-language preaching mission in Holland. Principals from the Holland Academy, which became Hope College in 1866, served as early ministers. In 1862 the mission became Hope Church, Second Protestant Dutch Reformed Church. The congregation's ten charter members were led by missionary preacher Philip Phelps, who later became the first president of Hope College. The church and college have been closely associated, sharing the same name and similar seals featuring an "anchor of hope." Through the years the congregation's progressive spirit has attracted people from diverse backgrounds.

Side Two

In 1860 the Reverend Albertus C. Van Raalte, founder of Holland, gave this congregation four village lots on this site. The original 1864 frame building burned in Holland's 1871 fire. In 1874 a simple brick Gothic Revival church, designed by Carl Pfeiffer of New York City, was built. When razed in 1981 to build the Parish Life Center, its bracketed belfry and thirty-one-foot spire were saved. Clark and Munger of Bay City designed the present Veneklasen brick Flemish stepped-gable sanctuary, which was dedicated in 1902. Major interior renovations were completed in 1947 and 1984. In 1962 an education wing was built. The exterior was restored in 1980.

77 West Eleventh Street, Holland; Hope Church; L1648A; April 20, 1989; 1991

Hope College

In 1851, four years after settlers from The Netherlands founded Holland, the Pioneer School was established to meet some of the educational needs of the young colony. This school, the predecessor of Hope College, received direction and financial support from the General Synod of the Reformed Church in America. The school evolved into the Holland Academy, which in 1862 enrolled its first college class. On May 14, 1866, the institution was chartered as Hope College, and on July 17, 1866, the first class of eight students was graduated. The college's name, seal and motto are derived from a statement of the founder of Holland, the Reverend Albertus C. Van Raalte, who said of the Pioneer School, "This is my Anchor of Hope for this people in the future." In the decades that followed, a strong college of arts and sciences was developed which continues to serve the church and the community.

Hope College Campus, Twelfth Street and College Avenue, Holland; Hope College; S231; January 16, 1962; 1962

The Netherlands Museum

Dr. and Mrs. Henry Kremers commissioned local builder George Dalman to design and construct this house for them. Completed in 1889, the modified Elizabethan-style dwelling was built primarily of native stone and locally manufactured brick. A prominent doctor, Kremers was elected mayor of the city in 1889. After his death in 1914, his wife, Alice Van Zwaluwenberg-Kremers, lived here until 1917, when she sold the house to the city of Holland for use as its first city hospital.

8 East Twelfth Street, Holland; Kremers House (Netherlands Museum); L622; July 26, 1978; 1985

Ninth Street Christian Reformed Church

Dedicated on June 25, 1856, this church was built under the leadership of the Reverend Albertus C. Van Raalte, founder and first pastor of the Holland colony. Jacobus Schrader designed the Greek Revival-style building using native hand-hewn oak for the sills and crossbeams. The copper rooster on the belfry, symbolizing Peter's denial and pride, is commonly found on Calvinist churches in The Netherlands. The city's oldest extant church, often referred to as the Pillar Church, was one of the few buildings in Holland to survive the devastating fire of 1871.

Side Two

The congregation of the Pillar Church was organized in 1847 and worshipped in a log church at the site of the Pilgrim Home Cemetery. Composed of immigrants in secession from the *Nederlandse Hervormde Kerk*, the church was without denominational ties until it joined the Reformed Church in America in 1850. A division occurred within its congregation in 1882 and the building was assumed by the seceding majority. The minority reestablished itself as the First Reformed Church. In December 1884 the Pillar Church affiliated with the Christian Reformed Church. Over the years its members, and those of daughter congregations, have sought to fulfill the ideals which inspired the founders to seek a new home in

This postcard of Holland, Michigan, was sent from Miss Minnie Meulekamp in Holland to a friend or relative in Amsterdam, The Netherlands, in September 1905. (*Dutch in Michigan*)

231

America; freedom of religion; purity of doctrine; and a Christian education for their children in home, school and church.

Intersection of Ninth Street and College Avenue, Holland; Ninth Street Christian Reformed Church (Pillar Church; Old First Church); HB18; February 19, 1958; 1975

Noordeloos

A continuous arrival of immigrants from the Netherlands in 1847 and 1848 dotted the Black River region with a number of distinct communities. Noordeloos, which was named for its first pastor's native village, provided rich soil for farming. Early settlers had previously worshipped in Zeeland, but a distance of five miles and poor roads prompted these parishioners to petition the Classis Holland on April 3, 1856, to organize their own Reformed church. The Reverend Koene van den Bosch, an influential "seceder," was invited to minister to area settlers. On May 16, 1856, he arrived from Noordeloos, the Netherlands, and was welcomed into the classis. He became the first pastor of the Noordeloos Reformed Church and preached his inaugural sermon from a farmer's wagon in the woods.

Noordeloos Christian Reformed Church

Religious discord in The Netherlands and antipathy with earlier religious leaders in the western Michigan settlements, inspired a secession movement in the Reformed church led by the Reverend Koene van den Bosch. At a meeting of the Classis Holland on April 8, 1857, the Reverend van den Bosch presented a letter of secession and, joined by three other churches, founded the Christian Reformed Church. This group, comprised of sixteen families, changed its name to Noordeloos Christian Reformed Church. The secession letter of March 14, 1857, was dated earlier than documents presented by fellow congregations, therefore Noordeloos claims the distinction of being the first congregation of the Christian Reformed Church denomination.

4075 112th Avenue, Holland; Noordeloos Church Informational Designation; L1744C; April 19, 1990; 1990

Third Reformed Church

Under the leadership of the Reverend Albertus C. Van Raalte, founder of the Holland colony, the Third Reformed Church was organized on September 9, 1867. The first house of worship, measuring ninety feet long, fifty-six feet wide and thirty-two feet high, was erected on this site. In the great Holland fire of October 8 and 9, 1871, the first structure was destroyed. On January 2, 1873, disaster struck again as the newly erected framework of a second building was demolished in a high wind. The present church, a structure of beauty and symmetry, was dedicated on November 25, 1874. The architectural style is known as Carpenter Gothic. The building is of balloon frame, battened perpendicularly on the outside, finished with buttresses towering in pinnacles above the roof. The steepled bell tower was added in 1891. The parish hall and education facilities were built in 1952. During the centennial observance of 1967-1968, the church building underwent extensive restoration so that it continues to stand as a significant historic landmark.

Side Two

From the time of its organization, a progressive spirit has marked the life of the Third Reformed Church. The congregation immediately organized a Sunday School with Isaac Cappon, Holland industrialist and the city's first mayor, as superintendent. In 1872 the church gave impetus to the establishment of a $30,000 endowment fund for Hope College. The missionary fervor of the Reformed Church in America caught hold quickly in the congregation. Miss Elizabeth Cappon went as a missionary teacher to Amoy, China, in 1891. Nearly 125 men and women have followed her in the work of Christian ministry at home and abroad. In recognition of changing language patterns, Third Church became the first Dutch-immigrant congregation in the community to use the English language exclusively. To express its activities and goals, the congregation chose for its motto "To know Him and to make Him known."

110 West Twelfth Street, SW corner of Pine Avenue, Holland; Third Reformed Church of Holland; HB49; December 6, 1976; 1976

Van Vleck Hall

This building was named for the Reverend John Van Vleck, principal of the Holland Academy from 1855 to 1859. After the Reverend Albertus C. Van Raalte raised the necessary funds for the building, Van Vleck designed and supervised its construction. Completed

Known as "Big Red," the Holland Harbor South Pierhead Light is a beacon, not only because of its lantern. The lighthouse was erected in 1907. (*Holland Harbor Lighthouse*)

in 1858, Van Vleck Hall initially contained dormitory, class and reading rooms, as well as a refectory, a chapel and the residence of the principal. It was a focal point for activity at the Holland Academy, which was chartered as Hope College in 1866.

Side Two

Van Vleck Hall has played a vital role in the history of Hope College. The building survived the great fire of 1871 and housed students and the library in the late nineteenth century. During both World Wars, it served as a dispensary and infirmary for student military training programs. Erected at the highest point on campus, this symmetrical building stands as a tribute to the educational ideals held by those Dutch-Americans who founded Hope College.

Hope College Campus, Holland; Van Vleck Hall; L464; August 6, 1976; 1976

Western Theological Seminary

Theological training began here in 1866 when seven of the first eight graduates of Hope College petitioned the General Synod of the Reformed Church in America for such training. The request was granted and classes were begun, using the facilities and staff of Hope College. In 1867 the Reverend Cornelius E. Crispell, D.D., was elected by the General Synod as the first professor. In 1869 the Reverend Albertus C. Van Raalte, founder of the Holland Colony, and the Reverend Philip Phelps, Jr., were also made professors. Financial difficulties, caused primarily by a national depression, forced the suspension of classes in 1877. The seminary was reorganized in 1885, and classes were resumed. It was then officially designated as Western Theological Seminary of the Reformed Church in America. Its purpose has been, and continues to be, the preparation of men and women to become ministers, missionaries and scholars in the service of Jesus Christ.

86 East Twelfth Street, SE corner of College Avenue, Holland; Western Theological Seminary; S276B; March 9, 1966; 1966

Jamestown Reformed Church

Completed in 1928, this church was designed by the Grand Rapids architectural firm of John and George Daverman that planned several Reformed and Christian Reformed churches in western Michigan in the early twentieth century. Jamestown's settlers originally traveled four miles to Forest Grove in order to attend services at the Reformed church. In 1889 the Classis of Holland approved a petition from the Jamestown parishioners to form their own congregation, which they named the Second Reformed Church of Jamestown. The first church building was dedicated in 1891 and it was used until December 24, 1927, when it burned. Rather than rebuild, the congregation decided to construct the present church, which in 1937 was reincorporated as the Jamestown Reformed Church.

2340 Riley Street, just west of Twenty-fourth Avenue, Jamestown Township; Second Reformed Church of Jamestown (Jamestown Reformed Church); L1520A; May 17, 1988; 1989

South Olive Christian Reformed Church

The South Olive Christian Reformed Church is a daughter congregation of the Noordeloos church. The Noordeloos church and three other local West Michigan congregations seceded from the Reformed Church in America in 1857 to form the Christian Reformed Church. In 1885 members of the Noordeloos church received permission to organize this church in the southern part of Olive Township. It was originally called the Holland Christian Reformed Church at New Holland.

Side Two

Completed in 1887, this church is the nucleus of this Dutch-Calvinist farming community. A. J. Baker of Hamilton, Michigan, was the contractor for the original forty-by-fifty-foot frame building. The structure was enlarged in 1897. The chapel, built in 1898, was moved and attached to the rear of the church in 1935. The full basement was completed in 1948. The simple design is accented with Gothic windows. The front tower, with its open belfry, houses a 1,033-pound bell cast in 1897.

6200 120th Avenue, eight miles north of Holland, Olive Township; Holland Christian Reformed Church of New Holland (South Olive Christian Reformed Church); L1177B; June 15, 1984; 1985

Holland Harbor Lighthouse

The first lighthouse built at this location was a small, square wooden structure erected in 1872. In 1880 the lighthouse service installed a new light atop a metal pole in a protective cage. The oil lantern was lowered by pulleys for service. At the turn of the century a steel tower was built for the light, and in 1907 the present structure was erected. Named the Holland Harbor South Pierhead Lighthouse, it has a gabled roof that reflects the Dutch influence in the area. The lighthouse, popularly referred to as "Big Red," was automated in 1932. When the U.S. Coast Guard recommended that it be abandoned in 1970, citizens circulated petitions to rescue it. The Holland Harbor Lighthouse Historical Commission was then organized to preserve and restore this landmark.

Holland Harbor

When seeking a location for his Netherlands emigrant followers in 1847, the Reverend A. C. Van Raalte was attracted by the potential of using Black Lake (Lake Macatawa) as a harbor. However, the lake's outlet to Lake Michigan was blocked by sandbars and silt. Van Raalte appealed to Congress for help. The channel was surveyed in 1849, but was not successfully opened due to inadequate appropriations. Frustrated, the Dutch settlers dug the channel themselves. On July 1, 1859, the small steamboat *Huron* put into port. Here, in 1886, the government established the harbor's first life-saving station. By 1899 the channel had been relocated and harbor work completed. This spurred business and resort expansion. In 1900 over 1,095 schooners, steamers and barges used the harbor.

South Pier, Holland Harbor, Holland State Park, Park Township; Holland Harbor South Pierhead Lighthouse (Holland Lighthouse); L394; January 16, 1976; 1987

Marigold Lodge

Built in 1913 for Egbert H. and Margaret Gold of Chicago, Marigold Lodge was one of the first large summer houses along Black Lake (now called Lake Macatawa). Mr. Gold named the estate in honor of his wife and daughter. In keeping with its Prairie School styling, the broad, low lodge is finished in stucco and simple weather-boarding. The house remained in the Gold family until 1969. Herman Miller, Incorporated later acquired title and refurbished the building and its grounds. The site was listed in the National Register of Historic Places in 1985.

Side Two

Egbert H. Gold (1858-1928), a Chicago industrialist and inventor, acquired over one hundred patents during his lifetime. President of the Chicago-based Vapor Car Company, he devised a heating system used by railroads. To build Marigold, he retained the architectural firm Tallmadge & Watson of Chicago, and in 1913 this elegant structure was begun. He had plantings from England and The Netherlands imported to landscape the grounds and turn the sandy, bramble-covered peninsula into a place of beauty.

1116 Hazel Avenue, Park Township; Gold, Egbert H., Estate (Marigold Lodge); S556A; June 23, 1983; 1985

Waukazoo Woods

In 1833 an Ottawa Indian village of about three hundred was located on Black Lake, now Lake Macatawa. The village was led by Chief Waukazoo, recognized by his followers as a prophet and by local settlers as an orator. The Ottawa adopted many of the customs of their white neighbors, such as dress and the use of oxen, carts, plows and axes. They built log buildings for storage, but preferred to live in their traditional wigwams. Many of these Indians were converted to Christianity. In 1839 the Protestants in the village established the "Old Wing Mission" southeast of here. The Catholics chose a site on the other side of Black Lake to build their church and consecrated a cemetery there in 1841. On June 1, 1849, the Waukazoo band moved to the Grand Traverse Bay area, founding the village of Waukazooville, which was annexed by Northport in 1852.

SW corner of Post Avenue and Waukazoo Drive, Park Township; Waukazoo Woods; L1236C; April 23, 1985; 1985

DeWitt School

Built in 1891, DeWitt School typifies the one-room schools of the turn of the century. It stands on an acre of land that was donated by the DeWitt and Bosch families. Classes for grades one through eight were held in it until 1957. At one time, a single teacher taught from twenty-five to forty students by holding one ten-minute session per subject for each of the eight grades. The original school district covered approximately four square miles, and many children walked more than two miles to and from school daily. Nearly two decades after the school closed, planning began for restoring it as a living museum for area school children. By 1979 the classroom resembled its 1891 appearance, featuring gas lights, a wood stove, an octagonal clock, a hanging globe, lunch pails and desks.

17710 West Taft Street, just west of Grand Haven Road, Spring Lake Township; Dewitt Bicentennial One-Room School (Little Red School House); L640A; January 29, 1979; 1982

Drenthe Christian Reformed Church

The village of Drenthe was settled by three groups of Dutch immigrants in 1847. Those from Staphorst settled to the west; those from the province of Drenthe, to the east; and the "Flakkenaars" from Zuid Holland, to the north. The settlers first worshiped in nearby Vriesland, but in 1848 they built a Reformed church east of the village. It was soon outgrown, and in 1875 this church was built. In 1882, following dissent over some practices of the Reformed denomination, the congregation voted to join the recently organized Christian Reformed Church. For many years services were conducted in Dutch, but by 1946 all were in English. Several additions have been made to the structure since 1875, but the main building has the original hand-hewn beams and fieldstone foundation.

6344 Adams Street, Zeeland; Drenthe Christian Reformed Church; L905B; March 16, 1981; 1981

First Reformed Church

Early in 1847 a group of Dutch families met in Goes, on the island of Zuid Beveland, and organized themselves into a congregation. With their pastor, the Reverend Cornelius Vander Meulen, the group sailed in three ships to America in search of freedom. They established their new homes in this forested area of Michigan and named it after their native province of Zeeland. The center of the community was the log church. In 1866 a wood frame structure, with fieldstone foundation, patterned on the church in Axel, The Netherlands, was built on this site. Use of the Dutch language was eliminated gradually and in May 1943 was discontinued. The present church, built around the old, remains as the physical evidence of the Dutch immigrant community founded upon a resolute faith in Almighty God.

148 East Central Avenue, SW corner of Church Street, Zeeland; First Reformed Church; L397A; May 14, 1975; 1976

1869 Vriesland Reformed Church

The congregation of the 1869 Vriesland Reformed Church was organized in 1846 in the Netherlands. Led by the Reverend Maarten Anne Ypma, forty-nine adults and their children emigrated to the United States in 1847. Attracted by the clay soil, these farmers settled this area and named it Vriesland for their native province of Friesland in The Netherlands. Many descendants of the community's original families still reside in the area, and Frisian names are prevalent.

1869 Vriesland Reformed Church Building

This edifice, built in 1869 during the ministry of the Reverend Henry Uiterwyk, is one of the oldest Reformed Church structures in Michigan. The first church on this site was a log cabin which was soon replaced by a clapboard building. The Colonial style of this third place of worship remains largely unchanged. The steeple, roof line and exterior walls and ornamentation are original. The congregation of the Vriesland Reformed Church worshipped here until 1973.

6641 Byron Road, NW corner of Sixty-fourth Avenue, two miles east of Zeeland, Zeeland Township; Vriesland Reformed Church; L482; December 14, 1976; 1979

Presque Isle
Lake Huron

This, the fifth largest lake in the world, was the first of the Great Lakes seen by white men. By following the Ottawa River route, Samuel de Champlain in 1615 came to the "Freshwater Sea." It was half a century before the French fully understood the lake's size. Lake shipping has swelled immensely since the *Griffin*'s solitary voyage in 1679. Much of the shore is still as wild as when the Huron Indians were the only travelers on the lake.

Roadside park on US-23, twenty-six miles north of Rogers City at Huron Beach, near Hammond Bay Refuge Harbor, Berringer Township; Lake Huron Informational Designation; S119; January 19, 1957; 1956

The Metz Fire

On October 15, 1908, raging fires swept the pine forests of Presque Isle County. When the

236

In 1908 fires raged through Presque Isle County's forests destroying acres of homes, farms and villages. (*The Metz Fire*)

General view of the Village of Metz after the great forest fires of 1908.

flames approached the village of Metz, a train jammed with women and children left for Posen, five miles away. At Nowicki's siding, two miles out of town, huge piles of blazing wood lined the track. As the engine raced past the siding, where the intense heat had warped the rails, the train left the track, leaving an open car full of refugees in the center of the flames. Sixteen were killed and dozens of others badly burned. Throughout this part of the state hundreds were left homeless, as many homes and farms were devastated. Supplies soon poured in so that shelters could be erected before the onset of the northern winter.

Metz Township Hall, Grambav Road, Metz Township; Metz Fire Informational Designation; S299; February 27, 1970; 1970

Presque Isle Electric Cooperative Monument

The first utility pole set by Presque Isle Electric Cooperative was erected near this site on September 22, 1937. Established in 1935, the Rural Electrification Administration (REA) was a New Deal program designed to help cooperatives provide low-cost power to rural areas. On December 22, 1937, the Presque Isle Electric Cooperative energized its first seventy miles of line, from Norway Dam in Alpena to Moltke Township in Presque Isle County, bringing electricity to eighty-two families.

Between 10957 and 10981 Michigan Street, Posen; Presque Isle Electric Cooperative Monument; L1469C; October 23, 1987; 1988

Old Presque Isle Lighthouse

Presque Isle Harbor is one of Lake Huron's safest harbors of refuge. Its name comes from this peninsula which, translating from the French, is "almost an island." Indians and Frenchmen portaged across the peninsula to avoid several miles of open lake. When vessels came to the harbor in increasing numbers, Congress in 1838 appropriated $5,000 for a lighthouse. Jeremiah Moors of Detroit in 1840 completed this lighthouse, which today is one of the oldest surviving lighthouses on the Great Lakes. Pat Garrity, the last keeper of this lighthouse, was appointed by President Lincoln. Four of Garrity's children, raised in the keeper's house, became lighthouse keepers. In 1870 a new lighthouse to the north was completed along with two range lights for the entrance to the harbor.

5295 East Grand Lake Road (Presque Isle Harbor), Presque Isle Township; Presque Isle Lighthouse (Old Presque Isle Lighthouse); L39; October 14, 1964; 1965

Presque Isle Light Station

This lighthouse, built in 1870 by Orlando M. Poe, is one of three Great Lakes towers built from the same plans. It replaced the smaller 1840 harbor light. The conical brick tower rises

Operations began at the Michigan Limestone and Chemical Company in 1912. Above a carrier docked at the Calcite port during the company's first season. (*World's Largest Limestone Quarry*)

113 feet from a limestone foundation. The Third Order Fresnel lens was made by Henri Le-Paute of Paris. Patrick Garrity, the keeper of the harbor light, lit the lamp for the first time at the opening of the 1871 navigation season. Garrity served here until 1885 when he became keeper of the Harbor Range Lights. His wife, Mary, sons Thomas, Patrick and John, and daughter Anna all served as light keepers in this area. In 1890 a steam-operated fog signal manufactured by Variety Iron Works of Cleveland, Ohio, was installed. The light was automated in 1970 by the U.S. Coast Guard.

4500 East Grand Lake Road, Presque Isle Township; Presque Isle Light Station (New Presque Isle Light Station); L1563A; June 30, 1988; 1990

World's Largest Limestone Quarry

Limestone is a mineral raw material essential in making steel, chemicals and cement. Henry H. Hindshaw, a geologist, established in 1908-1909 the commercial value of this area's limestone for industry. The high purity of this deposit and the availability of water transportation led to development here of a port and quarry. Both are named Calcite, after the principal ingredient of the stone. The Michigan Limestone and Chemical Company, founded in 1910, began operations in 1912. Purchased by Carl D. Bradley and the United States Steel Corporation in 1920, the company came under the sole ownership of U. S. Steel upon Bradley's death in 1928. In 1951 the company became a division of the corporation. Self-unloader vessels of the division's Bradley Transportation Line carry limestone from this, the world's largest limestone quarry, to industrial ports around the Great Lakes.

Michigan Limestone Operations, Calcite Plant Main Gate, 1035 Calcite Road, east of M-23, Rogers City; World's Largest Limestone Quarry Informational Designation; S214; May 1, 1959; 1960

Roscommon

Gerrish

Near this site on April 5, 1880, area residents met at the Gerrish Logging Camp to elect officers for their newly organized township. James Watson was chosen as the first supervisor. Originally the township embraced present-day Gerrish, Lyon and Markey townships. In 1920 the present boundary line was established. This structure, the second permanent town hall, was erected in 1970. The township borders on half of the shoreline of Michigan's sixth largest inland lake, Higgins Lake, and is primarily a resort area.

2997 East Higgins Lake Drive, Roscommon vicinity, Gerrish Township; Gerrish Township Informational Site (Gerrish Township Hall); L760B; December 12, 1979; 1980

Terney House

William J. Terney, lumber baron and Civil War veteran, moved to the Roscommon area in 1887 and erected this house in the late 1880s. Shortly afterwards, he began extensive lumbering operations here and was instrumental in bringing the railroad through the village. Near the turn of the century, Terney was appointed county treasurer. He was elected village president in 1904, and in later years, served as an officer for the Michigan State Fair. Terney engaged in a real estate business until his death in 1926. Local banker William B. Orcutt purchased this large Queen Anne residence from Terney in 1910. Its interior features white oak parquet flooring and ornate paneling, linking it to the once-booming lumbering epoch of Roscommon.

603 Lake Street (M-18), north of Third Street, Roscommon; Terney House; L631; August 24, 1978; 1980

Saginaw

George Nason House

George M. Nason (1859-1929) built this house in 1907-1908. The Nason family had emigrated from Northampton, England, to Buffalo, New York, in 1832. George's father, Robert (1831-1907), came to Chesaning in 1852 and engaged in farming and lumbering. In 1861 he purchased fifteen hundred acres of land about five miles from Chesaning and erected a sawmill. For over a decade, he also engaged in prosperous land speculative activities and by 1881, he was considered to be one of Chesaning's wealthiest men.

Side Two

George Nason (1859-1929) built this Georgian Revival-style house as a monument to his family's success in the lumbering business. Its exterior features stately Ionic columns. A grand circular opening between the first and second floor dominates the interior. Nason family members lived in the house until 1945. The building remained a private residence until 1980, when it was opened to the public as an elegant dining establishment called the Chesaning Heritage House.

605 West Broad Street (M-57), Chesaning; Nason, George, House (Chesaning Heritage House); L1035B; September 8, 1982; 1985

Leamington Stewart House

Leamington and Madeline Stewart built this Queen Anne house in 1895-1897. The house was based on Design No. 53 in George F. Barber's *The Cottage Souvenir No. 2*, a pattern book published in 1891. Barber advertised the house's cost at $5,250. Pattern books were popular in the late 1800s as a way to obtain contemporary house plans at bargain prices. An Ontario native, Stewart practiced medicine in Chesaning until his death in 1933.

505 West Broad Street, Chesaning; Stewart, Dr. Leamington B., House; L1432A; July 23, 1987; 1990

Frankenmuth Bavarian Inn

Theodore Fischer, a former bartender at the Exchange Hotel (now Zehnder's Restaurant), established the Union House Hotel in 1888. His son Herman and daughter-in-law Lydia are said to have begun the tradition of the "All You Can Eat" family-style chicken dinners served here. The William Zehnder, Sr., family, distant relatives of Fischer, purchased the restaurant in 1950 and continued the chicken dinner tradition. In 1959 the Zehnders extensively renovated, enlarged and redecorated the restaurant in a fantasy Bavarian motif. They also changed the name of the restaurant to the Bavarian Inn. The week-long grand opening celebration held in 1959 in honor of the new addition evolved into the annual Frankenmuth Bavarian Festival.

Side Two

The village of Frankenmuth began as a German community in 1845. Its first settlers were among the German immigrants who left their homeland because of poor farming conditions and political unrest. Frankenmuth also attracted people who wanted to convert the Indians to the Lutheran faith. The Zehnder family emigrated from Germany in 1846. A family trip back to Bavaria in the 1950s inspired them to redecorate their restaurant in the Bavarian

Ads like this one (top), which appeared in a German newspaper, inspired emigration to Michigan. This circa 1900 photo is of the Joseph Kaul family. (*Michigan's German Settlers*)

theme. The Bavarian Inn's motif, accented by a fifty-foot-high Glockenspiel, echoes Frankenmuth's German heritage. Over twenty million meals were served at the inn between 1888 and 1988. A record 5,470 meals were served on October 9, 1982. By the 1980s the Bavarian Inn was recognized as one of the ten largest restaurants in the United States.

713 South Main Street (M-83), Frankenmuth; Union House Hotel Informational Site (Bavarian Inn Restaurant); L1577C; July 21, 1988; 1988

Michigan's German Settlers

Fifteen German immigrants from Franconia, Bavaria, led by the Reverend August Craemer, founded Frankenmuth in 1845. They were advised to settle here by the Reverend Friedrich

Schmid, Lutheran pastor of Ann Arbor's German colony, founded in the 1820s. Other German agricultural villages were founded in the Saginaw Valley in the 1840s and 1850s. Here, as in many other areas of Michigan, German settlers have contributed greatly to the state's cultural heritage.

In front of Zehnder's Restaurant, Intersection of Old Main Street and Main Street (M-83), Frankenmuth; Germans in Michigan Informational Designation; S170; September 17, 1957; 1958

Presbyterian Church of South Saginaw

Begun in 1865 as a Sunday school for children of this area, the Presbyterian Church of South Saginaw was formally organized on November 10, 1866. Shortly afterwards, the congregation purchased a small building on the corner of Washington and Williamson. In 1872, Norman Miller of Saginaw City gave the congregation the lot across the street from the original church. The frame structure was moved to that site, and worship services were held there until 1885, when the present brick church was erected on the same lot. With the consolidation of the cities of East Saginaw and South Saginaw, the church became known as the Washington Avenue Presbyterian Church. The city's first Boy Scout troop was chartered at this church and one of its most outstanding members, Wilber M. Brucker, ruling elder of the congregation for many years, was governor of the state of Michigan from 1931 through 1932.

2312 South Washington Avenue, NE corner of Williamson, Saginaw; The Presbyterian Church of South Saginaw (Washington Avenue United Presbyterian Church); L921A; April 24, 1981; 1982

Saginaw Club

Organized April 18, 1889, the club's membership was comprised of most of the leading business and civic figures of Saginaw. One of the first items of business was preparation for a clubhouse. Architect W. T. Cooper furnished plans, and ground was broken on July 1, 1889. Described as a monument to "enterprise, sagacity, and liberality," the clubhouse was opened on May 29, 1890. The inaugural event was a full-dress ball attended by eight hundred guests. Only slightly modified from its original design, the Saginaw Club has graced the main street of town for over eighty years.

219 North Washington Avenue, Saginaw; Saginaw Club; L219; March 14, 1973; 1974

Saginaw Valley Lumbering Era

The Saginaw River Watershed has been crucial in the development of Michigan. In the 1830s when white settlers moved into the area, they discovered the rich timberlands and hundreds of miles of rivers, providing an excellent base for lumbering which soon thrived in the area. In 1834, Gardner and Ephraim Williams opened the first steam mill at the foot of Mackinaw Street in Saginaw. By 1854 the Saginaw Valley had become the leading producer of lumber in the state, a distinction it held for the next forty years. In 1869 the watershed area alone was earning $7 million yearly from lumbering, and Michigan was producing more lumber than any other state.

Side Two

This extraordinary output was possible because of a carefully organized process, which was constantly improved through invention and imagination. Cooperative boom companies were formed to collect the logs and float them downstream to the mouth of the tributaries. Using company marks, the logs were separated at this point into floating booms, and then formed into rafts, held together by rope and wedge-shaped oak pins. The Saginaw was one of the few rivers to use wooden pins extensively. The greatest impact on production, however, was made by saws. A series of refinements in blades and the introduction of gang saws increased capacity so dramatically, that, in one year, 1882, the Saginaw yielded one billion board feet of lumber. By the 1890s the loggers had depleted their raw material and much of mid-Michigan was cut-over, barren land. The Saginaw lumbering era had come to an end.

Saginaw County Government Building, 111 South Michigan, Saginaw; Saginaw Valley Lumbering Era Informational Designation; L415; August 15, 1975; 1976

St. Mary's Hospital

The need for medical facilities in fast-growing Saginaw Valley led Father Francis Van der Bom and Dr. Benjamin B. Ross to organize support for a hospital. It opened with the arrival

These Saginaw Valley riverhogs paused for a "Kodak moment" from unloading timber from trains into the Saginaw River. (*Saginaw Valley Lumbering Era*)

of four Daughters of Charity of St. Vincent de Paul on August 22, 1874. The original frame house proved inadequate; in 1875 a new building was begun on this site and the hospital incorporated as St. Mary's. Its first patients were principally injured lumbermen. The staff devised a health insurance plan of five dollars a year to raise funds. Over the years the hospital expanded and modernized to care for more patients, as well as to provide an increasing variety of medical and educational facilities. As it moves into its second century St. Mary's Hospital anticipates a future of continued care and service.

830 South Jefferson Avenue, Saginaw; St. Mary's Hospital; L289; July 26, 1974; 1974

Hess School

Spaulding Township was organized in 1858. Thirteen years later, Peter and Orissa Hess deeded this site to the first school district of the township for the sum of ten dollars. Local farmers erected the first school in 1875. That structure was replaced in 1915. Ten years later, fire destroyed the second building. However, in less than a year's time, the present red brick schoolhouse, the third to stand on this site, was erected and opened for use. This 1925 structure has served the community schools for over fifty years.

1520 Houlihan Road, NW corner of Cole Road, Saginaw vicinity, Spaulding Township; Hess School; L585; April 4, 1978; 1980

Saginaw Valley Coal

Coal was first mined in Michigan in the 1830s in Jackson County, and that area led in production through the 1880s. In the next decade dozens of mines were opened in Bay, Saginaw and Shiawassee counties, producing thousands of tons of coal annually. The hamlet of St. Charles, in the center of this new coal field, expanded rapidly, "touched by the magic hand of good luck." More than one thousand people were here by 1900, and the state coal mine inspector maintained his office here for years. After World War I a series of labor strikes and diminishing returns from the mines led to a decline in the state's coal production. Swan Creek mine, the last producing coal mine in Michigan, closed in 1952.

St. Charles Park, corner of M-52 and Parkway Drive, St. Charles; Saginaw Valley Coal Informational Designation; S362; December 10, 1971; 1975

Coal Mine No. 8

Coal was discovered in the St. Charles area in 1896. On this site in 1917 the Robert Gage Coal Company sunk a shaft two hundred feet beneath the surface. The main entry off the shaft was about three miles long. At times, the mine employed as many as four hundred men, who worked in pairs. In 1919 a miner earned sixty to seventy cents per ton. After undercutting and blasting coal from seams twenty-two to sixty-four inches thick, miners shoveled it into cars that were pulled by mules and electric motors to the cage, where it was lifted up the shaft to the tipple. It was then sorted, weighed and loaded into railroad cars. The highest grade of bituminous coal in Michigan was mined here until 1931, when the shift to other fuels and competition from higher grade coal in other states made it necessary to close.

Hartley Outdoor Education Center, 12633 Beaver Road, north of Townline and east of Orr roads, St. Charles vicinity, Swan Creek Township; Robert Gage Coal Company-Mine No. 8 (No. 8 Coal Mine Museum); L869A; December 3, 1980; 1982

Schroeder House

In 1896, John Schroeder built this one and one-half-story log home for his family on a farm about a mile west of Freeland. His son George resided there until 1968. Exhibiting hand-hewn, notched white pine logs, boarded gables and a wood shingled roof, the cabin was moved to the Hartley Outdoor Education Center in 1978. Equipped with furnishings from the late nineteenth century, the cabin is a pioneer heritage studies site where students can practice pioneer crafts and skills. The eighteen-by-twenty-six-foot log barn was built in 1981.

Hartley Outdoor Education Center, 12633 Beaver Road, north of Townline and east of Orr roads, St. Charles, Swan Creek Township; Schroeder, John and Fredricka, Cabin; L877B; January 8, 1981; 1982

Burt Opera House

In 1888 this settlement was named in honor of Wellington R. Burt, the lumber tycoon who arranged for the Cincinnati, Saginaw and Mackinaw Railroad to run through this village. During his 1888 gubernatorial campaign, Burt donated $1,000 for the construction of a township building. Henry Youmans, also seeking an office, supplied the bricks. Ironically, neither man carried this township in the election that year. Local resident Sarah A. Miller gave the land with a deed stipulating that any structure built be used for "education, social and wholesome amusements, and meetings," and public gatherings dedicated to "free thought, free speech and good government." Townspeople contributed labor and additional funds for the erection of this hall, dedicated in 1891. The Burt Opera House has hosted vaudeville shows, weddings, local fairs, township meetings and elections.

Wellington R. Burt

Wellington R. Burt (1831-1919) was a Saginaw businessman, civic leader and philanthropist. Born in New York State, he moved to a farm in Jackson County, Michigan. After two years in college, he traveled far and wide until returning to Michigan at the age of twenty-six and starting work in a lumber camp near St. Louis. In 1858 young Wellington became a lumber operator. In 1864 he built the sawmill community of Melbourne, seven miles north of Saginaw. Melbourne was destroyed by fire in 1876. A Democrat, Burt was elected to the state senate in 1892. He waged unsuccessful races for the governorship in 1888 and Congress in 1890. Involved in the lumber, salt and mining industries, as well as railroads, foreign bonds and banking investments, Burt ranked among the wealthiest men in America by the early twentieth century.

East Burt Road between Dorwood and Nichols roads, Taymouth Township; Burt Opera House; L406; July 17, 1975; 1979

St. Paul's Episcopal Mission

In the 1860s and 1870s, Scottish, Irish and English immigrants, attracted by the lumber boom, settled in Taymouth Township. In 1873 they established St. Paul's Episcopal Mission and the following year built this Gothic Revival-inspired church. The community's Episcopalian population soon declined and by 1893 services were being held monthly. The last service was held in 1909. Since 1920, Taymouth Township has owned the building, which retains its original form and trim.

Seymour Road south of East Burt Road, Morseville vicinity, Taymouth Township; St. Paul's Mission-Taymouth (St. Paul's Episcopal Mission); L494; December 14, 1976; 1990

St. Clair

Clay Township Library

This Greek Revival home was built by Charles H. Beers around 1849. In 1914 it became the home and office of Dr. Walter E. Bostwick, who died in 1943. His widow, Cordelia Sheill Bostwick, lived in the house until her death in 1948. In 1949 the building became the new home of the Clay Township Library, which was founded in 1929 by the Clay Township Library Association of Algonac. The building has also housed county health department and township offices.

1240 St. Clair River Drive, Algonac; Bostwick, Dr. Walter, House (Clay Township Library); L711A; August 3, 1979; 1985

Water Speed Capital

For more than a century, Algonac has played a leading role in ship building, from sailing cargo ships to large pleasure craft, racing boats and World War II landing craft. Between 1921 and 1932, Christopher Smith and Gar Wood built ten *Miss Americas* in Algonac. Smith and Wood worked together on the first; however, Wood was responsible for the rest. The *Miss Americas* held the Harmsworth trophy, symbol of the world's water speed supremacy, from 1921 to 1933. In 1932, Wood's *Miss America X* raced over a measured mile to establish the world's water speed record at 124.91 miles per hour. During the 1930s, Smith adopted the name Chris Craft Corporation. The firm became one of the world's largest builders of power pleasure boats. Headquartered in Algonac for many years, it had other manufacturing plants in Michigan, Ohio, Missouri, Tennessee, Florida and Italy.

City of Algonac Park, across the street from Algonac City Hall, 805 St. Clair River Drive, Algonac; America's Water Speed Supremacy Informational Designation; S537B; January 8, 1981; 1981

Cole United Methodist Church

The Cole United Methodist Church, formed in 1878, was named for Jesse and Adah Cole, who held services in their home during the 1860s. Beginning in 1870 church members worshipped in nearby schoolhouses, where the Reverend Lester Clark, a circuit rider, preached every other Sunday. The congregation's first church was erected in 1899. It served until July 10, 1984, when it was struck by lightning. The present church was dedicated on the same site on November 3, 1985.

7015 Carson Road, NE corner of Wilkes Road, Brockway Township; Cole Class-West Brockway Methodist Church Informational Designation ; L1568C; June 30, 1988; 1988

Harsen House

This house belonged to the family of Jacob Harsen. A gunsmith and fur trader who arrived here about 1778, Harsen was the first white settler on the island. On this site he built a log home, which was destroyed by a gunpowder explosion. The present structure, erected around 1800 and subsequently enlarged and altered, housed his descendents until the 1940s. The Harsen family once owned all of the island which bears their name.

2006 Golf Course Road, Harsens Island, Clay Township; Harsen Home; L511; February 7, 1977; 1977

North Channel Shooting Club

The North Channel Shooting Club was organized in 1869. Detroit sportsmen arrived at the club by ferryboat, interurban railroad and private yachts. After the 1920s automobiles increasingly allowed Detroiters to spend leisure time farther from the city. This trend, as well as the Depression and Prohibition, caused club membership to decline. The Chrysler Yacht Club purchased the property in 1967 and restored the decaying 1869 clubhouse. In 1981 the name was changed to the North Channel Yacht Club.

1001 North Channel on the St. Clair River, Clay Township; North Channel Shooting Club; L1488B; January 21, 1988; 1990

St. Clair River

Linking the upper and lower Great Lakes, this river has become one of the world's great marine highways. In the 1700s canoes passed by here with furs destined to adorn Europe's

Commissioned in 1921, the *Huron* served in northern Lake Michigan. In 1935 the *Huron* was assigned to the Corsica Shoals just north of Port Huron. (*Huron Lightship*)

royalty. Ships built at Marine City by Sam and Eber Brock Ward during the mid-1800s carried many immigrants up this river on their way to new homes in the West. By the 1900s mighty freighters returned from the north with iron ore, copper, grain—products of these settlers' labor.

*Two miles north of Algonac on M-29, Clay Township; St. Clair River Informational Designation (Algonac State Park); S124; January 19, 1957; 1957

Holy Cross Parish

Father Gabriel Richard received this triangular plot of land by way of a grant from President John Quincy Adams on April 1, 1825. This area, known as Catholic Point, contains, among other buildings, a church, a rectory, a convent, the former high school, a new high school and a grade school. The present church edifice, the second to stand on the site, was built in 1903. A bell, which formerly hung in the original church, was cast in Normandy, France, in 1825. The tracker organ in the church was built in 1861 and is one of the earliest American-built models in Michigan. Among former pastors of Holy Cross Parish, were the saintly missionary, Bishop Frederic Baraga, and a pioneer priest of St. Clair, Father Lawrence Kilroy. Holy Cross Parish has remained in continuous use and service to the people for over 150 years.

610 South Water Street, SE corner of Bridge Street, Marine City; Catholic Pointe (Holy Cross Historic District); L546; August 12, 1977; 1978

Marine City

Built in 1884 at a cost of $12,300, this edifice has served continuously as the seat of local government. Marine City was incorporated as the village of Marine in 1865. It became Marine City in 1867. The first village president was David Lester, a prominent shipbuilder. Shipbuilding was the principal industry for about a half century, employing several hundred men. During the era of wooden ships, this city was one of the largest shipbuilding centers in the Great Lakes area, with an output of nearly 250 vessels by 1900. The discovery of salt on Catholic Point in 1882 proved to be another prosperous business with major salt companies springing up as a result of this important find.

300 Broadway (M-29) at Main Street, Marine City; Marine City City Hall; L461; August 6, 1976; 1978

Newport Academy

Emily Ward established the Newport Academy about 1845 to provide educational opportunities for area children. Miss Ward was a niece of Samuel Ward, the founder of Newport (now Marine City), and the sister of Eber Brock Ward, a shipping magnate and wealthy steel industrialist. She conducted the academy for about twenty years. This structure, erected in 1847, was one of the first school buildings in the community. The city bought it in 1868 and moved it from a nearby corner to its present location in 1870. It has served as both a private and public school, a village hall and jail, a hose house and a church. The Marine City Public Library has occupied this structure since 1939.

405 South Main Street at the corner of St. Clair Street, Marine City; Newport Academy (Marine City Public Library); L683B; June 15, 1979; 1980

C. H. Wills & Company

C. Harold Wills (1878-1940) began working as a draftsman for Henry Ford in 1902. When the Ford Motor Company was organized in 1903, Wills was its chief engineer and metallurgist. He designed every Ford car until he resigned in 1919. Deciding to manufacture his own car, Wills selected Marysville, a hamlet of two hundred on the banks of the St. Clair River, as the site of C. H. Wills & Company. In 1921 the first overhead-cam, V-8 Wills Sainte Claire was produced. Remembered for its Flying Gray Goose radiator emblem, it utilized strong, lightweight molybdenum steel and was the first car to have back-up lights. Hydraulic brakes, balloon tires and a six-cylinder engine were added before the factory closed in 1926, having produced fourteen thousand cars. The property was purchased by the Chrysler Corporation in 1935.

840 Huron Avenue, east of the intersection of Huron Boulevard & M-29, Marysville; C. H. Wills and Company Informational Site (Chrysler Plant); L711A; August 3, 1979; 1985

Davidson House

This excellent Queen Anne-style house, completed in 1890, was the residence of Wilbur F. Davidson until his death in 1913. Born in Adrian in 1852, Davidson opened a Port Huron dry goods store in 1882. The next year he installed in the store the first electric light plant in St. Clair County. Much of the rest of his business career was with public and private electrical utilities. Davidson's daughter lived in the family home until 1951. In 1972 the building was entered on the National Register of Historic Places.

1707 Military Street at the corner of Oak Street, Port Huron; Davidson, Wilbur F., House; L220; May 17, 1973; 1973

First International Tunnel

At this point the Grand Trunk Western Railroad Tunnel, linking Port Huron with Canada, passes underneath Gratiot Avenue. This international submarine railway tunnel—first in the world—was opened in 1891. The tunnel's total length is 11,725 feet, with 2,290 feet underwater. The tunnel operations were electrified in 1908 and completely dieselized in 1958. Tracks were lowered in 1949 to accommodate larger freight cars. During World War I, a plot to blast the tunnel was foiled.

M-25 (Military Street), one block north of Beard, Port Huron; St. Clair River Tunnel, (Grand Trunk Tunnel); S81; August 23, 1956; 1962

Fort Gratiot Light

This lighthouse, oldest in Michigan, was built in 1829 to replace a tower destroyed by a storm. Lucius Lyon, the builder, was deputy surveyor general of the Northwest Territory and later a United States senator from Michigan. In the 1860s workers extended the tower to its present height of eighty-six feet. The light, automated in 1933, continues to guide shipping on Lake Huron into the narrow and swift-flowing St. Clair River.

Omar and Garfield streets, Port Huron; Fort Gratiot Lighthouse; S332; April 23, 1971; 1971

Fort St. Joseph

Built near here in 1686 by the French explorer Duluth, this fort was the second white settlement in lower Michigan. This post guarded the upper end of the vital waterway joining Lake Erie and Lake Huron. Designed to bar English traders from the upper lakes, the fort in 1687 was the mobilization center for a war party of French and Indians. In 1688 it was abandoned, but the site became part of Fort Gratiot in 1814.

Gratiot Park on M-25 (Gratiot Avenue) and Forest Street, under the Bluewater Bridge, Port Huron; Fort St. Joseph; S80; August 23, 1956; 1957

Huron Lightship

Commissioned in 1921, the *Huron* began service as relief vessel for other Great Lakes lightships. She is ninety-seven feet long, twenty-four feet in beam and carried a crew of eleven. On clear nights her beacon could be seen for fourteen miles. After serving in northern Lake Michigan the *Huron* was assigned to the Corsica Shoals in 1935. These shallow waters, six miles north of Port Huron, were the scene of frequent groundings by lake freighters in the late nineteenth century. A lightship station had been established there in 1893, since the manned ships were more reliable than lighted buoys. After 1940 the *Huron* was the only lightship on the Great Lakes. Retired from Coast Guard service in 1970, she was presented to the city of Port Huron in 1971.

Pine Grove Park on the St. Clair River, Port Huron; Huron Lightship No. 103 (Relief Lightship); S404; May 17, 1973; 1973

Port Huron High School

On September 9, 1908, the third Port Huron High School building opened here where two previous high schools had stood. Port Huron architect George Harvey designed this Second Renaissance Revival-style school, constructed of brick and limestone. A 1917 state law limited the establishment of junior colleges to communities of over thirty thousand residents. In May 1923 the population requirement was changed to twenty-five thousand and Port Huron qualified. In September 1923, Port Huron Junior College opened in temporary classrooms in the high school annex. The college moved to quarters in the Maccabee Building in 1928, and when a new high school was built in 1957 the junior college returned to the site of its founding. In 1967, by a vote of the people, the college separated from the school district and became St. Clair County Community College.

323 Erie Street, Port Huron; Port Huron High School (St. Clair Community College); L1609B; December 15, 1988; 1990

St. John's United Church of Christ

St. John's congregation was organized by German immigrants in 1864. The original wood-frame structure was erected here in 1869-1870 at a cost of $5,000. In 1904 it was enlarged and extensively remodeled to create this Romanesque-inspired structure with its handsome stained-glass windows. The church still has its original 1869-1870 steeple. St. John's is the oldest congregation of German origin in Port Huron, and its church is the oldest house of worship in the city.

710 Pine Street at Seventh Street, Port Huron; St. Johannes Evangelische Kirche (St. John's United Church of Christ); L796A; March 19, 1980; 1980

Tom Edison at Grand Trunk

The Grand Trunk Railroad Depot to the right is where twelve-year-old Tom Edison departed daily on the Port Huron-Detroit run. In 1859, the railroad's first year of operation, Tom persuaded the company to let him sell newspapers and confections on the daily trips. He became so successful that he soon placed two newsboys on other Grand Trunk runs to Detroit. He made enough money to support himself and to buy chemicals and other experimental materials.

500 Thomas Edison Parkway, Port Huron; Grand Trunk Western Railroad Depot (Port Huron-Fort Gratiot Thomas Edison Depot); S283; September 2, 1966; 1967

First Baptist Church

The Reverend E. K. Grout, pastor of the Baptist church in China Township, also held services in St. Clair's log courthouse. On November 5, 1848, Grout and seven other people organized a local congregation. Around 1852 the first meetinghouse was built here on land donated by the village board of supervisors. That church burned in 1870. The present Romanesque-inspired church was erected three years later. In 1974 citizens bought the church and gave it to the city of St. Clair for a community center.

308 South Fourth Street, St. Clair; First Baptist Church (City of St. Clair Community Center); L1456A; September 26, 1987; 1991

First Congregational Church

This red-brick stone-faced structure was built in 1879 by Samuel Hopkins on land donated by his son William. Founded in 1833, its congregation is the oldest continuing one in St. Clair County. The church's sixty-six-foot clock tower with its four back-lighted clock faces is visible from the Canadian shore. It appears on navigation charts of the St. Clair River and has long been the city clock.

300 Adams and Third Streets, St. Clair; Congregational Church (First Congregational Church-U.C.C); L712A; August 3, 1979; 1981

St. Mary's Church

In 1850 a Catholic Parish was established in St. Clair by Bishop Peter Paul LeFevre, who appointed Father Lawrence Kilroy as the first resident pastor. The parish completed a modest church at the intersection of Fifth and Pine in 1853. In 1864-1865, under the leadership of Father Francis VanderBom, the present brick church was completed at a cost of $13,000. Bricks for the church were hand formed and hauled to the site by church women. The present transept was added in 1921 during the pastorate of Father Edward J. Kromenaker (1917-1959).

St. Mary's Rectory

This picturesque red brick, Queen Anne-style structure was erected as a residence and office for St. Mary's parish priests in 1886, during the pastorate of Father C. M. B. Schenkelberg. The rectory archives contain the complete sacramental records of all of the early Catholic missionaries in the area, including those of Father Frederic Baraga. The rectory complex has been enlarged over the years with the addition of a garage in 1926, housekeeping quarters in 1953 and office space in 1959.

415 North Sixth Street between Vine and Orchard streets, St. Clair; St. Mary's Catholic Church and Rectory; L1270A; September 25, 1985; 1987

James McColl House

This Queen Anne-style structure was erected in 1899 by Scottish-born James Livingston. He gave the house to his daughter, Louise Livingston McColl. During the late nineteenth century, Livingston and his son-in-law, James McColl, produced linseed oil and twine in their flax mills in Michigan and Canada. At the time this house was built, McColl was also village president. The elaborate wood-frame home remained in the McColl family until 1980.

205 South Main Street, Yale; McColl, James, House; L870A; January 8, 1981; 1984

St. Joseph

St. Joseph County Courthouse

Michigan Territorial Governor George B. Porter proclaimed Centreville the St. Joseph County seat on November 22, 1831. On November 7, 1831, Robert Clark, Jr., Electra W. Dean, Charles Noble and Daniel B. Miller donated the public square and fifty-six additional lots to the county. The first courthouse, a Greek Revival structure with four large columns on its east portico, was built in the center of the square in 1842 by John Bryan. That building was removed in 1899, to make way for the present red brick and sandstone courthouse, whose construction began on September 8 of that year. Grand Rapids architect Sydney J. Osgood designed the Romanesque Revival structure, and Coldwater contractors Crookshank and Somers built it at a cost of $33,000.

Side Two

The present St. Joseph County courthouse was dedicated on August 1, 1900. Its Romanesque Revival design creates a commodious, well-lighted, solid building that echoes the justice and stability it represents. Marble floors, wide spacious stairs, ornately carved woodwork, frosted glass doors and three wall murals still grace the little-altered interior. The clock, whose faces are five and one-half feet in diameter, was purchased by the village of Centreville for $850 and placed in the seventy-five-foot tower prior to the completion of the courthouse. When the building became too small to accommodate all of the government offices, a new courts building was constructed on the south side of the public square. The courthouse, however, remains the seat of government.

*612 East Main Street, Centreville; St. Joseph County Courthouse; L1150A; March 20, 1984; 1988

Stewart House

This handsome L-shaped residence retains the characteristics of Greek Revival architecture and features symmetrically placed windows flanked by distinctive pilaster trim. It was constructed in the 1840s by Daniel and Alexander Stewart who were associated with the Denton Mills, Centreville's famous maker of sleeping garments. Although passing through

This 1934 poster advertised Harry Blackstone's appearance in Detroit during the peak of his popularity as a magician. (*Colon/Harry Blackstone*)

many hands, the house has remained with Frank Holtom's descendents since 1909 and has carried the name of "Lonelm Farms" for many years.

134 North Clark, Centreville; Stewart House; L248; July 26, 1973; 1978

Colon

Known as the "Magic Capital of the World," this small town has gained widespread recognition for the invention and manufacture of magic tricks. Colon's reputation as a magic mecca began after Australian Percy Abbott visited the famous American magician Harry Blackstone who lived in this area. Abbott subsequently returned to Colon and started the Abbott Magic Novelty Company in 1933. Mainly a mail-order operation, the company continues to devise tricks which baffle the human eye and mind. In 1934, Abbott sponsored the first "Magic Get-Together," now an annual event attracting thousands of professional and amateur devotees. Blackstone himself as well as other famous conjurers have performed at these festivals.

Harry Blackstone

One of America's most notable magicians, Harry Blackstone (1885-1965), lived in Colon. Born Harry Bouton, he began his professional wizardry career at the age of sixteen in his native city of Chicago. Blackstone's fame grew in the first three decades of the twentieth century when magic shows were a staple of vaudeville and Broadway. During World War II millions of servicemen watched him perform at gatherings of the USO (United Service Organizations). His shows often included the "dancing" handkerchief trick and rabbits which were given to young spectators. Blackstone utilized split-second timing and "misdirection" of the audience to create illusions. His colorful personality enhanced the drama of magic and endeared him to Colon, which in the early 1960s renamed Main Street in his honor.

Colon Village Library, corner of Blackstone and Main streets, Colon; Colon/Harry Blackstone Informational Designation; L526; April 15, 1977; 1977

Constantine United Methodist Church

Methodism began in Meek's Mill (Constantine) in 1829 when the Reverend Erastus Felton came from the Ohio Methodist Episcopal Conference as a circuit rider to the St. Joseph Mission. This congregation, the earliest in Constantine, was organized in 1831 under the ministry of the Reverend Leonard Gurley. In 1848 the congregation erected a small brick church, which served until the present Gothic-style structure was built. Dedicated on December 1, 1878, the church was remodeled in 1955.

285 White Pigeon Street, Constantine; Constantine Methodist Episcopal Church (Constantine United Methodist Church); L1190A; September 24, 1984; 1986

Mottville Bridge

The Great Sauk Trail, which connected Detroit, Chicago and Green Bay, Wisconsin, crossed the St. Joseph River at a shallow spot in this vicinity. Responding to the westward migration of pioneers, the federal government surveyed the trail and converted it into the Chicago Road (presently US-12) in 1825. The first Chicago Road bridge to cross the river near Mottville was a substantial timber structure constructed in 1833-1834 by contractor Hart L. Stewart. A pile-supported bridge replaced it in 1845. In 1867, Mahlon Thompson and Joseph Miller built a covered Burr arch truss. The ruins of its stone-block abutments are visible upstream from here. This three-span camelback bridge was built in 1922. In

This 1922 highway department photograph shows the intricacies of camelback bridge construction. (*Mottville Bridge*)

1990, US-12 was rerouted over a new bridge. The camelback bridge is now used for foot traffic.

Side Two

Constructed in 1922, this three-span, 270-foot-long bridge is the longest Michigan example of a reinforced concrete camelback bridge. These bridges are found primarily in Michigan and Ontario, Canada, and the Mottville Bridge is an excellent example of this design. It was built by contractors Smith and Nichols of Hastings under the direction of State Bridge Engineer C. A. Melick. The Michigan State Highway Department pioneered the use of standardized designs for concrete bridges. By the early 1920s the department had established standardized plans for camelback spans of 50, 60, 70, 75 and 90 feet. This bridge contains three identical 90-foot spans. It was preserved as an engineering landmark by the Michigan Department of Transportation when the present US-12 bridge was erected.

Old US-12 across the St. Joseph River, Mottville Township; US-12 St. Joseph River Bridge (Mottville Bridge); S576A; April 10, 1986; 1989

Langley Covered Bridge

This is the longest of Michigan's few remaining covered bridges. It is 282 feet long with three, ninety-four-foot spans of the Howe-truss construction. The bridge was built in 1887 by Pierce (?) Bodmer of Parkville, using the best quality white pine for the frame timbers. The bridge's name honors a pioneer Centreville family. When the Sturgis Dam was built in 1910, the Langley Bridge had to be raised eight feet. In 1950-1951 extensive repairs and replacement of parts on the bridge were carried out by the St. Joseph County Road Commission to preserve for the future this historic link with a bygone era.

Three miles north of Centreville on Covered Bridge Road, Nottawa Township; Langley Covered Bridge; L56; August 31, 1965; 1965

Historic District

The Downtown Three Rivers Commercial Historic District has one of the best-preserved Victorian street scapes in southwestern Michigan. Three Rivers, settled in the 1830s, grew with the development of local water power and a railroad in the 1850s. St. Joseph Street (North Main) and Penn Street (Portage) formed its business center. The district's oldest structures, built on North Main in the early 1850s, are the Kelsey Building (39-43) and the Crossett-Spencer-Millard Building (40-42). The district was listed in the National Register of Historic Places in 1982.

Located at 66 North Main Street, within the district bounded by North Main Street, Michigan and Portage avenues, Three Rivers; Downtown Three Rivers Historic District; L1315C; May 8, 1986; 1986

Old Three Rivers Public Library

Built in 1904, this structure served as a public library for seventy-five years. Financed by an Andrew Carnegie grant, it was designed by A. W. Rush & Company and built by H. V. Snyder & Son. Warren J. Sillits donated the site. The exterior pink granite and the interior wood came from the local area. A mosaic skylight and four Grecian columns adorn the entrance room. The building is part of the Downtown Three Rivers Commercial Historic District.

107 North Main Street, Three Rivers; Three Rivers Public Library (Carnegie Center for the Arts); L1044A; November 16, 1982; 1984

Sue Sillman House

This brick structure was built in the 1870s by Arthur Silliman, an early pioneer in the area, who came to Three Rivers in 1847. The lower level of the building served as Silliman's blacksmith shop and the upper stories housed his family. Near this site a Potawatomi Indian trail crossed the St. Joseph. The confluence of the St. Joseph, Portage and Rocky rivers at this site gave Three Rivers its name.

Side Two

Arthur Silliman deeded this property named "Riversby" to his daughter Sue in 1914. Sue Silliman was Three Rivers librarian and historian for forty-two years. During that time she also served on national, state and local boards of the Daughters of the American Revolution. Before she died in 1945, she left to the people of this area her papers, the books she wrote including *St. Joseph in Homespun*, her home, and the memory of a life dedicated to public service.

116 South Main Street, Three Rivers; Silliman, Arthur House (Sue Sillman House); L400; May 14, 1975; 1977

Three Rivers

Here the Rocky and Portage rivers join the winding St. Joseph River. Many centuries before the coming of the white man the junction of these water routes made this a favorite camping site for Indians. La Salle came through the region in 1680 on his way east, and in his wake came other Frenchmen who traded with the Indians. Three Rivers, founded in the 1830s, was as far as large boats could come up the St. Joseph. Flatboats and rafts were used to carry goods to and from Lake Michigan.

Scidmore Park on M-60 (West Michigan Avenue), Three Rivers; Three Rivers Informational Designation; S150; April 30, 1957; 1957

Sanilac

Brown City Community Schools

In 1884 the first school in this area was established on the Hughson farm site. About halfway through the 1886 school term, that building burned. The term was completed in a blacksmith shop. Before the year was out, however, a frame school had been built on a site called the Indian Sugar Bush. The frame school originally served students in grades one through eight. In 1895 five young women made up its first high-school graduating class. The present building replaced the frame school in 1915.

4290 Second Street, Brown City; Brown City Community Schools; 1986

Buel Methodist Episcopal Church

This handsome building was the first church erected in Buel Township. Known as the Buel United Methodist Church, it was dedicated on December 3, 1882. The founding trustees were Robert Jolley, David Chewings, Halver Hulverson, Nicholas Van Natter, Frank Chambers, James Van Camp and Isaac Horton. The 1910 addition of the Gothic-style stained-glass windows gave the church its present appearance. It received its current name in 1968.

Peck Road (M-90), five miles west of Croswell, Buel Township; Buel Methodist Episcopal Church (Buel United Methodist Church); L1187A; August 24, 1984; 1987

Trinity Church

This picturesque cobblestone building constructed in 1898 serves as the Croswell chapel of the Trinity Episcopal Church. Its interior features wooden arches and a rood screen between the nave and the chancel. This structure, formerly called Christ Church, replaced the county's first Episcopal church building erected nearby in 1870. Among the prominent citizens attending and supporting the present church were the families of lumber barons Wildman Mills, Truman Moss and Joseph Gaige.

*124 North Howard, Croswell; Croswell Chapel of Trinity Episcopal Church; L514; February 7, 1977; 1977

Old Town Hall & Masonic Temple

The village of Lexington and the local Masonic lodge combined their efforts and finances to build this three-story Italianate structure in 1876. The village owned the first two floors (the fire department and the opera house); the Masons, the third floor. The Masons maintained the roof, except for the fire bell's cupola. Village government remained here until 1982, when a new hall was erected. Restoration of the building to house retail shops began in 1986.

5475 Main Street, one-half block north of stop light, Lexington; Lexington Town Hall and Masonic Temple (Old Town Hall); L997A; February 18, 1982; 1987

Trinity Church

This tall stately Gothic-style church with its elegant wood interior was built in 1874 during Sanilac County's great lumbering era. The Reverend A. B. Flower came to Lexington as a missionary in 1869 and started this congregation known as the Church of the Good Shepherd. Among its active members was Mary Moore who married Albert Sleeper, governor of Michigan from 1917 to 1920. Sleeper served as vestryman and warden of the church until moving to Bad Axe. Since 1972 this has been the Lexington Chapel of Trinity Episcopal Church.

5646 Main Street (M-25), NW corner of Hubbard Street, Lexington; Church of the Good Shepherd (All Souls Trinity Episcopal Church); S421; April 5, 1974; 1977

The Marlette District Library

In 1914 the Marlette Research Club, composed of women in the community, decided to build a public library for Marlette. The club contacted the Carnegie Corporation for a grant to build the library. In compliance with the Carnegie Corporation's rules, Marlette raised funds and instituted a quarter-mil tax for maintenance of the library. In 1918 the Carnegie

Corporation agreed to fund the Research Club's library project. The simple brick building was constructed in 1921. The building has a hipped roof and a portico of classical design. The library was the last in the Midwest to receive a Carnegie library grant and the second to the last to do so in the country. The Marlette District Library is one of fifty-three Michigan libraries funded by the Carnegie Corporation.

3116 North Main, SW corner of Ervin Street, Marlette; Marlette District Library; L713A; August 3, 1979; 1987

Loop-Harrison House

This Second Empire-style mansion was built in the 1870s by Dr. Joseph Loop. A native of New York, Loop moved to Oakland County, Michigan, in 1843. He and his wife, Jane Gardner Loop, pioneered this land in Sanilac County in 1854, and after graduating from the University of Michigan's medical department in 1855, he opened a practice in Port Sanilac. When this home was built, he kept an office on the lower floor, and serviced a forty-mile circuit, bringing medical care to much of the county. Dr. Loop died in 1903 at the age of ninety-three, leaving the house to his only child, Ada. She and her husband, the Reverend Julius Harrison, passed it in turn to one of their sons, Captain Stanley Harrison. In 1964 he deeded it to the Sanilac County Historical Society for a museum.

228 South Ridge, just south of Mulberry Street, Port Sanilac; Loop, Joseph M., House (Sanilac Historical Museum); L172; December 10, 1971; 1975

The Great Storm of 1913

Sudden tragedy struck the Great Lakes on November 9, 1913, when a storm, whose equal veteran sailors could not recall, left in its wake death and destruction. The grim toll was 235 seamen drowned, ten ships sunk and more than twenty others driven ashore. Here on Lake Huron all 178 crewmen on the eight ships claimed by its waters were lost. For sixteen terrible hours gales of cyclonic fury made man and his machines helpless.

Roadside Park on M-25, one and one-half miles south of Port Sanilac, Sanilac Township; Great Lake Storm of 1913 Informational Designation; S110; November 27, 1956; 1957

Schoolcraft

Bishop Baraga's First Church

Near this site, on May 15, 1832, the Right Reverend Frederic Baraga, then a young Catholic missionary to the Indians, established and blessed his first church. A small building of logs and bark, it was built with the willing help of the Indians, and dedicated "to the honor of God under the name and patronage of His Virginal Mother Mary." Until his death in 1868, Father Baraga labored selflessly in an area from Minnesota to Sault Ste. Marie, from Grand Rapids to Eagle Harbor. World famous as a missionary, he became upper Michigan's first Roman Catholic Bishop in 1853.

Two and one-half miles north of Manistique on Leduc Road, less than one-quarter mile west of M-94, at Arrowhead Inn Point, Hiawatha Township; Bishop Baraga's First Mission Church Informational Site; S146; April 2, 1957; 1958

Father Frederick Baraga established his first mission in 1832. (*Bishop Baraga's First Church*)

Lime Kilns

These towers are the remains of kilns used by the White Marble Lime Company, founded by George Nicholson, Jr., in 1889. The kilns, which were fired by wood waste from the lumber industry, burned dolomite to produce quicklime for use as a building material and an ingredient in the manufacture of paper. As larger corporations were formed and the methods of producing lime were made more efficient, the company diversified; it established a sawmill and shingle mill and became a dealer in forest products, as well as crushed stone, cement and builders' supplies. Its operations here and in Manistique and Blaney once employed some 250 men.

253

In 1925 the company was reorganized as the Manistique Lime and Stone Company, and continued under that name until the Depression of 1929.

North of US-2 on Duck Inn Road, four and one-half miles east of Manistique, Manistique Township; White Marble Lime Company Kilns (Lime Kilns); L40; November 13, 1964; 1968

Shiawassee

Knaggs Bridge Area

Archaeological evidence indicates men lived in this area before the time of Christ. Chippewa Indians settled here sometime before 1790. Their village was called Kechewandaugoning, which is said to mean "Big Salt Lick." This was the birthplace of Okemos and the summer residence of Wasso, two of Michigan's best-known Indian chiefs. Henry Bolieu, a trader, the first white settler, built a cabin here on the Shiawassee River about 1817. When an Indian reservation was created in 1819, Peter Whitmore Knaggs built a trading post here, which he maintained for several years. Later, a relative John Knaggs operated a store and tavern at the same site until 1839. A bridge was first built here in 1838. In 1850 the reservation was opened to settlement. A dam, the remains of which can be seen, was built in 1856.

Cole Road, three miles SE of Bancroft, Burns Township; Knaggs Bridge Area Informational Site; L32; April 11, 1963; 1963

Byron

Samuel W. Dexter, of Dexter, Michigan, made the first purchase of land here in July 1824. Four men known as the Byron Company bought this land in 1836 and platted the village the next year. Named after the British poet Lord Byron, in the 1840s the town was one of the largest in the county. Incorporated as a village in 1873, throughout the last half of the nineteenth century Byron was a principal milling and agricultural supply center for the rich Shiawassee Valley.

Byron Area School, 312 West Maple Street, Byron; Byron Informational Designation; L287; May 30, 1974; 1974

Ellen May Tower

The daughter of Civil War Captain Samuel and Sarah Tower, Ellen May Tower was born May 8, 1868, in Byron. She attended Chaffee School, the Byron Village School and a nurse's training program at Detroit's Grace Hospital. She worked for several years at the Michigan School for the Blind. On April 21, 1898, Tower volunteered for service as an army nurse "in the event of war between the United States and Spain." War was declared by Spain three days later. She took her oath on September 1, 1898, and was sent to Camp Wikoff, located at Montauk Point, New York. Known as one of the "Camp Wikoff Angels," she cared for soldiers who had been returned to the United States to recover from injuries or disease. In late September 1898, she volunteered for duty in Puerto Rico where she died less than three months later.

Spanish-American War Nurse

During the Spanish-American War, approximately ninety percent of American casualties resulted from disease. On December 9, 1898, Ellen May Tower, an army nurse from Byron, died of typhoid fever in a hospital tent after only ten weeks abroad. Her remains arrived in Detroit on January 15, 1899, and her funeral took place in Byron two days later. The Owosso Evening Argus hailed the event as the first military funeral in Michigan for a woman. Thousands of servicemen, villagers and visitors attended. Dr. Sterling, who had awarded Tower's nursing diploma five years before to the day, delivered her eulogy. The Tower family had moved to Onaway in the 1880s. Nearby, the village of Tower was named for the nurse when it was founded in 1899.

Byron Sesquicentennial Park, 325 Maple Avenue, Byron; Ellen May Tower Informational Designation; L1619C; January 19, 1989; 1989

Michigan's First Coal Mine

Alexander McArthur of Corunna discovered coal on the banks of Coal Creek in 1839. It was part of a large vein that produced coal until after World War II. McArthur hauled his coal in

Beginning in 1873, the Corunna Coal Company mined a coal vein discovered in 1839. during the 1870s nearly one hundred tons of coal per day were excavated. (*Michigan's First Coal Mine*)

wagons, selling it to blacksmiths for ten cents a bushel. In 1841 this was the only mine in the state where coal was excavated for commercial use. It was reported that from an eight-by-nine-foot area McArthur mined 460 bushels of coal and shale in one year. In the 1860s a group of New York investors purchased McArthur's mining interests and land and on April 22, 1865, opened the McArthur Mining Company. The firm built a coal house, an office, an engine room and tramways. But within a year, the company had disbanded because transportation costs made shipping the coal unprofitable.

Side Two

The Corunna Coal Company opened here in 1873. It operated from the same coal vein that Alexander McArthur had mined in 1839. The Corunna Company dug a seventy-five-foot mine shaft and brought in skilled miners from Youngstown, Ohio. They mined nearly one hundred tons of coal a day. In 1877, Tod Kincaid began managing the coal operations and purchased an interest in the mines. In July 1891, Kincaid bought out his partners and began running the business himself. The construction in 1885 of a spur track to the mine by the Detroit, Milwaukee and Western Railroad had opened more markets for Kincaid's coal. The Kincaid Mine closed in the early 1900s; however, the coal vein continued to be mined sporadically until after World War II.

M-21, east of State Road near Michigan Brick Company, Caledonia Township; Coal Creek Vein Informational Site; L1470C; October 23, 1987; 1988

Corunna Public Schools

The Corunna School District was organized in 1842. Later that year a one-story frame schoolhouse was constructed. A teacher, Miss Cook, was hired in 1843 and received the "unprecedented salary of $2.50 per week" and the "privilege of boarding 'round'" in the community. In 1851 a two-story brick school was built to accommodate Corunna's growing population. A larger, three-story brick school was erected in 1866 just north of the schoolhouse. In the fall of 1882, both buildings burned. Another three-story brick school was constructed later that year to serve grades kindergarten through twelve. On April 14, 1908, that school burned. The present school was built that same year with funds from insurance policies and a city bond issue.

Shiawassee Street Bridge

Edwyn A. Bowd of Lansing, an architect popular in the early twentieth century for his plans of public buildings, designed the Shiawassee Street School, which opened in January 1909. Rickman and Son, who built the Shiawassee County Courthouse in 1903-1904, constructed this school at a cost of $31,000. The Georgian Revival-style school is trimmed in limestone. The bell in

Ellen May Tower (right) cared for U.S. soldiers during the Spanish-American War; she was buried in Byron (above). (*Ellen May Tower*)

the cupola was cast in 1882 and donated by the Corunna Presbyterian Church upon the school's completion. The building served as an elementary school between 1952 and 1976, when it became the home of Community Education courses and the Corunna Public Schools Administrative Offices. This was the fifth school built on this site since 1842.

106 South Shiawassee Street, south of State Street, Corunna; Corunna Public School (Shiawassee Street School); L1514B; April 25, 1988; 1989

First National Bank

This structure was built as a bank in 1903. It replaced an earlier three-story brick building that was destroyed by fire in December 1902. The present building was designed by architect Claire Allen of Jackson and built by Burnett and Baldwin of Corunna. It served as the site of Corunna's only bank from 1865 to 1969. In 1970 the building was purchased by Shiawassee County for use as administrative offices. It was restored in 1981 and in 1982 the name was changed in memory of Commissioner Devoist J. Surbeck.

201 North Shiawassee Street, NW corner of McArthur, Corunna; First National Bank of Corunna (Shiawassee County Annex); L1012A; April 29, 1982; 1987

Governor Parsons

Andrew Parsons was born in Hoosick, New York, in 1817. In 1836 he settled in Shiawassee County and at the age of nineteen was elected the first county clerk. After holding a number of county and state offices, Parsons in 1852 became a regent of the University of Michigan. The same year he was elected lieutenant-governor, and he became acting governor in March 1853 upon the resignation of Governor Robert McClelland. The formation of the Republican party in 1854 badly split the Democratic forces and perhaps accounted for Parsons's failure to receive the gubernatorial nomination. Instead, Parsons was elected to the state legislature from Shiawassee County. He fell ill during the legislative session of 1855 and returned to Corunna, where he died on June 6, 1855.

Andrew Parsons of Corunna was Michigan's governor from 1853 to 1854. (*Governor Parsons*)

318 McNeil Street, Corunna; Parsons, Governor Andrew, House; S295; June 27, 1969; 1969

Hugh McCurdy

Hugh McCurdy (1829-1908), a native of Scotland, immigrated with his parents to Birmingham, Michigan, in 1837. He first worked as a cooper's apprentice, and after reading the law was admitted to the Michigan bar in 1854 and practiced law in Pontiac. Soon after moving to Corunna in 1855, he was appointed Shiawassee County prosecutor. He was elected probate judge in 1860, state senator in 1864 and mayor of Corunna in 1880 and 1887. McCurdy established the First National Bank of Corunna in 1865. A member of the Free and Accepted Masons since 1850, he became grand master of the Grand Lodge of Michigan in 1873. In this capacity, he laid the cornerstone of the new state capitol on October 2, 1873. In 1892 he became grand master of the Knights Templar of the United States. In 1899, McCurdy and his wife, Emma, gave land to Corunna for a park.

Hugh McCurdy Park

"Corunna Has A Merry Christmas!" headlined the *Corunna Journal* on December 21, 1899. One week before Christmas, Judge Hugh McCurdy and his wife, Emma, donated thirty-four acres of their estate to the citizens of Corunna as a Christmas gift. The McCurdys continued to live in their house, nestled amid the parkland. Detroit landscape gardeners Rackham and Dilger designed the park with winding paths, rustic shelters and a casino. The casino burned in 1930, but was rebuilt later that year. A bridge gave park visitors access to Diana Island, located in a channel of the Shiawassee River that once flowed through the northern portion of the park. Over the years the park was the home of many animals including deer, raccoon and caged bears. The Shiawassee County Fair was held here from 1934 to 1987.

Corunna Avenue at Emma Avenue, Corunna; Hugh McCurdy Park Informational Site; L1734C; March 15, 1990; 1990

Shiawassee County Courthouse

Territorial Governor Lewis Cass established Shiawassee County in 1822, but as there were few white settlers in the area, its government was not organized until 1837. Two years later, the county commissioners designated this site in the village of Corunna as the public square. County offices occupied temporary facilities here until 1851, when a brick

During the early twentieth century, 135 trains a day passed through the Durand Depot. In 1911, 50 percent of Durand's population worked for Grand Trunk. (*Durand Union Station*)

courthouse was built. It was replaced in 1903-1904 by the present structure, designed by Claire Allen and costing $75,000. The cornerstone was laid on May 4, 1904, before the largest gathering in the county's history. The courthouse, with its elegant clock tower and columned facade, still houses most of the major county offices.

218 North Shiawassee Avenue (M-71), Corunna; Shiawassee County Courthouse; L366; November 14, 1974; 1974

Durand Railroad History

Durand's first settlers began farming here in 1837. Its first railroad, the Detroit and Milwaukee, arrived in 1856, thirty-one years before the village of Durand was officially organized. The settlement became a railroad center for the Grand Trunk and the Ann Arbor railroads. Trains passing through Durand ran to Toledo, Grand Rapids, Clare, Chicago, Port Huron and Detroit. Around the turn of the century, as many as thirty-five passenger trains, one hundred freight trains and three thousand passengers used the depot each day. Its yard facilities once included the only full-circle roundhouse on the Grand Trunk Western. In 1911 50 percent of Durand's population was employed by the Grand Trunk Western Railway Company.

The Knights Templar Special

In June 1923, the sixty-seventh annual conclave of the Grand Commandery of Michigan Knights Templar was held in Flint. Western Michigan Sir Knights traveling to the Masonic convention commissioned a Grand Trunk Western special train. The train left on June 5. At 9:30 A.M. it came upon a split track at Clark's Crossing in Durand. The engine and tender left the rails and turned over. The second passenger coach rammed the first; however, the rear cars remained upright. Four Knights Templar died in the accident: engineer Frank Persall and fireman Joseph Parker were members of Corunna Commandery No. 21 stationed at Durand; John Erickson and Heber D. Waldron were from Ionia Commandery No. 11. A. J. Fanning of Grand Rapids also died, and thirty-two persons were injured.

Iron Horse Park, near Durand Depot, 205 West Clinton, Durand; Knights Templar Special Informational Designation; S578C; May 8, 1986; 1986

Durand Union Station

Designed by Detroit architects Spier & Rohns, the 239-foot-long Grand Trunk Western Union Depot originally featured a spacious waiting room, a popular dining room, a lunch counter, areas for baggage and express mail and telegraph and railroad offices. It was built of Missouri granite brick and Bedford cut stone and originally roofed in slate. Later roofs were of red tile and, in more recent years of asphalt. Once the largest station in outstate Michigan, the depot is also one of the largest in a small town anywhere in the United States. On March 27, 1960, Grand Trunk Western train No. 56 left the depot for Detroit. It was the last regularly-scheduled passenger train in the United States to be pulled by a steam locomotive.

Side Two

The Detroit and Milwaukee Railway brought Durand its first rail service in 1856. In 1877 the Chicago & North Eastern Railroad reached the town, and in 1885 the Toledo, Ann Arbor and North Michigan (later the Ann Arbor Railroad) added its tracks. The Grand Trunk Railway System and the Ann Arbor Railroad built this depot in 1903, at a cost of $60,000 to serve the thousands of passengers who came to this railroad center. In 1905 the depot was nearly destroyed by fire; however, within six months this near-replica had been completed. The last Grand Trunk Western Railroad passenger train stopped here in 1971. Passenger service resumed in 1974 with Amtrak. The city of Durand acquired the depot in 1979.

200 Railroad Street, Durand; Grand Trunk Railroad Durand Depot (Durand Depot); S316; November 6, 1970; 1987

Birthplace of Thomas Edmund Dewey

Born here, above his grandfather's general store, on March 24, 1902, Thomas Dewey is known as one of Owosso's most famous sons. After attending the University of Michigan and Columbia University, he began a long and distinguished legal career. During the 1930s

Two-time Republican presidential candidate Thomas Dewey was born above his grandfather's Owosso store in 1902. (*Birthplace of Thomas Dewey*)

259

Lady with a Sunshade was painted by American Impressionist Frederick Frieseke in 1926. The painting hangs in the Owosso Public Library. (*Frederick Carl Frieseke*)

he achieved national prominence for his prosecution of organized crime in New York. Dewey was elected Governor of New York three times, serving from 1942 through 1954. Twice in 1944 and 1948, he received the Republican nomination for the presidency but was defeated in both elections. Retiring from active politics in the 1950s, Dewey devoted the rest of his life to the legal profession. He died March 16, 1971.

313 West Main Street, Owosso; Dewey, Thomas Edmund, Birthplace of (Calvin Building); S376; February 11, 1972; 1972

Comstock Cabin

Elias Comstock was the first pioneer to erect a permanent residence in Owosso. He moved here in 1836. Comstock was a merchant, school teacher, justice of the peace, township supervisor, judge and county clerk. This one-room structure was built for him in the mid-1830s. Though the cabin has been moved three times (the last in 1969), the original logs are still intact. It is now located just north of the Comstock homesite. Funds raised by the Owosso Bicentennial Committee help maintain the cabin and surrounding grounds.

Next to Curwood Castle, Curwood Castle Drive, Owosso; Comstock, Elias, Cabin; L773A; January 18, 1980; 1980

Curwood Castle

James Oliver Curwood was born in Owosso on June 12, 1878, and lived here most of his life. Writing and love of nature were his boyhood interests, and by 1908 Curwood was earning his living as a novelist. Most of his stories were adventure tales set in the Canadian north, where the author spent much of his time. During the 1920s his books were among the most popular in North America, and many were made into movies. The castle, built in 1922, was his writing studio, and a number of this later works were composed in the tower, overlooking the Shiawassee River. Curwood became a zealous conservationist, and in 1926 he was appointed to the Michigan Conservation Commission. He died at his nearby home on Williams Street on August 13, 1927.

Curwood Castle Drive, Owosso; Curwood Castle; HB59; April 24, 1970; 1970

Herman C. Frieseke

Herman C. Frieseke built this house in 1872. The bricks used were from the tile and brick factory that he and his brother, Julius, had opened in 1865 beside the tracks of the Detroit, Grand Haven and Milwaukee Railroad. Herman's son, Frederick Carl, who became a painter of the French Impressionist School, was born on April 7, 1874, and spent his childhood in this house. He died in France in 1939. One of his paintings, "Lady with a Sunshade," dedicated to the memory of his grandmother, Valetta Gould Graham, hangs in the Owosso Public Library.

Frederick Carl Frieseke

Born in Owosso, Frederick Carl Frieseke studied art at the Chicago Art Institute and the Art Students' League in New York before moving to France in 1898. Early in his career, Frieseke painted murals for Philadelphia and New York department store owner Rodman Wanamaker, who became his patron. In France, Frieseke, an impressionist, painted the landscapes, garden scenes and figures of his home in Giverny, Normandy. Frieseke exhibited selected paintings at the Paris Salon and won many awards, including a gold medal at the International Exhibition in Munich in 1904.

654 North Water Street, between King and Oliver streets, Owosso; Frieseke, Herman C., House (Boyhood Home of Frederick Carl Frieseke); L1419A; June 10, 1987; 1987

"Old Perry Centre"

The first settler in what is now Perry Township was Josiah Purdy, who in 1836 built a log cabin near an Indian trail. In 1841 the first township meeting was held at the home of Joseph Roberts. In 1987, the year of the Michigan sesquicentennial, that site was the Slocum farm on Miller Road. A coffee pot and tea kettle were used for the ballot boxes. James Titus was granted the first land abstract and built the first log cabin in "Old Perry Centre." In 1850, William Laing opened the town's first store and post office. The town was a stagecoach stop on the Owosso-Mason line. By 1880 the settlement of about three hundred inhabitants had a hotel, Methodist, Baptist and Congregational churches, two flour mills, a sawmill, several stores and a school.

Side Two

In 1877 the Chicago-Port Huron Railroad line was built about three quarters of a mile north of Perry Centre. Isaac Gale, developer of Morrice Village and vice-president of the railroad, promoted a railroad sidetrack and depot for Morrice, but not for Perry Centre. Taking matters into their own hands, Perry residents bought the materials and built their own sidetrack and depot in one weekend. With that accomplished, they moved the Methodist church and some of their dwellings closer to the sidetrack and established the current location of Perry. In 1913 a fire started when a spark from the railroad jumped to the grain elevator located next to the tracks and ignited the grain. Perry's business section, which was destroyed by the fire, has since been rebuilt and expanded.

M-52 at the junction of Ellsworth Road, Perry; Perry Centre Informational Designation; L1398C; March 19, 1987; 1987

Maple River

In 1837 four couples came to this area, known as Maple River, from Oakland County to claim their newly purchased acreage. They were soon followed by a dozen families. These pioneer farmers chose this vicinity because the very fertile land was well-adapted for grazing and crop production. The community church and octagonal schoolhouse were designed and built under the guidance of the Reverend George M. Reynolds, son of one of the pioneer settlers. Soon after several farmhouses of Greek Revival design were constructed and the cemetery was established. Mr. Reynolds served for many years as minister of the church and was also the first teacher when the school opened in 1850. Several of the early structures remain, and descendants of the original settlers still reside in this area.

540-1151 East Bennington and 5210 Colby Road, Shiawassee Township; Maple River Area (Maple River Historic Rural District); L595; April 4, 1978; 1979

Tuscola

Caro Masonic Temple

This two-story Italianate commercial building was erected in 1879. One of the first brick buildings on Caro's main street, the structure was built by businessman and philanthropist Charles Montague as a bank and general store. When the building was enlarged in 1887, the entire second story became the Masonic Temple. On December 27, 1887, Rufus C. Hatheway, Grand Master of the Free and Accepted Masons of Michigan, dedicated the temple during a gala ceremony.

156 North State Street, between East Frank and East Lincoln streets, Caro; Caro Masonic Temple; L1349B; October 23, 1986; 1987

First Presbyterian Church of Caro

Twelve persons organized the First Presbyterian Church of Caro in December 1878. The Reverend Edward P. Clark, the Presbyterian minister at Vassar, conducted the organizational meeting with the assistance of the Reverend R. P. Shaw of Bedford, Indiana. For the first year, this small group of Presbyterians held their worship and prayer services in the homes of members. Then in 1880, they erected their first house of worship on Lincoln and Pearl streets. The present limestone and brick church was begun in 1902 and dedicated on December 13, 1903. It has had no structural alterations since construction. A regal structure, it features a corner tower and stained-glass windows.

215 North Almer Street, Caro; First Presbyterian Church Informational Designation; L1257C; August 22, 1985; 1985

Peninsular Sugar Refining Company

The beet sugar industry in Michigan began growing rapidly in the late nineteenth century. The declining lumber industry had cleared thousands of acres of land suitable for the cultivation of sugar beets. In 1897 farmers were encouraged further to grow this new crop when the state legislature offered a bounty to producers of one cent for each pound of sugar made from Michigan beets. Soon numerous beet sugar factories appeared. Many of them were in the Saginaw Valley area where both climate and soil were satisfactory for growing sugar beets. One of the companies started in this era was the Peninsular Sugar Refining Company at Caro. Organized in 1898, it was first called the Caro Sugar Company. Today it is the oldest beet sugar factory still operating in Michigan.

Side Two

The Peninsular Sugar Refining Company owes its success in part to the willingness of area farmers to grow sugar beets. A German firm built the factory in 1899 on land donated by the community. A newspaper, the Tuscola County Advertiser, publicized the venture and Charles Montague, a local businessman, raised capital for it. Farmers hauled tons of beets to the Caro factory in horse-drawn wooden-wheeled wagons and sleighs. In October of 1899, the company embarked on its first season of beet sugar production. In 1906, Peninsular Sugar merged with several other companies to form the Michigan Sugar Company. With Charlie Sieland as superintendent, the Caro factory became known as a training ground for sugar craftsmen. Today Caro's modern automated equipment is housed in the original factory.

725 South Almer Street, Caro; Peninsular Sugar Refining Company (Michigan Sugar Company); S432; July 26, 1974; 1977

Trinity Episcopal Church

This skillfully designed board and batten Gothic Revival church, first served local Episcopalians in 1880. The congregation had been formed in 1871, the year the town was incorporated. During the 1870s, Caro grew to be a major commerce center for the Thumb area. By the 1920s, however, church membership dropped and the building was sold to the Nazarenes. In 1974 preservationists saved the church from demolition.

106 Joy Street, Caro; Trinity Episcopal Church (Trinity Nazarene Church); L359; December 18, 1974; 1975

Tuscola County Advertiser

The Tuscola County Advertiser began publishing on August 21, 1868. The city's oldest surviving business establishment, it was founded by Henry G. Chapin, a native of Conesus, New York.

Chapin edited and published the paper for twelve years. The paper began with a circulation of 300, and by 1986 it reached 14,200 readers. The newspaper has received over seventy Awards of Excellence from the Michigan Press Association and was honored as Michigan's outstanding weekly newspaper by the University of Michigan Press Club in 1983.

344 North State Street, Caro; *Tuscola Advertiser* Informational Designation; L1326C; July 17, 1986; 1986

Tuscola County Courthouse

Peter DeWitt Bush (1818-1913), the second permanent resident of the village of Caro, donated this site for the county courthouse square in 1866. Then he, along with two other pioneer settlers, moved an old frame church to the site to serve as the county's first court-house. In 1873 the county replaced the former church with a brick courthouse that served the community's needs until 1932, when the present Art Deco-style structure was completed. Designed by Detroit architect William H. Kuni and built by Cecil M. Kelly, a Caro native, the courthouse is faced with Indiana limestone. Situated on the same site as the old brick courthouse, this $180,000 structure was completely paid for when it was dedicated on January 24, 1933, by means of a one-mill, five-year tax levy.

440 North State Street (M-81), Caro; Tuscola County Courthouse; L1045A; November 16, 1982; 1984

Tuscola County Fair

On March 11, 1882, thirty-three years after the nation's first state fair was held in Detroit, the Tuscola County Fair was organized as the Caro District Agricultural Association. On September 19-22, 1882, the fair hosted its first agricultural and recreational exhibition. Always a primary agricultural attraction, the county fair has displayed new farming equipment and methods, animals, produce and handicrafts on this site for the past century.

700 South Almer Street, Caro; Tuscola County Fairgrounds (Village of Caro Fairgrounds); L928B; May 13, 1981; 1981

Elkland Township Hall

This hall was built in 1881 as the center of government activity for Elkland Township. Erected at a cost of $2,600, it was the first brick structure in Cass City. Local timber and brick supplied by the Depews Brick Kilns were used throughout the hall. Serving as the town's cultural center since 1965, this building has housed township gatherings, a newspaper office, lodge functions and a basketball court in years gone by.

One building east of the NE corner of West and Main streets, Cass City; Elkland Township Hall (Elkland Township Cultural Center); L714A; August 3, 1979; 1980

Frankenhilf

In 1849, Pastor Ferdinand Sievers of Bay County purchased over fifteen hundred acres of virgin forest here in Tuscola County to establish a colony of immigrants from revolution-torn Germany. A year later two families, under the leadership of pastor Herman Kuehn settled in this area. They named their community Frankenhilf, combining Franconia, a district of Bavaria, and *hilf* meaning assistance. Despite severe hardships, the colony slowly grew and in 1851 organized St. Michael's Lutheran Church. Vexed by the seemingly odd name of this fertile farm area, postal authorities referred to Frankenhilf as "Richville," which became the village's official name in 1862. St. Michael's Lutheran Church, the nucleus of the early colony, still holds worship services in both English and German.

3455 South Van Buren Street, Richville, Denmark Township; Community of Frankenhilf Informational Site; L540; June 6, 1977; 1977

Gilford United Methodist Church

In 1887 a camp meeting led by the Reverend David Arnold resulted in the establishment of the Gilford United Brethren in Christ Church. Henry Shannon and John Cragg had invited Arnold to preach to area settlers. In 1889, Charles and Naomi Phipps donated land for a church building. Church members laid the cornerstone later that year. In 1968, through a merger with the Methodist denomination, the name became the Gilford United Methodist Church.

35 North Bradleyville Road, north of West Gilford Road, Gilford, Gilford Township; Gilford United Methodist Church; L1614A; January 19, 1989; 1989

Watrous General Store

Aaron Watrous and his crew of loggers came here in 1852 to cut the virgin pine of the Cass River Valley. In 1860 he platted the town, naming it Watrousville, and a few years later constructed this building as a general store. The flagpole in front is thought to have been erected during the 1864 presidential campaign. Watrous died in 1868, and in 1882 the building became the Juniata Township Hall. Since 1972 it has been the museum of the Watrousville-Caro Area Historical Society.

4607 West Caro Road, Watrousville, Juniata Township; Watrous General Store, (Old Juniata Township Hall); L247; September 7, 1973; 1973

Watrousville United Methodist Church

Circuit riders, who traveled through local villages, served the Watrousville United Methodist Church, when it was established in 1856. The congregation became known as the Watrousville Charge in 1861. In 1865 the first trustees of the congregation, then called the First Methodist Society of Watrousville, were elected. Construction of the congregation's first church began in 1871 and was completed in 1873. The church burned on October 31, 1937, and a near replica was built in 1938 on the same site.

4446 West Caro Road (M-81), Watrousville, Juniata Township; Watrousville United Methodist Church Informational Designation; L1425C; June 10, 1987; 1987

Vassar's Logging Era

Here on the Cass River, March 1, 1849, four men led by Townsend North and James N. Edmunds found a suitable place to build a dam and start a town, which was named for Edmunds's uncle Matthew Vassar, later the founder of Vassar College, New York. The growth of the town for the next thirty years was based on lumbering and its many related industries. Cork pine, the best variety of white pine, grew in abundance along the Cass River and was much in demand. These kings of the forest grew to a height of 150 feet [and] a diameter of 3 or 4 feet. The wood was light, strong, easy to work with. Millions of board feet were marketed all over the world, especially in America's prairie states. With forests depleted, a diversified economy developed here—agriculture, manufacturing and commercial business.

In front of library, intersection of West Huron and West streets, Vassar; Vassar's Logging Era Informational Designation; L52; March 23, 1965; 1965

Indian Dave

Indian Dave was one of the last Chippewas to hunt, fish and trap in the old manner in the Tuscola County area. Dave was born around 1803 and given the name Ishdonquit. According to legend, in 1819 he attended the gathering at the Saginaw River where 114 Chippewa chiefs and braves signed the Treaty of Saginaw. The treaty ceded about six million acres of land in central eastern Michigan to the United States. Indian Dave fascinated youngsters with his tales and native customs. A mural portrait honoring him has hung in a Vassar bank for decades.

Side Two

The earliest recorded inhabitants of Tuscola County were Sauk Indians. But Chippewas occupied the area by the time of the first permanent white settlement in 1836. Exactly when Indian Dave settled here is not known. However, in 1866, in order to resolve the Vassar/Caro county-seat dispute, he and Peter Bush transported the county records to Caro by canoe. Dave was an expert at making bows and arrows, which he often sold for his livelihood. When he died in 1909, he was believed to be 106 years old. He is buried nearby in Wisner Cemetery.

Bay City-Forestville Road (M-25), east of Conger Road, Wisner Township; Indian Dave Stocker Informational Designation; L761B; December 12, 1979; 1981

Van Buren

Bloomingdale Depot

Originally called the Kalamazoo and South Haven Railroad Depot, this building was completed in December 1870. Harvey Howard, owner of the local sawmill, and his brothers Zenas and Joseph supplied the lumber and built the depot. Its original location was an acre of land donated by Augustus Haven. The park built on the depot grounds in 1912 is named in Haven's honor. The first passenger train arrived in Bloomingdale on July 4, 1970.

Kalamazoo and South Haven Railroad

On April 14, 1869, Kalamazoo businessmen filed articles of incorporation establishing the

Claire Allen designed many of Michigan's government buildings, including the Van Buren County Courthouse, which was dedicated in 1901. (*Van Buren Courthouse*)

Kalamazoo and South Haven Railroad Company. Final construction on the line was completed in December 1870. After a year of operation, the railroad became a division of the Michigan Central Railroad. The village of Bloomingdale was established along the line on May 23, 1870, by Lucius Kendall and Henry Killefer. Passenger service was discontinued in 1937; and all other rail service, in 1970.

NW corner of Kalamazoo and Van Buren streets, Bloomingdale; Kalamazoo and South Haven Railroad Bloomingdale Depot (Bloomingdale Depot); L1245A; June 20, 1985; 1987

Covert Library

This structure was the township's first commercial building and an integral part of Covert's development. In 1871, Packard and Sons Lumbering Company hired Will Frary to build a general store. Under George Michel's proprietorship from 1885 to 1915, the store became a gathering place for shopping, banking, worshipping and visiting. The community expressed interest in purchasing the building in the late 1930s. However, in 1940, Dr. and Mrs. O. M. Vaughn donated it to the city for use as a library, community center and Masonic lodge.

Main Street, Covert Township; Packard Hall [Michels Building] (Covert Township Library); L416; August 15, 1975; 1976

Decatur Township Hall

Constructed at the turn of the century, this building replaced the original 1870 township hall.

A Georgian Revival brick and stone structure, it was dedicated on September 19, 1901. Besides township activities, the hall has been the setting for traveling medicine shows, school plays and a greeting card factory. It is now used for township meetings and local elections. Since 1970 it has also housed the Decatur Community Museum.

103 East Delaware, east of Main Street, Decatur; Decatur Township Hall; L716A; August 3, 1979; 1981

Van Buren County Poorhouse

This two and a half-story brick building was constructed in 1884 as the county poorhouse and infirmary. Here lived the indigent and mentally retarded from Van Buren County. Able-bodied residents worked on the grounds and on the adjacent farm where they produced much of the food for the poorhouse. Operating from 1951 to 1958 as a county social welfare office, the building's altered function reflected society's changing methods of aiding the poor. The county historical museum now occupies the structure.

6215 Red Arrow Highway west of County Road 681, Hartford, Hartford Township; County Poor House (Van Buren County Historical Society Museum); L430; November 21, 1975; 1977

St. Mark's Church

St. Mark's parish, organized at the county courthouse on February 22, 1851, is Paw Paw's oldest Episcopal congregation. The Reverend Voltaire Spaulding conducted the first service in a vacant store. The present church's cornerstone was laid on the Feast of St. Mark, April 25, 1876. Joseph Davey built the church under the leadership of the Reverend Darius Barker. Bishop George Gillespie consecrated it on December 6, 1876. The bell tower with a bell donated by the Reverend George Schetky and his family was added in 1882.

The Reverend Darius Barker

The Reverend Darius Barker was born in 1805 at Unity, New Hampshire. He came to Michigan in 1839, living in Lenawee and Jackson counties. In 1866, Barker became the first resident rector of St. Mark's Episcopal Church. Barker used part of his house, located at the intersection of Oak and Van Buren streets, as a chapel until the present church was built in 1876. Barker extended his pastoral duties to include other Van Buren County communities. He died on May 29, 1892, and was buried in Prospect Cemetery in Paw Paw.

609 East Michigan Avenue, Paw Paw; St. Mark's Episcopal Church; L1375A; January 22, 1987; 1987

Territorial Road

One of the three great east-west routes of pioneer days, the Territorial Road from Detroit to St. Joe tapped the rich lands of the second "tier" of counties. Approved in 1829, the road was not surveyed through Van Buren County until 1835. Although at first it was only a "blaze and a name," the route soon was teeming with emigrants and travelers. The Dodge Tavern in Paw Paw, a famed stopping point, was so crowded at times that some weary persons, old-timers said, "offered a dollar for a post to lean against."

Old US-12, west of State Police Post, Paw Paw; Territorial Road Informational Designation ; S163; September 17, 1957; 1959

Van Buren County

Settlers attracted by lumbering came to this area in the 1830s. By the 1860s a mild climate, rich soil and easy access to the Chicago markets created a thriving fruit industry in Van Buren County. The county was one of thirteen platted by the territorial legislature in 1829, and one of six named for President Andrew Jackson's cabinet members. A gubernatorial commission chose Lawrence as the seat of government; however, when the county was set-off in 1837, the board of supervisors chose Paw Paw. When the board decided to build a new courthouse in 1900, it considered moving the county seat. South Haven, the county's largest town, Lawrence and Hartford all vied for the designation. In a county-wide election on April 1, 1901, citizens voted to keep the county seat in Paw Paw.

Van Buren County Courthouse

Van Buren County officials occupied the first county courthouse (the present Paw Paw City Hall) in 1845. On September 2, 1901, Frank O. Gilbert, the grand master of the Michigan Free and Accepted Masons, laid the cornerstone for the present courthouse. Members of the Grand Army of the Republic and fraternal organizations marched through town in celebration. The Paw Paw True Northerner estimated that between eight thousand and ten thousand people attended the ceremony. The monumental Classical Revival building, designed by Jackson architect Claire Allen, was dedicated on February 23, 1903. The Sheldon and Oradell Rupert memorial clock was installed in the tower in 1986. Both of Van Buren's courthouses are listed on the National Register of Historic Places.

Paw Paw Street, Paw Paw; Van Buren County Courthouse Complex; L556A; November 7, 1977; 1990

Warner Wine Haus

Completed in 1898, this structure was built as a waterworks station for the village of Paw Paw. Water from artesian wells powered the plant, first by steam and after 1908 by hydroelectricity. In the 1920s the wells were capped, and the structure soon fell into disrepair. Warner Vineyards purchased the structure in 1967. Using lumber from old wine casks and period materials, the firm remodeled the station as a tourist and education center, which opened in 1967.

706 South Kalamazoo Street, Paw Paw; Paw Paw Water Works Pumping Station (Warner Wine House); L939A; July 17, 1981; 1982

Hartman School

In 1906 the South Haven School District built this four-room school in Ward Two. The school, designed by Hussey and White of Lansing, was constructed at a cost of approximately $7,000. It was named for local businessman and school board president E. H. Hartman. On January 11, 1907, students moved into the new school. For over three-quarters of a century, Hartman School has served as a neighborhood school in Ward Two.

355 Hubbard Street, South Haven; Hartman School; L1095A; June 23, 1983; 1985

Haven Peaches

The Haven peach varieties were developed here by Michigan State University's South Haven Experiment Station, under the direction of Professor Stanley Johnston. From 1924 to 1963, eight yellow-fleshed freestone varieties were selected from more than twenty-one thousand cross-bred seedlings. They were named Halehaven, Kalhaven, Redhaven, Fairhaven, Sunhaven, Richhaven, Glohaven and Cresthaven. Redhaven was the first red-skinned commercial peach variety. It is now the most widely planted freestone peach variety in the world. The Haven peaches have provided an orderly supply of high quality peaches extending over a seven-week period. Prior to the development of Haven peaches, harvests had been restricted to a three-week period.

MSU South Haven Experimental Station, 802 St. Joseph Street, South Haven; Haven Peaches Informational Designation; S277; May 4, 1966; 1966

Indiana School

This school was built for Ward One of the South Haven School District in 1898. Constructed at a cost of nearly $5,000 by William Buck, the handsome two-story building was designed by Frank S. Allen. It later took its name from the street on which it is located. On December 5, 1898, some 115 students, kindergarten through sixth grade, moved into the structure. Since that time, Indiana School has remained a South Haven neighborhood school.

615 Indiana Avenue, South Haven; Ward School (Indiana School); L1173A; June 15, 1984; 1986

Liberty Hyde Bailey
1858-1954

The world-famous botanist and horticulturist, Liberty Hyde Bailey, was born in this frame house. Here in wilderness surroundings he learned of wild animals and plants and attended the local village school. He graduated from Michigan Agricultural College in 1882, served on its faculty and designed at that school the nation's first distinctively horticultural laboratory building. Bailey went on to be

Horticulturist and botanist Liberty Hyde Bailey was born in South Haven in 1858. (*Liberty Hyde Bailey*)

director of Cornell's College of Agriculture, retiring in 1913. Throughout his long life he made signal contributions to science.

903 Bailey Avenue, South Haven; Bailey, Liberty Hyde, Birthplace (Liberty Hyde Bailey Museum); S243; January 18, 1963; 1964

Scott Club

This federated women's club, founded as a reading circle in 1883 and named for Sir Walter Scott, merged with the Literary and Antiquarian Societies to build a clubhouse in 1892. John Cornelius Randall designed the sandstone Queen Anne structure, built by local artisans and completed in 1893. Two stained-glass windows created in Austria portray Sir Walter Scott and Henry Wadsworth Longfellow. This building has been in continuous use by the Scott Club as a cultural center providing fellowship for women of the area.

652 Phoenix Street, South Haven; Scott Club; L807A; April 21, 1980; 1982

Washtenaw

Antislavery Society

The founding meeting of the Michigan Antislavery Society was held in the First Presbyterian Church, located on this site, on November 10, 1836. Delegates from six counties elected officers and adopted fourteen resolutions denouncing slavery. This convention led to the establishment in Jackson in 1839 of the *American Freeman*, the state's first antislavery newspaper and its successor, Ann Arbor's *Signal of Liberty*, in 1841.

Ann Arbor News Building, 340 East Huron Street, Ann Arbor; Antislavery Society Informational Site; S488; August 6, 1976; 1976

Bethlehem United Church of Christ

In the late 1820s and early 1830s many German Protestant immigrants settled in the Ann Arbor area. Desiring to worship in German, they wrote Switzerland's Basel Mission to request a pastor. On August 20, 1833, the Reverend Friedrich Schmid arrived to help found one of Michigan's first German congregations. The church was formally organized on November 3, 1833, as the First German Evangelical Society of Scio. The next month, the congregation completed a modest log structure at the site of the present Bethlehem Cemetery. It built a second church at First and Washington in 1849, and in 1896 dedicated the present stone structure. From 1846 to 1916 the church conducted a parochial school. In 1945 the congregation became an Evangelical and Reformed church; it joined the United Church of Christ in 1958.

423 South Fourth Avenue, north of Packard Street, Ann Arbor; Bethlehem German Evangelical Church (Bethlehem United Church of Christ); L1046A; November 16, 1982; 1983

Central Title Service Building

On August 6, 1845, the first graduation ceremony for the University of Michigan was held in this building, which was then the First Presbyterian Church. Founded in 1817 in Detroit, the first university of the state moved to Ann Arbor in 1837, the year this building was constructed. Graduations were held here for the next eleven years and then moved to other church locations until the University of Michigan constructed a building large enough for this purpose.

213 East Washington Street between Fourth and Fifth avenues, Ann Arbor; First Presbyterian Church (Central Title Building); S584C; November 15, 1986; 1986

Governor Alpheus Felch

Born in Maine in 1804, Felch graduated from Bowdoin College in 1827. Entering the legal profession, he moved to Michigan in 1833 and after 1843 resided in Ann Arbor. A lifelong Democrat, Felch was governor in 1846-1847, serving previously as justice of the state supreme court and as a member of the first three legislatures. Rising to national prominence, he was U.S. senator in 1847-1853 and was then appointed to a commission to settle Spanish land claims in California. Returning to Ann Arbor in 1856 he resumed his law career, serving as Tappan Professor of Law at the University of Michigan in 1879-1883. On Felch's ninetieth birthday this park was named in his honor. He died two years later, in 1896.

121 Fletcher, SE corner of East Huron and Fletcher streets, Ann Arbor; Felch, Governor Alpheus, Park; S415; September 7, 1973; 1973

Listed in the National Register of Historic Places, Ann Arbor's Kempf House is one of the most pristine examples of Greek Revival architecture in Michigan. (*Kempf House*)

Kempf House

Cast iron grilles in an ancient Greek floral motif highlight the frieze of this temple-front Greek Revival house. Built in 1853 for Henry D. Bennett, secretary and steward of the University of Michigan, it became the home and studio of local musicians Reuben H. and Pauline Widenmann Kempf in 1890. Trained in Germany, Mr. Kempf (1859-1945) taught piano and organ. Mrs. Kempf (1860-1953), a graduate of the Cincinnati Conservatory, taught voice. The city of Ann Arbor purchased the house in 1969, and in 1983 it became the Kempf House Center of Local History.

312 South Division Street, south of East Liberty Street, Ann Arbor; Bennett, Henry, House (Reuben Kempf House); L236; May 17, 1973; 1988

Martha Cook Building

The Martha Cook Building first housed women students of the University of Michigan in 1915. New York lawyer William W. Cook, a Michigan alumnus, donated the building. The

Collegiate Gothic residence was named for Cook's mother, Martha W. Cook. New York architects York and Sawyer designed this building as well as the university Law Quadrangle, one of Cook's later donations. Paul Suttman's garden statue, known as "Eve," was a fiftieth anniversary gift of the building's alumnae.

Side Two

A statue of Portia, the heroine of Shakespeare's The *Merchant of Venice*, stands above the entrance of the Martha Cook Building. Gothic groin vaults frame the ground floor hallway, which houses a full-sized marble replica of the *Venus de Milo*. The Red Room, which connects to the Gold Room by a paneled alcove, displays a seventeenth century Flemish tapestry. William W. Cook's Steinway piano, commissioned in 1913, as well as a bust of Cook are exhibited in the Gold Room.

906 South University, SE corner of Tappan, Ann Arbor; Cook, Martha Building; S601A; October 10, 1989; 1990

Michigan Becomes a State

On this site, in 1836, delegates from all parts of Michigan met in Washtenaw County's first courthouse to consider a proposal by Congress for settling the boundary dispute between Michigan and Ohio. Both claimed a narrow strip of land, including the present city of Toledo. Congress proposed giving the greater part of the Upper Peninsula to Michigan while awarding the "Toledo Strip" to Ohio. In September the first "Convention of Assent" rejected this proposal. Support for the plan increased, and a second meeting was called. On a bitterly cold December 14 the famous "Frostbitten Convention" gave its assent to the Congressional plan. This action cleared the way for the admission of Michigan as a state into the Union on January 26, 1837.

Washtenaw County Building, NE corner of North Main and East Huron, Ann Arbor; Frost Bitten Convention Informational Designation; S261; September 18, 1964; 1966

Michigan Central Railroad Depot

Built in 1886, and conceived by Frederick Spier, the design of this granite block building was influenced by the great American architect Henry Hobson Richardson. The massive arch and two-foot thick walls are balanced by the simple, precise detailing. Carefully preserved, this depot is a symbol of the elegance and vitality of nineteenth century rail transportation.

401 Depot Street near the Broadway Bridge, between Division and State streets, Ann Arbor; Michigan Central Railroad Depot (Gandy Dancer); L339; July 26, 1974; 1975

Michigan's First Jewish Cemetery Site

At this site the first Jewish cemetery in Michigan was established in 1848-1849. The Jews Society of Ann Arbor acquired burial rights to this land adjacent to what was then the public cemetery. Several years earlier, immigrants from Germany and Austria had organized the first Jewish community in the state. Their first religious services were held in the homes of the five Weil brothers in the vicinity of the family tannery, J. Weil and Brothers. Members of the Jewish community participated in all aspects of the city's life. Jacob Weil served Ann Arbor as alderman from 1859 to 1861. By the 1880s this original Jewish community no longer existed. In 1900 the remains of those buried here were reinterred in Ann Arbor's Forest Hill Cemetery.

SW corner of East Huron and Fletcher streets, Ann Arbor; Michigan's First Jewish Cemetery Informational Site; L1039C; September 24, 1982; 1983

St. Thomas the Apostle Church

In 1831, Father Patrick O'Kelly came from Detroit to minister to the Irish Catholics in the Washtenaw area. He offered his first mass in Ann Arbor on July 12, 1835, in a home located on land bounded by Detroit, Kingsley and Fifth streets. St. Thomas parish took more permanent form in 1840, when under the leadership of Father Thomas Cullen it purchased land on Kingsley Street near Division Street and built Ann Arbor's first brick church. It established a parochial school in 1868. The church site was purchased in 1883. The present church, begun in 1896 under Father Edward D. Kelly, was dedicated in 1899. Its granite fieldstone and Bailey bluestone were donated and hauled to the site by parishioners and area farmers. The first hospital to serve the community and two additional Ann Arbor Catholic parishes emerged from St. Thomas parish.

NW corner of East Kingsley and North State streets, Ann Arbor; St. Thomas the Apostle Catholic Church; L1181A; July 20, 1984; 1985

Originally established in 1817 as the University of Michigania in Detroit, the University of Michigan was reestablished in Ann Arbor in 1837. (*The University of Michigan*)

Ticknor-Campbell House

In 1844, Benajah Ticknor, a U.S. naval surgeon from Connecticut, built this Classical Revival house on his 183-acre farm in Pittsfield Township. He used cobblestone construction, which originated in upstate New York. The rear wing includes a small frame house, first occupied in 1835 by his brother Heman Ticknor, farm manager and township leader. At Dr. Ticknor's death in 1858, his extensive medical and classical library was given to the University of Michigan. The home was listed in the Historic American Buildings Survey in 1936.

Side Two

In 1881, Scottish immigrant William Campbell, an educator from Ypsilanti, purchased this house on a 223-acre farm. He and his son Clair raised grain, hogs and purebred prize cattle. Farming continued on this site until 1955. For ninety-one years three generations of the Campbell family retained the house essentially unchanged. In 1972 the city of Ann Arbor purchased it for use as a pioneer farm museum, and it was placed on the national and Michigan historic registers.

2781 Packard Road, between Colony and Easy streets in Buhr Park, Ann Arbor; Ticknor, Dr. Benajah, House (Campbell House); L237; May 17, 1973; 1981

The University of Michigan

By legislative act in 1837, Ann Arbor was selected as the site for the University of Michigan. Near this point on the original forty-acre campus, classes were held in old Mason Hall in the fall of 1841. The student body numbered seven; the faculty had two members. Dr. Henry Philip Tappan's appointment in 1852 as the president of the university marked the beginning of the steady growth that has made it a world-famous institution.

NW corner of Graduate Library, near Tappan and South University streets, Ann Arbor; University of Michigan Informational Designation; S37; July 19, 1956; 1957

Bridgewater Town Hall

Bridgewater Township was set off from Hixon Township in 1832. The remainder became

271

Manchester Township in 1837. By 1850 there were two settlements, River Raisin and Bridgewater. Each had a railroad station and a post office. The River Raisin community no longer exists. In 1856 the first town hall opened on this site and was also used for "moral and scientific lectures and for funerals." The present hall was built in 1882 and has been in continuous use as the site of township meetings, elections and social functions.

10990 Clinton Road, NW corner of Braun Road, Bridgewater Township; Bridgewater Township Hall; L1486B; January 21, 1988; 1989

Chelsea Depot

In 1880, Chelsea was chosen by the Michigan Central Railroad for an experiment in upgrading the appearance of rural stations. Mason and Rice of Detroit were commissioned as the new station's architects. Their design was Victorian, characterized by numerous gables and gingerbread embellishments. This depot served patrons of the Michigan Central until 1975 when the company was taken over by Amtrak. In 1981, Amtrak discontinued service to Chelsea and closed the station. Fearing damage from prolonged neglect in 1985, area citizens formed the Chelsea Depot Association to restore the building. The group purchased the depot that year, and restoration began in 1986.

Chelsea

In the 1830s the Congdon brothers, Elisha and James, settled the land where Chelsea is located. In 1848 they offered the Michigan Central Railroad a free site on which to build a station. The first and succeeding structures were freight stations. The first shipment sent on May 2, 1850, was a barrel of eggs weighing 130 pounds. For a time more wool was shipped from Chelsea than from any other place in the state. Grain, apple, stock and meat shipments were also large. In 1880 the Michigan Central established Chelsea as a passenger service point. The depot was built with two waiting rooms—the east for women and children, the west for men.

NOTE: The Michigan Central Railroad was not taken over by Amtrak. 150 Jackson Street, Chelsea; Michigan Central Railroad Chelsea Depot (Chelsea Depot); L1356A; December 5, 1986; 1988

The Welfare Building

The Welfare Building was constructed in 1906 as a recreation facility for the workers of the Glazier Stove Company. It featured a swimming pool, a billiard hall, a basketball court, a theater and a reading room. Chelsea native Frank P. Glazier, who was the Michigan state treasurer from 1904 to 1908, founded the stove company in 1891. Because Chelsea, a predominantly rural community, lacked skilled labor, most of the company's workers commuted weekly via a special train from Detroit. In 1907, Glazier declared bankruptcy. The building was sold to the Lewis Spring & Axle Company, which manufactured the short-lived Hollier Eight automobile. Since 1960 the building has housed the *Chelsea Standard*.

300 North Main Street, near the Penn Railroad, Chelsea; Welfare Building; S524A; August 3, 1979; 1986

Dexter Depot

The Michigan Central Railroad reached Dexter from Detroit on July 4, 1841, just after Dexter's first depot was completed. Frederick H. Spier of Detroit designed the present depot, which was completed in record time. Work began on November 6, 1886, and at noon on January 19, 1887, the station opened. The plantings for the grounds came from railroad greenhouses at Niles and Ypsilanti. The depot had two waiting rooms, a ticket office and a baggage room. Passenger service ended at the Dexter Depot in 1953.

Track Pans

Kinnear, located two miles east of Dexter, was the site of Michigan's first railroad track water pans, which were built in 1901. The pans were situated between the rails and heated during cold weather. Steam locomotives scooped up the water as they moved over the pans. The Kinnear pans and telegraph station were named after Wilson S. Kinnear, chief engineer of the Detroit River Railroad Tunnel. In 1913 the pans were dismantled and moved to Four Mile Lake between Dexter and Chelsea.

3487 Broad, NW corner of Broad and Third streets, Dexter; Michigan Central Railroad Dexter Depot (Dexter Depot); L1303A; April 10, 1986; 1987

St. Joseph Catholic Church

The Catholic church in this village dates back to 1840 with Fathers Cullen, Hennesy and

Pulsers serving the predominately Irish parishioners for nearly thirty years. The present brick edifice, completed in 1874, is an example of simple Gothic style. Stained glass and carved woodwork enhance the interior. St. Joseph Catholic Church was dedicated on January 3, 1875, with almost seven hundred persons attending, and Bishop Caspar Henry Borgess performing the rite of consecration. The bell, weighing almost two tons, was placed in the belfry in 1885. One of St. Joseph's most notable resident pastors was Father Charles T. Walsh, who served the parish for thirty-five years. Associated with the church, the oldest in the village of this denomination, are a school, rectory and convent.

3430 Dover Street, corner of Fourth Street, Dexter; St. Joseph's Church; L626; July 26, 1978; 1978

Hudson Mills

This hamlet developed around the mills which were located here to utilize the great water power of the Huron River. Cornelius Osterhout built a sawmill here about 1827, followed in 1846 by a gristmill in which three men produced six thousand barrels of flour a year. Later a cider mill and plaster mill became part of the complex. In 1882 a wood pulp producer, the Birkett Manufacturing Company, acquired the mill property. Across the Huron the remains of the Birkett mill and dam are still visible.

Hudson Mills Metropolitan Park, south of North Territorial Road, just west of Huron River Drive, Dexter Township; Hudson Mills; L110; April 23, 1971; 1971

North Lake Methodist Church

The Reverend Charles Glenn organized the first Methodist class here in 1836, and for the next ten years the group met in the home of his brother, John. In 1846 the brothers presented the congregation with a building which served as both church and school until the present structure was erected in 1866. The former Grange Hall was added to the church in 1925 to serve as an educational and social center. With community help a new building for this purpose was begun in 1971.

14111 North Territorial Road, Dexter Township; North Lake Methodist Church; L193; February 11, 1972; 1972

Bethel Church

In 1840 the Reverend Friedrich Schmid of Ann Arbor organized the Evangelical German Bethel Congregation in Freedom Township. Schmid, a missionary pastor originally from Basil, Switzerland, frequently traveled to the township and held services in the Kuebler District School, one mile east of here. In 1849, Johannes and Louis Strieter deeded one acre of land to the congregation. Church members built a log church on the lot where they worshipped until 1857 when a frame building replaced it. That church stood just west of here. The church served until 1909 when the present structure was dedicated. Services were conducted only in German until 1926 when English was introduced into the Sunday school. German services officially ended in 1955. Today, Bethel Church is a member of the United Church of Christ.

Side Two

This Gothic Revival-style church, designed and built by Charles A. Sauer and Company of Ann Arbor, was dedicated on December 18, 1909. The *Manchester Enterprise* boasted that it was "one of the most complete church edifices in the state." Earlier that year the congregation had agreed to build a new church of native granite. The church was constructed of fieldstone gathered by local farmers and then shaped, given a rock-face finish and laid by the masons in random ashlar form. The square belfry contains a 2,000-pound bell from the previous church, made by the Buckeye Bell Foundry in Cincinnati, Ohio. The stained-glass windows were made by the Detroit Stained Glass Company. In 1965 the education wing was constructed.

10425 Bethel Church Road at Schneider Road, Freedom Township; Bethel Kirche (Bethel United Church of Christ); L1666A; June 15, 1989; 1990

Blacksmith Shop

In 1877 local masons built this shop in eight days. Its first owner, William F. Neebling, built wagons and followed the blacksmith trade until 1909, when he sold the business to Theodore Morschheuser. John F. Schneider apprenticed to Morschheuser in 1911 and bought the shop in 1922. Schneider worked as a blacksmith until his death in 1952. The building, one of Michigan's last intact main-street blacksmith shops, was purchased by the Manchester Area Historical Society in 1982.

324 East Main Street, Manchester; Neebling, William, Blacksmith Shop (John F. Schneider Blacksmith Shop); L1086A; April 18, 1983; 1983

The German Church

Many of Manchester's early settlers came from Wittenberg, Germany. Since there was no Evangelical church in Manchester, the immigrants worshipped at Bethel Church in Freedom Township. In 1862 the Reverend J. G. Hildner established an Evangelical congregation in Manchester. Services were conducted in German and held in houses until the congregation purchased an unused school in the 1870s. The Reverend S. Edelstein became the first resident pastor. In early 1882 the congregation purchased an entire city block and the present Gothic Revival church, designed by Detroit architect Carl Schmid, was built and named the Immanuel United Evangelical Church. In 1936 the congregation joined the Evangelical and Reformed Church and it became part of the United Church of Christ in the early 1960s.

324 West Main Street, west of McComb Street, Manchester; Emanuel German Evangelical Church (Emanuel United Church of Christ); L1404A; April 28, 1987; 1989

Manchester Township Library

In 1838, one year after Michigan attained statehood, Manchester Township established its library, one of the first township libraries in Michigan. During the early years the township clerk maintained the collection. In 1900 the township decided to rent quarters for the library and to hire a librarian. It was housed in various locations including the Mahrle Building on Adrian Street. In 1934 the township purchased the former James A. Lynch House as a permanent location.

James A. Lynch House

Junius Short constructed this house around 1867 for his eldest daughter, Elma (1844-1928), and his son-in-law, Dr. James A. Lynch (1837-1917), a physician. Lynch shared ownership of a pharmacy with John D. Van Duyn. The wood-frame house's cube shape, bracketed cornice and segmental- and round-arched windows reflect the Italianate style, popular in the 1870s. In 1934, Manchester Township purchased the house for $1,200 from descendants of Junius Short for use as a library.

202 West Main Street, Manchester; Lynch, James A., House (Manchester Township Library); L1384A; February 19, 1987; 1988

St. Patrick's Church

Catholicism in Northfield Township dates from the early nineteenth century. In 1829, Father Patrick O'Kelly, a native of Kilkenny, Ireland, was sent to the area to minister to the Irish Catholics who were settling in southwestern Michigan. The first parish church, a log structure, was completed on this site in 1831. Originally named St. Brigid, this is the oldest English-speaking Catholic parish in the state. The present Gothic Revival-style church was completed and dedicated in 1878. The parish was renamed St. Patrick's at that time. The rectory was completed in 1890. In 1917 the church and rectory were badly damaged by a cyclone; however, both were rebuilt in subsequent years. Serving the area for 150 years, the parish continues to reach out to the needs of the surrounding community.

Intersection of Northfield Church and Whitmore Lake roads, Northfield Township; St. Patrick's Parish Complex; S494; December 14, 1976; 1982

Davenport House

This handsome two and a half-story residence, constructed in 1875, was the home of William H. Davenport (1826-1909), prominent Saline citizen. In 1851, Davenport entered into partnership with H. J. Miller in a general store. He bought out Miller's interest in 1853 and became a leading city merchant. Later, Davenport started a private bank in 1885. Since 1902 this bank has been known as the Citizens' Bank of Saline. Well-known Detroit architect William Scott designed Davenport's elegant Second Empire home, built at a cost of $8,500.

300 East Michigan Avenue, Saline; Davenport, William H., House; L210; July 21, 1972; 1979

Webster Township Hall

In 1976, Webster Township Hall, built in 1871, was the sixth-oldest township hall in continuous use in the state. The structure, which replaced a building at Scully and North Territorial roads, was designed by Isaac Terry. Its cost of $1,758.17 included the land, fence and hitching posts. It relied on kerosene lamps as late as 1920 and on a wood burning stove until 1970. The room at the back of the hall was added in 1948. Among events celebrated at the hall was the 1933 Webster Township Centennial.

5001 Gregory Road (at Scully Road), Webster Township; Webster Township Hall; L1047A; November 16, 1982; 1983

This photograph of the Michigan State Normal School class of 1892 was taken for exhibit at the Columbian Exposition in Chicago, 1893. (*Eastern Michigan College*)

Webster United Church of Christ

In 1834 construction began on Webster Church, the oldest church building in continuous use in Washtenaw County. Built on land donated by Hannah Williams Kingsley, it was completed in 1835 after Moses Kingsley secured donations from Daniel Webster and others in the East. The church had been founded in 1833 under the leadership of the Reverend Charles G. Clark, a New York missionary to the Michigan frontier. Clark was pastor until 1858. Originally Presbyterian, the church polity changed to Congregational in 1860 and to United Church of Christ in 1961. Changes to the building have included the remodeling of the doors and windows, the loss of the spire due to lightning in 1914 and in 1954 the addition of the church school. The adjacent cemetery was founded in 1837.

5484 Webster Church Road, SE of Farrell Road, Webster Township; Webster Presbyterian Church (Webster United Church of Christ); L855A; November 2, 1980; 1983

Cleary College

In 1883, Irish immigrant Patrick Roger Cleary (1858-1948) founded Cleary's School of Penmanship. Starting with only two students, he soon attracted more by offering other business-related classes. In 1889 the school's name was changed to Cleary Business College and the facility moved to its third location on the corner of Michigan and Adams. The school was incorporated in 1891. In 1933 the Cleary family turned the physical assets of the college over to a board of trustees, establishing Cleary College as an independent nonprofit institution. The college moved to its present site in 1960. A branch college was opened in Livingston County in 1979. By 1982 the combined campuses served over one thousand students.

Side Two

Patrick Roger Cleary served as president of Cleary College from its inception in 1883 to his retirement in 1940. A graduate of Valparaiso University, he taught penmanship for several years prior to founding the college. He authored several books on profit and bookkeeping and served as business consultant to local merchants including J. L. Hudson. Succeeding Cleary as president was his son, Owen J., an Ypsilanti attorney who was Michigan's secretary of state from 1953 to 1954. During Patrick Cleary's administration, the college became one of the first in Michigan to train teachers in commercial subjects. It began granting associate and bachelor degrees in 1935. By 1979 one thousand bachelor degrees had been conferred by the college.

2170 Washtenaw Avenue, Ypsilanti; Cleary College Informational Designation; S553C; April 18, 1983; 1983

Eastern Michigan College

Founded by legislative action in 1849 as the Michigan State Normal School, it was the first state teacher education school west of Albany. Its aim was to provide instruction "in the art of teaching and in all the various branches that pertain to a good common school education." On this site the first building, old Pierce Hall, opened for classes in 1852. Built by the joint action of local citizens and the state, it stood here until 1948.

NW corner of College Place and Cross Street, between Pierce and Boone Halls, Ypsilanti; Eastern Michigan College Informational Designation (Eastern Michigan University); S94; September 25, 1956; 1957

Ladies' Literary Club House

This house, built prior to 1842 by Arden Ballard, has been recognized by the Historic American Building Survey as a model of Greek Revival architecture. The house was purchased by the Ladies' Literary Club in 1913.

218 North Washington Street, at the SE corner of Emmet Street, Ypsilanti; Davis, William M., House (Ladies' Literary Club Building); HB47; May 4, 1965; 1965

Michigan's Interurbans

Michigan's first interurban, the Ypsilanti and Ann Arbor, began operating in 1890. Pulled by a steam engine, the cars went west on Packard Road to the Ann Arbor city limits. Because of the low fares (ten cents one way) and frequent service (cars leaving every ninety minutes), the line was soon carrying over six hundred passengers daily. Electric power was adopted in 1896. In a few years a network of interurbans was built in southern Michigan. The "Ypsi-Ann" became part of a Detroit to Jackson road that carried fifty-three hundred passengers a day in 1902. It became possible to go from Detroit to Kalamazoo or from Bay City to Cincinnati on connecting lines. But the automobile, bus and truck put the interurbans out of business in Michigan in the 1920s. The last interurban from Ypsilanti ran in 1929.

Huron Valley School, northwest corner of Michigan Avenue and North Park Street, Ypsilanti; Michigan Interurbans Informational Designation; S128; January 19, 1957; 1958

Prospect Park

In 1842 this site became Ypsilanti's second cemetery, and at one time approximately 250 people were buried here. However, when Highland Cemetery opened in 1864, the use of this site began to decline. Inspired by a nationwide parks movement, in 1891 a group of local women began working to convert the by-then-neglected cemetery into the city's first park. Funds were raised, the remaining bodies were moved, the grounds were graded, trees were planted and walks were installed. Luna Lake, with its rustic fountain, was built. Completed in 1893, Prospect Park soon became noted for its floral carpet beds and its bandstand and dance pavilion. In 1902 a coastal defense cannon was purchased from Fort McCleary, Maine, and erected here. The park became an object of renewed community pride after a major 1982-1984 rejuvenation project.

Prospect Avenue and Cross Street, Ypsilanti; Prospect Park; L1137B; November 30, 1983; 1985

Ypsilanti

Located at the juncture of old Indian trails and the Huron River, this area was the camping and burying ground for several Indian tribes. In 1809, Gabriel Godfroy established an Indian trading post on the west bank of the Huron which he maintained for about ten years. Benjamin Woodruff and companions came up the river by boat in 1823 and settled one mile east of here at Woodruff's Grove. In 1825 a town was platted by Judge Augustus B. Woodward of Detroit and two local men, William Harwood and John Stewart. Situated on both sides of the Huron where the famous Chicago Road (now US-12) crossed the river, the town was named Ypsilanti in honor of the Greek war hero, Demetrius Ypsilanti. The home of Eastern Michigan University, the oldest state teachers college west of Albany, Ypsilanti is also the site of one of the state's very first publicly supported secondary schools. In World War II the Willow Run plant was erected to build B-24 bombers which were vitally important to the war effort. True to its heritage, Ypsilanti has grown in the mainstream of commerce, industry and education.

220 North Huron, between Michigan Avenue and Cross Street, Ypsilanti; Ypsilanti Area; S237; June 23, 1962; 1963

Ypsilanti Water Tower

The Ypsilanti Water Tower was designed by William R. Coats and constructed as part of an

276

The Ford Motor Company's Willow Run plant in Ypsilanti produced 8,685 B-24 Liberator Bombers during World War II. (*Willow Run*)

elaborate city waterworks project that began in 1889. Located on the highest point in Ypsilanti, the tower was completed in 1890. It is 147 feet high and has an 85-foot base constructed of Joliet limestone. The substructure walls taper from a thickness of forty inches at the bottom to twenty-four inches at the top. The reservoir holds a 250,000-gallon steel tank. To protect themselves from injury the builders made three stone crosses; one is visible over the west door. The Ypsilanti Community Utilities Authority has operated and maintained the structure since 1974. In 1975 this tower was designated by the American Water Works Association as an American Water Landmark. It was restored in 1976.

Side Two

Day laborers constructed this water tower which was completed in 1890 at a cost of $21,435.63. The tower and the city waterworks supplied 471 customers in the first year. An ordinance passed on April 14, 1898, established a yearly rate schedule. Rates were based on the number of faucets in use, the type of business that customers operated and the livestock they owned. A residence with one tap was charged $5.00; a private bathtub cost an extra $2.00. Saloon keepers paid $7.00 for one faucet, $3.00 for each additional faucet and $1.00 for each billiard table. Each cow a person owned cost $1.00. People who failed to pay their bill were subject to a $50.00 fine and ninety days in the county jail. Until 1956 this structure was the only water tower in the Ypsilanti water system.

Cross Street at Summit Street, Ypsilanti; Ypsilanti Water Works Stand Pipe (Ypsilanti Water Tower); L1591A; September 21, 1988; 1989

Willow Run (1941-1953)

After entering World War II in 1941, America desperately needed military equipment and supplies. The Ford Motor Company had begun building this factory in April 1941. Outstanding industrial architect Albert Kahn designed Willow Run, one of the largest manufacturing plants under one roof in the world. Completed in early 1942, this bulwark of the "Arsenal of Democracy" produced 8,685 B-24 Liberator Bombers and had a peak employment of forty-two hundred men and women. After the war, the newly formed Kaiser-Frazer Corporation—in an unsuccessful effort to create a large-scale automotive empire—occupied this plant. Here the company manufactured the first of 739,039 passengers cars, as well as military aircraft. In 1953, Kaiser-Frazer transferred its diminishing operations from Willow Run to Toledo, Ohio, and Argentina.

Willow Run (1953-Present)

"Willow Run" initially referred to the small stream running through this area. The name then identified the bomber factory, airport and community which sprung up around the wartime industry. Now this Willow Run plant is the General Motors Hydramatic Division, makers of automatic transmissions. First based in Detroit, this division moved to Livonia where fire destroyed its facilities on August 12, 1953. That September General Motors transferred the Hydramatic operations to Willow Run. Twelve weeks after the fire, transmissions again rolled off the totally retooled and rearranged assembly line—an amazing feat of industrial efficiency. This factory has known both war and peace. Continuing to make transmissions, the plant also manufactured military hardware during the Korean and Vietnam conflicts. Willow Run reflects the versatility of the auto industry.

Marker located in front of the Plant Administration Building; bounded by Airport Drive, Hudson Road and US-12, Ypsilanti Township; Willow Run Bomber Plant Informational Site (Hydramatic Division, General Motors Corporation); S509; August 24, 1978; 1978

Wayne

Aaron Greeley

In 1796, when the United States occupied Michigan, there existed many conflicting land claims along the Detroit and Rouge rivers. Congress in 1806 created a Board of Land Commissioners to adjust these claims. Aaron Greeley, an experienced surveyor, was appointed in 1808 to map this area. On April 23, 1812, Congress validated these claims surveyed by him.

St. Cosme Line Road

Southfield Road in this area was known for many years as the St. Cosme Line Road. This marker stands near the end of the northern boundary of a large tract of land, extending to the Detroit River, which was granted to Pierre Lawrence St. Cosme in 1776 by the Potawatomi Indians.

16850 Southfield, Allen Park; Greeley, Aaron, St. Cosme Line Road Informational Designation; S366; August 13, 1971; 1975

Old Rawsonville Village

Rawsonville, now a ghost town, was once a thriving village. On September 13, 1823, the first land patent in Van Buren Township was given to Henry Snow for this site, which was soon known as Snow's Landing. Called Rawsonville by 1838, the community reached its peak around the time of the Civil War. It then boasted sawmills, grist mills, two cooper shops, a stove factory, several drygoods and general stores, a wagon maker and three saloons. Rawsonville's failure to attract railroad service led to its decline. By the 1880s many of its businesses and mills had closed and its residents were moving away. In 1925 a dam erected on the Huron River covered most of the remaining structures with the newly formed Belleville Lake.

The Mosley-Bennett-Barlow Nature Preserve, Rawsonville Road, Belleville; Rawsonville Village Informational Designation; L1129C; October 27, 1983; 1985

Old Van Buren Township Hall

Van Buren Township was organized out of Huron Township by an act of the Legislative Council of the Territory of Michigan in 1835. Township business was conducted from homes until this building was completed in 1875. The original plans called for a one-story structure; however, shortly after construction began, the local Grange offered to pay for a second story to be used for its meetings. In a special election, township voters accepted the proposal. As the Grange declined in popularity, the second floor became a community meeting hall. For a short time during the 1930s, the basement served as a jail. In 1952 the Grange relinquished its portion to the township. The building served as the township hall until 1959.

405 Main Street, Belleville; Van Buren Township Hall; L255; November 15, 1973; 1983

Canton Center School

This one-room schoolhouse was constructed in 1884 by Hargreaze Sittlington. The school's arches and raised brickwork may have been modeled after the 1882 Cherry Hill United Methodist Church. Both buildings are typical of rural schoolhouses and churches of the period. The Canton Center School ceased operating as a grammar school in 1954. In 1977 the Plymouth-Canton School District donated the structure to the Canton Historical Society, which restored the building. It opened as a museum in 1982.

Adjacent to the Canton Township offices at 1150 Canton Center Road, Canton Township; Canton Center School District No. 4; L719A; August 3, 1979; 1989

Cherry Hill School

In 1876 this Italianate schoolhouse replaced a log school, built in 1836 and known officially as Canton Fractional No. 1 School. In 1944, Henry Ford, who operated a small factory in Cherry Hill, paid for an addition to this building as well as for the salary for a second

An Assembly Line
of the
Ford Motor Company

In 1927, Ford introduced a second edition of the Model A. This new Model A was the first car fully assembled at the Rouge Plant. (*Ford Rouge Plant*)

teacher. The school became part of Ford's Greenfield Village School System where students benefitted from art, music and dance curricula. Cherry Hill School was absorbed by the Plymouth School District in 1955.

50440 Cherry Hill Road, Canton Township; Canton Fractional School District No. 1 Schoolhouse (Cherry Hill School); L1638A; March 16, 1989; 1991

Cherry Hill United Methodist Church

When this pioneer church was organized in 1834, it was one of ten served by circuit rider Marcus Swift of the Detroit Methodist Conference. In 1848 its members raised $600 to build their first church, which served the community for thirty-four years. The present red brick Gothic-style church was completed in 1882. Its colorful stained-glass windows were donated by various families. The well-preserved church has been the setting for many community dinners and social gatherings as well as a religious focus for the community.

321 Ridge Road, between Cherry Hill and Geddes roads, Canton Township; Cherry Hill United Methodist Church; L829A; July 29, 1980; 1986

Sheldon's Corners

Timothy and Rachael Sheldon moved here from New York State in the early 1820s, after the Chicago Road (now US-12) was surveyed. The first people to purchase land in the area, they built an inn near here in 1825. In 1830, Timothy became postmaster of the area's post office. Eventually, the settlement of Sheldon's Corners supported a log schoolhouse, two general stores, two churches, a cobbler and a blacksmith. In 1834 this area became a part of the Township of Canton.

SE corner of Michigan Avenue and Sheldon Road, Canton Township; Sheldon's Corners Informational Designation; L1238C; May 21, 1985; 1987

Commandant's Quarters

This building was one of eleven built in 1833 for the United States Detroit Arsenal at Dearbornville. A walled compound, a 360-foot square, was erected to store military supplies on the frontier. Constructed of red brick in the Federal style, this arsenal was located on strategic Chicago Road, now Michigan Avenue. The quarters were a center for social and cultural events in Dearborn until they were closed in 1875. The Commandant's Quarters later became a fire station, police station, church, courthouse, school facility, library and meeting hall. The Dearborn Historical Commission acquired the building in 1949 and opened it as the city's Historical Museum on October 14, 1950.

21950 Michigan Avenue, Dearborn; Commandant's Quarters, Dearborn Arsenal (Dearborn Historical Museum); HB4; August 23, 1956; 1975

Dearborn Town Hall Complex

This municipal building opened on June 26, 1922, as the seat of government for the village of Springwells, which became a city in 1924, and in 1925 was renamed Fordson (for Henry and Edsel Ford). After Fordson consolidated with Dearborn in 1929, this structure became the center of municipal activities for the expanded city of Dearborn. Originally the two-and-a-half-story Georgian Revival structure housed all of the city departments. Included in the complex were a police and court facility, a communications center, a fire station and a maintenance garage. On May 23, 1981, the city dedicated a new addition, which linked the original building to the new quarters for the council chambers and the clerk's and treasurer's offices. The complex is now known as Town Hall.

Orville L. Hubbard

Orville Liscum Hubbard, LL.B. (1903-1982), was mayor of Dearborn from 1942 to 1978. Born near Union City, Hubbard enlisted in the U.S. Marine Corps in 1922. He graduated from the Detroit College of Law in 1932. Settling in Dearborn in 1929, he ran unsuccessfully for public office for ten years before becoming mayor. Often working twelve or more hours a day, Hubbard was an effective administrator who paid close attention to small details and the public's opinion. He made Dearborn known for punctual trash collection, speedy snow removal, Florida retirement facilities and a free recreational area, Camp Dearborn. Hubbard died in 1982, almost five years after his fifteenth term as Dearborn's mayor. At the time of his death, his administration was noted as having been one of the longest of any full-time U.S. mayor.

13615 Michigan Avenue, Dearborn; Springwells Municipal Building (Dearborn Town Hall); L1152A; March 20, 1984; 1984

Fair Lane

Here Henry and Clara Bryant Ford lived from 1915 until their deaths in 1947 and 1950. The eminent American auto magnate and inventor named Fair Lane after the road on which his father, William Ford, was born in County Cork, Ireland. The fifty-six room mansion made of marblehead limestone and concrete was completed in 1915. Inventor Thomas A. Edison, a frequent guest here, laid the cornerstone in 1914 for the powerhouse which supplied power for the entire estate. Ford's popularization of the automobile propelled America into an era of accelerated urbanization and industrialization. Yet the home of this man of controversy and varied interests reflects a love of nature and the countryside. Donated by the Ford Motor Company in 1957 to the University of Michigan for a Dearborn campus, Fair Lane's secluded acres shelter a national bird sanctuary and nature trails.

4901 Evergreen Road, Dearborn; Fair Lane (Henry Ford Estate); H17B; February 18, 1958; 1978

Ford Rouge Plant

Henry Ford began construction of this complex on the banks of the River Rouge in April 1917. Here the Ford Motor Company built World War I submarine chasers known as "Eagle" boats. By the mid-1920s this plant was the largest manufacturing center in the world. The transfer of the assembly line from nearby Highland Park to Dearborn in 1927 fulfilled Ford's vision of an industrial complex which encompassed all aspects of automotive production. The first automobile to be completely assembled here, the Model A, was introduced in December 1927. The Ford Trade School operated at this location for twenty years until 1946. During World War II, massive amounts of materiel for air, amphibious and land transport were produced. Beginning with raw materials, the Ford Rouge plant makes component parts and assembles vehicles.

Shaffer Highway, Gate No. 2, Miller Road, bounded by Dix Road, the Rouge River and Rotunda Drive, Dearborn; Ford River Rouge Complex; S493; December 14, 1976; 1977

Henry Ford Birthplace

At this intersection stood the home in which Henry Ford was born on July 30, 1863. The farmhouse was owned by Ford's parents, William and Mary Ford, and in 1944 it was moved to Greenfield Village. In a space of less than ten years at the beginning of this century, the founder of Ford Motor Company developed three separate and distinct concepts, any of which would have assured him an honored niche in history. He designed and built the Model T Ford car, "the car that put the world on wheels." He inaugurated the moving automotive assembly line and developed the process of mass production on which modern industry is based. By instituting a five-dollar wage for an eight-hour day, he promulgated a new economic concept that opened the door to mass distribution. Henry Ford was also a pioneer in the field of aviation and in the development of the farm tractor.

Ford and Greenfields roads, Dearborn; Ford, Henry, Birthplace Informational Site; S236; April 18, 1962; 1963

The Dearborn Hills Golf Club

During his long career Robert Herndon developed over fifty subdivisions and nine golf courses. In 1922 he opened the Dearborn Hills Golf Club. According to the *Dearborn Times Herald*, it was Michigan's first public golf course. Having been rejected by bankers who reminded him that "golf was for millionaires," Herndon financed the project with the aid of investors. The golf course was designed by three professional golfers including Walter Hagen. Construction of the golf course and the adjacent Dearborn Hills subdivision required extending Telegraph Road from Michigan Avenue to present-day Cherry Hill Road. This extension helped Telegraph become a major thoroughfare. Robert Herndon died in 1986 and, one year later, his widow deeded Dearborn Hills Golf Club to the city of Dearborn.

3001 South Telegraph Road, Dearborn; Dearborn Hills Golf Club Informational Designation; L1629B; February 16, 1989; 1989

The Dearborn Inn

Henry Ford built the Dearborn Inn in 1931 to accommodate overnight travelers arriving at the Ford Airport. Located opposite the inn on Oakwood Boulevard, the airport opened in 1924. The 179-room inn, designed by Albert Kahn, was the world's first airport hotel. The Georgian-style structure features a crystal-chandeliered ballroom and high ceilings. Its rooms are decorated with reproductions of furniture and fabrics of the eighteenth and nineteenth centuries. The guest quarters along Pilots Row originally were used by the airline's crews. The inn and the adjacent Colonial homes reflect Henry Ford's fondness for American history.

Colonial Homes and Adjacent Buildings

In 1937 the Dearborn Inn's accommodations were expanded with replicas of historically famous homes. Constructed on this twenty-three-acre wooded complex, the additions included the Barbara Fritchie House, the Patrick Henry House, the Oliver Wolcott House, the Edgar Allen Poe House and the Walt Whitman House. The homes are furnished with brass candlesticks on the mantles, English shaving mirrors, brass or pencil four-poster beds, traditional lighting fixtures and Dutch doors. In 1933 the dormitory building was added to house the inn's employees. It served this purpose until 1961. The fifty-four-unit Motor House was completed in 1960.

20301 Oakwood Boulevard, NW of Rotunda Drive, Dearborn; Dearborn Inn and Colonial Homes; L1070A; February 10, 1983; 1983

The Edison Institute

The Edison Institute, founded on this site by Henry Ford and dedicated to Thomas Alva Edison by President Herbert Hoover on October 21, 1929, the fiftieth anniversary of the invention of the incandescent lamp, has three divisions: Greenfield Village, America's first outdoor museum, contains some one hundred historic buildings moved here from many different areas to show how Americans lived and worked during the first three centuries of their history. The Henry Ford Museum exhibits Ford's vast collections of Americana which he began assembling as early as 1906. Together, the village and museum preserve historic objects and buildings of national significance. The Greenfield Village Schools were established by Henry Ford to carry out his "learning-by-doing" philosophy of education. Collectively, the Edison Institute's three divisions reflect the creative spirit that has built our nation from the time of the first settlers and demonstrate Henry Ford's concept of bringing American history to life.

Side Two

"I am collecting the history of our people as written into things their hands made and used. . . ."
"Education is the greatest force in civilization. . . ."
"I deeply admire the men who founded this country and I think we ought to know more about them and how they lived and the force and courage they had. . . ."
"The farther you look back, the farther you can look ahead. . . ."
"When we are through, we shall have reproduced American life as lived, and that, I think, is

Henry Ford revolutionized the auto industry with the Highland Park assembly line. Here, Ford poses in the first Ford automobile, a Model A. (*Birthplace of the Ford Automobile*)

the best way of preserving at least a part of our history and tradition. . . ."

29000 Oakwood Boulevard, bounded by Michigan Avenue, Village Road, Southfield Expressway and Oakwood Boulevard, Dearborn; Greenfield Village and Henry Ford Museum (Edison Institute); S251; September 13, 1963; 1962

The Ford Airport

At this airport, built by Henry Ford in 1924, world and national aviation history was made, ushering in a new era of flight embracing the all-metal airliner, radio control devices, air mail, scheduled flights and the airline services that the generation of the 1930s came to expect. For the first time in the *world*: A hotel, the Dearborn Inn, was designed and built for the air traveler; a guided flight of a commercial airliner was made by radio. For the first time in the *U.S.A.*: An all-metal, multi-engine, commercial airliner was built; a regularly scheduled passenger airline in continuous domestic service was inaugurated. Under the Kelly Act the first contract air mail for domestic routes was flown.

Ford Tri-Motor William B. Stout: 1880-1956

Born in Illinois, Stout came to Michigan as an automotive designer in 1914. During World War I he turned to aviation. In 1922 he produced America's first all-metal plane, a Navy torpedo plane. The same year he organized the Stout Metal Airplane Company. In the next two years he built America's first successful commercial metal planes. The company occupied the new airplane factory at the Ford Airport in 1924 and became a division of the Ford Motor Company in 1925. While he was the division's consulting engineer the Ford Tri-motor was developed. In 1926 he founded the Stout Air Services, this country's first regularly scheduled passenger airline. Later, in his Dearborn workshop, Stout designed the "Sky Car," a combination airplane and automobile; the "Rail Plane," a gas-driven railroad car; a collapsible "House Trailer," and the "Scarab Car," a spacious, rear-motor auto. An airline terminal for passenger use was constructed. The airport's closing in 1933 ended Ford's experimental work in aviation.

20301 Oakwood Boulevard at the Dearborn Inn, Dearborn; Ford Airport, William B. Stout Informational Site; S126; January 19, 1957; 1958

St. Joseph's Retreat

In 1885, Michigan's first private mental institution was located here under the guidance of the Daughters of Charity of St. Vincent de Paul. In 1855 the Sisters at St. Mary's Hospital in Detroit had begun the care of the mentally ill, formerly confined to prisons and poorhouses. In 1860 they opened a separate facility, the Michigan State Retreat, which was incorporated in 1883 as St. Joseph's Retreat. The original brick building situated on these 140 acres of farmland and lawns overlooking the River Rouge was enlarged and encircled by outer structures to accommodate four hundred patients. At first these included Civil War veterans; later alcoholics, drug addicts and other curables were rehabilitated. In 1962 the retreat was closed since it no longer met pressing needs; the impressive structure was subsequently razed.

23300 Michigan Avenue at Outer Drive, Dearborn; St. Joseph's Retreat Informational Site; S386; June 16, 1972; 1980

Wallaceville School

Constructed in 1824 as a church, the original log building on this site was the first school in Bucklin (later Dearborn) Township. In 1829 the building became a public school. When John B. Wallace donated the land and building to the school district, the school was named after him. The building burned in 1876, and was replaced by this brick structure. The building was used only intermittently after 1938, and in 1966 the city of Dearborn Heights converted it into a museum.

8050 North Gulley Road, Dearborn Heights; Wallaceville School; L67; February 17, 1967; 1967

Alpha House

Built about 1918, this Neo-Classical-style structure houses Gamma Lambda Chapter, third graduate chapter of the first black national Greek letter fraternity in the United States: Alpha Phi Alpha Fraternity, Incorporated. Founded in 1906 at Cornell University, the fraternity's aims are manly deeds, scholarship and love for all mankind. This local chapter, established in 1919, served as a focal point for black social, cultural, educational and community service activities in an era when there were few other outlets. The chapter continues civic and cultural work and involvement in nonprofit business enterprises that benefit the metropolitan Detroit community. Martin Luther King, Jr., W. E. B. Du Bois and Edward "Duke" Ellington, among others, are national members who have achieved prominence.

293 Eliot, between Brush and John R, Detroit; Alpha Phi Alpha Fraternity House (Alpha House); L549; August 30, 1977; 1977

American Academy of Pediatrics

The American Academy of Pediatrics was founded on June 24, 1930, by thirty-four physicians at Harper Hospital. Isaac A. Abt, M.D., was elected as its first president; John L. Morse, M.D., was chosen as the first vice-president; and Clifford G. Grulee, M.D., served as the first secretary-treasurer. The academy has always had as its primary purpose: "The attainment by all children of the Americas of their full potential for physical, emotional and social health." The academy conducts regular educational programs for child health professionals, encourages support of basic and applied research and sponsors numerous public information and child advocacy programs. By its golden anniversary in 1980, the American Academy of Pediatrics' membership roll included more than twenty thousand pediatricians.

3990 John R Street, at Alexandrine, Harper Grace Hospital, Detroit; American Academy of Pediatrics Informational Site (Harper Grace Hospital); S534B; July 27, 1980; 1980

The Battle of Bloody Run

Near this site, in late July 1763, the British and Indians fought the fiercest battle of Chief Pontiac's uprising. As Captain James Dalyell led about 260 soldiers across Parent's Creek, the Indians launched a surprise attack which devastated the British. Dalyell and some sixty of his men were killed, and the creek became known as Bloody Run. This battle marked the height of Pontiac's siege of Detroit, a struggle which he was forced to abandon three months later.

3321 East Jefferson Avenue, Detroit; Battle of Bloody Run Informational Designation; S70; August 23, 1956; 1977

Belle Isle

This island, a jewel in the hearts of Detroiters, has provided shining memories for visitors of all ages. About 1845, this site received its present name, Belle Isle, in honor of Governor Lewis Cass's daughter Isabella. On September 23, 1879, this island was purchased by the city of Detroit for $200,000. Early in the 1880s, the Board of Park Commissioners consulted with Frederick Law Olmsted, the designer of Central Park in New York City, to plan the development of Belle Isle as a public park. Belle Isle is now a unique island park covering

981 acres and attracting millions of visitors annually. Its most popular features include a beach, the Casino restaurant, beautiful formal gardens, Scott Fountain, riding stables, an aquarium, a conservatory, a nature interpretive center and the Dossin Great Lakes Museum.

Casino, Belle Isle, Detroit River, Detroit; Belle Isle [*Wahnabezee* (Swan Island), *Isle Au Cochon* (Hog Island)]; S529A; September 10, 1979; 1979

Bethel African Methodist Episcopal Church

In 1839 a group of black Detroit citizens formed the Colored Methodist Society, which became the core of the Bethel African Methodist Episcopal Church. The group held meetings in a hall which was donated by the Detroit Common Council. The society moved several times before a church was built on Lafayette in the 1840s. In 1841 the church assumed its present name and organization. From its inception, the church has served in a number of ways: it has provided a school for black children, an agency to assist southern migrants and a bureau for labor and housing. Today the church remains a focal point for community social services.

5050 St. Antoine (Richard Allen Boulevard), Detroit; Bethel African Methodist Episcopal Church; L388; April 4, 1975; 1976

Birth of Kiwanis

Kiwanis International, one of the great service organizations of the world, had its origin on January 21, 1915. On this date the state of Michigan issued a charter to a group of business and professional men who organized the first Kiwanis Club on this site in the Griswold Hotel. The club's name, Kiwanis, was an Indian term. The concept and principle which Kiwanis represents is symbolized by the slogan "We build." From this beginning, and within two years, Kiwanis became international in its scope.

Corner of Griswold Street and Grand River Avenue, Detroit; Kiwanis, Birth of/Griswold Hotel Informational Site; S254; January 24, 1964; 1965

Birthplace of Dr. Ralph J. Bunche

Undersecretary-General of the United Nations for the final sixteen years of his life, Ralph Bunche, grandson of a slave, was born in this neighborhood of Detroit on August 7, 1904, and lived here for the first decade of his life. Following the death of his parents in 1915, he spent the rest of his childhood in the West. After a brilliant career in political science at Harvard, Bunche collaborated in the late 1930s with Gunnar Myrdal in his monumental study of racism in America. Entering government service during World War II, he joined the State Department and was active in drafting the charter of the United Nations. Bunche's success as a UN mediator after the Arab-Israeli war of 1948 won for him the Nobel Peace Prize in 1950. He died in New York on December 9, 1971.

Mounted on store front on the south side of Fort Street, one-half block west of Junction, Detroit; Bunche, Ralph J., Birthplace, Informational Site; S363; February 11, 1972; 1972

Birthplace of Ford Automobile

This marker commemorates the birthplace of the Ford Motor car. Here in 1892, Henry Ford began experimenting with the motorized vehicle in his workshop, a small one-story brick structure, once located on this site. His invention was quite simple compared to today's automobiles. It consisted of a two-cylinder machine, mounted in a light frame geared to bicycle wheels. That unpretentious auto was the start of the Ford Motor Company, which played a major part in the automobile industry that changed the face of Michigan and the world.

220 Bagley Avenue, between Grand River and Clifford, Detroit; Ford Automobile Birthplace Informational Site (Michigan Theatre Building); S62; August 23, 1956; 1980

Cass Community United Methodist Church

This monumental structure typifies Richardsonian Romanesque ecclesiastic architecture. The original 1883 portion was designed by Mason and Rice for the Cass Avenue Methodist Episcopal Church, founded in 1880. The 1891 east addition is the work of Malcomson and Higginbotham. Of special significance are the colorful Tiffany stained-glass windows and the Johnson-Tracker church organ, thought to be the largest nineteenth-century pipe organ in Michigan. The congregation has a reputation for fostering community outreach programs since its founding.

3901 Cass Avenue at Selden, Detroit; Cass Avenue Methodist Episcopal Church (Cass Community United Methodist Church); L1224A; March 28, 1985; 1986

The conservatory, pictured here, is just one of many attractions at Belle Isle, named around 1845 for Isabella Cass, the daughter of Governor Lewis Cass. (*Belle Isle*)

Central United Methodist Church

Lewis Cass, governor of the Territory of Michigan, approved a constitution for the First Methodist Episcopal Society May 17, 1822. This church, a direct successor, was designed by Gordon W. Lloyd. It was completed in 1867 by the combined efforts of the First Methodist Episcopal Church and the Congress Street Society. When Woodward Avenue was widened in 1936, a thirty-foot section was removed from the nave, and the front and tower were subsequently relocated. The sanctuary was then rededicated. The stained-glass windows were installed in 1955. Maintaining the tradition of an open door and free pulpit, Central United Methodist Church has been called "the conscience of a city."

23 East Adams at Woodward Avenue, Detroit; Central United Methodist Church (Central Methodist Episcopal Church); L535; June 6, 1977; 1979

Chapoton House

Alexander Chapoton built this Queen Anne-style townhouse in the early 1870s. Chapoton, a builder, was one of the contractors for the state capitol in Lansing. A descendant of one of Detroit's oldest families, he was a state legislator and a member of the Detroit Board of Public Works. He built this house at a time when Beaubien Street consisted mostly of Victorian row houses. The house, which features a unique Queen Anne living hall, became an art gallery and studio in the 1980s.

511 Beaubien Street at Larned, Detroit; Chapoton, Alexander, House; L808A; April 21, 1980; 1987

Chicago Road

The Great Sauk Trail, the most important Indian trail in the Great Lakes region, was used later by French explorers, fur traders, missionaries and soldiers. After the 1760s the trail became a major road for British and American travelers. In the early 1800s, when a military road was needed to connect Detroit with Fort Dearborn (Chicago), Territorial Governor Lewis Cass and Father Gabriel Richard, an influential legislator, were leading supporters of the Great Sauk Trail route. With federal backing the road was surveyed in 1825 and built in 1829-1836. Many sections of the road were paved with huge oak logs, covered with a layer of dirt. Even before the road was improved, land-hungry settlers moved west from Detroit via the Chicago Road (now called Michigan Avenue).

Michigan Avenue and Washington Boulevard, Detroit; Chicago Road Informational Designation (Days Inn); S280; September 17, 1957; 1966

Church of Annunciation

The Annunciation (Evangelismos) Greek Orthodox Church was founded in 1910. It became the center of Detroit's Hellenic community, which dates back to the early 1890s. The first liturgy was held in a rented hall on Miami Boulevard (now Broadway). By 1913, Annunciation occupied a new edifice at 660 Macomb Avenue. In April 1968, six years after it was designated a Cathedral of the Detroit diocese, Annunciation moved to its present site.

707 East Lafayette Boulevard, Detroit; Church of Evangelismos Informational Designation; L774B; January 18, 1980; 1980

Conant Gardens

Conant Gardens reflects black settlement in Detroit's northeast side during the first of two large migrations of blacks to Detroit after World War I. The neighborhood was originally designed as a community for white collar employees of the Ford Motor Company. However, it was never developed. Around 1928 blacks began to build houses here and founded the Conant Gardens Homeowners' Association, which still exists. After 1934, Federal Housing Administration loans enabled blacks to buy property in Conant Gardens. The residents built houses in a variety of styles including Tudor Revival and the Craftsmen style. Conant Gardens was named for Shubael Conant, the original owner of the property. In 1837, Conant (1783-1867) became the founding president of the Detroit Anti-Slavery Society.

NE corner of Conant and Nevada, 18000 Conant, Detroit; Conant Gardens Informational Designation; L1694C; September 7, 1989; 1990

David Whitney, Jr. Residence

This mansion was once described as "an American palace enjoying the distinction of being the most pretentious modern home in the state and one of the most elaborate houses in the west." David Whitney, Jr. (1830-1900), its owner, was one of the wealthiest lumber barons in the Midwest. Begun in 1890, the house took four years to construct. Its exterior is made of pink jasper, mined in South Dakota. The luxurious interior is reminiscent of residences of Napoleonic Paris. Its features include silk-covered walls and ceilings, tapestries, extensive woodwork, leaded crystal and Tiffany windows.

4421 Woodward Avenue, Detroit; Whitney, David, House (The Whitney); S358; December 10, 1971; 1980

David Augustus Straker

Here stood the home of an eminent Detroit Negro who distinguished himself as a lawyer, politician and writer. A native of Barbados, Straker (1842-1908) came to America in 1867 and received a law degree from Howard University four years later. After a varied career in the South, he moved to Detroit and became counsel to William W. Ferguson, well-known black businessman. Straker won the celebrated 1890 case against the white owner of a saloon and restaurant who refused to serve Ferguson and a friend. Active in Republican politics as well as in legal affairs, Straker was elected circuit court commissioner. He wrote several books including a biography of Toussaint L'Ouverture and published and edited a weekly edition of the *Detroit Advocate*. Known as the "black Irish lawyer" because of his accent, Straker battled throughout his life for civil rights and racial pride.

*428 Temple, Detroit; Straker, D. Augustus Informational Site L374; January 16, 1976; 1977

Detroit Association of Women's Clubs

The Detroit Association of Colored Women's Clubs was organized on April 8, 1921, with eight clubs. This association reached its peak membership in 1945 with seventy-three clubs and three thousand members. Affiliated with the Michigan and the National Associations of Colored Women's Clubs, the Detroit association fosters educational, philanthropic and social programs. The association was incorporated in 1941. That same year, supported by a mortgage on its president's home, the association purchased its present clubhouse, a handsome Colonial Revival-style structure. The club members completely paid for the clubhouse in less than five years. The association sponsors girls' clubs, scholarships, annual clothing drives for needy school children and charitable programs for seniors and the dispossessed. Its motto is "Lifting As We Climb."

*5461 Brush Street, Detroit; Lennane, William, House (Detroit Association of Women's Clubs Clubhouse); L1207A; December 19, 1984; 1986

Detroit College of Law

Established in 1891, the Detroit College of Law was the first law school in the Detroit area and the second one in Michigan. The college, which opened in 1892 with sixty-nine students, was incorporated in 1893. Included in the first graduating class were men who became circuit court judges, a supreme court justice and an ambassador. Since its inception, the college has been a privately funded, coeducational institution devoted exclusively to professional education in law.

130 East Elizabeth Street, Detroit; Detroit College of Law Informational Designation; S554C; April 18, 1983, 1983

Detroit Copper & Brass

On this site, once owned by Christian Buhl—alderman, city mayor, police commissioner and banker—stands the former office of the Detroit Copper & Brass Rolling Mills Company. Buhl was the first president of the company, which was incorporated in 1880. Company owners erected this brick Georgian-style office building in 1906. Detroit Copper & Brass Rolling Mills was the largest fabricator of copper and brass in Michigan. As the primary provider of exterior ornamentation and brass engine parts for the Ford Motor Car Company, Detroit Copper & Brass played a major role in helping to build Detroit's reputation as "the city that put America on wheels." The company was absorbed by Anaconda Copper and Brass in 1927.

174 South Clark Street, Detroit; Detroit Copper and Brass Rolling Mills; L685A; June 15, 1979; 1980

Detroit Cornice and Slate Building

Designed by Harry J. Rill in 1897 for the Detroit Cornice and Slate Company, this building features a finely crafted facade of galvanized steel. The use of sheet metal in commercial buildings evolved from the cast iron structures built in New York in the 1850s. Metal permitted elegant ornamentation to be rendered quickly and cheaply. It was also convenient when, as in Detroit, there was a lack of stone quarries and skilled workers. The Detroit Cornice and Slate Company fashioned many of the building's simulated carvings on the friezes and tympanums in its shop here. Occupied by the company until 1972, the structure's exterior was then restored and its interior was renovated for office and commercial use.

733 St. Antoine Street at East Lafayette Street, Detroit; Detroit Cornice and Slate Company Building; L175; January 21, 1974; 1975

The *Free Press*

The *Detroit Free Press* began publishing as the *Democratic Free Press and Michigan Intelligencer* on the morning of May 5, 1831. Michigan's oldest daily newspaper, it supported the drive for statehood, helped establish the Associated Press and sent reporters to the battlefield to cover the Civil War. In 1853 the *Free Press* began publishing the state's first Sunday newspaper. By its 150th year its staff had earned five Pulitzer Prizes. The Lafayette Boulevard building, built in 1925, was designed by Albert Kahn.

321 West Lafayette on the SW corner of Washington Boulevard, Detroit; *Detroit Free Press* Building; S535A; January 8, 1981; 1981

The Detroit Medical College

Here in 1868 five young physicians, whose work with wounded during the Civil War had left them eager to improve the quality of medical education, founded the Detroit Medical College, the city's first such school. Like nearby Harper Hospital, it occupied the barracks-type buildings of a former military hospital. These were razed in 1884, but the school continued as the Detroit College of Medicine and became well-known for the variety and quality of its clinical instruction. In 1933 it was one of six city colleges to be consolidated into the institution now known as Wayne State University.

Between 3750 and 3800 Woodward at Martin Place, Detroit; Detroit Medical College (Detroit College of Medicine) Informational Site; S287; May 26, 1967; 1967

Detroit Memorial Hospital

In 1845 the Daughters of Charity founded St. Vincent's Hospital, the first in Michigan. They moved to the present site in 1850, renaming the hospital St. Mary's. Here charitable, non-sectarian care included attention to orphans, epidemic victims and the insane until separate

In 1918 thirty black physicians established Dunbar Hospital to provide quality healthcare for Detroit's black population. Above is the hospital staff of 1922. (*Dunbar Hospital*)

facilities were provided. During the Civil and Spanish-American wars, St. Mary's served as a military hospital. Gradually it expanded to provide 325 beds and a wide range of medical and teaching services. Extensive remodeling ensured patient comfort and modernized care. Its voluntary closing in 1949 promoted a non-profit corporation of St. Mary's physicians to purchase and rename the hospital Detroit Memorial. Thus, a long tradition of medical care continues on this site.

*Marker erected on St. Antoine Street, hospital at 1441 Chrysler Drive, Detroit; Detroit Memorial Hospital (Detroit's First Hospital); S424; July 26, 1974; 1974

The *Detroit News*

On August 23, 1873, James E. Scripps began publishing The *Evening News*, one of the first popular, low-priced evening newspapers in Michigan. The *News* specialized in short, local, human interest stories. Resolutely independent, it has continuously championed political and business reform. In 1917 the enterprise moved to this building designed by Albert Kahn. By its centenary, The *Detroit News* had attained the largest evening circulation in America.

615 Lafayette Boulevard at the SW corner of Second, Detroit; *Detroit News* Building; S459; February 21, 1975; 1976

Detroit *Plaindealer*

The office of the *Plaindealer*, Detroit's first successful black newspaper, was located on this site. Founded in 1883 by five young men, it served as an advocate of black interests in Michigan and throughout the Midwest. Especially concerned with developing racial pride, the paper preferred the designation Afro-American rather than Negro, and encouraged the support of black businessmen and politicans. Its managing editor, Robert Pelham, Jr., was perhaps the best-known black political figure in late-nineteenth-century Detroit. In 1889 he helped organize the Afro-American League, the first nationally prominent civil rights group. Later, he held the position of census clerk with the federal government. The *Plaindealer*, however, failed to receive sufficient financial support in the community, and ceased publication in 1894.

288

SW corner of Shelby and State, Detroit; Detroit *Plaindealer* Office Informational Site (Book-Cadillac Hotel); S450; November 14, 1974; 1975

Detroit Urban League

The Detroit Urban League began in 1916 with Forrester B. Washington as executive director, and Henry G. Stevens as president. The organization's initial purpose was the improvement of the social, moral and material status of the large number of blacks who migrated to the city during and directly after World War I. Its objectives expanded considerably under the leadership of John C. Dancy, executive director from 1918-1960. The league has responded flexibly to ever-changing contemporary problems. Seeking employment and housing opportunities for blacks, this institution has also offered a variety of social services including health care and recreational facilities. Responding to a maturing city, and its circumstances, the Detroit Urban League continues to serve Detroit's black community.

208 Mack Avenue at John R, Detroit; Kahn, Albert, House; L137; December 7, 1971 / Detroit Urban League Informational Designation; L443; March 2, 1976; 1978

Dunbar Hospital

At the time of World War I, health care for black Detroiters was inferior to that available for whites. Black physicians could not join the staffs of Detroit's white hospitals. On May 20, 1918, thirty black doctors, members of the Allied Medical Society (now the Detroit Medical Society) incorporated Dunbar Hospital, the city's first nonprofit community hospital for the black population. It also housed the first black nursing school in Detroit. Located in a reform-minded neighborhood, this area was the center of a social and cultural emergence of the black residents of the city during the 1920s. In 1928, Dunbar moved to a larger facility and was later renamed Parkside, operating under that name until 1962. In 1978 the Detroit Medical Society, an affiliate of the National Medical Association, purchased the site for their administrative headquarters and a museum.

*580 Frederick Street, Detroit; Dunbar Hospital (Detroit Medical Society Headquarters); 1979

Early Detroit: 1701-1760

Detroit was founded July 24, 1701, by Antoine de Lamothe Cadillac, who landed in this vicinity on that date. With him were one hundred Frenchmen and a like number of Indians. Cadillac took possession of the land in the name of Louis XIV. Here was built Fort Pontchartrain to prevent English traders from using the water route to the upper Great Lakes. The site was on a peninsula between the Detroit River and the Savoyard Creek. Huron, Ottawa and Potawatomi Indians accepted the invitation of Cadillac to settle near the fort. Detroit he wished to develop as an agricultural settlement. Mesdames Cadillac and de Tonty arrived later in 1701. Other families followed them. After Cadillac's removal in 1710, Detroit's growth was retarded for many years. In 1712 the French and their Indian allies fought and destroyed a band of Fox Indians camped north of the fort. The French crown encouraged the development of the colony in the 1740s by offering seed, livestock and farm equipment to settlers. The fort was enlarged in the 1750s. Detroit then had a French population of about one thousand, and farms lined the river above and below the fort as well as across the river.

*Erected at Cobo Hall, 151 West Jefferson Avenue, Detroit; Early Detroit: 1701-1760 Informational Designation (Detroit's Early History); S38; July 19, 1956; 1958

Elijah McCoy Homesite

Elijah McCoy, the noted black inventor, lived on this site for much of his adult life. Born in 1844 to fugitive slaves residing in Canada, McCoy was trained in Scotland as a mechanical engineer, and came to Michigan after the Civil War. Discrimination forced him to become a fireman on the Michigan Central Railroad. In 1872, McCoy patented his first automatic lubricating cup which oiled the locomotive while the train was in motion, thus eliminating frequent stops for oiling. He soon moved to Detroit where he improved his designs, and later set up a company to manufacture lubricators. These were installed in locomotives and steamships both here and abroad. McCoy died in 1929, honored for his important engineering innovations.

Elijah McCoy Drive at Lincoln Avenue, Detroit; McCoy, Elijah, Home Informational Site (Research Park); L362; November 14, 1974; 1974

Elmwood Cemetery

In 1846 when this was a farm on the outskirts of Detroit, a group of gentlemen formed a corporation and purchased the land for use as a public cemetery. The trustees patterned the grounds after Mount Auburn Cemetery in Cambridge, Massachusetts, and utilized the ideas of the famous nineteenth century landscape architect, Frederick Law Olmsted. Parent's Creek, renamed Bloody Run after the battle fought between Pontiac and the British in 1763, serves as the focus in the informal country garden landscape. Albert and Octavius Jordon designed the handsome Gothic Revival chapel, which opened for services in 1856. The chapel's limestone walls blend into the natural ravine and tree-shaded paths. Famous people buried here include General Russell Alger, geologist Douglass Houghton and Territorial Governor Lewis Cass.

Robert Bradley Drive, one block north of Lafayette, Detroit; Elmwood Cemetery; S453; February 21, 1975; 1976

Fannie Richards Homesite

Fannie Richards, Detroit's first black public school teacher, lived on this site. Born in Virginia about 1840, she moved to Detroit as a young woman. In 1863 she opened a private school for black children, and two years later was appointed to teach in the city's colored schools. In 1869 she helped sponsor a lawsuit against Detroit's racially segregated school system, and in a landmark decision, the Michigan Supreme Court ordered the schools integrated. An innovative teacher, Fannie Richards was transferred to the Everett Elementary school in 1871 where she taught the city's first kindergarten class. She retired from Everett in 1915, completing fifty years of service in Detroit schools. Fannie Richards died in 1922.

Rivard, between Lafayette Boulevard and Larned, Detroit; Richards, Fannie, Home Informational Site; L364; November 14, 1974; 1975

Finney Barn

Seymour Finney conducted one of the principal passenger depots of the underground railroad in the Detroit area. Finney, a tailor by trade, later became a hotel-keeper, and it was in this capacity that he assisted fugitive slaves in the era prior to 1861. In 1850 he purchased a site where in later years stood the Finney Hotel, and also erected a large barn which he operated along with his tavern. Strongly sympathetic with the abolitionist cause, Finney employed every means to assist escaping slaves across the river into Canada. Detroit was one of the most important "stations" en route to Canada; if a fugitive reached this city, he was comparatively safe. Finney Barn served as a hiding-place for runaways until they could reach the river bank and freedom.

NE corner of State and Griswold streets, across from Capitol Park, Detroit; Underground Railway/Finney Hotel Informational Site (Detroit Bank and Trust Building); S69; August 23, 1956; 1980

First Congregational Church of Detroit

In 1801, David Bacon and his wife Alice made the first attempt to establish Congregationalism in Detroit. Sent by a Connecticut Congregational society, the Bacons failed in their efforts to build a mission. It was not until 1844 that the First Congregational Society was formed in Detroit. The society erected a building which it soon outgrew. A second structure was dedicated in 1854. The third and present church known as the "Church of the Seven Arches" was completed in 1891. Designed by John L. Faxon, it has Byzantine and Romanesque features. The tower of the church is crowned by a statue of the angel Uriel. Both the exterior and interior of this church are rich in the colors and symbolism of the Christian religion.

33 East Forest Street, NE corner of Woodward Avenue, Detroit; First Congregational Church; L329; July 26, 1974; 1976

First Jewish Religious Services

Near this site in 1850, a small group of German-Jewish immigrants gathered at the home of Isaac and Sarah Cozens and formed the Bet El Society. Here Marcus Cohen, a layman, conducted the first Jewish religious service in Detroit. The following year, at the urging of Sarah Cozens, the society was incorporated under the name of "Beth El," meaning "House of God," and thus became the first Jewish congregation in Michigan, which is still in existence.

Corner of St. Antoine and East Congress, Detroit; First Jewish Religious Services Informational Designation; L516; April 1, 1977; 1977

First Michigan Colored Regiment

The First Michigan Colored Regiment was organized at Camp Ward, which originally stood on this location. Formed from August through October 1863, a year of draft riots and protests against the war, this Negro regiment consisted entirely of volunteers. During training, a regimental band was formed and toured southern Michigan to recruit additional volunteers. Mustered here as the 102nd U.S. Colored Troops, February 17, 1864, the nine hundred-man unit left Detroit March 28, 1864, for service in South Carolina, Georgia and Florida. More than fourteen hundred men served in the regiment during nineteen months in the field; ten percent of this number died in service. The regiment was disbanded in October 1865 in Detroit.

Duffield Public School grounds, Macomb Street east of Chene, Detroit; First Michigan Colored Regiment Informational Site; S288; March 1, 1968; 1968

The First Mile of Concrete Highway

In 1909, Wayne County built the first mile of concrete highway in the world here on Woodward between Six and Seven Mile roads. From far and near road builders came to see how concrete stood up under the heavy traffic of that period. The success of this experiment speeded the development of modern automobile highways. It cost $13,537, including $1,000 in state aid. The road was replaced in 1922 by a broad thoroughfare.

Woodward Avenue (US-10) between Six and Seven Mile roads in Palmer Park, Detroit; First Mile of Concrete Highway Informational Designation; S123; January 19, 1957; 1957

First Presbyterian Church

This building is the fourth home of the First Presbyterian Church, the continuing congregation of the First Protestant Society of Detroit, which was formally incorporated in 1821. The society was organized in 1816 by the Reverend John Monteith, a twenty-eight-year-old graduate of Princeton Theological Seminary, who in 1817 helped found and became the first president of what is now the University of Michigan. This Romanesque-style edifice, designed by George D. Mason and Zachariah Rice, was dedicated in 1891. Its congregation, one of the oldest Protestant ones in the state, established Detroit's Harper Hospital in 1861. In 1911 the adjoining "church house" was completed for educational and social activities.

2930 Woodward Avenue, Detroit; First Presbyterian Church, First Protestant Society of Detroit; S525A; August 3, 1979; 1980

First Unitarian Universalist Church

Perry W. McAdow and his wife Clara built this elaborate Victorian mansion in 1891. The McAdows, who had earned their fortune in the gold mines of Montana, lived here from 1891 to 1897. The house continued as a private residence until 1913, when it was sold to the Universalist congregation. It was used as a temporary church until 1916, when the congregation completed a new church in the former garden to the north. This structure then became the parish house. In 1934 the Universalist and Unitarian congregations merged acquiring the name, First Unitarian Universalist Church of Detroit. The group uses this structure as a place of meetings and worship for religious liberals. The house, with its notable frescos, paneling, plasterwork and stained glass was listed on the National Register of Historic Places in 1980.

4605 Cass Avenue at the corner of Forest Street, Detroit; McAdow, Perry, House (Unitarian Universalist Church); L497; December 14, 1976; 1986

Fisher Building

The golden tower of the Fisher Building has brightened the skyline of metropolitan Detroit since 1928. Called Detroit's largest art object, the edifice is a city landmark. The Fisher brothers, developers of the closed automobile, erected the building for their offices. Architect Albert Kahn received the Architectural League's Silver Medal designating this as the most beautiful commercial structure of the year. Outside metallic trim is solid bronze. Gold leaf dominates the hand-painted arcade ceiling, and marble from all over the world graces both the exterior and interior of the building. Shops, restaurants, art galleries, business offices and the renowned Fisher Theatre are housed within its walls. Underground walkways connect the Fisher Building to the General Motors World Headquarters and the New Center Building.

3011 West Grand Boulevard (lobby), NW corner of Second Boulevard, Detroit; Fisher Building; S474; October 21, 1975; 1978

This 1991 painting by Stewart Ashlee depicts the First Michigan Colored Regiment on a recruiting tour through southern Michigan in 1863. (*First Michigan Colored Regiment*)

Ford Motor Company

Ford Motor Company was incorporated as an automobile manufacturer on June 16, 1903. The articles of incorporation were drawn up and signed in the office of Alexander Y. Malcomson, who operated a coal yard once located on this site. Henry Ford gave the company its name and designed its first product, the 1903 Model A. The purpose of the company was to manufacture and sell motor cars and related parts. In addition to Ford and Malcomson, the original stockholders included other figures important in the history of Detroit: John S. Gray, John F. Dodge, Horace E. Dodge, Albert Strelow, Vernon C. Fry, Charles H. Bennett, Horace H. Rackham, John W. Anderson, James Couzens and Charles J. Woodall. Over the past seventy-five years the Ford Motor Company has become one of the leading auto producers of the world.

*149 Griswold, at Jefferson Avenue, Hart Plaza adjacent to Ford Auditorium, Detroit; Ford Motor Company Informational Site; L594; January 19, 1978; 1978

Fort Lernoult

This marks the site of the southwest bastion of Fort Lernoult. It was here, on July 11, 1796, that the American flag was first flown over Detroit. The fort was built by the British in 1778-1779 to protect Detroit against the possibility of attack by George Rogers Clark and the American army. Overlooking the stockaded village and named for its commander, Richard B. Lernoult, the fort controlled river traffic and land routes. The fort was not attacked during the American Revolution. However, it was then the foremost British military post in the West, a base for Indian raids against American frontier settlements and a guardian of the rich fur trade. Although the peace treaty of 1783 gave Michigan to the United States, the British did not evacuate the fort until 1796. In 1812, Fort Lernoult was surrendered to the British, but was regained by the Americans in 1813 and renamed Fort Shelby. The last troops were removed in 1826. The fort was leveled in the next two or three years.

Fort and Shelby streets, Detroit; Fort Lernoult (Comerica Bank); S71; August 23, 1956; 1964

Fort Pontchartrain

The first permanent French settlement in the Detroit region was built on this site in 1701. The location was recommended by Antoine de la Mothe Cadillac, who wished to move the fur trade center south from Michilimackinac. Cadillac's plan was approved by Count Jerome de Pontchartrain, minister of marine, for whom the fort was named. The term *le detroit* (the strait) was applied to the fort and surrounding area; after 1751 the post was known as Fort Detroit. In 1760, as a result of the French and Indian War, the British gained control of Detroit and other posts in the Great Lakes region. British troops enlarged Fort Detroit, but during the American Revolution they moved to nearby Fort Lernoult, built 1778-1779. The Americans occupied Fort Lernoult in 1796 and in 1813 renamed it Fort Shelby.

2 Washington Boulevard on Larned, Detroit; Fort Pontchartrain Informational Site (Hotel Pontchartrain); S27; February 18, 1956; 1967

Fort Street Presbyterian Church

Second Presbyterian Church was organized in 1849 by the Reverend Robert K. Kellogg and twenty-six charter members. The present limestone building, dedicated in 1855, was designed by Octavius and Albert Jordan in [the] Gothic Revival style. Renamed in 1859 as Fort Street Presbyterian Church, it has survived two severe fires, in 1876 and 1914. Still substantially unchanged, it is one of Detroit's oldest churches.

631 West Fort Street at Third Street, Detroit; Fort Street Presbyterian Church; L101; March 3, 1971; 1975

Fort Wayne

No hostile shots have ever been fired from this star-shaped fort built in the 1840s to guard against a British invasion from Canada which never came. This third bastion to protect the river approach to the city was named for General "Mad" Anthony Wayne who accepted the surrender of Detroit from the British in 1796. It was a mobilization center for Union troops during the Civil War. Regiments from Fort Wayne served in Indian conflicts, the Spanish-American War, the Philippine Insurrection and World War I. An active post in the 1920s, it housed a Civilian Conservation Corps during the Depression. Fort Wayne was a wartime supply depot in World War II and an induction center during the Korean and Vietnam conflicts. Deactivated by the federal government in 1967, it now operates as a military museum under the auspices of the Detroit Historical Commission.

On the grounds of Fort Wayne near the Visitors Center, 6325 West Jefferson Avenue, Detroit; Fort Wayne; S182; February 19, 1958; 1978

Frederick Douglass-John Brown Meeting

In the home of William Webb, two hundred feet north of this spot, two famous Americans met several Detroit Negro residents on March 12, 1859, to discuss methods of abolishing American Negro slavery. John Brown (1800-1859), fiery antislavery leader, ardently advocated insurrectionary procedures, and eight months later became a martyr to the cause. Frederick Douglass (c. 1817-1895), ex-slave and internationally recognized antislavery orator and writer, sought a solution through political means and orderly democratic processes. Although they differed on tactics to be used, they were united in the immortal cause of American Negro freedom. Among the prominent members of Detroit's Negro community reported to have been present were: William Lambert, George De Baptiste, Dr. Joseph Ferguson, Reverend William S. Monroe, Willis Wilson, John Jackson and William Webb.

633 East Congress at St. Antoine Street, Detroit; Webb, William, House Informational Site (Frederick Douglass, and John Brown Meeting Informational Site); S224; December 5, 1961; 1962

George De Baptiste Homesite

George De Baptiste, a long-time Mason, and one of Detroit's most active and impassioned black community leaders, lived on this site during the 1850s and 1860s. Born in Virginia about 1815, he moved to Madison, Indiana, in 1838 and became involved in the Underground Railroad. Forced to leave because of his antislavery activities, De Baptiste became the personal valet of General William Henry Harrison, whom he accompanied to the White House as a steward. In 1846, De Baptiste came to Detroit and conducted several successful businesses. At the same time he served as a delegate to the Cleveland National Convention of Colored Citizens, and as an agent for the Freedman's Aid Commission. During the Civil War, he was an organizer of Michigan's Colored Regiment. De Baptiste died in 1875.

SW corner of East Larned and Beaubien streets, Detroit; De Baptiste, George, Home Informational Site (Blue Cross-Blue Shield); L387; April 4, 1975; 1975

Henry Ford House

Henry and Clara Ford lived here from 1908 to 1915. The Fords were the first of a community of automobile magnates to reside in the Boston-Edison neighborhood. The Italian Renaissance Revival house, designed by Malcomson, Higginbotham and Clement of

Detroit, was completed in 1908. The elaborate gardens were designed by T. Glenn Phillips. The Fords built a machine shop above the garage for their son Edsel, who showed a keen interest in automobile design. The seven years in this house were the most creative of Mr. Ford's career. His Model T, mass production methods and wage-price theories, which revolutionized American life and industry and reverberated around the world, all commenced while he resided here. In 1915 the Fords moved to Fair Lane, their estate in Dearborn.

140 Edison Avenue, Detroit; Ford, Henry, House; L1323A; July 17, 1986; 1989

Hilberry Theatre

This structure was completed in 1917 for the First Church of Christ, Scientist. Field, Hinchman and Smith—predecessor to the architectural firm of Smith, Hinchman and Grylls—designed it in a Classical Roman Ionic style. In 1961, Wayne State University acquired the building and converted the auditorium into an open stage theater. Named after the president of the university, Clarence B. Hilberry, the theater was created to house a graduate repertory company, which opened its first season in 1964.

4743 Cass Avenue, Detroit; First Church of Christ Scientist (Hilberry Theatre); L1037A; September 8, 1982; 1982

Holy Family Church

In the early twentieth century, immigrants from southern Italy and Sicily settled in Detroit's northeast side. They first worshipped in a chapel at Saints Peter and Paul Church. In 1907, Father Giovanni Boschi arrived in Detroit and began a campaign to build a church for the Italian community. In 1908, Bishop John S. Foley canonized the church and named it Holy Family. Completed in November 1910, the Italian Renaissance basilica was designed by Edward A. Schilling of Detroit.

641 Walter P. Chrysler Highway, Detroit; Holy Family Roman Catholic Church (Church of the Holy Family); L1627A; February 16, 1989; 1990

Indian Village

Abraham Cook purchased the area, now known as Indian Village, from two French farmers, Gabriel St. Aubin and Francois Rivard, during the first decades of the nineteenth century. The vicinity, known as the Cook Farms, was a race track from 1836 to 1893. In 1894, Cook's heirs subdivided the property and named it Indian Village. The first home was built in 1895 and Indian Village developed into a distinctive single family residential community of over three hundred homes representing a diversity of popular styles of the late 1800s to early 1900s. Due to the unique combination of social and architectural history, Indian Village is one of the most significant neighborhoods in present-day Detroit. It was listed in the National Register of Historic Places in 1972.

District bounded by Mack, Burns, Jefferson, and Seminole avenues; marker on the NE corner of Iroquois and East Vernor, Detroit; Indian Village Historic District; S349; October 29, 1971; 1978

James A. Bailey

Circus entrepreneur James A. McGinnis was born near this site on July 4, 1847. At fourteen he joined a circus and adopted the name "Bailey." Developing a striking talent for advertising and management, he bought the Cooper & Bailey Shows which toured, under canvas, the world over. Further success came with Bailey's 1880 purchase of "Little America," the first elephant born in this country. The native Detroiter joined forces with celebrated showman Phineas T. Barnum in 1881. Overshadowed by his more flamboyant partner, Bailey guided the circus to many triumphs. Unlike Barnum who asserted, "The public likes to be humbugged," Bailey said, "Give the people the best . . . and they'll reward you." Barnum died in 1891, and Bailey ran the mammoth three-ring show until his death in 1906. The circus was then sold to Ringling Brothers which lives on as Ringling Brothers and Barnum & Bailey.

1 Washington Boulevard, Detroit; Bailey, James A., Home Informational Site (Cobo Arena); S504; January 19, 1978; 1978

Joe Muer's Oyster House

Built around 1880, this structure originally housed a shoe and grocery store. In 1894 it was purchased by William Malburg, an undertaker and the father-in-law of Joe Muer. In 1906, Muer founded the Swift Cigar Company. He manufactured cigars on this site until the Great

Depression. Muer started this popular restaurant on October 28, 1929, the day before the famous Wall Street crash. Despite a seemingly unfavorable beginning, the restaurant has continued to prosper for more than a half century and is still owned by the Muer family.

2000 Gratiot Avenue at East Vernor, Detroit; Muer's Oyster House, Inc. (Joe Muer's Restaurant); L720B; August 3, 1979; 1981

The Landing of Cadillac

After departing Montreal June 5, 1701, Antoine de la Mothe Cadillac and his convoy of twenty-five canoes sailed down this river and on the evening of July 23 camped sixteen miles below the present city of Detroit on what is now Grosse Ile. On the morning of July 24, Cadillac returned upriver and reached a spot on the shore near the present intersection of West Jefferson and Shelby. Pleased with the strategic features, the bank towering some forty feet above the level of the river, Cadillac landed and planted the flag of France, taking possession of the territory in the name of King Louis XIV. The erection of a fortress was immediately begun. The stockade, formed of fifteen-foot oak pickets set three feet in the ground, occupied an area of about an acre. The fortress was named Fort Pontchartrain du Detroit (the strait) in honor of Count Jerome de Pontchartrain, Minister of Marine. From this fort and settlement, Detroit, the Renaissance City, takes its origin.

Le débarquement de Cadillac

Après avoir quitté Montréal le 5 juin 1701, Antoine de la Mothe Cadillac descendit ce fleuve avec un convoi de vingt-cinq canoës. Le soir du 23 juillet, le détachement établit son camp à l'endroit qui s'appelle maintenant Grosse Ile, soit seize miles en aval de la position actuelle de la ville de Détroit. Le 24 juillet au matin, Cadillac revint en amont et atteignit le point de la rive qu'on peut situer aujourd'hui près du croisement des rues West Jefferson et Shelby. Séduit par la valeur stratégique du lieu qui dominait de quarante pieds le niveau de la rivière, Cadillac débarqua et planta le drapeau français, prenant ainsi possession du territoire au nom du Roi Louis XIV. La construction d'une forteresse commença immédiatement. Avec ses pieux de chêne qui faisaient quinze pieds de long et qui étaient enfoncés de trois pieds dans le sol, la palissade délimitait une superficie d'un arpent, soit environ une acre. On baptisa cet enclos Fort Pontchartrain du Détroit, en l'honneur du Comte Jérôme de Pontchartrain, ministre de la Marine. C'est de ce fort et de ce campement qu'est née la ville de Détroit, la Cité de la "Renaissance."

Hart Plaza, Jefferson Avenue at the foot of Woodward Avenue, Detroit; Landing of Cadillac Informational Site; S515A; May 22, 1979; 1979

L. B. King and Company Building

L. B. King and Company headquartered here from 1911 to 1932, and Annis Furs occupied the building from 1932 to 1983. Constructed in 1911 to the designs of James S. Rogers and Walter MacFarlane, it exemplifies the Chicago commercial style popular in the early twentieth century. The building features a steel frame, terra cotta skin, three-part vertical division and banks of "Chicago windows." It incorporates classical decorative elements in the cornice and the window details.

1274 Library Avenue at Grand River, Detroit; King, L. B., and Company Building (Annis Fur Building); L1376A; January 22, 1987; 1989

Le Cote Du Nord-Est

After founding Detroit in 1701 the Sieur de Cadillac divided the land northeast of Fort Pontchartrain into long, narrow "ribbon" farms each fronting on the river. The first settlers thus had easy access to the waterway for irrigation and transportation, and to the fort for defense. The Campaus, one of Detroit's prominent early families, were established along this *cote du nord-est*, or northeastern coast, for several generations. In 1874 the site became the headquarters of Parke, Davis & Company, established in 1866 by Dr. Samuel P. Duffield and Hervey C. Parke and joined in 1867 by George Davis. A subsidiary of Warner-Lambert Company since 1970, Parke-Davis is a major international pharmaceutical firm with laboratories and offices throughout the world.

Joseph Campau Street at the Detroit River, Detroit; *LeCote DuNord-Est* Informational Site (River Place Complex); S435; September 17, 1974; 1974

Lewis College of Business

This Colonial Revival structure was built in 1910 for James F. Murphy, treasurer of the

Heralded as America's first state fair, the Michigan State Fair convened for the first time in Detroit in September 1849. (*Michigan State Fair*)

Murphy Chair Company and a future director of the Murphy-Potter Company. In 1941 it became the office of the Lewis College of Business. Violet T. Lewis had established the college in Indianapolis in 1929 to train black women for business careers. Ten years later the Detroit Chamber of Commerce invited her to open a school here. The college was located at this site from 1941 to 1976, when its expansion required more spacious quarters. In its first fifty years, it educated over twenty thousand students. The United States Department of Education designated the Lewis College of Business a "Historically Black College" in 1987. It was the first college in the state to receive this designation.

*5450 John R Street, Detroit; Murphy, James F., House (Lewis College of Business); L1565A; June 30, 1988; 1988

Mackenzie House

This 1895 Queen Anne-style house, designed by Malcomson & Higginbotham, was the home of David Mackenzie. Educator, scholar and humanitarian, Mackenzie fostered higher education for Detroit students. While principal of Central High School, then housed in what is now "Old Main," he established the Detroit Junior College in 1917. Six years later that institution expanded to become the College of the City of Detroit with Mackenzie as its first dean. This was the nucleus from which Wayne State University grew.

4735 Cass between Forest and Hancock, Detroit; Mackenzie House; S514A; March 5, 1979; 1979

Martin Kundig

This site bears the name of Father Martin Kundig, Wayne County's first superintendent of the poor. Born in 1805 in Switzerland, Kundig was educated in Rome, and served in the Swiss Papal Guard, before coming to work in the Diocese of Detroit in 1833. A year later, a cholera epidemic broke out in the city, and the Catholic Female Association, organized by Kundig, assumed the burden of nursing, burying the dead and caring for the orphans. Kundig's medical skill, administrative ability and compassion was recognized, and in 1834 the county board of supervisors appointed him superintendent of the poor. Kundig organized the German Catholic School, helped build St. Mary's Church and was appointed a regent of the state university. In 1846 he moved to Wisconsin, where he died in 1879.

3300 Jefferies, SW corner of Martin Luther King Boulevard, Detroit; Kundig, Martin (Kundig Senior Center); L398; May 14, 1975; 1975

Michigan's Oldest Jewish Cemetery

Beth El, the first Jewish congregation in Michigan, was organized in Detroit on September 22, 1850, by twelve families. This half-acre cemetery, dedicated on January 1, 1851, was known then as "The Champlain Street Cemetery of Temple Beth El" because Lafayette was formerly called Champlain Street. The first interment was in fall of 1851, and in 1854 Samuel Marcus, the first rabbi of Beth El, was buried here. The cemetery, containing many graves of Jewish war veterans, was in active use until the 1950s.

3371 East Lafayette, between Elmwood Cemetery and Mount Elliott, Detroit; Champlain Street Cemetery of Temple Beth El (Beth El Cemetery); S241; August 14, 1962; 1973

Michigan State Fair

America's first state fair, conducted by the Michigan Agricultural Society with the support of the legislature and local citizens, was held in Detroit on September 25-27, 1849. About $800 in premiums were awarded for those "articles, productions and improvements" that were "best calculated to promote the agricultural and household manufacturing interests of the state." The site of this annual fair was often moved until 1905 when it was given a permanent home here at the fairgrounds.

1120 West State Fair Avenue, Woodard Avenue at Eight Mile Road, Detroit; Michigan State Fair Informational Site; S172; September 17, 1957; 1958

Michigan State Medical Society

Formation of the Michigan State Medical Society took place here, June 5, 1866, in the Supreme Court Room of Odd Fellows Hall. About one hundred physicians from all areas in Michigan were present. The society adopted the code of ethics of the American Medical Association. The state society, a voluntary, professional organization, provides postgraduate training for physicians and strives to improve the public health by its public service and

Incorporated in 1960, the Motown Record Corporation forever changed the course of music history. The Temptations (above) had the familiar Motown sound. (*Motown*)

educational activities.

85-87 Woodard Avenue, between Congress and Larned streets, Detroit; Michigan State Medical Society Informational Site; S270; June 11, 1965; 1965

Motown

The "Motown Sound" was created on this site from 1959 to 1972. The company was started with an $800 loan from the savings club of the Bertha and Berry Gordy, Sr., family. Originally called Tamla Records, the company's first national release was 'Money (That's What I Want),"in August 1959. The founder, choosing a name that reflected the Motor City, coined the word "Motown" for the company that was incorporated as the Motown Record Corporation on April 14, 1960. That same year it produced its first gold record, "Shop Around." In 1968 the company, which had grown from a family-oriented business to an international enterprise, moved its business operations to 2457 Woodward. Motown provided an opportunity for Detroit's inner-city youth to reach their full potential and become superstars.

Side Two

By the end of its first decade, Motown was the largest independent manufacturer of single 45 rpm records in the world. Among Motown's record labels were Tamla, Motown, Gordy, Soul, VIP, Rare Earth, Black Forum, Workshop Jazz, Divinity and others. In 1972, Motown moved its headquarters to Los Angeles, California. The company expanded its television productions and entered the motion picture industry. *Lady Sings the Blues*, Motown's first feature length film, received five Academy Award Nominations. By 1975, Motown Industries was the largest black-owned corporation in the world. In 1980 the Motown Historical Museum was established at Hitsville U.S.A. to commemorate the Motown Sound and to memorialize Motown's distinctive heritage and its global impact.

2648 West Grand Boulevard, Detroit; Motown Record Corporation Informational Site (Hitsville, U.S.A.); L1447C; August 21, 1987; 1987

Music Hall

Originally called the Wilson Theatre, this building was completed in 1928 with funds provided by Matilda Wilson (Mrs. Alfred G.). William E. Kapp of Smith, Hinchman & Grylls, an architectural firm whose works dominated the city's skyline of the 1920s, designed this Art Deco-style edifice. Terra cotta Greek masks adorn the exterior, and elaborate molded plaster and stenciling complement the interior. The theater's purpose of offering legitimate productions was initially fulfilled, but during the Depression its lights dimmed except for sporadic occasions. From 1946 to 1949, the Detroit Symphony Orchestra occupied the structure, which was renamed Music Hall. Area residents came here in the 1950s and 1960s to see Cinerama and other films. Now the home of the Music Hall Center and the Michigan Opera Theatre, Music Hall is restored to its original use and appearance.

350 Madison Avenue, Detroit; Wilson Theatre (Music Hall); L467; August 6, 1976; 1978

Old City Hall

For nearly a century this site on Campus Martius was the seat of Detroit's city government. City Hall was designed in 1860 by the firm of A. N. Jordan and James Anderson, but the Civil War forced postponement of construction until 1868. Impressive ceremonies marked the dedication of the building on the Fourth of July, 1871. An imposing structure with a mansard roof, City Hall was built of cream-colored Amherst sandstone, and the clock in the two-hundred-foot tower was said to be the largest in the nation. Statues of Cadillac, La Salle, Marquette and Richard were designed for the building by Julius Melchers to recall the city's French heritage. After a bitter public debate, City Hall was razed in 1961.

Woodward Avenue at Fort Street in Kennedy Square, Detroit; Detroit City Hall (Demolished); HB18; February 19, 1958; 1971

Omega Psi Phi

This Victorian structure, built in the early 1890s, houses the Detroit chapter of the first national Greek letter fraternity established at a Negro university. Omega Psi Phi was founded in 1911 at Howard University in Washington, D.C. The Greek letters symbolize the motto "Friendship is essential to the soul." DeWitt T. Burton, Francis Dent and O. T. Davis formed Nu Omega, the local chapter in 1923. Fifteen years later Nu Sigma, the undergraduate chapter, began at Wayne State University. Purchased in 1942 by Nu Omega, this house fulfilled the fraternity's initial purpose by creating an association of college men with similar ideals of manhood, scholarship, perseverance and uplift. Many members of this chapter achieved local or national prominence.

235 East Ferry Street, between John R and Brush, Detroit; Omega Psi Phi Fraternity House; L485; December 14, 1976; 1977

Orchestra Hall

This concert hall was built in 1919 as the home of the Detroit Symphony Orchestra. It was constructed to satisfy the demand of its music director, the internationally esteemed Ossip Gabrilowitsch, that a suitable hall be built. Architect Charles Howard Crane designed this brick and limestone structure which was completed in five months. The symphony moved to a larger facility in 1939. Two years later this hall became the Paradise Theatre featuring jazz and vaudeville until 1951. Scheduled for demoliton in 1970 the building was acquired by Save Orchestra Hall, Incorporated. These concerned citizens restored the badly deteriorated Orchestra Hall, which now continues its tradition of acoustical excellence and quality music in Detroit.

3711 Woodward Avenue at Parson, Detroit; Orchestra Hall; S323; February 11, 1970; 1979

Orsel McGhee House

In 1944 the Orsel McGhees, a black family, moved here into what was then an all-white neighborhood. A neighboring family won a court order revoking the McGhees' purchase of the house on the basis of a restrictive covenant forbidding non-white residents. The McGhees, aided by the NAACP and represented by Thurgood Marshall, appealed the case to the U.S. Supreme Court. The court's 1948 decision in favor of the McGhees upheld the principle of freedom from discrimination in the enjoyment of property rights.

4626 Seebaldt, Detroit; McGhee, Orsel, House; L486; December 14, 1976; 1983

Packard Motor Car Company

The Packard Motor Car Company, which built Detroit's first, and for many years most prestigious, luxury cars, produced over 1.5 million vehicles on this site from 1903 to 1954. The factory complex, designed by Albert Kahn, included the city's first use of reinforced concrete for industrial construction. At its opening, it was considered the most modern automobile manufacturing facility in the world. In it skilled craftsmen practiced over eighty trades.

*1580 East Grand Boulevard, Detroit; Packard Motor Car Company (Packard Properties Company); S546A; January 13, 1982; 1982

The Players

The Players, a Detroit gentlemen's amateur theatre club founded in 1911, opened this playhouse in 1926. The handsome building was created by club members William E. Kapp, architect; Corrado Parducci, stone sculptor; and Paul Honor, muralist. The playhouse, built in the style of the sixteenth-century English Renaissance, was one of the earliest major structures in the area to use cinder block laid in ashlar on its interior walls to give the appearance of cut stone. It has been in continual use as a playhouse since its completion.

3321 East Jefferson Avenue, Detroit; The Players (The Players Playhouse); L1262A; August 22, 1985; 1987

Recreation Park

In 1879, Recreation Park was established on the land surrounding this site. The park extended from Brady Street to Willis Avenue. It included the baseball field that was the home park of the Detroit Wolverines of the National League from 1881 to 1888. Here on May 2, 1881, the first major league baseball game in Detroit was played before 1,286 spectators. After that first game against Buffalo, more than four hundred major league games were played here over eight seasons. This marker stands in what was the left field. Home plate and a wooden grandstand were near Brady Street to the south. Fans strolled in a nearby grove of trees owned by Harper Hospital. Two Wolverines, Dan Brouthers and Sam Thompson, have been inducted into the Baseball Hall of Fame.

Side Two

At Mayor William G. Thompson's suggestion, the Detroit Wolverines were organized as a major league team to play at Recreation Park. In its first years the team finished from the middle to the bottom of the National League. It began to improve after it was purchased by pharmaceutical manufacturer Frederick K. Stearns in 1885. In 1887 it won the National League Pennant and the national championship, defeating St. Louis of the American Association in a fifteen-game series. Poor attendance caused the Wolverines to break up after the 1888 season. The franchise moved to Cleveland, where it finally disbanded in 1899. From 1889 to 1894 other baseball teams played at Recreation Park. In 1894 the park was closed, the grandstand torn down and the land was subdivided.

Brush Mall, Detroit Medical Center main campus, 3990 John R Street, Detroit; Recreation Park Informational Designation; L1426C; June 10, 1987; 1987

Redford Cemetery

In 1831, Israel Bell, a Pekin Village commissioner, gave one acre of land to the village for a cemetery. Originally called Bell Branch Cemetery after the river and the settlement founded by Bell in 1818, its name was changed to Redford Cemetery after Pekin's modern name, Redford Township. Additional acreage obtained in 1840, 1854 and 1883 expanded the cemetery to ten acres, of which half is in Redford Township and half is in Detroit. A wrought iron fence was built for the cemetery in 1886 with money contributed by Redford Township citizens. Among those buried here are Israel Bell and many war veterans, including two from the Revolutionary War and many from the War of 1812, the Civil War and World War I.

Telegraph Road between Five Mile Road and Puritan Avenue, Detroit; Redford Cemetery (Bell Branch Cemetery); L1317A; June 13, 1986; 1988

Redford Township School District No. 9

In 1874, Redford Township School District No. 9 bought an acre of land from Eugenius and Abigail Hodge and erected this school. Named Beech School, it served the Beech Park settlement that sprang up here adjacent to the Detroit, Lansing & Lake Michigan Railroad. The school was built to accommodate sixty children—although only fifty residents lived in the settlement at the time—and was the largest in the township. Classes were held in Beech School until 1952. The building has housed meetings of the Masonic lodge and the Boy Scouts of America, served as school offices and storage facilities and as the headquarters for the Association of Retarded Citizens. In 1988 the South Redford School District sold the property to a private developer.

12259 Beech-Daly Road at Southwestern and Capitol, Redford Township; Redford Township School District No. 9 Informational Designation (Beech School); L1826; May 16, 1991; 1991

Religious of the Sacred Heart

Responding to a request from the Antoine Beaubien family, five Religious of the Sacred Heart arrived in Detroit in 1851. The nuns opened a school on the north side of Jefferson Avenue, near this site. From 1851 to 1861 the school occupied three locations on Jefferson Avenue. The religious also taught in French-, Italian- and English-speaking parishes. In 1861 they erected a school on this site. It operated until 1918. It was relocated on Lawrence Avenue from 1918 to 1958, when it was moved to Bloomfield Hills.

South side of East Jefferson Avenue between Beaubien and Ste. Antoine streets, Detroit; Religious of the Sacred Heart Informational Designation; L1157C; March 20, 1984; 1984

Reverend John A. Lemke

John A. Lemke, the son of one of the founders of Detroit's first Polish Roman Catholic parish, was born in Detroit in 1866. In 1884 he entered St. Mary's Seminary in Baltimore, Maryland. Ordained March 10, 1889, he became the first native-born Detroiter of Polish descent to be ordained into the Catholic priesthood in the Diocese of Detroit. The ceremony was held at St. Albertus. Reverend Lemke died in 1890 at the age of twenty-four. He is buried at Mount Elliot Cemetery, Detroit.

St. Albertus Roman Catholic Church, 4231 St. Aubin Street, Detroit; Lemke, Father John A., Informational Designation; L800B; March 19, 1980; 1981

Robert Pauli Scherer

Robert Pauli Scherer (1906-1960) was a native of Detroit and a graduate of Detroit's public schools. In 1930, at the age of twenty-four, he invented the rotary die encapsulation machine in a workshop located in the basement of this structure. The building was then the home of his parents, Dr. and Mrs. Otto Scherer. R. P. Scherer's invention transformed the production of soft gelatin capsules used in the pharmaceutical industry into a commercial process that helped raise worldwide health and nutritional standards. In 1933 he founded the present-day R. P. Scherer Corporation. With eighteen plants in twelve countries the firm was the world's largest manufacturer of soft gelatin capsules in 1984. An ingenious inventor, Scherer received fifty-two patents during his lifetime. His experimental machine was placed in the Smithsonian Institution in 1955.

Children's Museum, 67 Kirby Street, Detroit; Scherer, Robert P., and R. P. Scherer Corporation Informational Designation; S563C; June 15, 1984; 1984

Sacred Heart Parish

Erected in 1875, this building was originally a German Catholic Church. As the social and ethnic composition of the neighborhood changed, so did the membership of the church. Many of the founding German parishioners moved away. Finally in 1938 the first black Catholic congregation in the city of Detroit moved to this edifice. That pioneer congregation, which had begun in 1911 as the St. Peter Claver Church on Eliot and Beaubien streets, still worships here. Affiliated with Sacred Heart Parish are a Sunday School, a choir, several church auxiliary organizations and numerous social, educational, and cultural functions which serve the people of this community. The church operated a high school until 1957 and an elementary school until 1965. This parish has served Detroit for over one hundred years.

1000 Eliot Street at Rivard, Detroit; Sacred Heart Roman Catholic Church Complex; L466; June 19, 1975; 1978

St. Albertus Church

Polish immigrants arrived in Detroit as early as the 1850s, but not until the Reverend Simon Wieczorek founded St. Albertus Roman Catholic Parish in 1872, did their community have a center. A neighborhood, called Wojciechowo, grew around the parish's first church. In 1885 the present Gothic Revival building replaced the original wooden frame structure. Inspired by the Reverend Dominic Kolasinski's concern for Polish traditions, it incorporates twelve lunette panels over the nave arcades, brick detailing and an octagonal tower common to churches in Poland. Although the community eventually dispersed, St. Albertus Church still stands as a symbol of the first Polish community in Detroit.

4231 St. Aubin Street at Canfield, Detroit; St. Albertus Roman Catholic Church; L333; July 26, 1974; 1975

Ste. Anne Church

On July 26, 1701, two days after his arrival, Antoine de la Mothe Cadillac, the founder of Detroit, built a chapel dedicated to Ste. Anne, patron saint of New France. Father Francois Vaillant, a Jesuit, and Father Nicholas Constantine Delhalle, a Franciscan, were instrumental in the founding of the parish. The church records, which date from 1704, are now the second oldest continuous Roman Catholic parish records in the nation. From 1833 to 1844, Ste. Anne's was the cathedral church for the diocese of Michigan and the northwest. The cornerstone for the present Gothic Revival building, the parish's eighth home, was laid in 1886. The handsome structure, designed by parishioner Leon Coquard, displays the oldest stained glass in the city. In the Gabriel Richard Chapel, enclosed in a marble tomb, lie the remains of Father Gabriel Richard.

Gabriel Richard

Father Gabriel Jacques Richard, S.S., (1767-1832)—pastor, educator and public servant—arrived in Detroit in 1798. In 1802 he became the pastor of Ste. Anne Church. He brought a printing press to the area and in 1809 printed Michigan's first newspaper, *The Michigan Essay or Impartial Observer*. In 1817, Richard and the Reverend John Monteith, a Presbyterian, became the first professors of the University of Michigania, the territory's pioneer educational establishment. Richard also established schools for girls and for Indian children. From 1823 to 1825, Richard was [the] Michigan Territory's delegate to the United States Congress. As a delegate, he was instrumental in gaining support for the Territorial Road, which lined Detroit and Chicago, opening Michigan to settlement. He died of cholera on September 13, 1832.

SE corner of Howard and Ste. Anne (Nineteenth) streets, Detroit; Ste. Anne Roman Catholic Church; S464; May 14, 1975; 1985

St. Anthony Church

During the early 1850s, the growing number of Catholic families of German and Alsatian descent on Detroit's east side necessitated the establishment of a new Catholic parish. The new congregation was originally founded as a mission church of St. Joseph parish. Named St. Anthony Mission, it completed its first frame church at a cost of $6,000 on July 5, 1857. The church was located at the corner of Gratiot and Centerline Road, now Field Avenue. Father Leopold Pawlowski was appointed as its first pastor. By the turn of the century, the congregation needed a larger church. On July 18, 1901, Bishop John Samuel Foley laid the cornerstone for the present red brick and terra cotta Romanesque church. The handsome structure, designed by Donaldson and Meier, features frescoed ceilings and an impressive white stone Romanesque altar.

Church at 5247 Sheridan Avenue, between Frederick Street and Gratiot Avenue, marker located on the corner of St. Anthony Place and Sheridan, Detroit; St. Anthony Catholic Church (St. Anthony Church); L1247A; June 20, 1985; 1986

St. Antoine YMCA Site

In 1909, Joseph L. Hudson, founder of mercantile establishments known through the nation, and Dr. Adolph G. Studer, General Secretary of the Young Men's Christian Association of Detroit, together with several leading black citizens, established the Douglass Institute, forerunner of the St. Antoine Street Branch YMCA. Organized in September 1920, the St. Antoine Branch provided community services through religious, educational and recreational activities. Construction of a building, which once stood here, began in 1924, just four blocks from the downtown YMCA where blacks were not allowed membership. The new building was well-equipped and on Sunday afternoons the gymnasium was set up for eminent national leaders to come and speak on current local and national problems. Many blacks of Detroit in the 1920s had roots in the St. Antoine "Y".

635 Elizabeth at St. Antoine, Detroit; St. Antoine YMCA (Demolished); L442; March 2, 1976; 1980

St. Elizabeth Church

In 1884 families of German descent, under the pastorate of Father Anthony Svensson, united to form a new parish. In 1885 they built a temporary church and school at McDougall and Willis, on land donated by Fannie Van Dyke. Detroit architects Donaldson and Meir designed the present red brick Romanesque Revival-style edifice, which was consecrated on February 14, 1892, by Bishop John Foley. The interior of the church contains wooden altar carvings by German craftsman Anthony Osebald. The parish's role as the center of spiritual growth for many ethnic groups was greatly enhanced with the advent of Vatican II in 1962, which advocated the change from Latin to the language of the people. In the church service the parish family continued to be multi-cultural with a strong sense of its black heritage.

3138 East Canfield Avenue at McDougall, Detroit; St. Elizabeth Church; L1061A; January 27, 1983; 1985

St. John's Episcopal Church

St. John's Episcopal parish, established in December 1958, served what was then a rural area of Detroit. Albert Jordan designed the original church (now St. John's Chapel), which was built in 1859. Henry Porter Baldwin, a former United States senator and future governor, donated the church lot and paid for the building. Two years later Jordan and his partner James Anderson, by then Detroit's ranking church architects, designed the present Victorian Gothic church. Known as the "Patriarch of Piety Hill," the limestone structure was constructed with a partial donation from Baldwin. The chancel was enlarged in 1892 and in 1936 the church and chapel (forty million pounds) were moved sixty feet eastward when Woodward Avenue was widened.

2326 Woodward Avenue, between the Fisher Freeway Service Drive and Montcalm, Detroit; St. John's Episcopal Church; L1421A; June 10, 1987; 1988

St. John's Presbyterian Church

On April 27, 1919, thirty-nine people met in the First Presbyterian Church on Woodward Avenue and organized St. John's Presbyterian Church. Reverend John W. Lee, a field missionary, led the formation of the church to serve Detroit's growing black population. St. John's was the first African-American Presbyterian congregation in Michigan. The first place of worship was located at Madison and Dubois streets. In 1936 churchwoman Anne Lewis led the establishment of the St. John's child care center. In 1940 the congregation moved to a church at Clinton and Joseph Campau streets. In the 1960s government-sponsored "urban renewal" projects forced the congregation to move to a new location. The first service in the present church was held on Christmas Day 1966.

1961 East Lafayette, Detroit; St. John's Presbyterian Church Informational Designation; L1781C; August 23, 1990; 1991

St. Josaphat Roman Catholic Church Complex

St. Josaphat's, founded on June 1, 1889, was the third Polish-speaking Roman Catholic parish established in Detroit. On February 2, 1890, it dedicated a combination church and school building. Within a decade plans were begun for a new church rectory and a convent. In 1901 this Late Victorian Romanesque-style church was completed at a cost of $100,000. The church was designed by Joseph G. Kastler and William E. N. Hunter. Local carpenters, Harcus & Lang and the Jermolowicz Brothers, were the builders. The stained glass was crafted by the Detroit Stained Glass Works. In 1907 the convent was completed. The complex was listed on the National Register of Historic Places in 1982.

715 East Canfield Avenue, west of I-75 service drive, Detroit; St. Josaphat's Roman Catholic Church Complex; L1281A; November 26, 1985; 1987

St. Joseph's Parish

Organized in 1855, St. Joseph's served a German Catholic neighborhood for generations. With schools and activities conducted in German, the parish sponsored a mutual benefit society to assist its immigrant flock. In 1873, led by Father Johann Friedland, the parish dedicated this limestone church, designed in the Gothic Revival style by Francis Himpler. No longer predominantly German, St. Joseph's continues as a neighborhood parish and still provides services in German.

1828 Jay Street, SE corner of Orleans Street, Detroit; St. Joseph's Roman Catholic Church; L204; June 16, 1972; 1973

St. Mary's Church

St. Mary's parish was founded by Father Martin Kundig in 1835 for the German-speaking Catholics in Detroit and is the third oldest Catholic parish in the city. The cornerstone for the original church was laid on the feast of Corpus Christi, June 19, 1841, and the church was consecrated in honor of the Immaculate Conception of the Blessed Virgin Mary on June 29, 1843. This High Victorian Romanesque-style structure was designed by German parishioner Peter Dederichs. The cornerstone was laid in 1884, and the edifice completed in 1885. St. Mary's founded the city's first black and Hispanic Catholic missions. Since 1893, this parish has been guided by the Fathers of the Congregation of the Holy Ghost, C.S.Sp.

St. Mary's Rectory

Constructed in 1876, this North Italian Banded Romanesque structure was designed by Swiss architect Julius Hess. It is the second rectory building of St. Mary's parish, which was organized in 1835 under the leadership of Father Martin Kundig (1835-1843). Following Father Kundig were the Redemptorist Fathers (1847-1872), the Franciscan Fathers (1872-1893) and the Holy Ghost Fathers, C.S.Sp. (1893 to the present). This edifice was completed under the guidance of the Franciscans. It also served as their monastery.

St. Mary's School

This structure, designed by Pius Daubner, was completed in 1868. It is one of the oldest Catholic school buildings in the state and the third in the history of St. Mary's. At the first school, built in 1844, laymen were the original instructors. In 1852 the "Christian Brothers" opened two classes with 180 pupils and the School Sisters of Notre Dame (a German order of teaching nuns) took charge of the girls and smaller boys. In 1855 a second school was built and used as a combination school, orphanage and sisters' residence. Prior to closing in 1966, St. Mary's Commercial School for Girls was the only one of its kind in Detroit. The building is now St. Mary's Community Center.

646 Monroe, Detroit; St. Mary's Roman Catholic Church (St. Mary's Downtown Complex); L686A; June 15, 1979; 1980

St. Matthew's Episcopal Church

Founded in 1846, St. Matthew's Church has served the prominent and well-established members of Detroit's black community. The combined influence of businessman William Lambert and William Monroe, first pastor of Second Baptist Church, drew members to the new congregation. St. Matthew's was forced to close during the Civil War due to declining membership. Many members had fled to Canada to escape the effects of the 1850 Fugitive Slave Act. The Reverend Monroe resigned and emigrated to Liberia. In 1881 the church reopened, becoming the center for reform groups and self-improvement clubs. Among St. Matthew's well-known ministers were former professor Charles Thompson and Robert Bagnall, organizer of Detroit's

Upon the death of Bernhard Stroh in 1882, the Lion Brewery became the B. Stroh Brewing Company; it remained so named until 1902. (*Stroh Brewery*)

chapter of the National Association for the Advancement of Colored People.

2019 St. Antoine, Detroit; St. Matthew's Episcopal Church; L447; March 2, 1976; 1976

St. Philip's Lutheran Church

St. Philip's Lutheran Church, founded in 1934, was the first black Lutheran church in Michigan. The Reverend H. J. Storm came to Detroit from his Windsor parish to lead the St. Philip's congregation each week until 1936, when the Reverend Raymond R. Pollatz be- came the church's first resident pastor. The parish soon moved from its one-room apart- ment to a school and later to a remodeled synagogue on King Street. The parish dedicated the building at this location on May 20, 1951.

Side Two

As the only black Lutheran church in Michigan in the 1930s, St. Philip's expanded quickly. Berea Lutheran, St. Titus and St. Matthias churches all grew from the original congregation. St. Philip's chose quality education for blacks as one of its missions. In 1944 it opened St. Philip's Day School in the basement of the church on King Street. The school was the first Lutheran school in Michigan open to black students, and many of Michigan's black leaders attended it.

*2884 East Grand Boulevard, Detroit; St. Philip's Lutheran Congregation Informational Designation; L1579C; July 21, 1988; 1988

SS. Peter and Paul Church

This is the oldest extant church in Detroit. Designed by Francis Letourno in the basilica form, it was built between 1844 and 1848 and served for twenty-nine years as the cathedral of the Detroit diocese under Bishop LeFevre. In 1877, Bishop Borgess gave the parish to the Jesuit Fathers to build a college here. This is now the University of Detroit. The church exterior retains its original simplicity and dignity.

629 East Jefferson Avenue, Detroit; Saints Peter and Paul Church; S325; January 22, 1971; 1974

Schwankovsky Temple of Music

Gordon W. Lloyd designed this massive structure as a music store for the F. J. Schwankovsky Company. The company, founded in 1879, operated a retail store for pianos, organs and musical merchandise, and later manufactured pianos. Completed in 1891, this six-story brick and brownstone structure, with cast-iron frame, was one of the first high-rise buildings on Woodward Avenue. It was also one of the first Detroit buildings whose initial construction included an electric elevator. The company held recitals in the second floor ballroom and brass concerts on the sixth floor balcony. By 1910, the F. J. Schwankovsky Company having ceased operations, the building became a jewelry store. From 1920 to 1978 it housed the Wright Kay jewelry firm. When sold in 1980, the structure was converted into the headquarters store for the House of Fabrics.

1500 Woodward Avenue at Clifford, Detroit; Schwankovsky Building (Wright Kay Building); L847A; October 2, 1980; 1982

Second Baptist Church

Founded in 1836 by thirteen former slaves, this is the oldest black congregation in Michigan. From its beginnings the church has occupied a prominent place in Detroit's black community. In 1839 it established the city's first school for black children, and its first pastor, the Reverend William C. Monroe, was a noted antislavery activist. In 1843 he presided over the first State Convention of Colored Citizens, which met at the Second Baptist Church. Delegates demanded the right to vote and an end to slavery. On January 6, 1863, Detroit's blacks celebrated the Emancipation Proclamation here. Located at this site since 1857, the church has expanded its facilities through the years.

441 Monroe Street, Detroit; Second Baptist Church of Detroit (Second Baptist Church); L346; September 17, 1974; 1974

Shrine Circus

Near this site, on February 26, 1906, some three thousand spectators watched the nation's first Shrine Circus. Detroit's Moslem Shrine Temple's one-ring show was the beginning of a major fund-raising venture for Shrine temples throughout the country. In 1907, Shrine temples in other cities began sponsoring circuses, and in 1925 the Shriners featured their first three-ring show. Originally operating for one week, Shrine Circuses appear across the nation throughout the year. Clyde Beatty and his wild animals were the main attraction in Detroit from 1925 to 1965. The Nelsons, aerialists and acrobats and the Romigs, clowns of Michigan were also featured performers during the early years. In the 1980s annual attendance at Shrine Circuses exceeded that of any other circus in America.

NW corner of Brush and Larned, parking lot of the Light Guard Armory, Detroit; Shrine Circus, Birthplace of American, Informational Designation; S552C; December 21, 1982; 1983

State Savings Bank

Completed in 1900, this is Michigan's preeminent example of design by the internationally renowned architects, McKim, Mead and White of New York. The three-story Neo-Classical structure features a white marble exterior with bronze window units. Among its superbly crafted interior features are carved Roman arched colonnades with bronze grill work and gold-leaf detail on the two-story-high ceiling of the main room. In 1907, Peoples Savings Bank (established in 1871) merged with the State Savings Bank (established in 1833) and made this structure its home. Having outgrown these quarters by 1914, Peoples State Bank commissioned Detroit architects Donaldson and Meier to design the Congress Street addition. The building became the world headquarters of Silver's Incorporated in 1980.

151 West Fort Street at the SW corner of Congress and Shelby, Detroit; State Savings Bank; S536A; January 8, 1981; 1982

Stearns Telephone

On September 22, 1877, a Bell telephone was installed on this site in the drugstore operated by Frederick Stearns. An iron wire strung along rooftops connected the store with the Stearns laboratory a half-mile away at the foot of Fifth Street. This service, only eighteen months after Alexander Graham Bell patented his invention, was the first to be offered by the organization which eventually developed into the Michigan Bell Telephone Company. A placard in the store window invited the public to drop in every hour on the hour to speak over the amazing new device. Other private lines followed, but it was a year before the first telephone exchange was constructed with fifteen or twenty subscribers on each party line.

511 Woodward Avenue, Detroit; Stearns Telephone Informational Site (Detroit Federal Savings); S303; April 24, 1970; 1972

Stroh Brewery

Leaving the chaos of the 1848 German Revolution, Bernhard Stroh emigrated from Kirn, Germany, to South America. He soon decided to try his fortune in another German settlement, and in 1850 he arrived in Detroit. Trained as a brewer, Stroh opened a brewery on

Catherine Street that same year. He developed a market for a new light lager beer among the larger German immigrant population. Pushing a cart through the city, he sold his beer from door to door. At his death in 1882 the Lion Brewery had become a thriving business to pass on to his sons, Julius and Bernhard, Jr. They expanded the company and in 1902 changed the name to The Stroh Brewery Company. Today members of the Stroh family still manage what is one of Michigan's major family businesses.

*Gratiot Avenue, SE of I-75, Detroit; Stroh's Brewery (demolished) S475; October 21, 1975; 1976

Sweetest Heart of Mary Catholic Church

During the late nineteenth century many Polish immigrants fleeing oppression came to Detroit. In 1886 a group of them organized the school that was the beginning of Sweetest Heart of Mary Parish. On December 8, 1888, the Reverend Dominic H. Kolasinski, former pastor and builder of neighboring St. Albertus Church, became their pastor without episcopal approval. Under his leadership, construction of this Late Victorian Gothic church began in July 1890. On February 18, 1894, the parish officially became part of the Diocese of Detroit. The church's windows, made by the Detroit Glass Works, won prizes at the 1893 Chicago Columbian Exposition. Its organ is one of the oldest Austin organs in existence. Its 217-foot spires house three large bells named St. Mary, St. Joseph and St. Barbara.

4440 Russell Street at Canfield, Detroit; Sweetest Heart of Mary Roman Catholic Church; L334; July 26, 1974; 1981

Thompson Home

This Victorian structure was completed in 1884. It was named for wealthy Detroit businessman David Thompson. In his will Thompson instructed his wife, Mary, to use part of his estate to found a charitable institution. She commissioned George DeWitt Mason, prominent local architect and leader in architectural education, to design the building. It stands as a distinctive example of his early work. The one-story addition was constructed in 1964.

4756 Cass Avenue between Forest and Hancock, Detroit; Thompson Home for Old Ladies; L358; November 14, 1974; 1976

Tiger Stadium

Baseball has been played on this site since before 1900 and it has been the home of the Detroit Tigers from their start as charter members of the American League in 1901. Standing on the location of an early haymarket, the stadium has been enlarged and renamed several times. Once called Bennett Park with wooden stands for ten thousand, it became Navin Field in 1912 when seating was increased to twenty-three thousand and home plate was moved from what is now right field to its present location. Major alterations later expanded its capacity to more than fifty-four thousand and in 1938 the structure became Briggs Stadium. Lights were installed in 1948 and in 1961 the name was changed to Tiger Stadium. The site of many championship sporting events, the evolution of this stadium is a tribute to Detroit's support of professional athletics.

2121 Trumbull Avenue at Michigan Avenue, Detroit; Navin Field/Briggs Stadium/Tiger Stadium; S470; September 15, 1975; 1976

Trinity Lutheran Church

Trinity Lutheran Church, one of the oldest of this denomination in Detroit, was founded in 1850. The Reverend Gottlieb Schaller conducted the early worship services, which were held in the former Mariners Church on Larned Street. In 1866 the congregation built a brick church on this site. After over sixty years of service, it was razed in 1929. The present Neo-Gothic-style church, designed by W. E. N. Hunter, was a gift of Charles Gauss. It was dedicated in 1931. Trinity Lutheran helped to establish many daughter congregations in Detroit. The church also established the Lutheran Institute for the Deaf, the Lutheran cemetery, and together with other congregations, the Detroit Lutheran High School, Valparaiso University of Indiana and the Lutheran radio hour.

1345 Gratiot Avenue at Russell, Detroit; Trinity Evangelical Lutheran Church Complex; L925A; April 24, 1981; 1982

War of 1812 Dead

Hardship struck soon after American troops regained Detroit on September 29, 1813, during the War of 1812. Soldiers' quarters were lacking, and food supplies became desperately short. Then a disease resembling cholera broke out among the soldiers. By

The Thompson Home for Old Ladies, designed by George Mason, was completed in 1884 as part of a bequest from Detroit businessman David Thompson. (*Thompson Home*)

December 1, 1813, nearly thirteen hundred officers and men were sick. Medical supplies were almost gone. Conditions worsened. When coffins became unobtainable, many soldiers were buried in a common grave at this site. Some seven hundred may have died before the epidemic ran its course.

SW corner of Washington Boulevard and Michigan Avenue, Detroit; War of 1812 Dead Informational Site; S242; November 17, 1962; 1963

Wayne State University

Here in the Central High building, completed in 1896, was founded in 1917 Detroit Junior College, from which grew a college of liberal arts. It united with other colleges, some begun here and some bearing notable histories in other parts of the city, to form a municipal institution, which in 1934 was named Wayne University. The oldest college, that of medicine, began in 1868. Wayne, with its ten colleges and schools, was sustained by the people of Detroit through their Board of Education until 1956, when it became a state university.

SW corner of Cass and Warren avenues in the historic district that includes 4735-4841 Cass Avenue, Detroit; Wayne State University Historic District; S116; January 19, 1957; 1958

West Canfield Historic District

In 1813, Territorial Governor Lewis Cass purchased the Macomb farm. By 1818 he had acquired "80 arpents in depth" of land extending almost three miles inland from the Detroit River in the form of a narrow French ribbon farm. Cass died in 1866. In 1869 his daughters

307

Matilda Cass Ledyard and Mary Cass Canfield subdivided block 98 and donated 100 feet for an avenue, which they named Canfield in memory of Mary's husband, Captain Augustus Canfield. Lewis Cass, Jr., subdivided block 100 on the north side of Canfield in 1871. Many of Detroit's most prominent attorneys, physicians, dentists and architects owned homes on West Canfield. In the 1880s the area became commonly known as Piety Hill because of the alleged social and moral character of its residents.

Side Two

The West Canfield Historic District encompasses one block of West Canfield Avenue extending from Second Boulevard to Third Street. All of the houses in the district were built in the 1870s through the 1890s. The elaborate houses, with ornately carved wood and stone trim, reflect a variety of architectural styles including Gothic Revival, Italianate, Second Empire and Queen Anne. Through the years the houses were being destroyed by neglect. In 1969 the Canfield West-Wayne Preservation Association organized to promote the purchase and restoration of the houses. The area became Detroit's first local historic district in 1970, and it was listed on the National Register of Historic Places in 1971.

Canfield Avenue between Second and Third streets, Detroit; West Canfield Historic District; S311; May 27, 1971; 1990

Wheeler Center

In 1919, Leon "Toy" Wheeler of Indianapolis, Indiana, became the first black recreation worker employed by the city of Detroit. Seven years later the Detroit Recreation Department acquired a building at Vernor Highway and Hastings Street which Wheeler managed. Knowledge of sports and leadership qualities made him an excellent choice for the job. In high school Wheeler had received four sports awards and then went on to become an outstanding college athlete. Wheeler was in charge of the Brewster Center which opened in 1929 in this two-story red brick building. Featuring a well-rounded athletic program, the center made significant progress in basketball, swimming, tennis, boxing and other sports. Today this organization, known as the Wheeler Center, is a pioneer in programs for the elderly.

Chrysler Service Drive, 637 Brewster, Detroit; Wheeler Center (Brewster-Wheeler Recreation Center); L441; March 2, 1976; 1978

William Ferguson Homesite

William Ferguson, Michigan's first black legislator, lived on this site. Born in 1857 to the family of one of the state's first black doctors, he was educated in Detroit schools. Successful in printing and real estate, he also became a lawyer and in 1889 when he was expelled from Gies' European Hotel Restaurant for refusing to eat in the colored section, he filed suit. Defeated in lower court, he and his lawyer, D. Augustus Straker, appealed to the Michigan Supreme Court. In Ferguson v. Gies (1890), the court ruled that separation by race in public places was illegal. The ruling propelled Ferguson to a prominent position in the black community, and he was elected to the Michigan House of Representatives in 1893 and 1895. He died in 1910.

On Alfred, between the Chrysler Service Drive and St. Antoine, Detroit; Ferguson, William, Informational Site; S451; November 14, 1974; 1975

William Lambert Homesite

William Lambert, a black leader in Michigan for almost fifty years, lived on this site. Born in New Jersey about 1817, he moved to Detroit as a young man and became active in the antislavery movement. In 1843 he helped organize the first State Convention of Colored Citizens and served as its chairman. Urging blacks to participate directly in the struggle for freedom and equality, he helped prepare an address to the citizens of Michigan outlining black grievances and demanding full civil rights. He was also prominent in the Underground Railroad and in early efforts to secure education for black children. After the Civil War, Lambert continued to work for black rights and operated a successful business. He died in 1890.

Larned, just east of St. Aubin, Detroit; Lambert, William, Homesite (Martin Luther King Housing Project); L363; November 14, 1974; 1975

Women's City Club of Detroit

William B. Stratton designed this building for the Women's City Club of Detroit—founded in 1919 "to promote a broad acquaintance among women" and to further civic and cultural activities. The club, which grew to be one of the largest women's clubs in the world with a membership of over eight thousand in the 1950s, occupied this building from 1924 to 1975. Mary Chase Perry Stratton's Pewabic tile is featured throughout.

2110 Park Street, west of Woodward, Detroit; Women's City Club of Detroit; L647A; April 29, 1979; 1980

Zion Lodge No. 1, F. & A. M.

On April 27, 1764, the Provincial Grand Master of the Free and Accepted Masons in New York issued a charter to a Masonic lodge in Detroit. The Royal American Regiment's Lieutenant John Christie was the master of the lodge, Michigan's first. The Detroit Masons first adopted the name Zion Lodge in 1794 when they began operating under a new charter from Quebec. With American occupation of Michigan, the lodge again came under the Grand Lodge of New York, which issued a new charter in 1806 to "Zion Lodge No. 1" of Detroit. This name was retained by the Grand Lodge of Michigan when it was formed in 1826. Zion Lodge suspended operations during the War of 1812 and during the anti-masonic agitation of 1829-1845, but each time its functions were resumed.

*500 Temple Avenue, Detroit; Detroit Masonic Temple; S255; January 24, 1964; 1964; *missing

Zion Lutheran Church

Blocks of limestone that once formed the old Detroit post office were used to construct the Zion Lutheran Church in 1933. This Neo-Gothic-style church, designed by the firm of Maul & Lentz of Detroit, was dedicated on May 27, 1933. In 1882, West Prussian immigrants had organized the congregation and built a frame church on this site. Services were conducted exclusively in German until 1925. It became an integrated congregation in 1961.

4305 Military Avenue, Detroit; Zion Evangelical Lutheran Church; L1626A; February 16, 1989; 1990

Henry Ford's Honeymoon House

Henry Ford and Clara Bryant were married on April 11, 1888. Soon afterwards, construction of this house, known as both the Honeymoon House and the Square House, began in Dearborn. Ford built the one-bedroom house himself using timber cut and sawed at his sawmill. The specifications for the kitchen, sitting room, parlor and bedroom were provided by his bride. Later, Ford added his workshop, where he often experimented with gasoline engines.

Side Two

In 1891 the Fords left this house for Detroit where Ford's career as an automaker began. They kept the house as a summer cottage until 1937. Ford then gave it to a friend, Robert Smith, now known for his soybean research. After the Fords died, the land on which the house stood was acquired by the Ford Land Development Corporation. Smith was told to move the house or tear it down. He moved it here on the anniversary of Ford's birthday, July 30, 1952. It was listed in the National Register of Historic Places in 1980.

29835 Beechwood Avenue, Garden City; Ford, Henry, Square House (Henry & Clara Ford Square House); S527A; August 3, 1979; 1981

A Nankin Pioneer

On May 10, 1825, Marcus Swift, from Palmyra, New York, bought the northwest quarter of Section 11 in Nankin Township from the United States government. He was the first to own land now part of Garden City. The Swift family's log cabin overlooked the River Rouge, a few rods from this site. The area was a dense hardwood forest. On May 28, 1827, Swift was elected as the first supervisor of Bucklin, which consisted of the present Redford, Dearborn, Livonia and Nankin townships and had a population of less than five hundred, not including a few Indians. Swift was appointed justice of the peace by Governor Lewis Cass in 1828. He was also a Methodist circuit rider and a vociferous opponent of slavery.

Warren Road and Sunset Drive, Garden City; Nankin Pioneer, A, Informational Designation; L41; January 22, 1965; 1965

Battle of Brownstown

In this vicinity on August 5, 1812, six weeks after the outbreak of war, an Indian force, led by the famous Shawnee chief, Tecumseh, ambushed about two hundred Americans under Major Thomas Van Horne who were on the way south to the River Raisin. There, supplies vitally needed by Hull's army in Detroit were awaiting an escort through the Indian blockade of the River Road. Tecumseh opened fire as the Americans forded Brownstown Creek. Van

Horne, overestimating the Indians' numbers, ordered his men to fall back. The retreat soon became a panic-stricken flight back to Fort Lernoult. Seventeen Americans were killed, twelve wounded and two captured and murdered. One Indian was killed.

Memorial Park, Parsons Elementary School, 14473 Middle Gibraltar Road, Gibraltar; Battle of Brownstown Informational Designation; S100; September 25, 1956; 1958

Angus Keith House

Angus Keith (1819-1899), a Great Lakes steamship captain, was born on Grosse Ile. In 1850 he purchased this property and later built this house. In 1858, Keith married Isabella Norvell, the daughter of John Norvell, who was one of Michigan's original U.S. senators. Keith's father, William Keith, commanded both naval and merchant ships. Angus Keith sailed the lakes for forty years and operated commercial vessels including lumber carriers for the Peshtigo Lumber Company.

9510 Horse Mill Road, Grosse Ile, Grosse Ile Township; Angus Keith House (Seven Gables); L1693B; November 16, 1989; 1991

Colonel Brodhead's Office

Colonel Thornton Fleming Brodhead (1822-1862) and his wife, Archange Macomb Abbott, lived on the hill just north of this site. This small stone office and library building was constructed around 1855. Colonel Brod-

William Ferguson became Michigan's first black legislator in 1893. (*William Ferguson*)

head was, at various times, editor and part owner of the *Detroit Free Press*, state senator and postmaster at Detroit. He served in the Mexican War and led the First Michigan Cavalry in the Civil War. The colonel was mortally wounded at the Second Battle of Bull Run.

20604 East River Road, Grosse Ile Township; Brodhead's, Colonel Thorton Fleming Office; L577; January 19, 1978; 1980

Eighteenth-Century Gristmill Site

From 1787 until about 1840 a horse-driven grist mill occupied the triangle of land north of Horsemill Road bounded by the river and Thorofare [*sic*]. Ten acres were cleared and enclosed as meadows for the mill horses. Equipped with "a pair of Stones 3 feet 3 inches in diameter," the mill was erected by William Macomb at a cost of 628 British pounds. He also maintained a "Cyder Press" near the shore and a shipping wharf.

East River Road, Grosse Ile Township; Eighteenth Century Gristmill Informational Site; L51; March 23, 1965; 1965

Mansion House and Survey Tree

Here, on high ground near the aged maple, an identification point in old surveys, stood the Mansion House built by William Macomb in 1783-1784. He died in 1796 leaving Grosse Ile to his three sons. Michigan's Governor William Hull and British Lieutenant Colonel James Grant met here September 12, 1807, to discuss border problems. William Macomb II lived here from 1809 to 1813 when the British ordered him out of the territory. His wife and infant son fled in November 1813 when Indians burned the house.

20722 East River Road, Grosse Ile, Grosse Ile Township; Mansion House and Survey Tree Informational Site; L35; December 10, 1963; 1964

Military Outpost 1815-1817

This point marked the northeast corner of the stockade of a post that was maintained on Grosse Ile by the United States Army for a short time after the War of 1812. The post was garrisoned by detachments of the Fifth Infantry Regiment which were quartered in seven log cabins. The troops protected the island's civilian population and their property from Indian raids.

East River Road, Grosse Ile, Grosse Ile Township; Grosse Ile Military Outpost (1815-1817); L23; May 4, 1962; 1962

The Rucker-Stanton House

This vernacular house was built by John A. Rucker, Jr., in 1848. Rucker was the great-grandson of William Macomb, who with his brother, Alexander, purchased Grosse Ile from four Indian tribes on July 6, 1776. In 1873, Robert Lee Stanton, Rucker's cousin, bought the house. Between 1897 and 1898 a large rear wing was added. The house was still owned and occupied by descendants of Alexander and William Macomb in 1987, the year of Michigan's sesquicentennial.

21719 West River Road, between Church and Lakeview roads, Grosse Ile, Grosse Ile Township; Rucker, John Anthony, House; L1280A; November 26, 1985; 1987

St. James Episcopal Chapel

Lisette Denison, a freed slave, willed her life savings to build Saint James Episcopal Chapel. With supplemental funds from her employer, William S. Biddle, and his brother James, this Gothic chapel was constructed in the summer of 1867. The architect was English-trained Gordon W. Lloyd of Detroit, who summered on Grosse Ile. The first rector was the Reverend Moses H. Hunter. James Biddle built a rough altar cross, a minister's kneeling bench, and a reading stand for the first services, which were held in 1868.

25150 East River Road, Grosse Ile, Grosse Ile Township; St. James Episcopal Church; L122; May 18, 1971; 1981

Grosse Pointe Academy

Owned by the Religious of the Sacred Heart from 1867-1969, this site is now an independent school. The narrow shape of the property reflects its original use as a French "ribbon farm" extending inland from Lake St. Clair. Situated at the Grosse Pointe Academy are an 1868 structure initially used as a public school for village children, the present academy building erected in 1929 and a place of worship modeled after a French convent chapel. Each of these edifices is still in use.

171 Lake Shore Drive west of Moran Road, Grosse Pointe Farms; Academy of the Sacred Heart (Grosse Pointe Academy); L523; April 15, 1977; 1977

The Grosse Pointe Memorial Church

This Neo-Gothic church was dedicated on May 15, 1927. Detroit architect W. E. N. Hunter designed the limestone structure, which contains stained-glass windows by the Willet Studios of Philadelphia, Pewabic tile from Detroit and wood carvings by German carver Alois Lang. The tower houses a forty-seven-bell carillon. In 1962 the education wing was erected. The church was dedicated to the founders, who organized the nondenominational Grosse Pointe Protestant Evangelical Church on September 7, 1865. In 1867 the first church was erected at Kerby Road and Lake Shore Drive. A stone and wood-frame building, referred to as the "ivy-covered church," was built on this site in 1894. In 1920 the congregation reorganized as a Presbyterian church.

16 Lakeshore Drive, Grosse Pointe Farms; Grosse Pointe Memorial Church; L1739A; April 19, 1990; 1991

Russell A. Alger House "The Moorings"

Russell A. Alger, Jr., (1873-1930) son of Michigan's Governor Russell Alger, built this Italian Renaissance-style mansion in 1910. Alger was one of the founders of the Packard Motor Car Company. Charles A. Platt of New York designed this elaborate structure, and Ellen Shipman of New York landscaped the grounds. The home, situated on Lake St. Clair, was referred to as "The Moorings." Alger lived here until his death in 1930. From 1936 to 1948, the house was used by the Detroit Institute of Arts as a branch museum. In 1949 it was deeded to the Grosse Pointe War Memorial Association in memory of those who served and died in our nation's wars and for facilitating the educational, cultural and civic needs of the community.

32 Lake Shore Drive, Grosse Pointe Farms; Alger, Russell A., Jr., House (Grosse Pointe War Memorial Association Building); S548A; February 18, 1982; 1983

Fox Indian Massacre

Encouraged by a potential alliance with the English, the Fox Indians besieged Fort Pontchartrain, Detroit, in 1712. Repulsed by the French and their Huron and Ottawa Indian allies, the Fox retreated and entrenched themselves in this area known as Presque Isle. The French pursued and defeated the Fox in the only battle fought in the Grosse Pointes. More than a thousand Fox Indians were killed in a fierce five-day struggle. Soon afterward French settlers began to develop the Grosse Pointes.

Corner of Lake Point and Windmill Point roads, Grosse Pointe Park; Fox Indian Massacre Informational Site; S502; April 11, 1977; 1977

Voigt-Kreit House

William Voigt, Jr., is thought to have designed this house as a summer home in the early 1900s. In 1889 his parents, who ran a butchering business, purchased the property for $1,850. French settler Joseph Tremble was granted the land by President James Madison in 1811. Paul Trombley later had title to the site. Voigt, Jr., a city engineer, owned The Home Brewing Company, and had studied architecture in Germany. As a member of the Detroit Board of Education, 1887-1893, he was instrumental in strengthening the compulsory education law and introducing physical culture into school programs. Voigt's sister Christine and her husband, Herman Kreit, D.D.S., were deeded the home in 1907. Dr. Kreit became a trustee and president of the village of Grosse Pointe Park. Christine taught German and science at the Liggett School from 1882 to 1900. The home remained in the family until 1969.

Voigt on Public Education

As a member of the Detroit Board of Education from 1887 to 1893, William Voigt, Jr., supported compulsory education laws and advocated providing free text books for students. Serving as president of the board in 1889 he defended the cost of public education in his annual report: "While the estimates asked by the Board of Education are undoubtedly large sums, and should be expended by the body with the utmost care and scrutiny, still . . . there is no purpose for which money should be so willingly given by the taxpayer as for our public schools, the one, of all our American institutions, which is the very foundation and base of the structure of our form of government. . . . American patriotism can well be measured by the love for our public schools."

16004 East Jefferson, Grosse Pointe Park; Kreit, Herman, House (Old Voigt House); L923A; April 24, 1981; 1982

Wardwell House

William Buck, an English immigrant farmer, built the main part of this house around 1849. It has fourteen-inch thick walls and is the oldest brick house in Grosse Pointe. The rear clapboard addition, built elsewhere, dates from the 1880s. Henry Russel, an attorney and businessman, bought the house in 1901. In 1912 it became the home of his daughter, Helen Wardwell, and her husband, Harold. She lived here for sixty-five years. In 1977 the property was acquired by the Grosse Pointe Memorial Church as a bequest of Helen Wardwell.

16109 Jefferson Avenue, Grosse Pointe Park; Seitz House; S487; August 6, 1976; 1981

Children's Home of Detroit

On May 18, 1836, following a cholera epidemic, thirteen civic-minded women met at the Woodward Avenue Presbyterian Church and founded the Ladies' Orphan Association of Detroit. The women adopted a constitution and began raising money to run a home for children orphaned by the epidemic. A house on St. Antoine Street was obtained, rent free, for one year. The home opened on February 1, 1837, and cared for eleven children during its first year. Now known as the Children's Home of Detroit, the home has had a number of names and locations. In 1950 it moved to this campus. As it celebrated its sesquicentennial in 1986, the Children's Home of Detroit continued to meet the challenge of serving children with special needs.

900 Cook Road, Grosse Pointe Woods; Children's Home of Detroit Informational Designation; L1237C; May 21, 1985; 1986

Colonel John Francis Hamtramck

John Francis Hamtramck was a native of Canada who dedicated his life to the new American nation. Born in 1756, Hamtramck fought in the American Revolution. He distinguished himself during and after the war fighting both Indian and British forces. In 1787 he was made commander of Post Vincennes in the Illinois Territory. There Major Hamtramck was instrumental in negotiating a peace treaty with area Indians.

Side Two

In 1793, Hamtramck was named lieutenant colonel in the forces led by General Anthony Wayne. The next year, Hamtramck was cited for bravery in Wayne's decisive victory at the Battle of Fallen Timbers. In 1796, Hamtramck, a newly appointed colonel, was further honored when he was given command of the fort at Detroit which had previously been in British hands. Except for two years, he remained there until his death in 1803. In 1798 one of the four townships in Wayne County was named for this military hero.

Veteran's Memorial Park, Berres and Dan, Hamtramck; Hamtramck, Colonel John, Burial Place Informational Site; S252; October 22, 1963; 1976

Chrysler Corporation

On June 6, 1925, the Chrysler Corporation was founded here after a reorganization of the Maxwell and Chalmers automotive companies by Walter P. Chrysler. The first cars to bear the Chrysler name were manufactured in the Maxwell plant, which was built here in 1909 and which is now the center of the corporation's worldwide administrative and engineering headquarters. Chrysler had its origin in some 130 auto companies founded as early as 1894 and today is one of the few survivors in an industry that has included approximately 1,500 companies. By 1930, Chrysler had become the world's third-largest producer of automobiles; during World War II its production of war materials helped make Detroit the world's "Arsenal of Democracy."

12000 Oakland Avenue, Highland Park; Chrysler Corporation S282; May 4, 1966; 1968

Home of the Model T

Here at his Highland Park Plant, Henry Ford in 1913 began the mass production of automobiles on a moving assembly line. By 1915, Ford built a million Model Ts. In 1925 over nine thousand were assembled in a single day. Mass production soon moved from here to all phases of American industry and set the pattern of abundance for twentieth century living.

15050 Woodward Avenue, Highland Park; Highland Park Plant, Ford Motor Company; S3; April 17, 1956; 1956

Livonia Revolutionary War Veterans

This marker commemorates three American Revolutionary War soldiers who lived and died in Livonia. David Dean was born in 1763 and enlisted in the New York militia in 1778. Dean settled in Livonia around 1836 where he died in 1838. A native of Connecticut, born in 1755, Salmon Kingsley belonged to a company of minutemen who aided in the defense of Boston. Kingsley came to Livonia in 1825 where he died two years later. Born in New York about 1763, Jeremiah Klumph was a messenger in Washington's army. Klumph lived in Livonia from 1836 until his death in 1855. These men were a few of the many Revolutionary veterans who settled in the west. All three journeyed with their families and settled in this area.

Intersection of Wayne and West Seven Mile roads, Livonia; Livonia Bicentennial Park Informational Designation; (Livonia Revolutionary War Soldiers); L395; January 16, 1976; 1976

Newburgh Cemetery

An organization, later known as the Newburgh Cemetery Society, was formed on November 23, 1832, to establish and maintain this cemetery, the first in the present city of Livonia. One grave, that of Salmon Kingsley, a veteran of the American Revolution who died in 1827, already existed here. In the century that followed, three other Revolutionary War veterans, more than fifty Civil War veterans and other early residents were buried here in these grounds, a treasured reminder of the pioneer era.

36000 Ann Arbor Trail, east of Newburgh Road, Livonia; Newburgh Cemetery; L36; January 24, 1964; 1964

Detroit's National League Wolverines played baseball in Recreation Park from 1881 to 1888. Later, the 1901 Tigers helped charter the American League. (*Recreation Park/Tiger Stadium*)

Wilson Barn

This barn was constructed in 1919 on the burnt-out foundation of an earlier structure built about 1888. It is a fine example of an increasingly rare bank barn style. Here, on the farm owned and operated by his family since 1847, Ira Wilson built a million-dollar enterprise which grew from dairy farming, to delivery, to full creamery operations. By his death in 1944 the business had become "one of the district's leading creameries." Wilson also held several local elective offices.

NE corner of Middlebelt and West Chicago roads, Livonia; Wilson Barn; L261; November 15, 1973; 1974

Reves-Wilhelm Cemetery

In this small cemetery are buried members of a pioneer family that settled this land in the 1820s. Many descendants still live in this area. Here lies Peter Wilhelm, who in 1827 or 1829 acquired Private Claim 49, an old French ribbon farm whose origins dated back into the 1700s. This land was part of that farm. Here are buried Peter's father, Nicholas, progenitor of the Wilhelm family in the United States; Peter's wife, Salome; their son Peter, Jr.; and their granddaughter Adeline Reves. Others are buried here, but their names are now unknown. Since 1948 this site has been maintained by Melvindale as a historic site, possibly the oldest in the immediate vicinity of Detroit unchanged from its original use.

Park area on Wall Street between Greenfield Road and Oakwood Boulevard, Melvindale; Reves-Wilhelm Cemetery; L25; August 14, 1962; 1963

First Presbyterian Church of Northville

In 1829 former members of the Farmington Church organized this church, originally named the First Presbyterian Society of Plymouth. In 1835-1836 a frame church was built here on land donated by D. L. Cady. A New England-inspired brick church opened in 1849 and was first remodeled under the Reverend James Dubuar who served from 1851-1875. Subsequent additions have included a new sanctuary, built in 1969. The original brick church is now undetectable within the present structure.

200 East Main Street, Northville; First Presbyterian Church of Plymouth Informational Site (First Presbyterian Church of Northville); L1665C; May 18, 1989; 1989

Mill Race Historical Village

In 1827, John Miller built a gristmill on this site. The structure was replaced by the Northville Mills in 1847. In 1919 mill owner Donald P. Yerkes sold the site to Henry Ford who razed the structure and built a valve factory across Griswold Street one year later. The factory was one of Ford's village industries, a group of rural plants that manufactured small automobile parts. The Ford Motor Company donated the land to the city of Northville in 1972 for use as a historical village.

Side Two

The Mill Race Historical Village was established in 1972 as a site for relocating buildings faced with demolition. That year the city of Northville donated the New School Church to the Northville Historical Society and it was the first structure moved to this site. The society's focus has been the preservation and display of architectural styles and furnishings of the nineteenth century. The Gazebo and Hirsch Blacksmith Shop are reproduction buildings.

Griswold Street, Northville; Mill Race Historical Village Informational Designation; L1427C; June 10, 1987; 1989

Baker House

Henry W. Baker (1833-1920) built this Italianate-style house in 1875. Born in Richmond, New York, Baker had moved to this area while still a boy. As a young man, he worked as a photographer, a merchant and a lumberman. At the age of forty-nine he helped found the Plymouth Iron Windmill Company, which in 1895 became the Daisy Manufacturing Company. The company, now best known for its BB guns, operated in Plymouth until 1958, when new owners moved it to Arkansas. Baker's descendants lived here until 1943.

233 South Main Street, Plymouth; Baker, Henry W., House; L874A; January 8, 1981; 1986

Plymouth

The village of Plymouth was settled in 1825, incorporated in 1867, and became a city in 1932. The Lord Mayor of Plymouth, England, came here in July 1967 to celebrate the centennial of Plymouth, Michigan's incorporation as a village. He and his aides presented this piece of rock from Plymouth, England, to the citizens of Plymouth, Michigan, some of who are descendants of the Pilgrims. This rock, taken from the Plymouth harbor from where the Mayflower sailed in 1620, stands as a symbol of friendship between the two cities.

City Hall, 201 South Main, Plymouth; Plymouth Informational Designation; L637; December 21, 1978; 1979

Sutherland House

This house was built for William Sutherland in 1921. A prefabricated semi-bungalow, it was constructed by the Lewis Manufacturing Company of Bay City, which built many such bungalows in Michigan between 1914 and 1940. Sutherland, a horticulturist and land developer, owned a large section of land in southwest Plymouth. After building this house, the first in this area, Sutherland sold the remaining lots to the city for the Sunshine Acres subdivision. Sutherland Street was named in his honor.

1142 South Main Street, Plymouth; Sutherland, William, House; L1377B; January 22, 1987; 1987

Pointe Mouillee Marsh

Pointe Mouillee provides a rich habitat for waterfowl and small game. Late Woodland Indians, attracted by the abundant wildlife resources, settled in this vicinity. The earliest white settlers in the area, French fur traders who sought beaver pelts, named the marsh "Pointe Mouillee," which means "wet point." In 1875 eight millionaire sportsmen organized the Big Eight Shooting Club, which was renamed the Pointe Mouillee Shooting Club in 1879. The marsh gradually receded over the years as Lake Erie's fluctuating waters eroded the protective barrier islands. In 1945 the Michigan Department of Conservation purchased the land with revenue from the federal Pittman-Robertson excise taxes and the state Game and Fish Protection Fund. During the 1980s the department initiated a major wildlife habitat project to restore the Mouillee marshes.

37205 Mouillee Road, Rockwood; Pointe Mouillee Marsh Informational Designation; L1722C; February 15, 1990; 1990

State Police Post

A Michigan State Police post has been located in this area since the early days of the department. In 1917 the first detachment in Monroe County was posted to South Rockwood, about one mile south of here. Close to both Detroit and the Canadian border, the original post was on the well-traveled Dixie Highway. The early troopers patrolled on horseback. Area headquarters were moved to this building, the first standardized state police post, in 1930. The building was purchased by the village of Rockwood for municipal offices in 1941, when the post was decommissioned.

Rockwood State Police Post, 32409 Fort Street, Rockwood; First Standardized State Police Post in Michigan Informational Designation; L1340C; September 16, 1986; 1987

Merrill-Morris House

Constructed in 1846, this Greek Revival residence was erected just nineteen years after Romulus was first settled. Originally the home of pioneer Harvey W. Merrill, the house is believed to be the oldest still standing in the city. Large walnut beams, hewn with an adz (a cutting tool), support the wood frame structure. Small frieze windows with grilles decorate the front entrance. This refined farmhouse became the home of Ray V. Morris and family in' 1912.

Side Two

The Morris family made several additions to the house and surrounding grounds, including a large barn, which was the center of many social activities for the community. Fire destroyed the barn in later years. In 1931 the family erected a fruit and vegetable stand on the southeast corner of the property. Produce, dairy products and maple syrup were available. During the 1930s, the family stand attracted hundreds of weekend visitors from Detroit.

13880 Huron River Drive South, Romulus; Merrill-Morris House; L606; May 17, 1978; 1980

Battle of Monguagon

On August 9, 1812, a force of about six hundred American troops, regulars and militia, moved down the River Road in an attempt to reach Frenchtown (Monroe) and bring back supplies needed desperately by the Americans in Detroit. At a point that cannot now be exactly located, near the Indian village of Monguagon, American scouts ran into a British and Indian force of about four hundred men, led by Captain Adam Muir and Tecumseh, blocking the road south. Lieutenant Colonel James Miller quickly brought up his Americans and, in a running battle drove the enemy back through present-day Trenton until the British pulled back across the river into Canada. Losses were heavy. Ironically, this, the only battle won by the Americans in Michigan during the War of 1812, was followed a week later by Hull's surrender of Detroit.

Elizabeth Park, Slocum and West Jefferson Avenues, Trenton; Battle of Monguagon Informational Designation; S199; September 25, 1956; 1962

French Landing Dam and Powerhouse

In 1910 the Eastern Michigan Edison Company, now the Detroit Edison Company, purchased most of the Van Buren Township land along the Huron River for a hydroelectric plant. The French Landing powerhouse and dam were completed in 1924-1925. The dam, the largest and last in a series of five constructed on the Huron River, created Belleville Lake, with its miles of beautiful residential and recreational lakefront lots. The dam generated up to 12.7 million kilowatt hours of electricity until it was decommissioned in 1962. It was eventually donated to the township. In 1981, Van Buren Township began a five-million-dollar project to restore the dam and powerhouse.

12100 Haggerty Road, Van Buren Township; French Landing Dam & Powerhouse; L998A; February 18, 1982; 1983

Johnson's Tavern

In 1824, George M. Johnson purchased eight acres of land from the government and erected a log tavern at this location, a day's journey from Detroit. Stephen G. Simmons bought the tavern from Johnson in 1825 and operated it until he was hanged for the murder of his wife in 1830. In 1832 the tavern, located on the new Detroit-Chicago military road, was purchased by Ezra Derby. He later subdivided some of his land and sold lots. A hamlet known as Derby's developed around the tavern, and in 1836 the name of the settlement was changed to Wayne, apparently to honor General Anthony Wayne. On April 12, 1869, forty-five years after George Johnson settled here, the village was incorporated.

35118 Michigan Avenue, Wayne; Johnson, George M., Tavern Informational Site (National Bank of Detroit); S296; June 27, 1969; 1969

The Henry W. Baker House is one of Plymouth's most prominent residences. Baker was one of the founders of the Daisy (air rifle) Manufacturing Company. (*Baker House*)

Old Wayne Village Hall

Since 1878 the Old Wayne Village Hall has served as the center of civic affairs in Wayne. It is one of the few surviving Second Empire-style buildings in Wayne County. The first meeting of the village took place on April 20, 1869. In the following years, meetings were held in rented quarters. In 1877, when the village's population had reached fourteen hundred, Wayne officials approved plans for a village hall and jail. James Lewis of Detroit received the building contract in January 1878. On August 19, 1878, the cornerstone was laid. The new village hall, built at a total cost of $1,415, was completed on November 19, 1878, and accepted for use on January 7, 1879. In 1916 quarters for the police and fire departments were added. The building became the home of the Wayne Historical Museum in 1969.

405 East Main Street, between Roys and Fourth streets, Wayne; Wayne Village Hall (Wayne Historical Museum); L1347A; October 23, 1986; 1987

Chief Tonquish Burial Site

Chief Tonquish and his son are buried nearby. Chief Tonquish led a band of Potawatomi Indians in this area in the early nineteenth century. In 1819 a series of clashes between these Indians and pioneers in the vicinity culminated in the death of a white man. Angry settlers pursued the Indians along the River Rouge to the point where it branches into what is now known as Tonquish Creek. Here Chief Tonquish was killed in a futile attempt to save his son's life. Their deaths marked the end of significant Indian skirmishes in southeastern Michigan. This event reflected many of the tensions and conflicts between Indians and settlers over such matters as food and territory which occurred during the westward movement in America.

Holliday Park Towne Houses, 34850 Fountain Boulevard, Westland; Chief Tonquish Informational Designation; L426; October 21, 1975; 1977

Cooper School

The original Cooper School was built sometime between 1836 and 1841 on a farm owned by Gilbert Cooper at the corner of present-day Ann Arbor Trail and Middlebelt Road. The Coopers were Nankin Township pioneers who owned a sawmill on the Rouge River. Cooper School became Fractional No. 1 of Nankin and Livonia in 1849. In 1865 the district built a one-room schoolhouse on land leased from Cooper's son, Loren. It was replaced in 1938 with a three-room brick structure. Over the years the school expanded to seventeen rooms and was annexed to the Livonia Public Schools in 1957. A fourth school was built in 1966. By this time, Cooper School's origins and the Cooper family had been forgotten. In 1987, as a Michigan sesquicentennial project, Cooper teachers and parents researched the school's history and discovered its pioneer namesakes.

28611 Ann Arbor Trail at the corner of Middlebelt Road, Westland; Cooper School Informational Site; L1578C; July 21, 1988; 1988

Nankin Mills

Two grist mills have occupied this site. The first was built between 1835 and 1842; the present was constructed soon after the Civil War. In 1918, Henry Ford purchased it as part of a plan to develop village mill industries along the Rouge and other small rivers. Equipped with a turbine generator, Nankin Mills produced engravings, carburetor parts, rivets and bearings. Ford believed that farmers working in an atmosphere of cleanliness and tranquility would restore a proper balance between the industrialized city and rural communities. Although his experiment intrigued American and European planners, it proved unprofitable. After World War II the mills closed. The Wayne County Road Commission acquired Nankin Mills, and in 1956 it was given new life as a nature center.

33175 Ann Arbor Trail, Westland; Nankin Mills Nature Center; L68; March 11, 1967; 1977

Perrinsville

The village of Perrinsville was established as a small commercial center during the 1830s. Abraham and Isaac Perrin started a successful sawmill where Merriman Road now crosses the Middle Rouge. Several businesses sprang up and the community became known as Perrinsville. About 1850 the village reached its peak of activity with flourishing enterprises on Ann Arbor Trail and Merriman Road. But a railroad built during this era by-passed Perrinsville to the south; in 1871, this railroad was intersected at what is now Wayne City by a rail line running from the north. Perrinsville's distance from these vital transportation lines led to its decline. It became an agricultural area. Absorbed by the city of Westland in 1966, one of Perrinsville's residential streets, a school and a store still exist.

Intersection of Ann Arbor Trail and Merriman Road, Westland; Perrinsville Informational Designation; L423; October 27, 1975; 1977

America's First Bessemer Steel Mill

Eber B. Ward, pioneer industrialist in many fields, built the Eureka Iron Works in Wyandotte in 1854. Here iron ore from Upper Michigan was smelted into iron in furnaces that were heated by charcoal made from wood cut in surrounding forests. Here in 1864 the first steel ingots were made by the Bessemer steel process, a method actually developed by the American, William Kelly, but named for Sir Henry Bessemer. The next year the first Bessemer steel rails were rolled at the Wyandotte mill. Once its value had been proven, Kelly's process was quickly adopted by other companies. Plagued by many difficulties, the Eureka Works was forced to cease operations in 1892.

NW corner of Van Alstyne Boulevard and Elm Street, Wyandotte; Eureka Iron Works (America's First Bessemer Steel Mill); S158; September 17, 1957; 1958

Wexford

Caberfae Ski Resort

Snow trains brought hundreds of ski enthusiasts to the Cadillac area to celebrate the opening of Caberfae on January 16, 1938. Caberfae, whose name comes from the Gaelic word meaning "stag's head," was a joint project of the U.S. Forest Service, the Civilian Conservation Corps (CCC), the Cadillac Chamber of Commerce and local volunteers. They cooperated to build a winter sports facility that would provide more than the existing snow shoe trails to the public. The CCC cleared ski and toboggan runs, and built a shelter and access roads. Skiers made five dollar contributions and volunteers used the money to construct the first rope tow in 1940. By the 1950s Caberfae had become one of the Midwest's largest ski resorts. Caberfae's success encouraged further growth of Michigan's winter sports industry.

Caberfae Road, Cadillac vicinity, South Branch Township; Caberfae Ski Resort Company Informational Site; L1601C; November 1, 1988; 1988

Cadillac Carnegie Library

Constructed with the joint support of an Andrew Carnegie grant and the Cadillac Literary Society, this Classical Revival-style building was completed at a cost of $30,000 in 1906. Built on land donated by Jacob and Wellington Cummer, it served as a public library until 1969. The structure housed the Cadillac Police Department for eight years before becoming the Wexford County Historical Society Museum in 1977. In 1978 the historical society began restoring the library to its original appearance.

127 Beech Street, one-half block east of Mitchell Street, Cadillac; Cadillac Carnegie Library (Wexford County Historical Society Museum); L856A; November 2, 1980; 1982

Charles T. Mitchell House

This Prairie-style building began as a Second Empire house built by George Mitchell in 1874. A lumberman and Cadillac's first mayor, Mitchell built the house with ornately carved woodwork and a mansard roof. His business partner, Wellington W. Cummer, occupied it from 1878 to 1922, when it was purchased by Mitchell's grand-nephew, Charles T. Mitchell. In 1926, Charles, a local industrialist, renovated the house to conform with current architectural trends. Totally redone in the Prairie style and clad with red brick, it lost its ornamentation and gained a low-pitched hipped roof. The extensive renovation was testimony to Charles Mitchell's wealth: his firms employed from one-fourth to one-third of Cadillac's work force.

118 North Shelby Street, Cadillac; Mitchell, Charles T., House; L1434A; July 23, 1987; 1988

Clam Lake Canal

In 1873 the Clam Lake Canal was constructed between Big and Little Clam lakes, present-day Lakes Mitchell and Cadillac. Lumbering was the major industry in the Clam Lake area, and sawmill owners needed an efficient means of transporting timber to the mills and railroad sites in Cadillac. Two years earlier George A. Mitchell, a prominent Cadillac banker and railroad entrepreneur, and Adam Gallinger, a local carpenter, formed the Clam Lake Canal Improvement and Construction Company. The company dug the canal at the narrowest point between the lakes through land owned by Mitchell. The channel is one-third mile long and was originally twenty feet wide. It has been widened at least six times, most recently in 1965, and is presently forty-eight feet wide. Today the channel serves the area's recreational boaters.

NE of 6093 M-115, Cadillac; Lake Cadillac-Lake Mitchell Canal; S1639A; March 16, 1989; 1990

Cobbs & Mitchell Building

In 1905, George D. Mason of Detroit designed this brick and limestone building as a showplace for the products of Cobbs & Mitchell, Incorporated, a nationally known lumber company. Completed in 1907, the building's interior is finished in nine varieties of native Michigan wood—elm, white maple, bird's-eye maple, sap birch, red birch, curly red birch, red beech, red oak and hemlock. The company was named for Jonathan W. Cobbs (1828-1898), and William W. Mitchell (1854-1915). Their families were prime movers in the growth of the city of Cadillac and developed much of northern Michigan's lumber industry. The building also housed the Mitchell Brothers Company and other lumbering interests before it was purchased by the State Highway Department in 1939.

100 East Chapin, west of Mitchell Street, Cadillac; Cobbs and Mitchell Incorporated Building (Michigan Department of Transportation District 3 Headquarters); L782A; February 27, 1980; 1981

Cobbs & Mitchell Mill No. 1

In June 1871, Cadillac's first sawmill began to operate on this site. Originally called the Pioneer Mill, it was built by an Indiana resident, John R. Yale. Jonathan W. Cobbs bought the mill in 1872 and took William W. Mitchell as his partner in lumbering operations on Lake Cadillac. The mill was then renamed Cobbs and Mitchell Mill No. 1. Enlarged several times, the mill cut pine, maple and later other hardwoods. By 1885 the mill was a major contributor to Cadillac's lumber production, having cut 5,679,000 feet of lumber. By 1940 it was Cadillac's only remaining sawmill. When it was razed that year, material salvaged from it was used to build an addition for the Wood Parts Company.

329 South Street at the lake, Cadillac; Cobbs & Mitchell Mill No. 1 Informational Site (Harbor View Apartments & Park); L1428C; June 10, 1987; 1987

Shay Locomotive

In the 1870s logging was a seasonal operation. Horses or oxen could drag logs over snow or ice trails to sawmills or rivers. But once the ground thawed, the logs could not be moved. Ephriam Shay (1839-1916), a logger from Haring, near Cadillac, was one of several people who decided that temporary railroad tracks and the right locomotive would allow lumbermen to haul logs year-round. Shay envisioned a small but powerful locomotive that could operate on tracks with steep grades and sharp curves. He used vertical pistons and a flexible drive shaft to transfer power via gears to all the wheels beneath the engine and tender. This produced more power, less wear on the tracks, and the ability to negotiate tight curves.

Side Two

Shay received patents for his geared locomotive in 1881. He had already granted the exclusive right of manufacture to Ohio's Lima Locomotive and Machine Company, which produced 2,770 Shay locomotives from 1880 to 1945. Before he developed his successful locomotive, Shay experimented with tramways that used cars pulled by horses. However, on a downgrade the horses were in danger of being run over by runaway cars. Later, with the help of William Crippen, a Cadillac machinist, Shay built a rigid-drive locomotive; however, it tore up the wooden tracks then in use. Finally, he produced the geared locomotive with pivot-mounted trucks that bears his name. This Shay Locomotive, built in 1898, was the last used by the Cadillac-Soo Lumber Company. It was restored in 1985.

Cass Street in the City Park, Cadillac; Shay Locomotive Informational Designation; S528A; August 3, 1979; 1987

Battle of Manton

In 1881, Manton became the Wexford County seat as a result of a compromise between Cadillac and Sherman. Those towns had quarreled over the issue for years. Cadillac partisans renewed the feud and won the county seat at an election in April 1882. After the election a sheriff's posse left Cadillac for Manton by special train to seize the county records. An angry crowd confronted the Cadillac men and drove them out of town. Collecting several hundred lumbermen, a supply of whiskey and a brass band, the sheriff returned to demand the records. Manton residents barricaded the courthouse, but the posse broke through doors and windows, seized the documents, and returned to Cadillac triumphant. Cadillac was victorious, but the battle of Manton left injuries and hard feelings.

Rotary Park, U.S.-131, south of Griswold Street, Manton; Battle of Manton Informational Designation; L79B; June 18, 1970; 1970

First Wexford County Courthouse

Wexford County was organized in 1869. The law organizing the county also specified that the county seat should be located "at or near what is called Manistee Bridge," where the Newaygo and Northport State Road crossed the Manistee River. In 1870 the village of Sherman was platted just south of the bridge. The first county courthouse, completed in 1872, was located about two hundred feet west of this marker. After a heated controversy, the county offices were transferred in 1880 to Manton, a small town in the eastern part of the county. The dispute was finally settled in 1882 when Cadillac was chosen as the county seat of Wexford County. The old courthouse in Sherman was used as a school until 1937.

NW corner of Fourteen Mile Road and M-37, Sherman, Wexford Township; First Wexford County Courthouse; L74; February 28, 1969; 1969

Out of State

Cadillac Museum

Antoine Laumet was born in this house on March 5, 1658. Laumet became le Sieur de la Mothe Cadillac. On July 24, 1701, he founded the settlement that became Detroit, Michigan, United States of America. Accompanied by one hundred troops of the Compagnie Franche de la Marine and nearly as many Indians, Cadillac claimed Detroit in the name of King Louis XIV, who had directed him to establish forts connecting Quebec and New Orleans. Cadillac brought his family to Detroit and remained there until 1710. In 1717, after serving as Governor of Louisiana, he returned to France. He died in Castelsarrasin in 1730. In 1972 the Detroit Historical Commission and Society gave the village of St. Nicolas-de-la-Grave twenty thousand dollars to purchase and help restore this house for use as a museum.

Musée Cadillac

C'est dans cette maison qu'est né Antoine Laumet le 5 mars 1658. Laumet devint le Sieur de la Mothe Cadillac. Le 24 juillet 1701, il fonda le petit village qui, plus tard, deviendra Détroit, Michigan, Etats-Unis d'Amérique. Accompagné d'une centaine de soldats de la Compagnie Franche de la Marine et de presque autant d'indiens, Cadillac revendiqua Détroit pour le compte du roi Louis XIV. Ce dernier lui avait assigné la tâche d'etablir des forts reliant Québec à la Nouvelle Orléans. Cadillac fit venir sa famille à Détroit et y resta jusqu'en 1710. En 1717, après avoir servi comme Gouverneur de la Louisiane, il revint en France. Il mourut à Castelsarrasin en 1730. En 1972, la Commission Historique et la Société Historique de Détroit firent don de 20.000,00 dollars US pour l'achat de cette maison afin qu'elle puisse servir de musée.

Lamothe Cadillac Avenue, St. Nicholas-de-la-Grave, France; Cadillac Museum Informational Site (Cadillac Homesite); S564C; June 15, 1984; 1984

Birth of Kiwanis

Kiwanis International, one of the great service organizations of the world, had its origin on January 21, 1915. On this date the state of Michigan issued a charter to a group of business and professional men who organized the first Kiwanis Club on this site in the Griswold Hotel. The club's name, Kiwanis, was an Indian term. The concept and principle which Kiwanis represents is symbolized by the slogan "We build." From its beginning, and within two years, Kiwanis became international in its scope.

Kiwanis International Museum, Indianapolis, Indiana; Birth Origins of Kiwanis (Kiwanis International); S254; January 24, 1964; 1982; *The original "Birth of Kiwanis" marker was erected in Detroit, Michigan, in 1965.

Michigan at Perryville

Among the sixty-one thousand Union soldiers who at the Battle of Perryville ended Confederate attempts to gain control of Kentucky were six Michigan units. The most heavily engaged of these were Coldwater's Loomis Battery (Battery A of the First Michigan Light Artillery), the Second Michigan Cavalry and the Twenty-first Michigan Infantry. During the course of the battle, Battery A, equipped with six ten-pounder Parrott guns, prevented the right flank of General Daniel McCook's corps from being turned and aided in the repulse of General Patrick Cleburne's Rebel brigade. At one point, Loomis was ordered to spike his guns and leave them. By refusing, he retained a key position. Battery A is reported to have fired the first and the last artillery rounds of the battle.

Side Two

The units from Michigan that fought in the Battle of Perryville were: the Thirteenth Michigan Infantry, mustered at Kalamazoo and commanded by Lieutenant Colonel Frederick W. Worden; the Twenty-first Michigan Infantry, mustered at Ionia and commanded by Colonel Ambrose A. Stevens; the Second Michigan Cavalry, mustered at Grand Rapids and commanded by Lieutenant Colonel Archibald P. Campbell; Battery A, First Michigan Light Artillery, mustered at Coldwater and commanded by Captain Cyrus O. Loomis; Battery D, First Michigan Light Artillery, mustered at Coldwater and commanded by Captain Josiah W. Church; the First Michigan Engineers and Mechanics, mustered at Marshall and commanded by Colonel William P. Innes.

Perryville Battlefield State Park, Boyle County, Kentucky; Battlefield at Perryville, Kentucky Informational Site; S555C; May 12, 1983; 1983

Michigan at Tebbs Bend

During the first week of July 1863, while the people of the North and the South focused their attention on Gettysburg and Vicksburg, five Michigan companies defended the bridge across the Green River here at Tebbs Bend. They were members of the Twenty-fifth Michigan Volunteer Infantry, (Colonel Orlando H. Moore commanding), First Brigade, Second Division, Twenty-third Army Corps, Army of the Ohio. On the morning of July 4, 1863, Confederate cavalry troops under the command of General John H. Morgan attacked the 260 well-entrenched Michigan volunteers. After the Michigan troops repelled eight attacks, Morgan retreated from this locale. However, his troops continued to raid through Kentucky and Indiana before the last remnants were captured in Ohio.

Side Two

The Twenty-fifth Michigan Volunteer Infantry was organized at Kalamazoo and mustered into service in September 1862 under the command of Colonel Orlando H. Moore. The companies of the regiment that fought here were: Company D, recruited at Three Rivers; Company E, recruited at Galesburg; Company F, recruited at Niles; Company I, recruited at Holland; and Company K, recruited at Buchanan. When ordered by General John H. Morgan to surrender, Colonel Moore replied, "This being the Fourth of July, I cannot entertain the proposition of surrender." Total casualties for the Twenty-fifth Infantry were six killed and twenty-four wounded. Eighty-one Confederate troops fell, including twenty-two commissioned officers.

Romine Loop Road, Taylor County, Kentucky; Tebbs Bend Informational Site (Michigan at Tebbs Bend); L1515C; April 25, 1988; 1988

Stonewall Regiment

More than ninety thousand Michigan men served in the Union Army and Navy during the Civil War. The Seventeenth Michigan Volunteer Infantry Regiment was mustered at the Detroit Barracks in August 1862 under the command of Colonel William H. Withington. The regiment consisted of raw recruits from field, workshop and schoolroom. One company was composed almost entirely of students from Ypsilanti Normal School, now Eastern Michigan University. With less than a month of military training, the Seventeenth left for Washington, DC, on August 27, 1862. From there it was sent to the Maryland campaign. On September 14, a little more than two weeks after leaving the state and just three days before the Battle of Antietam, the regiment engaged in battle here.

Side Two

The Seventeenth Michigan Volunteer Infantry Regiment was among the units of General Ambrose E. Burnside's Ninth Army Corps that were engaged in battle here on September 14, 1862. The fighting began around 9:00 A.M. just south of this site. Around noon a Confederate battery opened fire on the regiment, which was supporting Cook's Massachusetts Battery. The Seventeenth held its position for several hours. At 4:00 P.M. the command was given for an assault along the entire Union line. The Confederates came out of the woods to meet the charge at a fence line in the middle of the field, then moved back to the stone walls along the crest of the hill. The seventeenth advanced and captured the stone walls. Of the five hundred men of the "Stonewall Regiment" engaged in battle here, 27 were killed and 114 wounded, many mortally.

8629 Reno Monument Road, Braddock Heights, Maryland; Fox's Gap [Wise's Field] Informational Site (Braddock Heights); S580C; 1986

Michigan

THE STATE OF MICHIGAN HAS ERECTED THIS MARKER TO HER BRAVE AND COURAGEOUS SONS WHO FOUGHT AT STONES RIVER TO PRESERVE THE UNION.

Side Two

This marker is dedicated to all the Michigan soldiers engaged in this great battle, to the seventy-one men who lost their lives and to the six regiments which fought bravely for their country: Twenty-first Michigan Infantry, commanded by Lieutenant Colonel William B. McCreery (Flint), 18 killed, 89 wounded, 36 missing; Eleventh Michigan Infantry, commanded by Colonel William Stoughton (Sturgis), 30 killed, 84 wounded, 25 missing; Thirteenth Michigan Infantry, commanded by Colonel Michael Shoemaker (Jackson), 17 killed, 72 wounded; Fourth Michigan Cavalry, commanded by Colonel Robert H. G. Minty (Detroit), 1 killed, 7 wounded, 12 missing; First Michigan Engineers and Mechanics, commanded by Colonel William P. Innes (Grand Rapids), 2 killed, 9 wounded, 5 missing; First Michigan Artillery Battery, Company A, commanded by Colonel Cyrus O. Loomis (Coldwater), 1 killed, 10 wounded, 2 missing. Michigan men fought at Stones River for the preservation and perpetuity of the Union.

NOTE: The Ninth Michigan was also in the Battle of Stones River; Stones River Battlefield, Murfreesboro, Tennessee; Stones River Battlefield Informational Site; S279; March 9, 1966; 1966

Appendix

Properties listed in the State Register of Historic Sites that are marked with historical identification plaques are listed below. They are arranged alphabetically by county, municipality and historic site name.

Allegan

Goodrich, Dr. Asa, House, 112 Center Street, Douglas

Kirby, Sarah M., House, 294 West Center Street, Douglas

Ganges Fractional District No. 1 Schoolhouse, 6292 124th Avenue, Ganges Township

Saugatuck Engine House and Council Room, 102 Butler Street, Saugatuck

Antrim

Brown's School, Marsh Road at M-32, Jordan Township

Berrien

Pears Mill, 123 South Oak Street, Buchanan

Calhoun

Battle Creek Sanitarium, 74 North Washington Avenue, Battle Creek

Charlevoix

Harsha, Horace S., House, 103 State Street, Charlevoix

Cheboygan

Newton-Allaire House, 337 Dresser Street, Cheboygan

Clinton

Gunnisonville United Methodist Church [Gunnisonville Historic District], southeast and northeast corners of Clark and Wood roads, DeWitt Township

Eaton

Grand Ledge Chair Company Plant, 101 Perry Street, Grand Ledge

Genesee

Paterson, William S./ Sutherland, Dr. James K., House, 402 East Third, Street, Flint

Aitken, Robert P., Farmhouse, 1110 North Linden Road, Flint Township

Linden Presbyterian Church Informational Site, 119 West Broad Street, Linden

Gilbert, Horace/ Miller, Morgan and Enos, House, 5023 Holland Drive, Swartz Creek

Grand Traverse

Park Place Hotel, 300 East State Street, Traverse City

Ingham

Beck, Louis, House, 515 North Capitol Avenue, Lansing

Ferris, Edward, House, 3044 Onondaga Road, Onondaga Township

Ionia

Olry, John C., Farmstead, 3226 East Musgrove Highway, Sebewa Township

Jackson

Brown, William G., House, 6770 Brown Road, Parma Township

Timbers, John, House, 201 East Main Street, Spring Arbor Township

Kalamazoo

Hall, Festus, House, 114 South Main Street, Climax

Kent

Fallasburg School, Covered Bridge Road, Vergennes Township

Moseley School, southeast corner of Lincoln Lake Road and Four Mile Road, Vergennes Township

Odell, Orlando J., House / Vergennes Post Office, 10629 Bailey Drive, Vergennes Township

Vergennes District No. 1 Schoolhouse, 12980 Three Mile Road, Vergennes Township

Vergennes District No. 11 Schoolhouse, 1573 Parnell NE, Vergennes Township

Leelanau

Grand Traverse Light Station, northern point of Leelanau Peninsula, at the end of County Road 629, Leelanau Township

Luce

Newberry State Bank Building, 318 Newberry Avenue, Newberry

Mackinac

Wawashkamo Golf Club, British Landing Road, Mackinac Island

Macomb

Theisen, John, House, 12240 East Ten Mile Road, Warren

Shelby Fractional School District No. 4 Schoolhouse, 52650 Van Dyke, Shelby Township

Manistee

Douglas, William, House, 521 Pine Street, Manistee

Mason

First Mason County Courthouse, South Lakeshore Drive, Pere Marquette Township

Menominee

Pioneer Grange No. 1308 Hall, River Road, Stephenson

Monroe

Milan Old Village Hall and Fire Station, 153 East Main Street, Milan

Montcalm

Little Denmark Evangelical Lutheran Church, 1031 South Johnson Road (County Road 595) at intersection of Pakes Road, Montcalm Township

Montmorency

Calvary Episcopal Church, 330 North State Street, SE corner of Third Street, Hillman

Muskegon

Gerber, Cornelius, Cottage, 6480 West Cottage Grove, Fremont

Newaygo

Saint Mark's Episcopal Church, 30 Justice Street, Newaygo

Oakland

Lakeville Hall, 1469 Milmine Street, Addison Township

Ferndale School, 130 East Nine Mile Road, Ferndale

Orchard Lake Chapel, 5171 Commerce Road, between Hiller and Orchard Lake roads, Orchard Lake Village

Oceana

Benona Township Hall, 5400 West Woodrow, Benona Township

Mears, Charles, Silver Lake Boardinghouse, southeast corner of Lighthouse and Silver Lake Channel roads, Golden Township

Ottawa

Woman's Literary Club, 235 Central Avenue, Holland

Klanderman, Jacobus, Farmstead, 6091 Ninety-sixth Avenue, Olive Township

Bilz, Aloys, House, 107 South Division Street, Spring Lake

Saginaw

Fowler Schoolhouse, 13240 West Townline, Fremont Township

Freeland United Methodist Church, 205 East Washington Street, Tittabawassee Township

St. Clair

Woman's Benefit Association Building, 1338 Military Street, Port Huron

St. Joseph

Colon Public Library, 128 South Blackstone Avenue, Colon

Heywood, William, House, 180 East Third Street, Constantine

Messiah Lutheran Church, 185 West Fifth Street, Constantine

Sanilac

Divine, John, Law Office / Moore Public Library, 7239 Huron Avenue, Lexington

Tuscola

Lane House, 301 Prospect, Vassar

Washtenaw

Delta Upsilon Fraternity House, 1331 Hill Street, Ann Arbor

Phi Delta Theta Fraternity House, 1437 Washtenaw Avenue, Ann Arbor

Fountain-Bessac House, 102 West Main Street, Manchester

Wayne

Detroit Naval Armory, 7600 East Jefferson Avenue, Detroit

Esterling, Joseph H., House, 2245 Waubash, Detroit

Redford Theatre Building, 17354 Lahser Avenue, Detroit

Smith, James, Farm, 2015 Clements, Detroit

Wagstaff, Robert, House, 2576 Riverside Drive, Trenton

Wexford

Greenwood Disciples of Christ Church, 7303 North Thirty-five Mile Road, Greenwood Township

Photo Credits

Cover, Gary Boynton, Lansing; p. 20, Michigan Travel Bureau; p. 24, Historic Preservation Section (hereafter HPS); p. 26, HPS; p. 33, Dirk Bakker, Detroit; p. 37, Roger L. Rosentreter, Lansing; p. 41, U.S. Postal Service; p. 43, State Archives of Michigan (hereafter SAM); p. 44, Kellogg Company, Battle Creek; p. 49, Michigan State University Archives; p. 52, Susan Collins, Marshall; p. 56, Susan Collins, Marshall; p. 58, SAM; p. 63, SAM; p. 66, SAM; p. 69, SAM; p. 71, HPS; p. 73, David Kenyon, Department of Natural Resources; p. 74, SAM; p. 76, HPS; p. 79, SAM; p. 80, SAM; p. 81, Roger L. Rosentreter, Lansing; p. 85, Brian D. Conway, Lansing; p. 86, Department of Natural Resources; p. 89, SAM; p. 92, HPS; p. 93, SAM; p. 96, Dietrich Floeter, Traverse City; p. 97, Dietrich Floeter, Traverse City; p. 101, Lad Strayer, Adrian; p. 103, SAM; p. 104, Suomi College; p. 105, HPS; p. 109 Garfield Inn, Port Austin; p. 111 Michigan State University Archives; p. 115 SAM; p. 116; SAM; p. 119 Oldsmobile History Center; p. 121 Thomas Genhara, Lansing; p. 125, Roger L. Rosentreter, Lansing; p. 127, SAM; p. 130, SAM; p. 133, Lad Strayer, Adrian; p. 134, Jerry Roe, Lansing; p. 136, SAM; p. 138, HPS; p. 140, SAM; p. 141, Kalamazoo College Archives; p. 144, HPS (top), SAM (bottom); p. 148, HPS; p. 150, Grand Rapids Public Library; p. 152, SAM; p. 153, HPS; p. 156, (top) Michigan Travel Bureau, (bottom) SAM; p. 160, Scott Brooks-Miller, Lansing; p. 161, SAM; p. 164, Lad Strayer, Adrian; p. 165, SAM; p. 166, SAM; p. 169, SAM; p. 170, SAM; p. 172, SAM; p. 173, Mackinac Island State Park Commission (hereafter MISPC); p. 174, SAM; p. 175, MISPC; p. 176, Roger L. Rosentreter, Lansing; p. 177, Phil Porter, Cheboygan; p. 178 SAM; p. 179 SAM; p. 180 Roger L. Rosentreter, Lansing; p. 181, MISPC; p. 184, Norm Lorway, Mount Clemens; p. 185, SAM; p. 188, SAM; p. 189, SAM; p. 192, Dietrich Floeter, Traverse City; p. 193, Dietrich Floeter, Traverse City; p. 194, SAM; p. 196, Jack Deo; p. 197, SAM; p. 198, SAM; p. 200, Dietrich Floeter, Traverse City; p. 201, HPS; p. 205, Shannon Jones, Muskegon; p. 215, SAM; p. 217, Elizabeth Adams; p. 218, Elizabeth Adams; p. 222, Laura R. Ashlee, Lansing; p. 223, Michigan's Own Military Museum, Frankenmuth; p. 225, Michigan Travel Bureau; p. 229, (top) SAM, (bottom) HPS; p. 230, SAM; p. 231, SAM; p. 233, John and Ann Mahan; p. 237 SAM; p. 238, U.S. Steel Corporation; p. 240, SAM; p. 242, SAM; p. 245, John and Ann Mahan; p. 249, American Museum of Magic, Marshall; p. 250, SAM; p. 253, SAM; p. 255, SAM; p. 256, Kay Seward, Owosso; p. 257, SAM; p. 258, SAM; p. 259, SAM; p. 260, Owosso Public Library; p. 265, Roger L. Rosentreter, Lansing; p. 267, SAM; p. 269, Laura R. Ashlee, Lansing; p. 271, SAM; p. 275, SAM; p. 277, SAM; p. 279, SAM; p. 282, SAM; p. 285, Michigan Travel Bureau; p. 288, HPS; p. 292, Stewart Ashlee, Cheboygan; p. 296, SAM; p. 297, SAM; p. 304, Stroh Brewery Company, Detroit; p. 307, HPS; p. 310, SAM; p. 314, SAM; p. 317, Laura R. Ashlee, Lansing.

A

A Bygone Lumbering Town 196
A Nankin Pioneer 309
A. U. V. Auditorium 139
Aaron Greeley/St. Cosme Line Road 278
Academy of the Sacred Heart 207
Across the Peninsula 181
Ada Covered Bridge 146
Adrian College 162
Adrian Union Hall 162
Al Meyers Airport 168
Alabaster 128
Albion College 45
Aldrich House 209
Alexander Macomb 183
Alice B. Cowles House 111
All Saint's Episcopal Church/Gordon W. Lloyd 24
Allegan County 22
Alma College 99
Alpha House 283
Alpine Township Hall 147
Alton Pioneer Village 154
Alvah N. Belding Library 126
America's First Bessemer Steel Mill 318
American Academy of Pediatrics 283
American Museum of Magic 53
Andrews University 35
Angus Keith House 310
Ann Arbor Railroad 171
Antislavery Society 268
Aquinas College .148
Ardis Furnace, The 76
Armistice Day Storm 196
Austerlitz Port Office / William Hyser 154
Austin Blair, Eaton Rapids 80
Austin Blair, Jackson 133

B

Bagley Inn 207
Baker House 315
Barn Church 221
Barn Theatre 137
Barryville 28
Battle Alley 211
Battle Creek City Hall 46
Battle Creek House 46
Battle Creek Post Office 46
Battle Creek Sanitarium/Percy Jones Hospital 47
Battle of Bloody Run, The 283
Battle of Brownstown 309
Battle of Manton .320
Battle of Monguagon 316
Battlefield of 1814 174
Bay City 31
Bay Port Fishing District 108
Beaumont Memorial 174
Beckley Cemetery 47
Beckley School 47
Beet Sugar 33
Beet Sugar Industry 32
Beginning of State Reforestation 73
Bellaire—The Antrim County Seat 25
Belle Isle 283
Benzonia College 33
Benzonia Congregational Church 33
Berrien Springs Courthouse 35
Bertrand 36
Bethel African Methodist Episcopal Church 284
Bethel Church 273
Bethlehem United Church of Christ 268
Biddle House 174
Big Rock 203
Bigelow-Kuhn-Thomas House 111
Birth of Kiwanis, Detroit 284
Birth of Kiwanis, Indianapolis, Indiana 321
Birthplace of Dr. Ralph J. Bunche 284
Birthplace of Famed Song 45

Birthplace of Ford Automobile 284
Birthplace of "The Old Rugged Cross" 45
Birthplace of Thomas Edmund Dewey 259
Bishop Baraga's First Church 253
Blacksmith Shop .273
Blendon Landing .111
Bliss Pioneer Memorial Church 84
Blissfield Hotel 163
Bloomingdale Depot/Kalamazoo and
    South Haven Railroad 264
Blossom Heath Inn 187
Bois Blanc Island .173
Botsford Inn, The .209
Bottle House, The .190
Bowen's Mills 31
Box 23 Club, The/The Kerns Hotel Fire 114
Boyne City United Methodist Church 63
Brent Creek United Methodist Church 93
Bridgewater Town Hall 271
British Cannon 174
British Landing 174
Brooklyn Presbyterian Church 132
Brooklyn's Founder 132
Brown City Community Schools 252
Brown Trout 157
Bruce Catton 34
Bryant Farm 51
Buel Methodist Episcopal Church 252
Burnett's Post 40
Burt Opera House/Wellington R. Burt 251
Butler-Boyce House/W. D. Boyce 53
Byers Homestead .207
Byron 254
Byron Township Hall 147

C

C. H. Wills & Company 241
Caberfae Ski Resort 319
Cadillac Carnegie Library 319
Cadillac Museum/Musee Cadillac 321
Calhoun County Fair 53
Calumet Theater 102
Calvin College and Seminary 148
Canton Center School 278
Capitol Hill School 53
Cappon House, The/Isaac Cappon 228
Car Ferries on Lake Michigan 35
Carlton Township Hall 28
Carnegie Library, Iron Mountain 77
Carnegie Library, Mount Clemens 183
Caro Masonic Temple 262
Carpenter House 163
Cascade Christian Church 147
Cass Community United Methodist Church 284
Cass County Courthouse 61
Castle, The 149
Center Eaton United Methodist Church 81
Central Avenue Christian Reformed Church 228
Central Michigan University [marker 1] 131
Central Michigan University [marker 2] 131
Central Reformed Church 149
Central School 227
Central Title Service Building 268
Central United Methodist Church, Detroit 285
Central United Methodist Church, Lansing 112
Central United Methodist Church, Muskegon 204
Cereal Bowl of America 47
Chapin House, The / Henry Austin Chapin 37
Chapoton House 285
Chappee Rapids 200
Charles G. Learned 110
Charles T. Gorham 54
Charles T. Mitchell House 319
Charles W. Nash 87
Chelsea Depot/Chelsea 272
Cherry Hill School 278
Cherry Hill United Methodist Church 279

327

Chicago Road, Detroit 285
Chicago Road, The, Bronson Township 40
Chief Pontiac .213
Chief Shoppenagon/Shoppenagon's Homesite 73
Chief Tonquish Burial Site 318
Children's Home of Detroit 312
Chrysler Corporation 313
Church of Annunciation, Detroit 286
Church of the Resurrection/Monsignor John A. Gabriels,
    Lansing .113
City of Coldwater, The, 1861-1961 41
City Opera House 97
Civic Park 88
Clam Lake Canal 319
Clay Township Library 244
Cleary College 275
Cliffs Shaft Mine 193
Clinton 166
Clinton/Site of the Clinton Inn 166
Clinton United Methodist Church 166
Clinton Valley Center 214
Clinton Woolen Mill 166
Clinton-Kalamazoo Canal 218
Clio Depot 87
Coal Mine No. 8 251
Cobbs & Mitchell Building 319
Cobbs & Mitchell Mill No. 1 320
Cole United Methodist Church 239
College Baptist Church 100
Coldwater Regional Center/State Public School at
    Coldwater .42
Harry Blackstone 244
Colonel Brodhead's Office 310
Colonel John Francis Hamtramck 313
Colonel Samuel White/Samuel White Homestead . . . 213
Colonial Homes and Adjacent Buildings/
    The Dearborn Inn 281
Columbiaville Depot 157
Commandant's Quarters 279
Commerce Roller Mill 208
Commerce United Methodist Congregation 208
Community Library 145
Community Presbyterian Church 88
Comstock Cabin 260
Conant Gardens 286
Congregation Beth El 98
Congregation Shaarey Zedek 220
Congregational Church, Grand Blanc 93
Congregational Church, Hersey 226
Congregational Church of Litchfield 102
Congregational United Church of Christ 139
Constantine United Methodist Church 245
Cooper Congregational Church 137
Cooper School 318
Copper Country, The 107
Copper Peak Chippewa Hill 96
Cornish Pump .77
Corunna Public Schools/Shiawassee Street School . . 255
County Courthouse (Lenawee County), Adrian 162
County Courthouse (Livingston County), Howell . . .171
Courthouse, The/Oakland County 214
Court Street United Methodist Church (First Methodist) 88
Covert Library 265
Crapo Park 211
Crocker House 183
Curry House 95
Curved Dash Oldsmobile/Ransom Eli Olds 120
Curwood Castle 260

D

Daniel B. Eldred House 137
Davenport House 167
Davenport House 274
David Augustus Straker 286
David Kinsey Home 147
David S. Walbridge 139
David Simmons House 209

David Whitney, Jr. Residence 286
Davidson House 246
Davison Farmstead 93
Dearborn Hills Golf Club 281
Dearborn Inn, The/Colonial Homes and Adjacent Bldgs 281
Dearborn Town Hall Complex / Orville L. Hubbard . 280
Decatur Township Hall 265
Del Shannon/Runaway 47
DeLaro Homestead 137
Delta Center Methodist Church 78
Delta Mills 78
Delta Mills Schools 78
Delta Township/Delta Charter Township 79
Detroit Association of Women's Clubs 286
Detroit College of Law 287
Detroit Copper & Brass 287
Detroit Cornice and Slate Building 287
Detroit Medical College, The 287
Detroit Memorial Hospital 287
Detroit Memorial Park Cemetery 188
Detroit News, The 288
Detroit Plaindealer 288
Detroit Urban League 289
Dewey Cannon, The 40
Dewitt School 235
Dexter Depot/Track Pans 272
Dibbleville 87
District Schoolhouse 61
Dock Reserve .129
Doughty House 131
Drenthe Christian Reformed Church 236
Dryden Depot .158
Dunbar Hospital 289
Durand Railroad History/
    Knights Templar Special 258
Durand Union Station 258
Durant-Dort Carriage Company/
    William C. Durant 92
Durant-Dort Carriage Factory No. 1/Flint Road Car &
    Factory 88
Dutch in Michigan 229

E

Eagle River/Lake Shore Drive Bridge 156
Early Detroit: 1701-1760 289
Early Hastings .28
Early Missionary Bark Chapel 175
Early State Parks 160
East Hall 139
Eastern Michigan College 276
Eaton County .77
Ebenezer Reformed Church 22
Eber Durham House 209
Edison Institute, The 281
Edsel & Eleanor Ford House 182
Edward Israel Arctic Pioneer 139
Edwin B. Winans/Hamburg 169
1869 Vriesland Reformed Church 236
Eighteenth-Century Gristmill 310
Elijah McCoy Homesite 289
Elk Rapids Iron Company 25
Elkland Township Hall 263
Ella Sharp Museum 134
Ellen May Tower/Spanish-American
    War Nurse 254
Elmwood 66
Elmwood Cemetery 290
Emerson 68
Empire Lumber Company 160
Epaphroditus Ransom 139
Ephraim Shay .84
Episcopal Church/St. Paul's Church,
    Dowagiac .61
Episcopal Church of Good Shepherd, Allegan 22
Epoufette 174
Erie and Kalamazoo Railroad 163

Erin United Presbyterian Church 186
Escababa River: The Legend/
   Escanaba River: The Lumbermen 75
Evans House 167
Excelsior Town Hall 146

F

Fair Lane 280
Fallasburg Covered Bridge 155
Fallasburg Pioneer Village 155
Fannie Richards Homesite 290
Fanny M. Bair Library 146
Father Jerome MacEachin/St. Thomas Aquinas Roman
   Catholic Church, East Lansing 112
Father Marquette Park 194
Fenton House .87
Fenton United Methodist Church 87
Ferris State College 198
Ferry Street School 48
Finney Barn 290
Finnish Lutheran Church / Jacobsville 107
First Baptist Church, Battle Creek 48
First Baptist Church, Jackson 134
First Baptist Church, Kalamazoo 140
First Baptist Church, Marshall 54
First Baptist Church, Pontiac 215
First Baptist Church, St. Clair 242
First Baptist Church, Grand Blanc Township 93
First Baptist Church of Leslie 124
First Baptist Church of Royal Oak 219
First Congregational Church, Manistee 191
First Congregational Church, St. Clair 242
First Congregational Church, Vermontville 83
First Congregational Church of Charlotte 78
First Congregational Church of Detroit 290
First Congregational Church of Ovid/
   Village of Ovid 72
First Home, The 45
First International Tunnel, The 246
First Jewish Religious Services 290
First Methodist Episcopal Church, Pontiac 215
First Michigan Colored Regiment 291
First Mile of Concrete Highway, The 291
First National Bank 257
First (Park) Congregational Church 149
First Presbyterian Church, Coldwater 41
First Presbyterian Church, Blissfield 165
First Presbyterian Church, Detroit 291
First Presbyterian Church, Dimondale 79
First Presbyterian Church, Homer 52
First Presbyterian Church, Lansing 112
First Presbyterian Church, Pontiac 215
First Presbyterian Church, The, Richland 145
First Presbyterian Church of Caro 262
First Presbyterian Church of Northville 314
First Quaker Meeting 208
First Reformed Church 236
First Roadside Park 129
First State Prison 134
First Steam Railroad in Upper Peninsula 194
First Unitarian Universalist Church 291
First United Methodist Church, Big Rapids 198
First United Methodist Church, Holland 229
First United Methodist Church, Kalamazoo 140
First United Methodist Church, Mount Morris 94
First Wexford County Courthouse 320
First Women's Club in Michigan 140
Fisher Building 291
Fitch-Gorham-Brooks House/Harold C. Brooks 54
Fitzgerald Park 81
Flint Road Cart Factory/Durant-Dort Carriage
   Factory No. 1 88
Flint Sit-Down, The 88
Flint Sit-Down, The 89
Florence B. Dearing Museum 170
Floyd Starr/The Starr Commonwealth Schools 60
Ford Airport, The/Ford Tri-Motor - William B. Stout . 282

Ford Motor Company 292
Ford Rouge Plant 280
Fort Brady 66
Fort de Buade .182
Fort Drummond 65
Fort Gratiot Light 246
Fort Holmes .175
Fort Lernoult .292
Fort Miami 40
Fort Michilimackinac 86
Fort Pontchartrain 292
Fort St. Joseph, Niles 30
Fort St. Joseph, Port Huron 246
Fort Street Presbyterian Church 293
Fort Wayne 293
Fort Wilkins .156
Four Flags Hotel 38
Four Towns Methodist Church 208
Fox Indian Massacre 312
Frank Murphy .108
Frankenhilf 263
Frankenmuth Bavarian Inn 247
Franklin Boulevard Historic District 215
Franklin Village 210
Franklin Village School 211
Fred A. Aldrich/Jacob Smith 91
Fred A. Baker House 212
Fred W. Green 127
Frederick Douglass—John Brown Meeting 293
Fredrick Carl Frieseke/Herman C. Frieseke House . . .261
Free Press, The 287
French Landing Dam & Powerhouse 316
Fruit Belt, The 35
Furniture Industry 150

G

G.A.R. Hall/Grand Army of the
   Republic, Marshall 55
G.A.R. Hall, Sunfield 83
Gardner House Museum 45
General Squier Park 159
General Motors Sit-Down Strike, The 90
Genesee County Courthouse 90
George De Baptiste Homesite 293
George Nason House 247
German Church, The 274
Gerrish 238
Gilford United Methodist Church 263
Glen Oaks 209
Glenwood Cemetery 90
Gogebic Iron Range 95
Gordon W. Lloyd/All Saints Episcopal Church 24
Governor Alex J. Groesbeck 188
Governor Alpheus Felch 268
Governor Cyrus Gray Luce 41
Governor Frank D. Fitzgerald Home 82
Governor Fred M. Warner 209
Governor Kim Sigler 29
Governor Parsons 257
Governor's Mansion 54
Graafschap Christian Reformed Church 22
Grace Episcopal Church, Jonesville 101
Grace Episcopal Church, Mount Clemens 184
Grand Army of the Republic/The G.A.R. Hall 54
Grand Haven .227
Grand Hotel .176
Grand Marais 21
Grand River, The/Grand River History 114
Grand River Trail 126
Grand Traverse Bay 98
Grand Traverse County Courthouse 98
Grand Trunk Depot, Grand Haven 227
Grand Trunk Depot, Lansing 114
Gratiot County 99
Graveyard of Ships/Veterans Day Storm 225
Great Fire of 1871 192

Great Fire of 1881 108
Great Lakes Sport Fishery 161
Great Storm of 1913, The 253
Greenbush School 21
Greenbush United Methodist Church 71
Greensky Hill Mission 63
Greenville 203
Greilickville 159
Gresham United Methodist Church 78
Gros Cap and St. Helena Island 181
Grosse Pointe Academy 311
Grosse Pointe Memorial Church, The 311
Grosvenor House 102
Gunnisonville 70

H

Hackley House 204
Hackley Public Library 204
Hamburg/Edwin B. Winans 169
Harbour Inn 85
Harold C. Brooks/Fitch-Gorham-Brooks House . . . 54
Harriet Quimby 42
Harris Family 145
Harrison 68
Harrison Homestead 93
Harry Blackstone/Colon 245
Harry J. Eustace Hall 112
Harsen House 239
Hartland Music Hall 170
Hartman School 267
Harvey Randall House 60
Hasbrouck House 51
Haslett 125
Hastings Mutual Insurance Company 29
Hathaway-Hess Farm 224
Haven Peaches 267
The Hawkins Farm 52
Helmer House Inn 171
Henry Austin Chapin/The Chapin House 37
Henry Ford Birthplace 280
Henry Ford House 293
Henry Ford's Honeymoon House 309
Henry Howland Crapo/Willson Park 90
Herman C. Frieseke House/Frederick Carl Frieseke . . 261
Hermansville 201
Hess School 250
Hibbard Tavern 212
Highland Park Association 228
Hilberry Theatre 294
Hillsdale 100
Hillsdale College 100
Historic District 246
Historic Fort Mackinac 177
Historic Green 221
Holcombe Beach 187
Holland Harbor Lighthouse/Holland Harbor 234
Holly's Town Hall 211
Holy Ascension Orthodox Church 45
Holy Childhood of Jesus School 85
Holy Cross Parish 240
Holy Family Church 294
Holy Trinity Episcopal Church 191
Home of the Model T 313
Homer Fire Station 53
Honolulu House 55
Hope Church: Reformed Church in America 230
Hope College 230
Horton Bay 62
Houghton County/Houghton County Courthouse . . 105
Howard F. Young/Postmasters 57
Howarth School 213
Hudson Mills 273
Hugh McCurdy Park/Hugh McCurdy 257
Hume House 204
Huron Lightship 242

I

Indian Cemetery 131

Indian Dave 264
Indian Dormitory 177
Indian Fields 141
Indian Landing—Charlton Park 29
Indian Mission, The 110
Indian Trail 75
Indian Village, Detroit 294
Indian Village, Stambaugh Township 130
Indiana School 267
Ingham County Courthouse 124
Inland Waterway 65
Interlochen 96
Ionia Church of Christ 127
Ionia County Courthouse 127
Iron County 130
Iron Inn 130
Ironwood City Hall 95
Isaac Cappon/The Cappon House 228
Isaac Crary & John D. Pierce/State School System . . . 59
Isaac E. Crary House 55
Ishpeming: Historic Ski Center 193
Island House, The, Elk Rapids 26
Island House, Mackinac Island 177
Island Park 80
Italian Hall 103

J

Jackson Area, The 132
Jackson Mine 195
Jacob J. Post House 64
Jacob Smith/Fred A. Aldrich 91
Jacobsville/Finnish Lutheran Church 107
Jail & Sheriff's Residence 172
James A. Bailey 294
James A. Lynch House/Manchester Township Library 274
James A. Miner 55
James McColl House 243
James and Ellen White 48
Jameson Farm 136
Jamestown Reformed Church 234
Jean Baptiste Recollect Trading Post 206
Jenison Museum 227
Joe Muer's Oyster House 294
John Almon Starr/Saginaw Trail 219
John D. Pierce Homesite 55
John Isaac Cutler House 147
John Johnston House 66
John Rayner House 124
John T. Herrmann House 114
John W. Fallas/John Wesley Fallas House . . . 155
John Wesley Fallas House/John W. Fallas 154
Johnson's Tavern 316
Johnston Homesite 68
Joshua Simmons II 71

K

Kalamazoo and South Haven Railroad/
   Bloomingdale Depot 264
Kalamazoo Celery 141
Kalamazoo College 141
Kalamazoo Gazette 142
Kalamazoo Region, The 137
Kalamazoo School Case 142
Kalamazoo State Hospital 142
Kaleva 190
Kellogg Company/W. K. Kellogg 50
Kempf House 269
Kerns Hotel Fire, The/The Box 23 Club . . . 114
Ketchum Park 55
Keweenaw Bay 27
Kimball House Museum 48
Kingsley S. Bingham 169
Knaggs Bridge Area 254
Knights Templar Special/Durand
   Railroad History 258
The Kresge Foundation 221

L

L'Anse-Lac Vieux Desert Trail 27
L. B. King and Company Building 295
La Plaisance Bay Pike 167
Ladies Library Association 98
Ladies Library Hall 158
Ladies Literary Club, Grand Rapids 150
Ladies' Literary Club House, Ypsilanti 276
Lake County .157
Lake Erie 202
Lake Huron .236
Lake Michigan 181
Lake Orion Methodist Church 212
Lake Shore Drive Bridge/Eagle River 156
Lake St. Clair (Lac Sainte Claire) 187
Lake Superior .21
Lake Superior State College 66
Lawrence Institute of Technology 220
Lawrence Simmons House 210
Le Cote Du Nord-Est 295
Leamington Stewart House 247
Lebanon Lutheran Church 206
Leland Historic District(Fishtown) 161
Lemuel Botsford House 209
Lewis College of Business 295
Liberty Hyde Bailey 1858-1954 267
Lieutenant George A. Woodruff 55
Life Saving Station 172
Lime Kilns 253
Lincoln at Kalamazoo 142
Linden Mills 94
Linden Presbyterian Church 94
Little Bay De Noc 75
Little Stone Church 178
Little Traverse Bay 86
Livonia Revolutionary War Veterans 313
Lobb House 21
Logging Railroads 68
Log Schoolhouse, The 48
Loop-Harrison House 253
Louis Chevalier Claim, The 129
Ludington Hotel 75
Lumbering on the Huron Shore 129
Lumberjack Park 100

M

MacKinnon House 130
Mackenzie House 295
Mackinac Conference 179
Mackinac Island 179
Mackinac Straits 182
Mackinaw City 64
Malcolm X Homesite 116
Manchester Township Library/James A.
    Lynch House 274
Manistee Fire Hall 191
Mansion House and Survey Tree 310
Maple River .261
Marengo Pioneer Cemetery 53
Marigold Lodge 235
Marine City .240
Market Street 179
Marlette District Library, The 252
Marquette County Courthouse 194
Marquette Iron Range 195
Marquette's Death, Frankfort 34
Marquette's Death, Pere Marquette Township 197
Marshall 56
Marshall House/Sidney Ketchum (1797-1862) 59
Martha Cook Building 269
Martin Kundig 296
Mary Immaculate of Lourdes Church/Maria Santissima
    Immacolata 77
Mason's Tavern 94
Masonic Block 216
May House 151
McCabe-Marlowe House 151

McCain School 136
Meadow Brook Hall 218
Menominee Area 200
Menominee Iron Range 76
Merrill-Morris House 316
Methodism in Battle Creek 48
Methodist Episcopal Church of Highland Station . . .211
Methodist Indian Mission 67
Metz Fire, The 236
Michigan 324
Michigan Association of Counties/
    Michigan Education Association Building 117
Michigan At Perryville 321
Michigan At Tebbs Bend 323
Michigan Automobile Dealers Association 112
Michigan Becomes a State 270
Michigan Central Depot, Battle Creek 49
Michigan Central Depot, Wolverine 65
Michigan Central Railroad Depot 269
Michigan Dental Association 116
Michigan Education Association Building/
    Michigan Association of Counties 117
Michigan Grayling 74
Michigan: Historic Crossroads 202
Michigan Becomes A State 203
Michigan Library Association 42
Michigan Licensed Beverage Association 117
Michigan Manufacturers Assocation 117
Michigan Masonic Home 99
Michigan Millers Mutual Fire Insurance Company . .123
Michigan Pharmacists Association 117
Michigan Retail Hardware Association 118
Michigan School for the Blind/Administration Building 118
Michigan Sheriffs' Association 118
Michigan Society of Professional Engineers 118
Michigan State Fair 297
Michigan State Medical Society 297
Michigan State University—Founded 1855 112
Michigan Tech 106
Michigan's Capital 72
Michigan's First Coal Mine 254
Michigan's First Jewish Cemetery Site 270
Michigan's First Jewish Settler 86
Michigan's German Settlers 248
Michigan's Interurbans 276
Michigan's Oldest Jewish Cemetery 297
Michigan's Petroleum Industry 99
Midland County Courthouse 201
Military Outpost 1815-1817 311
Mill Race Historical Village 314
Mills Community House 34
Mineral Well .198
Mission Church 179
Moccasin Bluff 36
Monroe 203
Monsignor John A. Gabriels/Church of the
    Resurrection, Lansing 113
Montgomery Schuyler/Trinity Epis. Church., Marshall .59
Moravian Road 182
Morgan B. Hungerford House 119
Mormon Kingdom 63
Mormon Print Shop 63
Morris Chapel Church 36
Morton House, The 35
Mosherville Church / Mosherville School 102
Mother's Day In Albion/Mother's Day 46
Motown 298
Mottville Bridge 245
Mount Clemens Mineral Bath Industry 185
Musee Cadillac/Cadillac Museum 323
Music Hall 298
Muskegon Business College 205
Muskegon Log Booming Company 206

N

Nankin Mills .318
Nardin Park United Methodist Church 210

National House 56
Negro Settlers 199
The Netherlands Museum 231
New Baltimore/St. John's Lutheran Church 185
New Buffalo Welcome Center 37
New Fort Brady 67
Newburgh Cemetery 313
Newport Academy 241
Newport Hill 95
Newton House 62
Ninth Street Christian Reformed Church 231
Noordeloos/Noordeloos Christian Reformed Church . 232
Norrie Park 95
North Channel Shooting Club 239
North Evart United Methodist Church 226
North Lake Methodist Church 273
North Presbyterian Church 119
Northern Michigan University 195
The Northernmost Point of Lake Michigan 173
Norway Spring 77
Novotny's Saloon/Olde Towne Saloon 98

O

Oak Grove Cemetery 213
Oak Hill Cemetery 216
Oakland Christian Reformed Church 23
Oakland County/The Courthouse 214
Observatory, The 46
Officer's Club 74
Ogaukawning Church 31
Old Agency House 180
Old Cheboygan County Courthouse 64
Old City Hall 298
Old Indian Cemetery 205
Old Mackinac Point Lighthouse 64
Old Main/Suomi College 105
Old Mecosta County Jail 199
Old Mill Creek 65
Old Perry Centre 261
Old Presque Isle Lighthouse 190
Old Rawsonville Village 278
Old St. Joseph Neighborhood 40
Old Stone Barn, The 57
Old Three Rivers Public Library 246
Old Town Hall 168
Old Town Hall & Masonic Temple 252
Old Towne Saloon/Novotny's Saloon 237
Old Van Buren Township Hall 278
Old Wayne Village Hall 317
Old Wing Mission 23
Oliver C. Comstock, Jr. 57
Olivet College 82
Omega Psi Phi 298
Omena Presbyterian Church 161
Omer Masonic Hall 27
Opera House 83
Optometric Association 119
Orchestra Hall 299
Orsel McGhee House 299
Orson Starr Home 219
Ortonville Methodist Episcopal Church 214
Orville L. Hubbard/Dearborn Town Hall Complex . 280
Otsego County 226
Our Saviour's Lutheran Church 191
Overisel/Overisel Reformed Church 23
Owendale 109

P

Pacific Salmon 34
Packard Motor Car Company 299
Palmyra Presbyterian Church 167
Parc Aux Vaches—Madeline Bertrand Park 39
Paris Fish Hatchery 199
Parmalee United Methodist Church 30
Passenger Pigeons 85
Paulson House 21
Peninsula Building, The 142
Peninsular Sugar Refining Company 262

Perrinsville 318
Percy Jones Hospital/Battle Creek Sanitarium 47
Peter Seitz Tavern & Stagecoach Inn 203
Philip Orin Parmalee 70
Pier Cove 23
Pigeon Depot 110
Pinchtown 205
"Pine Grove" 216
Pioneer Bank 159
Pioneer Cemetery, Grant Township 129
Pioneer Cemetery, Kalamazoo 143
Pioneer Cemetery, Southfield 220
Pioneer Picnic Park 84
Pioneer School 57
Players, The 299
Plymouth 315
Plymouth Congregational Church 124
Poe's Corners 62
Pointe Mouillee Marsh 315
Polar Bears, The 222
Porcupine Mountains 225
Port Hope Chimney 110
Port Huron High School 242
Portage Prairie United Methodist Church 36
Post Office 68
Postmasters/Howard F. Young 57
Potterville United Methodist Church, The 82
Power House 132
Predmore House 212
Presbyterian Church of South Saginaw 249
Presque Isle Electric Cooperative Monument . . 237
Presque Isle Light Station 237
Prospect Park 276
Putnam Public Library 30

Q

Quincy Public Library 43

R

Railroad Depot 29
Railroad Union Birthplace 58
Ramsdell Theatre 192
Ransom Eli Olds/Curved Dash Oldsmobile . . . 120
Recreation Park 299
Red Ribbon Hall 80
Redford Cemetery 300
Redford Township School District No. 9 300
Religious of the Sacred Heart 300
Reverend Darius Barker, The/St. Mark's Church,
   Paw Paw 266
Reverend John A. Lemke 300
Reves-Wilhelm Cemetery 314
Richmond Center for the Performing Arts 186
Ring Lardner 38
Roadside Table, The 127
Robert J. Whaley/Whaley House 92
Robert Pauli Scherer 300
Robert W. Graham House 154
Rochester 217
Rochester Colony 70
Rochester Opera House 217
Rogers-Carrier House 120
Rose Township Hall 219
Roseland Park Mausoleum 207
Round Island Lighthouse 180
Rowe House 211
Royal Oak Methodist Episcopal Church 220
Royal Oak Woman's Club 220
Rucker-Stanton House, The 311
Rugg Pond Dam 146
"Runaway"/Del Shannon 47
Russell A. Alger House "The Moorings" 311

S

S. S. Kresge Company 222
S.S. *PERE MARQUETTE* 18 196
SS. Peter and Paul Church 304
Sacred Heart Academy 131

Sacred Heart Church 186
Sacred Heart Parish 301
Sacred Heart of Mary Catholic Church 62
Sage Public Library 32
Saginaw Bay 31
Saginaw Club 249
Saginaw Trail/John Almon Starr 219
Saginaw Valley Coal 250
Saginaw Valley Lumbering Era 249
St. Albertus Church, Detroit 301
Saint Andrew's Cemetery 151
St. Andrew's Episcopal Church, Big Rapids 190
St. Anthony Church, Detroit 301
St. Anthony's Catholic Church, Hillsdale 100
St. Antoine YMCA Site 302
St. Bernard Catholic Church, Alpena 25
St. Clair River 239
St. Cosme Line Road/Aaron Greeley 278
St. Elizabeth Church, Detroit 302
St. Ignace 182
St. Ignace Mission 182
St. Ignatius Loyola Church, Houghton 106
St. James Episcopal Chapel, Grosse Ile Township . . . 311
St. John the Baptist Catholic Church,
    Osceola Township 171
St. John's Church, Jackson 135
St. John's Church, St. Johns 72
St. John's Episcopal Church, Clinton 167
St. John's Episcopal Church, Detroit 302
St. John's Episcopal Church and Parish
    House, Ionia 128
Saint John's Episcopal Church, Mount Pleasant 131
St. John's Lutheran Church, Adrian 163
St. John's Lutheran Church/New Baltimore 186
St. John's Presbyterian Church, Detroit 302
St. John's United Church of Christ, Port Huron 242
St. Josaphat Roman Catholic Church
    Complex, Detroit 303
St. Joseph Catholic Church, Dexter 272
St. Joseph County Courthouse 243
St. Joseph Hospital and Home for the Aged 163
St. Joseph's Catholic Church, Adrian 163
St. Joseph's Church/St. Joseph's
    Shrine, Cambridge Township 165
St. Joseph's Mission, Niles Township 39
St. Joseph's Parish, Detroit 303
St. Joseph's Retreat, Dearborn 282
St. Katherine's Chapel, Williamston Township 126
St. Lawrence Parish of Utica, Utica 188
St. Mark's Church/The Reverend Darius
    Barker, Paw Paw 266
St. Mary Church, Cheboygan 64
St. Mary Star of the Sea Church, Jackson 135
St. Mary of Czestochowa Roman Catholic Church,
    Kinde 107
Saint Mary's, Niles 38
St. Mary's Church/St. Mary's Rectory,
    St. Clair 243
St. Mary's Hospital, Saginaw 249
St. Mary's Parish, Westphalia/Westphalia Settlement, .73
St. Mary's Pro-Cathedral, Sault Ste. Marie 68
St. Mary's School-Rectory-Church, Detroit 303
St. Matthew's Episcopal Church, Detroit 303
St. Michael Roman Catholic Church, Flint 91
St. Patrick Church, Ash Township 202
St. Patrick Church, White Lake 224
St. Patrick's Church, Northfield Township 274
St. Paul the Apostle Church, Calumet 103
St. Paul's, Brighton 168
St. Paul's Church/Episcopal Church, Dowagiac 61
St. Paul's Episcopal Church, Flint 91
St. Paul's Episcopal Church, Jackson 135
St. Paul's Episcopal Mission, Taymouth Township . . . 251
St. Philip's Lutheran Church, Detroit 304
St. Stephens, Hamburg Township 170
St. Thomas Aquinas Roman Catholic Church/
    Father Jerome MacEachin, East Lansing 112

St. Thomas Episcopal Church, Battle Creek 49
St. Thomas the Apostle Church, Ann Arbor 270
St. Vincent De Paul Catholic Church, Pontiac 216
St. Wenceslaus Church and Cemetery,
    Leelanau Township 161
Sam Cohodas Lodge/Sam Cohodas 195
Sam Hill House .58
Samuel White Homestead/Colonel Samuel White . . .213
Saranac 128
"Saratoga of the West," The 81
Sashabaw Cemetery 212
Sashabaw United Presbyterian Church 212
Sault Ste. Marie 67
Scales' Prairie .30
Schellenberger Tavern 58
Schoolhouse 132
Schroeder House 251
Schuler's 58
Schwankovsky Temple of Music 304
Scott Club 268
Scottville 197
Second Baptist Church 305
Second Island 82
Second Street Bridge, The 22
Seirn B. Cole House 50
Selfridge Field .183
Selinsky-Green House 187
Seventh-Day Adventists 50
Seymour Lake Methodist Episcopal Church 207
Shay Locomotive 320
Sheldon's Corners 279
Shelldrake 68
Shiawassee County Courthouse 257
Shiawassee Street School/Corunna Public Schools . . .255
Shoppenagon's Homesite/Chief Shoppenagon 74
Shrine Circus .305
Sidney Ketchum (1797-1862)/Marshall House 59
Simpson Park Campground 189
Singapore, Michigan 25
Site of the Clinton Inn/Clinton 166
Sixth Street Bridge 151
Skull Cave 180
Smith's Chapel .61
Smyrna 128
Sophie Turner House 120
South Olive Christian Reformed Church 234
South Street Historic District 143
Southfield Cemetery 221
Southfield Town Hall 221
Spanish-American War Nurse/Ellen May Tower 254
Spanish-American War Regiments 169
Spring Arbor College 135
Stafford's Bay View Inn 84
Stagecoaches 108
Starr Commonwealth Schools, The/Floyd Starr 60
State Bar of Michigan 120
State Capitol 121
State Police Post 315
State Public School at Coldwater/Coldwater
    Regional Center 42
State Savings Bank 305
State School System/Isaac Crary & John D. Pierce . . .59
Ste. Anne Church/Gabriel Richard 305
Stearns Telephone 305
Stephen Yerkes Rodgers House 21
Stewart House .243
Stockbridge Town Hall 126
Stonecrest 223
Stones River 323
Stonewall Regiment 323
Stoney Creek Village 218
Striker House 29
Stroh Brewery .305
Stuart House, The 143
Stuart Neighborhood 143
Sue Silliman House 246
Suomi College/Old Main 104

Suomi Synod 104
Sutherland House 315
Swedish Evangelical Lutheran Sion Church 32
Sweetest Heart of Mary Catholic Church 306

T

"Ten Hours or No Sawdust" Strike 32
Terney House 247
Territorial Road 266
Theron Murray House 210
"Thing," The 183
Third Reformed Church 232
32nd Red Arrow Division 74
Thomas Edison at Grand Trunk 242
Thomas Edison 185
Thomas J. O'Brien 59
Thomas' Mills 30
Thompson Home 306
Three Rivers 246
Ticknor-Campbell House 271
Tiger Stadium 306
Tom Edison at Grand Trunk 247
Tom Walker's Gristmill 171
Torrent House 206
Town of Michigan/Lansing 122
Township Hall, Rochester 217
Township Hall, Elk Rapids 27
Track Pans/Dexter Depot 272
Traverse City Regional Psychiatric Hospital 99
Trinity A.M.E. Church 122
Trinity Church, Croswell 252
Trinity Church, Lexington 252
Trinity Church, Mackinac Island 180
Trinity Church, Niles 39
Trinity Episcopal Church, Houghton 106
Trinity Episcopal Church, Caro 262
Trinity Episcopal Church/Montgomery Schuyler,
    Marshall 59
Trinity Lutheran Church, Detroit 306
Troy Corners 223
Turner-Dodge House 122
Tuscola County Advertiser 262
Tuscola County Courthouse 263
Tuscola County Fair 263
Tyrone Township Hall 171

U

Under The Oaks 135
Underground Railroad, The 62
Underhill Store 80
"Unto a New Land" 226
Union City Iron Furnace 44
Union Pump Company 50
United Methodist Church 158
University of Michigan, The 271
Upjohn Company, The/William E. Upjohn 144
Upper Bridge, The 202
Upton House 187

V

Valley City Milling Company 151
Van Buren County/Van Buren County Courthouse . . 266
Van Buren County Poorhouse 266
Van Vleck Hall 232
Vandenberg Center/Arthur H. Vandenberg 152
Vassar's Logging Era 264
"Vehicle City," The 91
Vergennes United Methodist Church 155
Vermontville Academy 83
Vermontville United Methodist Church 84
Veteran's Facility/Veteran's Cemetery 152
Veterans Day Storm/Graveyard of Ships 225
Veterans Hospital No. 100 50
Villa Maria 153
Village of Ovid/First Congregational Church of Ovid . 72
Village of Romeo 186
Village of Warren 189

Village of Wetzell 27
Voigt House 154
Voigt-Kreit House/Voigt on Public Education 312
Voiture 1116 - 40 et 8 94

W

W. D. Boyce/Butler-Boyce House 53
W. K. Kellogg/Kellogg Company 50
W. K. Kellogg House 145
Walker Tavern, The 165
Wallaceville School 283
War of 1812 Dead 306
Ward Mill Site/Ward Building Site 51
Wardwell House 312
Warner Wine Haus 267
Water Speed Capital 239
Watrous General Store 263
Watrousville United Methodist Church 263
Wattles House 223
Waukazoo Woods 235
Wawashkamo 180
Wayne State University 307
Webster Township Hall 274
Webster United Church of Christ 275
Welfare Building, The 272
Wellington R. Burt/Burt Opera House 251
Wellman General Store 133
Wesley United Methodist Church 39
West Canfield Historic District 307
Western Michigan University 145
Western Theological Seminary 234
Westphalia Settlement/St. Mary's Parish, Westphalia . 72
Whaley House/Robert J. Whaley 92
Wheatland Church of Christ 199
Wheeler Center 308
White Oak 126
White Rock School 87
White's Bridge 128
Whitefish Point Lighthouse 68
Whitefish Township 68
William Austin Burt 190
William C. Durant/Durant-Dort Carriage Company . . 92
William E. Upjohn/The Upjohn Company 144
William Ferguson Homesite 308
William Hyser/Austerlitz Post Office 154
William Lambert Homesite 308
William Peter Mansion, The 158
William Ray Perry House 94
William W. Cook 60
Williamston Center United Methodist Church 126
Willow Run (1941-1953)/Willow Run (1953-present) 277
Willson Park/Henry Howland Crapo 10
Wilson Barn 314
Wing House Museum 42
Winkler's Mill 219
"Witch's Hat" Depot 221
Wixom Cemetery 224
Wixom-Wire House 224
Wolverine Boys' State/Wolverine Girls' State 123
Women's City Club of Detroit 308
Woodberry-Kerns House 123
Wooden Stone School 167
Woodland Town Hall 30
Woodstock Manual Labor Institute 168
World's Largest Cement Plant 25
World's Largest Limestone Quarry 238

Y

Yankee Springs Inn 31
Ypsilanti 276
Ypsilanti Water Tower 276

Z

Zeba Indian United Methodist Church 28
Zion Church, Mount Pleasant 185
Zion Lodge No. 1, F. & A.M. 309
Zion Lutheran Church, Detroit 309